11-6 (b) Stockholders' equity, $833,000
11-7 (a) Stockholders' equity, $7,230,000;
(c) Stockholders' equity, $7,230,000
11-8 (b) Total assets, $1,167,000
11-9 No key figure
11-10 Stockholders' equity, Case A, $1,110,000;
Case B, $1,989,000
Bus. Dec. Prob. 11: Dividends paid on common stock by City Electric, $79,800,000

12-1 Income before extraordinary items, $540,000
12-2 (a) Net income, $350,000
12-3 Income before extraordinary items, $2,820,000
12-4 Book value per share, May 30, $30.20
12-5 (b) Retained earnings, Jan. 1, Year 12, as restated, $511,000
12-6 No key figure
12-7 (b) Total paid-in capital, $6,112,300
12-8 (a) Total paid-in capital, $2,800,000; (b) retained earnings, $369,000
Bus. Dec. Prob. 12: (a) Joseph's share of net assets, $480,000

13-1 (c) Closing entry, $375,000
13-2 (b) (1) Discount on bonds payable, $354,000
13-3 (b) Loss on retirement of bonds, $114,400
13-4 (c) (1) Premium on bonds payable, $124,000
13-5 (b) Net long-term liability, $4,125,850
13-6 (a) Carrying value of bonds, June 30, Year 11, $5,650,200
13-7 (c) Interest expense, issued at discount, $261,000; issued at premium, $248,000
13-8 (b) Gain on sale of bonds, $15,300
13-9 (d) Lease payment obligation, $40,184
13-10 (b) Payroll taxes expense, $1,248
13-11 (a) Net pay due, $5,525.80
Bus. Dec. Prob. 13: (a) Earnings per share, stock financing, $3.44

Appendix A
A-1 (c) Present value, $17,511
A-2 (b) Amortization of discount at Dec. 31, $15,710
A-3 (c) Net liability, Dec. 31, $23,197
A-4 (a) Present value under 5-year lease, $7,806,000
A-5 (b) Discount on notes receivable, $165,776

14-1 No key figure
14-2 No key figure
14-3 (b) Costs recovered during year, $84,000
14-4 (a) Profit under installment method, Year 1, $1 million
14-5 (a) Net income, as revised, $77,400

14-6 (d) Decline in purchasing power of owners' equity, $8,000
14-7 Total costs and expenses, (1) constant dollar basis, $424,500; (2) current cost basis, $413,000
Bus. Dec. Prob. 14: (b) (1) Net income, same accounting, Year 9, $60,000; (2) revised accounting, Year 9, $75,000

Appendix B
B-1 (b) Carrying value, beginning of Year 5, $324,000
B-2 Total assets, $3,120,000
B-3 Total assets, $3,804,000
B-4 (b) Percentage owned, 85%
B-5 Consolidated total assets, $1,121,000

15-1 No key figure
15-2 Increase in working capital, $88,000
15-3 Decrease in working capital, $12,000
15-4 Lower column totals, $156,000
15-5 (a) Decrease in working capital, $300,000; (c) Total sources of working capital, $468,000
15-6 (a) Decrease in working capital, $270,000; (c) Total sources of working capital, $109,500
15-7 (a) Decrease in working capital, $132,000; (c) Total sources of working capital, $692,700
15-8 (a) Cash outflow from operations, $32,500; (b) Decrease in working capital, $30,000
Bus. Dec. Prob. 15: (a) Projected decrease in working capital, $1,050,000

16-1 (d) Net income, Year 4, $21,000
16-2 (a) Net income, Harvest King, 7%
16-3 (e) Average stockholders' equity, $98,000
16-4 (e) Average stockholders' equity, $315,000
16-5 No key figure
16-6 (b) Current ratio, 3 to 1
16-7 (a) Times interest charges earned, Continental Transfer Co., 3.75 times
Bus. Dec. Prob. 16: (c) Percentage change in fourth quarter profits, decrease 10%

17-1 (c) Taxable income, $49,920
17-2 No key figure
17-3 (a) Capital loss deduction, $2,700
17-4 Adjusted gross income, $65,500
17-5 (a) Taxable income on revised basis, $193,750
17-6 Adjusted gross income, Case A, $72,000; Case B, $54,760
17-7 (c) Net income if new stock is used, $117,450
17-8 (b) Total income tax, $30,304
Bus. Dec. Prob. 17: Disposable income under single proprietorship form, $53,217

FINANCIAL ACCOUNTING

chpt 5?
3, 4, 8

Quiz 12/7

Test

McGraw-Hill Book Company

New York   St. Louis   San Francisco   Auckland   Bogotá   Hamburg   Johannesburg   London
Madrid   Mexico   Montreal   New Delhi   Panama   Paris   São Paulo   Singapore
Sydney   Tokyo   Toronto

FINANCIAL
ACCOUNTING

FOURTH EDITION

Walter B. Meigs
University of Southern California

Robert F. Meigs
San Diego State University

2 3 4 5 6 7 8 9 0   V N H V N H   8 9 8 7 6 5 4 3

ISBN 0-07-041534-X

Library of Congress Cataloging in Publication Data

Meigs, Walter B.
    Financial accounting.

    Includes index.
    1. Accounting.   I. Meigs, Robert F.   II. Title.
HF5635.M492 1983   657   82-18008
ISBN 0-07-041534-X

This book was set in Century Schoolbook by John C. Meyer & Son, Inc.
The editors were Donald G. Mason and Edwin Hanson;
the production supervisor was Phil Galea.
The cover was designed by Jo Jones.
The cover photograph was taken by Martin Bough.
Von Hoffmann Press, Inc., was printer and binder.

CONTENTS

transactions and related accounting entries. Sales taxes. Classified financial statements. The purpose of balance sheet classification. Classification and format of income statements.

The meaning of internal control. Strong internal control now required by law.

Organization plan to establish responsibility for every function. Control of transactions. Subdivision of duties strengthens internal control. Specific methods of achieving internal control. Limitations and cost of internal control.

Business documents and procedures. Purchase orders. Invoices. Debit and credit memoranda. Recording purchases at net price.

Streamlining the accounting process.

Sales journal. Controlling accounts and subsidiary ledgers. Purchases journal. Cash receipts journal. Cash payments journal. The general journal. Showing the source of postings in ledger accounts. Subsidiary ledger accounts. Ledger accounts. Proving the ledgers. Variations in special journals. Direct posting from invoices. Unit record for each transaction.

Internal control and the computer. Accounting applications of the computer.

Management responsibilities relating to cash. Basic requirements for internal control over cash. Cash receipts. Cash disbursements. The voucher system. Petty cash. Control features of bank checking accounts. Bank statements. Reconciling the bank account.

Securities exchanges. Marketable securities as current assets. Accounting for investments in marketable securities. Balance sheet valuation of marketable securities. Lower of cost or market (LCM). The argument for valuation at market value. Presentation of marketable securities in financial statements.

Depreciation and income taxes. Accelerated cost recovery system (ACRS). Inflation and depreciation. Historical cost versus replacement cost. FASB Statement No. 33—Disclosure of replacement cost.

Gains and losses on disposal of plant and equipment. Trading in used assets on new.

Accounting for natural resources. Percentage depletion versus cost depletion.

Characteristics. Operating expenses versus intangible assets. Amortization. Goodwill. Patents. Trademarks and trade names. Franchises. Copyrights. Other intangibles and deferred charges. Research and development (R&D) costs.

Accounting for the owner's equity in a single proprietorship. Closing the accounts. Financial statements for a single proprietorship.

Significant features of a partnership. Advantages and disadvantages of a partnership. Partnership accounting. Partnership profits and income taxes. Alternative methods of dividing partnership income. Other aspects of partnership accounting.

What is a corporation? Advantages of the corporate form of organization. Disadvantages of the corporate form of organization. Formation of a corporation. Authorization and issuance of capital stock. Par value. No-par stock. Preferred stock and common stock. Characteristics of preferred stock. The underwriting of stock issues. Market price of common stock. Stock issued for assets other than cash. Subscriptions to capital stock. Stockholder records in a corporation. Retained earnings or deficit. Donated capital. Balance sheet for a corporation illustrated.

Public misconceptions of the rate of corporate earnings. Developing predictive information. Discontinued operations. Extraordinary items. Earnings per share (EPS). Primary and fully diluted earnings per share. Presentation of earnings per share in the income statement. Cash dividends. Dividend dates. Liquidating dividends. Stock dividends. Stock splits. Retained earnings. Prior period adjustments to the Retained Earnings account. Statement of retained earnings. Appropriations and restrictions of retained earnings. Treasury stock. Recording purchases of treasury stock. Reissuance of treasury stock. Restriction of retained earnings when treasury stock is acquired. Book value per share of common stock. Illustration of stockholders' equity section.

and payment of the tax. Computation of individual income tax illustrated. Partnerships. Taxation of corporations. Computation of taxable income of corporations. Illustrative tax computation for corporation. Accounting income versus taxable income. Alternative accounting methods offering possible tax advantages. Interperiod income tax allocation.

PREFACE

The environment of accounting is changing fast, and these environmental changes, such as continued inflation and the critical financial problems of many cities, affect the goals and the content of an introductory text in accounting. In order to function intelligently as a citizen as well as in a business of any size or type, every individual needs more than ever before a clear understanding of basic accounting concepts. In this fourth edition, we have tried to reflect the impact of inflation on accounting measurements and to suggest the direction of needed changes in accounting concepts and methods. The importance of adequate disclosure in the system of financial reporting is stressed, and attention is drawn to the need for improved accounting controls in all sectors of society.

Our goal is to present accounting as an essential part of the decision-making process for the voter, the taxpayer, the government official, the business manager, and the investor. This edition, like the preceding one, is designed for the first college-level course in accounting. In this course, instructors often recognize three general groups of students: those who stand at the threshold of preparation for a career in accounting, students of business administration who need a good understanding of accounting as an important element of the total business information system, and students from a variety of other disciplines who will find the ability to use and interpret accounting information a valuable accomplishment. During the process of revision we have tried to keep in mind the needs and interests of all three groups.

A new edition provides authors with an opportunity to add new material, to condense the coverage of topics that have declined in relative importance, to reorganize portions of the book to improve instructional efficiency, and to refine and polish the treatment of basic subject matter. We have tried to do all these things in this fourth edition.

New features of this edition

Among the many new features of this edition are:

1 Illustrative cases—brief descriptions of interesting business situations which tie important concepts in the textbook to events in the "real world."
2 Learning objectives for each chapter, designed to focus students' attention upon the most important topics and concepts.
3 Increased flexibility through the use of optional appendixes (with separate problem material) to cover the specialized topics of present value computations and consolidated financial statements.
4 New, open text design to enhance readability, with an increased number of diagrams to present concepts visually.
5 An Instructor's Guide (separate from the Solutions Manual), with topical outlines of each chapter, an assignment guide indicating topics covered in each exercise and problem, and personal comments and observations by the authors on specific aspects of the text and of the introductory accounting course. Also included are solutions to the two parallel sets of Achievement Tests and Comprehensive Examinations.
6 Both printed and computer-based test banks with examination material arranged chapter-by-chapter for the entire text.
7 An increased number of single-concept problems and decision-oriented problems.
8 Thorough review of all problem material to assure emphasis of key topics and to eliminate unnecessary mathematical complexity.
9 A new appendix following Chapter 13 summarizing in one location the various applications of present value and demonstrating the use of present value tables.
10 A new appendix following Chapter 14 presenting an introductory level discussion of the basic concepts of consolidated financial statements.
11 Coverage of the accelerated cost recovery system (ACRS) now used to depreciate newly acquired assets for income tax purposes.
12 A discussion of the nature and purpose of reversing entries.
13 Perspective—careful effort throughout the text and problems to utilize current and realistic prices, interest rates, and profit levels.

Features carried forward from prior editions

Special qualities that are carried forward from prior editions include:

1 Depth of coverage. Topics are covered in a depth which will qualify the student for subsequent course work in accounting.
2 A reputation for accuracy in all problem material and solutions. All problems, solutions, and supplementary materials developed and tested first-hand by the authors in their own classes for introductory accounting students. This personal attention to accuracy is supplemented by independent testing by other accounting faculty.

3 People-oriented problems which depict the hard decisions that must be made by men and women acting as managers, investors, and in other roles.
4 For each chapter, a demonstration problem, a business decision problem, and a glossary of key terms introduced or emphasized in the chapter.
5 Emphasis on the impact of inflation upon accounting information.
6 The concept of present value, presented in clear and understandable terms, integrated into the discussions of the valuation of assets and liabilities.
7 Emphasis on internal control—how a business of any size can strengthen its system of internal control.
8 Evaluation of corporate profits. Are they adequate? Are they reasonable? What are the appropriate yardsticks?
9 Careful integration into the text and problems of the latest pronouncements of the Financial Accounting Standards Board.
10 The most comprehensive package of supplementary materials of any financial accounting textbook.

New topics and extensively revised chapters

Many new topics are discussed in this fourth edition. For example Chapter 4, entitled Completion of the Accounting Cycle, now includes coverage of reversing entries. Among the new topics in Chapter 5 on merchandising transactions are the net method of recording purchases, sales tax and corporate income tax accruals, and the distinction between the single-step and multiple-step formats of the income statement. In addition, this chapter has been carefully revised and reorganized. In its new form, the chapter is shorter, yet more clearly presents the basic topics of merchandising transactions and internal control.

Chapter 10 includes up-to-date coverage of the Accelerated Cost Recovery System (ACRS) and revised discussions of depreciation methods and accounting for natural resources. Two new appendixes cover the topics of accounting applications of present value and consolidated financial statements. Chapter 14, dealing with the effects of inflation, covers the constant dollar and current cost disclosure requirements of *FASB Statement No. 33*, with emphasis on the interpretation of this information by users of financial statements. Chapter 17, on income taxes, has been thoroughly revised to reflect the many recent changes in tax laws. Included are the important implications of the Economic Recovery Tax Act, the recent reductions in tax rates, the "marriage penalty," and the proposals for future indexing of tax brackets.

In addition to covering new topics, we have revised many chapters to better target our discussions to the needs and backgrounds of introductory students. For example our coverage of corporate income statements and stockholders' equity, formerly discussed in Chapters 7 and 8, has been moved to Chapters 11 and 12, where students are better prepared to deal with these topics. The discussions of discontinued operations, extraordinary items, and earnings per share have been revised to emphasize the interpretation of this information rather than the technical aspects of its presentation. Chapter 16, Analysis and

Interpretation of Financial Statements, includes real-world examples involving well-known corporations in order to acquaint students with realistic levels of business profits.

Supplementary materials

A full assortment of supplementary materials accompanies this text:

1 Solutions manual. A comprehensive manual containing answers to all review questions, exercises, problems, and Business Decision Problems contained in the text, along with a complete solution to the practice set.

In the development of problem material for this book, special attention has been given to the inclusion of problems of varying length and difficulty. By referring to the time estimates, difficulty ratings, and problem descriptions in the *Solutions Manual,* instructors can choose problems that best fit the level, scope, and emphasis of the course they are offering.

2 Two parallel sets of *Achievement Tests* and *Comprehensive Examinations.* Each set consists of four Achievement Tests with each test covering three or four chapters; the Comprehensive Examination covers the entire text and may be used as a final examination.

3 An instructor's guide. This new separate manual includes the following three sections for each chapter of the textbook:

a A brief topical outline of the chapter listing in logical sequence the topics the authors like to discuss in class.

b An assignment guide correlating specific exercises and problems with various topics covered in the chapter.

c Comments and observations.

The "Comments and observations" sections indicate the authors' personal views as to relative importance of topics and identify topics with which some students have difficulty. Specific exercises and problems are recommended to demonstrate certain points. Many of these sections include "Asides," introducing real-world situations (not included in the text) that are useful in classroom discussions. Also included are solutions to the parallel sets of Achievement Tests and Comprehensive Examination.

4 An examination question manual. With an abundance of test questions and exercises arranged chapter by chapter for the entire text, this examination booklet will be a most useful source for instructors who prefer to assemble their own examinations. The questions in this book are printed in an $8\frac{1}{2} \times 11$ format and can be torn out and copied to prepare individual examinations. All the questions and exercises in this manual are available on the EXAMINER system, a computerized test-generation system. Complete instructions for implementing the system are contained in the examination question manual.

5 A self-study guide. Written by the authors, the *Study Guide* enables students to measure their progress by immediate feedback. This self-study guide includes an outline of the most important points in each chapter, an abundance of objective questions, and several short exercises for each chapter. In the back of the self-study guide are answers to questions and solutions to exercises to help students evaluate their understanding of the subject. The self-study guide will also be useful in classroom discussions and for review by students before examinations.

6 *Working papers.* A soft-cover book of ***partially filled-in working papers*** for the problem material is published separately from the text. On these work sheets, the problem headings and some preliminary data have been entered to save students much of the mechanical pencil-pushing inherent in problem assignments.

7 *Practice set.* The practice set available with the preceding edition has been completely revised. Designed for use after completing Chapter 6 of the text, the practice set is now bound in two separate books, making it easier for students to journalize transactions, post entries, and prepare financial statements.

8 *Checklist of key figures for problems.* This list appears on the front and back inside covers of this book. The purpose of the checklist is to aid students in verifying their problem solutions and in discovering their own errors.

9 *Transparencies of problem solutions.* This is a visual aid prepared by the publisher for the instructor who wishes to display in a classroom the complete solutions to any or all problems.

10 *Visual classroom displays.* Sixteen special transparencies have been produced for use in the classroom to illustrate such concepts as closing entries, the preparation of a work sheet, and the use of controlling accounts and subsidiary ledgers.

Contributions by others

We want to express our sincere thanks to the many users of preceding editions who offered helpful suggestions for this edition. Especially helpful was the advice received from Professor Sarah L. Adams, California State University, Chico; Professor Harold L. Cannon, State University of New York at Albany; Professor Joseph M. Conder, Indiana University Southeast; Professor Richard E. Czarnecki, The University of Michigan-Dearborn; Professor Howard Felt, Temple University; Professor Tom Hallinan, Portland Community College; Professor Orville R. Keister, The University of Akron; Professor Hans E. Klein, University of Massachusetts-Boston; Professor John A. Miller, Jr., St. Louis Community College at Florissant Valley; Professor Phyllis L. Mirchin, Monclair State College; Professor G. Kenneth Nelson, Penn State University; and Professor Jean Tillery, Emory University.

We are keenly aware of the expert attention given this book and its many supplements by the editorial staff of McGraw-Hill, especially Ed Hanson and Don Mason.

Our special thanks go to Professor John A. Miller, Jr., St. Louis Community College at Florissant Valley, and Professor Gail Sergenian, Pace University, for assisting us in the proof stages of this edition by reviewing the end-of-chapter problems and text examples for accuracy.

The assistance of Nicholas Gikas and Steve Burns was most helpful in preparation of the manuscript.

We acknowledge with appreciation permission from the American Institute of Certified Public Accountants to quote from many of its pronouncements. All quotations are copyrighted by the American Institute of Certified Public Accountants.

We also are grateful to the Financial Accounting Standards Board which granted us permission to quote from FASB Statements, Discussion Memoranda, Interpretations, and Exposure Drafts. All quotations are copyrighted © by the Financial Accounting Standards Board, High Ridge Park, Stamford, Connecticut 06905, U.S.A. and are reprinted with permission. Copies of the complete documents are available from the FASB.

Walter B. Meigs

Robert F. Meigs

1

ACCOUNTING: THE LANGUAGE OF BUSINESS

After studying this chapter you should be able to:

- Explain the role of accounting in making business decisions.
- State the purpose of an accounting system.
- Describe the work of CPAs and other accountants.
- Explain the function of the FASB.
- State two financial objectives of a business.
- Describe a balance sheet; define assets, liabilities, and owners' equity.
- Discuss the accounting principles involved in asset valuation.
- Indicate the effects of various transactions upon the accounting equation and the balance sheet.

What is accounting? Many people think of accounting as a highly technical field which can be understood only by professional accountants. Actually, nearly everyone practices accounting in one form or another on an almost daily basis. Accounting is the art of measuring, communicating, and interpreting financial activity. Whether you are preparing a household budget, balancing your checkbook, preparing your income tax return, or running General Motors, you are working with accounting concepts and accounting information.

Accounting has often been called the "language of business." In recent years, corporate profits have become a topic of considerable public interest. What are "corporate profits"? What levels of corporate profits are necessary to finance the development of new products, new jobs, and economic growth? One cannot hope to answer such questions without understanding the accounting concepts and terms involved in the measurement of income.

1

Since a language is a means of social communication, it is logical that a language should change to meet the changing needs of society. In accounting, too, changes and improvements are continually being made. For example, as society has become increasingly interested in measuring the profitability of business organizations, accounting concepts and techniques have been changing to make such measurements more meaningful and more reliable.

We live in an era of accountability. Although accounting has made its most dramatic progress in the field of business, the accounting function is vital to every unit of our society. Individuals must account for their income. Large corporations are accountable to their stockholders, to governmental agencies, and to the public. The federal government, the states, the cities, the school districts: all must use accounting as a basis for controlling their resources and measuring their accomplishments. Accounting is equally essential to the successful operation of a business, a university, a fraternity, a social program, or a city.

In every election the voters must make decisions at the ballot box on issues involving accounting concepts; therefore, some knowledge of accounting is needed by all citizens if they are to act intelligently in meeting the challenges of our society. The objective of this text is to help you develop your knowledge of accounting and your ability to use accounting information in making economic decisions.

THE PURPOSE AND NATURE OF ACCOUNTING

The underlying purpose of accounting is to provide financial information about an economic entity. In this book the economic entity we concentrate upon is a business enterprise. The financial information provided by an accounting system is needed by managerial decision makers to help them plan and control the activities of the economic entity. Financial information is also needed by *outsiders*—owners, creditors, potential investors, the government, and the public— who have supplied money to the business or who have some other interest in the business that will be served by information about its financial position and operating results.

A system for creating accounting information

In order to provide useful financial information about a business enterprise, we need some means of keeping track of the daily business activities and then summarizing the results in accounting reports. The methods used by a business to keep records of its financial activities and to summarize these activities in periodic accounting reports comprise the *accounting system.*

The first function of an accounting system is to create a systematic record of the daily business activity, in terms of money. For example, goods and services are purchased and sold, credit is extended to customers, debts are incurred, and cash is received and paid out. These *transactions* are typical of business events which can be expressed *in monetary terms,* and must be entered in accounting records. The *recording* process may be performed in many ways: that is, by writing with pen or pencil, by printing with mechanical or electronic equipment, or by punching holes or making magnetic impressions on cards or tape. Of course, not all business events can be measured and described in monetary terms. Therefore, we do not show in the accounting records such events as the appointment of a new chief executive or the signing of a labor contract.

In addition to compiling a narrative record of events as they occur, we *classify* transactions and events into related groups or categories. Classification enables us to reduce a mass of detail into compact and usable form. For example, grouping all transactions in which cash is received or paid out is a logical step in developing useful information about the cash position of a business enterprise.

To organize accounting information in a useful form, we *summarize* the classified information into concise accounting reports designed to meet the information needs of decision makers.

These three steps we have described—recording, classifying, and summarizing—are the means of creating accounting information. It is important, however, to recognize that the accounting process is not limited to the function of *creating* information. It also involves *communicating* this information to interested parties and *interpreting* accounting information as it relates to specific business decisions.

Often we will want to compare the financial statements of Company A with those of Company B. From this comparison, we can determine which company is the more profitable, which is financially stronger, and which offers the better chance of future success. You can benefit personally by making this kind of analysis of a company you are considering going to work for—or investing in.

Communicating accounting information—Who uses accounting reports?

An accounting system must provide information to managers and also to a number of outsiders who have an interest in the financial activities of the business enterprise. The major types of accounting reports which are developed by the accounting system of a business enterprise and the parties receiving this information are illustrated in the diagram on page 4.

Accounting information is user-oriented

The persons receiving accounting reports are termed the *users* of accounting information. The type of information that a specific user will require depends upon the kinds of decisions that person must make. For example, managers need detailed information about daily operating costs for the purpose of controlling the operations of the business and setting reasonable selling prices. Outsiders, on the other hand, usually need summarized information concerning resources on hand and information on operating results for the past year to use in making investment decisions, levying income taxes, or making regulatory decisions.

Since the information needs of various users differ, it follows that the account-

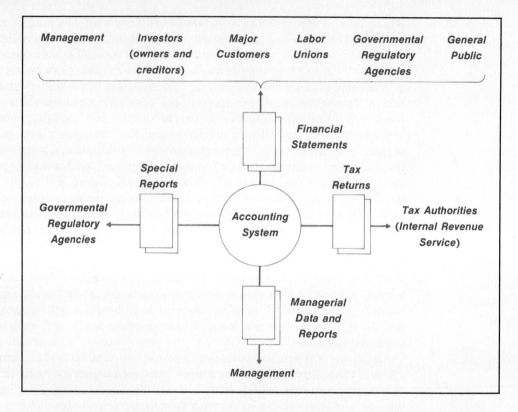

ing system of a business entity must be able to provide various types of accounting reports. The information in these reports must be presented in accordance with certain "ground rules" and assumptions, so that users of the reports will be able to interpret the information properly. For example, if a report indicates that a business owns land with an accounting value of $90,000, what does this dollar amount represent? Is it the original cost of the land to the business, the current market value of the land, or the assessed value for purposes of levying property taxes? Obviously the user of any accounting report needs to understand the standards and assumptions which have been used in preparing that report. In turn, the standards employed in the preparation of an accounting report must relate to the information needs of the user.

Financial statements   Among the most important types of accounting reports are financial statements. Financial statements are useful to management and also are the main source of financial information to persons outside the business enterprise. These statements are concise, perhaps only three or four pages for a large business. They summarize the business transactions of a specific time period such as a month or a year. Financial statements show the *financial position* of the business at the time of the report and also the *operating results* by which the business arrived at this position.

The basic purpose of financial statements is to assist decision makers in evaluating the financial strength, profitability, and future prospects of a business entity. Thus, managers, investors, major customers, and labor all have a direct interest in these reports. Every large corporation prepares annual financial statements which are distributed to all owners of the business. In addition, these financial statements are filed with various governmental agencies.

The accounting concepts used in the preparation of financial statements are called *generally accepted accounting principles.* These principles continually change and evolve in response to changes in the business environment.

Developing accounting information in conformity with generally accepted accounting principles is called *financial accounting,* because this information summarizes the financial position and operating results of a business entity. In the first part of this book we will emphasize financial accounting concepts rather than income tax rules, reports to regulatory agencies, or internal reports to management. As we shall see, financial accounting concepts apply to all types and sizes of business organizations. These concepts are useful to decision makers in both business and government in evaluating a wide range of economic issues.

Income tax returns   The Internal Revenue Service, as well as certain state and local tax authorities, requires businesses and individuals to file annual income tax returns designed to measure taxable income. *Taxable income* is a legal concept defined by laws originating in Congress (or in state legislatures). Since Congress uses the income tax laws to achieve various social objectives as well as to finance the government, income tax laws are frequently modified or changed. Thus the rules used in preparing income tax returns may vary from one year to the next. In general, however, there is a close parallel between income tax laws and financial accounting concepts.

Managerial data and reports   In addition to financial statements, management needs much detailed accounting data for use in planning and controlling the daily operations of the business. Management also needs specialized information for long-range planning and for major decisions such as the introduction of a new product or the closing of an older plant.

Reports to regulatory agencies   The activities of many business enterprises are regulated by governmental agencies. These regulatory agencies often require special types of accounting information specifically tailored to their needs. For example, when making a decision whether to allow a rate increase by an electric company, a state utilities commission might request information about the cost to the company of producing electricity and the company's need to accumulate funds to provide service to outlying areas. In large part, however, reports to regulatory agencies are based upon generally accepted accounting principles.

Using accounting information

Accounting extends beyond the process of creating records and reports. The ultimate objective of accounting is the *use* of this information, its analysis and interpretation. Accountants are always concerned with the significance of the figures they have produced. They look for meaningful relationships between events and financial results; they study the effect of various alternatives; and they search for significant trends that may throw some light on what will happen in the future.

Interpretation and analysis are not the sole province of the accountant. If managers, investors, and creditors are to make effective use of accounting information, they too must have some understanding of how the figures were put together and what they mean. An important part of this understanding is to recognize clearly the limitations of accounting reports. A business manager, an investor, or a creditor who lacks an understanding of accounting may not realize the extent to which accounting information is based upon *estimates* rather than upon precisely accurate measurements.

The distinction between accounting and bookkeeping   Persons with little knowledge of accounting may also fail to understand the difference between accounting and bookkeeping. *Bookkeeping* means the recording of transactions, the record-making phase of accounting. The recording of transactions tends to be mechanical and repetitive; it is only a small part of the field of accounting and probably the simplest part. *Accounting* includes the design of accounting systems, preparation of financial statements, audits, cost studies, development of forecasts, income tax work, computer applications to accounting processes, and the analysis and interpretation of accounting information as an aid to making business decisions. A person might become a reasonably proficient bookkeeper in a few weeks or months; however, to become a professional accountant requires several years of study and experience.

The work of accountants

Accountants tend to specialize in a given subarea of the discipline just as attorneys and members of other professions do. In terms of career opportunities, the field of accounting may be divided into three broad areas: (1) the public accounting profession, (2) private accounting, and (3) governmental accounting.

Public accounting

Certified public accountants are independent professional persons comparable to attorneys or physicians, who offer accounting services to clients for a fee. The *CPA certificate* is a license to practice granted by the state on the basis of a rigorous examination and evidence of practical experience. All states require that candidates pass an examination prepared and administered on a national basis twice each year by the American Institute of Certified Public Accountants. Requirements as to education and practical experience differ somewhat among the various states.

Auditing   The principal function of CPAs is auditing. How do people outside a business entity—owners, creditors, government officials, and other interested parties—know that the financial statements prepared by a company's management are reliable and complete? In large part, these outsiders rely upon *audits* performed by a CPA firm which is *independent* of the company issuing the financial statements.

To perform an audit of a business, a firm of certified public accountants makes a careful study of the accounting system and gathers evidence both from within the business and from outside sources. This evidence enables the CPA firm to express its professional *opinion* as to the fairness and reliability of the financial statements. Persons outside the business, such as bankers and investors who rely upon financial statements for information, attach great importance to the annual *audit report* by the CPA firm. The *independent* status of a CPA firm retained to make an annual audit is just as important as its technical competence in assuring outsiders that the financial statements prepared by management disclose all relevant information and provide a fair picture of the company's financial position and operating results.

Income tax services An important element of decision making by business executives is consideration of the income tax consequences of each alternative course of action. The CPA is often called upon for "tax planning," which will show how a future transaction such as the acquisition of new equipment may be arranged in a manner that will hold income taxes to a minimum amount. The CPA is also frequently retained to prepare the federal and state income tax returns. To render tax services, the CPA must have extensive knowledge of tax statutes, regulations, and court decisions, as well as a thorough knowledge of accounting.

Management advisory services In recent years many CPA firms have expanded into management consulting work. Separate departments, called management service departments, have been created to render advisory services to clients over a broad range of administrative and operating problems. For example, these services might include study of the desirability of a merger with another company, the creation of a pension plan for employees, or the researching of a foreign market for the company's products.

Private accounting

In contrast to the CPA in public practice who serves many clients, an accountant in private industry is employed by a single enterprise. The chief accounting officer of a medium-sized or large business is usually called the *controller,* in recognition of the fact that one of the primary uses of accounting data is to aid in controlling business operations. The controller manages the work of the accounting staff. He or she is also a part of the top management team charged with the task of running the business, setting its objectives, and seeing that these objectives are met.

The accountants in a private business, large or small, must record transactions and prepare periodic financial statements from accounting records. Within this broad area, a number of specialized phases of accounting have developed. Among the more important of these are:

Design of accounting systems   Although the same basic accounting principles are applicable to all types of business, each enterprise requires an individually tailored accounting system. This system includes accounting forms, records, instruction manuals, flow charts, computer programs, and reports to fit the particular needs of the business. Designing an accounting system and putting it into operation are thus specialized phases of accounting.

Cost accounting   Knowing the cost of a particular product is vital to the efficient management of a business. For example, an automobile manufacturer needs to know the cost of each type of car produced. Knowing the cost of each manufacturing process (such as painting an automobile) or the cost of any business operation (such as an employee training program) is also essential to making sound business decisions. The phase of accounting particularly concerned with collecting and interpreting cost data is called *cost accounting*.

Financial forecasting   A financial forecast (or budget) is a plan of financial operations for some future period, expressed in monetary terms. By using a forecast, management is able to make comparisons between *planned operations* and *actual results achieved*. A forecast is thus an attempt to preview operating results before the actual transactions have taken place. A forecast is a particularly valuable tool for the controller because it provides each division of the business with a specific goal, and because it gives management a means of measuring the efficiency of performance throughout the company.

Income tax accounting   As the income tax laws have become more complex, both internal accountants and independent public accountants have devoted more time to problems of taxation. Although many companies rely largely on CPA firms for tax planning and the preparation of income tax returns, larger companies also maintain their own tax departments.

Internal auditing   Most large corporations maintain staffs of *internal auditors* with the responsibility of evaluating the efficiency of operations and determining whether company policies are being followed consistently in all divisions of the corporation. The internal auditor, in contrast to the independent auditor or CPA, is not responsible for determining the overall fairness of the company's annual financial statements.

Management accounting   Keep in mind that the accounting system provides information for both external and internal use. The external reporting function has already been touched upon in our discussion of a CPA firm's independent audit of annual financial statements. The *internal* reporting function of an accounting system is sometimes called *management accounting;* it gives managers information needed for daily operations and also for long-range planning.

Management accounting utilizes the techniques of both cost accounting and forecasting to achieve its goal of helping executives formulate both short-range and long-range plans, to measure success in carrying out these plans, to identify problems requiring executive attention, and to choose among the alternative methods of attaining company objectives. At every organizational level of a company, specific problems arise for which accounting information is needed to help define the problem, identify alternative courses of action, and make a choice among these alternatives.

Certificate in Management Accounting   The Institute of Management Accounting offers a program leading to a Certificate in Management Accounting. This certificate is a recognition of an individual's knowledge and competence in management accounting. To qualify, one must pass a professional examination and meet specified standards as to education and professional experience.

Governmental accounting

Government officials rely on financial information to help them direct the affairs of their agencies just as the executives of corporations do. Many governmental accounting problems are similar to those applicable to private industry. In other respects, however, accounting for governmental affairs requires a somewhat different approach because the objective of earning a profit is absent from public affairs. Universities, hospitals, churches, and other not-for-profit institutions also follow a pattern of accounting that is similar to governmental accounting.

Internal Revenue Service   One of the governmental agencies which perform extensive accounting work is the Internal Revenue Service (IRS). The IRS handles the millions of income tax returns filed by individuals and corporations, and frequently performs auditing functions relating to these income tax returns and the accounting records on which they are based.

Securities and Exchange Commission   Another governmental agency deeply involved in accounting is the Securities and Exchange Commission (SEC). The SEC establishes requirements regarding the content of financial statements and the reporting standards to be followed. All corporations which offer securities for sale to the public must file annually with the SEC audited financial statements meeting these requirements.

Development of accounting standards—the FASB

Research to develop accounting principles and practices which will keep pace with changes in the economic and political environment is a major activity of professional accountants and accounting educators. In the United States four groups which have been influential in the improvement of financial reporting and accounting practices are the Financial Accounting Standards Board, the

American Institute of Certified Public Accountants, the Securities and Exchange Commission, and the American Accounting Association.

Of special importance in establishing generally accepted accounting principles is the Financial Accounting Standards Board, known as the FASB. The FASB consists of seven full-time members, including representatives from public accounting, industry, government, and accounting education. In addition to conducting extensive research, the FASB issues *Statements of Financial Accounting Standards,* which represent authoritative expressions of generally accepted accounting principles.

Note that the FASB is part of the private sector of the economy and not a government agency. The development of accounting standards in the United States has traditionally been carried on in the private sector although the government, acting through the SEC, has exercised great influence on the FASB and other groups concerned with accounting research and standards of financial reporting.

The contribution of the FASB and the other groups mentioned above will be considered in later chapters. At this point we merely want to emphasize that accounting is not a closed system or a fixed set of rules, but a constantly evolving body of knowledge. As we explore accounting principles and related practices in this book, you will become aware of certain problems and conflicts for which fully satisfactory answers are yet to be developed. The need for further research is apparent despite the fact that present-day American accounting practices and standards of financial reporting are by far the best achieved anywhere at any time.

Two primary business objectives

The management of every business must keep foremost in its thinking two primary objectives. The first is to earn a profit. The second is to stay solvent, that is, to have on hand sufficient cash to pay debts as they fall due. Profits and solvency, of course, are not the only objectives of business managers. There are many others, such as providing jobs for people, protecting the environment, creating new and improved products, and providing more goods and services at a lower cost. It is clear, however, that a business cannot hope to accomplish these objectives unless it meets the two basic tests of survival—operating profitably and staying solvent.

A business is a collection of resources committed by an individual or group of individuals, who hope that the investment will increase in value. Investment in any given business, however, is only one of a number of alternative investments available. If a business does not earn as large a profit as might be obtained from alternative investments, its owners will be well advised to sell or terminate the business and invest elsewhere. A business that continually operates at a loss will eventually exhaust its resources and be forced out of existence. Therefore, in order to operate successfully and to survive, the owners or managers of an enterprise must direct the business in such a way that it will earn a reasonable profit.

Business concerns that have sufficient cash to pay their debts promptly are said to be *solvent*. In contrast, a company that finds itself unable to meet its obligations as they fall due is called *insolvent*. Solvency must also be ranked as a primary objective of any enterprise, because a business that becomes insolvent may be forced by its creditors to stop operations and end its existence.

Accounting as the basis for business decisions

How do business executives know whether a company is earning profits or incurring losses? How do they know whether the company is solvent or insolvent, and whether it probably will be solvent, say, a month from today? The answer to both these questions in one word is *accounting*. Accounting is the process by which the profitability and solvency of a company can be measured. Accounting also provides information needed as a basis for making business decisions that will guide the company on a profitable and solvent course.

For specific examples of these decisions, consider the following questions. What prices should the firm set on its products? If production is increased, what effect will this have on the cost of each unit produced? Will it be necessary to borrow from the bank? How much will costs increase if a pension plan is established for employees? Is it more profitable to produce and sell product A or product B? Shall a given part be made or be bought from suppliers? Should an investment be made in new equipment? All these issues call for decisions that should depend, in part at least, upon accounting information. Suppose we turn the question around and ask: What business decisions could be made intelligently *without* the use of accounting information? Examples would be hard to find.

In large-scale business undertakings such as the manufacture of automobiles or the operation of nationwide chains of retail stores, the top executives cannot possibly have close physical contact with and knowledge of the details of operations. Consequently, these executives must depend to an even greater extent than the small business owner upon information provided by the accounting system.

We have already stressed that accounting is a means of measuring the results of business transactions and of communicating financial information. In addition, the accounting system must provide the decision maker with *predictive information* for making important business decisions in a changing world.

Internal control

Throughout this book we emphasize that business decisions of all types are based at least in part on accounting data. Management, therefore, needs assurance that the accounting data it receives are accurate and dependable. This assurance is provided in large part by developing a strong system of *internal control*. A basic principle of internal control is that no one person should handle all phases of a transaction from beginning to end. When business operations are so organized that two or more employees are required to participate in every transaction, the possibility of fraud is reduced and the work of one employee gives assurance of the accuracy of the work of another.

A system of internal control comprises all the measures taken by an organization for the purpose of (1) protecting its resources against waste, fraud, and inefficiency; (2) ensuring accuracy and reliability in accounting and operating data; (3) securing compliance with company policies; and (4) evaluating the level of performance in all divisions of the company.

A CPA firm in conducting an audit of a company will evaluate the adequacy of internal control in each area of the company's operations. The stronger the system of internal control, the more confidence the CPA can place in the integrity of the company's financial statements and accounting records. Consequently, the audit work can be performed more rapidly, with less detailed investigation of transactions, when internal controls are strong. The internal auditors also regard the study of internal control as a major part of their work. If internal controls are weak, the usual consequences are waste, fraud, inefficiency, and unprofitable operations.

Forms of business organization

A business enterprise may be organized as a *single proprietorship,* a *partnership,* or a *corporation.*

Single proprietorship A business owned by one person is called a single proprietorship. Often the owner also acts as the manager. This form of business organization is common for small retail stores and service enterprises, for farms, and for professional practices in law, medicine, and public accounting. The owner is personally liable for all debts incurred by the business. From an accounting viewpoint, however, the business is an entity separate from the proprietor.

Partnership A business owned by two or more persons voluntarily associated as partners is called a partnership. Partnerships, like single proprietorships, are widely used for small businesses and professional practices. As in the case of a single proprietorship, a partnership is not legally an entity separate from its owners; consequently, a partner is personally responsible for the debts of the partnership. From an accounting standpoint, however, a partnership is a business entity separate from the personal activities of the partners.

Corporation A business organized as a separate legal entity with ownership divided into transferable shares of capital stock is called a corporation. Capital stock certificates are issued by the corporation to each stockholder showing the number of shares he or she owns. The stockholders are free to sell all or part of these shares to other investors at any time, and this ease of transfer adds to the attractiveness of investing in a corporation.

Persons wanting to form a new corporation must file an application with state officials for a corporate charter. When this application has been approved, the corporation comes into existence as a *legal entity* separate from its owners. The important role of the corporation in our economy is based on such advantages as the ease of gathering large amounts of money, transferability of shares in ownership, limited liability of owners, and continuity of existence.

Accounting principles apply to all three forms of business organization, but are most carefully defined to aid corporations in making satisfactory financial reports to public investors. In this book we shall use the corporate form of organization as our basic model, along with some specific references to single proprietorships and partnerships.

FINANCIAL STATEMENTS:
THE STARTING POINT IN THE STUDY OF ACCOUNTING

The preparation of financial statements is not the first step in the accounting process, but it is a convenient point to begin the study of accounting. The financial statements are the means of conveying to management and to interested outsiders a concise picture of the profitability and financial position of the business. Since these financial statements are in a sense the end product of the accounting process, the student who acquires a clear understanding of the content and meaning of financial statements will be in an excellent position to appreciate the purpose of the earlier steps of recording and classifying business transactions.

The two most widely used financial statements are the *balance sheet* and the *income statement*.[1] Together, these two statements (perhaps a page each in length) summarize all the information contained in the hundreds of thousands of pages comprising the detailed accounting records of a business. In this introductory chapter and in Chapter 2, we shall explore the nature of the balance sheet, or statement of financial position, as it is sometimes called. Once we have become familiar with the form and arrangement of the balance sheet and with the meaning of technical terms such as *assets, liabilities,* and *owners' equity,* it will be as easy to read and understand a report on the financial position of a business as it is for an architect to read the blueprint of a proposed building. (We shall discuss the income statement in Chapter 3.)

The balance sheet

The purpose of a balance sheet is to show the financial position of a business *at a particular date.* Every business prepares a balance sheet at the end of the year, and most companies prepare one at the end of each month. A balance sheet consists of a listing of the assets and liabilities of a business and of the owners' equity. The following balance sheet portrays the financial position of Westside Cleaners, Inc., at December 31.

---

[1]A third financial statement, called a *statement of changes in financial position,* will be discussed later.

WESTSIDE CLEANERS, INC.
Balance Sheet
December 31, 19___

Assets		Liabilities & Stockholders' Equity		
Cash	$ 20,500	Liabilities:		
Accounts receivable	65,000	Notes payable		$ 26,000
Supplies	1,500	Accounts payable.............		36,000
Land...........................	68,000	Income taxes payable		18,000
Building	133,500	Total liabilities..............		$ 80,000
Cleaning equipment	39,000	Stockholders' equity:		
Delivery equipment	22,500	Capital stock.........	$225,000	
		Retained earnings....	45,000	270,000
Total	$350,000	Total		$350,000

Note that the balance sheet sets forth in its heading three items: (1) the name of the business, (2) the name of the financial statement "Balance Sheet," and (3) the date of the balance sheet. Below the heading is the body of the balance sheet, which consists of three distinct sections: assets, liabilities, and stockholders' equity. The remainder of this chapter is largely devoted to making clear the nature of these three sections.

Another point to note about the form of a balance sheet is that cash is always the first asset listed; it is followed by receivables, supplies, and any other assets that will soon be converted into cash or consumed in operations. Following these items are the more permanent assets, such as land, buildings, and equipment.

The liabilities of a business are always listed before the owners' equity. Each liability (such as notes payable, accounts payable, and income taxes payable) should be listed separately, followed by a total figure for liabilities.

The business entity The illustrated balance sheet refers only to the financial affairs of the business entity known as Westside Cleaners, Inc., and not to the personal financial affairs of the owners. Individual stockholders may have personal bank accounts, homes, automobiles, and investments in other businesses; but since these personal belongings are not part of the cleaning company business, they are not included in the balance sheet of this business unit.

In brief, *a business entity is an economic unit which enters into business transactions that must be recorded, summarized, and reported. The entity is regarded as separate from its owner or owners;* the entity owns its own property and has its own debts. Consequently, for each business entity there should be a separate set of accounting records. A balance sheet and an income statement are intended to portray the financial position and the operating results of a single business entity. If the owners were to intermingle their personal affairs with the transactions of the business, the resulting financial statements would be misleading and would fail to describe clearly the activities of the business entity.

Assets

Assets are economic resources which are owned by a business and are expected to benefit future operations. Assets may have definite physical form such as buildings, machinery, or merchandise. On the other hand, some assets exist not in physical or tangible form, but in the form of valuable legal claims or rights; examples are amounts due from customers, investments in government bonds, and patent rights.

One of the most basic and at the same time most controversial problems in accounting is determining the dollar values for the various assets of a business.

The cost principle   Assets such as land, buildings, merchandise, and equipment are typical of the many economic resources that will be used in producing income for the business. The prevailing accounting view is that such assets should be recorded at their cost. When we say that an asset is shown in the balance sheet at its *historical cost,* we mean the dollar amount originally paid to acquire the asset; this amount may be very different from what we would have to pay today to replace it.

For example, let us assume that a business buys a tract of land for use as a building site, paying $100,000 in cash. The amount to be entered in the accounting records as the value of the asset will be the cost of $100,000. If we assume a booming real estate market, a fair estimate of the sales value of the land 10 years later might be $250,000. Although the market price or economic value of the land has risen greatly, the accounting value as shown in the accounting records and on the balance sheet would continue unchanged at the cost of $100,000. This policy of accounting for assets at their cost is often referred to as the *cost principle* of accounting.

In reading a balance sheet, the user should bear in mind that the dollar amounts listed do not indicate the prices at which the assets could be sold, nor the prices at which they could be replaced. One useful generalization to be drawn from this discussion is that a balance sheet does not show "how much a business is worth."

The going-concern assumption   It is appropriate to ask *why* accountants do not change the recorded values of assets to correspond with changing market prices for these properties. One reason is that the land and building used to house the business are acquired for *use* and not for resale; in fact, these assets ordinarily cannot be sold without disrupting the business. The balance sheet of a business is prepared on the assumption that the business is a continuing enterprise, a "going concern." Consequently, the present estimated prices at which the land and buildings could be sold are of less importance than if these properties were intended for sale.

The objectivity principle   Another reason for using cost rather than current market values in accounting for assets is the need for a definite, factual basis for valuation. The cost for land, buildings, and many other assets purchased for cash can be rather definitely determined. Accountants use the term *objective* to describe asset valuations that are factual and can be verified by independent experts. For example, if land is shown on the balance sheet at cost, any CPA who performed an audit of the business would be able to find objective evidence that the land was actually valued at the cost incurred in acquiring it. Estimated market values, on the other hand, for assets such as buildings and specialized machinery are not factual and objective. Market values are constantly changing and estimates of the prices for which assets could be sold are largely a matter of personal opinion. Of course at the date an asset is acquired, the cost and market value are usually the same because the buyer would not pay more than the asset was worth and the seller would not take less than current market value. The bargaining process which results in the sale of an asset serves to establish both the current market value of the property and the cost to the buyer. With the passage of time, however, the current market value of assets is likely to differ considerably from the cost recorded in the owner's accounting records.

Accounting for inflation   Severe worldwide inflation in recent years has raised serious doubts as to the adequacy of the conventional cost basis in accounting for assets. When inflation becomes very severe, historical cost values for assets simply lose their relevance as a basis for making business decisions. Proposals for adjusting recorded dollar amounts to reflect changes in the value of the dollar, as shown by a price index, have been considered for many years. However, stronger interest is being shown at present in balance sheets which would show assets at *current appraised values* or *replacement costs* rather than at historical cost. The British government hs experimented extensively with the revision of corporate accounting to reflect inflation. The British approach proposes that year-end balance sheets show assets at their current value rather than at historical or original cost. Many companies in the Netherlands are now using some form of current-value accounting. In the United States, the Financial Accounting Standards Board requires that large corporations disclose the *current replacement cost* of certain assets as *supplementary information* to conventional cost-based financial statements.

Accounting concepts are not as exact and unchanging as many persons assume. To serve the needs of a fast-changing economy, accounting concepts and methods also must undergo continuous evolutionary change. As of today, however, the cost basis of valuing assets is still the generally accepted method.

The problem of valuation of assets is one of the most complex in the entire field of accounting. It is merely being introduced at this point; in later chapters we shall explore carefully some of the valuation principles applicable to the major types of assets.

Liabilities

Liabilities are debts. All business concerns have liabilities; even the largest and most successful companies find it convenient to purchase merchandise and supplies on credit rather than to pay cash at the time of each purchase. The liability arising from the purchase of goods or services on credit is called an *account payable,* and the person or company to whom the account payable is owed is called a *creditor.*

A business concern frequently finds it desirable to borrow money as a means of supplementing the funds invested by the owners, thus enabling the business to expand more rapidly. The borrowed funds may, for example, be used to buy merchandise which can be sold at a profit to the firm's customers. Or, the borrowed money might be used to buy new and more efficient machinery, thus enabling the company to turn out a larger volume of products at lower cost. When a business borrows money for any reason, a liability is incurred and the lender becomes a creditor of the business. The form of the liability when money is borrowed is usually a *note payable,* a formal written promise to pay a certain amount of money, plus interest, at a definite future time. An *account payable,* as contrasted with a *note payable,* does not involve the issuance of a formal written promise to the creditor, and it does not call for payment of interest. When a business has both notes payable and accounts payable, the two types of liabilities are shown separately in the balance sheet, with notes payable listed first. Another important form of liability for corporations is *income taxes payable.* This type of liability does not appear in the balance sheet of a single proprietorship or partnership because an unincorporated business is not a taxable entity. A figure showing the total of the liabilities should also be inserted, as shown in the balance sheet on page 14.

Owners' equity

The owners' equity in a corporation is called *stockholders' equity.* In the following discussion, we will use the broader term "owners' equity" because the concepts being presented are equally applicable to the ownership equity in corporations, partnerships, and single proprietorships.

The owners' equity in a business represents the resources invested by the owners. The equity of the owners is a *residual claim* because the claims of the creditors legally come first. If you are the owner of a business, you are entitled to whatever remains after the claims of the creditors are fully satisfied. Thus, owners' equity is equal to the total assets minus the liabilities. For example:

Westside Cleaners, Inc., has total assets of	*$350,000*
And total liabilities amounting to	*80,000*
Therefore, the owners' equity must equal	*$270,000*

Suppose that Westside Cleaners, Inc., borrows $20,000 from a bank. After recording the additional asset of $20,000 in cash and recording the new liability of $20,000 owed to the bank, we would have the following:

Westside Cleaners, Inc., now has total assets of	*$370,000*
And total liabilities are now.	*100,000*
Therefore, the owners' equity still is equal to	*$270,000*

It is apparent that the total assets of the business were increased by the act of borrowing money from a bank, but the increase in total assets was exactly offset by an increase in liabilities, and the owners' equity remained unchanged. The owners' equity in a business *is not increased* by the incurring of liabilities of any kind.

Increases in owners' equity   The owners' equity in a business comes from two sources:

1 Investment by the owners
2 Earnings from profitable operation of the business

Only the first of these two sources of owners' equity is considered in this chapter. The second source, an increase in owners' equity through earnings of the business, will be discussed in Chapter 3.

Decreases in owners' equity   Decreases in owners' equity also are caused in two ways:

1 Distribution of cash or other assets by the business to its owners
2 Losses from unprofitable operation of the business

Both causes of decreases in owners' equity will be considered in Chapter 3.

Owners' equity in corporations and single proprietorships   The ownership equity of a corporation consists of two elements: capital stock and retained earnings, as shown in the following illustration.

For a Corporation

Equity of stockholders . . .

Stockholders' equity:		
Capital stock	$1,000,000	
Retained earnings.	278,000	
Total stockholders' equity.		$1,278,000

The $1,000,000 shown under the caption *capital stock* represents the amount invested in the business by its owners. The $278,000 of *retained earnings* represents the portion of owners' equity which has been accumulated through profitable operation of the business. The corporation has chosen to retain this $278,000 in the business rather than to distribute these earnings to the stockholders as *dividends*. The total earnings of the corporation may have been considerably more than $278,000, because any earnings which were paid to stockholders as dividends would not appear on the balance sheet. The term *retained earnings* describes only the earnings which were *not* paid out in the form of dividends.

A single proprietorship is not required to maintain a distinction between invested capital and earned capital. Consequently, the balance sheet of a single proprietorship will have only one item in the owner's equity section, as illustrated on the next page.

For a Single Proprietorship

*. . . equity of a
single proprietor*

Owner's equity:

John Smith, capital *$30,000*

What is capital stock?

As previously mentioned, the caption *capital stock* in the balance sheet of a corporation represents the amount invested by the owners of the business. When the owners of a corporation invest cash or other assets in the business, the corporation issues in exchange shares of capital stock as evidence of the investor's ownership equity. Thus, the owners of a corporation are termed *stockholders.*

The basic unit of capital stock is called a *share,* but a corporation may issue capital stock certificates in denominations of 1 share, 100 shares, or any other number. The total number of shares of capital stock outstanding at any given time represents 100% ownership of the corporation. Outstanding shares are those in the hands of stockholders. The number of shares owned by an individual investor determines the extent of his or her ownership of the corporation.

Assume, for example, that Draper Corporation issues a total of 5,000 shares of capital stock to investors in exchange for cash. If we assume further that Thomas Draper acquires 500 shares of the 5,000 shares outstanding, we may say that he has a 10% interest in the corporation. Suppose that Draper now sells 200 shares to Evans. The total number of shares outstanding remains unchanged at 5,000, although Draper's percentage of ownership has declined to 6% and a new stockholder, Evans, has acquired a 4% interest in the corporation. The transfer of 200 shares from Draper to Evans had *no effect* upon the corporation's assets, liabilities, or amount of stock outstanding. The only way in which this transfer of stock affects the corporation is that the list of stockholders must be revised to show the number of shares held by each owner.

The accounting equation

A fundamental characteristic of every balance sheet is that the total figure for assets always equals the total of liabilities plus owners' equity. This agreement or balance of total assets with the total of liabilities and owners' equity is one reason for calling this financial statement a *balance sheet.* But *why* do total assets equal total equities? The answer can be given in one short paragraph:

The dollar totals on the two sides of the balance sheet are always equal because these two sides are *merely two views of the same business property.* The listing of assets shows us what things the business owns; the listing of liabilities and owners' equity tells us who supplied these resources to the business and how much each group supplied. Everything that a business owns has been supplied to it by the creditors or by the owners. Therefore, the total claims of the creditors plus the claims of the owners equal the total assets of the business.

The equality of assets on the one hand and of the claims of the creditors and the owners on the other hand is expressed in the equation:

*Fundamental
accounting
equation*

Assets = Liabilities + Owners' Equity
$350,000 = $80,000 + $270,000

The amounts listed in the equation were taken from the balance sheet illustrated on page 14. A balance sheet is simply a detailed statement of this equation. To emphasize this relationship, compare the balance sheet of Westside Cleaners, Inc., with the above equation.

To emphasize that the owners' equity is a residual element, secondary to the claims of creditors, it is often helpful to transpose the terms of the equation, as follows:

Alternative form of accounting equation

$$\textbf{Assets} - \textbf{Liabilities} = \textbf{Owners' Equity}$$
$$\$350,000 - \$80,000 = \$270,000$$

Every business transaction, no matter how simple or how complex, can be expressed in terms of its effect on the accounting equation. A thorough understanding of the equation and some practice in using it are essential to the student of accounting.

Regardless of whether a business grows or contracts, this equality between the assets and the claims against the assets is always maintained. Any increase in the amount of total assets is necessarily accompanied by an equal increase on the other side of the equation, that is, by an increase in either the liabilities or the owners' equity. Any decrease in total assets is necessarily accompanied by a corresponding decrease in liabilities or owners' equity. The continuing equality of the two sides of the balance sheet can best be illustrated by taking a brand-new business as an example and observing the effects of various transactions upon its balance sheet.

Effects of business transactions upon the balance sheet

Assume that John Green, Susan Green, and R. J. Hill organized a corporation called Greenhill Real Estate. A charter was obtained from the state authorizing the new corporaton to issue 18,000 shares of capital stock with a par value of $10 a share.[2] John and Susan Green each invested $72,000 cash and R. J. Hill invested $36,000. The entire authorized capital stock of $180,000 was therefore issued as follows: 7,200 shares to John Green, 7,200 shares to Susan Green, and 3,600 shares to R. J. Hill. The three stockholders each received a stock certificate as evidence of his or her ownership equity in the corporation.

The planned operations of the new business call for obtaining listings of houses and commercial property being offered for sale by property owners, advertising these properties, and showing them to prospective buyers. The listing agreement signed with each property owner provides that Greenhill Real Estate shall receive at the time of sale a commission equal to 6% of the sales price of the property.

The new business was begun on September 1 with the deposit of $180,000 in a bank account in the name of the business, Greenhill Real Estate. The initial balance sheet of the new business then appeared as follows:

---

[2]Par value is the amount assigned to each share of stock in accordance with legal requirements. The concept of par value is more fully explained in Chapter 11.

GREENHILL REAL ESTATE
Balance Sheet
September 1, 19___

Assets		Stockholders' Equity	
Cash	$180,000	Capital stock....................	$180,000

Beginning balance sheet of a new business

Purchase of an asset for cash   The next transaction entered into by Greenhill Real Estate was the purchase of land suitable as a site for an office. The price for the land was $141,000, and payment was made in cash on September 3. The effect of this transaction on the balance sheet was twofold: first, cash was decreased by the amount paid out; and second, a new asset, Land, was acquired. After this exchange of cash for land, the balance sheet appeared as follows:

GREENHILL REAL ESTATE
Balance Sheet
September 3, 19___

Assets		Stockholders' Equity	
Cash	$ 39,000	Capital stock....................	$180,000
Land..........................	141,000		
Total	$180,000	Total	$180,000

Balance sheet totals unchanged by purchase of land for cash

Purchase of an asset and incurring of a liability   On September 5 an opportunity arose to buy a complete office building which had to be moved to permit the construction of a freeway. A price of $36,000 was agreed upon, which included the cost of moving the building and installing it upon Greenhill Real Estate's lot. As the building was in excellent condition and would have cost approximately $60,000 to build, it was considered a very fortunate purchase.

The terms provided for an immediate cash payment of $15,000 and payment of the balance of $21,000 within 90 days. Cash was decreased $15,000, but a new asset, Building, was recorded at cost in the amount of $36,000. Total assets were thus increased by $21,000, but the total of liabilities and owners' equity was also increased as a result of recording the $21,000 account payable as a liability. After this transaction had been recorded, the balance sheet appeared as follows:

GREENHILL REAL ESTATE
Balance Sheet
September 5, 19___

Assets		Liabilities & Stockholders' Equity	
Cash	$ 24,000	Liabilities:	
Land..........................	141,000	Accounts payable.............	$ 21,000
Building	36,000	Stockholders' equity:	
		Capital stock.................	180,000
Total	$201,000	Total	$201,000

Totals increased equally by purchase of building on credit

Note that the building appears in the balance sheet at $36,000, its cost to Greenhill Real Estate. The estimate of $60,000 as the probable cost to construct such a building is irrelevant. Even if someone should offer to buy the building from Greenhill for $60,000 or more, this offer, if refused, would have no bearing on the balance sheet. Accounting records are intended to provide a historical record of *costs actually incurred;* therefore, the $36,000 price at which the building was purchased is the amount to be recorded.

Sale of an asset After the office building had been moved to Greenhill Real Estate's lot, the company decided that the lot was larger than was needed. The adjoining business, Carter's Drugstore, wanted more room for a parking area; so, on September 10, Greenhill sold a small, unused corner of the lot to Carter's Drugstore for a price of $11,000. Since the selling price was computed at the same amount per foot as the corporation had paid for the land, there was neither a profit nor a loss on the sale. No down payment was required, but it was agreed that the full price would be paid within three months. By this transaction a new asset in the form of an account receivable was acquired, but the asset Land was decreased by the same amount; consequently, there was no change in the amount of total assets. After this transaction, the balance sheet appeared as shown below:

GREENHILL REAL ESTATE
Balance Sheet
September 10, 19___

	Assets		Liabilities & Stockholders' Equity	
No change in totals by sale of land at cost	Cash	$ 24,000	Liabilities:	
	Accounts receivable	11,000	Accounts payable.............	$ 21,000
	Land...........................	130,000	Stockholders' equity:	
	Building	36,000	Capital stock.................	180,000
	Total	$201,000	Total	$201,000

In the illustration thus far, Greenhill Real Estate has an account receivable from only one debtor and an account payable to only one creditor. As the business grows, the number of debtors and creditors will increase, but the Accounts Receivable and Accounts Payable accounts will continue to be used. The additional records necessary to show the amount receivable from each debtor and the amount owing to each creditor will be explained in Chapter 6.

Purchase of an asset on credit A complete set of office furniture and equipment was purchased on credit from General Equipment, Inc., on September 14. The amount of the transaction was $5,400, and it was agreed that payment should be made later. As the result of this transaction the business owned a new asset, Office Equipment, but it also had incurred a new liability. The increase in total assets was exactly offset by the increase in liabilities. After this transaction the balance sheet appeared as follows:

GREENHILL REAL ESTATE
Balance Sheet
September 14, 19___

Assets		Liabilities & Stockholders' Equity	
Cash	$ 24,000	**Liabilities:**	
Accounts receivable	11,000	Accounts payable	$ 26,400
Land	130,000	**Stockholders' equity:**	
Building	36,000	Capital stock	180,000
Office equipment	5,400		
Total	$206,400	Total	$206,400

Totals increased by acquiring asset on credit

Collection of an account receivable On September 20, cash in the amount of $1,500 was received as partial settlement of the account receivable from Carter's Drugstore. This transaction caused cash to increase and the accounts receivable to decrease by an equal amount. In essence, this transaction was merely the exchange of one asset for another of equal value. Consequently, there was no change in the amount of total assets. After this transaction the balance sheet appeared as follows:

GREENHILL REAL ESTATE
Balance Sheet
September 20, 19___

Assets		Liabilities & Stockholders' Equity	
Cash	$ 25,500	**Liabilities:**	
Accounts receivable	9,500	Accounts payable	$ 26,400
Land	130,000	**Stockholders' equity:**	
Building	36,000	Capital stock	180,000
Office equipment	5,400		
Total	$206,400	Total	$206,400

Totals unchanged by collection of a receivable

Payment of a liability On September 30 Greenhill paid $3,000 in cash to General Equipment, Inc. This payment caused a decrease in cash and an equal decrease in liabilities. Therefore the totals of assets and equities were still in balance. After this transaction, the balance sheet appeared as follows:

GREENHILL REAL ESTATE
Balance Sheet
September 30, 19___

Assets		Liabilities & Stockholders' Equity	
Cash	$ 22,500	**Liabilities:**	
Accounts receivable	9,500	Accounts payable	$ 23,400
Land	130,000	**Stockholders' equity:**	
Building	36,000	Capital stock	180,000
Office equipment	5,400		
Total	$203,400	Total	$203,400

Totals decreased by paying a liability

The transactions which have been illustrated for the month of September were merely preliminary to the formal opening for business of Greenhill Real Estate on October 1. During September no sales were arranged by the company and no commissions were earned. Consequently, the stockholders' equity at September 30 is shown in the above balance sheet at $180,000, unchanged from the original investment on September 1. September was a month devoted exclusively to organizing the business and not to regular operations. In succeeding chapters we shall continue the example of Greenhill Real Estate by illustrating operating transactions and considering how the net income of the business can be determined.

Effect of business transactions upon the accounting equation

A balance sheet is merely a detailed expression of the accounting equation, Assets = Liabilities + Owners' Equity. To emphasize the relationship between the accounting equation and the balance sheet, let us now repeat the September transactions of Greenhill Real Estate to show the effect of each transaction upon the accounting equation. Briefly restated, the seven transactions were as follows:

Sept. **1** Issued capital stock in exchange for $180,000 cash invested in the business by the stockholders.

3 Purchased land for $141,000 cash.

5 Purchased a building for $36,000, paying $15,000 cash and incurring a liability of $21,000.

10 Sold part of the land at a price equal to cost of $11,000, collectible within three months.

14 Purchased office equipment on credit for $5,400.

20 Received $1,500 cash as partial collection of the $11,000 account receivable.

30 Paid $3,000 on accounts payable.

In the table below, each transaction is identified by date; the effect of each transaction on the accounting equation is shown, and also the new dollar balance of each item is listed. Each of the lines labeled Balances contains the same items as the balance sheet previously illustrated for the particular date. The final line in the table corresponds to the amounts in the balance sheet at the end of September. Note that the equality of the two sides of the equation was maintained throughout the recording of the transactions.

	Assets					= Liabil-ities +	Owners' Equity
	Cash +	Accounts Receiv-able +	Land +	Building +	Office Equip-ment	= Accounts + Payable	Capital Stock
Sept. 1	+$180,000						+$180,000
Sept. 3	−141,000		+$141,000				
Balances	$39,000		$141,000				$180,000
Sept. 5	−15,000			+$36,000		+$21,000	
Balances	$24,000		$141,000	$36,000		$21,000	$180,000
Sept. 10		+$11,000	−11,000				
Balances	$24,000	$11,000	$130,000	$36,000		$21,000	$180,000
Sept. 14					+$5,400	+5,400	
Balances	$24,000	$11,000	$130,000	$36,000	$5,400	$26,400	$180,000
Sept. 20	+1,500	−1,500					
Balances	$25,500	$ 9,500	$130,000	$36,000	$5,400	$26,400	$180,000
Sept. 30	−3,000					−3,000	
Balances	$22,500 +	$ 9,500 +	$130,000 +	$36,000 +	$5,400 =	$23,400 +	$180,000

USE OF FINANCIAL STATEMENTS BY OUTSIDERS

Through careful study of the financial statements of a company, it is possible for an outsider with a knowledge of accounting to obtain a fairly complete understanding of the financial position of the business and to become aware of significant changes that have occurred since the date of the preceding balance sheet. Bear in mind, however, that financial statements have limitations. As stated earlier, only those factors which can be reduced to monetary terms appear in the balance sheet. Let us consider for a moment some important business factors which are not set forth in financial statements. Perhaps a competing store has just opened for business across the street; the prospect of intensified competition in the future will not be described in the balance sheet. As another example, the health, experience, and managerial skills of the key people in the management group are extremely important in the success of a business, but these qualities cannot be measured and expressed in dollars in the balance sheet.

Bankers and other creditors

Bankers who have loaned money to a business or who are considering making such a loan are vitally interested in the balance sheet of the business. By studying the amount and kinds of assets in relation to the amount and payment dates of the liabilities, a banker can form an opinion as to the ability of the business to pay its debts promptly. The banker gives particular attention to the amount of cash and of other assets (such as accounts receivable) which will soon be converted into cash, and then compares the amount of these assets with the amount of liabilities falling due in the near future. The banker is also interested in the amount of the owners' equity, as this ownership capital serves as a protecting buffer between the banker and any losses which may befall the business. Bankers seldom are willing to make a loan unless the balance sheet and other information concerning the prospective borrower offer reasonable assurance that the loan can and will be repaid promptly at the maturity date.

Another important group making constant use of balance sheets consists of the credit managers of manufacturing and wholesaling firms, who must decide whether prospective customers are to be allowed to buy merchandise on credit. The credit manager, like the banker, studies the balance sheets of customers and prospective customers for the purpose of appraising their debt-paying ability. Credit agencies such as Dun & Bradstreet, Inc., make a business of obtaining financial statements from virtually all business concerns and appraising their debt-paying ability. The conclusions reached by these credit agencies are available to business managers willing to pay for credit reports about prospective customers.

Owners

The financial statements of corporations listed on the stock exchanges are eagerly awaited by millions of stockholders. A favorable set of financial statements may cause the market price of the company's stock to rise dramatically; an unfavorable set of financial statements may cause the bottom to fall out of the market price. Current dependable financial statements are one of the essential ingredients for successful investment in securities. Of course, financial statements are equally important in a business organized as a single proprietorship or as a partnership. The financial statements tell the owners just how successful the business has been and also summarize in concise form its present financial position.

Others interested in accounting information

In addition to owners, managers, bankers, and merchandise creditors, some other groups making use of accounting data are financial analysts, governmental agencies, employees, potential investors, and writers for business periodicals. In this chapter we have indicated the extent to which a modern industrial society depends upon accounting. Even more important, however, is a clear understanding at the outset of your study that accounting does not exist just for the sake of keeping a record or in order to fill out income tax returns and various other regulatory reports. These are but auxiliary functions. If you gain an understanding of accounting concepts, you will have acquired an analytical skill essential to the field of professional management. *The prime and vital purpose of accounting is to aid decision makers in choosing among alternative courses of action.*

KEY TERMS INTRODUCED IN CHAPTER 1

Accounting equation   Assets equal liabilities plus owners' equity. $A = L + OE$.

American Institute of Certified Public Accountants (AICPA)   The national professional association of certified public accountants (CPAs). Carries on extensive research and is influential in improving accounting standards and practices.

Assets   Economic resources owned by a business which are expected to benefit future operations.

Audit report   A report issued by the CPA firm expressing an independent professional opinion on the fairness and reliability of the financial statements of a business.

Auditing   The principal activity of a CPA. Consists of an independent examination of the accounting records and other evidence relating to a business to support the expression of an impartial expert opinion about the reliability of the financial statements.

Balance sheet   A financial statement which shows the financial position of a business entity by summarizing the assets, liabilities, and owners' equity at a specific date.

Business entity   An economic unit that enters into business transactions. For accounting purposes, the activities of the entity are regarded as separate from those of its owners.

Certificate in Management Accounting (CMA)   A designation granted to persons who have demonstrated competence in management accounting by passing an examination and meeting educational requirements.

Certified Public Accountants (CPAs)   Independent professional accountants licensed by a state to offer auditing and accounting services for a fee.

Corporation   A business organized as a separate legal entity and chartered by a state, with ownership divided into transferable shares of capital stock.

Cost accounting   A specialized field of accounting concerned with determining and controlling the cost of particular products or processes.

Cost principle   The widely used concept of valuing assets for accounting purposes at their original cost to the business.

Creditor   The person or company to whom a liability is owed.

Dividend   A distribution of cash by a corporation to its stockholders.

Financial accounting   The area of accounting which emphasizes measuring and reporting the financial position and operating results of a business entity in conformity with generally accepted accounting principles.

Financial Accounting Standards Board (FASB)   An independent group which conducts research in accounting and issues authoritative statements as to proper accounting principles and methods for reporting financial information.

Financial statements   Reports which summarize the financial position and operating results of a business (balance sheet and income statement).

Generally accepted accounting principles   The accounting concepts, measurement techniques, and standards of presentation used in financial statements. Examples include the cost principle, the going-concern assumption, and the objectivity principle.

Going-concern assumption   An assumption by accountants that a business will continue to operate indefinitely unless specific evidence to the contrary exists, as, for example, impending bankruptcy.

Internal control   All measures used by a business to guard against errors, waste, and fraud; to assure the reliability of accounting data; and to promote compliance with all company policies.

Liabilities   Debts or obligations of a business. The claims of creditors against the assets of a business.

Management accounting   The area of accounting which emphasizes developing and interpreting accounting information relevant to specific managerial decisions.

Notes payable   Liabilities evidenced by a formal written promise to pay a certain amount of money plus interest at a future date. Usually arise from borrowing.

Owners' equity   The excess of assets over liabilities. The amount of the owners' investment in a business plus profits from successful operations which have been retained in the business.

Partnership   A business owned by two or more persons voluntarily associated as partners.

Retained earnings   That portion of stockholders' equity resulting from profits which have been retained in the business rather than distributed as dividends.

Securities and Exchange Commission (SEC)   A governmental agency which reviews the financial statements and other reports of corporations which offer securities for sale to the public. Works closely with the FASB and the AICPA to improve financial reporting practices.

Single proprietorship   An unincorporated business owned by one person.

Solvency   Having enough money to pay debts as they fall due.

Stockholders' equity   The owners' equity in a corporation.

Transactions   Business events which can be measured in money and which are entered in accounting records.

DEMONSTRATION PROBLEM FOR YOUR REVIEW

The accounting data (listed alphabetically) for the Crystal Auto Wash as of August 31, 19___, are shown below. The figure for Cash is not given but it can be determined when all the available information is assembled in the form of a balance sheet.

Accounts payable..................	$ 9,000	Land.............................	$40,000
Accounts receivable	800	Machinery & equipment..........	85,000
Buildings	60,000	Notes payable	29,000
Capital stock	50,000	Retained earnings	99,400
Cash............................	?	Supplies	400
Income taxes payable	3,000		

On September 1, the following transactions occurred:
(1) Additional capital stock was issued for $15,000 cash.
(2) The accounts payable of $9,000 were paid in full. (No payment was made on the notes payable.)
(3) One-quarter of the land was sold at cost. The buyer gave a promissory note for $10,000. (Interest applicable to the note may be ignored.)
(4) Washing supplies were purchased at a cost of $2,000, to be paid for within 10 days. Washing supplies were also purchased for $600 cash from another car-washing concern which was going out of business. These supplies would have cost $1,000 if purchased through regular channels.

Instructions

a Prepare a balance sheet at August 31, 19___.

b Prepare a balance sheet at September 1, 19___.

SOLUTION TO DEMONSTRATION PROBLEM

a

CRYSTAL AUTO WASH
Balance Sheet
August 31, 19___

Assets		Liabilities & Stockholders' Equity		
Cash	$ 4,200	Liabilities:		
Accounts receivable	800	Notes payable		$ 29,000
Supplies	400	Accounts payable.............		9,000
Land..........................	40,000	Income taxes payable		3,000
Buildings	60,000	Total liabilities..............		$ 41,000
Machinery & equipment.........	85,000	Stockholders' equity:		
		Capital stock........	$50,000	
		Retained earnings ...	99,400	149,400
Total	$190,400	Total		$190,400

b

CRYSTAL AUTO WASH
Balance Sheet
September 1, 19___

Assets		Liabilities & Stockholders' Equity		
Cash	$ 9,600	Liabilities:		
Notes receivable................	10,000	Notes payable		$ 29,000
Accounts receivable	800	Accounts payable.............		2,000
Supplies	3,000	Income taxes payable		3,000
Land..........................	30,000	Total liabilities..............		$ 34,000
Buildings	60,000	Stockholders' equity:		
Machinery & equipment.........	85,000	Capital stock........	$65,000	
		Retained earnings ...	99,400	164,400
Total	$198,400	Total		$198,400

REVIEW QUESTIONS

1 In broad general terms, what is the purpose of accounting?

2 Why is a knowledge of accounting terms and concepts useful to persons other than professional accountants?

3 What is meant by the term *business transaction?*

4 What are financial statements and how do they relate to the accounting system?

5 Explain briefly why each of the following groups is interested in the financial statements of a business:

   a Creditors

   b Potential investors

   c Labor unions

6 Distinguish between *accounting* and *bookkeeping*.

7 What is the principal function of certified public accountants? What other services are commonly rendered by CPA firms?

8 Private accounting includes a number of subfields or specialized phases, of which cost accounting is one. Name four other such specialized phases of private accounting.

9 One primary objective of every business is to operate profitably. What other primary objective must be met for a business to survive? Explain.

10 Not all the significant happenings in the life of a business can be expressed in monetary terms and entered in the accounting records. Identify two or more significant events affecting a business which could not be satisfactorily measured and entered in its accounting records.

11 Information available from the accounting records provides a basis for making many business decisions. List five examples of business decisions requiring the use of accounting information.

12 State briefly the purpose of a balance sheet.

13 Define assets. List five examples.

14 State briefly two proposals which have been made to enable accounting to function better during a period of inflation.

15 Define liabilities. List two examples.

16 Mint Corporation was offered $500,000 cash for the land and buildings occupied by the business. These assets had been acquired five years ago at a price of $300,000. Mint Corporation refused the offer, but is inclined to increase the land and buildings to a total valuation of $500,000 in the balance sheet in order to show more accurately "how much the business is worth." Do you agree? Explain.

17 Explain briefly the concept of the *business entity.*

18 State the accounting equation in two alternative forms.

19 The owners' equity in a business arises from what two sources?

20 Why are the total assets shown on a balance sheet always equal to the total of the liabilities and the owners' equity?

21 Can a business transaction cause one asset to increase or decrease without affecting any other asset, liability, or the owners' equity?

22 If a transaction causes total liabilities to decrease but does not affect the owners' equity, what change, if any, will occur in total assets?

23 Give examples of transactions that would:

   a Cause one asset to increase and another asset to decrease without any effect on the liabilities or owners' equity.

   b Cause both total assets and total liabilities to increase without any effect on the owners' equity.

24 Is the Financial Accounting Standards Board (FASB) a government agency? What is its principal function?

EXERCISES

Ex. 1-1 Listed below in random order are the balance sheet items of Rivero Corporation. You are to prepare a balance sheet for the company using a similar sequence for assets as in the illustrated balance sheet on page 14. You must compute the amount for retained earnings.

Land............................	$ 90,000	Office equipment...............	$ 10,200
Accounts payable...............	43,800	Building	210,000
Accounts receivable	56,700	Capital stock..................	75,000
Retained earnings	?	Notes payable	213,600
Cash	36,300	Income taxes payable	11,400

Ex. 1-2 **a** Brick Company has total assets of $680,000 and stockholders' equity of $305,000. What is the amount of the liabilities?

b The balance sheet of Metals Corporation shows retained earnings of $70,000. The assets amount to $400,000 and are twice as large as the liabilities. What is the amount of capital stock?

c The assets of Wolf Company amounted to $600,000 on December 31 of Year 1 but increased to $750,000 by December 31 of Year 2. During the same period, liabilities increased by $20,000. The stockholders' equity at December 31 of Year 1 amounted to $100,000. What was the amount of stockholders' equity at December 31 of Year 2? Explain the basis for your answer.

Ex. 1-3 Indicate the effect of each of the following transactions upon the total assets of a business by use of the appropriate phrase: "increase total assets," "decrease total assets," "no change in total assets."
(a) Issued capital stock in exchange for land.
(b) Collected an account receivable.
(c) Made payment of a liability.
(d) Purchased an office desk on account (on credit).
(e) Borrowed money from a bank.
(f) Sold land on account (on credit) for a price equal to its cost.
(g) Sold land for cash at a price equal to its cost.
(h) Sold land for cash at a price below its cost.
(i) Sold land for cash at a price above its cost.
(j) Purchased a delivery truck at a price of $7,000, terms $1,000 cash and the balance to be paid in 30 equal monthly installments.

Ex. 1-4 For each of the following, describe a transaction that will have the required effect on elements of the accounting equation.
a Increase an asset and increase owners' equity.
b Increase an asset and increase a liability.
c Increase one asset and decrease another asset.
d Decrease an asset and decrease a liability.
e Increase one asset, decrease another asset, and increase a liability.

Ex. 1-5 List four column headings on a sheet of notebook paper as follows:

Transaction	Total Assets	Liabilities	Owners' Equity

Next, you are to identify each of the following transactions by letter on a separate line in the first column. Then indicate the effect of each transaction on the total assets, liabilities, and owners' equity by placing a plus (+) for an increase, a minus sign (−) for a decrease, or the letters (NC) for no change in the appropriate column.

(a) Purchased a typewriter on credit.
(b) Issued capital stock to a creditor in settlement of a liability.
(c) Purchased office equipment for cash.
(d) Collected an account receivable.
(e) Distributed cash as a dividend to stockholders.
(f) Paid a liability.
(g) Returned for credit some of the office equipment previously purchased on credit but not yet paid for.
(h) Sold land for a price in excess of cost.

As an example, transaction (a) would be shown as follows:

Transaction	Total Assets	Liabilities	Owners' Equity
(1)	+	+	NC

Ex. 1-6   The total assets of Skyway, Inc. amounted to $1.4 million, and its total liabilities amounted to $600,000. During the five years of its existence, Skyway, Inc., has been quite successful and has earned total profits equal to exactly one-half the $640,000 originally invested by stockholders. Of the profits earned, one-half has been distributed as dividends to stockholders; the other half has been retained in the business. Prepare the stockholders' equity section of the balance sheet, including dollar amounts.

Ex. 1-7   Certain transactions relating to Crest Corporation are listed below. For each transaction you are to determine the effect on the total assets, total liabilities, and owners' equity of Crest Corporation. Prepare your answer in tabular form, identifying each transaction by letter and using the symbols (+) for increase, (−) for decrease, and (NC) for no change. An answer is provided for the first transaction to serve as an example. Note that some of the transactions concern the personal affairs of the owner of the business, John Crest, rather than being strictly transactions of the corporation.

	Total Assets	Liabilities	Owners' Equity
a Issued capital stock to John Crest in exchange for cash..	+	NC	+
b Purchased office equipment on credit..................			
c Purchased a delivery truck for cash			
d Distributed cash as dividend to John Crest, the only stockholder...			
e Paid a liability of the business			
f Returned for credit some defective office equipment which had been purchased on credit but not yet paid for.......			
g Obtained a loan from the bank for business use			
h John Crest obtained a personal bank loan and used the money to buy additional shares of capital stock in Crest Corporation..			
i John Crest sold some shares of stock in Crest Corporation to another investor at a price in excess of cost			

Ex. 1-8   The following balance sheet of Solar Corporation is incorrect because of improper headings and the misplacement of several accounts. Prepare a corrected balance sheet.

SOLAR CORPORATION
March 31, 19___

Assets		Owners' Equity	
Retained earnings	$ 78,600	Accounts receivable	$113,400
Cash	32,700	Notes payable	206,400
Building	144,000	Supplies	4,200
Capital stock	120,000	Land..........................	81,000
Automobiles	49,500	Income taxes payable	19,800
Total	$424,800	Total	$424,800

PROBLEMS

1-1   A list of balance sheet items in random order appears below for Sugarloaf Chalet at October 31, 19___. You are to prepare a balance sheet at October 31 using a sequence for assets similar to that in the balance sheet on page 14. Include a figure for total liabilities. The figure for notes payable must be computed.

Accounts payable...............	$ 50,250	Snowmobiles...................	$ 36,900
Capital stock	240,000	Notes payable	?
Buildings	234,000	Equipment	114,500
Accounts receivable	50,625	Land..........................	110,500
Cash	43,875	Retained earnings	204,150
Income taxes payable	22,860		

1-2   Five transactions of Fremont Corporation are summarized below in equation form, with each of the five transactions identified by a letter. For each of the transactions (*a*) through (*e*), write a separate sentence explaining the nature of the transaction.

	Cash	+	Accounts Receivable	+	Land	+	Building	+	Office Equipment	=	Accounts Payable	+	Capital Stock
Balances	$3,100		$6,400		$21,000		$57,100				$ 9,100		$78,500
a	+500		−500										
Balances	$3,600		$5,900		$21,000		$57,100				$ 9,100		$78,500
b	−1,200								+$1,200				
Balances	$2,400		$5,900		$21,000		$57,100		$1,200		$ 9,100		$78,500
c	+6,000												+6,000
Balances	$8,400		$5,900		$21,000		$57,100		$1,200		$ 9,100		$84,500
d									+1,600		+1,600		
Balances	$8,400		$5,900		$21,000		$57,100		$2,800		$10,700		$84,500
e	−800								+2,400		+1,600		
Balances	$7,600	+	$5,900	+	$21,000	+	$57,100	+	$5,200	=	$12,300	+	$84,500

Column group headers: Assets = Liabilities + Owners' Equity

1-3 Shown below is a list of balance sheet items in random order for Ruby Red Farms at September 30, 19___. You are to prepare a balance sheet by using these items and computing the amount of retained earnings. Use a similar sequence of assets as in the balance sheet illustrated on page 14. Include a figure for total liabilities.

Land............................	$325,000	Fences & gates	$ 18,650
Buildings	43,500	Irrigation system................	32,180
Notes payable	295,000	Income taxes payable	5,640
Accounts receivable	12,425	Cash	9,045
Retained earnings	?	Livestock	67,100
Notes receivable................	6,029	Farm machinery	23,872
Accounts payable...............	42,830	Capital stock...................	50,000
Property taxes payable..........	4,675	Wages payable	1,010

1-4 During the period of organizing World Health Spas, Inc., a balance sheet was prepared after each transaction. By studying these successive balance sheets, you can determine what transactions have occurred. You are to prepare a list of these transactions by date of occurrence. For example, the transaction leading to the balance sheet of July 1, 19___, could be described as follows: "On July 1, 19___, issued $320,000 par value capital stock for cash."

(1)

WORLD HEALTH SPAS, INC.
Balance Sheet
July 1, 19___

Assets		**Stockholders' Equity**	
Cash	$320,000	Capital stock...................	$320,000

(2)

WORLD HEALTH SPAS, INC.
Balance Sheet
July 5, 19___

Assets		**Liabilities & Stockholders' Equity**	
Cash	$169,600	Liabilities:	
Land..........................	180,000	Notes payable	$295,000
Building	265,400	Stockholders' equity:	
		Capital stock.................	320,000
Total	$615,000	Total	$615,000

(3)

WORLD HEALTH SPAS, INC.
Balance Sheet
July 18, 19___

Assets		**Liabilities & Stockholders' Equity**	
Cash	$ 77,000	Liabilities:	
Land..........................	180,000	Notes payable	$295,000
Building	265,400	Stockholders' equity:	
Equipment.....................	92,600	Capital stock.................	320,000
Total	$615,000	Total	$615,000

(4)

WORLD HEALTH SPAS, INC.
Balance Sheet
July 31, 19___

Assets		Liabilities & Stockholders' Equity	
Cash	$ 50,700	Liabilities:	
Land..........................	180,000	Notes payable	$290,000
Building	265,400	Stockholders' equity:	
Equipment....................	113,900	Capital stock.................	320,000
Total	$610,000	Total	$610,000

1-5 The balance sheet items for Hernando's Hideaway (arranged in alphabetical order) were as follows at August 1, 19___. (You are to compute the figure for cash.)

Accounts payable................	$ 7,800	Income taxes payable	$ 3,400
Accounts receivable	630	Land..........................	77,000
Building	82,000	Notes payable	75,800
Capital stock...................	55,000	Retained earnings	62,300
Cash..........................	*31ᵀᴾ* ?	Supplies	6,100
Furniture......................	35,400		

During the next two days, the following transactions occurred: *CASH +17200*

Aug. 2 Additional capital stock was issued for $25,000 cash. The accounts payable were paid in full. (No payment was made on the notes payable or income taxes payable.)

Aug. 3 Furniture was purchased at a cost of $8,900 to be paid within 10 days. Supplies were purchased for $1,250 cash from a restaurant supply center which was going out of business. These supplies would have cost $1,890 if purchased through normal channels.

Instructions

a Prepare a balance sheet at August 1, 19___.

b Prepare a balance sheet at August 3, 19___.

1-6 From the accounts listed below, prepare a balance sheet as of June 1, 19___, for Blueline Printers, Inc. Also prepare a new balance sheet after the transaction on June 2 and a third balance sheet after the transactions on June 10.

Capital stock...................	$140,000	Printing equipment	$139,500
Retained earnings	134,000	Notes payable	75,000
Cash	18,000	Supplies	4,900
Income taxes payable	?	Accounts payable...............	14,500
Land..........................	114,000	Building	118,500

June 2 One-half the land was sold to a contractor at a price of $57,000. A down payment of $14,250 was received and the buyer signed a note agreeing to pay the balance within 10 days. (The note did not bear interest.)

June 10 Cash in the amount of $42,750 was received from the buyer of the land in final settlement of the June 2 transaction. Also on this date, all the accounts payable were paid in cash.

1-7 Hollywood Scripts is a service-type enterprise in the entertainment field. It was organized as a single proprietorship by Bradford Jones, who operates the business but has only a limited knowledge of accounting. Jones prepared the following balance sheet, which, although arranged satisfactorily, contains certain errors with respect to the concepts of business entity and asset valuation.

HOLLYWOOD SCRIPTS
Balance Sheet
November 30, 19___

Assets		Liabilities & Owner's Equity	
Cash	$ 1,150	Liabilities:	
Notes receivable................	5,000	Notes payable	$ 65,000
Accounts receivable	3,565	Accounts payable.............	36,000
Land...........................	60,000	Total liabilities..............	$101,000
Building	51,025		
Office furniture.................	6,953	Owner's equity:	
Other assets	19,265	Bradford Jones, capital	45,958
Total	$146,958	Total	$146,958

In discussion with Jones and by inspection of the accounting records, you discover the following facts.

(1) One of the notes receivable amounting to $3,000 is an IOU which Jones received in a poker game about ten years ago. The IOU bears only the initials B.K. and Jones does not know the name or address of the maker.

(2) Office furniture includes an antique desk purchased November 29 of the current year at a cost of $1,800. Jones explains that he is not required to pay for the desk until January and therefore he has not included this debt among the liabilities.

(3) Also included in the amount for office furniture is a typewriter which cost $425 but is not on hand, because Jones gave it to his son as a birthday present.

(4) The "Other assets" of $19,265 represents the total amount of income taxes Jones has paid the federal government over a period of years. Jones explains that he considers the income tax law to be unconstitutional and that a friend who attends law school will help Jones recover the taxes paid as soon as he completes his legal education.

(5) The asset land was acquired at a cost of $40,000, but was increased to a valuation of $60,000 when a friend of Jones offered to pay that much for it if Jones would move the building off the lot.

Instructions

a Prepare a corrected balance sheet at November 30, 19___. (Since the business is organized as a single proprietorship, the owner's equity section of the balance sheet should contain only one account, entitled Bradford Jones, capital.)

b For each of the five numbered items above, use a separate numbered paragraph to explain whether the treatment followed by Jones is in accord with generally accepted accounting principles.

1-8   Linda Shields and Mark Ryan own all the capital stock of Seaview Apartment Service, Inc. Both stockholders also work full time in the business. The company performs management services for apartment house owners, including finding tenants, collecting rents, and doing maintenance and repair work.

When the business was organized, Shields and Ryan invested a total of $50,000 to acquire the capital stock. At December 31, Year 1, a partial list of the corporation's balance sheet items included cash of $14,900, office equipment of $5,300, accounts payable of $15,300, and income taxes payable of $2,100. Additional information concerning the corporation's financial position and operations appears in the following six numbered paragraphs. Some of this information should be included in the balance sheet; some should not.

(1) Earlier in Year 1, the corporation purchased an office building from Shields at a price of $37,000 for the land and $62,000 for the building. Shields had acquired the property several years ago at a cost of $20,000 for the land and $45,000 for the building. At December 31, Year 1, Shields and Ryan estimated that the land was worth $42,000 and the building was worth $65,000. The corporation owes Shields a $44,000 note payable in connection with the purchase of the property.

(2) While working, Shields drives her own automobile, which cost $7,600. Ryan uses a car owned by the corporation, which cost $5,200.

(3) One of the apartment houses managed by the company is owned by Ryan. Ryan acquired the property at a cost of $90,000 for the land and $180,000 for the building.

(4) Company records show a $1,400 account receivable from Ryan and $18,400 accounts receivable from other clients.

(5) Shields has a $10,000 bank account in the same bank used by the corporation. She explains that if the corporation should run out of cash, it may use that $10,000 and repay her later.

(6) Company records have not been properly maintained, and the amount of retained earnings is not known. (You can compute this amount as a final step in preparing the balance sheet.)

Instructions

a Prepare a balance sheet for the business entity Seaview Apartment Service, Inc., at December 31, Year 1.

b For each of the notes numbered (1) through (5) above, explain your reasoning in deciding whether or not to include the items on the balance sheet and in determining the proper dollar valuation.

BUSINESS DECISION PROBLEM 1

Mile Corporation and Lee Corporation are in the same line of business and both were recently organized, so it may be assumed that the recorded costs for assets are close to current market values. The balance sheets for the two companies are as follows at July 31, 19____:

MILE CORPORATION
Balance Sheet
July 31, 19___

Assets		Liabilities & Stockholders' Equity		
Cash	$20,000	Liabilities:		
Accounts receivable	28,000	Notes payable (due in		
Land	27,200	60 days)		$14,400
Building	18,000	Accounts payable		9,600
Office equipment	1,200	Total liabilities		$24,000
		Stockholders' equity:		
		Capital stock	$60,000	
		Retained earnings ...	10,400	70,400
Total	$94,400	Total		$94,400

LEE CORPORATION
Balance Sheet
July 31, 19___

Assets		Liabilities & Stockholders' Equity		
Cash	$ 4,800	Liabilities:		
Accounts receivable	9,600	Notes payable (due in		
Land	96,000	60 days)		$ 62,400
Building	60,000	Accounts payable		43,200
Office equipment	12,000	Total liabilities		$105,600
		Stockholders' equity:		
		Capital stock	$72,000	
		Retained earnings ..	4,800	76,800
Total	$182,400	Total		$182,400

Instructions

a Assume that you are a banker and that each company had applied to you for a 90-day loan of $12,000. Which would you consider to be the more favorable prospect? Explain your answer fully.

b Assume that you are an investor considering purchasing all the capital stock of one or both of the companies. For which business would you be willing to pay the higher price? Do you see any indication of a financial crisis which you might face shortly after buying either company? Explain your answer fully. (It is recognized that for either decision, additional information would be useful, but you are to reach your decision on the basis of the information available.)

2

Recording Changes in Financial Position

After studying this chapter you should be able to:

- Describe a ledger and a ledger account. List the elements that comprise a T account.
- State the rules of debit and credit for balance sheet accounts.
- Explain the double-entry system of accounting.
- Explain the purpose of a journal and its relationship to the ledger.
- Prepare journal entries to record common business transactions affecting balance sheet accounts.
- Transfer (post) information from the journal to ledger accounts.
- Prepare a trial balance and explain its uses and limitations.

Many business concerns have several hundred or even several thousand business transactions each day. It would obviously be impracticable to prepare a balance sheet after each transaction, and it is quite unnecessary to do so. Instead, the many individual transactions are recorded in the accounting records and, at the end of the month or other accounting period, a balance sheet is prepared from these records. The purpose of this chapter is to demonstrate how business transactions are analyzed, entered in the accounting records, and stored for use in preparing balance sheets and other financial reports.

The use of "accounts" for recording transactions

An accounting system includes a separate record for each item that appears in the balance sheet. For example, a separate record is kept for the asset Cash, showing all the increases and decreases in cash which result from the many transactions in which cash is received or paid. A similar record is kept for every other asset, for every liability, and for every element of owners' equity. The form of record used to record increases and decreases in a single balance sheet item is called an *account,* or sometimes a *ledger account.* All these separate accounts are usually kept in a loose-leaf binder, and the entire group of accounts is called a *ledger.*

Many businesses use computers for maintaining accounting records and store data on magnetic tapes rather than in ledgers. Nevertheless, an understanding of accounting concepts is most easily acquired by study of a manual accounting system. The knowledge gained by working with manual accounting records is readily transferable to any type of automated accounting system. For these reasons, we shall use standard written accounting records, such as ledger accounts, in our study of basic accounting concepts. These written records continue to be used by a great many businesses, but for our purposes they should be viewed as conceptual devices rather than as fixed components of an accounting system.

THE LEDGER

A ledger account is a means of bringing together in one place all the information about changes in a specific asset, a liability, or an element of owners' equity. For example, a ledger account for the asset *cash* provides a record of the amount of cash receipts, cash payments, and the current cash balance. By maintaining a Cash account, management can keep track of the amount of cash available for meeting payrolls and for making current purchases of assets or services. This record of cash is also useful in planning future operations and in advance planning of applications for bank loans. The development of the annual budget requires estimating in advance the expected receipts and payments of cash; these estimates of cash flow are naturally based to some extent on the ledger accounts showing past cash receipts and payments.

In its simplest form, an account has only three elements: (1) a title, consisting of the name of the particular asset, liability, or owners' equity; (2) a left side, which is called the *debit* side; and (3) a right side, which is called the *credit* side. This form of account, illustrated below, is called a *T account* because of its resemblance to the letter T. More complete forms of accounts will be illustrated later.

Title of Account	
Left or debit side	*Right or credit side*

T account: a ledger account in simplified form

Debit and credit entries

An amount recorded on the left or debit side of an account is called a *debit,* or a *debit entry;* an amount entered on the right or credit side is called a *credit,* or a *credit entry.* Accountants also use the words debit and credit as verbs. The act of recording a debit in an account is called *debiting* the account; the recording of a credit is called *crediting* the account.

Students beginning a course in accounting often have preconceived but erroneous notions about the meanings of the terms debit and credit. For example, to some people unacquainted with accounting, the word credit may carry a more favorable connotation than does the word debit. Such connotations have no validity in the field of accounting. Accountants use *debit* to mean an entry on the left-hand side of an account, and *credit* to mean an entry on the right-hand side. The student should therefore regard debit and credit as simple equivalents of left and right, without any hidden or subtle implications.

To illustrate the recording of debits and credits in an account, let us go back to the cash transactions of Greenhill Real Estate as illustrated in Chapter 1. When these cash transactions are recorded in an account, the receipts are listed in vertical order on the debit side of the account and the payments are listed on the credit side. The dates of the transactions may also be listed, as shown in the following illustration:

Cash

Cash transactions	9/1		180,000	9/3	141,000
entered in ledger	9/20	*22,500*	1,500	9/5	15,000
account			*181,500*	9/30	3,000
					159,000

Note that the total of the cash receipts, $181,500 is in small-size figures so that it will not be mistaken for a debit entry. The total of the cash payments (credits), amounting to $159,000, is also in small-size figures to distinguish it from the credit entries. These *footings,* or memorandum totals, are merely a convenient step in determining the amount of cash on hand at the end of the month. The difference in dollars between the total debits and the total credits in an account is called the *balance.* If the debits exceed the credits the account has a *debit balance;* if the credits exceed the debits, the account has a *credit balance.* In the illustrated Cash account, the debit total of $181,500 is larger than the credit total of $159,000; therefore, the account has a debit balance. By subtracting the credits from the debits ($181,500 − $159,000), we determine that the balance of the Cash account is $22,500. This debit balance is noted on the debit (left) side of the account. The balance of the Cash account represents the amount of cash owned by the business on September 30; in a balance sheet prepared at this date, Cash in the amount of $22,500 would be listed as an asset.

Debit balances in asset accounts   In the preceding illustration of a cash account, increases were recorded on the left or debit side of the account and decreases were recorded on the right or credit side. The increases were greater than the decreases and the result was a debit balance in the account.

All asset accounts normally have debit balances. In fact, the ownership by a business of cash, land, or any other asset indicates that the increases (debits) to that asset have been greater than the decreases (credits). It is hard to imagine an account for an asset such as land having a credit balance, as this would indicate that the business had disposed of more land than it had acquired and had reached the impossible position of having a negative amount of land.

The balance sheets previously illustrated in Chapter 1 showed all the assets on the left side of the balance sheet. The fact that assets are located on the *left* side of the balance sheet is a convenient means of remembering the rule that an increase in an asset is recorded on the *left* (debit) side of the account, and also that an asset account normally has a debit *(left-hand)* balance.

<table>
<tr><td></td><td colspan="2" align="center">*Any Asset Account*</td></tr>
<tr><td>**Asset accounts
normally have
debit balances**</td><td>*(Debit)*
Increase</td><td>*(Credit)*
Decrease</td></tr>
</table>

Credit balances in liability and owners' equity accounts   Increases in liability and owners' equity accounts are recorded by credit entries, and decreases in these accounts are recorded by debits. The relationship between entries in these accounts and their position on the balance sheet may be summed up as follows: (1) Liabilities and owners' equity belong on the *right* side of the balance sheet; (2) an increase in a liability or an owners' equity account is recorded on the *right* side of the account; and (3) liability and owners' equity accounts normally have credit *(right-hand)* balances.

<table>
<tr><td></td><td colspan="2" align="center">*Any Liability Account
or Owners' Equity Account*</td></tr>
<tr><td>**Liability accounts
and owners'
equity accounts
normally have
credit balances**</td><td>*(Debit)*
Decrease</td><td>*(Credit)*
Increase</td></tr>
</table>

The diagram on page 43 emphasizes again the relationship between the position of an account in the balance sheet and the method of recording an increase or decrease in the account. The accounts used are those previously shown in the balance sheet (page 23) prepared for Greenhill Real Estate.

Balance Sheet Accounts

Diagram of balance sheet accounts

(Left side of balance sheet) Assets	=	*(Right side of balance sheet)* Liabilities + Owners' Equity

Cash

(Debit) Increase	*(Credit)* Decrease

Accounts Payable

(Debit) Decrease	*(Credit)* Increase

Accounts Receivable

(Debit) Increase	*(Credit)* Decrease

Capital Stock

(Debit) Decrease	*(Credit)* Increase

Land

(Debit) Increase	*(Credit)* Decrease

Building

(Debit) Increase	*(Credit)* Decrease

Office Equipment

(Debit) Increase	*(Credit)* Decrease

Concise statement of the rules of debit and credit   The rules of debit and credit, which have been explained and illustrated in the preceding sections, may be concisely summarized as follows:

Mechanics of debit and credit

Asset Accounts	Liability & Owners' Equity Accounts
Increases are recorded by debits	*Increases are recorded by credits*
Decreases are recorded by credits	*Decreases are recorded by debits*

Equality of debits and credits   Every business transaction affects two or more accounts. The *double-entry system,* which is the system in almost universal use, takes its name from the fact that *equal debit and credit entries are made for every* *transaction.* If only two accounts are affected (as in the purchase of land for cash), one account, Land, is debited and the other account, Cash, is credited for the same amount. If more than two accounts are affected by a transaction, the sum of the debit entries must be equal to the sum of the credit entries. This situation was illustrated when Greenhill Real Estate purchased a building for a price of $36,000. The $36,000 debit to the asset account, Building, was exactly equal to the total of the $15,000 credit to the Cash account plus the $21,000 credit to the liability account, Accounts Payable. Since every transaction results in an equal amount of debits and credits in the ledger, it follows that the total of *all* debit entries in the ledger is equal to the total of *all* the credit entries.

Recording transactions in ledger accounts: illustration

The procedure for recording transactions in ledger accounts will be illustrated by using the September transactions of Greenhill Real Estate. Each transaction will first be analyzed in terms of increases and decreases in assets, liabilities, and stockholders' equity. Then we shall follow the rules of debit and credit in entering these increases and decreases in T accounts. Asset accounts will be shown on the left side of the page, liability and stockholders' equity accounts on the right side. For convenience in following the transactions into the ledger accounts, the letter used to identify a given transaction will also appear opposite the debit and credit entries for that transaction. This use of identifying letters is for illustrative purposes only and is not used in actual accounting practice.

Transaction (a)   The sum of $180,000 cash was invested in the business on September 1, and 18,000 shares of $10 par value capital stock were issued.

	Analysis	Rule	Entry
Recording an investment in the business	The asset Cash was increased	Increases in assets are recorded by debits	Debit: Cash, $180,000
	The stockholders' equity was increased	Increases in stockholders' equity are recorded by credits	Credit: Capital Stock, $180,000

Cash		**Capital Stock**	
9/1 (a) 180,000			9/1 (a) 180,000

Transaction (b)   On September 3, Greenhill Real Estate purchased land for cash in the amount of $141,000.

	Analysis	Rule	Entry
Purchase of land for cash	The asset Land was increased	Increases in assets are recorded by debits	Debit: Land, $141,000
	The asset Cash was decreased	Decreases in assets are recorded by credits	Credit: Cash, $141,000

Cash

9/1	180,000	9/3 (b)	141,000

Land

9/3 (b)	141,000	

Transaction (c)   On September 5, Greenhill Real Estate purchased a building from OK Company at a total price of $36,000. The terms of the purchase required a cash payment of $15,000 with the remainder of $21,000 payable within 90 days.

	Analysis	Rule	Entry
Purchase of an asset, with partial payment	A new asset, Building, was acquired	Increases in assets are recorded by debits	Debit: Building, $36,000
	The asset Cash was decreased	Decreases in assets are recorded by credits	Credit: Cash, $15,000
	A new liability, Accounts Payable, was incurred	Increases in liabilities are recorded by credits	Credit: Accounts Payable, $21,000

Cash

9/1	180,000	9/3	141,000
		9/5 (c)	15,000

Accounts Payable

	9/5 (c)	21,000

Building

9/5 (c)	36,000	

Transaction (d)   On September 10, Greenhill Real Estate sold a portion of its land on credit to Carter's Drugstore for a price of $11,000. The land was sold at its cost, so there was no gain or loss on the transaction.

	Analysis	Rule	Entry
Sale of land on credit	A new asset, Accounts Receivable, was acquired	Increases in assets are recorded by debits	Debit: Accounts Receivable, $11,000
	The asset Land was decreased	Decreases in assets are recorded by credits	Credit: Land, $11,000

Accounts Receivable

9/10	(d) 11,000		

Land

9/3	141,000	9/10	(d) 11,000

Transaction (e)   On September 14, Greenhill Real Estate purchased office equipment on credit from General Equipment, Inc., in the amount of $5,400.

	Analysis	Rule	Entry
Purchase of an asset on credit	A new asset, Office Equipment, was acquired	Increases in assets are recorded by debits	Debit: Office Equipment, $5,400
	A new liability, Accounts Payable, was incurred	Increases in liabilities are recorded by credits	Credit: Accounts Payable, $5,400

Office Equipment

9/14	(e) 5,400	

Accounts Payable

	9/5	21,000
	9/14	(e) 5,400

Transaction (f)   On September 20, cash of $1,500 was received as partial collection of the account receivable from Carter's Drugstore.

	Analysis	Rule	Entry
Collection of an account receivable	The asset Cash was increased	Increases in assets are recorded by debits	Debit: Cash, $1,500
	The asset Accounts Receivable was decreased	Decreases in assets are recorded by credits	Credit: Accounts Receivable, $1,500

Cash

9/1	180,000	9/3	141,000
9/20 (f)	1,500	9/5	15,000

Accounts Receivable

9/10	11,000	9/20 (f)	1,500

Transaction (g) A cash payment of $3,000 was made on September 30 in partial settlement of the amount owing to General Equipment, Inc.

	Analysis	Rule	Entry
Payment of a liability	**The liability Accounts Payable was decreased**	**Decreases in liabilities are recorded by debits**	**Debit: Accounts Payable, $3,000**
	The asset Cash was decreased	**Decreases in assets are recorded by credits**	**Credit: Cash, $3,000**

Cash

9/1	180,000	9/3	141,000
9/20	1,500	9/5	15,000
		9/30 (g)	3,000

Accounts Payable

9/30 (g)	3,000	9/5	21,000
		9/14	5,400

Running balance form of ledger account

The T form of account used thus far is very convenient for illustrative purposes. Details are avoided and we can concentrate on basic ideas. T accounts are also often used in advanced accounting courses and by professional accountants for preliminary analysis of a transaction. In other words, the simplicity of the T account provides a concise conceptual picture of the elements of a business transaction. In formal accounting records, however, more information is needed, and the T account is replaced in many manual accounting systems by a ledger account with special rulings, such as the following illustration of the Cash account for Greenhill Real Estate.

Ledger account with a balance column

Cash   Account No.

Date	Explanation	Ref	Debit	Credit	Balance
19— Sept. 1			180 000 00		180 000 00
3				141 000 00	39 000 00
5				15 000 00	24 000 00
20			1 500 00		25 500 00
30				3 000 00	22 500 00

The *Date* column shows the date of the transaction—which is not necessarily the same as the date the entry is made in the account. The *Explanation* column is needed only for unusual items, and in many companies it is seldom used. The *Ref* (Reference) column is used to list the page number of the journal in which the transaction is recorded, thus making it possible to trace ledger entries back to their source (a journal). The use of a *journal* is explained later in this chapter. In the *Balance* column of the account, the new balance is entered each time the account is debited or credited. Thus the current balance of the account can always be observed at a glance.

Although we shall make extensive use of this three-column running balance form of account in later chapters, there also will be many situations in which we shall continue to use T accounts to achieve simplicity in illustrating accounting principles and procedures.

The normal balance of an account

The running balance form of ledger account does not indicate specifically whether the balance of the account is a debit or credit balance. However, this causes no difficulty because we know that asset accounts normally have debit balances and that accounts for liabilities and owners' equity normally have credit balances.

The balance of any account normally results from recording more increases than decreases. In asset accounts, increases are recorded as debits, so asset accounts normally have debit balances. In liability and owners' equity accounts, increases are recorded as credits, so these accounts normally have credit balances.

Occasionally an asset account may temporarily acquire a credit balance, either as the result of an accounting error or because of an unusual transaction. For example, an account receivable may acquire a credit balance because a customer overpays his account. However, a credit balance in the Building account could be created only by an accounting error.

Sequence and numbering of ledger accounts

Accounts are usually arranged in the ledger in *financial statement order;* that is, assets first, followed by liabilities, owners' equity, revenue, and expenses. The number of accounts needed by a business will depend upon its size, the nature of its operations, and the extent to which management and regulatory agencies want detailed classification of information. An identification number is assigned to each account. A *chart of accounts* is a listing of the account titles and account numbers being used by a given business.

In the following list of accounts, certain numbers have not been assigned; these numbers are held in reserve so that additional accounts can be inserted in the ledger in proper sequence whenever such accounts become necessary. In this illustration, the numbers from 1 to 29 are used exclusively for asset accounts; numbers from 30 to 49 are used for liabilities; numbers in the 50s signify owners' equity accounts; numbers in the 60s represent revenue accounts; and numbers from 70 to 99 designate expense accounts. Revenue and expense accounts are discussed in Chapter 3. The balance sheet accounts with which we are concerned in this chapter are numbered as shown in the following brief chart of accounts.

	Account Title	Account Number
System for numbering ledger accounts	*Assets:*	
	Cash..	*1*
	Accounts Receivable...	*2*
	Land..	*20*
	Building	*22*
	Office Equipment...	*25*
	Liabilities:	
	Accounts Payable..	*30*
	Stockholders' Equity:	
	Capital Stock..	*50*
	Retained Earnings	*51*

In large businesses with many more accounts, a more elaborate numbering system would be needed. Some companies use a four-digit number for each account; each of the four digits carries special significance as to the classification of the account.

Flow of information through the accounting system

The term *transaction* was explained in Chapter 1, but a concise definition at this point may be a helpful reminder. *A transaction is a business event which can be expressed in money and must be recorded in the accounting records.* Common examples are the payment or collection of cash, a purchase or sale on credit, and the payment of dividends to stockholders. Note that a transaction has an accounting value and has an influence on the financial statements. Events such as the opening of a competing business or the retirement of an employee, although possibly of importance to the business, are not considered to be transactions and are not entered in the accounts.

Business transactions are evidenced by *source documents* such as a check, a sales ticket, or a cash register tape. These source documents are the starting point for the flow of accounting information through the accounting system into the financial statements. In our description of the accounting process thus far, emphasis has been placed on the analysis of transactions in terms of debits and credits to ledger accounts. Although transactions *could* be entered directly in ledger accounts, it is much more convenient and efficient in a manual accounting system to record the information shown on source documents first in a *journal* and later to transfer the debits and credits to ledger accounts.

THE JOURNAL

Occurrence of a business transaction

Preparation of a business document

Information entered in journal

Debits and credits posted from journal to ledger

Financial statements prepared from ledger

The journal, or book of original entry, is a chronological (day-by-day) record, showing for each transaction the debit and credit changes caused in specific ledger accounts. A brief explanation is also included for each transaction. At convenient intervals, the debit and credit entries recorded in the journal are transferred to the accounts in the ledger. The updated ledger accounts, in turn, serve as the basis from which the balance sheet and other financial statements are prepared. The flow chart on the left side of this page illustrates the sequence of steps by which information flows through an accounting system.

The unit of organization for the journal is the *transaction,* whereas the unit of organization for the ledger is the *account.* By making use of both a journal and a ledger, we achieve several advantages which would not be possible if transactions were recorded directly in ledger accounts:

1 *The journal shows all information about a transaction in one place and also provides an explanation of the transaction.* In a journal entry, the debits and credits for a given transaction are recorded together, but when the transaction is recorded in the ledger, the debits and credits are entered in different accounts. Since a ledger may contain hundreds of accounts, it would be very difficult to locate all the facts about a particular transaction by looking in the ledger. The journal is the record which shows the complete story of a transaction in one entry.

2 *The journal provides a chronological record of all the events in the life of a business.* If we want to look up the facts about a transaction of some months or years back, all we need is the date of the transaction in order to locate it in the journal.

3 *The use of a journal helps to prevent errors.* If transactions were recorded directly in the ledger, it would be very easy to make errors such as omitting the debit or the credit, or entering the debit twice or the credit twice. Such errors are not likely to be made in the journal, since the offsetting debits and credits appear together for each transaction.

The general journal: illustration of entries

Many businesses maintain several types of journals. The nature of operations and the volume of transactions in the particular business determine the number and type of journals needed. The simplest type of journal is called a *general journal* and is illustrated on page 51.

General Journal Page 1

Date		Account Titles and Explanations	LP	Debit	Credit
September journal entries for Greenhill Real Estate	19__				
Sept.	1	Cash.....................................	1	180,000	
		Capital Stock........................	50		180,000
		Issued 18,000 shares of $10 par value capital stock in exchange for cash.			
	3	Land.....................................	20	141,000	
		Cash..............................	1		141,000
		Purchased land for office site.			
	5	Building................................	22	36,0000	
		Cash..............................	1		15,000
		Accounts Payable...................	30		21,000
		Purchased building to be moved to our lot. Paid part cash; balance payable within 90 days to OK Company.			
	10	Accounts Receivable.....................	2	11,000	
		Land..............................	20		11,000
		Sold the unused part of our lot at cost to Carter's Drugstore. Due within three months.			
	14	Office Equipment	25	5,400	
		Accounts Payable...................	30		5,400
		Purchased office equipment on credit from General Equipment, Inc.			
	20	Cash.....................................	1	1,500	
		Accounts Receivable...............	2		1,500
		Collected part of receivable from Carter's Drugstore.			
	30	Accounts Payable.........................	30	3,000	
		Cash..............................	1		3,000
		Made partial payment of the liability to General Equipment, Inc.			

A general journal has only two money columns, one for debits and the other for credits; it may be used for all types of transactions. The process of recording a transaction in a journal is called *journalizing* the transaction. We have illustrated above the use of the general journal to journalize the transactions of Greenhill Real Estate which have previously been discussed.

Efficient use of a general journal requires two things: (1) ability to analyze the effect of a transaction upon assets, liabilities, and owners' equity and (2) familiarity with the standard form and arrangement of journal entries. Our primary interest is in the analytical phase of journalizing; the procedural steps can be learned quickly by observing the following points in the illustrated journal entries.

1 The year, month, and day of the first entry on the page are written in the date column. The year and month need not be repeated for subsequent entries until a new page or a new month is begun.

2 The name of the account to be debited is written on the first line of the entry and is customarily placed at the extreme left next to the date column. The amount of the debit is entered on the same line in the left-hand money column.

3 The name of the account to be credited is entered on the line below the debit entry and is indented, that is, placed about 1 inch to the right of the date column. The amount credited is entered on the same line in the right-hand money column.

4 A brief explanation of the transaction is usually begun on the line immediately below the title of the last account credited. The explanation need not be indented.

5 A blank line is left after each entry. This spacing causes each journal entry to stand out clearly as a separate unit and makes the general journal easier to read.

6 An entry which includes more than one debit or more than one credit (such as the entry on September 5) is called a *compound journal entry.* Regardless of how many debits or credits are contained in a compound journal entry, all the debits are entered before any credits are listed.

7 The LP (ledger page) column just to the left of the debit money column is left blank at the time of making the journal entry. When the debits and credits are later transferred to ledger accounts, the numbers of the ledger accounts are listed in this column to provide a convenient cross reference with the ledger.

In journalizing transactions, remember to use the exact title of the ledger accounts to be debited and credited. For example, in recording the purchase of office equipment for cash, *do not* prepare a journal entry debiting "Office Equipment Purchased" and crediting "Cash Paid Out." There are no ledger accounts with such titles. The proper journal entry would consist of a debit to *Office Equipment* and a credit to *Cash.*

A familiarity with the general journal form of describing transactions is just as essential to the study of accounting as a familiarity with plus and minus signs is to the study of mathematics. The journal entry is a *tool* for *analyzing* and *describing* the impact of various transactions upon a business entity. The ability to describe a transaction in journal entry form requires a complete understanding of the nature of the transaction and its effects upon the financial position of the business.

Posting

The process of transferring the debits and credits from the general journal to the proper ledger accounts is called *posting*. Each amount listed in the debit column of the journal is posted by entering it on the debit side of an account in the ledger, and each amount listed in the credit column of the journal is posted to the credit side of a ledger account.

The mechanics of posting may vary somewhat with the preferences of the individual. The following sequence is commonly used:

1 Locate in the ledger the first account named in the journal entry.
2 Enter in the debit column of the ledger account the amount of the debit as shown in the journal.
3 Enter the date of the transaction in the ledger account.
4 Enter in the reference column of the ledger account the number of the journal page from which the entry is being posted.
5 The recording of the debit in the ledger account is now complete. As evidence of this fact, return to the journal and enter in the LP (ledger page) column the number of the ledger account or page to which the debit was posted.
6 Repeat the posting process described in the preceding five steps for the credit side of the journal entry.

Illustration of posting   To illustrate the posting process, the journal entry for the first transaction of Greenhill Real Estate is repeated on page 54, along with the two ledger accounts affected by this entry.

Note that the Ref (Reference) column of each of the two ledger accounts illustrated contains the number 1, indicating that the posting was made from page 1 of the general journal. Entering the journal page number in the ledger account and listing the ledger page in the journal provide a cross reference between these two records. The audit of accounting records always requires looking up some journal entries to obtain more information about the amounts listed in ledger accounts. A cross reference between the ledger and journal is therefore essential to efficient audit of the records. Another advantage gained from entering in the journal the number of the account to which a posting has been made is to provide evidence throughout the posting work as to which items have been posted. Otherwise, any interruption in the posting might leave some doubt as to what had been posted.

Journalizing and posting by hand is a useful method for the study of accounting, both for problem assignments and for examinations. The manual approach is also followed in many small businesses. One shortcoming is the opportunity for error that exists whenever information is being copied from one record to another. In businesses having a large volume of transactions, the posting of ledger accounts is performed by accounting machines or by a computer, which speeds up the work and reduces errors. In these more sophisticated systems, transactions may be recorded simultaneously in both the journal and the ledger.

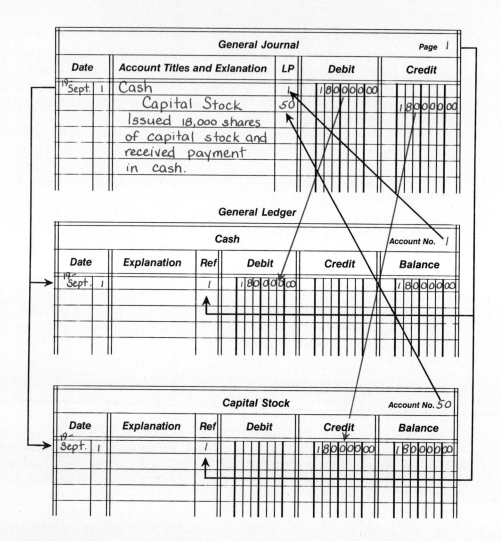

Ledger accounts after posting

After all the September transactions have been posted, the ledger of Greenhill Real Estate appears as shown on pages 55 and 56. The accounts are arranged in the ledger in balance sheet order, that is, assets first, followed by liabilities and stockholders' equity.

To conserve space in this illustration, several ledger accounts appear on a single page. In actual practice, each account occupies a separate page in the ledger.

Since equal dollar amounts of debits and credits are entered in the accounts for every transaction recorded, the sum of all the debits in the ledger must be equal to the sum of all the credits. If the computation of account balances has been accurate, it follows that the total of the accounts with debit balances must be equal to the total of the accounts with credit balances.

Ledger showing September transactions

Cash — Account No. 1

Date		Explanation	Ref	Debit	Credit	Balance
19— Sept	1		1	18000000		18000000
	3		1		14100000	3900000
	5		1		1500000	2400000
	20		1	150000		2550000
	30		1		300000	2250000

Accounts Receivable — Account No. 2

Date		Explanation	Ref	Debit	Credit	Balance
19— Sept	10		1	1100000		1100000
	20		1		150000	950000

Land — Account No. 20

Date		Explanation	Ref	Debit	Credit	Balance
19— Sept	3		1	14100000		14100000
	10		1		1100000	13000000

Building — Account No. 22

Date		Explanation	Ref	Debit	Credit	Balance
19— Sept	5		1	3600000		3600000

Office Equipment — Account No. 25

Date		Explanation	Ref	Debit	Credit	Balance
19— Sept	14		1	540000		540000

Accounts Payable					Account No. 30
Date	Explanation	Ref	Debit	Credit	Balance
19—Sept. 5		1		21 000 00	21 000 00
14		1		5 400 00	26 400 00
30		1	3 000 00		23 400 00

Capital Stock					Account No. 50
Date	Explanation	Ref	Debit	Credit	Balance
19—Sept. 1		1		180 000 00	180 000 00

THE TRIAL BALANCE

Before using the account balances to prepare financial statements, it is desirable to *prove* that the total of accounts with debit balances is in fact equal to the total of accounts with credit balances. This proof of the equality of debit and credit balances is called a *trial balance*. A trial balance is a two-column schedule listing the names and balances of all the accounts *in the order in which they appear in the ledger*. The debit balances are listed in the left-hand column and the credit balances in the right-hand column. The totals of the two columns should agree. A trial balance taken from the ledger of Greenhill Real Estate appears below.

GREENHILL REAL ESTATE
Trial Balance
September 30, 19___

Trial balance at month-end proves ledger is in balance

Cash	$ 22,500	
Accounts receivable	9,500	
Land	130,000	
Building	36,000	
Office equipment	5,400	
Accounts payable		$ 23,400
Capital stock		180,000
	$203,400	$203,400

Uses and limitations of the trial balance

The trial balance provides proof that the ledger is in balance. The agreement of the debit and credit totals of the trial balance gives assurance that:

1 Equal debits and credits have been recorded for all transactions.

2 The debit or credit balance of each account has been correctly computed.
3 The addition of the account balances in the trial balance has been correctly performed.

Suppose that the debit and credit totals of the trial balance do not agree. This situation indicates that one or more errors have been made. Typical of such errors are (1) the entering of a debit as a credit or vice versa; (2) arithmetical mistakes in balancing accounts; (3) clerical errors in copying account balances into the trial balance; (4) listing a debit balance in the credit column of the trial balance, or vice versa; and (5) errors in addition of the trial balance.

The preparation of a trial balance does *not* prove that transactions have been correctly analyzed and recorded in the proper accounts. If, for example, a receipt of cash were erroneously recorded by debiting the Land account instead of the Cash account, the trial balance would still balance. Also, if a transaction were completely omitted from the ledger, the error would not be disclosed by the trial balance. In brief, *the trial balance proves only one aspect of the ledger, and that is the equality of debits and credits.*

Despite these limitations, the trial balance is a useful device. It not only provides assurance that the ledger is in balance, but it also serves as a convenient stepping-stone for the preparation of financial statements. As explained in Chapter 1, the balance sheet is a formal statement showing the financial position of the business, intended for distribution to managers, owners, bankers, and various outsiders. The trial balance, on the other hand, is merely a working paper, useful to the accountant but not intended for distribution to others. The balance sheet and other financial statements can be prepared more conveniently from the trial balance than directly from the ledger, especially if there are a great many ledger accounts.

Locating errors

In the illustrations given thus far, the trial balances have all been in balance. Every accounting student soon discovers in working problems, however, that errors are easily made which prevent trial balances from balancing. The lack of balance may be the result of a single error or a combination of several errors. An error may have been made in adding the trial balance columns or in copying the balances from the ledger accounts. If the preparation of the trial balance has been accurate, then the error may lie in the accounting records, either in the journal or in the ledger accounts. What is the most efficient approach to locating the error or errors? There is no single technique which will give the best results every time, but the following procedures, done in sequence, will often save considerable time and effort in locating errors.

1 Prove the addition of the trial balance columns by adding these columns in the opposite direction from that previously followed.
2 If the error does not lie in addition, next determine the exact amount by which the schedule is out of balance. The amount of the discrepancy is often a clue to the source of the error. If the discrepancy is *divisible by 9,* this suggests either a *transposition* error or a *slide.* For example, assume that the Cash account

has a balance of $2,175, but in copying the balance into the trial balance the figures are **transposed** and written as $2,157. The resulting error is $18, and like all transposition errors is divisible by 9. Another common error is the slide, or incorrect placement of the decimal point, as when $2,175.00 is copied as $21.75. The resulting discrepancy in the trial balance will also be an amount divisible by 9.

To illustrate another method of using the amount of a discrepancy as a clue to locating the error, assume that the Office Equipment account has a **debit** balance of $420 but that it is erroneously listed in the **credit** column of the trial balance. This will cause a discrepancy of two times $420, or $840, in the trial balance totals. Since such errors as recording a debit in a credit column are not uncommon, it is advisable, after determining the discrepancy in the trial balance totals, to scan the columns for an amount equal to exactly **one-half** of the discrepancy. It is also advisable to look over the transactions for an item of the **exact amount** of the discrepancy. An error may have been made by recording the debit side of the transaction and forgetting to enter the credit side.

3 Compare the amounts in the trial balance with the balances in the ledger. Make sure that each ledger account balance has been included in the correct column of the trial balance.

4 Recompute the balance of each ledger account.

5 Trace all postings from the journal to the ledger accounts. As this is done, place a check mark in the journal and in the ledger after each figure verified. When the operation is completed, look through the journal and the ledger for unchecked amounts. In tracing postings, be alert not only for errors in amount but for debits entered as credits, or vice versa.

Dollar signs

Dollar signs are not used in journals or ledgers. Some accountants use dollar signs in trial balances; some do not. In this book, dollar signs are used in trial balances. Dollar signs should always be used in the balance sheet, the income statement, and other formal financial reports. In the balance sheet, for example, a dollar sign is placed by the first amount in each column and also by the final amount or total. Many accountants also place a dollar sign by each subtotal or other amount listed below an underlining. In the published financial statements of large corporations, such as those illustrated in the appendix of this book, the use of dollar signs is often limited to the first and last figures in a column.

When dollar amounts are being entered in the columnar paper used in journals and ledgers, commas and decimal points are not needed. On unruled paper, commas and decimal points should be used. Most of the problems and illustrations in this book are in even dollar amounts. In such cases the cents column can be left blank or, if desired, zeros or dashes may be used.

Accounting records in perspective

We have emphasized in this chapter the purpose of the journal and ledger and have explained how these accounting records are used. Now we need to consider how these records fit into the accounting process as a whole. It is important to keep in mind that accounting records are not an end in themselves. Just as the physician uses symbols and cryptic notation to write a prescription in the course of providing medical services, the accountant uses symbols and concise notations to interpret business transactions and to classify information about them. Although the prescription order written by the physician and the records created by the accountant are important and must be accurate and complete, they are only a means to an end. The goal of the physician is to restore the health of the patient. The goal of the accountant is to communicate accounting information to persons who will use this information as a basis for business decisions. These persons include managers, owners, potential investors, creditors, financial analysts, labor unions, and governmental agencies. They want to know the financial position of the business as shown by the balance sheet. What resources (assets) does the business have and what debts (liabilities) does it owe? These persons also want to know how profitable the business has been, as shown by the income statement. Finally, they would like to know about the future prospects of the business. Looking into the future of a business involves much uncertainty, but the accumulating and interpreting of accounting information are vitally important elements of financial forecasting.

The use of journals and ledgers, along with the double-entry system and the various symbols and technical terms, has developed over a long period of time because these devices constitute an efficient information system. On a daily basis, this information system absorbs the economic essence of many business transactions. After classifying and summarizing this mass of data, the accounting process produces concise financial statements for the use of decision makers. Remember that your study of the accounting model in the early chapters of this book will equip you to read financial statements with understanding and to make better decisions because you will be familiar with the underlying accounting concepts and processes.

KEY TERMS INTRODUCED IN CHAPTER 2

Account A record used to summarize all increases and decreases in a particular asset, such as Cash, or any other type of asset, liability, owners' equity, revenue, or expense.

Account balance The difference in dollars between the total debits and total credits in an account.

Credit An amount entered on the right-hand side of an account. A credit is used to record a decrease in an asset and an increase in a liability or owners' equity.

Credit balance The balance of an account in which the total amount of credits exceeds the total amount of debits.

Debit   An amount entered on the left-hand side of an account. A debit is used to record an increase in an asset and a decrease in a liability or in owners' equity.

Debit balance   The balance of an account in which the total amount of debits exceeds the total amount of credits.

Double-entry method   In recording transactions, the total dollar amount of debits must equal the total dollar amount of credits.

Financial statement order   The usual sequence of accounts in a ledger; that is, assets first, followed by liabilities, owners' equity, revenue, and expenses.

Footing   The total of amounts in a column.

Journal   A chronological record of transactions, showing for each transaction the debits and credits to be entered in specific ledger accounts.

Ledger   A loose-leaf book, file, or other record containing all the separate accounts of a business.

Posting   The process of transferring information from the journal to individual accounts in the ledger.

Source documents   Original evidence of transactions as, for example, checks, sales tickets, and cash register tapes.

Trial balance   A two-column schedule listing the names and the debit or credit balances of all accounts in the ledger.

DEMONSTRATION PROBLEM FOR YOUR REVIEW

Auto Parks, Inc., was organized on July 1 to operate a parking lot near a new sports arena. The following transactions occurred during July prior to the corporation beginning its regular business operations.

July   1 Issued 20,000 shares of $10 par value capital stock to the owners of the corporation in exchange for their investment of $200,000 cash.

July   2 Purchased land to be used as the parking lot for a total price of $250,000. A cash down payment of $120,000 was made and a note payable was issued for the balance of the purchase price.

July   5 Purchased a small portable building for $36,000 cash. The purchase price included installation of the building on the parking lot.

July 12 Purchased office equipment on credit from Suzuki & Co. for $6,000.

July 28 Paid $2,000 of the amount owed to Suzuki & Co.

   The account titles and account numbers used by Auto Parks, Inc., to record these transactions are:

Cash..................................	1		Notes payable.........................	30
Land..................................	20		Accounts payable......................	32
Building	22		Capital stock..........................	50
Office equipment.....................	25			

Instructions

a Prepare journal entries for the month of July.

b Post to ledger accounts of the three-column running balance form.

c Prepare a trial balance at July 31.

SOLUTION TO DEMONSTRATION PROBLEM

a   *General Journal*   Page 1

Date		Account Titles and Explanations	LP	Debit	Credit
19__					
July	1	Cash.....................................	1	200,000	
		Capital Stock........................	50		200,000
		Issued 20,000 shares of $10 par value capital stock for cash.			
	2	Land.....................................	20	250,000	
		Cash................................	1		120,000
		Notes Payable	30		130,000
		Purchased land. Paid part cash and issued a note payable for the balance.			
	5	Building.................................	22	36,000	
		Cash................................	1		36,000
		Purchased a small portable building for cash. The price included installation on the company's lot.			
	12	Office Equipment	25	6,000	
		Accounts Payable....................	32		6,000
		Purchased office equipment on credit from Suzuki & Co.			
	28	Accounts Payable.........................	32	2,000	
		Cash................................	1		2,000
		Paid part of account payable to Suzuki & Co.			

		Cash				Account No. 1
Date		Explanation	Ref	Debit	Credit	Balance
19__ July	1		1	200,000 00		200,000 00
	2		1		120,000 00	80,000 00
	5		1		36,000 00	44,000 00
	28		1		2,000 00	42,000 00

Land					Account No. 20
Date	Explanation	Ref	Debit	Credit	Balance
19— July 2		1	250000 00		250000 00

Building					Account No. 22
Date	Explanation	Ref	Debit	Credit	Balance
19— July 5		1	36000 00		36000 00

Office Equipment					Account No. 25
Date	Explanation	Ref	Debit	Credit	Balance
19— July 12		1	6000 00		6000 00

Notes Payable					Account No. 30
Date	Explanation	Ref	Debit	Credit	Balance
19— July 2		1		130000 00	130000 00

Accounts Payable					Account No. 32
Date	Explanation	Ref	Debit	Credit	Balance
19— July 12		1		6000 00	6000 00
28		1	2000 00		4000 00

Capital Stock					Account No. 50
Date	Explanation	Ref	Debit	Credit	Balance
19— July 1		1		200000 00	200000 00

AUTO PARKS, INC.
Trial Balance
July 31, 19___

Cash	$ 42,000	
Land	250,000	
Building	36,000	
Office equipment	6,000	
Notes payable		$130,000
Accounts payable		4,000
Capital stock		200,000
	$334,000	$334,000

REVIEW QUESTIONS

1 Is it true that favorable events are recorded by credits and unfavorable events by debits? Explain.

2 What is an account and how does it differ from a ledger?

3 In its simplest form, an account has only three elements or basic parts. What are these three elements?

4 What requirement is imposed by the double-entry method in the recording of any business transaction?

5 How does a T account differ from a three-column running balance form of ledger account?

6 Does the term *debit* mean increase and the term *credit* mean decrease? Explain.

7 State briefly the rules of debit and credit as applied to asset, liability, and owners' equity accounts.

8 What relationship exists between the position of an account on the balance sheet and the rules for recording increases in that account?

9 For each of the following accounts, state whether it is an asset, a liability, or owners' equity; also state whether it would normally have a debit or a credit balance: **(a)** Office Equipment, **(b)** Capital Stock, **(c)** Accounts Receivable, **(d)** Accounts Payable, **(e)** Cash, **(f)** Notes Payable, **(g)** Retained Earnings.

10 A student beginning the study of accounting prepared a trial balance in which two unusual features appeared. The Buildings account showed a credit balance of $20,000, and the Accounts Payable account a debit balance of $100. Considering each of these two abnormal balances separately, state whether the condition was the result of an error in the records or could have resulted from proper recording of an unusual transaction.

11 Explain precisely what is meant by each of the phrases listed below. Whenever appropriate, indicate whether the left or right side of an account is affected and whether an increase or decrease is indicated.

a A debit of $200 to the Cash account

b Credit balance

c Credit side of an account

d A debit of $600 to Accounts Payable

e Debit balance

f A credit of $50 to Accounts Receivable

g A debit to the Land account

12 For each of the following transactions, indicate whether the account in parentheses should be debited or credited, and give the reason for your answer.

   a Purchased a typewriter on credit, promising to make payment in full within 30 days. (Accounts Payable)

   b Purchased land for cash. (Cash)

   c Sold an old, unneeded typewriter on 30-day credit. (Office Equipment)

   d Obtained a loan of $5,000 from a bank. (Cash)

   e Issued 1,000 shares of $25 par value capital stock for cash of $25,000. (Capital Stock)

13 Compare and contrast a *journal* and a *ledger.*

14 What is the primary purpose of journal entries from the point of view of *(a)* a business entity and *(b)* an accounting student?

15 During the first week of an accounting course, one student expressed the opinion that a great deal of time could be saved if a business would record transactions directly in ledger accounts rather than entering transactions first in a journal and then posting the debit and credit amounts from the journal to the ledger. Student B agreed with this view but added that such a system should not be called double-entry bookkeeping since each transaction would be entered only once. Student C disagreed with both A and B. He argued that the use of a journal and a ledger was more efficient than entering transactions directly in ledger accounts. Furthermore, he argued that the meaning of double-entry bookkeeping did not refer to the practice of maintaining both a journal and a ledger. Evaluate the statements made by all three students.

16 Which step in the recording of transactions requires greater understanding of accounting principles: **(a)** the entering of transactions in the journal or **(b)** the posting of entries to ledger accounts?

17 What is a *compound* journal entry?

18 State two facts about the sequence of accounts in a journal entry and the use of indentation which make it easy to distinguish between a debit and a credit.

19 What purposes are served by the preparation of a trial balance?

20 List the following five items in a logical sequence to illustrate the flow of accounting information through the accounting system:

   a Information entered in journal

   b Preparation of a business document

   c Financial statements prepared from ledger

   d Occurrence of a business transaction

   e Debits and credits posted from journal to ledger

EXERCISES

Ex. 2-1   Analyze separately each of the following transactions, using the format illustrated at the end of the exercise. In each situation, explain the debit portion of the transaction before the credit portion.

   a On February 1, Ginger Denton organized a corporation to conduct business under the name of Flair Decorating Services, Inc. The corporation issued 30,000 shares of $2 par value capital stock to Denton in exchange for $60,000 cash which she invested in the business.

b On February 23, the corporation purchased an office building in an industrial park for a total price of $114,000, of which $68,000 was applicable to the land and $46,000 to the building. A cash down payment of $28,500 was made and a note payable was issued for the balance of the purchase price.

c On February 25, office equipment was purchased on credit from ADR Company at a price of $4,600. The account payable was to be paid on March 25.

d On February 28, a portion of the office equipment purchased on February 25 was found to be defective and was returned to ADR Company. ADR Company agreed that Flair Decorating Services would not be charged for the defective equipment, which had cost $750.

e On March 25, the remaining liability to ADR Company was paid in full.

Note: The type of analysis to be made is shown by the following illustration, using transaction **(a)** as an example.

a (1) The asset Cash was increased. Increases in assets are recorded by debits. Debit Cash, $60,000.

    (2) The owners' equity was increased. Increases in owners' equity are recorded by credits. Credit Capital Stock, $60,000.

Ex. 2-2   Enter the following transactions in T accounts drawn on ordinary notebook paper. Label each debit and credit with the letter identifying the transaction. Prepare a trial balance at May 31.

a On May 10, the Bluegrass Corporation was organized and issued 6,400 shares of $10 par value capital stock in exchange for $64,000 cash.

b On May 13, land was acquired for $32,000 cash.

c On May 18, a prefabricated building was purchased from E-Z Built Corporation at a cost of $38,400. A cash payment of $9,600 was made and a note payable was issued for the balance.

d On May 20, office equipment was purchased at a cost of $8,200. A cash down payment of $2,050 was made, and it was agreed that the balance should be paid within 30 days.

e On May 30, $3,200 of the amount due E-Z Built Corporation was paid.

Ex. 2-3   The first six transactions of a newly organized company appear in the following T accounts.

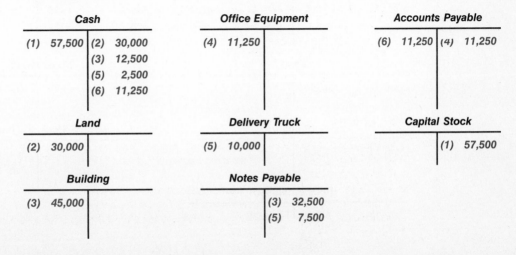

For each of the six transactions in turn, indicate the type of accounts affected (asset, liability, or owners' equity) and whether the account was increased or decreased. Arrange your answers in the form illustrated for transaction (1), shown here as an example.

	Account Debited		Account Credited	
Transaction	**Type of Account**	**Increase or Decrease**	**Type of Account**	**Increase or Decrease**
(1)	Asset	Increase	Owners' equity	Increase

Ex. 2-4 Enter the following transactions in the two-column journal of Blue Water Service Company. Include a brief explanation of the transaction as part of each journal entry. Do not include in the explanation any amounts or account titles since these are shown in the debit-credit portion of the entry.

June 1 Acquired office equipment from Bell Company for $850 cash.

June 3 Collected an account receivable of $2,000 from a customer, William Rinehart.

June 4 Issued a check for $360 in full payment of an account payable to Chemical Supply Company.

June 8 Issued an additional 1,000 shares of $5 par value capital stock in exchange for $5,000 cash.

June 8 Borrowed $50,000 cash from the bank by signing a 90-day note payable.

June 9 Purchased an adjacent vacant lot for use as parking space. The price was $90,000, of which $10,000 was paid in cash; a note payable was issued for the balance.

Ex. 2-5 Transactions are recorded first in a journal and then posted to ledger accounts. In this exercise, however, your understanding of the relationship between journal and ledger is tested by asking you to study some ledger accounts and determine the journal entries which were probably made by the company's accountant to produce these ledger entries. The following accounts show the first six transactions of the Greenbriar Corporation. Prepare a journal entry (including written explanation) for each transaction.

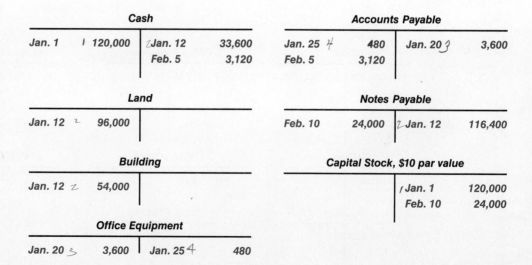

Cash			
Jan. 1	120,000	Jan. 12	33,600
		Feb. 5	3,120

Accounts Payable			
Jan. 25	480	Jan. 20	3,600
Feb. 5	3,120		

Land	
Jan. 12	96,000

Notes Payable			
Feb. 10	24,000	Jan. 12	116,400

Building	
Jan. 12	54,000

Capital Stock, $10 par value			
		Jan. 1	120,000
		Feb. 10	24,000

Office Equipment			
Jan. 20	3,600	Jan. 25	480

Ex. 2-6 Some of the following errors would cause the debit and credit columns of the trial balance to have unequal totals. For each of the four paragraphs, write a statement explaining with reasons whether the error would cause unequal totals in the trial balance. Each paragraph is to be considered independently of the others.

a A $540 payment for a new typewriter was recorded by a debit to Office Equipment of $54 and a credit to Cash of $54.

b A payment of $400 to a creditor was recorded by a debit to Accounts Payable of $400 and a credit to Cash of $40.

c An account receivable in the amount of $800 was collected in full. The collection was recorded by a debit to Cash for $800 and a debit to Capital Stock for $800.

d An account payable was paid by issuing a check for $350. The payment was recorded by debiting Accounts Payable $350 and crediting Accounts Receivable $350.

Ex. 2-7 The trial balance prepared by Studio Patrol Service at December 31 was not in balance. In searching for the error, an employee discovered that a transaction for the purchase of a typewriter on credit for $530 had been recorded by a *debit* of $530 to the Office Equipment account and a *debit* of $530 to Accounts Payable. The Accounts Payable account had a large credit balance both before and after this $530 debit posting. The credit column of the incorrect trial balance had a total of $85,300.

In answering each of the following five questions, explain briefly the reasons underlying your answer and state the dollar amount of the error if any.

a Was the Office Equipment account overstated, understated, or correctly stated in the trial balance?

b Was the total of the debit column of the trial balance overstated, understated, or correctly stated? because Accts Payable has a credit balance

c Was the Accounts Payable account overstated, understated, or correctly stated in the trial balance?

d Was the total of the credit column of the trial balance overstated, understated, or correctly stated?

e How much was the total of the debit column of the trial balance before correction of the error? 86,360

PROBLEMS

2-1 Opinion Research Service was organized to conduct polls on various issues of interest to political candidates. The following alphabetical list shows the account balances at February 28, 19___.

Accounts payable................	$ 6,930	Land...........................	$ 86,900
Accounts receivable	4,625	Notes payable	275,000
Automobiles	12,600	Notes receivable...............	10,000
Cameras........................	2,200	Office building	120,200
Capital stock...................	66,820	Stationery & office supplies	765
Cash............................	?	Tape recorders	3,800
Computer.......................	36,800	Taxes payable	3,100
Furniture & fixtures	12,250	Technical library...............	1,800
Garage building	48,000		

Instructions Prepare a trial balance with the accounts arranged in the usual financial statement order. (Compute the balance for the Cash account so that the ledger will be in balance. In listing the relatively permanent assets used in the business, remember that land and buildings are listed before the other plant assets, such as cameras and automobiles, which may be in any order you prefer.)

2-2 Kahala Secretarial Service is located in a suburban office building and provides typing, duplicating, and other services to the tenants of the building and to other clients. As of March 31, the ledger accounts contained entries as follows:

Cash				Notes Payable	
1,890.70	518.60			1,000.00	14,000.00
561.50	1,000.00				
2,465.00	595.00				
315.00	360.00				

Accounts Receivable				Accounts Payable	
3,798.00	260.00			318.60	232.35
263.00	55.00			200.00	318.60
55.00				360.00	890.00
190.50					267.00
2,105.00					595.75

Office Supplies				Taxes Payable	
1,500.00				265.00	1,465.00
250.00				330.00	
250.00					

Office Equipment				Capital Stock	
13,240.00					15,000.00

Delivery Equipment	
6,200.00	

Instructions Determine the balances of the accounts and prepare a trial balance at March 31, 19___.

2-3 After several seasons of professional tennis competition, Anne Peckham had saved enough money to start her own tennis school, to be known as Winners' Tennis College, Inc. During June, while organizing the business, Peckham kept only an informal record of transactions in the form of T accounts which she maintained on a large blackboard. Peckham asks you to develop from the T accounts a ledger using the standard three-column running balance form of accounts. She says that she will prepare journal entries for June from some rough notes she has kept but that she will need some assistance in establishing the running balance form of ledger accounts. The T accounts reflecting all June transactions are as follows:

	Cash	1				**Tennis Equipment**	25
6/2	35,000	6/4	21,600	6/7	1,240		
		6/18	212	6/13	650		
		6/23	650				

	Office Supplies	9			**Notes Payable**	30
6/8	212				6/4	75,600

	Land	20				**Accounts Payable**	31
6/4	25,200			6/18	212	6/7	1,240
				6/23	650	6/8	212
						6/13	650

	Tennis Courts	22			**Capital Stock**	50
6/4	72,000				6/2	35,000

Instructions

a Transfer the information shown by the T accounts to ledger accounts of the three-column running balance form.

b Prepare a trial balance at June 30 from the ledger accounts completed in part **(a).**

2-4   Pacific Rentals, Inc., a small corporation, had the following transactions during October:

Oct. 1 Issued 10,000 shares of $10 par value capital stock and received $100,000 cash as full payment for the stock.

Oct. 3 Purchased a small office building located on a large lot for a total price of $240,000, of which $200,000 was applicable to the land and $40,000 to the building. A cash payment of $60,000 was made and a note payable was issued for the remainder of the purchase price.

Oct. 8 Purchased a used typewriter for $400 cash.

Oct. 9 Purchased office equipment from James Office Supply at a cost of $3,600. A cash down payment of $900 was made, the balance to be paid in three equal installments due October 28, November 28, and December 28. The purchase was on open account and did not require signing a promissory note.

Oct. 10 A portion of the land purchased October 3 was sold for $50,000 to Raybar, Inc. The buyer made a down payment of $20,000 and agreed to pay for the balance within 20 days. Since the land was sold at the same price per square foot that Pacific Rentals paid for it, there was no gain or loss on the transaction.

Oct. 28 Paid James Office Supply $900 cash as the first installment due on the account payable for office equipment.

Oct. 30 Received $30,000 cash from Raybar, Inc., in full settlement of the account receivable created in the transaction of October 10.

Instructions

a Prepare a journal entry (including explanation) for each of the preceding transactions, then post to ledger accounts. Use the running balance form of ledger account. The account titles and the account numbers to be used are

Cash..............................	10	Office equipment	23
Accounts receivable	16	Notes payable	32
Land..............................	20	Accounts payable...................	35
Building	22	Capital stock	50

b Prepare a trial balance at October 31, 19___.

2-5 Property Management Corporation was started on November 1 by Chris Evans to provide managerial services for the owners of apartment buildings. The organizational period extended throughout the month of November and included the transactions listed below.
   The account titles and account numbers to be used are

Cash..............................	11	Office equipment	25
Accounts receivable	15	Notes payable	31
Land..............................	21	Accounts payable...................	32
Building	23	Capital stock	51

Nov. **1** The corporation issued 5,600 shares of capital stock to its owner, Chris Evans, in exchange for her investing $56,000 cash in the business.

Nov. **4** Purchased land and an office building for a price of $80,000, of which $38,400 was considered applicable to the land and $41,600 attributable to the building. A cash down payment of $24,000 was made and a note payable for $56,000 was issued for the balance of the purchase price.

Nov. **7** Purchased office equipment on credit from Harvard Office Equipment, $4,400.

Nov. **9** A typewriter (cost $560), which was part of the November 7 purchase of office equipment, proved defective and was returned for credit to Harvard Office Equipment.

Nov. 11 Sold to Regent Pharmacy at cost one-third of the land acquired on November 4. No down payment was required. The buyer promised to pay one-half the purchase price of $12,800 within 10 days and the remainder by December 12.

Nov. 18 Paid $1,600 in partial settlement of the liability to Harvard Office Equipment.

Nov. 21 Received cash of $6,400 as partial collection of the account receivable from Regent Pharmacy.

Instructions

a Prepare journal entries for the month of November.

b Post to ledger accounts of the three-column running balance form.

c Prepare a trial balance at November 30.

2-6 George Harris, after several seasons of professional football, had saved enough money to start his own business, to be known as Number One Auto Rentals, Inc. The business transactions during March while the new corporation was being organized are listed on page 71.

Mar. 1 George Harris invested $140,000 cash in the business, in exchange for which the corporation issued 14,000 shares of its $10 par value capital stock.

Mar. 3 The new company purchased land and a building at a cost of $120,000, of which $72,000 was regarded as applicable to the land and $48,000 to the building. The transaction involved a cash payment of $41,500 and the issuance of a note payable for $78,500.

Mar. 5 Purchased 20 new automobiles at $5,600 each from Fleet Sales Company. Paid $32,000 cash, and agreed to pay another $32,000 by March 26 and the remaining balance by April 15.

Mar. 7 Sold an automobile at cost to Harris's father-in-law, Howard Facey, who paid $2,400 in cash and agreed to pay the balance within 30 days.

Mar. 8 One of the automobiles was found to be defective and was returned to Fleet Sales Company. The amount payable to this creditor was thereby reduced by $5,600.

Mar. 20 Purchased office equipment at a cost of $4,480 cash.

Mar. 26 Issued a check for $32,000 in partial payment of the liability to Fleet Sales Company.

Instructions

a Journalize the above transactions, then post to ledger accounts. Use the running balance form of ledger account rather than T accounts. The account titles and the account numbers to be used are as follows:

Cash..................................	10	Automobiles	22
Accounts receivable	11	Notes payable	31
Land.................................	16	Accounts payable.....................	32
Buildings	17	Capital stock	50
Office equipment	20		

b Prepare a trial balance at March 31, 19___.

2-7 Educational TV, Inc., was organized in February, 19___, to operate as a local television station. The account titles and numbers used by the corporation are listed below:

Cash.................................	11	Telecasting equipment	24
Accounts receivable	15	Film library...........................	25
Supplies	19	Notes payable	31
Land.................................	21	Accounts payable.....................	32
Building	22	Capital stock	51
Transmitter..........................	23		

The transactions for February, 19___, were as follows:

Feb. 1 A charter was granted to Paul and Alice Marshal for the organization of Educational TV, Inc. The Marshals invested $288,000 cash and received 28,800 shares of stock in exchange.

Feb. 3 The new corporation purchased the land, buildings, and telecasting equipment previously used by a local television station which had gone bankrupt. The total purchase price was $249,000, of which $90,000 was attributable to the land,

$75,000 to the building, and the remainder to the telecasting equipment. The terms of the purchase required a cash payment of $179,000 and the issuance of a note payable for the balance.

Feb. 5 Purchased a transmitter at a cost of $195,000 from AC Mfg. Co., making a cash down payment of $60,000. The balance, in the form of a note payable, was to be paid in monthly installments of $11,250, beginning February 15. (Interest expense is to be ignored.)

Feb. 9 Purchased a film library at a cost of $31,995 from Modern Film Productions, making a down payment of $14,000 cash, with the balance on account payable in 30 days.

Feb. 12 Bought supplies costing $2,925, paying cash.

Feb. 15 Paid $11,250 to AC Mfg. Co. as the first monthly payment on the note payable created on February 5. (Interest expense is to be ignored.)

Feb. 25 Sold part of the film library to City College; cost was $8,000 and the selling price also was $8,000. City College agreed to pay the full amount in 30 days.

Instructions

a Prepare journal entries for the month of February.

b Post to ledger accounts of the three-column running balance form.

c Prepare a trial balance at February 28, 19___.

2-8   Julie Austin and Tom Miller have operated as independent real estate agents in Portland, Oregon, for many years. Early in January they agree to combine their separate businesses into a corporation. The balance sheets for Austin and Miller before they combine their businesses follow:

	Austin	Miller
Cash......	$ 2,400	$ 6,100
Accounts receivable	17,200	23,600
Land......	47,000	26,000
Buildings......	35,000	57,400
Office equipment	10,400	16,100
Total	$112,000	$129,200
Notes payable	$ 58,000	$ 49,500
Accounts payable......	14,000	19,700
Owners' capital......	40,000	60,000
Total	$112,000	$129,200

The A & M Realty Corporation was organized on January 20, with authority to issue 25,000 shares of capital stock with a par value of $5 each. Asset values stated on the records of each realtor are to be retained by the corporation. Miller's books will be used to record all transactions of the corporation. Accordingly, assets and liabilities shown in Austin's records are transferred to the corporation and $40,000 of capital stock is issued to Austin. Miller's capital account is closed out; and $60,000 of capital stock is issued to him. Thus, capital stock is received by Austin and Miller in proportion to the capital (assets less liabilities) each has invested.

During the remainder of January the following transactions are completed by the A & M Realty Corporation:

Jan. 21 Sold surplus office equipment on account for $3,800. The equipment is carried in the accounting records at $3,800.

Jan. 24 Purchased a vacant lot for $24,500. Paid $2,450 down; balance is due on February 28 of the current year.

Jan. 26 Collected $6,900 on accounts receivable.

Jan. 29 Paid $6,600 on accounts payable and $5,600 on notes payable.

Jan. 31 Issued an additional 2,400 shares of stock to employees for a total consideration of $12,000 in cash.

Instructions

a Prepare journal entries to record the issuance of capital stock to Austin and Miller on Miller's books (which are retained by the corporation). The entry for issuance of stock to Austin should include a debit for each asset being acquired and a credit for each liability assumed.

b Prepare journal entries for the transactions from January 21 through January 31.

c Post to ledger accounts of the three-column running balance form and determine the account balances on January 31. Account numbers need not be assigned to the ledger accounts. (Remember that the ledger accounts used by the corporation contain balances from Miller's business prior to incorporation.)

d Prepare a balance sheet at January 31. (Note: In order to avoid excessive length, this problem does not require preparation of a trial balance.)

BUSINESS DECISION PROBLEM 2

Richard Fell, a college student with several summers' experience as a guide on canoe camping trips, decided to go into business for himself. He considered incorporating, but decided instead to operate as a single proprietorship for the first year. To start this guide service, Fell estimated that at least $4,800 cash would be needed. On June 1, 19___, Fell organized Wilderness Canoe Trails by depositing $1,600 of personal savings in a bank account in the name of the business. Also on June 1, the business borrowed an additional $3,200 cash from John Fell (Richard's father) by issuing a three-year note payable. To help the business get started, John Fell agreed that no interest would be charged on the loan. The following transactions were also carried out by the business on June 1:

(1) Bought a number of canoes at a total cost of $6,200; paid $1,700 cash and agreed to pay the balance within 60 days.

(2) Bought camping equipment at a cost of $3,400 payable in 60 days.

(3) Bought supplies for cash, $800.

After the close of the season on September 10, Fell asked another student, Sharon Lee, who had taken a course in accounting, to help determine the financial position of the business.

The only record Fell had maintained was a checkbook with memorandum notes written on the check stubs. From this source Lee discovered that Fell had invested an additional $1,200 of savings in the business on July 1, and also that the accounts payable arising from the purchase of the canoes and camping equipment had been paid in full. A bank statement received from the bank on September 10 showed a balance on deposit of $2,840.

Fell informed Lee that all cash received by the business had been deposited in the bank and all bills had been paid by check immediately upon receipt; consequently, as of September 10 all bills for the season had been paid. However, nothing had been paid on the note payable.

The canoes and camping equipment were all in excellent condition at the end of the season and Fell planned to resume operations the following summer. In fact he had already accepted reservations from many customers who wished to return.

Lee felt that some consideration should be given to the wear and tear on the canoes and equipment but she agreed with Fell that for the present purpose the canoes and equipment should be listed in the balance sheet at the original cost. The supplies remaining on hand had cost $40 and Fell felt that a refund for this amount could be obtained if they were returned to the supplier.

Lee suggested that two balance sheets be prepared, one to show the condition of the business on June 1 and the other showing the condition on September 10. She also recommended to Fell that a complete set of accounting records be established.

Instructions

a Use the information in the first paragraph (including the three numbered transactions) as a basis for preparing a balance sheet dated June 1. (As illustrated in Chapter 1, the owner's equity section of the balance sheet for this unincorporated business should consist of only one account, entitled *Richard Fell, Capital.*)

b Prepare a balance sheet at September 10. (Because of the incomplete information available, it is not possible to determine the amount of cash at September 10 by adding cash receipts and deducting cash payments throughout the season. The amount on deposit as reported by the bank at September 10 is to be regarded as the total cash belonging to the business at that date.)

c By comparing the two balance sheets, compute the change in owner's equity. Explain the sources of this change in owner's equity and state whether you consider the business to be successful. Also comment on the cash position at the beginning and end of the season. Has the cash position improved significantly? Explain.

3

MEASURING BUSINESS INCOME

After studying this chapter you should be able to:

- Explain the role of profits in an expanding economy.
- Define revenue and expenses and explain the matching principle.
- Apply the rules of debit and credit to revenue and expense transactions.
- Define and record depreciation expense.
- Prepare an income statement and a statement of retained earnings. Explain how these statements provide a link between two balance sheets.
- Prepare closing entries.
- Describe the sequence of procedures in the accounting cycle.
- Distinguish between the accrual basis and the cash basis of accounting.

In this chapter you will be introduced to the challenge of measuring income. Some people mistakenly assume that measuring income is a matter of simple arithmetic. In fact, no topic in accounting is more complex and controversial than measuring the net income of a specific business for a specific year. We will be concerned with one aspect or another of measuring and reporting income throughout this book.

The earning of net income, or profits, is a major goal of almost every business enterprise, large or small. Profit is the *increase in the owners' equity resulting from operation of the business.* This increase usually is accompanied by an increase in total assets. The opposite of profit, a decrease in owners' equity resulting from operation of the business, is termed a *loss.* If you were to organize a small business of your own, you would do so with the hope and expectation that the business would operate at a profit, thereby increasing your ownership equity.

Individuals who invest in the capital stock of large corporations also expect the business to earn a profit which will increase the value of their investment.

The resources generated by profitable operations may be retained in the business to finance expansion, or they may be distributed as dividends to the stockholders. Some of the largest corporations have become large by retaining their profits in the business and using these profits for growth. Retained profits may be used, for example, to acquire new plant and equipment, to carry on research leading to new and better products, and to extend sales operations into new territories.

Profits: public image versus economic function

In recent years, business profits have become a controversial issue. Critics often call corporate profits "excessive" and charge that profits are a major cause of rising prices. Such charges have received considerable publicity, and as a result many people have come to believe that business profits can cause harm to society. Actually, business profits perform a vital economic function in our economy; a satisfactory level of business profits is generally associated with high employment, an improving standard of living, and an expanding national economy.

In a free market economy, profits assist in the efficient allocation of resources. When the demand for a particular product is much greater than the supply, the price consumers will pay for the product tends to rise. As the price rises, investors are attracted to that industry by the opportunity to earn greater than normal profits. The inflow of capital into the industry results in greater productive capacity, and the supply of the product increases to meet demand.

Corporate profits may be viewed as the "return" to stockholders for having invested their resources in a particular company. When creditors lend money to a company, they expect to earn a reasonable rate of interest. When employees invest their time and labor, they expect to earn a reasonable wage. It is equally logical that stockholders, who supply financial resources to a business, should expect to earn a satisfactory return on their investment.

If business profits were reduced to insignificant levels, prices probably would rise rather than fall. Investors would stop providing capital to those industries in which profit opportunities were unsatisfactory. The resulting capital shortages would leave businesses unable to produce enough goods, causing production shortages, higher prices, and unemployment. Thus, a satisfactory level of business profits is essential to maintaining high levels of production and to financing economic growth.

When competition is restricted, profits may become "excessive." Excessive profits, just as excessive wages or excessive materials costs, can be harmful to the economy. Profits are excessive when they become unreasonably large in relation to the amounts of money invested and the degree of risk being taken by the owners of a business. The risk taken by owners of a business is the chance that future losses may decrease or even wipe out their investment. Once we have completed our study of how business profits are measured, we shall discuss some ways of appraising their adequacy.

Retained earnings

The increase in owners' equity resulting from profitable operations is credited to an account called *Retained Earnings,* which appears in the stockholders' equity section of the balance sheet. If a business has sufficient cash, a distribution of profits may be made to the stockholders. Distributions of this nature are termed *dividends* and decrease both total assets and total stockholders' equity. The decrease in stockholders' equity is reflected by a decrease in the Retained Earnings account. Thus, the balance of the Retained Earnings account represents only the earnings which have *not* been distributed as dividends.

Some people mistakenly believe that retained earnings represent a fund of cash available to a corporation. *Retained earnings is not an asset; it is an element of stockholders' equity.* Although the amount of retained earnings indicates the portion of total assets which were *financed* by earning and retaining net income, it does *not* indicate the *form* in which these resources are currently held. The resources generated by retaining profits may have been invested in land, buildings, equipment, or any other kind of asset. The total amount of cash owned by a corporation is shown by the balance of the Cash account, which appears in the asset section of the balance sheet.

Net income

Since the drive for profits underlies the very existence of business organizations, it follows that a most important function of an accounting system is to provide information about the profitability of a business. Before we can measure the profits of a business, we need to establish a sharp, clear meaning for *profits.* Economists often define profits as the amount by which an entity becomes *better off* during a period of time. Unfortunately, how much "better off" an entity has become is largely a matter of personal opinion and cannot be measured *objectively* enough to provide a useful definition for accountants.

For this reason, accounts usually look to actual business transactions to provide objective evidence that a business has been profitable or unprofitable. For example, if an item which cost a business $60 is sold for $100 cash, we have objective evidence that the business has earned a profit of $40. Since business managers and economists use the word *profits* in somewhat different senses, accountants prefer to use the alternative term *net income,* and to define this term very carefully. *Net income is the excess of the price of goods sold and services rendered over the cost of goods and services used up during a given time period.* At this point, we shall adopt the technical accounting term *net income* in preference to the less precise term *profits.*

To determine net income, it is necessary to measure for a given time period (1) the price of goods sold and services rendered and (2) the cost of goods and services used up. The technical accounting terms for these items comprising net income are *revenue* and *expenses.* Therefore, we may state that *net income equals revenue minus expenses.* To understand why this is true and how the measurements are made, let us begin with the meaning of revenue.

Revenue

Revenue is the price of goods sold and services rendered during a given time period. When a business renders services to its customers or delivers merchandise to them, it either receives immediate payment in cash or acquires an account receivable which will be collected and thereby become cash within a short time. The revenue for a given period is equal to the inflow of cash and receivables from sales made in that period. For any single transaction, the amount of revenue is a measurement of the asset values received from the customer.

Revenue causes an increase in owners' equity. The inflow of cash and receivables from customers increases the total assets of the company; on the other side of the accounting equation, the liabilities do not change, but owners' equity is increased to match the increase in total assets. Thus revenue is the gross increase in owners' equity resulting from business activities.

Various terms are used to describe different types of revenue; for example, the revenue earned by a real estate broker may be called *Commissions Earned.* In the professional practice of lawyers, physicians, dentists, and CPAs, the revenue is called *Fees Earned.* A business which sells merchandise rather than services (General Motors, for example) will use the term *Sales* to describe the revenue earned. Many businesses also receive revenue by leasing a part of their property to others; the amounts received from a tenant are called *Rent Earned.* Another type of revenue is *Interest Earned,* which means the amount received as interest on notes receivable, bank deposits, government bonds, or other securities.

Realization or recognition of revenue   Revenue is recognized and entered in the accounting records at the time services are rendered to a customer or when goods sold to a customer are delivered. The amount of revenue is equal to the cash received plus the accounts receivable acquired from customers buying on credit. Thus the *point of sale* is the time to recognize revenue, regardless of whether the customer pays cash or promises to pay later.

To illustrate the recognition of revenue, let us assume that a business begins operations in March and makes sales of merchandise or services to its customers in March as follows: sales for cash, $25,000; sales on credit (to be collected in April), $15,000. The revenue for March is $40,000, an amount equal to the *cash received and to be received* from March sales. When the accounts receivable of $15,000 are collected during April, they must not be counted a second time in measuring revenue for April. The act of collection causes an increase in the asset, Cash, and a corresponding decrease in the asset, Accounts Receivable. The amount of total assets remains unchanged, and, of course, there is no change in liabilities or owners' equity.

Another example of a cash receipt that does not represent revenue comes from borrowing. A business may obtain cash by borrowing from a bank. This increase in cash is offset by an increase in liabilities in the form of a note payable to the bank. The owners' equity is not affected by the borrowing transaction.

Expenses

Expenses are the cost of the goods and services used up in the process of obtaining revenue. Examples include salaries paid employees, charges for newspaper advertising and for telephone service, and the wearing out (depreciation) of the building and office equipment. All these items are necessary to attract and serve customers and thereby to obtain revenue. Expenses are sometimes referred to as the "cost of doing business," that is, the cost of the various activities necessary to carry on a business.

Expenses cause the owners' equity to decrease. Revenue may be regarded as the positive factor in creating net income, expenses as the negative factor. The relationship between expenses and revenue is a significant one; the expenses of a given month or other period are incurred in order to generate revenue *in that same period.* The salaries earned by sales employees waiting on customers during July are applicable to July revenue and should be treated as July expenses, even though these salaries may not actually be paid to the employees until sometime in August.

As previously explained, revenue and cash receipts are not one and the same thing; similarly, expenses and cash payments are not identical. Examples of cash payments which are not expenses of the current period include the purchase of an office building for cash, the purchase of merchandise for later sale to customers, the repayment of a bank loan, and the distribution of cash dividends by the business to the stockholders. In deciding whether a given item should be regarded as an expense of the current period, it is often helpful to pose the following questions:

1 Was the alleged "expense" incurred in order to produce revenue of the current period?
2 Does the item in question reduce owners' equity?

If the answer to both questions is Yes, the transaction does represent an expense.

Dividends

A dividend is a distribution of assets (usually cash) by a corporation to its stockholders. Although the payment of a dividend reduces the owners' equity in the corporation, a dividend is not an expense. Unlike payments for advertising, rent, and salaries, the payment of dividends does not serve to generate revenue.

Since the declaration and payment of a dividend reduces the stockholders' equity, the dividend could be recorded by debiting the Retained Earnings account. However, a clearer record is created if a separate *Dividends* account is debited for all amounts distributed as dividends to stockholders. The disposition of the Dividends account when financial statements are prepared will be illustrated later in this chapter.

Matching revenue and expenses

To prepare an income statement and determine the net income for any particular time period, we use the *matching principle*. The word *matching* refers to the close relationship that exists between certain expenses and the revenue realized as a result of incurring those expenses. For example, assume that a real estate broker earned revenue of $30,000 in the form of commissions during a given year. Earning these commissions required the making of a great many telephone calls to clients, and the telephone bill for the year amounted to $1,500. Clearly the telephone expense is closely associated with the revenue realized and must be deducted along with other operating expenses such as advertising and office rent in determining net income for the year.

Note that timing is an important factor in matching revenue and expenses. Expenses are incurred in order to produce revenue. This year's expenses are associated with this year's revenue. We do not compare this year's expenses with last year's revenue because there is no close relationship between the two. To carry out the matching principle and achieve a valid measurement of each period's net income, our accounting system must ensure that revenue is recognized when it is earned and that expenses are recorded in the period they are incurred.

In summary, revenue must be matched with the related expenses incurred in producing that revenue. In matching revenue and expenses in the income statement, we show first all the revenue earned and then deduct from the revenue all the expenses incurred in producing that revenue.

Relating revenue and expenses to time periods

A balance sheet shows the financial position of the business at a given date. An income statement, on the other hand, shows the results of operations over *a period of time*. In fact, the concept of income is meaningless unless it is related to a period of time. For example, if a business executive says, "My business produces net income of $5,000," the meaning is not at all clear; it could be made clear, however, by relating the income to a time period, such as "$5,000 a week," "$5,000 a month," or "$5,000 a year."

The accounting period   Every business concern prepares a yearly income statement, and most businesses prepare quarterly and monthly income statements as well. Management needs to know from month to month whether revenue is rising or falling, whether expenses are being held to the level anticipated, and how net income compares with the net income of the preceding month and with the net income of the corresponding month of the preceding year. The term *accounting period* means *the span of time covered by an income statement*. It may consist of a month, a quarter of a year, a half year, or a year.

Many income statements cover the calendar year ended December 31, but an increasing number of companies are adopting an annual accounting period ending with a month other than December. Generally a business finds it more convenient to end its annual accounting period during a slack season rather than during a time of peak activity. Any 12-month accounting period adopted by a business is called its *fiscal year*. A fiscal year ending at the annual low point of seasonal activity is said to be a *natural business year*. The fiscal year selected by the federal government for its accounting purposes begins on October 1 and ends 12 months later on September 30.

Transactions affecting two or more accounting periods   The operation of a business entails an endless stream of transactions, many of which begin in one accounting period but affect several succeeding periods. Fire insurance policies, for example, are sometimes issued to cover a period of three years. In this case, the apportionment of the cost of the policy by months is an easy matter. If the policy covers three years (36 months) and costs, for example, $360, the insurance expense each month is $10.

Not all transactions can be so precisely divided by accounting periods. The purchase of a building, furniture and fixtures, machinery, a typewriter, or an automobile provides benefits to the business over all the years in which such an asset is used. No one can determine in advance exactly how many years of service will be received from such long-lived assets. Nevertheless, in measuring the net income of a business for a period of one year or less, the accountant must estimate what portion of the cost of the building and other long-lived assets is applicable to the current year. Since the apportionments for these transactions which overlap two or more accounting periods are in the nature of estimates rather than precise measurements, it follows that income statements should be regarded as *useful approximations* of annual income rather than as absolutely accurate determinations.

If we assume a stable price level, the time period for which the measurement of net income can be most accurate is the entire life span of the business. When a business concern sells all its assets, pays its debts, and ends its existence, it would then theoretically be possible to determine with precision the net income for the time period from the date of organization to the date of termination. Such a theoretically precise measurement of net income, however, would be too late to be of much use to the owners or managers of the business. The practical needs of business enterprise are well served by income statements of reasonable accuracy that tell managers and owners each month, each quarter, and each year the results of business operation.

Rules of debit and credit for revenue and expenses

Our approach to revenue and expenses has stressed the fact that revenue increases the owners' equity and that expenses decrease the owners' equity. The rules of debit and credit for recording revenue and expenses follow this relationship, and therefore the recording of revenue and expenses in ledger accounts requires only a slight extension of the rules of debit and credit presented in

Chapter 2. The rule previously stated for recording increases and decreases in owners' equity was as follows:

Increases in owners' equity are recorded by credits.
Decreases in owners' equity are recorded by debits.

This rule is now extended to cover revenue and expense accounts:

Revenue increases owners' equity; therefore revenue is recorded by a credit.
Expenses decrease owners' equity; therefore expenses are recorded by debits.

Ledger accounts for revenue and expenses

During the course of an accounting period, a great many revenue and expense transactions occur in the average business. To classify and summarize these numerous transactions, a separate ledger account is maintained for each major type of revenue and expense. For example, almost every business maintains accounts for Advertising Expense, Telephone Expense, and Salaries Expense. At the end of the period, all the advertising expenses appear as debits in the Advertising Expense account. The debit balance of this account represents the total advertising expense of the period and is listed as one of the expense items in the income statement.

Revenue accounts are usually much less numerous than expense accounts. A small business such as Greenhill Real Estate in our continuing illustration may have only one or two types of revenue, such as commissions earned from arranging sales of real estate and fees earned from managing properties in behalf of clients. In a business of this type, the revenue accounts might be called Sales Commissions Earned and Management Fees Earned.

Recording revenue and expense transactions: illustration The organization of Greenhill Real Estate during September has already been described in Chapters 1 and 2. The illustration is now continued for October, during which month the company earned commissions by selling several residences for its clients. Bear in mind that the company does not own any residential property; it merely acts as a broker or agent for clients wishing to sell their houses. A commission of 6% of the selling price of the house is charged for this service. During October the company not only earned commissions but incurred a number of expenses.

Note that each illustrated transaction which affects an income statement account also affects a balance sheet account. This pattern is consistent with our previous discussion of revenue and expenses. In recording revenue transactions, we debit the assets received and credit a revenue account. In recording expense transactions, we debit an expense account and credit the asset Cash, or perhaps a liability account if payment is to be made later. The transactions for October were as follows:

Oct. 1 Paid $360 for publication of newspaper advertising describing various houses offered for sale.

Advertising expense incurred and paid

Analysis	Rule	Entry
The cost of advertising is an expense	Expenses decrease the owners' equity and are recorded by debits	Debit: Advertising Expense, $360
The asset Cash was decreased	Decreases in assets are recorded by credits	Credit: Cash, $360

Oct. 6 Earned and collected a commission of $2,250 by selling a residence previously listed by a client.

Revenue earned and collected

Analysis	Rule	Entry
The asset Cash was increased	Increases in assets are recorded by debits	Debit: Cash, $2,250
Revenue was earned	Revenue increases the owners' equity and is recorded by a credit	Credit: Sales Commissions Earned, $2,250

Oct. 16 Newspaper advertising for October was ordered at a price of $270, payment to be made within 30 days.

Advertising expense incurred but not paid

Analysis	Rule	Entry
The cost of advertising is an expense	Expenses decrease the owners' equity and are recorded by debits	Debit: Advertising Expense, $270
An account payable, a liability, was incurred	Increases in liabilities are recorded by credits	Credit: Accounts Payable, $270

Oct. 20 A commission of $8,390 was earned by selling a client's residence. The sales agreement provided that the commission would be paid in 60 days.

Revenue earned, to be collected later

Analysis	Rule	Entry
An asset in the form of an account receivable was acquired	Increases in assets are recorded by debits	Debit: Accounts Receivable, $8,390
Revenue was earned	Revenue increases the owners' equity and is recorded by a credit	Credit: Sales Commissions Earned, $8,390

Oct. 30 Paid salaries of $7,100 to employees for services rendered during October.

	Analysis	Rule	Entry
Salaries expense incurred and paid	Salaries of employees are an expense	Expenses decrease the owners' equity and are recorded by debits	Debit: Salaries Expense, $7,100
	The asset Cash was decreased	Decreases in assets are recorded by credits	Credit: Cash, $7,100

Oct. 30 A telephone bill for October amounting to $144 was received. Payment was required by November 10.

	Analysis	Rule	Entry
Telephone expense incurred, to be paid later	The cost of telephone service is an expense	Expenses decrease the owners' equity and are recorded by debits	Debit: Telephone Expense, $144
	An account payable, a liability, was incurred	Increases in liabilities are recorded by credits	Credit: Accounts Payable, $144

Oct. 30 A dividend was declared and paid to the owners of the 18,000 shares of capital stock. The amount of the dividend was 10 cents per share, or a total of $1,800. (As explained on page 79, a dividend is not an expense.)

	Analysis	Rule	Entry
Payment of a dividend	Payment of a dividend decreases the owners' equity	Decreases in owners' equity are recorded by debits	Debit: Dividends, $1,800
	The asset Cash was decreased	Decreases in assets are recorded by credits	Credit: Cash, $1,800

The journal entries to record the October transactions are as follows:

October journal entries for Greenhill Real Estate

	General Journal			Page 2
Date	**Account Titles and Explanation**	**LP**	**Debit**	**Credit**
19__ Oct. 1	Advertising Expense	70	360	
	Cash..............................	1		360
	Paid for newspaper advertising.			
6	Cash.....................................	1	2,250	
	Sales Commissions Earned	61		2,250
	Earned and collected commission by selling residence for client.			
16	Advertising Expense	70	270	
	Accounts Payable...................	30		270
	Ordered newspaper advertising; payable in 30 days.			
20	Accounts Receivable......................	2	8,390	
	Sales Commissions Earned	61		8,390
	Earned commission by selling residence for client; commission to be received in 60 days.			
30	Salaries Expense..........................	72	7,100	
	Cash..............................	1		7,100
	Paid salaries for October.			
30	Telephone Expense	74	144	
	Accounts Payable...................	30		144
	To record liability for October telephone service.			
30	Dividends	51	1,800	
	Cash..............................	1		1,800
	Paid dividend to stockholders (18,000 shares at 10 cents per share).			

The column headings at the top of the illustrated journal page *(Date, Account Titles and Explanation, LP, Debit,* and *Credit)* are seldom used in practice. They are included here as an instructional guide but will be omitted from some of the later illustrations of journal entries.

Sequence of accounts in the ledger

Accounts are located in the ledger in financial statement order; that is, the balance sheet accounts first (assets, liabilities, and owners' equity) followed by the income statement accounts (revenue and expenses). The usual sequence of accounts within these five groups is shown by the following list.

Balance Sheet Accounts	Income Statement Accounts
Assets:	**Revenue:**
Cash	Commissions earned (fees earned, rent earned, sales, etc.)
Marketable securities	
Notes receivable	**Expenses:** (No standard sequence of listing exists for expense accounts.)
Accounts receivable	
Inventory (discussed in Chapter 5)	Advertising
Office supplies (unexpired insurance, pre-paid rent, and other prepaid expenses discussed in Chapter 4)	Salaries
	Rent
	Telephone
Land	Depreciation
Buildings	Various other expenses
Equipment	
Other assets	
Liabilities:	
Notes payable	
Accounts payable	
Salaries payable (and other short-term liabilities discussed in Chapter 4)	
Stockholders' equity:	
Capital stock	
Retained earnings	

Why are ledger accounts arranged in financial statement order?

Remember that a trial balance is prepared by listing the ledger account balances shown in the ledger, working from the first ledger page to the last. Therefore, if the accounts are located in the ledger in *financial statement order,* the same sequence will naturally be followed in the trial balance, and this arrangement will make it easier to prepare the balance sheet and income statement from the trial balance. Also, this standard arrangement of accounts will make it easier to locate any account in the ledger.

Ledger accounts for Greenhill Real Estate: illustration

The ledger of Greenhill Real Estate after the October transactions have been posted is now illustrated. The accounts appear in the ledger in financial statement order, as illustrated.

Cash — Account No. 1

Date		Explanation	Ref	Debit	Credit	Balance
Sept.	1		1	180000 00		180000 00
	3		1		141000 00	39000 00
	5		1		15000 00	24000 00
	20		1	1500 00		25500 00
	30		1		3000 00	22500 00
Oct.	1		2		360 00	22140 00
	6		2	2250 00		24390 00
	30		2		7100 00	17290 00
	30		2		1800 00	15490 00

Accounts Receivable — Account No. 2

Date		Explanation	Ref	Debit	Credit	Balance
Sept.	10		1	11000 00		11000 00
	20		1		1500 00	9500 00
Oct.	20		2	8390 00		17890 00

Land — Account No. 20

Date		Explanation	Ref	Debit	Credit	Balance
Sept.	3		1	141000 00		141000 00
	10		1		11000 00	130000 00

Building — Account No. 22

Date		Explanation	Ref	Debit	Credit	Balance
Sept.	5		1	36000 00		36000 00

Office Equipment — Account No. 25

Date		Explanation	Ref	Debit	Credit	Balance
19— Sept.	14		1	5400 00		5400 00

Accounts Payable — Account No. 30

Date		Explanation	Ref	Debit	Credit	Balance
19— Sept.	5		1		21000 00	21000 00
	14		1		5400 00	26400 00
	30		1	3000 00		23400 00
Oct.	16		2		270 00	23670 00
	30		2		144 00	23814 00

Capital Stock — Account No. 50

Date		Explanation	Ref	Debit	Credit	Balance
19— Sept.	1		1		180000 00	180000 00

Dividends — Account No. 51

Date		Explanation	Ref	Debit	Credit	Balance
19— Oct.	30		2	1800 00		1800 00

Sales Commissions Earned — Account No.

Date		Explanation	Ref	Debit	Credit	Balance
19— Oct.	6		2		2250 00	2250 00
	20		2		8390 00	10640 00

Advertising Expense					Account No. 70
Date	Explanation	Ref	Debit	Credit	Balance
19— Oct. 1		2	360 00		360 00
16		2	270 00		630 00

Salaries Expense					Account No. 72
Date	Explanation	Ref	Debit	Credit	Balance
19— Oct. 30		2	7100 00		7100 00

Telephone Expense					Account No. 74
Date	Explanation	Ref	Debit	Credit	Balance
19— Oct. 30		2	144 00		144 00

Trial balance

A trial balance was prepared from Greenhill's ledger accounts, as follows:

GREENHILL REAL ESTATE
Trial Balance
October 31, 19___

Proving the equality of debits and credits

Cash	$ 15,490	
Accounts receivable.................................	17,890	
Land	130,000	
Building...	36,000	
Office equipment.....................................	5,400	
Accounts payable		$ 23,814
Capital stock...		180,000
Dividends...	1,800	
Sales commissions earned...........................		10,640
Advertising expense..................................	630	
Salaries expense	7,100	
Telephone expense...................................	144	
	$214,454	$214,454

Recording depreciation at the end of the period

This trial balance includes all the October expenses requiring cash payments such as salaries, advertising, and telephone service, but it does not include any depreciation expense. Our definition of expense is *the cost of goods and services used up in the process of obtaining revenue.* Some of the goods used up are purchased in advance and used up gradually over a long period of time. Buildings and office equipment, for example, are used up over a period of years. Each year, a portion of these assets *expires,* and a portion of their total cost should be recognized as *depreciation expense.* The term depreciation means the systematic allocation of the cost of an asset to expense over the accounting periods making up its useful life.

Depreciation expense does not require monthly cash outlays; in effect, it is *paid in advance* when the related asset is originally acquired. Nevertheless, depreciation is an inevitable and continuing expense. Failure to record depreciation would result in *understating* total expenses of the period and consequently *overstating* the net income.

Building The office building purchased by Greenhill Real Estate at a cost of $36,000 is estimated to have a useful life of 20 years. The purpose of the $36,000 expenditure was to provide a place in which to carry on the business and thereby to obtain revenue. After 20 years of use the building will be worthless and the original cost of $36,000 will have been entirely consumed. In effect, the company has purchased 20 years of "housing services" at a total cost of $36,000. A portion of this cost expires during each year of use of the building. If we assume that each year's operations should bear an equal share of the total cost (straight-line depreciation), the annual depreciation expense will amount to ¹⁄₂₀ of $36,000, or $1,800. On a monthly basis, depreciation expense is $150 ($36,000 cost ÷ 240 months). There are alternative methods of spreading the cost of a depreciable asset over its useful life, some of which will be considered in Chapter 10.

The journal entry to record depreciation of the building during October follows:

General Journal
Page 2

Date		Account Titles and Explanation	LP	Debit	Credit
19—					
Oct.	31	Depreciation Expense: Building............	76	150	
		Accumulated Depreciation: Building	23		150
		To record depreciation for October. Cost of			
		$36,000 ÷ 240 months = $150 a month.			

Recording depreciation of the building

The depreciation expense account will appear in the income statement for October along with the other expenses of salaries, advertising, and telephone expense. The Accumulated Depreciation: Building account will appear in the balance sheet as a deduction from the Building account, as shown by the following illustration of a *partial* balance sheet:

GREENHILL REAL ESTATE
Partial Balance Sheet
October 31, 19___

Showing accumulated depreciation in the balance sheet

Building (at cost)...	$36,000	
Less: Accumulated depreciation..	150	$35,850

The end result of crediting the Accumulated Depreciation: Building account is much the same as if the credit had been made to the Building account; that is, the net amount shown on the balance sheet for the building is reduced from $36,000 to $35,850. Although the credit side of a depreciation entry *could* be made directly to the asset account, it is customary and more efficient to record such credits in a separate account entitled Accumulated Depreciation. The original cost of the asset and the total amount of depreciation recorded over the years can more easily be determined from the ledger when separate accounts are maintained for the asset and for the accumulated depreciation.

Accumulated Depreciation: Building is an example of a *contra-asset account,* because it has a credit balance and is offset against an asset account (Building) to produce the proper balance sheet valuation for the asset.

Office equipment   Depreciation on the office equipment of Greenhill Real Estate must also be recorded at the end of October. This equipment cost $5,400 and is assumed to have a useful life of 10 years. Monthly depreciation expense on the straight-line basis is, therefore, $45, computed by dividing the cost of $5,400 by the useful life of 120 months. The journal entry is as follows:

		General Journal			*Page 2*

Date		**Account Titles and Explanation**	**LP**	**Debit**	**Credit**
19__					
Oct.	31	Depreciation Expense: Office Equipment ...	78	45	
		Accumulated Depreciation: Office			
		Equipment	26		45
		To record depreciation for October. Cost of			
		$5,400 ÷ 120 months = $45 a month.			

Recording depreciation of office equipment

No depreciation was recorded on the building and office equipment for September, the month in which these assets were acquired, because regular operations did not begin until October. Generally, depreciation is not recognized until the business begins active operation and the assets are placed in use. Accountants often use the expression *matching costs and revenue* to convey the idea of writing off the cost of an asset to expense during the time periods in which the business uses the asset to generate revenue.

The journal entry by which depreciation is recorded at the end of the month is called an *adjusting entry.* The adjustment of certain asset accounts and related expense accounts is a necessary step at the end of each accounting period so that the information presented in the financial statements will be as accurate and complete as possible. In the next chapter, adjusting entries will be shown for some other items in addition to depreciation.

The adjusted trial balance

After all the necessary adjusting entries have been journalized and posted, an *adjusted trial balance* is prepared to prove that the ledger is still in balance. It also provides a complete listing of the account balances to be used in preparing the financial statements. The following adjusted trial balance differs from the trial balance shown on page 89 because it includes accounts for depreciation expense and accumulated depreciation.

GREENHILL REAL ESTATE
Adjusted Trial Balance
October 31, 19__

Adjusted trial balance

Cash	$ 15,490	
Accounts receivable	17,890	
Land	130,000	
Building	36,000	
Accumulated depreciation: building		$ 150
Office equipment	5,400	
Accumulated depreciation: office equipment		45
Accounts payable		23,814
Capital stock		180,000
Dividends	1,800	
Sales commissions earned		10,640
Advertising expense	630	
Salaries expense	7,100	
Telephone expense	144	
Depreciation expense: building	150	
Depreciation expense: office equipment	45	
	$214,649	$214,649

FINANCIAL STATEMENTS

Now that Greenhill Real Estate has been operating for a month, managers and outside parties will want to know more about the company than just its financial position. They will want to know the results of Greenhill's operations—whether the company's activities have been profitable or unprofitable. To provide this additional information, we will prepare a more complete set of financial statements, including an income statement, a statement of retained earnings, and a balance sheet.[1]

The income statement

When we measure the net income earned by a business we are measuring its economic performance—its success or failure as a business enterprise. Stockholders, prospective investors, managers, bankers, and other creditors are anxious to see the latest available income statement and thereby to judge how well the company is doing. The October income statement for Greenhill Real Estate appears as follows:

GREENHILL REAL ESTATE
Income Statement
For the Month Ended October 31, 19___

Income statement for October

Sales commissions earned		$10,640
Expenses:		
Advertising expense	$ 630	
Office salaries expense	7,100	
Telephone expense	144	
Decpreciation expense: building.......................................	150	
Depreciation expense: office equipment..............................	45	8,069
Net income		$ 2,571

This income statement consists of the last six accounts in the adjusted trial balance shown above. It shows that the revenue during October exceeded the expenses of the month, thus producing a net income of $2,571. Bear in mind, however, that our measurement of net income is not absolutely accurate or precise, because of the assumptions and estimates involved in the accounting process. We have recorded only those economic events which are *evidenced by accounting transactions.* Perhaps during October Greenhill Real Estate has developed a strong interest on the part of many clients who are on the verge of buying or selling homes. This accumulation of client interest is an important step toward profitable operation, but is not reflected in the October income statement because it is not subject to objective measurement. Remember also that in determining the amount of depreciation expense we had to estimate the useful life of the building and office equipment. Any error in our estimates is reflected in the net income reported for October. Despite these limitations, the income statement is of vital importance and indicates that the new business has been profitable during the first month of its operation.

---

[1]A complete set of financial statements also includes a statement of changes in financial position, which will be discussed in Chapter 15.

At this point we are purposely ignoring income taxes on corporations. Corporate income taxes will be introduced in Chapter 5 and considered more fully in Chapters 11 and 17.

Alternative titles for the income statement include *earnings statement, statement of operations,* and *profit and loss statement.* However, *income statement* is by far the most popular term for this important financial statement. In brief, we can say that an income statement is used to summarize the *operating results* of a business by matching the revenue earned during a given time period with the expenses incurred in obtaining that revenue.

Statement of retained earnings

Retained earnings is that portion of the stockholders' equity created by earning and retaining net income. The *statement of retained earnings,* which covers the same time period as the related income statement, shows the sources of increase and decrease in retained earnings for that period.

GREENHILL REAL ESTATE
Statement of Retained Earnings
For the Month Ended October 31, 19___

Statement of retained earnings for October

Retained earnings, Sept. 30, 19___	$ –0–
Net income for October	2,571
Subtotal	$2,571
Dividends	1,800
Retained earnings, Oct. 31, 19___	$ 771

In this example the company had no retained earnings at the beginning of the period. The statement for the following month (November) would show a beginning balance of $771.

The balance sheet

In preparing a balance sheet for Greenhill Real Estate at October 31, we can obtain the balances of the asset, liability, and capital stock accounts from the adjusted trial balance on page 92. The amount of retained earnings at October 31 does not appear in the adjusted trial balance, but has been determined in the statement of retained earnings.

Previous illustrations of balance sheets have been arranged in the *account form,* that is, with the assets on the left side of the page and the liabilities and stockholders' equity on the right side. The following balance sheet is presented in *report form,* that is, with the liabilities and stockholders' equity sections listed below rather than to the right of the asset section. Both the account form and the report form are widely used.

GREENHILL REAL ESTATE
Balance Sheet
October 31, 19___

Assets

Balance sheet at
October 31:
report form

Cash		$ 15,490
Accounts receivable		17,890
Land		130,000
Building	$ 36,000	
Less: Accumulated depreciation	150	35,850
Office equipment	$ 5,400	
Less: Accumulated depreciation	45	5,355
Total assets		$204,585

Liabilities & Stockholders' Equity

Liabilities:		
Accounts payable		$ 23,814
Stockholders' equity:		
Capital stock	$180,000	
Retained earnings	771	180,771
Total liabilities & stockholders' equity		$204,585

If we compare the October 31 balance sheet to the one prepared at September 30 (page 23), we see that the stockholders' original investment of $180,000 appears unchanged under the caption of Capital Stock. The amount of retained earnings, however, has changed between the two balance sheet dates. The Retained Earnings account had a zero balance at September 30, but as explained in the statement of retained earnings, it was increased by the $2,571 net income earned during October and decreased by the $1,800 dividend paid, leaving a balance of $771 at October 31.

The amount of the Retained Earnings account at any balance sheet date represents the total earnings of the company since the date of incorporation, minus any losses and minus all dividends distributed to stockholders. One reason for maintaining a distinction between capital stock and retained earnings is that a corporation usually cannot legally pay dividends greater than the amount of retained earnings. The separation of these two elements of ownership may also be informative because it shows how much of the total stockholders' equity resulted from the investment of funds by stockholders and how much was derived from earning and retaining net income.

In the Greenhill Real Estate illustration, we have shown the two common ways in which the stockholders' equity may be increased: (1) investment of cash or other assets by the owners and (2) operating the business at a profit. There are also two common ways in which the stockholders' equity may be decreased: (1) payment of dividends and (2) operating the business at a loss.

Income statement and retained earnings statement: a link between two balance sheets

A set of financial statements becomes easier to understand if we recognize that the balance sheet, income statement, and statement of retained earnings are all related to one another. The balance sheet prepared at the end of the previous accounting period and the one prepared at the end of the current period each show the amount of retained earnings at the respective balance sheet dates. The statement of retained earnings summarizes the factors (net income and dividends) which have caused the amount of retained earnings to change between these two balance sheet dates. The income statement explains in greater detail the change in retained earnings resulting from profitable operation of the business. Thus, the income statement and the retained earnings statement provide an informative link between successive balance sheets.

CLOSING THE ACCOUNTS

The accounts for revenue, expenses, and dividends are *temporary owners' equity accounts* used during the accounting period to classify changes affecting the owners' equity. At the end of the period, we want to transfer the net effect of these various increases and decreases into retained earnings, which is a permanent owners' equity account. We also want to reduce the balances of the temporary owners' equity accounts to zero, so that these accounts will again be ready for use in accumulating information during the next accounting period. These objectives are accomplished by the use of *closing entries*.

Revenue and expense accounts are closed at the end of each accounting period by transferring their balances to a summary account called *Income Summary*. When the credit balances of the revenue accounts and the debit balances of the expense accounts have been transferred into one summary account, the balance of this Income Summary will be the net income or net loss for the period. If the revenue (credit balances) exceeds the expenses (debit balances), the Income Summary account will have a credit balance representing net income. Conversely, if expenses exceed revenue, the Income Summary will have a debit balance representing net loss. This is consistent with the rule that increases in owners' equity are recorded by credits and decreases are recorded by debits.

A journal entry made for the purpose of closing a revenue or expense account is called a *closing entry*. This term is also applied to the journal entries (to be explained later) used in closing the Income Summary account and the Dividends account into the Retained Earnings account.

A principal purpose of the year-end process of closing the revenue and expense accounts is to reduce their balances to zero. Since the revenue and expense accounts provide the information for the income statement of *a given accounting period,* it is essential that these accounts have zero balances at the beginning of each new period. The closing of the accounts has the effect of "wiping the slate clean" and preparing the accounts for the recording of revenue and expenses during the succeeding accounting period.

It is common practice to close the accounts only once a year, but for illustration, we shall now demonstrate the closing of the accounts of Greenhill Real Estate at October 31 after one month's operation.

Closing entries for revenue accounts   Revenue accounts have credit balances. Therefore, closing a revenue account means transferring its credit balance to the Income Summary account. This transfer is accomplished by a journal entry debiting the revenue account in an amount equal to its credit balance, with an offsetting credit to the Income Summary account. The only revenue account of Greenhill Real Estate is Sales Commissions Earned, which had a credit balance of $10,640 at October 31. The journal entry necessary to close this account is as follows:

General Journal

Page 3

Closing a revenue account

Date		Account Titles and Explanation	LP	Debit	Credit
19___					
Oct.	31	Sales Commissions Earned	61	10,640	
		Income Summary	53		10,640
		To close the Sales Commissions Earned account.			

After this closing entry has been posted, the two accounts affected will appear as shown below. Arrows have been added to indicate the debit and credit parts of the closing entry.

	Sales Commissions Earned				61		Income Summary					53
Date	Exp.	Ref	Debit	Credit	Balance	Date	Exp.	Ref	Debit	Credit	Balance
Oct. 6		2		2,250	2,250	Oct. 31		3		10,640	10,640
20		2		8,390	10,640						
31	To close	3	10,640		–0–						

Closing entries for expense accounts   Expense accounts have debit balances. Closing an expense account means transferring its debit balance to the Income Summary account. The journal entry to close an expense account, therefore, consists of a credit to the expense account in an amount equal to its debit balance, with an offsetting debit to the Income Summary account.

There are five expense accounts in the ledger of Greenhill Real Estate. Five separate journal entries could be made to close these five expense accounts, but the use of one *compound journal entry* is an easier, timesaving method of closing all five expense accounts. A compound journal entry is an entry that includes debits to more than one account or credits to more than one account.

General Journal — Page 3

Date		Account Titles and Explanation	LP	Debit	Credit
19__					
Oct.	31	Income Summary	53	8,069	
		Advertising Expense	70		630
		Salaries Expense.	72		7,100
		Telephone Expense	74		144
		Depreciation Expense: Building	76		150
		Depreciation Expense: Office Equip-	78		45
		ment.			
		To close the expense accounts.			

Closing the various expense accounts by use of a compound journal entry

After this closing entry has been posted, the Income Summary account has a credit balance of $2,571, and the five expense accounts have zero balances, as shown on page 99.

Closing the Income Summary account   The five expense accounts have now been closed and the total amount of $8,069 formerly contained in these accounts appears in the debit column of the Income Summary account. The commissions of $10,640 earned during October appear in the credit column of the Income Summary account. Since the credit entry of $10,640 representing October revenue is larger than the debit of $8,069 representing October expenses, the account has a credit balance of $2,571—the net income for October.

The net income of $2,571 earned during October causes the owners' equity to increase. The *credit* balance of the Income Summary account is, therefore, transferred to the Retained Earnings account by the following closing entry:

General Journal — Page 3

Date		Account Titles and Explanation	LP	Debit	Credit
19__					
Oct.	31	Income Summary	53	2,571	
		Retained Earnings	51		2,571
		To close the Income Summary account for			
		October by transferring the next income to			
		the Retained Earnings account.			

Net income earned increases the owners' equity

Income Summary   *Account No. 53*

Date		Explanation	Ref	Debit	Credit	Balance
19__						
Oct.	31		3		10,640	10,640
	31		3	8,069		2,571

Expense accounts have zero balances after closing entries have been posted

Advertising Expense   *Account No. 70*

Date		Explanation	Ref	Debit	Credit	Balance
19__						
Oct.	2		2	360		360
	16		2	270		630
	31	To close	3		630	–0–

Salaries Expense   *Account No. 72*

Date		Explanation	Ref	Debit	Credit	Balance
19__						
Oct.	30		2	7,100		7,100
	31	To close	3		7,100	–0–

Telephone Expense   *Account No. 74*

Date		Explanation	Ref	Debit	Credit	Balance
19__						
Oct.	30		2	144		144
	31	To close	3		144	–0–

Depreciation Expense: Building   *Account No. 76*

Date		Explanation	Ref	Debit	Credit	Balance
19__						
Oct.	31		2	150		150
	31	To close	3		150	–0–

Depreciation Expense: Office Equipment   *Account No. 78*

Date		Explanation	Ref	Debit	Credit	Balance
19__						
Oct.	31		2	45		45
	31	To close	3		45	–0–

After this closing entry has been posted, the Income Summary account has a zero balance, and the net income earned during October appears in the Retained Earnings account as shown below:

Income Summary   Account No. 53

19__						
Oct.	31	Revenue	3		10,640	10,640
	31	Expenses	3	8,069		2,571
	31	To close	3	2,571		–0–

Retained Earnings   Account No. 51

19__						
Oct.	31	Net income for October	3		2,571	2,571

In our illustration the business has operated profitably with revenue in excess of expenses. Not every business is so fortunate; if the expenses of a business are larger than its revenue, the Income Summary account will have a debit balance. In that case, the closing of the Income Summary account would require a debit to the Retained Earnings account and an offsetting credit to the Income Summary account. A debit balance in the Retained Earnings account is referred to as a *deficit;* it is shown as a deduction from Capital Stock in the balance sheet.

Note that the Income Summary account is used only at the end of the period when the accounts are being closed. The Income Summary account has no entries and no balance except during the process of closing the accounts at the end of the accounting period.

Closing the Dividends account   As explained earlier in this chapter, the payment of dividends to the owners is not considered as an expense of the business and, therefore, is not taken into account in determining the net income for the period. Since dividends do not constitute an expense, the Dividends account is closed not into the Income Summary account but directly to the Retained Earnings account, as shown by the following entry:

General Journal   Page 3

Dividends account is closed to Retained Earnings

Date		Account Titles and Explanation	LP	Debit	Credit
19__					
Oct.	31	Retained Earnings	51	1,800	
		Dividends	52		1,800
		To close the Dividends account.			

After this closing entry has been posted, the Dividends account will have a zero balance, and the dividends distributed during October will appear as a deduction or debit entry in the Retained Earnings account, as follows:

Dividends

19__						
Oct.	30	Declaration and payment	2	1,800		1,800
	31	To close	3		1,800	–0–

Retained Earnings

19__						
Oct.	31	Net income for October	3		2,571	2,571
	31	Dividends	3	1,800		771

The closing process—in summary The closing of the accounts may be illustrated graphically by the use of T accounts as shown below:

Diagram showing closing of the accounts

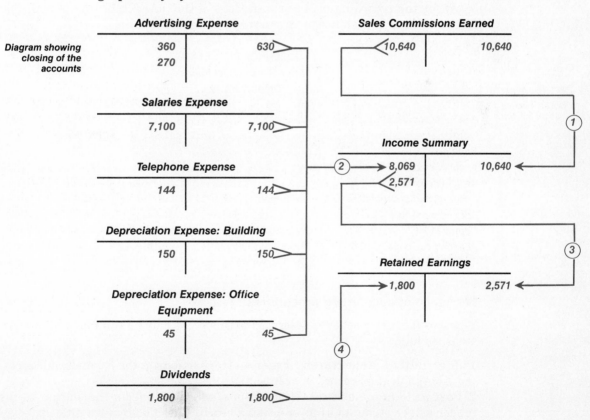

As illustrated in the preceding diagram, the closing process consists of four steps:

1 Close the various revenue accounts by transferring their balances into the Income Summary account.
2 Close the various expense accounts by transferring their balances into the Income Summary account.
3 Close the Income Summary account by transferring its balance into the Retained Earnings account.
4 Close the Dividends account by transferring its balance into the Retained Earnings account.

After-closing trial balance

After the revenue and expense accounts have been closed, it is desirable to prepare an *after-closing trial balance,* which of course will consist solely of balance sheet accounts. There is always the possibility that an error in posting the closing entries may have upset the equality of debits and credits in the ledger. The after-closing trial balance, or *post-closing trial balance* as it is often called, is prepared from the ledger. It gives assurance that the accounts are in balance and ready for the recording of the transactions of the new accounting period. The after-closing trial balance of Greenhill Real Estate follows:

GREENHILL REAL ESTATE
After-Closing Trial Balance
October 31, 19——

Only the balance sheet accounts remain open

Cash	$ 15,490	
Accounts receivable	17,890	
Land	130,000	
Building	36,000	
Accumulated depreciation: building		$ 150
Office equipment	5,400	
Accumulated depreciation: office equipment		45
Accounts payable		23,814
Capital stock		180,000
Retained earnings, Oct. 31		771
	$204,780	$204,780

Sequence of accounting procedures

The accounting procedures described to this point may be summarized in eight steps, as follows:

1 **Journalize transactions**   Enter all transactions in the journal, thus creating a chronological record of events.
2 **Post to ledger accounts**   Post debits and credits from the journal to the proper ledger accounts, thus creating a record classified by accounts.

3 Prepare a trial balance   Prove the equality of debits and credits in the ledger.

4 Prepare end-of-period adjustments   Enter adjusting entries in the general journal, and post to ledger accounts.

5 Prepare an adjusted trial balance   Prove again the equality of debits and credits in the ledger.

6 Prepare financial statements   An income statement shows the results of operation for the period. A statement of retained earnings shows the changes in retained earnings during the period and the closing balance. A balance sheet shows the financial position of the business at the end of the period.

7 Journalize and post the closing entries   The closing entries clear the revenue, expense, and dividends accounts, making them ready for recording the events of the next accounting period, and also bring the Retained Earnings account up-to-date.

8 Prepare an after-closing trial balance   This step ensures that the ledger remains in balance after posting of the closing entries.

Dividends—declaration and payment

Earlier in this chapter the declaration and the payment of a cash dividend were treated as a single event recorded by one journal entry. A small corporation with only a few stockholders may choose to declare and pay a dividend on the same day. In large corporations with thousands of stockholders and constant transfers of shares, an interval of a month or more will separate the date of declaration from the later date of payment.

Assume for example that on April 1 the board of directors of Universal Corporation declares the regular quarterly dividend of $1 per share on the 1 million shares of outstanding capital stock. The board's resolution specifies that the dividend will be payable on May 10 to stockholders of record on April 25. To be eligible to receive the dividend, an individual must be listed on the corporation's records as a stockholder on April 25, the date of record. Two entries are required: one on April 1 for the declaration of the dividend and one on May 10 for its payment, as shown below.

Dividends declared and . . .	*Apr. 1*	Dividends	1,000,000	
		Dividends Payable....................................		1,000,000
		Declared dividend of $1 per share payable May 10 to stockholders of record Apr. 25.		
. . . Dividends paid	*May 10*	Dividends Payable.......................................	1,000,000	
		Cash		1,000,000
		Paid the $1 per share dividend declared on Apr. 1.		

The Dividends Payable account is a liability which comes into existence when the dividend is declared and is discharged when the dividend is paid.

Accrual basis of accounting versus cash basis of accounting

A business which recognizes revenue in the period in which it is earned and which deducts in the same period the expenses incurred in generating this revenue is using the *accrual basis of accounting.*

The alternative to the accrual basis of accounting is the *cash basis.* Under cash basis accounting, revenue is not recorded until received in cash; expenses are assigned to the period in which cash payment is made. Most business concerns use the accrual basis of accounting, but individuals, professionals (such as physicians and lawyers), and many small service-type companies, usually maintain their accounting records on a cash basis.

The cash basis of accounting does not give a good picture of profitability. For example, it ignores uncollected revenue which has been earned and expenses which have been incurred but not paid. However, the cash basis does offer several advantages in the preparation of income tax returns. Throughout this book we shall be working with the accrual basis of accounting, except for that portion of Chapter 17 dealing with the income tax returns of individuals.

KEY TERMS INTRODUCED OR EMPHASIZED IN CHAPTER 3

Accounting period   The span of time covered by an income statement. One year is the accounting period for much financial reporting, but financial statements are also prepared by most companies for each quarter of the year and also for each month.

Accrual basis of accounting   Calls for recording revenue in the period in which it is earned and recording expenses in the period in which they are incurred. The effect of events on the business is recognized as services are rendered or consumed rather than when cash is received or paid.

Accumulated depreciation   A contra-asset account shown as a deduction from the related asset account in the balance sheet. Depreciation taken throughout the useful life of an asset is accumulated in this account.

Adjusted trial balance   A listing of all ledger account balances after the amounts have been changed to include the adjusting entries made at the end of the period.

Adjusting entries   Entries required at the end of the period to update the accounts before financial statements are prepared. Adjusting entries serve to apportion transactions properly between the accounting periods affected and to record any revenue earned or expenses incurred which have not been recorded prior to the end of the period.

After-closing trial balance   A trial balance prepared after all closing entries have been made. Consists only of accounts for assets, liabilities, and owners' equity.

Cash basis of accounting   Revenue is recorded when received in cash and expenses are recorded in the period in which cash payment is made. Fails to match revenue with related expenses and therefore does not lead to a logical measurement of income. Use is limited mostly to individual income tax returns and to accounting records of physicians and other professional firms.

Closing entries   Journal entries made at the end of the period for the purpose of closing temporary accounts (revenue, expense, and dividends accounts) and bringing the Retained Earnings account up to date.

Contra-asset account   An account with a credit balance which is offset against or deducted from an asset account to produce the proper balance sheet valuation for the asset.

Depreciation   The systematic allocation to expense of the cost of an asset (such as a building) during the periods of its useful life.

Dividend   A distribution of cash by a corporation to its stockholders.

Dividends payable   The ledger account which is credited at the date of declaring a dividend. Classified in the balance sheet as a liability.

Expenses   The cost of the goods and services used up in the process of obtaining revenue.

Financial statement order   Sequence of accounts in the ledger; balance sheet accounts first (assets, liabilities, and owners' equity), followed by income statement accounts (revenue and expenses).

Fiscal year   Any 12-month accounting period adopted by a business.

Income statement   A report used to evaluate the performance of a business by matching its revenue and related expenses for a particular accounting period. Shows the net income or net loss.

Income Summary account   The summary account in the ledger to which revenue and expense accounts are closed at the end of the period. The balance (credit balance for a net income, debit balance for a net loss) is transferred to the Retained Earnings account.

Matching principle   In the measurement of net income, revenue earned during the accounting period is offset with all expenses incurred in generating that revenue whether or not these expenses were paid during the accounting period.

Net income   The excess of revenue earned over the related expenses for a given period.

Report form balance sheet   A balance sheet in which the sections for liabilities and owners' equity are listed below the section for assets.

Retained earnings   That portion of stockholders' equity resulting from profits earned and retained in the business.

Revenue   The price of goods sold and services rendered by a business. Equal to the inflow of cash and receivables in exchange for services rendered or goods delivered during the period.

Temporary owners' equity accounts   The accounts for revenue, expenses, and dividends used during the accounting period to classify changes affecting the owners' equity.

DEMONSTRATION PROBLEM FOR YOUR REVIEW

Key Insurance Agency was organized on September 1, 19___. Assume that the accounts are closed and financial statements prepared each month. The company occupies rented office space but owns office equipment estimated to have a useful life of 10 years from date of acquisition, September 1. The trial balance for Key Insurance Agency at November 30 is shown on page 106.

Cash	$ 3,750	
Accounts receivable	1,210	
Office equipment	4,800	
Accumulated depreciation: office equipment		$ 80
Accounts payable		1,640
Capital stock		6,000
Retained earnings		1,490
Dividends	500	
Commissions earned		6,220
Advertising expense	800	
Salaries expense	3,600	
Rent expense	770	
	$15,430	$15,430

Instructions

a Prepare the adjusting journal entry to record depreciation of the office equipment for the month of November.

b Prepare an adjusted trial balance at November 30, 19___.

c Prepare an income statement and a statement of retained earnings for the month ended November 30, 19___, and a balance sheet in report form at November 30, 19___.

SOLUTION TO DEMONSTRATION PROBLEM

a Adjusting journal entry:

Depreciation Expense: Office Equipment	40	
Accumulated Depreciation: Office Equipment		40
To record depreciation for November ($4,800 ÷ 120 months).		

b

KEY INSURANCE AGENCY
Adjusted Trial Balance
November 30, 19___

Cash	$ 3,750	
Accounts receivable	1,210	
Office equipment	4,800	
Accumulated depreciation: office equipment		$ 120
Accounts payable		1,640
Capital stock		6,000
Retained earnings		1,490
Dividends	500	
Commissions earned		6,220
Advertising expense	800	
Salaries expense	3,600	
Rent expense	770	
Depreciation expense: office equipment	40	
Totals	$15,470	$15,470

c

KEY INSURANCE AGENCY
Income Statement
For the Month Ended November 30, 19___

Commissions earned		$6,220
Expenses:		
Advertising expense	$ 800	
Salaries expense..	3,600	
Rent expense...	770	
Depreciation expense: office equipment.............................	40	5,210
Net income...		$1,010

KEY INSURANCE AGENCY
Statement of Retained Earnings
For the Month Ended November 30, 19___

Retained earnings, Oct. 31, 19___	$1,490
Net income for the month	1,010
Subtotal..	$2,500
Dividends	500
Retained earnings, Nov. 30, 19___	$2,000

KEY INSURANCE AGENCY
Balance Sheet
November 30, 19___

Assets

Cash..		$3,750
Accounts receivable		1,210
Office equipment	$4,800	
Less: Accumulated depreciation	120	4,680
Total assets		$9,640

Liabilities & Stockholders' Equity

Liabilities:		
Accounts payable..		$1,640
Stockholders' equity:		
Capital stock	$6,000	
Retained earnings	2,000	8,000
Total liabilities & stockholders' equity		$9,640

REVIEW QUESTIONS

1 What is the meaning of the term *revenue?* Does the receipt of cash by a business indicate that revenue has been earned? Explain.

2 What is the meaning of the term *expenses?* Does the payment of cash by a business indicate that an expense has been incurred? Explain.

3 Explain the effect of operating profitably upon the balance sheet of a business entity.

4 Does the Retained Earnings account represent a supply of cash which could be distributed to stockholders? Explain.

5 Does a well-prepared income statement provide an exact and precise measurement of net income for the period or does it represent merely an approximation of net income? Explain.

6 For each of the following financial statements, indicate whether the statement relates to a single date or to a period of time:
a Balance sheet
b Income statement
c Statement of retained earnings

7 Explain the rules of debit and credit with respect to transactions recorded in revenue and expense accounts.

8 Supply the appropriate term (debit or credit) to complete the following statements.
a The Capital Stock account, Retained Earnings account, and revenue accounts are increased by _____ entries.
b Asset accounts and expense accounts are increased by _____ entries.
c Liability accounts and owners' equity accounts are decreased by _____ entries.

9 Supply the appropriate term (debit or credit) to complete the following statements.
a When a business is operating profitably, the journal entry to close the Income Summary account will consist of a _____ to that account and a _____ to Retained Earnings.
b When a business is operating at a loss, the journal entry to close the Income Summary account will consist of a _____ to that account and a _____ to Retained Earnings.
c The journal entry to close the Dividends account consists of a _____ to that account and a _____ to Retained Earnings.

10 How does depreciation expense differ from other operating expenses?

11 Assume that a business acquires a delivery truck at a cost of $9,600. Estimated life of the truck is four years. State the amount of depreciation expense per year and per month. Give the adjusting entry to record depreciation on the truck at the end of the first month, and explain where the accounts involved would appear in the financial statements.

12 All ledger accounts belong in one of the following five groups: asset, liability, owners' equity, revenue, and expense. For each of the following accounts, state the group in which it belongs. Also indicate whether the normal balance would be a debit or a credit.
a Fees Earned   **e** Building
b Notes Payable   **f** Depreciation Expense
c Telephone Expense   **g** Accumulated Depreciation: Building
d Retained Earnings

13 A service enterprise performs services in the amount of $500 for a customer in May and receives payment in June. In which month is the $500 of revenue recognized? What is the journal entry to be made in May and the entry to be made in June?

14 Which of the following accounts should be closed by a debit to Income Summary and a credit to the account listed?

Dividends	Salaries Expense
Fees Earned	Accounts Payable
Advertising Expense	Depreciation Expense
Accounts Receivable	Accumulated Depreciation

15 Supply the appropriate terms to complete the following statements. _____ and _____ accounts are closed at the end of each accounting period by transferring their balances to a summary account called _____ _____. A _____ balance in this summary account represents net income for the period; a _____ balance represents a net loss for the period.

16 Which of the ten accounts listed below are affected by closing entries at the end of the accounting period?

Cash	Capital Stock
Fees Earned	Dividends
Income Summary	Accumulated Depreciation
Accounts Payable	Accounts Receivable
Telephone Expense	Depreciation Expense

17 How does the accrual basis of accounting differ from the cash basis of accounting? Which gives a more accurate picture of the profitability of a business? Explain.

18 Remington Corporation pays dividends regularly. Should these dividends be considered an expense of the business? Explain.

EXERCISES

Ex. 3-1 Hillcrest Corporation, a firm of real estate brokers, carried out the following transactions during September. Which of these transactions represented revenue to the firm during the month of September? Explain.

a Hillcrest Corporation received $25,000 cash from the issuance of additional shares of its capital stock.

b Collected $1,500 rent for September from a dentist to whom Hillcrest Corporation rented part of its building.

c Arranged a sale of an apartment building owned by a client, Stephen Roberts. The commission for making the sale was $14,400, but this amount would not be received until November 20.

d Collected cash of $2,400 from an account receivable. The receivable originated in August from services rendered to a client.

e Borrowed $15,000 from Century Bank to be repaid in three months.

Ex. 3-2 During July the Columbus Company carried out the following transactions. Which of these transactions represented expenses for July? Explain.

a Paid a garage $640 for automobile repair work performed in May.

b Declared and paid a $1,000 dividend to shareholders.

c Paid $24,000 in settlement of a loan obtained three months earlier.

d Purchased a typewriter for $960 cash.

e Paid $192 for gasoline purchases for the delivery truck during July.

f Paid $1,800 salary to an employee for time worked during July.

Ex. 3-3 Label each of the following statements as true or false. Explain the reasoning underlying your answer and give an example of a transaction which supports your position.

a Every transaction that affects a balance sheet account also affects an income statement account.

b Every transaction that affects an income statement account also affects a balance sheet account.

c Every transaction that affects an expense account also affects an asset account.

d Every transaction that affects a revenue account also affects another income statement account.

e Every transaction that affects an expense account also affects a revenue account.

Ex. 3-4 Total assets and total liabilities of Mannix Corporation as shown by the balance sheets at the beginning and end of the year were as follows:

	Beginning of Year	End of Year
Assets	$155,000	$200,000
Liabilities	95,000	110,000

Compute the net income or net loss from operations for the year in each of the following independent cases:

a No dividends were declared or paid during the year and no additional capital stock was issued.

b No dividends were declared or paid during the year, but additional capital stock was issued at par in the amount of $25,000.

c Dividends of $10,000 were declared and paid during the year. No change occurred in capital stock.

d Dividends of $3,000 were declared and paid during the year, and additional capital stock was issued at par in the amount of $18,000.

Ex. 3-5 Supply the missing figures in the following independent cases:

a Capital stock (no change during year)... $150,000
Dividends for the year.. 18,000
Retained earnings at beginning of year... 72,000
Net income for the year 53,500
Total stockholders' equity at end of year.. _____

b Retained earnings at end of year... $251,700
Dividends for the year... 37,400
Net income for the year 93,200
Retained earnings at beginning of year... _____

c Net income for the year .... $ _____
Retained earnings at end of year.. 143,000
Retained earnings at beginning of year... 127,000
Dividends for the year... 36,000

d Dividends for the year.. $ _59._

   Retained earnings at end of year... 299,000

   Net income for the year 85,000

   Retained earnings at beginning of year....................................... 273,000

e Total stockholders' equity at beginning of year............................... $214,000

   Total stockholders' equity at end of year..................................... 265,000

   Amount received from additional capital stock issued during year............... 21,000

   Net income for the year .... _53_

   Dividends for the year... 23,000

Ex. 3-6   Martin Corporation's income statement showed net income of $25,380 for the month of October. In recording October transactions, however, certain transactions were incorrectly recorded. Study the following list of selected October transactions, and identify any which were incorrectly recorded. Also give the journal entry as it should have been made, and compute the correct amount of net income for October.

   a Made an error in computing depreciation on the building for October. Recorded as $25. The correct amount of depreciation was $250.

   b Recorded the payment on October 31 of a $4,000 dividend by debiting Salaries Expense and crediting Cash. The dividend had been declared on October 2.

   c Earned a commission of $2,500 by selling a residence for a client. Commission to be received in 60 days. Recorded by debiting Commissions Earned and crediting Accounts Receivable.

   d A payment of $250 for newspaper advertising was recorded by debiting Advertising Expense and crediting Accounts Receivable.

   e Received but did not pay a bill of $285 for October telephone service. Recorded by debiting Telephone Expense and crediting Commissions Earned.

Ex. 3-7   When beginning operations, Land Company established its ledger with the accounts arranged in alphabetical order, but found this sequence inconvenient for preparing financial statements. You are to rearrange the following alphabetical list of 21 ledger accounts in *financial statement order* so that Land Company may improve the organization of its ledger.

Accounts payable	Electricity expense
Accounts receivable	Interest payable
Accumulated depreciation:	Land
Buildings	Notes payable
Accumulated depreciation:	Notes receivable
Office equipment	Office equipment
Advertising expense	Capital stock
Buildings	Retained earnings
Cash	Rent expense
Commissions earned	Salaries expense
Depreciation expense: buildings	Telephone expense
Depreciation expense:	
Office equipment	

Ex. 3-8 An employee of Lawn Care Corporation prepared the following closing entries at the year-end. **(a)** Identify any errors which the employee made and **(b)** prepare correct closing entries for the business.

Entry 1

Lawn service revenue	*78,000*	
Accumulated Depreciation	*8,000*	
Retained Earnings	*27,000*	
Income Summary		*113,000*
To close accounts with credit balances.		

Entry 2

Income Summary	*73,000*	
Salaries Expense		*56,000*
Dividends		*11,000*
Advertising Expense		*4,000*
Depreciation Expense		*2,000*
To close accounts with debit balances.		

Entry 3

Income Summary	*40,000*	
Capital Stock		*40,000*
To close Income Summary account.		

PROBLEMS

3-1 The March transactions of Madison Motors, an automobile repair shop, included the following:

(1) On March 1, paid rent for the month of March, $1,200.

(2) On March 3, at request of National Insurance, Inc., made repairs on car of Stanley West. Sent bill for $610 for services rendered to National Insurance, Inc. (Credit Repair Service Revenue.)

(3) On March 9, made repairs to car of H. F. Smith and collected in full the charge of $430.

(4) On March 14, placed advertisement in *Daily Star* to be published in issue of March 16 at cost of $150, payment to be made within 30 days.

(5) On March 25, received a check for $610 from National Insurance, Inc., representing collection of the receivable of March 3.

(6) On March 31, declared and paid a dividend of $3,600.

Instructions

a Write an analysis of each transaction. An example of the type of analysis desired is as follows:

(1) (a) Rent is an operating expense. Expenses are recorded by debits. Debit Rent Expense, $1,200.

(b) The asset Cash was decreased. Decreases in assets are recorded by credits. Credit Cash, $1,200.

b Prepare a journal entry (including explanation) for each of the above transactions.

3-2 City flights provides transportation by helicopter between a major airport and various business centers of a large city. Among the ledger accounts used by the company are the following:

Cash	Passenger fare revenue
Accounts payable	Advertising expense
Dividends payable	Fuel expense
Capital stock	Rent expense
Retained earnings	Repair & maintenance expense
Dividends	Salaries expense

Some of the January transactions of City Flights are listed below.

Jan. 3 Paid $1,600 rent for the building for January.

Jan. 4 Placed advertising in local newspapers for publication during January. The agreed price of $540 was payable within 10 days after the end of the month.

Jan. 15 Cash receipts from passengers for the first half of January amounted to $9,650.

Jan. 16 Declared a dividend of $3,000 payable March 15 to stockholders of record March 1.

Jan. 16 Paid salaries to employees for services rendered in first half of January, $5,500.

Jan. 29 Received a bill from Western Oil Co. for fuel used in January, amounting to $1,970, and payable by February 10.

Jan. 31 Paid $1,686 to Stevens Motors for repair and maintenance work during January.

Instructions Prepare a journal entry (including an explanation) for each of the above transactions.

3-3 An adjusted trial balance for Marina Center at December 31 appears below.

MARINA CENTER
Adjusted Trial Balance
December 31, 19___

Cash	$ 8,600	
Accounts receivable	42,000	
Office equipment	15,000	
Accumulated depreciation: office equipment		$ 3,000
Accounts payable		6,000
Capital stock		24,600
Retained earnings		30,000
Dividends	18,000	
Sales commissions earned		172,000
Advertising expense	41,500	
Rent expense	30,000	
Salaries expense	63,000	
Utilities expense	16,000	
Depreciation expense: office equipment	1,500	
	$235,600	$235,600

Instructions

a Prepare journal entries to close the accounts. Use four entries: (1) to close the revenue account, (2) to close the expense accounts, (3) to close the Income Summary account, and (4) to close the Dividends account.

b Does the amount of net income or net loss appear in the closing entries? Explain fully.

3-4 Mountain Air Service, Inc., was organized on January 1 for the purpose of flying skiers among neighboring ski areas and to remote mountaintops. The following transactions were completed during January.

Jan. 1 Issued 26,000 shares of $10 par value capital stock for cash of $260,000.

Jan. 2 Purchased a helicopter for $240,000 and spare parts for $4,800, paying cash.

Jan. 3 Paid $1,720 cash to rent a building for January.

Jan. 15 Cash receipts from passengers for the first half of January amounted to $14,560.

Jan. 16 Paid $12,970 to employees for services rendered during the first half of January.

Jan. 24 Placed advertising in local newspapers for publication during January. The agreed price of $270 was payable within ten days after the end of the month.

Jan. 28 Paid $936 to J. J. Motors for maintenance and repair service during January.

Jan. 29 Received a bill from Indian Oil Co. for fuel used in January, amounting to $1,732 and payable by February 10.

Jan. 31 Paid $12,970 to employees for services rendered during the last half of January.

Jan. 31 Cash receipts from passengers during the last half of January amounted to $14,992.

The useful life of the helicopter for depreciation purposes was estimated to be 10 years. Depreciation should not be recorded on the spare parts; these are allocated to expense when they are used. The account titles and account numbers used by the company included the following:

Cash	11	Passenger fare revenue	51
Spare parts	14	Advertising expense	61
Helicopter	21	Depreciation expense: helicopter	63
Accumulated depreciation:		Fuel expense	65
helicopter	23	Rent expense	67
Accounts payable	31	Repair & maintenance expense	69
Capital stock	41	Salaries expense	71

Instructions

a Prepare journal entries for the operating transactions in January and also the month-end adjusting entry for depreciation of the helicopter. Number the general journal pages as Page 1 and Page 2.

b Post to ledger accounts.

c Prepare an adjusted trial balance at January 31.

3-5 Ryan Radio Repair was organized on May 1, 19___. The accounts were closed and financial statements prepared each month. An adjusted trial balance as of the succeeding July 31 follows.

RYAN RADIO REPAIR
Adjusted Trial Balance
July 31, 19___

Cash	$ 8,820	
Accounts receivable	3,640	
Land	73,500	
Building	126,000	
Accumulated depreciation: building		$ 1,260
Repair equipment	16,800	
Accumulated depreciation: repair equipment		840
Notes payable		70,000
Accounts payable		2,100
Capital stock		140,000
Retained earnings		14,000
Dividends	10,500	
Repair service revenue		23,800
Advertising expense	420	
Depreciation expense: building	420	
Depreciation expense: repair equipment	280	
Repair parts expense	1,820	
Utilities expense	350	
Wages expense	9,450	
	$252,000	$252,000

Instructions

a Prepare journal entries to close the accounts at July 31. Use four entries: (1) to close the revenue account, (2) to close the expense accounts, (3) to close the Income Summary account, and (4) to close the Dividends account.

b Prepare financial statements (income statement, statement of retained earnings, and a balance sheet in report form).

c What were the estimated lives of the building and equipment as assumed by the company in setting the depreciation rates?

3-6 J. D. Rand, Inc., offers investment counseling and brokerage services to its clients and earns revenue in the form of commissions, dividends on securities owned, and interest on loans made to customers for the purchase of securities. The adjusted trial balance of the corporation was as follows at August 31, 19___, the end of the fiscal year:

J. D. RAND, INC.
Adjusted Trial Balance
August 31, 19___

Cash	$ 82,000	
Marketable securities	88,600	
Accounts receivable	104,000	
Land	300,000	
Building	496,000	
Accumulated depreciation: building		$ 54,600
Furniture & equipment	144,000	
Accumulated depreciation: furniture & equipment		37,800
Notes payable		276,000
Miscellaneous payables		25,600
Capital stock		600,000
Retained earnings, Sept. 1, prior year		254,000
Dividends	12,000	
Commissions earned		349,600
Dividends earned		9,600
Interest earned		13,500
Advertising expense	26,700	
Office expense	50,700	
Interest expense	36,000	
Depreciation expense	41,900	
Salaries and bonuses expense	226,600	
Miscellaneous expense	12,200	
	$1,620,700	$1,620,700

Instructions From the adjusted trial balance and supplementary data given, prepare the following at August 31:

a Income statement for the year

b Statement of retained earnings

c Balance sheet in report form

d Closing entries

e After-closing trial balance

3-7 On November 1, 19___, Continental Moving Co. was organized to provide transportation of household furniture. During November the following transactions occurred:

Nov. 1 Cash of $1,000,000 was received in exchange for 100,000 shares of $10 par value capital stock.

Nov. 2 Purchased land for $250,000 and building for $360,000, paying $210,000 cash and signing a $400,000 mortgage payable bearing interest at 9%.

Nov. 3 Purchased six trucks from Willis Motors at a total cost of $432,000. A cash down payment of $200,000 was made, the balance to be paid by January 12.

Nov. 6 Purchased office equipment for cash, $24,000.

Don't Forget Heading!

Nov. 6 Moved furniture for Mr. and Mrs. Don Fitch from New York to Los Angeles for $6,850. Collected $4,850 in cash, balance to be paid within 30 days (credit Moving Service Revenue).

Nov. 9 Moved furniture for various clients for $32,350. Collected $18,350 in cash, balance to be paid within 30 days.

Nov. 15 Paid salaries to employees for the first half of the month, $15,100.

Nov. 25 Moved furniture for various clients for a total of $37,000. Cash collected in full.

Nov. 30 Salaries expense for the second half of November amounted to $13,250.

Nov. 30 Received a gasoline bill for the month of November from Lucier Oil Company in the amount of $17,500, to be paid by December 10.

Nov. 30 Received bill of $1,250 for repair work on trucks during November by Newport Repair Company.

Nov. 30 Paid $5,000 to the holder of the mortgage payable. This $5,000 payment included $3,000 interest expense for November and $2,000 reduction in the liability.

Nov. 30 Declared a $10,000 dividend, payable December 15.

Estimated useful life of the building was 20 years, trucks 4 years, and office equipment 10 years.

The account titles to be used and the account numbers are as follows:

Cash	1	Retained earnings	41
Accounts receivable	3	Dividends	45
Land	11	Income summary	50
Building	12	Moving service revenue	60
Accumulated depreciation: building	13	Salaries expense	70
		Gasoline expense	71
Trucks	15	Repairs & maintenance expense	72
Accumulated depreciation: trucks	16	Interest expense	73
Office equipment	18	Depreciation expense: building	74
Accumulated depreciation: office equipment	19	Depreciation expense: trucks	75
Accounts payable	30		
Dividends payable	31	Depreciation expense: office equipment	76
Mortgage payable, 9%	32		
Capital stock	40		

Instructions

a Prepare journal entries. (Number journal pages to permit cross reference to ledger.)

b Post to ledger accounts. (Number ledger accounts to permit cross reference to journal.)

c Prepare a trial balance at November 30, 19___.

d Prepare adjusting entries and post to ledger accounts.

e Prepare an adjusted trial balance.

f Prepare an income statement for November, and a balance sheet at November 30, 19___, in report form. (A statement of retained earnings is not required.)

g Prepare closing entries and post to ledger accounts.

h Prepare an after-closing trial balance.

BUSINESS DECISION PROBLEM 3

John Bell, owner of a small business called Top-Notch Company, has accepted a salaried position overseas and is trying to interest you in buying his business. He describes the operating results of the business as follows: "The business has been in existence for only 18 months, but the growth trend is very impressive. Just look at these figures."

	Cash Collections from Customers
First six-month period..	$60,000
Second six-month period...	80,000
Third six-month period..	90,000

"I think you'll agree those figures show real growth," Bell concluded.

You then asked Bell whether sales were made only for cash or on both a cash and credit basis. He replied as follows:

"At first we sold both for cash and on open account. In the first six months we made total sales of $100,000 and 70% of those sales were made on credit. We had $40,000 of accounts receivable at the end of the first six-month period.

"During the second six-month period, we tried to discourage selling on credit because of the extra paper work involved and the time required to follow up on slow-paying customers. Our sales on credit in that second six-month period amounted to $35,000, and our total accounts receivable were down to $30,000 at the end of that period.

"During the third six-month period we made sales only for cash. Although we prefer to operate on a cash basis only, we did very well at collecting receivables. We collected in full from every customer to whom we ever sold on credit and we don't have a dollar of accounts receivable at this time."

Instructions

a To facilitate your reaching a decision, prepare a schedule comparing cash collections and sales data for each of the three six-month periods under review. Use the following column headings:

	(1) Sales on Credit	(2) Collections on Accounts Receivable	(3) Ending Balance of Accounts Receivable	(4) Total Cash Collections from Customers	(5) Sales for Cash	(6) (1) + (5) Total Sales
First six months						
Second six months						
Third six months						

b Based upon your analysis in part **a**, do you consider Bell's explanation of the "growth trend" of cash collections to be a well-founded portrayal of the progress of his business? Explain fully any criticism you may have of Bell's line of reasoning.

4

COMPLETION OF
THE ACCOUNTING
CYCLE

After studying this chapter you should be able to:

- Explain how accounting periods of uniform length are useful in measuring the income of a business.
- Explain the purpose of adjusting entries.
- Discuss the basic types of adjusting entries.
- Prepare a work sheet and explain its usefulness.
- Describe the steps in the accounting cycle.
- Explain when and why reversing entries may be used.

Accounting periods and financial statements

For the purpose of making accounting measurements and preparing financial statements, the life of a business is divided into accounting periods of equal length. Because accounting periods are equal in length, we can compare the revenue and expenses of the current period with the revenue and expenses of prior periods and determine whether our operating results are improving or declining. As explained in Chapter 3, the *accounting period* means the span of time covered by an income statement. The usual accounting period for which complete financial statements are prepared and distributed to investors, bankers, and government agencies is one year. However, most businesses also prepare quarterly and monthly financial statements so that management will be informed on the profitability of the business from month to month.

In this chapter we will emphasize two important steps necessary to the completion of the accounting cycle. One of these steps is the preparation of adjusting entries as a means of achieving a precise cutoff of revenue earned and expenses incurred through the last day of an accounting period. The other key step is the preparation of a work sheet to arrange in convenient form all of the accounting data required at the end of the period.

At the end of an accounting period, adjustments of some of the account balances in the ledger must be made before financial statements are prepared. Adjusting entries for depreciation are necessary, for example, because the recorded costs of buildings and office equipment are gradually expiring with the passage of time. Before financial statements are prepared, the accounts must be brought up to date with respect to depreciation and several other items.

To serve the needs of management, investors, bankers, and other groups, financial statements must be as complete and accurate as possible. The balance sheet must contain all the assets and liabilities at the close of business on the last day of the period. The income statement must contain all the revenue and expenses applicable to the period covered but must not contain any revenue or expenses relating to the following period. In other words, a precise *cutoff* of transactions at the end of the period is essential to the preparation of reliable financial statements. Adjusting entries make possible an accurate cutoff of revenue and expense at the end of an accounting period.

Apportioning transactions between accounting periods

Some business transactions are begun and completed within a single accounting period, but many other transactions are begun in one accounting period and concluded in a later period. For example, a building purchased this year may last for 25 years; during each of those 25 years a fair share of the cost of the building should be recognized as expense. The use of *adjusting entries* to record depreciation expense applicable to a given accounting period was illustrated in the preceding chapter. Let us now consider all types of transactions which overlap two or more accounting periods and therefore require adjusting entries.

PRINCIPAL TYPES OF ADJUSTING ENTRIES

The various adjusting entries required at the end of the period may be classified into the following groups:

1 Recorded costs which must be apportioned between two or more accounting periods. Example: the cost of a building.
2 Recorded revenue collected in advance which must be apportioned between two or more accounting periods. Example: management fees collected in advance for services to be rendered this period and also in future periods.
3 Unrecorded expenses. Example: wages earned by employees after the last payday in an accounting period.
4 Unrecorded revenue. Example: management fees earned but not yet collected or billed to customers.

All these adjusting entries involve the recognition of either revenue or expense and, therefore, represent a change in owners' equity. Owners' equity, however, cannot change by itself; there must also be a corresponding change in either assets or liabilities. Thus, every adjusting entry must involve both an income statement account (either a revenue or an expense) *and* a balance sheet account (either an asset or a liability).

To demonstrate these various types of adjusting entries, the illustration of Greenhill Real Estate will be continued for November. We shall consider in detail only those November transactions related to adjusting entries.

Recorded costs apportioned between accounting periods

When a business makes an expenditure that will benefit more than one accounting period, the amount is usually debited to an asset account. At the end of each period which benefits from the expenditure, an appropriate portion of the cost is transferred from the asset account to an expense account. For example, let us consider payments for insurance and for office supplies.

Prepaid expenses   Payments in advance are often made for such items as insurance, rent, and office supplies. At the end of the accounting period, a portion of the services or supplies probably will have expired or will have been consumed, but another portion will be unexpired or unused. That portion of the economic benefits from the expenditure which *has expired or has been consumed is an expense of the current period*. However, the *unexpired or unused portion of the economic benefits from the expenditure represents an asset* at the balance sheet date and will not become expense (expired cost) until a later accounting period.

Insurance   On November 1, Greenhill Real Estate paid $540 for a three-year fire insurance policy covering the building. This expenditure was debited to an asset account by the following journal entry:

Expenditure for insurance policy recorded as asset

Unexpired Insurance	540	
Cash		540

Purchased three-year fire insurance policy.

Since this expenditure of $540 will protect the company against fire loss for three years, the cost of protection each year is ⅓ of $540, or $180. The insurance expense applicable to each month's operations is 1⁄12 of the annual expense, or $15. In order that the accounting records for November show insurance expense of $15, the following *adjusting entry* is required at November 30:

Adjusting entry. Portion of asset expires (becomes expense)

Insurance Expense	15	
Unexpired Insurance..		15

To record insurance expense for November.

This adjusting entry serves two purposes: (1) it apportions the proper amount of insurance expense to November operations and (2) it reduces the asset account to $525 so that the correct amount of unexpired insurance will appear in the balance sheet at November 30. What would be the effect on the income statement for November if the above adjustment were not made? The expenses would be understated by $15 and consequently the net income would be overstated by $15. The balance sheet also would be affected by failure to make the adjustment: the assets would be overstated by $15 and so would the owners' equity. The overstatement of the owners' equity would result from the overstated amount of net income transferred to the Retained Earnings account when the accounts were closed at November 30.

Office supplies   On November 2, Greenhill Real Estate purchased enough stationery and other office supplies to last for several months. The cost of the supplies was $720, and this amount was debited to an asset account by the following journal entry:

Expenditure for office supplies recorded as asset

Office Supplies.	720	
Cash		720

Purchased office supplies.

No entries were made during November to record the day-to-day usage of office supplies, but on November 30 a careful count was made of the supplies still on hand. This count, or physical inventory, showed unused supplies with a cost of $600. It is apparent, therefore, that supplies costing $120 were used during November. On the basis of the November 30 count, an adjusting entry is made debiting an expense account $120 (the cost of supplies consumed during November), and reducing the asset account by $120 to show that only $600 worth of office supplies remained on hand at November 30. The *adjusting entry* follows:

Adjusting entry. Portion of supplies used represents expense

Office Supplies Expense	120	
Office Supplies		120

To record consumption of office supplies in November.

The Office Supplies account will appear in the balance sheet as an asset; the Office Supplies Expense account will be shown in the income statement. How would failure to make this adjustment affect the financial statements? In the income statement for November, the expenses would be understated by $120 and the net income overstated by the same amount. Since the overstated amount for net income in November would be transferred into the Retained Earnings account in the process of closing the accounts, the owners' equity section of the balance sheet would be overstated by $120. Assets also would be overstated because Office Supplies would be listed at $120 too much.

When payments for insurance, office supplies, and rent are expected to provide economic benefits for more than one accounting period, the advance payment is usually recorded by a debit to an asset account such as Unexpired Insurance, Office Supplies, or Prepaid Rent. However, the advance payment *could* be recorded by debiting an expense account such as Insurance Expense. At the end of the period, the adjusting entry would then consist of a debit to Unexpired Insurance and a credit to Insurance Expense. This alternative method would lead to the same amounts in the balance sheet and income statement as the method previously illustrated. Under both procedures, we would be treating as an expense of the current period the cost of the economic benefits consumed, and carrying forward as an asset the cost of the economic benefits applicable to future periods.

Depreciation of building   The November 30 adjusting entry to record depreciation of the building used by Greenhill Real Estate is exactly the same as the October 31 *adjusting entry* explained in Chapter 3.

Adjusting entry. Cost of building is gradually converted to expense

Depreciation Expense: Building 150
    Accumulated Depreciation: Building 150
To record depreciation for November.

This allocation of depreciation expense to November operations is based on the following facts: the building cost $36,000 and is estimated to have a useful life of 20 years (240 months). Using the straight-line method of depreciation, the portion of the original cost which expires each month is $\frac{1}{240}$ of $36,000, or $150.

The Accumulated Depreciation: Building account now has a credit balance of $300 as a result of the October and November credits of $150 each. The book value of the building is $35,700, that is, the original cost of $36,000 minus the accumulated depreciation of $300. The term *book value* means the net amount at which an asset is shown in the accounting records, as distinguished from its market value. *Carrying value* is an alternative term, with the same meaning as book value.

Depreciation of office equipment   The November 30 adjusting entry to record depreciation of the office equipment is the same as the *adjusting entry* for depreciation a month earlier, as shown in Chapter 3.

Adjusting entry. Cost of office equipment gradually converted to expense

Depreciation Expense: Office Equipment 45
    Accumulated Depreciation: Office Equipment 45
To record depreciation for November.

Original cost of the office equipment was $5,400, and the estimated useful life was 10 years (120 months). Depreciation each month under the straight-line method is therefore $\frac{1}{120}$ of $5,400, or $45. What is the book value of the office equipment at this point? Original cost of $5,400 minus accumulated depreciation of $90 for two months leaves a book value of $5,310.

What would be the effect on the financial statements if the adjusting entries for depreciation of the building and office equipment were omitted at November 30? In the income statement the expenses would be understated by $195 ($150 depreciation of building and $45 depreciation of office equipment), and net income for the month would be overstated by $195. In the balance sheet the assets would be overstated by $195; the owners' equity would be overstated the same amount because of the $195 overstatement of the net income added to the Retained Earnings account. If depreciation had not been recorded in either October or November, the overstatement in the balance sheet at November 30 would amount to $390 with respect both to assets and to owners' equity.

Recorded revenue collected in advance apportioned between accounting periods

On November 1, Greenhill Real Estate agreed to act as manager of some rental properties for a monthly fee of $300. The owner of the properties, Frank Day, was leaving the country on an extended trip and therefore paid the company for six months' service in advance. The journal entry to record the transaction on November 1 was

Management fee collected but not yet earned

Cash	1,800	
Unearned Management Fees		1,800

Collected in advance six months' fees for management of properties owned by Frank Day.

This receipt of cash does not represent revenue. By collecting in advance from the client, Greenhill Real Estate becomes obligated to render services in the future. Revenue is earned only by the actual *rendering* of services to customers, or by the *delivery* of goods to them. This management fee will be earned gradually over a period of six months as Greenhill performs the required services. The $1,800 collected in advance is therefore credited to an *unearned revenue* account. Some accountants prefer the term *deferred revenue.* At the end of each month, an amount of $300 will be transferred from unearned revenue to a revenue account by means of an adjusting entry. The first in this series of transfers will be made at November 30 by the following *adjusting entry.*

Adjusting entry. To recognize earning of a part of management fee

Unearned Management Fees	300	
Management Fees Earned		300

Fee earned by managing Frank Day property during November.

The $1,500 credit balance remaining in the Unearned Management Fees account represents an obligation to render $1,500 worth of services in five future months; therefore, it belongs in the balance sheet in the liability section. An unearned revenue account differs from other liabilities because it ordinarily will be settled by rendering services rather than by making a cash payment, but it nevertheless is a liability. The Management Fees Earned account is shown as revenue in the income statement for November.

Unrecorded expenses

Adjusting entries are necessary at the end of each accounting period to record any expenses which have been incurred but not recognized in the accounts. Salaries of employees and interest on borrowed money are common examples of expenses which accumulate day by day but which may not be recorded until the end of the period. These expenses are said to *accrue,* that is, to grow or accumulate.

Accrual of interest On November 1, Greenhill Real Estate borrowed the sum of $3,000 from a bank. Banks require every borrower to sign a *promissory note,* that is, a formal, written promise to repay the amount borrowed plus interest at an agreed future date. (Various forms of notes in common use and the accounting problems involved will be discussed more fully in Chapter 8.) The note signed by John Green, with certain details omitted, is shown below.

Note payable issued to bank

$3,000	Los Angeles, California	November 1, 19___

Three months .... **after date** .... I .... **promise to pay**

to the order of .... American National Bank ....

.... ———Three thousand and no/100——— ....**dollars**

for value received, with interest at........................... 12 percent per year ....

Greenhill Real Estate

By .... *John Green* ....
President

The note payable is a liability of Greenhill Real Estate, similar to an account payable but different in that a formal written promise to pay is required and interest is charged on the amount borrowed. A Notes Payable account is credited when the note is issued; the Notes Payable account will be debited three months later when the note is paid. Interest accrues throughout the life of the note payable, but it is not payable until the note matures on February 1. To the bank making the loan, the note signed by Greenhill is an asset, a note receivable. The revenue earned by banks consists largely of interest charged to borrowers.

The journal entry made on November 1 to record the borrowing of $3,000 from the bank was as follows:

Entry when bank loan is obtained

Cash 3,000
    Notes Payable 3,000
Obtained from bank three-month loan with interest at 12% a year.

Three months later, Greenhill Real Estate must pay the bank $3,090, representing repayment of the $3,000 note payable plus $90 interest ($3,000 × .12 × 3/12). The $90 is the total interest expense for the three months. Although no payment will be made for three months, one-third of the interest expense ($30) is *incurred* each month, as shown below.

Accrual of interest

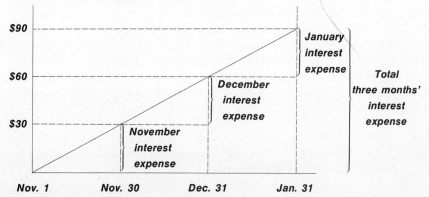

The following *adjusting entry* is made at November 30 to charge November operations with one month's interest expense and also to record the amount of interest owed to the bank at the end of November.

<table>
<tr><td>*Adjusting entry for interest expense incurred in November*</td><td>Interest Expense ....</td><td>30</td><td></td></tr>
<tr><td></td><td>Interest Payable ....</td><td></td><td>30</td></tr>
<tr><td></td><td>*To record interest expense applicable to November ($3,000 × .12 × ¹/₁₂).*</td><td></td><td></td></tr>
</table>

The debit balance in the Interest Expense account will appear in the November income statement; the credit balances in the Interest Payable and Notes Payable accounts will be shown in the balance sheet as liabilities. These two liability accounts will remain in the records until the maturity date of the loan, at which time a cash payment to the bank will wipe out both the Notes Payable account and the Interest Payable account.

Accrual of salary On November 20, Greenhill hired Carl Nelson as a part-time salesperson whose duties were to work evenings calling on property owners to secure listings of property for sale or rent. The agreed salary was $225 for a five-evening week, payable each Friday; payment for the first week was made on Friday, November 24. Personal income taxes and other taxes relating to payroll are ignored in this illustration.

Assume that the last day of the accounting period, November 30, fell on Thursday. Nelson had worked four evenings since being paid the preceding Friday and therefore had earned $180 (⅘ × $225). In order that this $180 of November salary expense be reflected in the accounts before the financial statements are prepared, and *adjusting entry* is necessary at November 30.

<table>
<tr><td>*Adjusting entry for salaries expense incurred but unpaid at November 30*</td><td>Salaries Expense ....</td><td>180</td><td></td></tr>
<tr><td></td><td>Salaries Payable ....</td><td></td><td>180</td></tr>
<tr><td></td><td>*To record salary expense and related liability to salesperson for last four evenings' work in November.*</td><td></td><td></td></tr>
</table>

The debit balance in the Salaries Expense account will appear as an expense in the November income statement; the credit balance of $180 in the Salaries Payable account is the amount owing to the salesman for work performed during the last four days of November and will appear among the liabilities in the balance sheet at November 30.

The next regular payday for Nelson will be Friday, December 1, which is the first day of the new accounting period. Since the accounts were adjusted and closed on November 30, all the revenue and expense accounts have zero balances at the beginning of business on December 1. The payment of a week's salary to Nelson will be recorded by the following entry on December 1:

<table>
<tr><td>*Payment of salary overlapping two accounting periods*</td><td>Salaries Payable ....</td><td>180</td><td></td></tr>
<tr><td></td><td>Salaries Expense ....</td><td>45</td><td></td></tr>
<tr><td></td><td>Cash ....</td><td></td><td>225</td></tr>
<tr><td></td><td>*Paid weekly salary to salesperson.*</td><td></td><td></td></tr>
</table>

Note that the net result of the November 30 accrual entry has been to split the weekly salary expense between November and December. Four days of the work week fell in November, so four days' pay, or $180, was recognized as November expense. One day of the work week fell in December so $45 was recorded as December expense.

No accrual entry is necessary for other salaries in Greenhill Real Estate because everyone except Nelson is paid regularly on the last working day of the month.

Unrecorded revenue

The treatment of unrecorded revenue is similar to that of unrecorded expenses. Any revenue which has been earned but not recorded during the accounting period should be recognized in the accounts by means of an adjusting entry, debiting an asset account and crediting a revenue account. *Accrued revenue* is a term often used to describe revenue which has been accumulating during the period but which has not been recorded prior to the closing date.

On November 16, Greenhill Real Estate entered into a management agreement with Angela Clayton, the owner of two small office buildings. The company agreed to manage the Clayton properties for a fee of $240 a month, payable on the fifteenth of each month. No entry is made in the accounting records at the time of signing a contract, because no services have yet been rendered and no change has occurred in assets or liabilities. The managerial duties are to begin immediately, but the first monthly fee will not be received until December 15. The following *adjusting entry* is therefore necessary at November 30:

Adjusting entry for fees earned but uncollected

Management Fees Receivable	*120*	
Management Fees Earned		*120*

To record accrued revenue from services rendered to Angela Clayton during November.

The debit balance in the Management Fees Receivable account will be shown in the balance sheet as an asset. The credit balance of the Management Fees Earned account, including earnings from both the Day and Clayton contracts, will appear in the November income statement.

The collection of the first monthly fee from Clayton will occur in the next accounting period (December 15, to be exact). Of this $240 cash receipt, half represents collection of the asset account, Management Fees Receivable, created at November 30 by the adjusting entry. The other half of the $240 cash receipt represents revenue earned during December; this should be credited to the December revenue account for Management Fees Earned. The entry on December 15 is as follows:

Management fee applicable to two accounting periods

Cash	*240*	
Management Fees Receivable		*120*
Management Fees Earned		*120*

Collected commission for month ended December 15.

The net result of the November 30 accrual entry has been to divide the revenue from managing the Clayton properties between November and December in accordance with the timing of the services rendered.

Adjusting entries and the accrual basis of accounting

Adjusting entries help make accrual basis accounting work successfully. By preparing adjusting entries, we can recognize revenue in the accounting period in which it is earned and also bring into the accounts any unrecorded expenses which helped to produce that revenue. For example, an adjusting entry to record revenue which has been earned but has not been recorded or collected prior to the end of the period helps achieves our goal of an income statement which includes all the revenue earned in a given time period. Other adjusting entries cause expenses to be recorded in the accounting period in which the benefits from the expenditures are received, even though cash payment is made in an earlier or later period.

THE WORK SHEET

The work necessary at the end of an accounting period includes construction of a trial balance, journalizing and posting of adjusting entries, preparation of financial statements, and journalizing and posting of closing entries. So many details are involved in these end-of-period procedures that it is easy to make errors. If these errors are recorded in the journal and in the ledger accounts, considerable time and effort can be wasted in correcting them. Both the journal and the ledger are formal, permanent records. They may be prepared manually in ink, produced on accounting machines, or printed by a computer. One way of avoiding errors in the permanent accounting records and also of simplifying the work to be done at the end of the period is to use a *work sheet.*

A work sheet is a large columnar sheet of paper, especially designed to arrange in a convenient systematic form all the accounting data required at the end of the period. The work sheet is not a part of the permanent accounting records; it is prepared in pencil by accountants for their own convenience. If an error is made on the work sheet, it may be erased and corrected much more easily than an error in the formal accounting records. Furthermore, the work sheet is designed to reduce errors by automatically bringing to light many types of discrepancies which otherwise might be entered in the journal and posted to the ledger accounts. Dollar signs, decimal points, and commas are not used with the amounts entered on work sheets, although commas are shown on this example. A work sheet for Greenhill Real Estate appears on page 129.

The work sheet may be thought of as a testing ground on which the ledger accounts are adjusted, balanced, and arranged in the general form of financial statements. The satisfactory completion of a work sheet provides considerable assurance that all the details of the end-of-period accounting procedures have

GREENHILL REAL ESTATE
Work Sheet
For the Month Ended November 30, 19___

	Trial Balance Dr	Trial Balance Cr	Adjustments Dr	Adjustments Cr	Adjusted Trial Balance Dr	Adjusted Trial Balance Cr	Income Statement Dr	Income Statement Cr	Balance Sheet Dr	Balance Sheet Cr
Cash	21,800									
Accounts receivable	16,990									
Unexpired insurance	540									
Office supplies	720									
Land	130,000									
Building	36,000									
Accumulated depreciation:building		150								
Office equipment	5,400									
Accumulated depreciation: office equipment		45								
Notes payable		3,000								
Accounts payable		23,595								
Unearned management fees		1,800								
Capital stock		180,000								
Retained earnings, Oct. 31, 19___		771								
Dividends	1,500									
Sales commissions earned		15,484								
Advertising expense	1,275									
Salaries expense	9,425									
Telephone expense	1,195									
	224,845	224,845								

1. Enter ledger account balances before adjustments in Trial Balance columns on work sheet

been properly brought together. After this point has been established, the work sheet then serves as the source from which the formal financial statements are prepared and the adjusting and closing entries are made in the journal.

Preparing the work sheet

Note that the heading of the work sheet illustrated for Greenhill Real Estate consists of three parts: (1) the name of the business, (2) the title *Work Sheet,* and (3) the period of time covered. The body of the work sheet contains five pairs of money columns, each pair consisting of a debit and a credit column. The procedures to be followed in preparing a work sheet will now be illustrated in five simple steps.

1 Enter the ledger account balances in the Trial Balance columns   The titles and balances of the ledger accounts at November 30 are copied into the Trial Balance columns of the work sheet. In practice these amounts may be taken directly from the ledger. It would be a duplication of work to prepare a trial balance as a separate schedule and then to copy this information into the work sheet. As soon as the account balances have been listed on the work sheet, these two columns should be added and the totals entered.

2 Enter the adjustments in the Adjustments columns   The required adjustments for Greenhill Real Estate were explained earlier in this chapter; these same adjustments are now entered in the Adjustments columns of the work sheet. (See page 131.)

As a cross reference, the debit and credit parts of each adjustment are keyed together by placing a key letter to the left of each amount. For example, the adjustment debiting Insurance Expense and crediting Unexpired Insurance is identified by the key letter (a). The use of the key letters makes it easy to match a debit entry in the Adjustments columns with its related credit. The identifying letters also key the debit and credit entries in the Adjustments columns to the brief explanations which appear at the bottom of the work sheet.

The titles of any accounts debited or credited in the adjusting entries but not listed in the trial balance should be written on the work sheet below the trial balance. For example, Insurance Expense does not appear in the trial balance; therefore it should be written on the first available line below the trial balance totals. After all the adjustment debits and credits have been entered in the Adjustments columns, this pair of columns must be totaled. Proving the equality of debit and credit totals helps to detect any arithmetical errors and to prevent them from being carried over into other columns of the work sheet.

3 Enter the account balances as adjusted in the Adjusted Trial Balance columns   The work sheet as it appears after completion of the Adjusted Trial Balance columns is illustrated on page 132. Each account balance in the first pair of columns is combined with the adjustment, if any, in the second pair of columns, and the combined amount is entered in the Adjusted Trial Balance columns. This

GREENHILL REAL ESTATE
Work Sheet
For the Month Ended November 30, 19___

	Trial Balance Dr	Trial Balance Cr	Adjustments* Dr	Adjustments* Cr	Adjusted Trial Balance Dr	Adjusted Trial Balance Cr	Income Statement Dr	Income Statement Cr	Balance Sheet Dr	Balance Sheet Cr
Cash	21,800									
Accounts receivable	16,990									
Unexpired insurance	540			(a) 15						
Office supplies	720			(b) 120						
Land	130,000									
Building	36,000									
Accumulated depreciation: building		150		(c) 150						
Office equipment	5,400									
Accumulated depreciation: office equipment		45		(d) 45						
Notes payable		3,000								
Accounts payable		23,595								
Unearned management fees		1,800	(e) 300							
Capital stock		180,000								
Retained earnings, Oct. 31, 19___		771								
Dividends	1,500									
Sales commissions earned		15,484								
Advertising expense	1,275									
Salaries expense	9,425		(g) 180							
Telephone expense	1,195									
Totals	224,845	224,845								
Insurance expense			(a) 15							
Office supplies expense			(b) 120							
Depreciation expense: building			(c) 150							
Depreciation expense: office equipment			(d) 45							
Management fees earned				(e) 300						
				(h) 120						
Interest expense			(f) 30							
Interest payable				(f) 30						
Salaries payable				(g) 180						
Management fees receivable			(h) 120							
			960	960						

*Adjustments:
(a) Portion of insurance cost which expired during November
(b) Office supplies used during November
(c) Depreciation of building during November
(d) Depreciation of office equipment during November
(e) Earned one-sixth of the commission collected in advance on the Day properties
(f) Interest expense accrued during November on note payable
(g) Salesman's salary for last four days of November
(h) Rental commission accrued on Clayton contract in November

GREENHILL REAL ESTATE
Work Sheet
For the Month Ended November 30, 19___

Enter the adjusted amounts in columns 5 and 6 of work sheet

	Trial Balance Dr	Trial Balance Cr	Adjustments* Dr	Adjustments* Cr	Adjusted Trial Balance Dr	Adjusted Trial Balance Cr	Income Statement Dr	Income Statement Cr	Balance Sheet Dr	Balance Sheet Cr
Cash	21,800				21,800					
Accounts receivable	16,990				16,990					
Unexpired insurance	540			(a) 15	525					
Office supplies	720			(b) 120	600					
Land	130,000				130,000					
Building	36,000				36,000					
Accumulated depreciation: building		150		(c) 150		300				
Office equipment	5,400				5,400					
Accumulated depreciation: office equipment		45		(d) 45		90				
Notes payable		3,000				3,000				
Accounts payable		23,595				23,595				
Unearned management fees		1,800	(e) 300			1,500				
Capital stock		180,000				180,000				
Retained earnings, Oct. 31, 19___		771				771				
Dividends	1,500				1,500					
Sales commissions earned		15,484				15,484				
Advertising expense	1,275				1,275					
Salaries expense	9,425		(g) 180		9,605					
Telephone expense	1,195				1,195					
Totals	224,845	224,845								
Insurance expense			(a) 15		15					
Office supplies expense			(b) 120		120					
Depreciation expense: building			(c) 150		150					
Depreciation expense: office equipment			(d) 45		45					
Management fees earned				(e) 300 (h) 120		420				
Interest expense			(f) 30		30					
Interest payable				(f) 30		30				
Sales salaries payable				(g) 180		180				
Management fees receivable			(h) 120		120					
			960	960	225,370	225,370				

*Explanatory notes relating to adjustments are the same as on page 131 process of combining the items on each line throughout the first four columns of the work sheet requires horizontal addition or subtraction. It is called *cross footing,* in contrast to the addition of items in a vertical column, which is called *footing* the column.

For example, the Office Supplies account has a debit balance of $720 in the Trial Balance columns. This $720 debit amount is combined with the $120 credit appearing on the same line in the Adjustments column; the combination of a $720 debit with a $120 credit produces an adjusted debit amount of $600 in the Adjusted Trial Balance debit column. As another example, consider the Office Supplies Expense account. This account had no balance in the Trial Balance columns but shows a $120 debit in the Adjustments debit column. The combination of a zero starting balance and $120 debit adjustment produces a $120 debit amount in the Adjusted Trial Balance.

Many of the accounts in the trial balance are not affected by the adjustments made at the end of the month; the balances of these accounts (such as Cash, Land, Building, or Notes Payable in the illustrated work sheet) are entered in the Adjusted Trial Balance columns in exactly the same amounts as shown in the Trial Balance columns. After all the accounts have been extended into the Adjusted Trial Balance columns, this pair of columns is totaled to prove that no arithmetical errors have been made up to this point.

4 Extend each amount in the Adjusted Trial Balance columns into the Income Statement columns or into the Balance Sheet columns Assets and liabilities are entered in the Balance Sheet columns. The owners' equity accounts (Capital Stock, Retained Earnings, and Dividends) are also entered in the Balance Sheet columns. The revenue and expense accounts are entered in the Income Statement columns.

The process of extending amounts horizontally across the work sheet should begin with the account at the top of the work sheet, which is usually Cash. The cash figure is extended to the Balance Sheet debit column. Then the accountant goes down the work sheet line by line, extending each account balance to the appropriate column. The work sheet as it appears after completion of this sorting process is illustrated on page 134. Note that each amount in the Adjusted Trial Balance columns is extended to one *and only one* of the four remaining columns.

5 Total the Income Statement columns and the Balance Sheet columns. Enter the net income or net loss as a balancing figure in both pairs of columns, and again compute column totals The work sheet as it appears after this final step is shown on page 135.

The net income or net loss for the period is determined by computing the difference between the totals of the two Income Statement columns. In the illustrated work sheet, the credit column total is the larger and the excess represents net income:

Income Statement credit column total (revenue) **$15,904**
Income Statement debit column total (expenses) 12,435
Difference: net income for period .... **$ 3,469**

GREENHILL REAL ESTATE
Work Sheet
For the Month Ended November 30, 19____

Extend each adjusted amount to columns for income statement or balance sheet

	Trial Balance		Adjustments*		Adjusted Trial Balance		Income Statement		Balance Sheet	
	Dr	Cr	Dr	Cr	Dr	Cr	Dr	Cr	Dr	Cr
Cash	21,800				21,800				21,800	
Accounts receivable	16,990				16,990				16,990	
Unexpired insurance	540			(a) 15	525				525	
Office supplies	720			(b) 120	600				600	
Land	130,000				130,000				130,000	
Building	36,000				36,000				36,000	
Accumulated depreciation: building		150		(c) 150		300				300
Office equipment	5,400				5,400				5,400	
Accumulated depreciation: office equipment		45		(d) 45		90				90
Notes payable		3,000				3,000				3,000
Accounts payable		23,595				23,595				23,595
Unearned management fees		1,800	(e) 300			1,500				1,500
Capital stock		180,000				180,000				180,000
Retained earnings, Oct. 31, 19____		771				771				771
Dividends	1,500				1,500				1,500	
Sales commissions earned		15,484				15,484		15,484		
Advertising expense	1,275				1,275		1,275			
Salaries expense	9,425		(g) 180		9,605		9,605			
Telephone expense	1,195				1,195		1,195			
Totals	224,845	224,845								
Insurance expense			(a) 15		15		15			
Office supplies expense			(b) 120		120		120			
Depreciation expense: building			(c) 150		150		150			
Depreciation expense: office equipment			(d) 45		45		45			
Management fees earned				(e) 300 (h) 120		420		420		
Interest expense			(f) 30		30		30			
Interest payable				(f) 30		30				30
Sales salaries payable				(g) 180		180				180
Management fees receivable			(h) 120		120				120	
Totals			960	960	225,370	225,370				

*Explanatory notes relating to adjustments are the same as on page 131.

Completed work sheet

GREENHILL REAL ESTATE
Work Sheet
For the Month Ended November 30, 19___

	Trial Balance		Adjustments*		Adjusted Trial Balance		Income Statement		Balance Sheet	
	Dr	Cr	Dr	Cr	Dr	Cr	Dr	Cr	Dr	Cr
Cash	21,800				21,800				21,800	
Accounts receivable	16,990				16,990				16,990	
Unexpired insurance	540			(a) 15	525				525	
Office supplies	720			(b) 120	600				600	
Land	130,000				130,000				130,000	
Building	36,000				36,000				36,000	
Accumulated depreciation: building		150		(c) 150		300				300
Office equipment	5,400				5,400				5,400	
Accumulated depreciation: office equipment		45		(d) 45		90				90
Notes payable		3,000				3,000				3,000
Accounts payable		23,595				23,595				23,595
Unearned management fees		1,800	(e) 300			1,500				1,500
Capital stock		180,000				180,000				180,000
Retained earnings, Oct. 31, 19___		771				771				771
Dividends	1,500				1,500				1,500	
Sales commissions earned		15,484				15,484		15,484		
Advertising expense	1,275				1,275		1,275			
Salaries expense	9,425		(g) 180		9,605		9,605			
Telephone expense	1,195				1,195		1,195			
Totals	224,845	224,845								
Insurance expense			(a) 15		15		15			
Office supplies expense			(b) 120		120		120			
Depreciation expense: building			(c) 150		150		150			
Depreciation expense: office equipment			(d) 45		45		45			
Management fees earned				(e) 300 (h) 120		420		420		
Interest expense			(f) 30		30		30			
Interest payable				(f) 30		30				30
Sales salaries payable				(g) 180		180				180
Management fees receivable			(h) 120		120				120	
			960	960	225,370	225,370	12,435	15,904	212,935	209,466
Net income							3,469			3,469
Totals							15,904	15,904	212,935	212,935

*Explanatory notes relating to adjustments are the same as on page 131.

Note that the net income of $3,469 is entered in the Income Statement *debit* column as a balancing figure and also on the same line as a balancing figure in the Balance Sheet *credit* column. The caption Net Income is written in the space for account titles to identify and explain this item. New totals are then computed for both the Income Statement columns and the Balance Sheet columns. Each pair of columns is now in balance.

The reason for entering the net income of $3,469 in the Balance Sheet *credit column* is that the net income accumulated during the period in the revenue and expense accounts causes an increase in the owners' equity. If the balance sheet columns did not have equal totals after the net income had been recorded in the credit column, the lack of agreement would indicate that an error had been made in the work sheet.

Let us assume for a moment that the month's operations had produced a loss rather than a profit. In that case the Income Statement debit column would exceed the credit column. The excess of the debits (expenses) over the credits (revenue) would have to be entered in the *credit column* in order to bring the two Income Statement columns into balance. The incurring of a loss would decrease the owners' equity; therefore, the loss would be entered as a balancing figure in the Balance Sheet *debit column*. The Balance Sheet columns would then have equal totals.

Self-balancing nature of the work sheet   Why does the entering of the net income or net loss in one of the Balance Sheet columns bring this pair of columns into balance? The answer is short and simple. All the accounts in the Balance Sheet columns have November 30 balances with the exception of the Retained Earnings account, which still shows the October 31 balance of $771. By bringing in the current month's net income of $3,469 and the Dividends of $1,500, the total owners' equity is brought up to date as of November 30. The Balance Sheet columns now prove the familiar proposition that assets are equal to the total of liabilities and owners' equity.

Uses for the work sheet

Preparing financial statements   Preparing the formal financial statements from the work sheet is an easy step. All the information needed for both the income statement and the balance sheet has already been sorted and arranged in convenient form in the work sheet. For example, compare the amounts on the following income statement with the amounts listed in the Income Statement columns of the completed work sheet.

GREENHILL REAL ESTATE
Income Statement
For the Month Ended November 30, 19___

Revenue:		
Sales commissions earned		$15,484
Management fees earned		420
Total revenue		$15,904
Expenses:		
Advertising	$1,275	
Office supplies	120	
Salaries	9,605	
Telephone	1,195	
Insurance	15	
Depreciation: building	150	
Depreciation: office equipment	45	
Interest	30	
Total expenses		12,435
Net income		$ 3,469

As noted in Chapter 3, we are purposely ignoring income taxes on corporations at this stage of our study. Corporate income taxes are introduced in Chapter 5 and considered more fully in Chapters 7 and 17.

The statement of retained earnings can also be compiled directly from the work sheet. Compare the following statement of retained earnings with amounts shown on the completed work sheet for November. The October 31 balance of $771 in retained earnings plus the $3,469 of net income earned in November and minus the $1,500 of dividends paid lead to a new balance of $1,755 in retained earnings at November 30.

GREENHILL REAL ESTATE
Statement of Retained Earnings
For the Month Ended November 30, 19___

Retained earnings, Oct. 31, 19___	$ 771
Net income for November	3,469
Subtotal	$4,240
Less: Dividends	1,500
Retained earnings, Nov. 30, 19___	$2,740

Finally, the Greenhill balance sheet illustrated for the month of November contains the amounts for assets, liabilities, and capital stock listed in the Balance Sheet columns of the work sheet, along with the new balance of retained earnings.

GREENHILL REAL ESTATE
Balance Sheet
November 30, 19___

Assets

Compare these amounts with figures in Balance Sheet columns of work sheet

Cash		$ 21,800
Accounts receivable..		16,990
Management fees receivable		120
Unexpired insurance		525
Office supplies..		600
Land		130,000
Building	$ 36,000	
Less: Accumulated depreciation...........................	300	35,700
Office equipment..	$ 5,400	
Less: Accumulated depreciation...........................	90	5,310
Total assets		$211,045

Liabilities & Stockholders' Equity

Liabilities:

Notes payable...		$ 3,000
Accounts payable		23,595
Interest payable		30
Salaries payable..		180
Unearned management fees		1,500
Total liabilities		$ 28,305
Stockholders' equity:		
Capital stock...	$180,000	
Retained earnings..	2,740	182,740
Total liabilities & stockholders' equity		$211,045

Recording adjusting entries in the accounting records   After the financial statements have been compiled from the work sheet at the end of the period, adjusting journal entries are prepared to bring the ledger accounts into agreement with the financial statements. This is an easy step because the adjustments have already been computed on the work sheet. The amounts appearing in the Adjustments columns of the work sheet and the related explanations at the bottom of the work sheet provide all the necessary information for the adjusting entries, as shown in the journal illustration on page 139. These adjusting entries are first entered in the journal and then posted to the ledger accounts.

General Journal Page 5

Adjustments on
work sheet are
entered in
general journal

Date		Account Titles and Explanation	LP	Debit	Credit
19__ Nov.	30	Insurance Expense.......................... Unexpired Insurance .... Insurance expense for November.		15	15
	30	Office Supplies Expense................... Office Supplies .... Office supplies used during November.		120	120
	30	Depreciation Expense: Building............ Accumulated Depreciation: Building Depreciation for November.		150	150

	30	Depreciation Expense: Office Equipment ...
		     Accumulated Depreciation: Office
		        Equipment ....
		 Depreciation for November.
				45	45

	30	Unearned Management Fees.............. Management Fees Earned .... Earned one-sixth of fee collected in advance for management of the properties owned by John Day.		300	300
	30	Interest Expense .... Interest Payable..................... Interest expense accrued during November on note payable ($3,000 × .12 × 1/12).		30	30
	30	Salaries Expense........................... Salaries Payable .... To record expense and related liability to salesman for last four evenings' work in November.		180	180
	30	Management Fees Receivable.............. Management Fees Earned .... To record the receivable and related revenue earned for managing properties owned by Angela Clayton.		120	120

Closing entries When the financial statements have been prepared from the work sheet, the revenue and expense accounts have served their purpose for the current period and should be closed. These accounts will then have zero balances and will be ready for the recording of revenue and expenses during the next fiscal period.

The journalizing and posting of closing entries were illustrated in Chapter 3. The point to be emphasized now is that the completed work sheet provides in convenient form all the information needed to make the closing entries. The preparation of closing entries from the work sheet may be summarized as follows:

1 To close the accounts listed in the Income Statement credit column, debit the revenue accounts and credit Income Summary.
2 To close the accounts listed in the Income Statement debit column, debit Income Summary and credit the expense accounts.
3 To close the Income Summary account, transfer the balancing figure in the Income Statement columns of the work sheet ($3,469 in the illustration) to the Retained Earnings account. A profit is transferred by debiting Income Summary and crediting the Retained Earnings account; a loss is transferred by debiting the Retained Earnings account and crediting Income Summary.
4 To close the Dividends account, debit the Retained Earnings account and credit the Dividends account.

The entries to close the revenue and expense accounts, as well as the Dividends account, at November 30 are shown on page 141.

The accounting cycle

As stated at the beginning of this chapter, the life of a business is divided into accounting periods of equal length. In each period we repeat a standard sequence of accounting procedures beginning with the journalizing of transactions and concluding with an after-closing trial balance.

Because the work sheet includes the trial balance, the adjusting entries in preliminary form, and an adjusted trial balance, the use of a work sheet will modify the sequence of procedures given in Chapter 3, as follows:

1 Journalize transactions Analyze business transactions as they occur and record them promptly in a journal.

2 Post to ledger accounts Transfer debits and credits from journal entries to ledger accounts.

3 Prepare a work sheet Begin with a trial balance of the ledger, enter all necessary adjustments, sort the adjusted account balances between income statement accounts and balance sheet accounts, and determine the net income or net loss.

Closing entries derived from work sheet

			General Journal			Page 6
Date			Account Titles and Explanation	LP	Debit	Credit
19__						
Nov.	30		Sales Commissions Earned		15,484	
			Management Fees Earned		420	
			Income Summary			15,904
			To close the revenue accounts.			
	30		Income Summary		12,435	
			Advertising Expense			1,275
			Salaries Expense			9,605
			Telephone Expense			1,195
			Insurance Expense			15
			Office Supplies Expense			120
			Depreciation Expense: Building			150
			Depreciation Expense: Office			
			Equipment			45
			Interest Expense			30
			To close the expense accounts.			
	30		Income Summary		3,469	
			Retained Earnings			3,469
			To close the Income Summary account.			
	30		Retained Earnings		1,500	
			Dividends			1,500
			To close the Dividends account.			

4 Prepare financial statements Utilize the information in the work sheet to prepare an income statement, a statement of retained earnings, and a balance sheet.

5 Adjust and close the accounts Using the information in the work sheet as a guide, enter the adjusting entries in the journal. Post these entries to ledger accounts. Prepare and post journal entries to close the revenue and expense accounts into the Income Summary account and to transfer the net income or net loss to the Retained Earnings account. Also prepare and post a journal entry to close the Dividends account into the Retained Earnings account.

6 Prepare an after-closing trial balance Prove that equality of debit and credit balances in the ledger has not been upset by the adjusting and closing procedures.

The above sequence of accounting procedures constitutes a complete accounting process. The regular repetition of this standardized set of procedures in each accounting period is often referred to as the *accounting cycle*. The procedures of a complete accounting cycle are illustrated below.

Illustration of the accounting cycle

Note that the preparing of financial statements (Step 4) comes before entering adjusting and closing entries in the journal and posting these entries to the ledger (Step 5). This sequence reflects the fact that *management wants the financial statements as soon as possible.* Once the work sheet is complete, all information required for the financial statements is available. Top priority then goes to preparation of the financial statements.

In most business concerns the accounts are closed only once a year; for these companies the accounting cycle is one year in length. For purposes of illustration in a textbook, however, it is often convenient to assume that the entire accounting cycle is performed within the time period of one month. The completion of the accounting cycle is the occasion for preparing financial statements and closing the revenue and expense accounts.

Preparing monthly financial statements without closing the accounts

Many companies which close their accounts only once a year nevertheless prepare *monthly* financial statements for managerial use. These monthly statements are prepared from work sheets, but the adjustments indicated on the work sheets are not entered in the accounting records and no closing entries are made. Under this plan, the time-consuming operation of journalizing and posting adjustments and closing entries is performed only at the end of the fiscal year, but the company has the advantage of monthly financial statements. Monthly and quarterly financial statements are often referred to as *interim statements,* because they are in between the year-end statements. The annual or year-end statements are usually audited by a firm of certified public accountants; interim statements are usually unaudited.

Reversing entries

Reversing entries are an optional bookkeeping procedure which may be carried out at year-end to simplify the recording of certain routine cash receipts and payments in the following period. As the name suggests, a *reversing entry* is the exact reverse of an adjusting entry. It contains the same account titles and dollar amounts as the related adjusting entry, but the debits and credits are the reverse of those in the adjusting entry and the date is the first day of the next accounting period.

Let us use as an example a small company on a five-day work week which pays its employees each Friday. Assume that the payroll is $600 a day or $3,000 for a five-day week. Throughout the year, the company's bookkeeper makes a journal entry each Friday as follows:

Regular weekly entry for payroll

Salaries Expense	*3,000*	
Cash		*3,000*
To record payment of salaries for the week.		

Next, let us assume that December 31, the last working day of Year 1, falls on Wednesday. All expenses of Year 1 must be recorded before the accounts are closed and financial statements prepared at December 31. Therefore, an adjusting entry must be made to record the salaries expense and the related liability to employees for the three days they have worked since the last payday. The adjusting entry for $1,800 (computed as 3 × $600 daily salary expense) is shown below:

Adjusting entry at end of year

Salaries Expense	*1,800*	
Salaries Payable		*1,800*
To record salaries expense and the related liability to employees for last three days worked in December.		

The closing of the accounts on December 31 will reduce the Salaries Expense account to zero, but the liability account, Salaries Payable, will remain open with its $1,800 credit balance at the beginning of the new year. On the next regular payday, Friday, January 2, the company's bookkeeper can record the $3,000 payroll by a debit of $1,800 to Salaries Payable, a debit of $1,200 to Salaries Expense, and a credit of $3,000 to Cash. However, splitting the debit side of the entry in this manner ($1,800 to the liability account and $1,200 to expense) requires more understanding and alertness from the bookkeeper than if the entry were identical with the other 51 payroll entries made during the year.

By making a reversing entry as of the first day of the new accounting period, we can simplify the recording of routine transactions and avoid the need for the company's employees to refer to prior adjusting entries for guidance. The reversing entry for the $1,800 year-end accrual of salaries would be dated January 1, Year 2, and would probably be made under the direction of the accountant responsible for the year-end closing of the accounts and preparation of financial statements. The entry would be as follows:

Reversing entry makes possible . . .

Jan. 1   Salaries Payable 1,800

          Salaries Expense 1,800

        To reverse the accrual of salaries made on Dec. 31, Year 1.

This reversing entry closes the Salaries Payable account by transferring the $1,800 liability to the credit side of the Salaries Expense account. Thus, the Salaries Expense account begins the new year with an abnormal credit balance of $1,800. On Friday, January 2, the normal payroll entry for $3,000 will be made to the same accounts as on every other Friday during the year.

. . . regular payroll entry for first payday of new year

Salaries Expense 3,000

    Cash 3,000

Paid salaries for week ended Jan. 2, Year 2.

After this January 2 entry has been posted, the ledger account for Salaries Expense will show a debit balance of $1,200, the result of this $3,000 debit and the $1,800 credit from the reversing entry on January 1. The amount of $1,200 is the correct expense for the two workdays of the new year at $600 a day. The results, of course, are exactly the same as if no reversing entry had been used and the company's bookkeeper has split the debit side of the January 2 payroll entry between Salaries Payable and Salaries Expense.

The ledger accounts for Salaries Expense and for Salaries Payable are shown below to illustrate the effect of posting the adjusting entry and the reversing entry.

Salaries Expense

Year 1		Debit	Credit	Balance
Various	(51 weekly entries of $3,000)			153000
Dec. 31	Adjusting entry (3 days @ $600)	1800		154800
31	To close at year-end		154800	-0-
Year 2				
Jan. 1	Reversing entry		1800	1800 cr
2	Weekly payroll	3000		1200

Salaries Payable

Year 1		Debit	Credit	Balance
Dec. 31	Adjusting entry (3 days @ $600)		1800	1800
Year 2				
Jan. 1	Reversing entry	1800		-0-

Which adjusting entries may be reversed? Reversing entries may be used for *any adjusting entry that accrues an expense* (for example, interest expense, utilities expense, taxes expense, and salaries expense). Reversing entries also may be used for *any adjusting entry that accrues revenue* (for example, commissions earned but not yet collected or billed to customers, interest earned but not yet collected, and rent earned but not yet collected). Adjustments which accrue expenses or revenue bring liabilities or assets (receivables) into the records and *are followed by payments or receipts of cash*. This characteristic is helpful in identifying those adjusting entries which may be reversed.

Adjusting entries for depreciation *are not reversed.* Neither is the adjusting entry to apportion part of the cost of unexpired insurance to expense, nor the entry to apportion part of any asset to expense. Reversing entries which recognize that a portion of revenue collected in advance has now been earned at the year-end are not reversed. Finally, remember that reversing entries are optional. They are a convenience in carrying out the accounting process, but are not essential to the application of accounting principles or the preparation of good financial statements.

KEY TERMS INTRODUCED OR EMPHASIZED IN CHAPTER 4

Accounting cycle The sequence of accounting procedures performed during an accounting period. The procedures include journalizing transactions, posting, preparation of a work sheet and financial statements, adjusting and closing the accounts, and preparation of an after-closing trial balance.

Accrued expenses Expenses such as salaries of employees and interest on notes payable which have been accumulating day-by-day but are unrecorded and unpaid at the end of the period. Also called *unrecorded expenses.*

Accrued revenue Revenue which has been earned during the accounting period but has not been recorded or collected prior to the closing date. Also called *unrecorded revenue.*

Book value The net amount at which an asset is shown in accounting records. For depreciable assets, book value equals cost minus accumulated depreciation. Also called *carrying value.*

Carrying value See book value.

Deferred revenue An obligation to render services or deliver goods in the future because of advance receipt of payment. Also called *unearned revenue.*

Interim statements Financial statements prepared at intervals of less than one year. Usually quarterly and monthly statements.

Prepaid expenses Advance payments for such expenses as rent and insurance. The portion which has not been used up at the end of the accounting period is included in the balance sheet as an asset.

Promissory note A formal written promise to repay an amount borrowed plus interest at a future date.

Reversing entries An optional year-end bookkeeping technique consisting of the reversal on the first day of the new accounting period of those year-end adjusting entries which accrue expenses or revenue and thus will be followed by later cash payments or receipts. Purpose is to permit company personnel to record routine transactions in a standard manner without referring to prior adjusting entries.

Unearned revenue See deferred revenue.

Unrecorded expenses   See accrued expenses.

Unrecorded revenue   See accrued revenue.

Work sheet   A large columnar sheet designed to arrange in convenient form all the accounting data required at the end of the period. Facilitates preparation of financial statements and the work of adjusting and closing the accounts.

DEMONSTRATION PROBLEM FOR YOUR REVIEW

Reed Geophysical Company adjusts and closes its accounts at the end of the calendar year. At December 31, 198X the following trial balance was prepared from the ledger:

REED GEOPHYSICAL COMPANY
Trial Balance
December 31, 198X

Cash	$12,540	
Prepaid office rent	8,400	
Prepaid dues and subscriptions	960	
Supplies on hand	1,300	
Equipment	20,000	
Accumulated depreciation: equipment		$ 1,200
Notes payable		5,000
Unearned consulting fees		35,650
Capital stock		10,000
Retained earnings, Jan. 1, 198X		12,950
Dividends	7,000	
Consulting fees earned		15,200
Salaries expense	26,900	
Telephone expense	550	
Miscellaneous expenses	2,350	
	$80,000	$80,000

Other data

(a) On January 1, 198X the Prepaid Office Rent account had a balance of $2,400, representing the prepaid rent for the months from January to June 198X inclusive. On July 1, the lease was renewed and office rent for one year at $500 per month was paid in advance.

(b) Dues and subscriptions expired during the year in the total amount of $710.

(c) A count of supplies on hand was made at December 31; the cost of the unused supplies was $450.

(d) The useful life of the equipment has been estimated at 10 years from date of acquisition.

(e) Accrued interest on notes payable amounted to $100 at year-end. Set up a separate Interest Expense account.

SOLUTION TO DEMONSTRATION PROBLEM

Account	TB Dr	TB Cr	Adj Dr	Adj Cr	Adj TB Dr	Adj TB Cr	Income Stmt Dr	Income Stmt Cr	Balance Sheet Dr	Balance Sheet Cr
Cash	12,540				12,540				12,540	
Prepaid office rent	8,400			(a) 5,400	3,000				3,000	
Prepaid dues and subscriptions	960			(b) 710	250				250	
Supplies on hand	1,300			(c) 850	450				450	
Equipment	20,000				20,000				20,000	
Accumulated depreciation: equipment		1,200		(d) 2,000		3,200				3,200
Notes payable		5,000				5,000				5,000
Unearned consulting fees		35,650	(f) 32,550			3,100				3,100
Capital stock		10,000				10,000				10,000
Retained earnings, Jan. 1, 198X		12,950				12,950				12,950
Dividends	7,000				7,000				7,000	
Consulting fees earned		15,200		(f) 32,550 (g) 3,000		50,750		50,750		
Salaries expense	26,900		(h) 200		27,100		27,100			
Telephone expense	550				550		550			
Miscellaneous expenses	2,350				2,350		2,350			
	80,000	80,000								
Rent expense			(a) 5,400		5,400		5,400			
Dues and subscriptions expense			(b) 710		710		710			
Supplies expense			(c) 850		850		850			
Depreciation expense: equipment			(d) 2,000		2,000		2,000			
Interest expense			(e) 100		100		100			
Interest payable				(e) 100		100				100
Consulting fees receivable			(g) 3,000		3,000				3,000	
Salaries payable				(h) 200		200				200
			44,810	44,810	85,300	85,300	39,060	50,750	46,240	34,550
Net income							11,690			11,690
Totals							50,750	50,750	46,240	46,240

(f) Consulting services valued at $32,550 were rendered during the year for clients who had made payment in advance.

It is the custom of the firm to bill clients only when consulting work is completed or, in the case of prolonged engagements, at six-month intervals.

(g) December 31, engineering services valued at $3,000 had been rendered to clients but not yet billed. No advance payments had been received from these clients.

(h) Salaries earned by staff engineers but not yet paid amounted to $200 at December 31.

Instructions Prepare a work sheet for the year ended December 31, 198X.

REVIEW QUESTIONS

1 Which of the following statements do you consider most acceptable?

a Adjusting entries affect balance sheet accounts only.

b Adjusting entries affect income statement accounts only.

c An adjusting entry may affect two or more balance sheet accounts or two or more income statement accounts, but cannot affect both a balance sheet account and an income statement account.

d Every adjusting entry affects both a balance sheet account and an income statement account.

2 The recording of depreciation involves two ledger accounts: Depreciation Expense and Accumulated Depreciation. Explain the purpose of each account; indicate whether it normally has a debit balance or a credit balance; and state where it appears in the financial statements.

3 At the end of the currect year, the adjusted trial balance of the Midas Company showed the following account balances, among others:

Building, $31,600

Depreciation Expense: Building, $1,580

Accumulated Depreciation: Building, $11,060

Assuming that straight-line depreciation has been used, what length of time do these facts suggest that the Midas Company has owned the building?

4 The Ryan Company has a five-day work week. The weekly payroll for salespeople amounts to $1,250. All salespeople are paid up to date at the close of business each Friday. If December 31 falls on Wednesday, what year-end adjusting entry is needed?

5 The Marvin Company purchased a three-year fire insurance policy on August 1 and debited the entire cost of $540 to Unexpired Insurance. The accounts were not adjusted or closed until the end of the year. Give the adjusting entry at December 31.

6 The net income reported by the Haskell Company for Year 2 was $21,400, and the Retained Earnings account stood at $36,000. However, the company had failed to recognize that interest amounting to $1,000 had accrued on a note payable to the bank. State the corrected figures for net income and retained earnings. In what other respect was the balance sheet of the company in error?

7 Office supplies on hand in the Melville Company amounted to $642 at the beginning of the year. During the year additional office supplies were purchased at a cost of $1,561 and charged to the asset account. At the end of the year a physical count showed that supplies on hand amounted to $812. Give the adjusting entry needed at December 31.

8 The X Company at December 31 recognized the existence of certain unexpired costs which would provide benefits to the company in future periods. Give examples of such unexpired costs and state where they would be shown in the financial statements.

9 In performing the regular end-of-period accounting procedures, does the preparation of the work sheet precede or follow the posting of adjusting entries to ledger accounts? Why?

10 List in order the procedures comprising the accounting cycle when a work sheet is used.

11 Explain why the amount of net income is entered in the Income Statement debit column on a work sheet.

12 Do the totals of the balance sheet ordinarily agree with the totals of the Balance Sheet columns of the work sheet?

13 Is a work sheet ever prepared when there is no intention of closing the accounts? Explain.

14 The Adjustments columns of the work sheet for Davis Company contained only three adjustments, as follows: depreciation of building, $3,600; expiration of insurance, $500; and salaries accrued at year-end, $4,100. If the Trial Balance columns showed totals of $600,000, what would be the totals of the Adjusted Trial Balance columns?

15 Should the Adjusted Trial Balance columns be totaled before or after the adjusted amounts are carried to the Income Statement and Balance Sheet columns? Explain.

16 In extending adjusted account balances from the Adjusted Trial Balance columns to the Income Statement and Balance Sheet columns, is there any particular sequence to be followed in order to minimize the possibility of errors? Explain.

17 At year-end the adjusting entry to reduce the Unexpired Insurance account by the amount of insurance premium applicable to the current period was accidentally omitted. Which items in the income statement will be in error? Will these items be overstated or understated? Which items in the balance sheet will be in error? Will they be overstated or understated?

18 The weekly payroll of Stevens Company, which has a five-day work week, amounts to $15,000 and employees are paid up to date every Friday. On January 1 of the current year, the Salaries Expense account showed a credit balance of $9,000. Explain the nature of the accounting entry or entries which probably led to this balance.

EXERCISES

Ex. 4-1 On September 1, Bar Company purchased a one-year fire insurance policy and recorded the payment of the full yearly premium of $4,800 by debiting Unexpired Insurance. The accounts were not adjusted or closed until the end of the calendar year. Prepare the necessary adjusting entry at December 31.

Ex. 4-2 Mill Corporation adjusts and closes its accounts at the end of the calendar year. Prepare the adjusting entries required at December 31 based on the following information. (Not all of these items may require adjusting entries.)

     a A bank loan had been obtained on October 1. Accrued interest on the loan at December 31 amounts to $1,200. No interest expense has been recorded.

     b Depreciation of office equipment is based on estimated life of 10 years. The balance in the Office Equipment account is $26,400; no change has occurred in the account during the year.

     c Interest receivable on United States Government bonds owned at December 31 amounts to $1,920. This accrued interest has not been recorded.

     d On December 31, an agreeement was signed to lease a truck for 12 months beginning January 1 at a rate of 30 cents a mile. Usage is expected to be 1,500 miles per month and the contract specifies a minimum payment equivalent to 10,000 miles a year.

Ex. 4-3 On Friday of each week, Ozark Company pays its employees weekly salaries amounting to $100,000 for a five-day work week.

     a Prepare the necessary adjusting entry at year-end, assuming that December 31 falls on Tuesday.

     b Prepare the journal entry for payment by Ozark Company of a week's salaries to its employees on Friday, January 3, the first payday of the new year. (Assume that no reversing entry was made.)

Ex. 4-4 Among the ledger accounts used by Cottonwood Speedway are the following: Prepaid Rent, Rent Expense, Unearned Admissions Revenue, Admissions Revenue, Prepaid Printing, Printing Expense, Concessions Receivable, and Concessions Revenue. For each of the following items, write first the journal entry (if one is needed) to record the external transaction and secondly the adjusting entry, if any, required on March 31, the end of the fiscal year.

     a On March 1, paid rent for the next four months at $25,000 per month.

     b On March 2, sold season tickets for a total of $600,000. The season includes 60 racing days: 15 in March, 25 in April, and 20 in May.

     c On March 3, an agreement was reached with Snack-Bars, Inc., allowing that company to sell refreshments at the track in return for 10% of the gross receipts from refreshment sales.

     d On March 5, schedules for the 15 racing days in March and the first 10 racing days in April were printed and paid for at a cost of $10,000.

     e On March 31, Snack-Bars, Inc., reported that the gross receipts from refreshment sales in March had been $135,000 and that the 10% owed to Cottonwood Speedway would be remitted on April 10.

Ex. 4-5 Property Management Company manages apartment buildings for various owners who wish to be relieved of this responsibility. Among the ledger accounts in use are Cash, Unearned Management Fees, Management Fees, and Management Fees Receivable. On December 1, the company received a check for $12,000 from a client, Susan Hart, who was leaving for a six-month stay abroad. This check represented payment in advance for management of Hart's real estate properties during the six months of her absence. Explain how this transaction would be recorded, the adjustment, if any, to be made at December 31, and how this information would be shown in the year-end financial statements.

Ex. 4-6 The following amounts are taken from consecutive balance sheets of Jensen Company.

	December 31	
	Year 1	Year 2
Unexpired insurance	$ –0–	$1,200
Unearned rental revenue	5,500	4,000
Interest payable	100	800

The income statement for Year 2 of the Jensen Company shows the following items:

Insurance expense	$ 700
Rental revenue	18,000
Interest expense	1,000

Instructions Determine the following amounts:
a Cash paid during Year 2 on insurance policies
b Cash received during Year 2 as rental revenue
c Cash paid during Year 2 for interest

Ex. 4-7 The trial balances of Fisher Insurance Agency, as of September 30, 19___, before and after the posting of adjusting entries, are shown below:

	Before Adjustments		After Adjustments	
	Dr	Cr	Dr	Cr
Cash	$ 6,180		$ 6,180	
Commissions receivable			800	
Office supplies	600		360	
Office equipment	6,220		6,220	
Accumulated depreciation: office equipment		$ 2,150		$ 2,240
Accounts payable		1,550		1,550
Salaries payable				450
Unearned commissions		400		140
Capital stock		4,500		4,500
Retained earnings		2,500		2,500
Commissions earned		3,900		4,960
Salaries expense	2,000		2,450	
Office supplies expense			240	
Depreciation expense: office equipment			90	
	$15,000	$15,000	$16,340	$16,340

Instructions By comparing the two trial balances shown above, it is possible to determine which accounts have been adjusted. You are to prepare the adjusting journal entries which must have been made to cause these changes in account balances. Include an explanation as part of each adjusting entry.

Ex. 4-8 Milo Company closes its accounts at the end of each calendar year. The company operates on a five-day work week and pays its employees up to date each Friday. The weekly payroll is regularly $5,000. On Tuesday, December 31, Year 1, an adjusting entry was made to accrue $2,000 salaries expense for the two days worked since the last payday. The company did not make a reversing entry. On Friday, January 3, Year 2, the regular weekly payroll of $5,000 was paid and recorded by the usual entry debiting Salaries Expense $5,000 and crediting Cash $5,000.

Were Milo Company's accounting records correct for Year 1? For Year 2? Explain two alternatives the company might have followed with respect to payroll at year-end. One of the alternatives should include a reversing entry.

PROBLEMS

Group A

4-1 Sierra Ski Bowl maintains its accounting records on a calendar-year basis. Using the year-end information shown below, you are to prepare all necessary adjusting journal entries at December 31.

(a) A one-year fire insurance policy had been purchased and paid for in full at a total premium of $1,800 on December 1 of the current year. The payment was debited to Unexpired Insurance.

(b) On December 31, Sierra Ski Bowl signed an agreement to lease a truck from Olympic Rentals for the period of one year beginning January 1 at a rate of 24 cents per mile, with a minimum monthly charge of $240.

(c) Depreciation on the building for the year ended December 31 was $3,600.

(d) A portion of the land owned had been leased to an amusement park at a yearly rental of $14,400. One year's rent had been collected in advance at the date of the lease (December 16) and credited to Unearned Rental Revenue. (Recognize one-half month's rent as earned.)

(e) Another portion of the land owned had been rented on December 1 to a service station operator at an annual rate of $2,880. No rent had as yet been collected from this tenant.

(f) Accrued wages payable, $5,520.

(g) Accrued interest receivable on United States government bonds owned amounts to $990 as of December 31.

(h) A six-month bank loan in the amount of $72,000 had been obtained on October 31. No interest had been paid and no interest expense recorded. Accrued interest at December 31 amounted to $1,200.

(i) Accrued property taxes, $3,470.

Instructions From the information given above, draft the adjusting entries (including explanations) required at December 31.

4-2 Gary Smith organized Safe Storage on January 1 for the purpose of leasing a large vacant building and renting space in this building to others for storage of industrial materials. The accounting policies of the company call for making adjusting entries and closing the accounts each month. Shown below is a trial balance and other information for use in preparing adjusting entries at January 31.

SAFE STORAGE
Trial Balance
January 31, 19___

Cash	$ 8,105	
Unexpired insurance	4,080	
Office supplies	405	
Office equipment	7,200	
Notes payable		$ 3,000
Unearned storage fees		1,350
Capital stock		12,000
Storage fees earned		8,850
Rent expense	1,800	
Telephone expense	135	
Salaries expense	3,475	
	$25,200	$25,200

Other data

(a) The monthly insurance expense amounted to $400.

(b) The amount of office supplies on hand, based on a physical count on January 31, was $195.

(c) A $3,000 one-year note payable was signed on January 1. Interest accrued at January 31 was $45.

(d) The useful life of office equipment was estimated at eight years.

(e) Certain clients chose to pay several months' storage fees in advance. It was determined that $480 of such fees was still unearned as of January 31.

(f) Several clients neglected to send in storage fees amounting to $330 for the month of January. These amounts have not been recorded but are considered collectible.

(g) Salaries earned by employees but not yet paid amounted to $240.

Instructions

Based on the above trial balance and other information, prepare the adjusting entries (with explanations) needed at January 31.

4-3 Kingspoint Motel maintains its accounting records on the basis of a calendar year. The following information is available as a source for adjusting entries at December 31.

(a) Salaries earned by employees but not yet paid amount to $10,860.

(b) As of December 31 the motel has earned $5,040 rental revenue from current guests who will not be billed until they are ready to check out.

(c) On December 16, a suite of rooms was rented to a guest for six months at a monthly rental of $1,500. Rent for the first three months was collected in advance and credited to Unearned Rental Revenue.

(d) A one-year bank loan in the amount of $90,000 had been obtained on November 1 at an annual interest rate of 9%. No interest has been paid and no interest expense has been recorded.

(e) Depreciation on the motel for the year ended December 31 was $43,800.

(f) Depreciation on a station wagon owned by the motel was based on a four-year life. The station wagon, purchased new on September 1 of the current year, cost $10,800.

(g) On December 31, Kingspoint Motel entered into an agreement to host the National Building Suppliers Convention in June of next year. The motel expects to earn rental revenue of at least $15,000 from the convention.

Instructions

a From the information given, draft the adjusting entries (including explanations) required at December 31.

b Assume that all necessary adjusting entries at December 31 have been recorded and that net income for the year is determined to be $300,000. How much net income would have been indicated by the accounting records if the company had failed to make the above adjusting entries? Show computations.

4-4 Pacific Beach Motor Camp obtains revenue from camping fees and also from a contract with a concessionaire who sells refreshments on the premises. The books are closed at the end of each calendar year; at December 31 the data for adjustments were compiled and a work sheet was prepared. The first four columns of the work sheet contained the account balances and adjustments shown below.

	Trial Balance		Adjustments*	
	Dr	Cr	Dr	Cr
Cash	24,100			
Unexpired insurance	2,100			(a) 700
Prepaid advertising........................	1,000			(b) 300
Land	375,000			
Equipment.................................	48,000			
Accumulated depreciation:				
equipment..............................		8,000		(f) 4,000
Notes payable.............................		110,000		
Unearned revenue from				
concessions		7,500	(d) 5,000	
Capital stock.............................		263,000		
Retained earnings.........................		5,000		
Revenue from camping fees.................		174,500		
Advertising expense	5,500		(b) 300	
Water expense	10,400			
Salaries expense	78,900		(e) 1,100	
Repairs and maintenance expense...........	17,500			
Miscellaneous expense	5,500			
	568,000	568,000		
Insurance expense			(a) 700	
Interest expense...........................			(c) 400	
Interest payable				(c) 400
Revenue from concessions..................				(d) 5,000
Salaries payable...........................				(e) 1,100
Depreciation expense:				
equipment..............................			(f) 4,000	
			11,500	11,500

*Adjustments:
(a) $700 insurance expired during year.
(b) $300 prepaid advertising expired at end of year.
(c) $400 accrued interest expense on notes payable.
(d) $5,000 concession revenue earned during year.
(e) $1,100 of salaries earned but unpaid at Dec. 31, 19____.
(f) $4,000 depreciation expense for year.

Instructions Complete the work sheet by listing the appropriate amounts in the remaining six columns. Follow the format of the work sheet illustrated on page 135.

4-5 Green Valley Golf Club began operations on March 1 of the current year on a site rented from the county. The company's accounting policy is to adjust and close its accounts each month. Before adjustments on October 31, the account balances were as follows:

Cash	$ 54,530	
Unexpired insurance	4,060	
Prepaid rent	105,000	
Equipment	336,000	
Accumulated depreciation: equipment		$ 24,500
Accounts payable		56,000
Dividends payable		14,000
Unearned greens fees		28,000
Capital stock		350,000
Retained earnings		28,630
Dividends	14,000	
Greens fees earned		89,600
Salaries expense	54,600	
Repairs and maintenance expense	13,440	
Water expense	9,100	
	$590,730	$590,730

Other data
(a) The unexpired insurance represents a three-year fire insurance policy purchased on March 1 for $5,040.
(b) Monthly rent expense amounted to $35,000.
(c) The equipment was being depreciated over an eight-year life.
(d) On October 10, a local corporation purchased 7,000 special price tickets for $28,000. Each ticket was good for one round of golf. During October, 2,170 of the tickets were used.
(e) The Elks' Club reserved the entire golf course for the last two days of October and the first day of November for a golf tournament, agreeing to pay greens fees of a flat $7,000 per day at the conclusion of the tournament.
(f) Salaries earned by employees but not paid were $4,900 at October 31.

Instructions Based on the trial balance and other data, prepare a 10-column work sheet for the month ended October 31, 19___. Use a pair of columns for each of the following: Trial Balance, Adjustments, Adjusted Trial Balance, Income Statement, and Balance Sheet.

4-6 White Water Taxi was organized to transport tourists to a nearby resort island. The company adjusts and closes its accounts at the end of each month. Selected account balances appearing on the June 30 *adjusted* trial balance are as follows:

Prepaid rent	$ 2,700
Unexpired insurance	720
Boats	28,800
Accumulated depreciation: boats	$2,100
Unearned passenger revenue	750

Other data
(1) Four months' rent had been prepaid on June 1.
(2) The unexpired insurance is a 36-month fire insurance policy purchased on January 1.
(3) The boats are being depreciated over an eight-year estimated useful life, with no residual value.
(4) The unearned passenger revenue represents tickets good for future rides sold to a resort hotel for $6 per ticket on June 1. During June, 175 of the tickets were used.

Instructions
a Determine:
(1) The monthly rent expense
(2) The original cost of the 36-month fire insurance policy
(3) The age in months of the boats
(4) How many $6 tickets for future rides were sold to the resort hotel on June 1
b Prepare the adjusting entries which were made on June 30.

4-7 County Lines, Inc., is a bus company in a suburban area. The company adjusts and closes its accounts each month. At December 31, the following trial balance was prepared from the ledger.

Cash	$ 200,625	
Prepaid rent	27,000	
Unexpired insurance	31,200	
Spare parts on hand	85,500	
Buses	1,215,000	
Accumulated depreciation: buses		$ 232,875
Unearned passenger revenue		90,000
Capital stock, $10 par value		1,050,000
Retained earnings		171,900
Dividends	18,000	
Passenger revenue		284,700
Fuel expense	38,700	
Repairs & maintenance expense	3,300	
Salaries expense	202,050	
Advertising expense	8,100	
	$1,829,475	$1,829,475

Other data

(a) Monthly rent amounted to $4,500.

(b) Insurance expense for December was $6,300.

(c) Maintenance work costing $7,800 was done on the buses by City Garage in late December. No bill has yet been received, and the expense has not been recorded.

(d) Spare parts used in connection with maintenance work during December amounted to $5,550.

(e) The buses are being depreciated over a useful life of 10 years.

(f) Early in December 15,000 special books of bus tickets were sold to the public for $6 per book. Each ticket book contained 10 bus tickets. As of December 31, 45,000 tickets had been used.

(g) Salaries earned by employees but not paid were $4,950 at December 31.

Instructions

a Prepare a 10-column work sheet for the month ended December 31, 19____.

b Prepare an income statement, a statement of retained earnings, and a balance sheet (in report form).

c Prepare adjusting and closing entries at December 31.

4-8 Blue Lagoon Airline provides passenger and freight service among some Pacific Islands. The accounts are adjusted and closed each month. At June 30, the following trial balance was prepared from the ledger.

BLUE LAGOON AIRLINE
Trial Balance
June 30, 19____

Cash	$ 190,500	
Prepaid rent expense	54,000	
Unexpired insurance	46,800	
Prepaid maintenance expense	22,500	
Spare parts	57,000	
Airplanes	2,000,000	
Accumulated depreciation: airplanes		$ 577,000
Unearned passenger revenue		60,000
Capital stock		1,390,000
Retained earnings		277,700
Dividends	12,000	
Passenger revenue earned		184,000
Gasoline expense	13,800	
Salaries expense	86,700	
Advertising expense	5,400	
	$2,488,700	$2,488,700

Other data

(a) Monthly rent amounted to $3,000.

(b) Insurance expense for June was $3,900.

(c) All necessary maintenance work was provided by Reese Air Service at a fixed charge of $7,500 a month. Service for three months had been paid for in advance on June 1.

(d) Spare parts used in connection with maintenance work amounted to $3,750 during the month.

(e) The airplanes were several years old when purchased. Their remaining useful life at the time of purchase was estimated to be 10,000 hours of flying time. Depreciation expense is computed on the basis of hours of flying time each month. During June, total flying time amounted to 200 hours.

(f) The Chamber of Commerce purchased 2,000 special tickets for $60,000. Each ticket allowed the holder one flight normally priced at $45. During the month 400 tickets were used by the holders.

(g) Salaries earned by employees but not paid amounted to $3,300 at June 30.

Instructions

a Prepare a 10-column work sheet for the month ended June 30, 19___.

b Prepare an income statement and a statement of retained earnings for the month of June and a balance sheet at June 30, 19___.

c Prepare adjusting and closing entries.

4-9   Financial Consultants, Inc., is in the business of performing research and preparing financial analyses for business organizations and government agencies. Much of its work is done through a computer service center for which payment is made on an hourly basis. The company adjusts and closes its accounts monthly. At October 31, the account balances were as follows *before* adjustments were made.

Cash	$ 71,760
Research fees receivable	–0–
Prepaid office rent	28,800
Prepaid computer rental expense	42,960
Office supplies	4,200
Office equipment	25,200
Accumulated depreciation: office equipment	600
Notes payable	24,000
Accounts payable	8,760
Interest payable	–0–
Salaries payable	–0–
Unearned research fees	114,600
Capital stock	50,000
Retained earnings	33,820
Dividends	2,400
Research fees earned	16,200
Office salaries expense	5,040
Research salaries expense	58,320
Telephone expense	2,640
Travel expense	6,660
Office rent expense	–0–
Computer rental expense	–0–
Office supplies expense	–0–
Depreciation expense: office equipment	–0–
Interest expense	–0–

Other data

(a) The amount in the Prepaid Office Rent account represented office rent for eight months paid in advance on October 1, 19___ when the lease was renewed.

(b) During October, 220 hours of computer time were used at a cost of $180 an hour.

(c) Office supplies on hand October 31 were determined by count to amount to $840.

(d) Office equipment was estimated to have a useful life of seven years from date of purchase.

(e) Accrued interest on notes payable amounted to $96 on October 31.

(f) Services to clients amounting to $76,440 performed during October were chargeable against the Unearned Research Fees account.

(g) Services to clients who had not made advance payments and had not been billed amounted to $35,280 at October 31.

(h) Salaries earned by research staff but not paid amounted to $5,160 on October 31.

Instructions

a Prepare a 10-column work sheet for the month of October.

b Prepare financial statements consisting of an income statement and statement of retained earnings for the month of October and a balance sheet at October 31, 19___.

4-10 The following events relating to salaries occurred in King Company near December 31, the end of the fiscal year.

Dec. 27 Recorded payment of regular weekly salaries of $3,000.

Dec. 31 Prepared an adjusting entry for accrued salaries of $1,200.

Jan. 1 Made a reversing entry for accrued salaries.

Jan. 3 Recorded payment of regular weekly salaries of $3,000.

King Company rents a portion of its building to a tenant for $2,100 a month payable in advance on the twenty-first of each month. The tenant is often late in making the payments. Year-end transactions relating to rent revenue were as follows.

Dec. 31 Recorded accrued rent revenue of $700 for the period December 21– December 31.

Jan. 1 Made a reversing entry for accrued rent revenue.

Jan. 4 Recorded collection of $2,100 rent for period December 21–January 21.

Instructions

a Prepare journal entries (with explanations) for the four events relating to salaries.

b How much of the $3,000 in salaries paid on January 3 represents a January expense? Explain.

c Assume that no reversing entry was made by King Company; prepare the journal entry for payment of salaries on January 3.

d Prepare journal entries (with explanations) for the three events relating to rent revenue.

e How much of the $2,100 rent received on January 4 represents January revenue? Explain.

f Assume that no reversing entry was made by King Company with respect to rent; prepare the journal entry to record collection of $2,100 rent on January 4.

BUSINESS DECISION PROBLEM 4

Seven Souls Marina rents 50 slips in a large floating dock to owners of pleasure boats in the area. The marina also performs repair services on small craft.

Bob Mathews, a friend of yours, is convinced that recreational boating will become increasingly popular in the area and has entered into negotiations to buy Seven Souls Marina.

Bob does not have quite enough cash to purchase the business at the price the owner has demanded. However, the owner of the marina has suggested that Bob might purchase the marina with what cash he does have, and turn the net income of the business over to the retiring owner until the balance of the purchase price has been paid. A typical month's income for Seven Souls Marina is determined as follows:

Revenue:		
Slip rentals		$2,520
Repairs		3,180
Total revenue		$5,700
Operating expenses:		
Wages	$1,920	
Insurance	36	
Depreciation expense: docks	960	
Depreciation expense: equipment	180	
Other expenses	240	3,336
Net income		$2,364

Bob is concerned about turning the whole net income of the business over to the former owner for the next several months, because he estimates that he and his family will need to keep at least $960 a month to meet their living expenses. In coming to you for advice, Bob explains that all revenue of Seven Souls Marina is collected when earned and that both wages and "other" expenses are paid when incurred. Bob does not understand, however, when depreciation expense must be paid or why there is any insurance expense when the insurance policies of the business have more than two years to run before new insurance must be purchased.

Instructions

a Advise Bob as to how much cash the business will generate each month. Will this amount of cash enable Bob to withdraw $960 per month to meet his living expenses and pay $2,364 per month to the former owner?

b Explain why insurance expense appears on the income statement of the business if no new policies will be purchased within the next two years.

5

ACCOUNTING FOR PURCHASES AND SALES OF MERCHANDISE

After studying this chapter you should be able to:

- Account for purchases and sales of merchandise.
- Determine the cost of goods sold by the periodic inventory method.
- Prepare a work sheet and closing entries for a merchandising company.
- Prepare a classified balance sheet and either a single-step or multiple-step income statement.
- Discuss the basic means of achieving internal control.
- Describe the typical business documents involved in purchase transactions.
- Explain the advantage of recording purchase invoices by the net-price method.

The preceding four chapters have illustrated step by step the complete accounting cycle for a business rendering personal services. Service-type companies represent an important part of our economy. They include, for example, airlines, railroads, motels, travel agencies, theaters, golf courses, ski resorts, and professional football clubs. These enterprises receive commissions or fees for the services they provide and their net income is equal to the excess of commissions or fees earned over operating expenses incurred.

In contract to the service-type business, merchandising companies, both wholesalers and retailers, earn revenue by selling goods or merchandise. The term *merchandise* means goods acquired by a business for resale to customers. Net income results if the revenue from sales exceeds (1) the cost of the goods sold and (2) the operating expenses, as shown in the following income statement.

CORNER STORE
Income Statement
For the Year Ended December 31, 19___

Revenue from sales	$1,000,000
Less: Cost of goods sold	700,000
Gross profit on sales	$ 300,000
Less: Operating expenses	250,000
Net income	$ 50,000

In this simplified example of an income statement, Corner Store sold for $1,000,000 goods which cost $700,000. Thus the store earned a $300,000 gross profit on sales. Operating expenses, such as store rent and salaries, are subtracted from the gross profit to produce net income of $50,000.

Revenue from sales

If merchandising companies are to succeed or even to survive, they must sell their goods at prices higher than they pay to the vendors or suppliers from whom they buy. The selling prices charged by a retail store must cover three things: (1) the cost of the merchandise to the store; (2) the operating expenses of the business such as advertising, store rent, and salaries of the sales staff; and (3) a net income to the business.

Revenue from sales equals the gross amount of sales minus sales returns and allowances and sales discounts, as shown in the following partial income statement.

Partial Income Statement

Revenue from sales:		
Gross sales		$506,000
Less: Sales returns and allowances	$4,000	
Sales discounts	2,000	6,000
Net sales		$500,000

The $506,000 of gross sales in the partial income statement represents the total of both cash and credit sales for the year. When a business sells merchandise to its customers, it either receives immediate payment in cash or acquires an account receivable which soon will be collected in cash. As explained in Chapter 3, the inflow of cash and receivables from sales of the current period is equal to the revenue for that period. Each cash sale is rung up on a cash register before the merchandise is handed to the customer. At the end of the day, the total shown by the cash register represents cash sales for the day and is recorded by a journal entry, as follows:

Journal entry for cash sales	Cash	900	
	Sales		900
	To record the sale of merchandise for cash.		

For a sale of merchandise on credit, a typical journal entry would be:

*Journal entry for
sale on credit*

Accounts Receivable *500*

    Sales *500*

Sold merchandise on credit to Kay's Gift Shop; payment due within 30 days.

Revenue from the sale of merchandise is considered as earned in the period in which the merchandise is delivered to the customer, even though payment in cash is not received for a month or more after the sale. Consequently, the revenue earned in a given accounting period may differ considerably from the cash receipts of that period.

The amount and trend of sales are watched very closely by management, investors, and others interested in the progress of a company. A rising volume of sales is evidence of growth and suggests the probability of an increase in earnings. A declining trend in sales, on the other hand, is often the first signal of reduced earnings and of financial difficulties ahead. The amount of sales for each year is compared with the sales of the preceding year; the sales of each month may be compared with the sales of the preceding month and also with the corresponding month of the preceding year. These comparisons bring to light significant trends in the volume of sales.

Sales returns and allowances

Most merchandising companies allow customers to obtain a refund by returning merchandise which is found to be unsatisfactory. When customers find that merchandise purchased has minor defects, they may agree to keep such merchandise if an allowance is made on the sales price. Refunds and allowances have the effect of reversing previously recorded sales and reducing the amount of revenue earned by the business. The journal entry to record sales returns and allowances is shown below:

*Journal entry for
sales returns and
allowances*

Sales Returns and Allowances *100*

    Cash (or Accounts Receivable) *100*

Made refund for merchandise returned by customer.

At the end of the accounting period, the amount accumulated in the Sales Returns and Allowances account will be shown in the income statement as a deduction from sales.

The use of a Sales Returns and Allowances account rather than recording refunds by direct debits to the Sales account is advisable because the accounting records then show both the total amount of sales and the amount of sales returns. Management is interested in the percentage relationship between goods sold and goods returned as an indication of customer satisfaction with the merchandise.

Credit terms

For all sales of merchandise on credit, the terms of payment should be clearly stated, so that buyer and seller can avoid any misunderstanding as to the time and amount of the required payment. One common example of credit terms is "net 30 days" or "n/30," meaning that the net amount of the invoice or bill is due in 30 days. Another common form of credit terms is "10 e.o.m.," meaning payment is due 10 days after the end of the month in which the sale occurred.

Sales discounts

Manufacturers and wholesalers often sell goods on credit terms of 30 to 60 days or more, but offer a discount for earlier payment. For example, the credit terms may be "2% 10 days, net 30 days." These terms mean that the authorized credit period is 30 days, but that the customer company may deduct 2% of the amount of the invoice if it makes payment within 10 days. On the invoice, these terms would appear in the abbreviated form "2/10, n/30"; this expression is read "2, 10, net 30." The 10-day period during which the discount is available is called the *discount period*. Because a sales discount provides an incentive to the customer to make an early cash payment, it is often referred to as a *cash discount*.

For example, assume that Adams Company on November 3 sells merchandise for $1,000 on credit to Zipco, Inc., terms 2/10, n/30. At the time of the sale, the seller does not know if the buyer will take advantage of the discount by paying within the discount period; therefore, Adams Company records the sale at the full price by the following entry.

Nov. 3 *Accounts Receivable* *1,000*
              Sales *1,000*
        To record sale to Zipco, Inc., terms 2/10, n/30.

The customer now has a choice between saving $20 by paying within the discount period, or waiting a full 30 days and paying the full price. If Zipco mails its check on or before November 13, it is entitled to deduct 2% of $1,000 or $20, and settle the obligation for $980. If Zipco decides to forgo the discount, it may postpone payment an additional 20 days until December 3 but must then pay $1,000.

Assuming that payment is made by Zipco on November 13, the last day of the discount period, the entry by Adams Company to record collection of the receivable is

Nov. 13 *Cash* *980*
     Sales Discount *20*
          Accounts Receivable *1,000*
        Collected from Zipco, Inc., for our sale of Nov. 3, less 2% cash discount.

If a customer returns a portion of the merchandise before making payment, the discount applies only to the portion of the goods kept by the customer. In the above example, if Zipco had returned $300 worth of goods out of the $1,000 purchase, the discount would have been applicable only to the $700 portion of the order which the customer kept.

At the end of the year the debit balance accumulated in the Sales Discount ledger account is deducted from gross sales to determine the revenue from sales. This treatment reflects the fact that allowing a cash discount reduces the amount received from sales.

Cost of goods sold

The cost of the merchandise sold during the year appears in the income statement as a deduction from the sales of the year. The merchandise which is *available for sale but not sold* during the year constitutes the *inventory* of merchandise on hand at the end of the year. The inventory is included in the year-end balance sheet as an asset.

How can the manager determine, at the end of a year, a month, or other accounting period, the quantity and the cost of the goods remaining on hand? How can management determine the cost of the goods sold during the period? These amounts must be determined before either a balance sheet or an income statement can be prepared. In fact, the determination of inventory value and of the cost of goods sold may be the most important single step in measuring the profitability of a business. The two alternative approaches to the determination of inventory and of cost of goods sold are called the *perpetual inventory system* and the *periodic inventory system.*

The perpetual inventory system

Automobile dealers and television stores sell merchandise of *high unit value* and make a relatively small number of sales each day. Because sales transactions are few and of substantial amount, it is easy to look up the cost of the individual automobile or television set being sold. Thus a cost figure can be recorded as the *cost of goods sold* for each sales transaction. Under this system, the records show the cost of each article in stock. Units added to inventory and units removed for delivery to customers are recorded on a daily basis—hence the name *perpetual inventory system.* When financial statements are to be prepared, the total cost of goods sold during the accounting period is easily determined by adding the costs recorded from day to day for the units sold.

The perpetual inventory system will be discussed in Chapter 9; at present we are concentrating upon the *periodic inventory system* used by many companies dealing in merchandise of low unit value.

The periodic inventory system

In a business selling a variety of merchandise with low unit prices, the periodic inventory system may be more suitable than attempting to maintain perpetual inventory records of all items in stock. A business such as a drugstore may sell a customer a bottle of aspirin, a candy bar, and a tube of toothpaste. It is not practicable to look up in the records at the time of each sale the cost of such small items. Instead, stores which deal in merchandise of low unit value usually wait until the end of the accounting period to determine the cost of goods sold. To do this, the store must have information on three things: (1) the beginning inventory, (2) the cost of goods purchased during the period, and (3) the ending inventory or cost of goods unsold and on hand at the end of the period. This information enables the store to compute the cost of goods sold during the period as shown on the next page.

Computing cost of goods sold	*Inventory of merchandise at beginning of year*	$ 50,000
	Purchases	250,000
	Cost of goods available for sale	$300,000
	Less: Inventory at end of year	60,000
	Cost of goods sold	$240,000

In this example the store had $50,000 of merchandise at the beginning of the year. During the year it purchased an additional $250,000 worth of merchandise. Thus it had available for sale merchandise costing $300,000. By the end of the year all but $60,000 worth of merchandise had been sold. Consequently, the cost of the goods sold during the year must have been $240,000.

In more general terms, we can say that every merchandising business has *available for sale* during an accounting period the merchandise on hand at the beginning of the period *plus* the merchandise purchased during the period. If all these goods were sold during the period, there would be no ending inventory, and cost of goods sold would be equal to the cost of goods available for sale. Normally, however, some goods remain unsold at the end of the period; *cost of goods sold is then equal to the cost of goods available for sale minus the ending inventory of unsold goods.*

The cost of goods sold is an important concept which requires careful attention. To gain a thorough understanding of this concept, we need to consider the nature of the accounts used in determining the cost of goods sold.

Beginning inventory and ending inventory

An inventory of merchandise consists of the goods on hand and available for sale to customers. The goods on hand at the beginning of an accounting period are called the *beginning inventory;* the goods on hand at the end of the period are called the *ending inventory.* Since a new accounting period begins as soon as the old one ends, the *ending inventory of one accounting period is the beginning inventory of the following period.*

A business using the periodic inventory system will determine the amount of the ending inventory by taking a physical inventory. Taking inventory includes three steps. First, all items of merchandise in the store and stockrooms are counted; second, the quantity of each item is multiplied by the cost per unit; and third, the costs of the various kinds of merchandise are added together to get a total cost figure for all goods on hand.

The cost figure for ending inventory appears as an asset in the balance sheet and as a deduction in the cost of goods sold section of the income statement. It is brought into the accounting records by *a closing entry debiting Inventory and crediting Income Summary.* (This entry will be illustrated and explained more fully later in this chapter.) After the ending inventory has been recorded in the ledger, the Inventory account remains unchanged throughout the next accounting period. It represents both the ending inventory of the completed accounting period and the beginning inventory of the following period. Keep in mind that the Inventory account is not debited or credited as goods are purchased or sold. The balance in the Inventory account during the year shows the amount of goods which were on hand at the beginning of the present period.

Cost of merchandise purchased for resale

Under the periodic inventory system, the cost of merchandise purchased for resale is recorded by debiting an account called Purchases, as shown below.

Journal entry for purchase of merchandise

Nov. 3	Purchases	10,000	
	Accounts Payable		10,000
	Purchased merchandise from ABC Supply Co. Credit terms 2/10, n/30.		

The Purchases account *is used only for merchandise acquired for resale;* assets acquired for use in the business (such as a delivery truck, a typewriter, or office supplies) are recorded by debiting the appropriate asset account, not the Purchases account. The Purchases account does not indicate whether the purchased goods have been sold or are still on hand.

At the end of the accounting period, the balance accumulated in the Purchases account represents the total cost of merchandise purchased during the period. This amount is used in preparing the income statement. The Purchases account has then served its purpose and it is closed to the Income Summary account. Since the Purchases account is closed at the end of each period, it has a zero balance at the beginning of each succeeding period.

Purchase discounts   As explained earlier, manufacturers and wholesalers frequently grant a cash discount to customers who will pay promptly for goods purchased on credit. The selling company regards a cash discount as a *sales discount;* the buying company calls the discount a *purchase discount.*

If the $10,000 purchase of November 3 shown above is paid for on or before November 13, the last day of the discount period, the purchasing company will save 2% of the price of the merchandise, or $200, as shown by the following entry:

Nov. 13	Accounts Payable	10,000	
	Purchase Discounts		200
	Cash		9,800
	Paid ABC Supply Co. for purchase of Nov. 3, less 2% cash discount.		

The effect of the discount was to reduce the cost of the merchandise to the buying company. The credit balance of the Purchase Discounts account should therefore be deducted in the income statement from the debit balance of the Purchases account.

If the buying company chooses to postpone payment rather than take the discount, it will have the use of $9,800 for an additional 20 days. However, the extra $200 expense is a high penalty to incur for the use of $9,800 for 20 days. (A 20-day period is approximately $\frac{1}{18}$ of a year; 18 times 2% amounts to 36%.[1]) Although interest rates vary widely, most businesses are able to borrow money from banks at an annual interest rate of 20% or less. Well-managed businesses, therefore, generally pay all invoices within the discount period even though this policy necessitates borrowing from banks in order to have the necessary cash available.

---

[1]A more accurate estimate of interest expense on an annual basis can be obtained as follows: ($200 × 18) ÷ $9800 = 36.7%.

Purchase returns and allowances   When merchandise purchased from suppliers is found to be unsatisfactory, the goods may be returned, or a request may be made for an allowance on the price. A return of goods to the supplier is recorded as follows:

Accounts Payable *1,200*
    Purchase Returns and Allowances *1,200*
To reduce liability to Jet Supply Co. by the cost of goods returned for credit.

It is preferable to credit Purchase Returns and Allowances when merchandise is returned to a supplier rather than crediting the Purchases account directly. The accounts then show both the total amount of purchases and the amount of purchases which required adjustment or return. Management is interested in the percentage relationship between goods purchased and goods returned, because the returning of merchandise for credit is an expensive, time-consuming process. Excessive returns suggest inefficiency in the operation of the purchasing department and a need to find more dependable suppliers.

The Transportation-in account

The cost of merchandise acquired for resale logically includes any transportation charges necessary to bring the goods to the purchaser's place of business. A separate ledger account is used to accumulate transportation charges on merchandise purchased. The journal entry to record transportation charges on inbound shipments of merchandise is as follows:

Transportation-in *125*
    Cash (or Accounts Payable) *125*
Air freight charges on merchandise purchased from Miller Brothers, Kansas City.

Since transportation charges are part of the *delivered cost* of merchandise purchased, the Transportation-in account is combined with the Purchases account in the income statement to determine the cost of goods available for sale.

Transportation charges on inbound shipments of merchandise must not be confused with transportation charges on outbound shipments of goods to customers. Freight charges and other expenses incurred in making deliveries to customers are regarded as selling expenses; these outlays are debited to a separate account entitled Delivery Expense and are not included in the cost of goods sold.

F.O.B. shipping point and F.O.B. destination

The agreement between the buyer and seller of merchandise includes a provision as to which party shall bear the cost of transporting the goods. The term *F.O.B. shipping point* means that the seller will place the merchandise "free on board" the railroad cars or other means of transport, and that the buyer must pay transportation charges from that point. In most merchandise transactions involving wholesalers or manufacturers, the buyer bears the transportation cost. Sometimes, however, as a matter of convenience, the seller prepays the freight and includes this cost in the amount billed to the buyer.

F.O.B. destination means that the seller agrees to bear the freight cost. If the seller prepays the truckline or other carrier, the agreed terms have been met and no action is required of the buyer other than to pay the agreed purchase price of the goods. If the seller does not prepay the freight, the buyer will pay the carrier and deduct this payment from the amount owed the seller when making payment for the merchandise.

Inventory theft and other losses

Under the periodic inventory system, it is assumed that all goods available for sale during the year are either sold or are on hand at year-end for the ending inventory. As a result of this assumption, the cost of merchandise lost because of shoplifting, employee theft, or spoilage will be included automatically in cost of goods sold. For example, assume that a store has goods available for sale which cost $600,000. Assume that shoplifters steal $10,000 worth of goods and that the ending inventory is $100,000. (If the thefts had not occurred, the ending inventory would have been $10,000 larger.) The cost of goods sold is computed at $500,000 by subtracting the $100,000 ending inventory from the $600,000 cost of goods available for sale. The theft loss is not shown separately in the income statement. In reality, cost of goods *sold* was $490,000, and cost of goods *stolen* was $10,000.

Although the periodic inventory system causes inventory losses to be included automatically in cost of goods sold, accountants have devised a method of estimating losses of merchandise from theft. This method is explained in Chapter 9.

Income statement for a merchandising company

To bring together the various concepts discussed thus far in the chapter, we need to look at a classified income statement for a merchandising business. The income statement of Olympic Sporting Goods shown on the next page has three major sections: (1) a revenue section, (2) a cost of goods sold section, and (3) an operating expenses section. We have already discussed the various accounts used in the first two sections. Note that the amount of *gross profit on sales,* $200,000, is determined by subtracting the cost of goods sold from net sales. If the business is to be successful, the gross profit on sales must be sufficient to cover the operating expenses such as salaries, advertising, and depreciation.

The operating expenses in the third major section of the income statement are classified either as selling expenses or as general and administrative expenses. Selling expenses include all expenses of storing and displaying merchandise for sale, advertising, sales salaries, and delivering goods to customers. General and administrative expenses include the expenses of the general offices, accounting department, personnel office, and credit and collection departments.

OLYMPIC SPORTING GOODS
Income Statement
For the Year Ended December 31, Year 11

This income statement consists of three major sections

Gross sales			$506,000
Less: Sales returns and allowances		$ 4,000	
Sales discounts		2,000	6,000
Net sales			$500,000
Cost of goods sold:			
Inventory, Jan. 1		$ 60,000	
Purchases	$300,000		
Less: Purchase returns and allowances	$2,000		
Purchase discounts	1,000	3,000	
Net purchases		$297,000	
Add: Transportation-in		13,000	
Cost of goods purchased		310,000	
Cost of goods available for sale		$370,000	
Less: Inventory, Dec. 31		70,000	
Cost of goods sold			300,000
Gross profit on sales			$200,000
Operating expenses:			
Selling expenses:			
Sales salaries		$ 76,000	
Delivery service		4,000	
Advertising		16,000	
Depreciation		9,000	
Total selling expenses		105,000	
General & administrative expenses:			
Office salaries		$ 60,000	
Telephone		2,000	
Depreciation		8,000	
Total general & administrative expenses		70,000	
Total operating expenses			175,000
Income from operations			$ 25,000
Income taxes expense			5,000
Net income			$ 20,000

In many companies certain expenses, such as depreciation of the building, need to be divided, part to selling expense and part to general and administrative expenses. Olympic Sporting Goods divided its $17,000 of depreciation expense by allocating $9,000 to selling expenses and $8,000 to general and administrative expenses. This allocation can conveniently be made when the income statement is prepared from the work sheet; thus no additional ledger accounts are required. The account for Telephone Expense, $2,000, was not divided because management did not consider the amount large enough to warrant such treatment.

Note that the final deduction on the income statement is for income taxes expense. A corporation is a legal entity subject to corporation income tax; consequently, the ledger of a corporation must contain accounts for recording income taxes. No such accounts are needed for a business organized as a single proprietorship or partnership. Income taxes are based on a corporation's earnings and are recorded by an adjusting entry such as the following.

Recording corporate income taxes

Income Taxes Expense	5,000	
Income Taxes Payable		5,000

To record income taxes payable.

The account debited in this entry, Income Taxes Expense, is shown as the last deduction on the income statement to arrive at the "bottom line" figure for net income. The account for Income Taxes Payable is a current liability.

Analyzing the income statement   How does this income statement compare in form and content with the income statement of the service-type business presented in preceding chapters? The most important change is the inclusion of the section entitled Cost of Goods Sold. Note how large the cost of goods sold is in comparison with other figures on the statement. The cost of merchandise sold during the year amounts to $300,000, or 60% of the year's net sales of $500,000. Another way of looking at this relationship is to say that for each dollar the store receives by selling goods to customers, the sum of 60 cents represents a recovery of the cost of the merchandise. This leaves a *gross profit* of 40 cents from each sales dollar, out of which the store must pay its operating expenses. In our illustration the operating expenses for the year were $175,000, that is, 35% of the net sales figure of $500,000. Therefore, the gross profit of 40 cents contained in each dollar of sales was enough to cover the operating expenses of 35 cents and leave a pretax income of 5 cents from each dollar of sales. After the deduction of income taxes expense, the net income amounted to $20,000, or 4 cents from each dollar of net sales.

Of course the percentage relationship between sales and cost of goods sold will vary from one type of business to another, but, in all types of merchandising companies the cost of goods sold is one of the largest elements in the income statement. Accountants, investors, bankers, and business managers in general have the habit of mentally computing percentage relationships when they look at financial statements. Formation of this habit will be helpful throughout the study of accounting, as well as in many business situations.

In analyzing an income statement, we compare each item in the statement with the amount of net sales. The amount of net sales is regarded as 100%, and every other item or subtotal on the statement is expressed as a percentage of net sales. The cost of goods sold in most types of business will be between 60 and 80% of net sales. Conversely, the *gross profit on sales* (sales minus cost of goods sold) usually will vary between 40 and 20% of net sales.

Work sheet for a merchandising business

A merchandising company, like the service business discussed in Chapter 4, uses a work sheet at the end of the period to organize the information needed to prepare financial statements and to adjust and close the accounts. The new elements in the work sheet for Olympic Sporting Goods on page 173 are the beginning inventory, the ending inventory, and the other merchandising accounts. The inventory accounts are shown in a distinctive color to help focus your attention on their treatment.

Trial balance columns   The Trial Balance columns were prepared by listing the ledger account balances at December 31, Year 11. Notice that the Inventory account in the Trial Balance debit column shows a balance of $60,000, the cost of merchandise on hand at the end of the prior year. No entries were made in the Inventory account during the current year despite the various purchases and sales of merchandise. The significance of the Inventory account in the trial balance is that it shows the amount of merchandise with which Olympic Sporting Goods began operations on January 1 of the current year.

Adjustments on the work sheet   Only two adjustments were necessary at December 31: one to record depreciation of the building and the other to record the income taxes expense for the year. (The amount of income taxes is given as $5,000. We are not concerned at this point with the procedures for computing income taxes expense.) After these two adjustments were recorded, the Adjustments columns were then totaled to prove the equality of the adjustment debits and credits.

Income Statement columns   The accounts to be carried from the Adjusted Trial Balance columns to the Income Statement columns are the revenue accounts, the cost of goods sold accounts, and the operating expense accounts.

Recording the ending inventory on the work sheet   The key point to be observed in this work sheet is the method of recording the *ending inventory*. On December 31, a physical inventory was taken of all merchandise on hand. The entire inventory, priced at cost, amounted to $70,000. This ending inventory, dated December 31, does not appear in the trial balance; it is therefore written on the first available line below the trial balance totals. The amount of $70,000 is listed in the Income Statement credit column and also in the Balance Sheet debit column. By entering the ending inventory in the Income Statement *credit* column, we are in effect deducting it from the total of the beginning inventory, the purchases, and the transportation-in, all of which are extended from the adjusted trial balance to the Income Statement *debit* column.

One of the functions of the Income Statement columns is to bring together all the accounts involved in determining the cost of goods sold. The accounts with debit balances are the beginning Inventory, Purchases, and Transportation-in; these accounts total $373,000. Against this total the three credit items of Purchase Returns and Allowances, $2,000, Purchase Discounts, $1,000, and ending Inventory, $70,000, are offset. The three accounts with debit balances exceed in total the three credit balances by an amount of $300,000; this amount is the cost of goods sold, as shown in the income statement on page 170.

OLYMPIC SPORTING GOODS
Work Sheet
For the Year Ended December 31, Year 11

	Trial Balance Dr	Trial Balance Cr	Adjustments* Dr	Adjustments* Cr	Adjusted Trial Balance Dr	Adjusted Trial Balance Cr	Income Statement Dr	Income Statement Cr	Balance Sheet Dr	Balance Sheet Cr
Cash	19,000				19,000				19,000	
Accounts receivable	25,000				25,000				25,000	
Inventory, Jan. 1	60,000				60,000		60,000			
Land	123,000				123,000				123,000	
Building	120,000				120,000				120,000	
Accumulated depreciation: building		61,000		(a) 17,000		78,000				78,000
Notes payable		20,000				20,000				20,000
Accounts payable		30,000				30,000				30,000
Capital stock		150,000				150,000				150,000
Retained earnings, Dec. 31, Year 10		64,000				64,000				64,000
Dividends	10,000				10,000				10,000	
Sales		506,000				506,000		506,000		
Sales returns and allowances	4,000				4,000		4,000			
Sales discounts	2,000				2,000		2,000			
Purchases	300,000				300,000		300,000			
Purchase returns and allowances		2,000				2,000		2,000		
Purchase discounts		1,000				1,000		1,000		
Transportation-in	13,000				13,000		13,000			
Advertising expense	16,000				16,000		16,000			
Sales salaries	76,000				76,000		76,000			
Office salaries	60,000				60,000		60,000			
Telephone expense	2,000				2,000		2,000			
Delivery service	4,000				4,000		4,000			
	834,000	834,000								
Depreciation expense: building			(a) 17,000		17,000		17,000			
Income taxes expense			(b) 5,000		5,000		5,000			
Income taxes payable				(b) 5,000		5,000				5,000
			22,000	22,000	856,000	856,000				
Inventory, Dec. 31								70,000	70,000	
							559,000	579,000	367,000	347,000
Net income							20,000			20,000
Totals							579,000	579,000	367,000	367,000

Note the treatment of the beginning inventory

Note the treatment of the ending inventory

*Adjustments: (a) Depreciation of building during the year.
(b) To accrue income taxes.

The ending inventory is also entered in the Balance Sheet debit column of the work sheet, because this inventory of merchandise on December 31 will appear as an asset in the balance sheet bearing this date.

Completing the work sheet   When all the accounts on the work sheet have been extended into the Income Statement or Balance Sheet columns, the final four columns should be totaled. The net income is computed and the work sheet completed in the same manner as illustrated in Chapter 4 for a service business.

Financial statements

The work to be done at the end of the period is much the same for a merchandising business as for a service-type firm. First, the work sheet is completed; then, financial statements are prepared from the data in the work sheet; next, the adjusting and closing entries are entered in the journal and posted to the ledger accounts; and finally, an after-closing trial balance is prepared.[2] This completes the periodic accounting cycle.

The income statement on page 170 was prepared from the information in the income statement columns of the Olympic Sporting Goods work sheet. The statement of retained earnings and the balance sheet appear below and on the next page. Note that the final amount in the statement of retained earnings also appears in the stockholders' equity section of the balance sheet as the new balance of retained earnings.

OLYMPIC SPORTING GOODS
Statement of Retained Earnings
For the Year Ended December 31, Year 11

Retained earnings, Dec. 31, Year 10	$64,000
Net income for Year 11	20,000
Subtotal	$84,000
Less: Dividends	10,000
Retained earnings, Dec. 31, Year 11	$74,000

Closing entries

The entries used in closing revenue and expense accounts have been explained in preceding chapters. The important new elements in this illustration of closing entries for a trading business are the entries showing the *elimination* of the beginning inventory and the *recording* of the ending inventory. The beginning inventory is cleared out of the Inventory account by a debit to Income Summary and a credit to Inventory. A separate entry could be made for this purpose, but we can save time by making one compound entry which will debit the Income Summary account with the balance of the beginning inventory and with the

---

[2]The journalizing of the two adjusting entries for Olympic Sporting Goods is not illustrated here because these entries are similar to those demonstrated in previous chapters.

OLYMPIC SPORTING GOODS
Balance Sheet
December 31, Year 11

Assets

Cash		$ 19,000
Accounts receivable		25,000
Inventory		70,000
Land		123,000
Building	$120,000	
Less: Accumulated depreciation	78,000	42,000
Total assets		$279,000

Liabilities & Stockholders' Equity

Liabilities:		
Notes payable		$ 20,000
Accounts payable		30,000
Income taxes payable		5,000
Total liabilities		$ 55,000
Stockholders' equity:		
Capital stock	$150,000	
Retained earnings	74,000	224,000
Total liabilities & stockholders' equity		$279,000

balances of all temporary owners' equity accounts having debit balances. The *temporary owners' equity accounts* are those which appear in the income statement. As the name suggests, the temporary owners' equity accounts are used during the period to accumulate temporarily the increases and decreases in the owners' equity resulting from operation of the business. The entry to close out the beginning inventory and temporary owners' equity accounts with debit balances is illustrated below. (For emphasis, the accounts unique to a merchandising business are shown in black.)

Closing temporary owners' equity accounts with debit balances	Dec. 31	Income Summary	559,000	
		Inventory (Jan. 1)		60,000
		Purchases		300,000
		Sales Returns and Allowances		4,000
		Sales Discounts		2,000
		Transportation-in		13,000
		Advertising Expense		16,000
		Sales Salaries Expense		76,000
		Office Salaries Expense		60,000
		Telephone Expense		2,000
		Delivery Service		4,000
		Depreciation Expense		17,000
		Income Taxes Expense		5,000
		To close out the beginning inventory and the temporary owners' equity accounts with debit balances.		

The preceding closing entry closes all the operating expense accounts and Income Taxes Expense, as well as the accounts used to accumulate the cost of goods sold. It also closes the accounts for Sales Returns and Allowances and for Sales Discounts. Although the accounts for Sales Returns and Allowances and for Sales Discounts have debit balances, they are not expense accounts. In terms of account classification, they belong in the revenue group of accounts because they are offsets to the Sales account and appear in the income statement as deductions from Sales. After this first closing entry, the Inventory account has a zero balance. Therefore, it is time to record in this account the new inventory of $70,000 determined by count at December 31.

To bring the ending inventory into the accounting records after the stocktaking on December 31, we could make a separate entry debiting Inventory and crediting the Income Summary account. It is more convenient, however, to combine this step with the closing of the Sales account and any other temporary proprietorship accounts having credit balances, as illustrated in the following closing entry.

Closing temporary proprietorship accounts with credit balances	Dec. 31	Inventory (Dec. 31)	70,000	
		Sales	506,000	
		Purchase Returns and Allowances	2,000	
		Purchase Discounts	1,000	
		Income Summary		579,000
		To record the ending inventory and to close all temporary owners' equity accounts with credit balances.		

The remaining closing entries serve to transfer the balance of the Income Summary account to the Retained Earnings account and to close the Dividends account, as follows:

Closing Income Summary account and Dividends account	Dec. 31	Income Summary	20,000	
		Retained Earnings		20,000
		To close the Income Summary account.		
	31	Retained Earnings	10,000	
		Dividends		10,000
		To close the Dividends account.		

After the preceding four closing entries have been posted to the ledger, the only accounts left with dollar balances will be balance sheet accounts. An after-closing trial balance should be prepared to prove that the ledger is in balance after the year-end entries to adjust and close the accounts.

Summary of merchandising transactions and related accounting entries

The transactions regularly encountered in merchandising operations and the related accounting entries may be concisely summarized as follows:

Transactions during the Period	Related Accounting Entries	
	Debit	Credit

	Transactions during the Period	Debit	Credit
Customary journal entries relating to merchandise	Purchase merchandise for resale	Purchases	Cash (or Accounts Payable
	Incur transportation charges on merchandise purchased for resale	Transportation-in	Cash (or Accounts Payable)
	Return unsatisfactory merchandise to supplier, or obtain a reduction from original price	Cash (or Accounts Payable)	Purchase Returns and Allowances
	Pay for merchandise within discount period	Accounts Payable	Cash and Purchase Discounts
	Sell merchandise to customers	Cash (or Accounts Receivable)	Sales
	Permit customers to return merchandise, or grant them a reduction from original price	Sales Returns and Allowances	Cash (or Accounts Receivable)
	Collect account receivable within discount period	Cash and Sales Discounts	Accounts Receivable
	Inventory Procedures at End of Period		
	Transfer the balance of the beginning inventory to the Income Summary account	Income Summary	Inventory
	Take a physical inventory of goods on hand at the end of the period, and price these goods at cost	Inventory	Income Summary

Sales taxes

Sales taxes are levied by many states and cities on retail sales. Usually certain classes of sales are exempt, notably food and some commodities, such as gasoline and cigarettes, that are already subject to special excise taxes. To discourage residents from avoiding the tax by making purchases outside the state, some states levy a supplementary *use tax,* applicable to goods purchased outside the state and brought in.

Typically a sales tax is imposed on the consumer, but the seller must collect the tax, file tax returns at times specified by law, and remit a percentage of the reported sales. The actual tax collected by the selling company from its customers may be greater or less than the amount paid to the government because no tax is collected on sales under a certain amount, and due to rounding of pennies, the tax collected on a given sale may be slightly more than the specified percentage.

A sales tax is collected when a cash sale is made or is included in the charge to the customer's account on a credit sale. The liability to the governmental unit for sales taxes may be recorded at the time the sale is made as follows:

Sales tax recorded at time of sale

Accounts Receivable (or Cash)	1,050	
Sales Tax Payable		50
Sales		1,000

To record sale of $1,000 subject to 5% sales tax.

Instead of recording the sales tax liability at the time of sale, some businesses prefer to credit the Sales account with the entire amount collected, including the sales tax, and to make an adjustment at the end of each period to reflect sales tax payable. For example, suppose that the total recorded sales for the period under this method were $315,000. Since the Sales account includes both the sales price and the sales tax (say, 5%), it is apparent that $315,000 is 105% of the actual sales figure. Actual sales are $300,000 ($315,000 ÷ 1.05) and the amount of sales tax due is $15,000. (Proof: 5% of $300,000 = $15,000.) The entry to record the liability for sales taxes would be

Sales tax recorded as adjustment of sales

Sales	15,000	
Sales Tax Payable		15,000

To remove sales taxes of 5% on $300,000 of sales from the Sales account, and reflect as a liability.

Any discrepancy between the tax due and the amount actually collected from customers, under this method, would be absorbed automatically in the net sales figure. If certain of the products being sold (such as food) are not subject to the tax, it is necessary to keep a record of taxable and nontaxable sales.

Classified financial statements

The financial statements illustrated up to this point have been rather short and simple because of the limited number of accounts used in these introductory chapters. Now let us look briefly at a more comprehensive balance sheet for a merchandising business.

In the balance sheet of Skymart Corporation illustrated on the next page, the assets are classified into three groups: (1) current assets, (2) plant and equipment, and (3) other assets. The liabilities are classified into two types: (1) current liabilities and (2) long-term liabilities. This classification of assets and liabilities is virtually a standard one throughout American business.

The purpose of balance sheet classification

The purpose underlying a standard classification of assets and liabilities is to aid management, owners, creditors, and other interested persons in understanding the financial position of the business. Bankers, for example, would have a difficult time in reading the balance sheets of all the companies which apply to them for loans, if each of these companies followed its own individual whims as to the sequence and arrangement of accounts comprising its balance sheet. Standard practices as to the order and arrangement of a balance sheet are an important means of saving the time of the reader and of giving a fuller comprehension of the company's financial position. Some of the major balance sheet classifications are discussed briefly in the following section.

SKYMART CORPORATION
Balance Sheet
December 31, 19___

Assets

Current assets:

Cash		$ 145,000
U.S. government bonds		100,000
Notes receivable		124,000
Accounts receivable		261,000
Inventory		352,000
Prepaid expenses		12,000
Total current assets		$ 994,000

Plant and equipment:

Land		$100,000	
Building	$240,000		
Less: Accumulated depreciation	19,200	220,800	
Store equipment	$ 94,000		
Less: Accumulated depreciation	18,800	75,200	
Delivery equipment	$ 28,000		
Less: Accumulated depreciation	7,000	21,000	
Total plant and equipment			417,000

Other assets:

Land (future building site)	165,000
Total assets	$1,576,000

Liabilities & Stockholders' Equity

Current liabilities:

Notes payable		$ 115,000
Accounts payable		180,400
Income taxes payable		20,000
Accrued expenses payable		10,000
Unearned revenue		5,100
Total current liabilities		$ 330,500

Long-term liabilities:

Mortgage payable (due in 10 years)		250,000
Total liabilities		$ 580,500

Stockholders' equity:

Capital stock	$600,000	
Retained earnings	395,500	995,500
Total liabilities & stockholders' equity		$1,576,000

Current assets   Current assets include cash, government bonds and other marketable securities, receivables, inventories, and prepaid expenses. To qualify for inclusion in the current asset category, an asset must be capable of being converted into cash within a relatively short period without interfering with the normal operation of the business. The period is usually one year, but it may be longer for those businesses having an operating cycle in excess of one year.

The term *operating cycle* means the average time period between the purchase of merchandise and the conversion of this merchandise back into cash. The series of transactions comprising a complete cycle often runs as follows: (1) purchase of merchandise, (2) sale of the merchandise on credit, (3) collection of the account receivable from the customer. The word *cycle* suggests the circular flow of capital from cash to inventory to receivables to cash again. This cycle of transactions in a merchandising business is portrayed in the following diagram.

The operating cycle repeats continuously

In a business handling fast-moving merchandise (a supermarket, for example) the operating cycle may be completed in a few weeks; for most merchandising businesses the operating cycle requires several months but less than a year.

The sequence in which current assets are listed depends upon their liquidity; the closer an asset is to becoming cash the higher is its liquidity. The total amount of a company's current assets and the relative amount of each type give some indication of the company's short-run, debt-paying ability.

Current liabilities   Liabilities that must be paid within one year or the operating cycle (whichever is longer) are called *current liabilities*. Among the more common types of current liabilities are notes payable, accounts payable, taxes payable, salaries payable, interest payable, and unearned revenue. Notes payable are usually listed first, followed by accounts payable; any sequence of listing is acceptable for other current liabilities.

Settlement of most types of current liabilities requires writing a check to the creditor; in other words, use of the current asset cash. A somewhat different procedure for settlement is followed for the current liability of unearned revenue. As explained in Chapter 4, unearned revenue is a liability which arises when money is received from customers in advance for goods or services to be delivered in the future. To meet such obligations usually will require using up current assets either through delivering merchandise to the customer or making payments to employees or others to provide the agreed services.

The key point to recognize is the relationship between current liabilities and current assets. Current liabilities must be paid in the near future and current assets must be available to make these payments. Comparison of the amount of current liabilities with the amount of current assets is an important step in appraising the ability of a company to pay its debts in the near future.

Current ratio   Many bankers and other users of financial statements believe that for a business to qualify as a good credit risk, the total current assets should be about twice as large as the total current liabilities. In studying a balance sheet, a banker or other creditor will compute the *current ratio* by dividing total current assets by total current liabilities. The current ratio is a convenient measure of the short-run debt-paying ability of a business.

In the illustrated balance sheet of Skymart Corporation the current assets of $994,000 are approximately three times as great as the current liabilities of $330,500; the current ratio is therefore 3 to 1, which would generally be regarded as a very strong current position. The current assets could shrink by two-thirds and still be sufficient for payment of the current liabilities. Although a strong current ratio is desirable, an extremely high current ratio (such as 4 to 1 or more) may signify that a company is holding too much of its resources in cash, marketable securities, and other current assets and is not pursuing profit opportunities as aggressively as it might.

Working capital   The excess of current assets over current liabilities is called *working capital;* the relative amount of working capital is another indication of short-term financial strength. In the illustrated balance sheet of Skymart Corporation, working capital is $663,500, computed by subtracting the current liabilities of $330,500 from the current assets of $994,000. The importance of solvency (ability to meet debts as they fall due) was emphasized in Chapter 1. Ample working capital permits a company to buy merchandise in large lots, to carry an adequate stock of goods, and to sell goods to customers on favorable credit terms. Many companies have been forced to suspend business because of inadequate working capital, even though total assets were much larger than total liabilities.

Classification and format of income statements

There are two common forms of income statements: the *multiple-step income statement* and the *single-step income statement.* The multiple-step statement is more convenient in illustrating accounting principles and has been used consistently in our illustrations thus far. The income statement for Olympic Sporting Goods on page 170 is in multiple-step form. It is also a *classified* income statement because the various items of expense are classified into significant groups. The single-step form of income statement is illustrated on page 182.

Multiple-step income statement   The multiple-step income statement is so named because of the series of steps in which costs and expenses are deducted from revenue. As a first step, the cost of goods sold is subtracted from net sales to produce an amount for gross profit on sales. As a second step, operating expenses are deducted to obtain a figure for income from operations. As a final step, income taxes expense is subtracted to determine net income. The multiple-step statement is noted for its numerous sections and significant subtotals. It is widely used by small businesses.

The classification of expenses between selling on the one hand and general and administrative on the other hand was illustrated for Olympic Sporting Goods in the income statement on page 170. This classification aids management in controlling expenses by emphasizing that certain expenses are the responsibility of the executive in charge of sales, and that other types of expenses relate to the business as a whole. Of course, many small companies are not organized into departments; consequently they do not subdivide operating expenses on the income statement.

Single-step income statement   The income statements prepared by large corporations for distribution to thousands of stockholders often are greatly condensed because the public presumably is more interested in a concise report than in the details of operations. The single-step form of income statement takes its name from the fact that the total of all expenses (including the cost of goods sold) is deducted from total revenue in a single step. All types of revenue, such as sales, interest earned, and rent revenue, are added together to show the total revenue. Then all expenses are grouped together and deducted in one step without the use of subtotals. A condensed income statement in single-step form is shown below for National Corporation, a large merchandising company.

NATIONAL CORPORATION
Income Statement
For the Year Ended December 31, 19___

Condensed single-step income statement

Revenue:		
Net sales		$90,000,000
Interest earned		1,800,000
Total revenue		$91,800,000
Expenses:		
Cost of goods sold	$60,000,000	
Selling expenses	14,400,000	
General & administrative expenses	9,750,000	
Income taxes expense	3,150,000	
Total expenses		87,300,000
Net income		$ 4,500,000

Use of the single-step income statement has increased in recent years, perhaps because it is relatively simple and easy to read. A disadvantage of this format is that useful concepts such as the gross profit on sales are not readily apparent.

THE SYSTEM OF INTERNAL CONTROL

The meaning of internal control

In this section we shall round out our discussion of a merchandising business by considering the *system of internal control* by which management maintains control over the purchasing, receiving, storing, and selling of merchandise. Strong internal controls are needed not only for purchases and sales transactions, but for all other types of transactions as well. In fact, the concept of internal control affects all the assets of a business, all liabilities, the revenue and expenses, and every aspect of operations. The purpose of internal control is to provide assurance that the entire business operates in accordance with management's plans and policies.

As defined in Chapter 1, the system of internal control includes all the measures taken by an organization for the purpose of *(1)* protecting its resources against waste, fraud, and inefficiency; *(2)* ensuring accuracy and reliability in accounting and operating data; *(3)* securing compliance with company policies; and *(4)* evaluating the level of performance in all divisions of the company.

Many people think of internal control as a means of safeguarding cash and preventing fraud. Although internal control is an important factor in protecting assets and preventing fraud, this is only a part of its role. Remember that business decisions are based on accounting data: and the system of internal control provides assurance of the *dependability of the accounting data used in making decisions*.

The decisions made by management are communicated throughout the organization and become company policy. The results of the policies—the consequences of managerial decisions—must be reported back to management so that the soundness of company policies can be evaluated. Among the means of communication included in the system of internal control are organization charts, manuals of accounting policies and procedures, flow charts, financial forecasts, purchase orders, receiving reports, invoices, and many other documents. The term *documentation* refers to all the charts, forms, reports, and other business papers that guide and describe the working of a company's system of accounting and internal control.

Administrative controls and accounting controls Internal controls fall into two major classes: administrative controls and accounting controls. *Administrative controls* are measures that increase operational efficiency and compliance with policies in all parts of the organization. For example, an administrative control may be a requirement that traveling salespersons submit reports showing the number of calls made on customers each day. Another example is a directive requiring airline pilots to have an annual medical examination. These internal administrative controls have no direct bearing on the reliability of the financial statements. Consequently, administrative controls are not of direct interest to accountants and independent auditors.

Internal accounting controls are measures that relate to protection of assets and to the reliability of accounting and financial reports. An example is the requirement that a person whose duties involve handling cash shall not also maintain accounting records. More broadly stated, the accounting function must be kept separate from the custody of assets. Another *accounting control* is the requirement that checks, purchase orders, and other documents be serially numbered. Still another example is the rule that a person who orders merchandise and supplies should not be the one to receive them and should not sign checks to pay for them.

Strong internal control now required by law

Some American corporations in past years made payments to foreign officials which could have been interpreted as bribes. These payments in many cases were legal under the laws of the countries in which they were made, although they were not in conformity with American business ethics. The top executives of the corporations involved sometimes were not aware that these questionable transactions were taking place.

To put an end to such practices, the United States Congress passed the Foreign Corrupt Practices Act. This act requires every publicly owned corporation in the United States to maintain a system of internal control sufficient to provide reasonable assurance that transactions are executed only with the knowledge and authorization of management. The system of internal control also must limit the use of corporate assets to those purposes approved by management. Finally, the act requires that accounting records of assets be compared at reasonable intervals with the assets actually on hand. Thus a strong system of internal control, long recognized as vital to the operation of a large business, is now required by federal law.

GUIDELINES TO STRONG INTERNAL CONTROL

Organization plan to establish responsibility for every function

An organization plan should indicate clearly the departments or persons responsible for such functions as purchasing, receiving incoming shipments, maintaining accounting records, approving credit to customers, and preparing the payroll. When an individual or department is assigned responsibility for a function, authority to make decisions should also be granted. The lines of authority and responsibility can be shown on an organization chart, as illustrated on the next page.

Control of transactions

If management is to direct the activities of a business according to plan, every transaction should go though four steps: It should be *authorized, approved, executed,* and *recorded.* For example, consider the sale of merchandise on credit. The top management of the company may *authorize* the sale of merchandise on

Portion of an Organization Chart

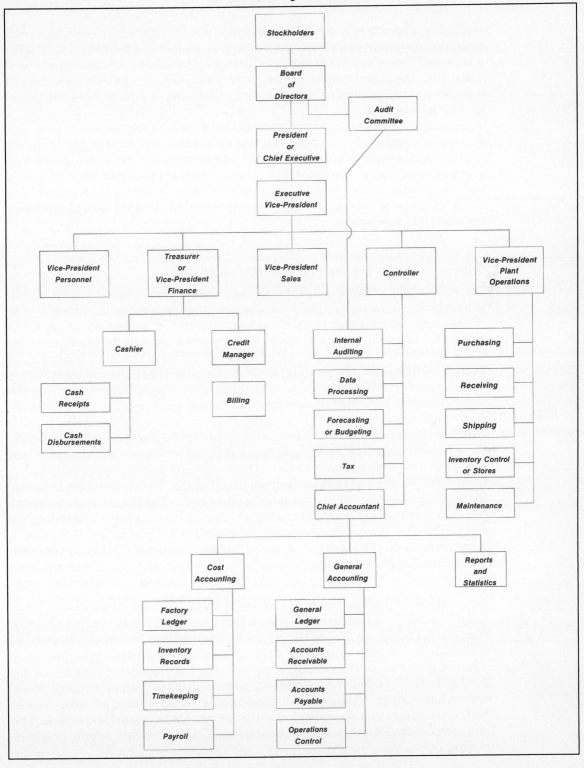

credit to customers who meet certain standards. The manager of the credit and collection department may *approve* a sale of given dollar amount to a particular customer. The sales transaction is *executed* by preparing a sales invoice and delivering the merchandise to the credit customer. The sales transaction is *recorded* in the accounting department by debiting Accounts Receivable and crediting Sales.

Consider for a moment the losses that would probably be incurred if this internal control of transactions did not exist. Assume, for example, that all employees in a store were free to sell on credit any amount of merchandise to any customer, and responsibility for recording the sales transactions was not fixed on any one person or department. The result no doubt would be many unrecorded sales; of those sales transactions that were recorded, many would represent uncollectible receivables.

Subdivision of duties strengthens internal control

The subdivision of duties within a company should be designed so that no one person or department handles a transaction completely from beginning to end. When duties are divided in this manner, the work of one employee serves to verify that of another and any errors which occur tend to be detected promptly.

To illustrate the development of internal control through subdivision of duties, let us review the procedures for a sale of merchandise on account by a wholesaler. The sales department of the company is responsible for securing the order from the customer; the credit department must approve the customer's credit before the order is filled; the stock room assembles the goods ordered; the shipping department packs and ships the goods; and the accounting department records the transaction. Each department receives written evidence of the action of the other departments and reviews the documents describing the transaction to see that the actions taken correspond in all details. The shipping department, for instance, does not release the merchandise until after the credit department has approved the customer as a credit risk. The accounting department does not record the sale until it has received documentary evidence that (1) the goods were ordered, (2) the extension of credit was approved, and (3) the merchandise was shipped to the customer.

Accounting function separate from custody of assets   An employee who has custody of an asset or access to an asset should not maintain the accounting record of that asset. The person having custody of an asset will not be inclined to waste it, steal it, or give it away if he or she is aware that another employee is maintaining a record of the asset. The employee maintaining the accounting record does not have access to the asset and therefore has no incentive to falsify the record. If one person has custody of assets and also maintains the accounting records, there is both opportunity and incentive to falsify the records to conceal a shortage. The diagram below illustrates how separation of duties creates strong internal control.

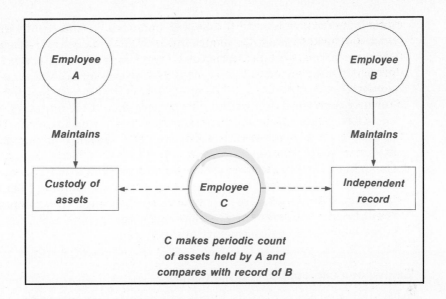

C makes periodic count
of assets held by A and
compares with record of B

In this diagram Employee A has custody of assets and Employee B maintains an accounting record of the assets. Employee C periodically counts the assets and compares the count with the record maintained by B. This comparison should reveal any errors made by either A or B unless the two have collaborated to conceal an error or irregularity.

Prevention of fraud If one employee is permitted to handle all aspects of a transaction, the danger of fraud is increased. Studies of fraud cases suggest that many individuals may be tempted into dishonest acts if given complete control of company property. Most of these persons, however, would not engage in fraud if doing so required collaboration with another employee. Losses through employee dishonesty occur in a variety of ways: merchandise may be stolen; payments by customers may be withheld; suppliers may be overpaid with a view to kickbacks to employees; and lower prices may be allowed to favored customers. The opportunities for fraud are almost endless if all aspects of a sale or purchase transaction are concentrated in the hands of one employee.

Specific methods of achieving internal control

Among the more important internal control devices are the following:

1 Internal auditing. Virtually every large organization has an internal auditing staff. The internal auditors study both administrative controls and accounting controls in all units of the organization and prepare reports to top management on their findings.
2 Financial forecasts. A plan of operations is prepared each year setting goals for each division of the business, as, for example, the expected volume of sales,

amounts of expenses, and future cash balances. Actual results are compared with forecasted amounts month by month. This comparison strengthens actual controls because variations from planned results are investigated promptly and may reveal accounting errors or other breakdowns in company policies.

3 Serially numbered documents. The printer should include serial numbers on such documents as checks, purchase orders, and sales invoices. If a document is misplaced or concealed, the break in the sequence of numbers will call attention to the discrepancy.

4 Competent personnel. Even the best-designed system of internal control will not work well unless the people using it are competent. Competence and integrity of employees are in part developed through training programs, but they also are related to the policies for selection of personnel, the adequacy of supervision, and the complexity of the system.

Limitations and cost of internal control

Although internal control is highly effective in increasing the reliability of accounting data and in protecting against fraud, no system of internal control is foolproof. Two or more dishonest employees working in collusion can defeat the system—temporarily. Carelessness by employees and misunderstanding of instructions can cause a breakdown in controls. Finally, the question of cost of controls cannot be ignored. Too elaborate a system of internal control may entail greater expense than is justified by the protection gained. For this reason, a system of internal control must be tailored to meet the needs of an individual business.

INTERNAL CONTROLS OVER THE PURCHASE AND SALE OF MERCHANDISE

Business documents and procedures

Carefully designed business documents and procedures for using them are necessary to ensure that all transactions are properly authorized, approved, executed, and recorded. Some of the more important of these business documents and the procedures related to them are shown in the following table.

Business Document	Initiated by	Sent to
Purchase requisition Issued when quantity of goods on hand falls below established reorder point	Departmental sales managers or inventory control department	Purchasing department

Business Document	Initiated by	Sent to
Purchase order Specifies prices, quantities, and method of transportation	Purchasing department	Original to selling company (vendor, supplier), copies to buyer's accounting, receiving, and finance departments
Invoice Confirms that goods have been shipped and requests payment	Seller (supplier)	Accounting department of buying company
Receiving report Based on count and inspection of goods received	Receiving department of buying company	Original to accounting department, copies to purchasing department and to department requisitioning goods
Invoice approval form	Accounting department of buying company	Finance department, to support issuance of check. Returned to accounting department with carbon copy of check.

Purchase orders

In many businesses and especially in large organizations, the buying company uses its own purchase order forms. A purchase order of the Zenith Company issued to Adams Manufacturing Company is illustrated below.

Serially numbered purchase order

PURCHASE ORDER   **Order No. 999**

ZENITH COMPANY
10 Fairway Avenue, San Francisco, California

To: Adams Manufacturing Company   **Date** Nov. 10, 19___

       19 Union Street   **Ship via** Jones Truck Co.

       Kansas City, Missouri   **Terms:** 2/10, n/30

Please enter our order for the following:

Quantity	Description	Price	Total
15 sets	Model S irons	$60.00	$900.00
50 dozen	X3Y Shur—Par golf balls	7.00	350.00

Zenith Company

By *D. D. McCarthy*

Several copies of a purchase order are usually prepared. The original is sent to the supplier; it constitutes an authorization to deliver the merchandise and to submit a bill based on the prices listed.

The issuance of a purchase order does not call for any debit or credit entries in the accounting records of either the prospective buyer or seller. The company which receives an order does not consider (for accounting purposes) that a sale has been made until the merchandise is delivered. At that point ownership of the goods changes, and both buyer and seller should make accounting entries to record the transaction.

Invoices

When a manufacturer or wholesaler receives an order for its products, it takes two actions. One is to ship the goods to the customer and the other is to send the customer an invoice. By the act of shipping the merchandise, the seller is giving up ownership of one type of asset, inventory; by issuing the invoice the seller is recording ownership of another form of asset, an account receivable.

An invoice contains a description of the goods being sold, the quantities, prices, credit terms, and method of shipment. The illustration below shows an invoice issued by Adams Manufacturing Company in response to the previously illustrated purchase order from Zenith Company.

Invoice is basis for accounting entry

INVOICE

ADAMS MANUFACTURING COMPANY
19 Union Street
Kansas City, Missouri

Sold to: Zenith Company
10 Fairway Avenue
San Francisco, Calif.

Shipped to: Same

Terms: 2/10, n/30

Invoice no. 777
Invoice date Nov. 15, 19___
Your order no. 999
Date shipped Nov. 15, 19___
Shipped via Jones Truck Co.

Quantity	Description	Price	Amount
15 sets	Model S irons	$60.00	$ 900.00
50 dozen	X3Y Shur-Par golf balls	7.00	350.00
			$1,250.00

From the viewpoint of the seller, an invoice is a *sales invoice;* from the buyer's viewpoint it is a *purchase invoice*. The invoice is the basis for an entry in the accounting records of both the seller and the buyer because it evidences the transfer of ownership of goods. At the time of issuing the invoice, the selling company makes an entry debiting Accounts Receivable and crediting Sales. The buying company however, does not record the invoice as a liability until after verifying the following aspects of the transaction:

1 The invoice agrees with the purchase order as to prices, quantities, and other provisions.
2 The invoice is arithmetically correct in all extensions of price times quantity and in the addition of amounts.
3 The goods covered by the invoice have been received and are in satisfactory condition.

Evidence that the merchandise has been received in good condition must be obtained from the receiving department. It is the function of the receiving department to receive all incoming goods, to inspect them as to quality and condition, and to determine the quantities received by counting, measuring, or weighing. The receiving department should prepare a serially numbered report for each shipment received; one copy of this *receiving report* is sent to the accounting department for use in verifying the invoice.

The verification of the invoice in the accounting department is accomplished by comparing the purchase order, the invoice, and the receiving report. Comparison of these documents establishes that the merchandise described in the invoice was actually ordered, has been received in good condition, and was billed at the prices specified in the purchase order.

When these verification procedures have been completed, the invoice is recorded as a liability by an entry debiting the Purchases account and crediting Accounts Payable.

Debit and credit memoranda (debit memos, credit memos)

If merchandise purchased on account is unsatisfactory and is to be returned to the supplier (or if a price reduction is agreed upon), a *debit memorandum* may be prepared by the purchasing company and sent to the supplier. The debit memorandum informs the supplier that his or her account is being debited (reduced) by the buyer and explains the circumstances.

The supplier upon being informed of the return of damaged merchandise (or having agreed to a reduction in price) will issue a *credit memorandum* as evidence that the account receivable from the purchaser is being credited (reduced) by the supplier.

Recording purchase invoices at net price

Most well-managed companies have a firm policy of taking all purchase discounts offered. The recording of purchase invoices at their gross amount and making payment of a reduced amount within the discount period was described earlier in this chapter. Some companies which regularly take advantage of all available purchase discounts prefer the alternative method of recording purchase invoices at the net amount after discount rather than at the gross amount. If the amount which the buyer intends to pay is the invoice amount minus a cash discount, why not record this net amount as the liability at the time the invoice is received? For example, if Zenith Company receives a $10,000 purchase invoice bearing terms of 2/10, n/30, the entry could be

Entry for purchase: net price method

Nov. 3	Purchases	9,800	
	Accounts Payable		9,800

To record purchase invoice from Adams Manufacturing Company less 2% cash discount available.

Assuming that the invoice is paid within 10 days, the entry for the payment is as follows:

Entry for payment: net price method

Nov. 13	Accounts Payable	9,800	
	Cash		9,800

To record payment of $10,000 invoice from Adams Manufacturing Company less 2% cash discount.

Through oversight or carelessness, the purchasing company occasionally may fail to make payment of an invoice within the 10-day discount period. If such a delay occurred in paying the invoice from Adams Manufacturing Company, the full amount of the invoice would have to be paid rather than the recorded liability of $9,800. The journal entry to record the late payment on, say, December 3, is as follows:

Entry for payment after discount period: net price method

Dec. 3	Accounts Payable	9,800	
	Purchase Discounts Lost	200	
	Cash		10,000

To record payment of invoice and loss of discount by delaying payment beyond the discount period.

Under this method the cost of goods purchased is properly recorded at $9,800, and the additional payment of $200 caused by failure to pay the invoice promptly is placed in a special expense account designed to attract the attention of management. The gross-price method of recording invoices described earlier in this chapter shows the amount of purchase discounts *taken* each period; the *net-price method* now under discussion shows the amount of purchase discounts *lost* each period. The latter method has the advantage of drawing the attention of management to a breakdown in internal control. The fact that a purchase discount has been taken does not require attention by managment, but a discount lost because of inefficiency in processing accounts payable does call for managerial investigation.

As previously suggested, inefficiency and delay in paying invoices should not be concealed by adding the penalty of lost discount to the cost of merchandise purchased. The purchases should be stated at the net price available by taking cash discounts; the Purchase Discounts Lost account should be shown in the income statement as an operating expense.

KEY TERMS INTRODUCED OR EMPHASIZED IN CHAPTER 5

Beginning inventory   Goods on hand and available for sale to customers at the beginning of the accounting period.

Cash discount   A reduction in price (usually 2% or less) offered by manufacturers and wholesalers to encourage customers to pay invoices within a specified discount period.

Cost of goods sold   A computation appearing as a separate section of an income statement showing the cost of goods sold during the period. Computed by adding net delivered cost of merchandise purchases to beginning inventory to obtain cost of goods available for sale, and then deducting from this total the amount of the ending inventory. Usually equal to between 60 and 80% of net sales.

Credit memorandum   A document issued to show a reduction in the amount owed by a customer because of goods returned, a defect in the goods or services provided, or an error.

Current assets   Cash and other assets that can be converted into cash within one year or the operating cycle (whichever is longer) without interfering with the normal operation of the business.

Current ratio   Current assets divided by current liabilities. A measure of short-run debt-paying ability.

Ending inventory   Goods still on hand and available for sale to customers at the end of the accounting period.

Financial forecast   A plan of operations for a future period with expected results expressed in dollars.

Fraud   Dishonest acts intended to deceive, often involving the theft of assets and falsification of accounting records and financial statements.

Gross profit on sales   Revenue from sales minus cost of goods sold.

Internal auditing   An activity carried on in large organizations by a professional staff to investigate and evaluate the system of internal control on a year-round basis. Also to evaluate the efficiency of individual departments within the organization.

Internal control   All measures used by a business to guard against errors, waste, or fraud and to assure the reliability of accounting data. Designed to aid in the efficient operation of a business and to encourage compliance with company policies.

Inventory (merchandise)   Goods acquired and held for sale to customers.

Invoice   An itemized statement of goods being bought or sold. Shows quantities, prices, and credit terms. Serves as the basis for an entry in the accounting records of both seller and buyer because it evidences the transfer of ownership of goods.

Multiple-step income statement   An income statement in which cost of goods sold and expenses are subtracted from revenue in a series of steps, thus producing significant subtotals prior to net income.

Net-price method   A policy of recording purchase invoices at amounts net of (reduced by) cash discounts.

Operating cycle   The average time period from the purchase of merchandise to its sale and conversion back into cash.

Organization chart   A diagram showing organizational lines of authority and responsibility, with emphasis on separation of functions.

Periodic inventory system   A system of accounting for merchandise in which inventory at the balance sheet date is determined by counting and pricing the goods on hand. Cost of goods sold is computed by subtracting the ending inventory from the cost of goods available for sale.

Perpetual inventory system A system of accounting for merchandise that provides a continuous record showing the quantity and cost of all goods on hand.

Physical inventory The process of counting and pricing the merchandise on hand at a given date, usually the end of the accounting period.

Purchase order A serially numbered document sent by the purchasing department of a business to a supplier or vendor for the purpose of ordering materials or services.

Purchases An account used to record the cost of merchandise purchased for the purpose of sale to customers.

Receiving report An internal form prepared by the receiving department for each incoming shipment showing the quantity and condition of goods received.

Sales tax A tax levied by most states and many cities on certain retail sales. Typically the seller must collect the tax and file returns with the taxing agency.

Single-step income statement An income statement in which the cost of goods sold and all expenses are combined and deducted from total revenue in a single step to determine net income.

Working capital Current assets minus current liabilities. Another measure of short-run debt-paying ability.

DEMONSTRATION PROBLEM FOR YOUR REVIEW

Village Supply completed the following merchandising transactions during May. The company's policy calls for taking advantage of all cash discounts available to it from suppliers; purchase invoices are recorded at the *net amount*. In making sales, the company grants credit terms of 2/10, n/30, and strictly enforces the 10-day limitation. The amounts listed as cash sales below are net of sales discounts.

May   3 Sold merchandise to Rich Company for cash, $32,880.

May 16 Sold merchandise on account to Riverside Company, $14,820.

May 16 Purchased merchandise from Hilton Supply Company, $18,900; terms 2/10, n/30 (to be recorded at the net amount).

May 17 Paid transportation charges on goods received from Hilton Supply Company, $726.

May 18 Issued credit memorandum no. 102 to Riverside Company for allowance on damaged goods, $420.

May 24 Purchased merchandise from Pete Construction Co., $17,100; terms 1/10, n/30 (to be recorded at the net amount).

May 25 Returned defective goods with invoice price of $900 to Pete Construction Co., accompanied by debit memorandum no. 122.

May 26 Received cash from Riverside Company in full payment of account.

May 26 Paid Hilton Supply Company account in full.

Instructions

a Journalize the above transactions, recording purchase invoices at the net amount.

b Prepare a partial income statement for May showing sales and cost of goods sold (in detail), and gross profit on sales. Assume the inventory at April 30 to be $11,400 and the inventory at May 31 to be $13,920.

c What is the amount of accounts payable at May 31? What would be the amount of accounts payable at May 31 if the company followed a policy of recording purchase invoices at the gross amount?

SOLUTION TO DEMONSTRATION PROBLEM

a

Journal entries

May	3	Cash	32,880	
		Sales		32,880
		To record the sale of merchandise for cash.		
	16	Accounts Receivable	14,820	
		Sales		14,820
		To record sale to Riverside Co.		
	16	Purchases	18,522	
		Accounts Payable		18,522
		To record $18,900 purchase invoice from		
		Hilton Supply Company less 2% cash		
		discount available (terms 2/10, n/30).		
	17	Transportation-in	726	
		Cash		726
		Paid transportation charges on goods		
		purchased from Hilton Supply Company.		
	18	Sales Returns & Allowances	420	
		Accounts Receivable		420
		Issue credit memo No. 102 to customer,		
		Riverside Co. for damaged goods.		
	24	Purchases	16,929	
		Accounts Payable		16,929
		To record $17,100 purchase invoice from Pete		
		Construction Co., less 1% cash discount		
		available (terms 1/10, n/30).		
	25	Accounts Payable	891	
		Purchase Returns & Allowances		891
		To reduce liability to Pete Construction Co.,		
		for net amount of defective goods returned.		
		Invoice price $900 − 1% discount = $891		
		recorded liability. Debit memo No. 122.		
	26	Cash	14,112	
		Sales Discount	288	
		Accounts Receivable		14,400
		Collected from Riverside Company for our		
		May 16 sale, $14,820 − return of $420 and 2%		
		discount on balance of $14,400.		
	26	Accounts Payable	18,522	
		Cash		18,522
		Paid $18,900 purchase invoice from Hilton		
		Supply Company less 2% discount.		

b

VILLAGE SUPPLY
Partial Income Statement
For the Month Ended May 31, 19___

Gross sales			$47,700
Less: Sales returns & allowances		$ 420	
Sales discounts		288	708
Net sales			$46,992
Cost of goods sold:			
Inventory, Apr. 30, 19___		$11,400	
Purchases	$35,451		
Transportation-in	726		
Delivered cost of purchases	$36,177		
Less: Purchase returns & allowances	891		
Net purchases		35,286	
Cost of goods available for sale		$46,686	
Less: Inventory, May 31, 19___		13,920	
Cost of goods sold			32,766
Gross profit on sales			$14,226

c Accounts payable (net), $16,038; accounts payable (gross), $16,200. Computed as $16,038 ÷ .99 = $16,200, or $17,100 purchase − $900 return = $16,200.

REVIEW QUESTIONS

1 During the current year, Green Bay Company made all sales of merchandise at prices in excess of cost. Will the business necessarily report a net income for the year? Explain.

2 The income statement for Stereo West showed gross profit on sales of $144,000, operating expenses of $130,000, and cost of goods sold of $216,000. What was the amount of net sales?

3 Valley Mart during its first year of operations had cost of goods sold of $90,000 and a gross profit equal to 40% of sales. What was the dollar amount of sales for the year?

4 Is the normal balance of the Sales Returns and Allowances account a debit or a credit? Is the normal balance of the Purchase Returns and Allowances account a debit or a credit?

5 Which of the following expenditures by Southside Drugstore should be recorded by a debit to the Purchases account?
  a Purchase of a new delivery truck
  b Purchase of a three-year insurance policy
  c Purchase of merchandise from drug manufacturer
  d Purchase of advertising space in local newspaper
  e Payment in advance for three months' guard service by Security Patrol, Inc.

6 Supply the proper terms to complete the following statements:
  a Net sales − cost of goods sold = _?_
  b Beginning inventory + purchases − purchase returns and allowances − purchase discounts + transportation-in = _?_

    c Cost of goods sold + ending inventory = ?
    d Cost of goods sold + gross profit on sales = ?
    e Net income + operating expenses = ?

7 During the current year, Davis Corporation purchased merchandise costing $200,000. State the cost of goods sold under each of the following alternative assumptions:
    a No beginning inventory; ending inventory $40,000
    b Beginning inventory $60,000; no ending inventory
    c Beginning inventory $58,000; ending inventory $78,000
    d Beginning inventory $90,000; ending inventory $67,000

8 Zenith Company uses the periodic inventory system and maintains its accounting records on a calendar-year basis. Does the beginning or the ending inventory figure appear in the trial balance prepared from the ledger on December 31?

9 Compute the amount of cost of goods sold, given the following account balances: beginning inventory $40,000, purchases $84,000, purchase returns and allowances $4,500, purchase discounts $1,500, transportation-in $1,000, and ending inventory $36,000.

10 In which columns of the work sheet for a merchandising company does the ending inventory appear?

11 State briefly the difference between the *perpetual* inventory system and the *periodic* inventory system.

12 When the periodic inventory method is in use, how is the amount of inventory determined at the end of the period?

13 What is the purpose of a closing entry consisting of a debit to the Income Summary account and a credit to the Inventory account?

14 Tireco is a retail store in a state that imposes a 5% sales tax. Would you expect to find an account entitled Sales Tax Expense and another account entitled Sales Tax Payable in Tireco's ledger? Explain your answer.

15 Explain the terms *current assets, current liabilities,* and *current ratio.*

16 Madison Corporation has current assets of $540,000 and current liabilities of $300,000. Compute the current ratio and the amount of working capital.

17 Barnes Imports has a current ratio of 3 to 1 and working capital of $60,000. What are the amounts of current assets and current liabilities?

18 What is the purpose of a system of internal control? List four specific objectives which the measures included in a system of internal control are designed to achieve.

19 Criticize the following statement: "Internal control may be defined as all those measures which a business uses to prevent fraud."

20 Suggest a control device to protect a business against the loss or nondelivery of invoices, purchase orders, and other documents which are routed from one department to another.

21 Criticize the following statement: "In our company we get things done by requiring that a person who initiates a transaction follow it through in all particulars. For example, an employee who issues a purchase order is held responsible for inspecting the merchandise upon arrival, approving the invoice, and preparing the check in payment of the purchase. If any error is made, we know definitely whom to blame."

22 Explain why the operations and custodianship functions should be separate from the accounting function.

23 A system of internal control is often said to include two major types of controls: administrative controls and accounting controls. Explain the nature of each group and give an example of each.

24 How does a single-step income statement differ from a multiple-step income statement?

25 Company A sells merchandise to B on credit and two days later agrees that B can return a portion of the merchandise. B does so. What document should Company A issue to record the return? What accounts on Company A's records are affected by this return of merchandise?

26 What accounting entry, if any, is required on the part of the company issuing a purchase order? On the part of the company receiving the purchase order?

27 Name three documents (business papers) which are needed by the accounting department to verify that a purchase of merchandise has occurred and that payment of the related liability should be made.

EXERCISES

Ex. 5-1 From the following list, select the appropriate items and compute the *cost of goods available for sale.*

Purchases	$215,000	Purchase returns & allowances ...	$ 8,000
Sales	420,000	Purchase discounts	7,000
Transportation-in	10,000	Sales returns & allowances	12,000
Sales discounts	6,000	Beginning inventory	45,000

Ex. 5-2 This exercise stresses the sequence and relationship of items in a multiple-step income statement for a merchandising business. Each of the five horizontal lines in the table represents a separate set of income statement items. You are to copy the table and fill in the missing amounts. A net loss in the right-hand column is to be indicated by placing brackets before and after the amount, as for example, in line *e* (10,000).

	Net Sales	Begin-ning Inventory	Net Purchases	Ending Inventory	Cost of Goods Sold	Gross Profit	Expenses	Net Income or (Loss)
a	100,000	27,000	65,000	22,000	?	30,000	35,000	?
b	400,000	80,000	260,000	?	240,000	?	?	30,000
c	500,000	45,000	?	120,000	325,000	175,000	140,000	?
d	700,000	?	500,000	125,000	?	175,000	200,000	?
e	?	100,000	?	110,000	640,000	160,000	?	(10,000)

Ex. 5-3 Give the journal entry, if any, to be prepared for each of these events:

a Received a telephone order from a customer for $1,800 worth or merchandise.

b Issued a purchase order to Mack Company for merchandise costing $2,500.

c Received the merchandise ordered from Mack Company and an invoice for $2,500; credit terms 2/10, n/30. (Record at gross amount.)

d Delivered the $1,800 of merchandise ordered in (a) above to the customer and mailed an invoice; credit terms 10 e.o.m.

e Mailed check to Mack Company in full settlement of amount owed after taking allowable discount.

f Customer returned $400 of goods delivered in (**d**) above, which were unsatisfactory. A credit memorandum was issued for that amount.

Ex. 5-4 Hudson Company sold merchandise to River Company for $3,000; terms 2/10, n/30. River Company paid for the merchandise within the discount period. Both companies record invoices at the gross amounts.

a Give the journal entries by Hudson Company to record the sale and the subsequent collection.

b Give the journal entries by River Company to record the purchase and the subsequent payment.

Ex. 5-5 The balance sheet of Hunt Company contained the following items, among others:

Cash	*$ 37,600*
Accounts receivable	*148,000*
Inventory	*198,400*
Store equipment (net)	*192,000*
Other assets	*28,800*
Mortgage payable (due in 3 years)	*48,000*
Notes payable (due in 10 days)	*15,200*
Accounts payable	*138,400*
Bob Hunt, capital	*220,800*

Instructions

a From the above information compute the amount of current assets and the amount of current liabilities.

b How much working capital does Hunt Company have?

c Compute the current ratio.

Ex. 5-6 Taft Company received purchase invoices during July totaling $42,000, all of which carried credit terms of 2/10, n/30. It was the company's regular policy to take advantage of all available cash discounts, but because of employee vacations during July, there was confusion and delay in making payments to suppliers, and none of the July invoices was paid within the discount period.

a Explain briefly two alternative ways in which the amount of purchases might be presented in the July income statement.

b What method of recording purchase invoices can you suggest that would call to the attention of the Taft Company management the inefficiency of operations in July?

Ex. 5-7 Jet Auto Supply Store received from a manufacturer a shipment of 200 gasoline cans. Harold Abbott, who handles all purchasing activities, telephoned the manufacturer and explained that only 100 cans were ordered. The manufacturer replied that two separate purchase orders for 100 cans each had recently been received from Jet Auto Supply Store. Harold Abbott is sure that the manufacturer is in error and is merely trying to justify an excess shipment, but he can find no means of proving the point. What is the missing element in internal control over purchases by Jet Auto Supply Store?

Ex. 5-8 The Hasagami General Store operates in an area in which a 6% sales tax is levied on all products handled by the store. On cash sales, the salesclerks include the sales tax in the amount collected from the customer and ring up the entire amount on the cash register without recording separately the tax liability. On credit sales, the customer is charged for the list price of the merchandise plus 6%, and the entire amount is debited to Accounts Receivable and credited to the Sales account. On sales of less than one dollar, the tax collected is rounded to the nearest cent.

Sales tax must be remitted to the government quarterly. At March 31 the Sales account showed a balance of $152,360 for the three-month period ended March 31.

a What amount of sales tax is owed at March 31? (Round to nearest dollar.)

b Give the journal entry to record the sales tax liability on the books.

Ex. 5-9 Robert Hale, president of Hale Equipment, a merchandising business, explains to you how duties have been assigned to employees. Hale states: "In order to have clearly defined responsibility for each phase of our operations, I have made one employee responsible for the purchasing, receiving, and storage of merchandise. Another employee has been charged with responsibility for maintaining the accounting records and for making all collections from customers. I have assigned to a third employee responsibility for maintaining personnel records for all our employees and for timekeeping, preparation of payroll records, and distribution of payroll checks. My goal in setting up this organization plan is to have a strong system of internal control."

You are to evaluate Hale's plan of organization and explain fully the reasoning underlying any criticism you may have.

PROBLEMS

5-1 Carleton Company uses the periodic inventory system. Sales are made on a variety of credit terms to various customers, and some sales are for cash. The company completed the following transactions among others during the month of January.

Jan. 2 Sold merchandise on credit to Cable, Inc., $6,000. Terms, 2/10, n/30.

Jan. 3 Purchased merchandise for cash, $1,065.

Jan. 4 Sold merchandise to Tucker Company on credit, $1,200. Terms, 10 e.o.m.

Jan. 6 Paid transportation charges on shipment to Tucker Company, $375.

Jan. 8 Purchased office equipment from ABC Corporation for cash, $8,250.

Jan. 12 Received check for $5,880 from Cable, Inc., as settlement within discount period for goods sold them on Jan. 2.

Jan. 14 Permitted Tucker Company to return for credit $630 of the merchandise purchased on Jan. 4 (no reduction in the transportation charges paid on Jan. 6).

Jan. 15 Sold merchandise for cash, $6,450.

Jan. 16 Refunded $390 to a customer who had made a cash purchase on Jan. 15.

Jan. 20 Purchased merchandise from Selzer Company on credit, $4,950. Terms 2/10, n/30. (Record purchase invoices at gross amount.)

Jan. 21 Paid by check transportation charges on merchandise purchased from Selzer Company in the amount of $240.

Jan. 23 Returned for credit of $450 merchandise purchased from Selzer Company (no reduction was allowed with respect to the transportation charges paid Jan. 21).

Jan. 25 Purchased stationery and miscellaneous office supplies on open account, $705.

Jan. 30 Made payment within discount period to Selzer Company for merchandise purchased Jan. 20. (Note that a portion of goods were returned for credit on Jan. 21.)

Instructions Prepare a separate journal entry (including an explanation) for each of the preceding transactions.

5-2 Newport Beach is in the wholesale merchandise field and relies on the periodic inventory system. The income statement of the company for the first year ended June 30, 19___, contained the following items.

Income taxes expense	$ 12,000	Transportation-in	$ 6,000
Depreciation expense	33,600	Purchases	559,100
Utilities expense	21,400	Ending inventory	68,000
Beginning inventory	110,000	Salaries expense	125,300
Sales returns & allowances	12,500	Insurance expense	3,700
Purchase returns & allowances	2,100	Miscellaneous expense	11,600
Advertising expense	26,400	Sales discounts	10,000
Sales	922,500	Purchase discounts	2,000

Instructions

a Prepare a multiple-step income statement utilizing all the accounts listed above. Use the format illustrated on page 170, but do not divide operating expenses between selling and general administrative.

b Compute the gross profit percentage (gross profit on sales divided by net sales).

c Compute the percentage of net sales represented by the cost of goods sold (cost of goods sold divided by net sales).

d Compute the percentage of net sales represented by net income (net income divided by net sales).

5-3 A four-column schedule consisting of the first four columns of a 10-column work sheet for Motorsport Supplies appears on the next page. The company uses the periodic inventory system and maintains its accounting records on a calendar-year basis. A physical inventory taken at December 31 showed the ending inventory to be $66,000. The completed Adjustments columns have been included in the work sheet to minimize the detail work involved. These adjustments were derived from the following information available at December 31.

(1) Depreciation expense for the year on store equipment, $2,200.

(2) Income taxes, $1,400.

MOTORSPORT SUPPLIES

	Trial Balance		Adjustments	
	Debit	Credit	Debit	Credit
Cash	6,400			
Accounts receivable	16,000			
Inventory, Jan. 1	60,000			
Prepaid rent	4,400			
Equipment	22,000			
Accumulated depreciation: equipment		6,600		(a) 2,200
Accounts payable		20,400		
Capital stock		60,000		
Retained earnings		22,800		
Dividends	20,000			
Sales		529,000		
Sales returns & allowances	21,000			
Sales discounts	8,000			
Purchases	368,000			
Purchase returns & allowances		18,000		
Purchase discounts		6,000		
Transportation-in	12,000			
Advertising expense	32,000			
Rent expense	25,000			
Salaries expense	68,000			
	662,800	662,800		
Depreciation expense			(a) 2,200	
Income taxes expense			(b) 1,400	
Income taxes payable				(b) 1,400
			3,600	3,600

Instructions   Prepare a 10-column work sheet utilizing the trial balance and adjusting data provided. Follow the format illustrated on page 173. Include at the bottom of the work sheet a legend consisting of a brief explanation keyed to each adjusting entry.

5-4   Grant Company, a small merchandising business, uses a periodic inventory system and maintains its accounts on a calendar-year basis. The adjusted trial balance of Grant Company, after all necessary adjustments had been made, appeared as shown on page 203.

GRANT COMPANY
Adjusted Trial Balance
December 31, 198X

Cash	$ 57,000	
Accounts receivable	102,000	
Inventory, Jan. 1	86,700	
Prepaid insurance	2,100	
Office supplies	3,600	
Furniture & fixtures	60,000	
Accumulated depreciation: furniture & fixtures		$ 3,600
Notes payable		21,000
Accounts payable		24,900
Income taxes payable		40,000
Capital stock		140,000
Retained earnings		76,440
Dividends	30,000	
Sales		879,000
Sales returns & allowances	10,000	
Sales discounts	2,000	
Purchases	574,575	
Purchase returns & allowances		2,600
Purchase discounts		2,035
Transportation-in	30,000	
Sales salaries expense	90,000	
Advertising expense	20,000	
Rent expenses	24,000	
Depreciation expense: furniture & fixtures	4,800	
Office salaries expense	46,200	
Office supplies expense	4,200	
Insurance expense	1,400	
Telephone expense	1,000	
Income taxes expense	40,000	
Totals	$1,189,575	$1,189,575

The inventory on December 31, as determined by count, amounted to $107,640.

Instructions

a Prepare a multiple-step income statement for Grant Company. Use the format illustrated on page 170. Divide operating expenses into two groups: (1) selling expenses and (2) general and administrative expenses. The company allocates rent expense and depreciation expense 75% to selling expense and 25% to general and administrative expense. Insurance expense and telephone expense are considered to be too small to require allocation and are to be classified under general and administrative expenses.

b Prepare the necessary journal entries to close the accounts on December 31. (*Suggestion:* Use four separate closing entries. The first entry may be used to close the beginning inventory and all nominal accounts having debit balances; the second entry to record the ending inventory and to close nominal accounts having credit balances; the third entry to close the Income Summary account; and the fourth entry to close the Dividends account.)

5-5 On September 30, the close of the fiscal year for Border Corporation, the company's accountant prepared the following trial balance from the ledger.

Cash	$ 37,260	
Accounts receivable	37,827	
Inventory, beginning	67,032	
Unexpired insurance	1,296	
Office supplies	909	
Land	54,792	
Buildings	122,400	
Accumulated depreciation: buildings		$ 34,416
Equipment	35,640	
Accumulated depreciation: equipment		20,880
Accounts payable		19,548
Capital stock		180,000
Retained earnings, beginning of year		47,826
Dividends	18,000	
Sales		386,469
Sales returns & allowances	4,922	
Sales discounts	1,000	
Purchases	260,820	
Purchase returns & allowances		1,861
Purchase discounts		2,000
Transportation-in	5,337	
Salaries expense	44,532	
Property taxes expense	1,233	
	$693,000	$693,000

Other data

(1) Depreciation for the year was $4,896 on buildings and $2,970 on equipment.
(2) Accrued salaries payable as of September 30 were $5,040.
(3) Examination of policies showed $810 unexpired insurance on September 30.
(4) Office supplies on hand at September 30 were estimated to amount to $378.
(5) Income taxes expense for the year was determined to be $10,000.
(6) Inventory of merchandise on September 30 was $54,000.

Instructions

a Prepare a work sheet at September 30.

b Prepare a multiple-step income statement for the year. (Show all operating expenses in one group.)

c Prepare a classified balance sheet as of September 30.

d Prepare a statement of retained earnings for the year.

e Prepare closing journal entries.

5-6 Some of the year-end ledger account balances of Mainline Station are listed below.

Delivery equipment	$ 31,552
Interest payable	1,024
Advance payments from customers	5,760
Notes payable (due in 90 days)	64,000
U.S. government bonds	19,200
Accounts receivable	90,560
Accounts payable	59,200
Interest receivable	192
Inventory	244,640
Accumulated depreciation: delivery equipment	3,155
Salaries payable	2,560
Cash	43,040
Land	95,000
Furniture & fixtures	11,200
Mortgage payable (due in 20 years)	60,000
Retained earnings	301,000

Instructions

a Prepare a partial balance sheet for Mainline Station consisting of the current asset section and the current liability section *only*. Select the appropriate items from the above list.

b Compute the current ratio and the amount of working capital. Explain how each of these measurements is computed. State with reasons whether you consider the company to be in a strong or weak current position.

5-7 At December 31 the year-end work sheet prepared by Dairy Center contained the following amounts in the Income Statement columns.

	Debit	Credit
Inventory, Jan. 1.	312,000	
Sales		948,000
Sales returns & allowances	16,000	
Sales discounts	6,000	
Purchases	620,000	
Purchase returns & allowances		16,000
Purchase discounts		4,000
Transportation-in	15,000	
Sales salaries	110,000	
Store rent	24,000	
Advertising expense	38,000	
Depreciation expense: store fixtures	2,400	
Delivery service	5,600	
Office salaries	62,000	
Depreciation expense: office equipment	2,000	
Office supplies	1,000	
Utilities expense (70% selling, 30% gen. & adm.)	3,000	
Income taxes expense	20,000	
Inventory, Dec. 31		320,000
Subtotals	1,237,000	1,288,000
Net income	51,000	
Totals	1,288,000	1,288,000

Instructions

a Prepare a classified, multiple-step income statement. Show in detail the items making up cost of goods sold, and separate the operating expenses between selling expenses and general and administrative expenses.

b Prepare a *condensed,* single-step income statement along the lines of those published by large corporations. Use the format illustrated on page 182.

5-8 At the Uptown Theater, the cashier is located in a box office at the front of the building. The cashier receives cash from customers and operates a ticket machine which ejects serially numbered tickets. The serial number appears on each end of the ticket. The tickets come from the printer in large rolls which fit into the ticket machine and are removed at the end of each cashier's working period.

After purchasing a ticket from the cashier, in order to be admitted to the theater a customer must hand the ticket to a doorman stationed some 50 feet from the box office at the entrance to the theater lobby. The doorman tears the ticket in half, opens the door for the customer, and returns the ticket stub to the customer. The other half of the ticket is dropped by the doorman into a locked box.

Instructions

a Describe the internal controls present in Uptown Theater's method of handling cash receipts.

b What steps should be taken regularly by the theater manager or other supervisor to make these internal controls work most effectively?

c Assume that the cashier and the doorman decided to collaborate in an effort to abstract cash receipts. What action might they take?

d On the assumption made in **c** of collaboration between the cashier and the doorman, what features of the control procedures would be most likely to disclose the embezzlement?

5-9 After spending several years as an executive for a large nationwide finance company, Charles Bell resigned in order to open his own finance business, called Happy Loan Company. The business consists of four very small offices in four cities a few miles apart. The activity of each office consists of making small loans to individual borrowers. The borrowers agree to repay the amount borrowed plus interest in monthly installments over a period of 36 months or less.

Charles Bell has his own office at one of the four loan offices and makes fairly frequent trips to the other offices to provide general supervision and to perform some internal auditing work. Early in the current year Bell called upon a firm of certified public accountants, explained that he was worried about the honesty of his employees, and made the following statement: "In the large nationwide loan company where I worked before starting my own business, we had over 500 offices scattered over 10 states. The system of accounting and internal control in that company made fraud absolutely impossible. I can describe the system to you in detail and I want you to install that system in my own company."

Instructions

a Explain how the CPA firm would probably respond to Bell's request that it install the large finance company's system of internal control in his new business.

b Comment on Bell's statement that the new system would make fraud absolutely impossible.

5-10 Dave Smith, an employee of Jones Company, is responsible for preparing checks to suppliers in payment for purchases of merchandise. Before submitting the checks to the treasurer for signature, Smith receives a copy of the purchase order, the receiving report, and the supplier's invoice. After determining that all three documents are in agreement and that no arithmetical errors exist, he fills in an invoice approval form and then prepares a check complete except for the treasurer's signature. Smith files the documents (purchase order, purchase invoice, receiving report, and invoice approval form) alphabetically by supplier. As a final step, he forwards the check to the treasurer for signature.

While trying to finish work early on Friday, December 31, Smith accidentally prepared for the treasurer's signature a check payable to Miller Company, a regular supplier, for $96,420, although the invoice and other documents indicated the amount payable was actually $69,420. Smith had previously made another error in recording the invoice, debiting the Purchases account when the debit should have been to Office Equipment because the invoice was for a computer and other equipment to be used in the business and not to be sold to customers. The amount of this accounting entry agreed with the invoice but not with the check. The entry was as follows:

Purchases *69,420*

    Accounts Payable *69,420*

To record purchase invoice from Miller Company. Terms, cash upon delivery.

The check for $96,420 was forwarded to the treasurer, promptly signed, and entered in the accounting records as a debit to Accounts Payable and a credit to Cash in the amount of $96,420. The treasurer mailed the check to the supplier. The supplier did not notice the overpayment and deposited the check.

A physical inventory was taken at the close of business Dec. 31, and financial statements were prepared by Jones Company without discovery of the error. Net income for the year was $100,000 and the retained earnings at December 31 appeared in the balance sheet as $204,000.

On January 20, Smith was processing another invoice from Miller Company and discovered the previous overpayment error. Smith processed the new invoice in a normal manner and then informed Miller Company by telephone of the December overpayment, requesting that a refund check be mailed and the envelope marked for his attention. After receiving the refund check for $27,000, Smith went to a nearby town, opened a new bank account in the name of Jones Company, and deposited the check. A short time later he withdrew the amount deposited, closed the bank account, and moved out of town leaving no forwarding address.

Instructions

a Were the figures for net income and retained earnings correct as shown in the financial statements? Explain fully. If you consider these amounts incorrect, compute corrected amounts. Income taxes are to be ignored.

b Assuming that the facts about the overstated check, the refund, and the theft by Smith all came to light late in January, prepare the necessary adjusting entry or entries. Include a full explanation as part of such entries.

c Identify any weaknesses in the system of internal control indicated by the above events and make recommendations for improvements.

5-11 Jane Miller, an experienced engineer, is considering buying the Eastern Engineering Company at year-end from its current owner, Jack Peterson. Eastern Engineering Company, a single proprietorship, has been a profitable business, earning about $54,000 each year. Jane Miller is certain she could operate the business just as profitably. The principal activity of the business has been the performance of engineering studies for government agencies interested in the development of air and water pollution control programs. Jane Miller comes to you with the balance sheet of Eastern Engineering Company shown below and asks your advice about buying the business.

EASTERN ENGINEERING COMPANY
Balance Sheet
December 31, 19___

Assets		Liabilities & Owners' Equity	
Cash	$ 36,000	Notes payable	$ 50,000
U.S. government contract		Accounts payable	20,200
receivable	90,000	Wages payable	5,400
Other contracts receivable ..	25,200	J. Peterson, capital	210,600
Equipment			
(net of depreciation)	81,000		
Patents	54,000		
	$286,200		$286,200

Miller immediately points out, as evidence of the firm's solvency, that the current ratio for Eastern Engineering is 2 to 1. In discussing the specific items on the balance sheet, you find that the patents were recently purchased by Eastern, and Miller believes them to be worth their $54,000 cost. The notes payable liability consists of one note to the manufacturer of the equipment owned by Eastern, which Peterson had incurred five years ago to finance the purchase of the equipment. The note becomes payable, however, in February of the coming year. The accounts payable all will become due within 30 to 60 days.

Since Miller does not have enough cash to buy Peterson's equity in the business, she is considering the following terms of purchase: (1) Peterson will withdraw all the cash from the business, thus reducing his equity to $174,600, (2) Peterson will also keep the $90,000 receivable from the U.S. government, leaving his equity in the business at $84,600, and (3) by borrowing heavily, Miller thinks she can raise $84,600 in cash, which she will pay to Peterson for his remaining equity. Miller will assume the existing liabilities of the business.

Instructions

a Prepare a classified balance sheet for Eastern Engineering Company as it would appear immediately after Miller acquired the business, assuming that the purchase is carried out immediately on the proposed terms.

b Compute the current ratio and the working capital position of Eastern Engineering Company after Miller's purchase of the business.

c Write a memorandum to Miller explaining what problems she might encounter if she purchases the business as planned.

5-12 Jim Brown, long-time office manager of North Building Materials, prepares all purchase orders for merchandise in which the company deals. Brown personally owns a large waterfront lot and during the current year was having a marina constructed on this lot. The construction plans included boat slips, a large dock, a restaurant, and a marine supply store.

To obtain building materials for this project, Brown fraudulently issued purchase orders in the name of North Building Materials and instructed the suppliers to deliver the materials at his waterfront site. The suppliers did not question the propriety of these orders since they were accustomed to receiving from North Building Materials purchase orders signed by Brown. When purchase invoices from the suppliers relating to these materials reached North Building Materials, Brown entered them in the accounting records as debits to Purchases and credits to Accounts Payable. On the appropriate dates, he prepared company checks payable to the suppliers and presented them to the treasurer of North Building Materials for signature. Since the checks were payable to suppliers from whom North Building Materials regularly made purchases, the treasurer signed and mailed the checks without question.

The accounting system used by North Building Materials required that duplicate copies of purchase orders be attached to the related receiving reports and purchase invoices, and then be filed alphabetically by vendor. Since there were no receiving reports for the materials delivered to the marina, Brown removed from the files the purchase orders and related purchase invoices for these materials and concealed these documents in his desk. During the year, the billed price of the materials which Brown ordered and diverted to his marina totaled $110,000. Of this total, all but $10,000 had been paid for at year-end by North Building Materials and cash discounts of $2,000 had been taken. The remaining $10,000 in unpaid invoices were included in the year-end balance of accounts payable at the gross amount.

North Building Materials uses the periodic inventory system. A complete physical inventory was taken on December 31. In an effort to prevent the theft of materials from having a conspicuous effect on the year's reported earnings, Brown changed figures on the inventory count sheets, thereby causing the ending inventory to be overstated by $100,000.

Condensed financial statements for the company at December 31 of the current year appeared as follows:

NORTH BUILDING MATERIALS
Balance Sheet
December 31, 19___

Assets		Liabilities & Stockholders' Equity		
Cash	$ 32,000	Notes payable		$320,000
Accounts receivable	280,000	Accounts payable		260,000
Inventory	625,000	Accrued salaries		20,000
Office equipment (net)	5,000	Total liabilities		$600,000
Trucks (net)	36,000	Stockholders' equity:		
		Capital stock	$100,000	
		Retained earnings	278,000	378,000
	$978,000			$978,000

NORTH BUILDING MATERIALS
Income Statement
For the Year Ended December 31, 19___

Net sales				$3,661,000
Cost of goods sold:				
Beginning inventory			$ 520,000	
Purchases		$3,225,000		
Less: Purchase returns & allow..............	$72,000			
Purchase discounts	60,000	132,000	3,093,000	
Cost of goods available for sale			$3,613,000	
Less: Inventory, Dec. 31, 19___..............			625,000	
Cost of goods sold				2,988,000
Gross profit on sales				$ 673,000
Operating expenses:				
Selling			$ 409,000	
General and administrative			265,000	674,000
Net loss				$ 1,000

At an office party on New Year's Eve, Jim Brown became somewhat intoxicated and confided to a secretary how he had acquired "free materials" to build a marina. The secretary reported this information to Lee North, president of the company, who immediately demanded an explanation from Brown. Jim Brown confessed to his dishonest actions and returned the purchase orders and purchase invoices he had removed from the files. Also on New Year's Eve, the marina being constructed by Brown was completely destroyed by fire. There was no insurance in force, and Brown had no other assets. Lee

North discharged Brown, who left town without any forwarding address. Lee North considers that the entire problem was caused by his failure to establish a satisfactory system of internal control. He does not attach any blame to the suppliers.

Instructions

a Compute the loss to North Building Materials from Jim Brown's dishonest actions. Show how you arrived at this amount. (Income taxes are not to be considered.)

b Prepare a corrected balance sheet and income statement. Omit from the balance of the Purchases account the cost of the materials which were never in the possession of the company. After deducting operating expenses, show Income from Operations followed by the nonoperating item, Loss from Material Shortages.

c Explain the weaknesses in the system of internal control which made possible concealment of the thefts by Brown and recommend any appropriate improvements in the system.

BUSINESS DECISION PROBLEM 5

Bell Company and Harte Corporation are both merchandising companies applying for nine-month bank loans in order to finance the acquisition of new equipment. Both companies are seeking to borrow the amount of $210,000 and have submitted the following balance sheets with their loan applications:

BELL COMPANY
Balance Sheet
January 31, 19___

Assets

Current assets:			
Cash			$ 57,000
Accounts receivable			153,000
Inventories			162,000
Short-term prepayments			6,000
Total current assets			$ 378,000
Plant and equipment:			
Land		$150,000	
Building	$600,000		
Less: Accumulated depreciation	90,000	510,000	
Store equipment	$180,000		
Less: Accumulated depreciation	45,000	135,000	
Total plant and equipment			795,000
Total assets			$1,173,000

Liabilities & Stockholders' Equity

Current liabilities:		
Accounts payable		$ 135,000
Income taxes payable		45,000
Total current liabilities		$ 180,000
Long-term liabilities:		
Mortgage payable (due in 13 months)		330,000
Total liabilities		$ 510,000
Stockholders' equity:		
Capital stock	$300,000	
Retained earnings	363,000	663,000
Total liabilities & stockholders' equity		$1,173,000

HARTE CORPORATION
Balance Sheet
January 31, 19___

Assets

Current assets:			
Cash			$ 384,000
U.S. government bonds			210,000
Accounts receivable			603,000
Inventories			567,000
Total current assets			$1,764,000
Plant & equipment:			
Land		$ 180,000	
Building and equipment	$1,230,000		
Less: Accumulated depreciation	180,000	1,050,000	
Total plant & equipment			1,230,000
Total assets			$2,994,000

Liabilities & Stockholders' Equity

Current liabilities:		
Notes payable		$ 600,000
Accounts payable		520,000
Income taxes payable		140,000
Total current liabilities		$1,260,000
Long-term liabilities:		
Mortgage payable (due in 10 years)		420,000
Total liabilities		$1,680,000
Stockholders' equity:		
Capital stock	$750,000	
Retained earnings	564,000	1,314,000
Total liabilities & stockholders' equity		$2,994,000

Instructions

a Compute the current ratio and amount of working capital for each company as of January 31, 19___.

b Compute the current ratio and amount of working capital that each company would have *after* obtaining the bank loan and investing the borrowed cash in new equipment (assuming no other transactions affecting current accounts).

c From the viewpoint of a bank loan officer, to which company would you prefer to make a $210,000 nine-month loan? Explain. Include in your answer a discussion of the ability of each company to meet its obligations in the near future, and also make a comparison of the relative liquidity of the various current assets held by each company.

6

ACCOUNTING SYSTEMS: MANUAL AND EDP

After studying this chapter you should be able to:

- Explain the purpose and characteristics of special journals.
- Use special journals to record sales on credit, purchases on account, and cash transactions.
- Explain the usefulness of a subsidiary ledger and its relationship to a controlling account in the general ledger.
- Post entries in special journals to the general ledger and sudsidiary ledgers.
- Discuss accounting applications of computers and means of achieving internal control in EDP systems.

Streamlining the accounting process

In the early chapters of an introductory accounting book, basic accounting principles can be discussed most conveniently in terms of a small business with only a few customers and suppliers. This simplified model of a business has been used in preceding chapters to demonstrate the analysis and recording of the more common types of business transactions.

The recording procedures illustrated thus far call for recording each transaction by an entry in the general journal, and then posting each debit and credit from the general journal to the proper account in the ledger. We must now face the practical problem of streamlining and speeding up this basic accounting system so that the accounting department can keep pace with the rapid flow of transactions in a modern business.

Accounting systems in common use range from manual systems, which use special journals to streamline the journalizing and posting processes, to sophisticated computer systems which maintain accounting records on magnetic tape. The accounting system in use in any given company will be specially tailored to the size and information needs of the business.

MANUAL ACCOUNTING SYSTEMS

In a large business there may be hundreds or even thousands of transactions every day. To handle a large volume of transactions rapidly and efficiently, it is helpful to group the transactions into like classes and to use a specialized journal for each class. This will greatly reduce the amount of detailed recording work and will also permit a division of labor, since each special-purpose journal can be handled by a different employee. The great majority of transactions (perhaps as much as 90 or 95%) usually fall into four types. These four types and four corresponding special journals are as follows:

Type of Transaction	Name of Special Journal
Sales of merchandise on credit	Sales journal
Purchases of merchandise on credit	Purchases journal
Receipts of cash	Cash receipts journal
Payments of cash	Cash payments journal

In addition to these four special journals, a *general journal* will be used for recording transactions which do not fit into any of the above four types. The general journal is the same book of original entry illustrated in preceding chapters; the adjective "general" is added merely to distinguish it from the special journals.

Sales journal

Illustrated below is a sales journal containing entries for all sales on account made during November by the Seaside Company. Whenever merchandise is sold on credit, several copies of a sales invoice are prepared. The information listed on a sales invoice usually includes the date of the sale, the serial number of the invoice, the customer's name, the amount of the sale, and the credit terms. One copy of the sales invoice is used by the seller as the basis for an entry in the sales journal.

Sales Journal   Page 1

Date		Account Debited	Invoice No.	✓	Amount
19 ——					
Nov	2	John Adams	301	✓	450
	4	Harold Black	302	✓	1,000
	5	Robert Cross	303	✓	975
	11	H. R. Davis	304	✓	620
	18	C. D. Early	305	✓	900
	23	John Frost	306	✓	400
	29	D. H. Gray	307	✓	11.850
					16.195
					(5) (41)

Entries for sales on credit during November

Note that the illustrated sales journal contains special columns for recording each of these aspects of the sales transaction, except the credit terms. If it is the practice of the business to offer different credit terms to different customers, a column may be inserted in the sales journal to show the terms of sale. In this illustration it is assumed that all sales are made on terms of 2/10, n/30; consequently, there is no need to write the credit terms as part of each entry. *Only sales on credit are entered in the sales journal.* When merchandise is sold for cash, the transaction is recorded in a *cash receipts* journal, which is illustrated later in this chapter.

Advantages of the sales journal   Note that each of the above seven sales transactions is recorded on a single line. Each entry consists of a debit to a customer's account; the offsetting credit to the Sales account is understood without being written, because sales on account are the only transactions recorded in this special journal.

An entry in a sales journal need not include an explanation; if more information about the transaction is desired it can be obtained by referring to the file copy of the sales invoice. The invoice number is listed in the sales journal as part of each entry. The one-line entry in the sales journal requires much less writing than would be necessary to record a sales transaction in the general journal. Since there may be several hundred or several thousand sales transactions each month, the time saved in recording transactions in this streamlined manner becomes quite important.

Every entry in the sales journal represents a debit to a customer's account. Charges to customers' accounts should be posted daily so that each customer's account will always be up-to-date and available for use in making decisions relating to collections and to the further extension of credit. A check mark (✔) is placed in the sales journal opposite each amount posted to a customer's account, to indicate that the posting has been made.

Another advantage of the special journal for sales is the great saving of time in posting credits to the Sales account. Remember that every amount entered in the sales journal represents a credit to Sales. In the illustrated sales journal on page 215, there are seven transactions (and in practice there might be 700). Instead of posting a separate credit to the Sales account for each sales transaction, we can wait until the end of the month and make one posting to the Sales account for the total of the amounts recorded in the sales journal.

In the illustrated sales journal for November, the sales on account totaled $16,195. On November 30 this amount is posted as a credit to the Sales account, and the ledger account number for Sales (41) is entered under the total figure in the sales journal to show that the posting operation has been performed. The total sales figure is also posted as a debit to ledger account no. 5, Accounts Receivable. To make clear the reason for this posting to Accounts Receivable, an explanation of the nature of controlling accounts and subsidiary ledgers is necessary.

Controlling accounts and subsidiary ledgers

In preceding chapters all transactions involving accounts receivable from customers have been posted to a single account entitled Accounts Receivable. Under this procedure, however, it is not easy to look up the amount receivable from a given customer. In practice, businesses which sell goods on credit *maintain a separate account receivable for each customer.* If there are 4,000 customers, this would require a ledger with 4,000 accounts receivable, in addition to the accounts for other assets, and for liabilities, owners' equity, revenue, and expenses. Such a ledger would be cumbersome and unwieldy. Also, the trial balance prepared from such a large ledger would be a very long one. If the trial balance showed the ledger to be out of balance, the task of locating the error or errors would be most difficult. All these factors indicate that it is not desirable to have too many accounts in one ledger. Fortunately, a simple solution is available; this solution is to divide the ledger into several separate ledgers.

In a business which has a large number of customers and a large number of creditors, it is customary to divide the ledger into three separate ledgers. All the accounts with *customers* are placed in alphabetical order in a separate ledger, called the *accounts receivable ledger.* All the accounts with *creditors* are arranged alphabetically in another ledger called the *accounts payable ledger.* Both of these ledgers are known as *subsidiary ledgers,* because they support and are controlled by the general ledger.

After thus segregating the accounts receivable from customers in one subsidiary ledger and placing the accounts payable to creditors in a second subsidiary ledger, we have left in the original ledger all the revenue and expense accounts and also all the balance sheet accounts except those with individual customers and individual creditors. This ledger is called the *general ledger,* to distinguish it from the subsidiary ledgers.

When the numerous individual accounts receivable from customers are placed in a subsidiary ledger, an account entitled Accounts Receivable continues to be maintained in the general ledger. This account shows the *total amount due from all customers;* in other words, this single *controlling account* in the general ledger takes the place of the numerous customers' accounts which have been removed to form a subsidiary ledger. The general ledger is still in balance because the controlling account, Accounts Receivable, has a balance equal to the total of the customers' accounts which were removed from the general ledger. Agreement of the controlling account with the sum of the accounts receivable in the subsidiary ledger also provides assurance of accuracy in the subsidiary ledger.

A controlling account entitled Accounts Payable is also kept in the general ledger in place of the numerous accounts with creditors which have been removed to form the accounts payable subsidiary ledger. Because the two controlling accounts represent the total amounts receivable from customers and payable to creditors, a trial balance can be prepared from the general ledger alone. The illustration below shows the relationship of the subsidiary ledgers to the controlling accounts in the general ledger:

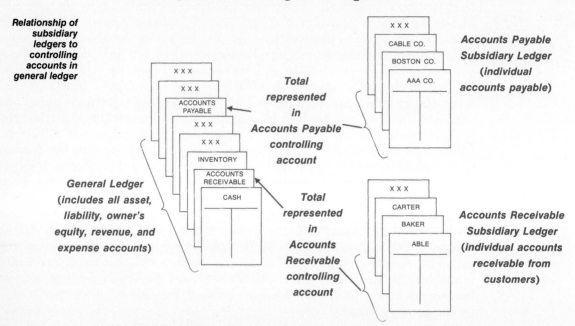

Relationship of subsidiary ledgers to controlling accounts in general ledger

Posting to subsidiary ledgers and to controlling accounts   To illustrate the posting of subsidiary ledgers and of controlling accounts, let us refer again to the sales journal illustrated on page 215. Each debit to a customer's account is posted currently during the month from the sales journal to the customer's account in the accounts receivable ledger. The accounts in this subsidiary ledger are usually kept in alphabetical order and are not numbered. When a posting is made to a customer's account, a check mark (✔) is placed in the sales journal as evidence that the posting has been made to the subsidiary ledger.

At month-end the sales journal is totaled. The total amount of sales for the month, $16,195, is posted as a credit to the Sales account and also as a debit to the controlling account, Accounts Receivable, in the general ledger. The controlling account will, therefore, equal the total of all the customers' accounts in the subsidiary ledger.

The diagram on page 219 shows the day-to-day posting of individual entries from the sales journal to the subsidiary ledger. The diagram also shows the month-end posting of the total of the sales journal to the two general ledger accounts affected, Accounts Receivable and Sales. Note that the amount of the monthly debit to the controlling account is equal to the sum of the debits posted to the subsidiary ledger.

Subsidiary ledger posted daily; general ledger posted monthly

Purchases journal

The handling of purchase transactions when a purchases journal is used follows a pattern quite similar to the one described for the sales journal.

Assume that the purchases journal illustrated on the next page contains all purchases of merchandise on credit during the month by the Seaside Company. The invoice date is shown in a separate column because the cash discount period begins on this date.

The five entries are posted as they occur during the month as credits to the creditors' accounts in the subsidiary ledger for accounts payable. As each posting is completed a check mark (✔) is placed in the purchases journal.

At the end of the month the purchases journal is totaled and ruled as shown in

			Purchases Journal			*Page 1*
Date		**Account Credited**		**Invoice Date**	✔	**Amount**
19__				19__		
Nov	2	Alabama Supply Co. (net 30)		Nov 2	✔	3,325
	4	Barker & Bright (2/10, n/30)		4	✔	700
	10	Canning & Sons (net 30)		9	✔	500
	17	Davis Co. (2/10, n/30)		16	✔	900
	27	Excelsior, Inc. (net 30)		25	✔	1,825
						7,250
						(50) (21)

Entries for purchases on credit during November

the above illustration. The total figure, $7,250, is posted to two general ledger accounts as shown on the next page:

1 As a debit to the Purchases account
2 As a credit to the Accounts Payable controlling account

The account numbers for Purchases (50) and for Accounts Payable (21) are then placed in parentheses below the column total of the purchases journal to show that the posting has been made.

Under the particular system being described, the only transactions recorded in the purchases journal are *purchases of merchandise on credit.* The term *merchandise* means goods acquired for resale to customers. If merchandise is purchased for cash rather than on credit, the transaction should be recorded in the cash payments journal, as illustrated on pages 224 and 225.

The diagram on the next page illustrates the day-to-day posting of individual entries from the purchases journal to the accounts with creditors in the subsidiary ledger for accounts payable. The diagram also shows how the column total of the purchases journal is posted at the end of the month to the general ledger accounts, Purchases and Accounts Payable. One objective of this diagram is to emphasize that the amount of the monthly credit to the control account is equal to the sum of the credits posted to the subsidiary ledger.

When assets other than merchandise are being acquired, as, for example, a delivery truck or an office desk for use in the business, the journal to be used depends upon whether a cash payment is made. If assets of this type are purchased for cash, the transaction should be entered in the cash payments journal; if the transaction is on credit, the general journal is used. The purchases journal is not used to record the acquisition of these assets because the total of this journal is posted to the Purchases account and this account (as explained in Chapter 5) is used in determining the cost of goods sold.

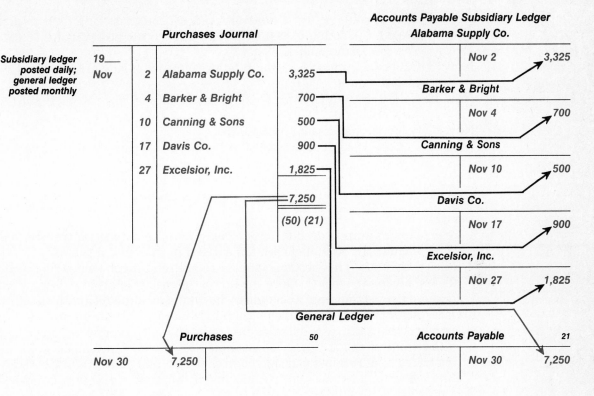

Subsidiary ledger posted daily; general ledger posted monthly

Cash receipts journal

All transactions involving the receipt of cash are recorded in the cash receipts journal. One common example is the sale of merchandise for cash. As each cash sale is made, it is rung up on a cash register. At the end of the day the total of the cash sales is computed by striking the total key on the register. This total is entered in the cash receipts journal, which therefore contains one entry for the total cash sales of the day. For other types of cash receipts, such as the collection of accounts receivable from customers, a separate journal entry may be made for each transaction. The cash receipts journal illustrated on pages 222 and 223 contains entries for selected November transactions, all of which include the receipt of cash.

Nov. **1** R. B. Jones organized Seaside Company by investing $75,000 cash in exchange for 7,500 shares of $10 par value capital stock.

Nov. **4** Sold merchandise for cash, $300.

Nov. **5** Sold merchandise for cash, $400.

Nov. **8** Collected from John Adams for sales invoice of Nov. 2, $450 less 2% cash discount.

Nov. 10 Sold a small portion of land not needed in business for a total price of $7,000, consisting of cash of $1,000 and a note receivable for $6,000. The cost of the land sold was $5,000.

Nov. 12 Collected from Harold Black for sales invoice of Nov. 4, $1,000 less 2% cash discount.

Nov. 20 Collected from C. D. Early for sales invoice of Nov. 18, $900 less 2% cash discount.

Nov. 27 Sold merchandise for cash, $125.

Nov. 30 Obtained $4,000 loan from bank. Issued a note payable in that amount.

Note that the cash receipts journal illustrated below and on page 223 has three debit columns and three credit columns as follows:

Debits:

1 Cash. This column is used for every entry, because only those transactions which include the receipt of cash are entered in this special journal.

2 Sales discounts. This column is used to accumulate the sales discounts allowed during the month. Only one line of the cash receipts book is required to record a collection from a customer who takes advantage of a cash discount.

3 Other accounts. This third debit column is used for debits to any and all accounts other than cash and sales discounts, and space is provided for writing in the name of the account. For example, the entry of November 10 in the illustrated cash receipts journal shows that cash and a note receivable were obtained when land was sold. The amount of cash received, $1,000, is entered in the Cash debit column; the account title Notes Receivable is written in the

Cash Receipts Journal

	Date		Explanation	Debits		Other Accounts		
				Cash	Sales Discounts	Name	LP	Amount
Includes all transactions involving receipt of cash	19___							
	Nov	1	Issued capital stock	75,000				
		4	Cash sales	300				
		5	Cash sales	400				
		8	Invoice Nov. 2, less 2%	441	9			
		10	Sale of land	1,000		Notes Receivable	3	6,000
		12	Invoice Nov. 4, less 2%	980	20			
		20	Invoice Nov. 18, less 2%	882	18			
		27	Cash sales	125				
		30	Obtained bank loan	4,000				
				83,128	47			6,000
				(1)	(43)			(X)

Other Accounts debit column along with the amount of the debit to this account, $6,000. These two debits are offset by credit entries to Land, $5,000, and to Gain on Sale of Land, $2,000, in the Other Accounts credit column.

Credits:

1 Accounts receivable. This column is used to list the credits to customers' accounts as receivables are collected. The name of the customer is written in the space entitled Account Credited to the left of the Accounts Receivable column.
2 Sales. The existence of this column will save posting by permitting the accumulation of all sales for cash during the month and the posting of the column total at the end of the month as a credit to the Sales account (41).
3 Other accounts. This column is used for credits to any and all accounts other than Accounts Receivable and Sales. In some instances, a transaction may require credits to two accounts. Such cases are handled by using two lines of the special journal, as illustrated by the transaction of November 10, which required credits to both the Land account and to Gain on Sale of Land.

Posting the cash receipts journal   It is convenient to think of the posting of a cash receipts journal as being divided into two phases. The first phase consists of the daily posting of individual amounts throughout the month; the second phase consists of the posting of column totals at the end of the month.

Posting during the month   Daily posting of the Accounts Receivable credit column is desirable. Each amount is posted to an individual customer's account in

Page 1

		Credits			
	Accounts Receivable			**Other Accounts**	
Account Credited	✓	**Amount**	**Sales**	**LP**	**Amount**
Capital Stock, $10 par				30	75,000
			300		
			400		
John Adams	✓	450			
Land				11	5,000 ⎱
Gain on Sale of Land				40	2,000 ⎰
Harold Black	✓	1,000			
C. D. Early	✓	900			
			125		
Notes Payable				20	4,000
		2,350	825		86,000
		(5)	(41)		(X)

the accounts receivable subsidiary ledger. A check mark (✔) is placed in the cash receipts journal alongside each item posted to a customer's account to show that the posting operation has been performed. When debits and credits to customers' accounts are posted daily, the current status of each customer's account is available for use in making decisions as to further granting of credit and as a guide to collection efforts on past-due accounts.

The debits and credits in the Other Accounts sections of the cash receipts journal may be posted daily or at convenient intervals during the month. If this portion of the posting work is done on a current basis, less detailed work will be left for the busy period at the end of the month. As the postings of individual items are made, the number of the ledger account debited or credited is entered in the LP (ledger page) column of the cash receipts journal opposite the item posted. Evidence is thus provided in the special journal as to which items have been posted.

Posting column totals at month end At the end of the month, the cash receipts journal is ruled as shown on pages 222 and 223. Before posting any of the column totals, it is first important to prove that *the sum of the debit column totals is equal to the sum of the credit column totals.*

After the totals of the cash receipts journal have been crossfooted, the following column totals are posted:

1 Cash debit column. Posted as a debit to the Cash account.
2 Sales Discounts debit column. Posted as a debit to the Sales Discounts account.

Cash Payments Journal

				Credits		Other Accounts		
Date	Check No.	Explanation	Cash	Purchase Discounts	Name	LP	Amount
19__								
Nov 1	101	Paid November rent	800				
2	102	Purchased merchandise	500				
8	103	Invoice of Nov. 4, less 2%	686	14			
9	104	Bought land and building	70,000		Notes Payable	20	30,000
17	105	Paid sales salaries	3,600				
26	106	Invoice of Nov. 17, less 2%	882	18			
27	107	Purchased merchandise	400				
28	108	Purchased merchandise	650				
29	109	Newspaper advertisement	50				
29	110	Three-year ins. policy	720				
			78,288	32			30,000
			(1)	(52)			(X)

Includes all transactions involving payment of cash

3 Accounts Receivable credit column. Posted as a credit to the controlling account, Accounts Receivable.
4 Sales credit column. Posted as a credit to the Sales account.

As each column total is posted to the appropriate account in the general ledger, the ledger account number is entered in parentheses just below the column total in the special journal. This notation shows that the column total has been posted and also indicates the account to which the posting was made. The totals of the Other Accounts columns in both the debit and credit sections of the special journal are not posted, because the amounts listed in the column affect various general ledger accounts and have already been posted as individual items. The symbol (X) is placed below the totals of these two columns to indicate that no posting is made.

Cash payments journal

Another widely used special journal is the cash payments journal, sometimes called the *cash disbursements journal,* in which all payments of cash are recorded. Among the more common of these transactions are payments of accounts payable to creditors, payment of operating expenses, and cash purchases of merchandise.

The cash payments journal illustrated below contains entries for all November transactions of the Seaside Company which required the payment of cash.

Nov. **1** Paid rent on store building for November, $800.
Nov. **2** Purchased merchandise for cash, $500.

Page 1

		Debits			
Account Debited	Accounts Payable		Purchases	Other Accounts	
	✔	Amount		LP	Amount
Store Rent expense				54	800
			500		
Barker & Bright	✔	700			
Land				11	65,000 ⎱
Building				12	35,000 ⎰
Sales Salaries Expense				53	3,600
Davis Co.	✔	900			
			400		
			650		
Advertising Expense				55	50
Unexpired Insurance				6	720
		1,600	1,550		105,170
		(21)	(50)		(X)

Nov. 8 Paid Barker & Bright for invoice of Nov. 4, $700 less 2%.

Nov. 9 Bought land, $65,000, and building, $35,000, for future use in business. Paid cash of $70,000 and signed a promissory note for the balance of $30,000. (Land and building were acquired in a single transaction.)

Nov. 17 Paid salesmen's salaries, $3,600.

Nov. 26 Paid Davis Co. for invoice of Nov. 16, $900 less 2%.

Nov. 27 Purchased merchandise for cash, $400.

Nov. 28 Purchased merchandise for cash, $650.

Nov. 29 Paid for newspaper advertising, $50.

Nov. 29 Paid for three-year insurance policy, $720.

Note in the illustrated cash payments journal that the three credit columns are located to the left of the three debit columns; any sequence of columns is satisfactory in a special journal as long as the column headings clearly distinguish debits from credits. The Cash column is often placed first in both the cash receipts journal and the cash payments journal because it is the column used in every transaction.

Good internal control over cash disbursements requires that all payments be made by check. The checks are serially numbered and as each transaction is entered in the cash payments journal, the check number is listed in a special column provided just to the right of the date column. An unbroken sequence of check numbers in this column gives assurance that every check issued has been recorded in the accounting records.

The use of the six money columns in the illustrated cash payments journal parallels the procedures described for the cash receipts journal.

Posting the cash payments journal The posting of the cash payments journal falls into the same two phases already described for the cash receipts journal. The first phase consists of the daily posting of entries in the Accounts Payable debit column to the individual accounts of creditors in the accounts payable subsidiary ledger. Check marks (✓) are entered opposite these items to show that the posting has been made. If a creditor telephones to inquire about any aspect of his account, information on all purchases and payments made to date is readily available in the accounts payable subsidiary ledger.

The individual debit and credit entries in the Other Accounts columns of the cash payments journal may be posted daily or at convenient intervals during the month. As the postings of these individual items are made, the number of the ledger account debited or credited is entered in the LP (ledger page) column of the cash payments journal opposite the item posted.

The second phase of posting the cash payments journal is performed at the end of the month. When all the transactions of the month have been journalized, the cash payments journal is ruled as shown on pages 224 and 225, and the six money columns are totaled. The equality of debits and credits is then proved before posting.

After the totals of the cash payments journal have been proved to be in balance, the totals of the columns for Cash, Purchase Discounts, Accounts

Payable, and Purchases are posted to the corresponding accounts in the general ledger. The numbers of the accounts to which these postings are made are listed in parentheses just below the respective column totals in the cash payments journal. The totals of the Other Accounts columns in both the debit and credit section of this special journal are not to be posted, and the symbol (X) is placed below the totals of these two columns to indicate that no posting is required.

The general journal

When all transactions involving cash or the purchase and sale of merchandise are recorded in special journals, only a few types of transactions remain to be entered in the general journal. Examples include the declaration of dividends, the purchase or sale of plant and equipment on credit, the return of merchandise for credit to a supplier, and the return of merchandise by customers for credit to their accounts. The general journal is also used for adjusting and closing entries at the end of the accounting period.

The following transactions of the Seaside Company during November could not conveniently be handled in any of the four special journals and were therefore entered in the general journal.

Nov. 25 A customer, John Frost, was permitted to return for credit $50 worth of merchandise that had been sold to him on Nov. 23.

Nov. 28 The Seaside Company returned to a supplier, Excelsior, Inc., for credit $300 worth of the merchandise purchased on Nov. 27.

Nov. 29 Purchased for use in the business office equipment costing $1,225. Agreed to make payment within 30 days to XYZ Equipment Co.

			General Journal			Page 1
Date			Account Titles and Explanation	LP	Dr	Cr
19__ Nov	25		Sales Returns and Allowances	42	50	
			Accounts Receivable, John Frost	5/✓		50
			Allowed credit to customer for return of merchandise from sale of Nov. 23.			
	28		Accounts Payable, Excelsior, Inc.	21/✓	300	
			Purchase Returns and Allowances	51		300
			Returned to supplier for credit a portion of merchandise purchased on Nov. 27.			
	28		Office Equipment	14	1,225	
			Accounts Payable, XYZ Equipment Co.	21/✓		1,225
			Purchased office equipment on 30-day credit.			

Transactions which do not fit any of the four special journals

Each of the preceding three entries includes a debit or credit to a controlling account (Accounts Receivable or Accounts Payable) and also identifies by name a particular creditor or customer. When a controlling account is debited or credited by a *general journal entry,* the debit or credit must be posted twice: one posting to the controlling account in the general ledger and another posting to a customer's account or a creditor's account in a subsidiary ledger. This double posting is necessary to keep the controlling account in agreement with the subsidiary ledger.

For example, in the illustrated entry of November 25 for the return of merchandise by a customer, the credit part of the entry is posted twice:

1 To the Accounts Receivable controlling account in the general ledger; this posting is evidenced by listing the account number (5) in the LP column of the general journal.
2 To the account of John Frost in the subsidiary ledger for accounts receivable; this posting is indicated by the check mark (✔) placed in the LP (ledger page) column of the general journal.

Showing the source of postings in ledger accounts

When a general journal and several special journals are in use, the ledger accounts should indicate the book of original entry from which each debit and credit was posted. An identifying symbol is placed opposite each entry in the reference column of the account. The symbols used in this text are as follows:

S1 meaning page 1 of the sales journal
P1 meaning page 1 of the purchases journal
CR1 meaning page 1 of the cash receipts journal
CP1 meaning page 1 of the cash payments journal
J1 meaning page 1 of the general journal

Subsidiary ledger accounts

The following illustration shows a customer's account in a subsidiary ledger for accounts receivable.

Name of Customer

Date			Ref	Debit	Credit	Balance
19__						
July	1		S1	400		400
	20		S3	200		600
Aug	4		CR7		400	200
	15		S6	120		320

Subsidiary ledger: account receivable

The advantage of this three-column form of account is that it shows at a glance the present balance receivable from the customer. The current amount of a customer's account is often needed as a guide to collection activities, or as a basis for granting additional credit. In studying the above illustration note also that the Reference column shows the source of each debit and credit.

Accounts appearing in the accounts receivable subsidiary ledger are assumed to have debit balances. If one of these customers' accounts should acquire a credit balance by overpayment or for any other reason, the word *credit* should be written after the amount in the Balance column.

The same three-column form of account is also generally used for creditors' accounts in an accounts payable subsidiary ledger, as indicated by the following illustration:

Name of Creditor

Date			Ref	Debit	Credit	Balance
19___						
July	10		P1		625	625
	25		P2		100	725
Aug	8		CP4	725		0
	12		P3		250	250

Subsidiary ledger: account payable

Accounts in the accounts payable subsidiary ledger normally have credit balances. If by reason of payment in advance or accidental overpayment, one of these accounts should acquire a debit balance, the word *debit* should be written after the amount in the Balance column.

As previously stated, both the accounts receivable and accounts payable subsidiary ledgers are customarily arranged in alphabetical order and account numbers are not used. This arrangement permits unlimited expansion of the subsidiary ledgers, as accounts with new customers and creditors can be inserted in proper alphabetical sequence.

Ledger accounts

The general ledger   The general ledger accounts of the Seaside Company illustrated next indicate the source of postings from the various books of original entry. The subsidiary ledger accounts appear on pages 232–233. To gain a clear understanding of the procedures for posting special journals, you should trace each entry in the illustrated special journals into the general ledger accounts and also to the subsidiary ledger accounts where appropriate. The general ledger accounts are shown in T-account form in order to distinguish them more emphatically from the accounts in the subsidiary ledgers.

Note that the Cash account contains only one debit entry and one credit entry, although there were many cash transactions during the month. The one debit, $83,128, represents the total cash received during the month and was posted from the cash receipts journal on November 30. Similarly, the one credit entry of $78,288 was posted on November 30 from the cash payments journal and represents the total of all cash payments made during the month.

General ledger accounts

Cash — 1

19__ Nov	30		CR1	83,128	19__ Nov	30		CP1	78,288

Notes Receivable — 3

19__ Nov	10		CR1	6,000					

Accounts Receivable — 5

19__ Nov	30		S1	16,195	19__ Nov	25		J1	50
						30		CR1	2,350

Unexpired Insurance — 6

19__ Nov	29		CP1	720					

Land — 11

19__ Nov	9		CP1	65,000	19__ Nov	10		CR1	5,000

Building — 12

19__ Nov	9		CP1	35,000					

Office Equipment — 14

19__ Nov	29		J1	1,225					

Notes Payable — 20

					19__ Nov	9		CP1	30,000
						30		CR1	4,000

Accounts Payable   21

19__					19__				
Nov	28		J1	300	Nov	29		J1	1,225
	30		CP1	1,600		30		P1	7,250

Capital Stock   30

					19__				
					Nov	1		CR1	75,000

Gain on Sale of Land   40

					19__				
					Nov	10		CR1	2,000

Sales   41

					19__				
					Nov	30		CR1	825
						30		S1	16,195

Sales Returns and Allowances   42

19__									
Nov	25		J1	50					

Sales Discounts   43

19__									
Nov	30		CR1	47					

Purchases   50

19__									
Nov	30		CP1	1,550					
	30		P1	7,250					

Purchase Returns and Allowances   51

					19__				
					Nov	28		J1	300

Purchase Discounts   52

					19__				
					Nov	30		CP1	32

Sales Salaries Expense   53

19__									
Nov	17		CP1	3,600					

Store Rent Expense   54

19__									
Nov	1		CP1	800					

Advertising Expense   55

19__									
Nov	29		CP1	50					

Accounts receivable ledger The subsidiary ledger for accounts receivable appears as follows after the posting of the various journals has been completed.

John Adams

Customers' accounts

19__						
Nov	2		S1	450		450
	8		CR1		450	0

Harold Black

19__						
Nov	4		S1	1,000		1,000
	12		CR1		1,000	0

Robert Cross

19__						
Nov	5		S1	975		975

H. R. Davis

19__						
Nov	11		S1	620		620

C. D. Early

19__						
Nov	18		S1	900		900
	20		CR1		900	0

John Frost

19__							
Nov	23			S1	400		400
	25			J1		50	350

D. H. Gray

19__							
Nov	29			S1	11,850		11,850

Accounts payable ledger   The accounts with creditors in the accounts payable subsidiary ledger are as follows:

Alabama Supply Co.

Creditors' accounts

19__							
Nov	2			P1		3,325	3,325

Barker & Bright

19__							
Nov	4			P1		700	700
	8			CP1	700		0

Canning & Sons

19__							
Nov	10			P1		500	500

Davis Co.

19__							
Nov	17			P1		900	900
	26			CP1	900		0

Excelsior, Inc.

19__							
Nov	27			P1		1,825	1,825
	28			J1	300		1,525

XYZ Equipment Co.

19__							
Nov	29			J1		1,225	1,225

Proving the ledgers

At the end of each accounting period, proof of the equality of debits and credits in the general ledger is established by preparation of a trial balance, as illustrated in preceding chapters. When controlling accounts and subsidiary ledgers are in use, it is also necessary to prove that each subsidiary ledger is in agreement with its controlling account. This proof is accomplished by preparing a schedule of the balances of accounts in each subsidiary ledger and determining that the totals of these schedules agree with the balances of the corresponding controlling accounts. The Seaside Company's trial balance and schedules of accounts receivable and accounts payable appear on page 235.

Variations in special journals

The number of columns to be included in each special journal and the number of special journals to be used will depend upon the nature of the particular business and especially upon the volume of the various kinds of transactions. For example, the desirability of including a Sales Discounts column in the cash receipts journal depends upon whether a business offers discounts to its customers for prompt payment.

A retail store may find that customers frequently return merchandise for credit. To record efficiently this large volume of sales returns, the store may establish a sales returns and allowances journal. A purchase returns and allowances journal may also be desirable if returns of goods to suppliers occur frequently.

Special journals should be regarded as laborsaving devices which may be designed with any number of columns appropriate to the needs of the particular business. A business will usually benefit by establishing a special journal for any type of transaction that occurs quite frequently.

Direct posting from invoices

In many business concerns the efficiency of data processing is increased by posting sales invoices directly to the customers' accounts in the accounts receivable ledger rather than copying sales invoices into a sales journal and then posting to accounts in the subsidiary ledger. If the sales invoices are *serially numbered,* a file or binder of duplicate sales invoices arranged in numerical order may take the place of a formal sales journal. By accounting for each *serial number,* it is possible to be certain that all sales invoices are included. At the end of the month, the invoices are totaled on a calculator, and a general journal entry is made debiting the Accounts Receivable controlling account and crediting Sales for the total of the month's sales invoices.

Direct posting may also be used in recording purchase invoices. As soon as purchase invoices have been verified and approved, credits to the creditors' accounts in the accounts payable ledger may be posted directly from the purchase invoices.

SEASIDE COMPANY
Trial Balance
November 30, 19___

General ledger trial balance

Cash	$ 4,840	
Notes receivable	6,000	
Accounts receivable (see schedule below)	13,795	
Unexpired insurance	720	
Land	60,000	
Building	35,000	
Office equipment	1,225	
Notes payable		$ 34,000
Accounts payable (see schedule below)		6,575
Capital, stock, $10 par		75,000
Gain on sale of land		2,000
Sales		17,020
Sales returns and allowances	50	
Sales discounts	47	
Purchases	8,800	
Purchase returns and allowances		300
Purchase discounts		32
Sales salaries expense	3,600	
Store rent expense	800	
Advertising expense	50	
	$134,927	$134,927

Schedule of Accounts Receivable
November 30, 19___

Subsidiary ledgers in balance with control accounts

Robert Cross	$ 975
H. R. Davis	620
John Frost	350
D. H. Gray	11,850
Total (per balance of controlling account)	$13,795

Schedule of Accounts Payable
November 30, 19___

Alabama Supply Co.	$3,325
Canning & Sons	500
Excelsior, Inc.	1,525
XYZ Equipment Co.	1,225
Total (per balance of controlling account)	$6,575

The trend toward direct posting from invoices to subsidiary ledgers is mentioned here as further evidence that accounting records and procedures can be designed in a variety of ways to meet the individual needs of different business concerns.

Unit record for each transaction

Our discussion has thus far been limited to a manual accounting system. One of the points we have emphasized is that an immediate record should be made of every business transaction. The *medium* used to make this record is usually a document or form, such as an invoice or a check. This concept of a unit record for each transaction is an important one in every type of accounting system. Regardless of whether we use mechanical or electronic equipment, the document representing a single transaction is a basic element of the accounting process.

EDP ACCOUNTING SYSTEMS

The term *electronic data processing* (EDP) refers to the processing of data by electronic computers. A computer-based accounting system processes data in basically the same manner as does a manual or mechanical system. Transactions are initially recorded manually on source documents. The data from these source documents are then entered into punched cards or a magnetic device such as a tape or disc which can be read by the computer. The computer processes the information and performs such routine tasks as printing journals (called transaction summaries), posting to ledger accounts, determining account balances, and printing financial statements and other reports.

The primary advantage of the computer is its incredible speed. The number of computations made by an electronic computer is measured in millions per second. In one minute, an electronic printer can produce as much printed material as the average typist in a full day. Because of this speed, ledger accounts may be kept continually up to date and current reports may be prepared quickly at any time to assist executives in making decisions.

Internal control and the computer

EDP equipment itself is highly reliable and the possibility of errors caused by the hardware is very small. However, the use of reliable equipment does not eliminate entirely the possibilities of errors in the accounting records. Human beings create the information that goes into a computer, and human beings make mistakes. Errors may still be made in the preparation of source documents, such as invoices, checks, and credit memos. The process of entering information (keypunching data into punched cards or keyboarding data into a tape or disc at a terminal) is comparable to using a typewriter, and some errors are likely. Also, the computer program may contain errors which may cause the data to be processed improperly. To reduce the possibility of these types of errors, an EDP system should include both *input controls* and *program controls.*

Input controls Input controls are the precautions taken to ensure that the data being entered into the computer are correct. One important input control is the manual preparation of *control totals,* representing the total dollar amount of all source documents sent to the EDP department for processing. The computer will add up the total dollar amount of all data processed and print this total as part of the computer output. The manually prepared control totals may then be compared to the total printed by the computer to ensure that all source douments sent to the EDP department have been processed.

Another input control is the use of a *verifier.* When data are entered at the keyboard, there is always the possibility of striking a wrong key, causing an error in the input. In the verifier step, a second operator enters the same data; the computer's processing unit compares both entries and any differences cause the machine to signal that an error has been made.

Program controls Program controls are error-detecting measures built into the computer program. An example of a program control is a *limit test,* which compares every item of data processed by the computer to a specified dollar limit. In the event an amount exceeds the dollar limit, the computer does not process that item and prints out an error report. A limit test is particularly effective in such computer applications as preparing paychecks, when it is known that none of the paychecks should be for more than a specified amount, such as $1,000.

Another example of a program control is an *item count.* The total number of data items to be processed by the computer is determined, and that total is entered as part of the input to the computer. The computer then counts the number of items it processes, and if this number differs from the predetermined total, an error report is printed. This item count ensures that all the data are actually processed by the computer.

Separation of duties to prevent computer-related fraud In Chapter 6 we emphasized that subdivision of duties is essential to strong internal control. If related duties are all lodged in the hands of one person, internal control is destroyed. Some spectacular fraud cases involving the use of computers have made clear the danger of having one person design the system and serve as both programmer and operator.

ILLUSTRATIVE CASE John Jones, a bank employee, developed a computer program which would identify all overdrawn checking accounts and prepare a list showing the depositors' names, account numbers, and the dollar amounts overdrawn. Jones was later assigned to work as operator of the bank's computer. While working in this capacity, he made a change in the program which caused the computer to ignore overdrafts in his own personal checking account. After inserting this patch in the computer program, Jones was able to overdraw his account in any amount without the overdraft coming to the attention of the bank's management. His fraud was discovered only when the computer broke down and a list of overdrawn accounts was prepared manually by other bank employees.

Accounting applications of the computer

The use of electronic data processing equipment is possible for virtually every phase of accounting operations. Even a CPA firm, in conducting an annual audit, may use the computer as an audit tool. For this purpose the auditors may employ specially written computer programs to aid in their work of sampling and analyzing data to determine the fairness of the financial statements.

The most common application of the computer, however, is to process large masses of accounting data relating to routine repetitive operations such as recording retail sales, maintaining perpetual inventory records, preparing payroll, and posting to ledger accounts.

Electronic cash registers The electronic cash registers now prominent in most large department stores greatly reduce the work involved in accounting for sales transactions. When these registers are in use, the price tags on merchandise have a special magnetic code that can be read by an electronic "wand" attached to the register. A sales clerk touches the "wand" to the price tag, and the code is sent instantaneously to the computer. From the code number, the computer is able to identify the item being sold, record the amount of the sale, and transfer the cost of the item from the Inventory account to the Cost of Goods Sold account. If the transaction is a credit sale, the sales clerk enters the customer's credit card number in the electronic register. This number enables the computer to update instantly the customer's account in the subsidiary ledger.

Note that all of the accounting is done automatically as the sales clerk rings up the sale. Thus any number of transactions can be recorded and posted with virtually no manual work. At the end of each day, the computer prints a complete sales journal along with up-to-date balances for the general ledger and subsidiary ledger accounts relating to sales transactions.

Payrolls In a manual accounting system the preparation of payroll checks is usually separate from the maintenance of records showing pay rates, positions, time worked, payroll deductions, and other personnel data. An EDP system, however, has the capability of maintaining all records relating to payroll as well as turning out the required paychecks. Payroll processing is usually one of the first accounting operations to be placed on the computer.

The payroll procedure consists of determining for each employee the gross earnings, making deductions, computing net pay, preparing the payroll check, and maintaining a record of each individual's earnings. Also, the company needs a payroll summary for each period and usually a distribution of payroll costs by department, by product, or classified by the various productive processes. The payroll function has become increasingly complex and time-consuming in recent years because of the advent of social security taxes, income tax withholding, and other payroll deductions. Each employee must receive not only a payroll check but a statement showing the gross earnings, deductions, and net pay. The company's records must be designed to facilitate filing regular payroll reports to the federal and state governments showing amounts withheld for income taxes, unemployment insurance, and social security. The time and the expense required to prepare payrolls has risen in proportion to the need for more information. The demands by governments, labor unions, credit unions, and other outside agencies have added to the problem.

An EDP payroll system will not only maintain the necessary records, print the checks, and print these reports, but it can also keep management informed of the costs of various functions within the business. For example, data can be produced showing the work-hours and labor costs on each job, labor cost by department for each salesclerk, or the time required by different employees to perform similar work. In other words, much current information can be developed without significant extra expense that will provide management with a detailed breakdown of labor costs. The comparison below illustrates the efficiency of processing payrolls by EDP rather than manually:

Payroll may be prepared either manually or by EDP

Function	Payroll Prepared Manually	Payroll Prepared by EDP
1 Timekeeping	Fill in new set of records each period, making extensions manually.	Enter raw data on appropriate forms.
2 Computation of gross pay	Compute gross pay for each employee, perhaps with desk calculator, and enter manually in records.	Performed electronically.
3 Calculation of deductions	For each employee, refer to charts and make computations; enter manually in records.	Performed electronically.
4 Preparation of checks, earnings statements, and payroll register	Write by hand or type checks. Proofread and maintain controls.	Performed electronically.
5 Bank reconciliation	Reconcile payroll bank account per accounting records with monthly bank statement.	Performed electronically.
6 Reports to government	Prepare quarterly reports showing for each employee and in total amounts earned, deducted, and paid. Reconcile individual data with controls.	Performed electronically.
7 Managerial control data	Prepare distribution of hours and labor cost by department or by job. Other analyses may be needed.	Performed electronically.

Computer-based journals and ledgers As mentioned earlier in this chapter, computers also may be used to maintain the journals and ledgers and to prepare financial statements. Transactions and end-of-period adjustments still must be analyzed by persons possessing a knowledge of accounting principles. However, after these transactions have been analyzed and prepared in computer input form, the computer can be used to print the journals, post to the ledger accounts, and print the financial statements and other financial reports. The advantage of maintaining accounting records by computer is that the possibility of mathematical errors is greatly reduced, and the speed of the computer permits the records to be kept continuously up-to-date.

Other accounting applications of computers include forecasting the profit possibilities inherent in alternative courses of action, analyzing gross profit margins by department or by product line, and determining future cash requirements long in advance. Recent developments of accounting applications of the computer provide much more information about business operations than was available to management in the past.

KEY TERMS INTRODUCED OR EMPHASIZED IN CHAPTER 6

Accounts payable ledger   A subsidiary ledger containing an account with each supplier or vendor. The total of the ledger agrees with the general ledger controlling account, Accounts Payable.

Accounts receivable ledger   A subsidiary ledger containing an account with each credit customer. The total of the ledger agrees with the general ledger controlling account, Accounts Receivable.

Cash payments journal   A special journal used to record all payments of cash.

Cash receipts journal   A special journal used to record all receipts of cash.

Controlling account   A general ledger account which is supported by detailed information in a subsidiary ledger.

Input controls   Internal control measures to ensure accuracy of data entered into a computer (such as control totals, the total dollar amount of documents to be processed).

Program   Instructions to a computer consisting of a series of steps planned to carry out a certain process (such as payroll preparation).

Program controls   Error-detecting measures built into a computer program (such as a limit test setting a maximum dollar amount, or item counts specifying the number of items to be processed).

Purchases journal   A special journal used exclusively to record purchases of merchandise on credit.

Sales journal   A special journal used exclusively to record sales of merchandise on credit.

Subsidiary ledger   A supplementary record used to provide detailed information for a control account in the general ledger. The total of accounts in a subsidiary ledger equals the balance of the related control account in the general ledger.

DEMONSTRATION PROBLEM FOR YOUR REVIEW

The Signal Corporation began operations on November 1, 19___. The chart of accounts used by the company included the following accounts, among others:

Cash	10	Purchases	60
Marketable securities	15	Purchase returns & allowances	62
Office supplies	18	Purchase discounts	64
Notes payable	30	Salaries expense	70
Accounts payable	32	Utilities expense	71

November transactions relating to the purchase of merchandise and to accounts payable are listed below, along with selected other transactions.

Nov.   **1** Purchased merchandise from Moss Co. for $3,000. Invoice dated today; terms 2/10, n/30.

Nov.   **3** Received shipment of merchandise from Wilmer Co. and invoice dated November 2 for $7,600; terms 2/10, n/30.

Nov. 6 Purchased merchandise from Archer Company at cost of $5,600. Invoice dated November 5; terms 2/10, n/30.

Nov. 9 Purchased marketable securities, $1,200.

Nov. 10 Issued check to Moss Co. in settlement of invoice dated November 1, less discount.

Nov. 12 Received shipment of merchandise from Cory Corporation and an invoice dated November 11 in amount of $7,100; terms net 30 days.

Nov. 14 Issued check to Archer Company in settlement of invoice of November 5.

Nov. 16 Paid cash for office supplies, $110.

Nov. 17 Purchased merchandise for cash, $950.

Nov. 19 Purchased merchandise from Klein Co. for $11,500. Invoice dated November 18; terms 2/10, n/30.

Nov. 21 Purchased merchandise from Belmont Company for $8,400. Invoice dated November 20; terms 1/10, n/30.

Nov. 24 Purchased merchandise for cash, $375.

Nov. 26 Purchased merchandise from Brooker Co. for $6,500. Invoice dated today; terms 1/10, n/30.

Nov. 28 Paid utilities, $150.

Nov. 30 Paid salaries for November, $2,900.

Nov. 30 Paid $2,600 cash to Wilmer Co. and issued 12%, 90-day promissory note for $5,000 in settlement of invoice dated November 2.

Instructions

a Record the transactions in the appropriate journals. Use a single-column purchases journal and a six-column cash payments journal.

b Indicate how postings would be made by placing ledger account numbers and check marks in the appropriate columns of the journals.

c Prepare a schedule of accounts payable at November 30 to prove that the subsidiary ledger is in balance with the controlling account.

SOLUTION TO DEMONSTRATION PROBLEM

a & b   *Purchases Journal*   *Page 1*

Date		Account Credited		Invoice Date		✔	Amount
19—				19—			
Nov	1	Moss Co.	(terms 2/10, n/30)	Nov	1	✔	3,000
	3	Wilmer Co.	(terms 2/10, n/30)		2	✔	7,600
	6	Archer Company	(terms 2/10, n/30)		5	✔	5,600
	12	Cory Corporation	(terms net 30)		11	✔	7,100
	19	Klein Co.	(terms 2/10, n/30)		18	✔	11,500
	21	Belmont Company	(terms 1/10, n/30)		20	✔	8,400
	26	Brooker Co.	(terms 1/10, n/30)		26	✔	6,500
							$49,700
							(60)(32)

Cash Payments Journal

Date	Explanation	Cash (Credit)	Purchase Discounts (Credit)	Other Accounts (Credit) Name	LP	Amount	Account Debited	✓	Accounts Payable (Debit)	Purchases (Debit)	Other Accounts (Debit) LP	Amount
19— Nov 9	Bought securities	1,200					Marketable Securities				15	1,200
10	Invoice, Nov. 1, less 2%	2,940	60				Moss Co.	✓	3,000			
14	Invoice, Nov. 5, less 2%	5,488	112				Archer Company	✓	5,600			
16	Purchased office supplies	110					Office Supplies				18	110
17	Cash purchases	950								950		
24	Cash purchases	375								375		
28	Paid utilities	150					Utilities Expense				71	150
30	Paid salaries	2,900					Salaries Expense				70	2,900
30	Invoice, Nov. 2, note issued for unpaid balance	2,600		Notes Payable	30	5,000	Wilmer Co.	✓	7,600			
		16,713	172			5,000			16,200	1,325		4,360
		(10)	(64)			(X)			(32)	(60)		(X)

c

SIGNAL CORPORATION
Schedule of Accounts Payable
November 30, 19___

Belmont Company	$ 8,400
Brooker Co.	6,500
Cory Corporation	7,100
Klein Co.	11,500
Total (per general ledger controlling account)	$33,500

REVIEW QUESTIONS

1 What advantages are offered by the use of special journals?

2 The column total of one of the four special journals described in this chapter is posted at month-end to two general ledger accounts. One of these two accounts is Accounts Payable. What is the name of the special journal? What account is debited and what account is credited with this total?

3 Pine Hill General Store makes about 500 sales on account each month, using only a two-column general journal to record these transactions. What would be the extent of the work saved by using a sales journal?

4 When accounts receivable and accounts payable are kept in subsidiary ledgers, will the general ledger continue to be a self-balancing ledger with equal debits and credits? Explain.

5 Explain how, why, and when the cash receipts journal and cash payments journal are crossfooted.

6 During November the sales on credit made by the Hardy Company actually amounted to $41,625, but an error of $1,000 was made in totaling the amount column of the sales journal. When and how will the error be discovered?

7 Considerable copying work may be performed in preparing a sales invoice, a sales journal, and a receivables ledger. Is this step-by-step sequence, with its related opportunity for errors, a characteristic of all types of accounting systems? Explain.

8 What are the principal advantages of electronic data processing in the accounting department of a company?

9 In which phases or areas of accounting can EDP equipment be used to advantage? Which phases can most conveniently and advantageously be converted to electronic data processing?

10 Explain the meaning of the term *computer program*.

11 Explain the meaning of the term *input control* and give an example.

12 Explain the meaning of the term *program control* and give an example.

13 English Corporation uses a general journal and four special journals: **(a)** sales journal, **(b)** purchases journal, **(c)** cash receipts journal, and **(d)** cash payments journal. Which journal should the company use to record (1) the declaration of a dividend, and (2) the later payment of this dividend? Explain the reasoning underlying your answer.

14 For a large modern department store, such as a Sears or J. C. Penney, is it necessary to maintain a manual single-column sales journal? Explain.

EXERCISES

Ex. 6-1 True or false.

    a The use of special journals aids in keeping all general ledger accounts posted up-to-date throughout the month.

    b An advantage of special journals is that many different types of business transactions can be recorded in a single journal.

    c The sale for cash of additional shares of capital stock should be recorded in the general journal.

    d Some of the column totals in the cash payments journal are not posted to ledger accounts.

    e Some of the column totals in the cash receipts journal are not posted until the end of the month.

    f When a firm's payroll is processed by a computer, it will still be necessary to prepare manually the reports which must be filed with the government showing for each employee the amounts earned, deducted, and paid.

Ex. 6-2 Fall River Company uses a cash receipts journal, a cash payments journal, a sales journal, a purchases journal, and a general journal. Indicate which journal should be used to record each of the following transactions.

    a Adjusting entry to record depreciation

    b Purchase of delivery truck for cash

    c Purchase of merchandise on account

    d Return of merchandise by a customer company for credit to its account

    e Payment of property taxes

    f Purchase of typewriter on account

    g Sale of merchandise on account

    h Sale of merchandise for cash

    i Cash refund to a customer who returned merchandise

    j Return of merchandise to a supplier for credit

Ex. 6-3 The accounting system used by Adams Company includes a general journal and also four special journals for cash receipts, cash payments, sales, and purchases of merchandise. On January 31, after all January posting had been completed, the Accounts Receivable controlling account in the general ledger had a debit balance of $160,000, and the Accounts Payable controlling account had a credit balance of $48,000.

    The February transactions recorded in the four special journals can be summarized as follows:

Sales journal	*Total transactions, $96,000*
Purchases journal	*Total transactions, $56,000*
Cash receipts journal	*Accounts Receivable column total, $76,800 (credit)*
Cash payments journal	*Accounts Payable column total, $67,200 (debit)*

    a What posting would be made of the $76,800 total of the Accounts Receivable column in the cash receipts journal at February 28?

    b What posting would be made of the $96,000 total of the sales journal at February 28?

    c What posting would be made of the $56,000 total of the purchases journal at February 28?

d What posting would be made of the $67,200 total of the Accounts Payable column in the cash payments journal at February 28?

e Based on the above information, state the balances of the Accounts Receivable controlling account and the Accounts Payable controlling account in the general ledger after completion of posting at February 28?

Ex. 6-4 Island Company, a merchandising concern, uses a cash receipts journal, a cash payments journal, a sales journal, a purchases journal, and a general journal.

a In which of the five journals would you expect to find the smallest number of transactions recorded?

b At the end of the accounting period, the total of the sales journal should be posted to what account or accounts? As a debit or credit?

c At the end of the accounting period, the total of the purchases journal should be posted to what account or accounts? As a debit or credit?

d Name two subsidiary ledgers which would probably be used in conjunction with the journals listed above. Identify the journals from which postings would regularly be made to each of the two subsidiary ledgers.

e In which of the five journals would adjusting and closing entries be made?

Ex. 6-5 Collins Company uses a sales journal to record all sales of merchandise on credit. During July the transactions in this journal were as follows:

Sales Journal

Date		Account Debited	Invoice No.	Amount
July	6	Robert Baker		3,600
	15	Minden Company		8,610
	17	Pell & Warden		1,029
	26	Stonewall Corporation		17,500
	27	Robert Baker		3,000
				33,739

Entries in the general journal during July include one for the return of merchandise by a customer, as follows:

July	18	Sales Returns and Allowances	500	
		Accounts Receivable, Minden Company		500
		Allowed credit to customer for return of		
		merchandise from sale of July 15.		

a Prepare a subsidiary ledger for accounts receivable by opening a T account for each of the four customers listed above. Post the entries in the sales journal to these individual customers' accounts. From the general journal, post the credit to the account of Minden Company.

b Prepare general ledger accounts in T form as follows: a controlling account for Accounts Receivable, a Sales account, and a Sales Returns and Allowances account.

Post to these accounts the appropriate entries from the sales journal and general journal.

c Prepare a schedule of accounts receivable at July 31 to prove that this subsidiary ledger is in agreement with its controlling account.

Ex. 6-6 A check for $13,230 was received from a customer within 10 days from the date of sending a sales invoice of $13,500, with terms of 2/10, n/30. In recording the receipt of the check, Robert Hall, the employee maintaining the cash receipts journal, entered $13,230 in the Cash column and $13,500 in the Accounts Receivable column, but made no entry in the Sales Discounts column. What procedure should bring this error to light?

Ex. 6-7 Jason Company maintains its sales journal and accounts receivable ledger on a computer. Each day the accounting department prepares a control total of total credit sales and sends the sales invoices to the EDP department. The sales data are keypunched in the EDP department, and the punched cards and a control figure representing the total number of sales transactions (per the invoices) are entered into the computer.

The computer prepares the sales journal, posts to the accounts receivable ledger (maintained on magnetic tape), and performs an item count. Any discrepancy in the item count is printed out on an error report. A copy of the sales journal for each day is sent back to the accounting department for comparison with the daily control totals.

What control procedure will first detect the following independent errors?

a A sales invoice of $760 is accidentally keypunched as $7,600.

b A sales invoice is lost on the way from the accounting department to the EDP department.

c Several punched cards are lost before being processed by the computer.

PROBLEMS

6-1 A manual accounting system similar to the one illustrated in Chapter 6 is used by Barnes Company. At September 30, the subsidiary ledger for accounts receivable included the following accounts with individual customers. Note that these accounts include postings from three different journals.

The purpose of this problem is to show the relationship between a controlling account and a subsidiary ledger. By studying the following subsidiary ledger accounts, you can determine what amounts should appear in the controlling account. (In actual practice, of course, both the controlling account and the subsidiary ledger would be completed by posting amounts from the various journals.)

D. Anderson

Date	Explanation	Ref	Debit	Credit	Balance
19–					
Sept 3		S4	560		560
9		S4	1 040		1 600
27		CR2		960	640

K. Brown

Date		Explanation	Ref	Debit	Credit	Balance
19–						
Aug.	31	Balance				5 184
Sept.	8		CR1		3 200	1 984
	8		J1		640	1 344
	28		CR2		1 344	-0-

J. Cathway

Date		Explanation	Ref	Debit	Credit	Balance
19–						
Aug.	31	Balance				3 520
Sept.	10		J1		800	2 720
	11		S4	2 000		4 720
	30		CR2		2 560	2 160

R. Davis

Date		Explanation	Ref	Debit	Credit	Balance
19–						
Sept.	4		S4	7 040		7 040
	29		S4	1 920		8 960
	29		CR2		7 040	1 920

Instructions You are to prepare the general ledger controlling account, Accounts Receivable, for the month of September. Remember that a controlling account is posted on a daily basis for transactions recorded in the general journal, but is posted only at the end of the month for the *monthly totals* of special journals such as the sales journal and the cash receipts journal.

Include in the controlling account the balance of accounts receivable at August 31, the September transactions from the general journal in chronological order, and the running balance of the account after each entry. Finally, make one posting to record total sales on credit for September and one posting to record total cash collections from customers during September. For each amount you enter in the Accounts Receivable controlling account, you should list the date and source (name of journal and journal page). Use the symbols shown on page 228 to identify the various journals. When the controlling account is completed, it should contain in summary form the information shown above in the customers' accounts in the subsidiary ledger.

6-2 Frost Center uses multicolumn cash receipts and cash payments journals similar to those illustrated in this chapter. The cash activities for the month of May are presented below:

May 1 R. J. Lopez, president and sole stockholder of Frost Center, invested additional cash of $45,000 in the business in exchange for an additional 4,500 shares of $10 par value capital stock.

May 1 Purchased U.S. government bonds, $9,000. (Debit U.S. Government Bonds.)

May 2 Paid May rent, $3,600. (Debit expense account.)

May 2 Cash sales of merchandise, $12,300.

May 4 Purchased fixtures, $10,500, making a down payment of $1,500 and issuing a note payable for the balance.

May 9 Received $2,100 as partial collection of our $6,300 sales invoice to Bee Co. Received a note receivable for the balance.

May 12 Paid Dallas Co. invoice, $9,000 less 2% purchase discount.

May 13 Sold land costing $7,500 for $8,850 cash. (Credit Gain on Sale of Land, $1,350.)

May 15 Received $3,822 cash in settlement of our invoice to Bing Company after allowing 2% discount.

May 19 Cash purchase of merchandise, $7,200.

May 20 Paid note payable due today, $5,100, and accrued interest amounting to $102.

May 21 Sold U.S. government bonds costing $3,000 for $2,925. (Debit Loss on Sale of Bonds, $75.)

May 23 Paid installment on note payable due today, $1,440, of which $702 represented interest expense.

May 25 Cash sales of merchandise, $9,045.

May 25 Paid Post Company invoice, $9,900 less 2%.

May 26 Purchased three-year fire insurance policy, $1,170.

May 28 Cash purchase of merchandise, $6,450.

May 30 Received cash in settlement of our sales invoice to Baker Company, $7,800, less 2%.

May 31 Paid monthly salaries, $8,034.

Instructions   Enter the above transactions in a six-column journal for cash receipts and a six-column journal for cash payments. Compute column totals and rule the journals. Determine the equality of debits and credits in column totals.

6-3   The chart of accounts used by the Hunt Corporation included the following accounts, among others:

Cash	10	Sales	50
Notes receivable	15	Sales returns & allowances	52
Accounts receivable	17	Sales discounts	54
Land	20	Purchases	60
Office equipment	25	Purchase returns & allowances	62
Notes payable	30	Interest revenue	82
Accounts payable	32	Gain on sale of land	85

The sales activity, cash receipts, and certain other transactions for the month of June are presented below:

June 1 Sold merchandise to Miley Company for cash, $7,725.

June 4 Sold merchandise to Presto Company, $26,500. Invoice no. 618; terms 2/10, n/30.

June 5 Received cash refund of $3,400 for merchandise returned to a supplier.

June 8 Sold merchandise to Topper Company for $13,500. Invoice no. 619; terms 2/10, n/30.

June 9 Received a check from Hartman Company in payment of a $7,500 invoice, less 2% discount.

June 11 Received $3,500 from Gray Company in payment of a past-due invoice.

June 13 Received check from Presto Company in settlement of invoice dated June 4, less discount.

June 16 Sold merchandise to Mexical Company, $13,000. Invoice no. 620; terms 2/10, n/30.

June 16 Returned $3,000 of merchandise to supplier, ICM Corporation, for reduction of account payable.

June 18 Purchased office equipment at a cost of $9,500; signing a 15%, 90-day note payable for the full amount.

June 20 Sold merchandise to Johnston Company for $24,000. Invoice no. 621; terms 2/10, n/30.

June 21 Mexical Company returned for credit $2,000 of merchandise purchased on June 16.

June 23 Borrowed $75,000 cash from a local bank, signing a six-month note payable.

June 25 Received payment in full from Mexical Company in settlement of invoice dated June 16, less return and discount.

June 29 Sold land costing $95,000 for a price of $140,000. Terms of sale were $35,000 cash and a 12%, two-year note receivable for $105,000. (Credit Gain on Sale of Land for $45,000.)

June 30 Collected from Johnston Company amount of invoice dated June 20, less 2% discount.

June 30 Collected $40,600 in full settlement of a $40,000, 9%, 60-day note receivable held since May 1. (No interest revenue had been recorded on the note prior to this date.)

June 30 Received a 60-day, non-interest-bearing note from Topper Company in settlement of invoice dated June 8.

Instructions Record the above transactions in the appropriate journals. Use a single-column sales journal, a six-column cash receipts journal, and a two-column general journal. Foot and rule the special journals and indicate how postings would be made by placing ledger account numbers and check marks in the appropriate columns of the journals.

6-4 Ozark Corporation has a chart of accounts which includes the following accounts, among others.

Cash	10	Accounts payable	30
Office supplies	18	Purchases	50
Land	20	Purchase returns & allowances	52
Building	22	Purchase discounts	53
Notes payable	28	Salaries expense	60

The December transactions relating to the purchase of merchandise for resale and to accounts payable are listed below along with selected other transactions.

Dec. 1 Purchased merchandise from Sawyer Company at a cost of $9,380. Invoice dated today; terms 2/10, n/30.

Dec. 4 Purchased merchandise from Bright Company for $30,200. Invoice dated December 3; terms 2/10, n/30.

Dec. 5 Returned for credit to Sawyer Company defective merchandise having a list price of $2,880.

Dec. 6 Received shipment of merchandise from Trojan Co. and their invoice dated December 5 in amount of $20,520. Terms net 30 days.

Dec. 8 Purchased merchandise from Wayne Associates, $24,480. Invoice dated today with terms 1/10, n/60.

Dec. 10 Purchased merchandise from King Corporation, $30,000. Invoice dated December 9; terms 2/10, n/30.

Dec. 10 Issued check to Sawyer Company in settlement of balance resulting from purchase of December 1 and purchase return of December 5.

Dec. 11 Issued check to Bright Company in payment of December 3 invoice.

Dec. 18 Issued check to King Corporation in settlement of invoice dated December 9.

Dec. 20 Purchased merchandise for cash, $1,080.

Dec. 21 Bought land, $64,800, and building, $144,000, for expansion of business. Paid cash of $36,000 and signed a promissory note for the balance of $172,800. (Land and building were acquired in a single transaction from R. M. Wilson.)

Dec. 23 Purchased merchandise for cash, $900.

Dec. 26 Purchased merchandise from Taper Company for $32,400. Invoice dated December 26; terms 2/10, n/30.

Dec. 28 Paid cash for office supplies, $270.

Dec. 29 Purchased merchandise for cash, $1,890.

Dec. 31 Paid salaries for December, $7,920.

Instructions

a Record the transactions in the appropriate journals. Use a single-column purchases journal, a six-column cash payments journal, and a two-column general journal. Foot and rule the special journals. Make all postings to the proper general ledger accounts and to the accounts payable subsidiary ledger.

b Prepare a schedule of accounts payable at December 31 to prove that the subsidiary ledger is in balance with the controlling account for accounts payable.

6-5 Skyline, Inc., began operations on May 1, and established an accounting system using the following accounts:

Cash	10	Sales	50
Marketable securities	13	Sales returns & allowances	52
Notes receivable	14	Sales discounts	54
Accounts receivable	15	Purchases	60
Inventory	17	Purchase returns & allowances	62
Unexpired insurance	19	Purchase discounts	64
Land	20	Transportation-in	66
Building	21	Rent expense	70
Furniture and fixtures	24	Salaries expense	72
Notes payable	30	Taxes expense	74
Accounts payable	32	Supplies expense	76
Mortgage payable	36	Insurance expense	78
Capital stock	40	Interest earned	80
Retained earnings	42	Interest expense	83
Income summary	45	Loss on sale of securities	84

The transactions for the month of May are listed below.

May 1 Sold capital stock for $180,000, and deposited this amount in the bank under the name Skyline, Inc.

May 3 Purchased land and building on contract, paying $90,000 cash and signing a mortgage for the remaining balance of $285,000. Estimated value of the land was $165,000.

May 6 Purchased merchandise from Fast Company, $18,300. Invoice dated today; terms 2/10, n/30.

May 7 Sold merchandise to W. B. Allen, $9,000. Invoice no. 1; terms 2/10, n/60.

May 7 Sold merchandise for cash, $2,220.

May 7 Paid $810 for a two-year fire insurance policy.

May 10 Paid freight charges of $615 on Fast Company purchase of May 6.

May 12 Sold merchandise to Connors Company, $14,700. Invoice no. 2; terms 2/10, n/60.

May 13 Purchased merchandise for cash, $4,260.

May 15 Received payment in full from W. B. Allen; Invoice no. 1, less 2% discount.

May 15 Purchased marketable securities for cash, $4,800.

May 16 Issued credit memorandum no. 1 to Connors Company, $1,200 for goods returned today.

May 16 Paid Fast Company invoice of May 6, less discount.

May 18 Purchased merchandise from Hope Corporation, $11,100. Invoice dated today; terms 2/10, n/30.

May 20 A portion of merchandise purchased from Hope Corporation was found to be substandard. After discussion with the vendor, a price reduction of $300 was agreed upon and debit memorandum no. 1 was issued in that amount.

May 22 Received payment in full from Connors Company; Invoice no. 2, less returns and discount.

May 23 Purchased merchandise from Fast Company, $12,600. Invoice dated today; terms 2/10, n/30.

May 25 Sold for $4,260 the securities purchased on May 15.

May 27 Sold merchandise for cash, $1,545.

May 28 Borrowed $9,000 from the bank, issuing a 60-day, 10% note payable as evidence of indebtedness.

May 28 Paid Hope Corporation invoice dated May 18, less discount and return of $300.

May 30 Paid first installment on mortgage, $3,300. This payment included interest of $2,070.

May 30 Purchased merchandise for cash, $2,760.

May 30 Paid monthly salaries of $6,345.

May 31 Sold merchandise to J. Jones, $8,250. Invoice no. 3; terms 2/10, n/60.

Instructions

Enter the May transactions in the following journals:

    Two-column general journal
    One-column sales journal
    One-column purchases journal
    Six-column cash receipts journal
    Six-column cash payments journal

Foot and rule all special journals and show how postings would be made by placing ledger account numbers and check marks in the appropriate columns of the journals.

6-6 Sand Castle Company uses the following accounts (among others) in recording transactions:

Cash	10	Dividends	53
Notes receivable	14	Sales	60
Accounts receivable	16	Sales returns and allowances	62
Supplies	17	Sales discounts	64
Unexpired insurance	18	Purchases	70
Equipment	26	Purchase returns and allowances	72
Accumulated depreciation:		Purchase discounts	74
equipment	28	Transportation-in	76
Notes payable	30	Salaries expense	80
Accounts payable	32	Supplies expense	84
Dividends payable	34	Insurance expense	86
Mortgage payable	40	Depreciation expense: equipment	88
Capital stock	50	Gain on sale of equipment	90
Retained earnings	52	Interest expense	92

The schedules of accounts receivable and accounts payable for the company at October 31, 19___, are shown below:

Schedule of Accounts Receivable October 31, 19___		Schedule of Accounts Payable October 31, 19___	
Ace Contractors	$20,800	Durapave, Inc.	$30,000
Reliable Builders, Inc.	8,750		
Total	$29,550		

The November transactions of Sand Castle Company were as follows:

Nov. 2 Purchased merchandise on account from Durapave, Inc., $28,000. Invoice was dated today with terms of 2/10, n/30.

Nov. 3 Sold merchandise to Ace Contractors $16,000. Invoice no. 428; terms 2/10, n/30.

Nov. 4 Purchased supplies for cash, $875. (Debit the asset account, Supplies.)

Nov. 5 Sold merchandise for cash, $5,600.

Nov. 7 Paid the Durapave, Inc., invoice for $30,000, representing October purchases. No discount was allowed by Durapave, Inc., as the discount period had expired.

Nov. 10 Purchased merchandise from Tool Company, $32,500. Invoice dated November 9 with terms of 1/10, n/30.

Nov. 10 Collected from Ace Contractors for invoice no. 428 for $16,000 less 2%, and for October sales of $20,800 on which the discount had lapsed.

Nov. 12 Sold merchandise to Rex Company, $21,750. Invoice no. 429; terms 2/10, n/30.

Nov. 14 Paid freight charges of $2,050 on goods purchased November 10 from Tool Company.

Nov. 14 Sold equipment for $9,000, receiving cash of $1,500 and a 30-day, 10% note receivable for the balance. Equipment cost $20,000 and accumulated depreciation was $13,000. (Debit Accumulated Depreciation: Equipment for $13,000 and credit Gain on Sale of Equipment for $2,000.)

Nov. 15 Issued credit memorandum no. 38 in favor of Rex Company upon return of $1,000 of merchandise.

Nov. 18 Paid for one-year fire insurance policy, $1,425. (Debit Unexpired Insurance.)

Nov. 18 Purchased merchandise for cash, $7,625.

Nov. 19 Paid the Tool Company invoice dated November 9, less the 1% discount.

Nov. 20 Sold merchandise on account to Vincent Co., $13,650; invoice no. 430. Required customer to sign a 30-day, non-interest-bearing note. (Record this sale by a debit to Accounts Receivable, then transfer from Accounts Receivable to Notes Receivable by means of an entry in the general journal.)

Nov. 22 Purchased merchandise for cash, $4,050.

Nov. 22 Sold merchandise for cash, $4,675.

Nov. 22 Received payment from Rex Company for invoice no. 429. Customer made deduction for credit memorandum no. 38 issued November 15, and a 2% discount.

Nov. 23 Sold merchandise on account to Waite, Inc., $9,950. Invoice no. 431; terms 2/10, n/30.

Nov. 24 Declared a dividend of $37,500 on capital stock, payable December 20, 19___.

Nov. 25 Purchased merchandise from Smith Company, $26,500. Invoice dated November 24 with terms of 2/10, n/60.

Nov. 26 Issued debit memorandum no. 42 to Smith Company in connection with merchandise returned today amounting to $2,125.

Nov. 27 Purchased equipment having a list price of $60,000. Paid $10,000 down and signed a promissory note for the balance of $50,000.

Nov. 30 Paid monthly salaries of $14,800 for services rendered by employees during November.

Nov. 30 Paid monthly installment on mortgage, $3,500, of which $1,020 was interest.

Instructions

a Record the November transactions in the following journals:

    General journal—2 columns

    Sales journal—1 column

    Purchases journal—1 column

    Cash receipts journal—6 columns

    Cash payments journal—6 columns

Foot and rule all special journals and show how postings would be made by placing ledger account numbers and check marks in the appropriate columns of the journals.

b Prepare a schedule of accounts receivable and accounts payable as of November 30. You may want to use T accounts to compile the accounts receivable from customers and amounts payable to suppliers at November 30. Begin with the October 31 balances. You can verify your November 30 totals by computing the balances of the controlling accounts determined by posting of totals from the special journals and individual transactions from the general journal.

6-7 Star Valley, a successful retail business, had the following transactions during November.

Nov. 2 Purchased merchandise on account from Dunlop Co., $13,000. Invoice was dated today with terms of 2/10, n/30.

Nov. 3 Sold merchandise to Filmore Company, $8,300. Invoice no. 428; terms 2/10, n/30.

Nov. 4 Purchased supplies for cash, $300. (Debit Supplies.)

Nov. 5 Sold merchandise for cash, $2,000.

Nov. 9 Paid the Dunlop Co. invoice dated November 2.

Nov. 10 Purchased merchandise from Burton Company, $11,700. Invoice dated November 9 with terms of 1/10, n/30.

Nov. 10 Collected from Filmore Company for invoice no. 428, dated November 3.

Nov. 12 Sold merchandise to Payless, Inc., $7,360. Invoice no. 429; terms 2/10, n/30.

Nov. 14 Paid freight charges of $740 on goods purchased November 9 from Burton Company.

Nov. 14 Sold land for $90,000, receiving cash of $20,000 and a note receivable for the balance. The land had been acquired at a cost of $75,000 for use in the business, but due to a change of plans was no longer needed. (Credit Gain on Sale of Land, $15,000.)

Nov. 15 Issued credit memorandum no. 38 in favor of Payless, Inc., upon their return of $360 of merchandise.

Nov. 18 Paid for one-year fire insurance policy, $1,400. (Debit Unexpired Insurance.)

Nov. 18 Purchased merchandise for cash, $2,700.

Nov. 19 Paid the Burton Company invoice dated November 9.

Nov. 20 Sold merchandise on account to Peat Brothers, $7,000. Invoice no. 430. Required customer to sign a 30-day, non-interest-bearing note. (Record this sale by a charge to Accounts Receivable, then transfer from Accounts Receivable to Notes Receivable by means of an entry in the general journal.)

Nov. 22 Purchased merchandise for cash, $1,500.

Nov. 22 Sold merchandise for cash, $1,800.

Nov. 22 Received payment from Payless, Inc., for invoice no. 429. Customer made deduction for credit memorandum no. 38 issued November 15.

Nov. 25 Purchased merchandise from Amber Company, $9,500. Invoice dated November 24, with terms 2/10, n/30.

Nov. 26 Issued debit memorandum no. 42 to Amber Company in connection with merchandise returned today to Amber amounting to $300.

Nov. 27 Purchased equipment having a list price of $21,600. Paid $3,600 down and signed a promissory note for the balance of $18,000.

Nov. 30 Paid monthly salaries of $5,300 for services rendered by employees during November.

Nov. 30 Paid monthly installment on mortgage, $1,260, of which $370 was interest.

Listed below are some of the ledger accounts used by Star Valley.

Cash	10	Sales	60
Notes receivable	14	Sales returns & allowances	62
Accounts receivable	16	Sales discounts	64
Supplies	17	Purchases	70
Unexpired insurance	18	Purchase returns & allowances	72
Land	20	Purchase discounts	74
Equipment	26	Transportation-in	76
Accumulated depreciation:		Salaries expense	80
equipment	28	Supplies expense	84
Notes payable	30	Insurance expense	86
Accounts payable	32	Depreciation expense:	
Mortgage payable	40	equipment	88
Capital stock	50	Gain on sale of land	90
Retained earnings	52	Interest expense	92

Instructions

a Record the November transactions in the following journals:
   General journal—two columns
   Sales journal—one column
   Purchases journal—one column
   Cash receipts journal—six columns
   Cash payments journal—six columns

b Foot and rule all special journals.

c Show how postings would be made by placing ledger account numbers and check marks in the appropriate columns of the journals.

BUSINESS DECISION PROBLEM 6

Leisure Clothing is a mail-order company which sells clothes to the public at discount prices. Recently Leisure Clothing initiated a new policy allowing a 10-day free trial on all clothes bought from the company. At the end of the 10-day period, the customer may either pay cash for the purchase or return the goods to Leisure Clothing. The new policy caused such a large boost in sales that, even after considering the many sales returns, the policy appeared quite profitable.

The accounting system of Leisure Clothing includes a sales journal, purchases journal, cash receipts journal, cash payments journal, and a general journal. As an internal control procedure, an officer of the company reviews and initials every entry in the general journal before the amounts are posted to the ledger accounts. Since the 10-day free trial policy has been in effect, hundreds of entries recording sales returns have been entered in the general journal each week. Each of these entries has been reviewed and initialed by an officer of the firm, and the amounts have been posted to Sales Returns & Allowances and to the Accounts Receivable control account in the general ledger, and also to the customer's account in the accounts receivable subsidiary ledger.

Since these sales return entries are so numerous, it has been suggested that a special journal be designed to handle them. This could not only save time in journalizing and posting the entries, but also eliminate the time-consuming individual review of each of these repetitive entries by an officer of the company.

Instructions

a How many amounts are entered in the general journal to describe a single sales return transaction? Are these amounts the same?

b Explain why these sales return transactions are suited to the use of a special journal. Explain in detail how many money columns the special journal should have, and what postings would have to be done either at the time of the transaction or at the end of the period.

c Assume that there were 3,000 sales returns during the month. How many postings would have to be made during the month if these transactions were entered in the general journal? How many postings would have to be made if the special journal you designed in **b** were used? (Assume a one-month accounting period.)

7

CASH AND MARKETABLE SECURITIES

After studying this chapter you should be able to:

- Explain the objectives of efficient cash management.
- Discuss means of achieving internal control over cash receipts and disbursements.
- Describe the operation of a petty cash fund and of a voucher system.
- Prepare a bank reconciliation.
- Account for investments in stocks and bonds.
- Apply the lower-of-cost-or-market rule to a portfolio of marketable equity securities.

CASH

Accountants define cash as money on deposit in banks and any items that banks will accept for immediate deposit. These items include not only coins and paper money, but also checks and money orders. On the other hand, notes receivable, IOUs, and postdated checks are not accepted for immediate deposit and are not included in the accountants' definition of cash.

In the balance sheet, cash is listed first among the current assets, because it is the most current and liquid of all assets. The banker, credit manager, or investor who studies a balance sheet critically is always interested in the total amount of cash as compared with other balance sheet items, such as accounts payable. These outside users of a company's financial statements are not interested, however, in such details as the number of separate bank accounts, or in the distinction between cash on hand and cash in banks. A business that carries checking accounts with several banks will maintain a separate ledger account for each bank account. On the balance sheet, however, the entire amount of cash on hand and cash on deposit with the several banks will be shown as a single amount. One objective in preparing financial statements is to keep them short, concise, and easy to read.

Some bank accounts are restricted as to their use, so that they are not available for making payments to meet normal operating needs of the business. An example (discussed in Chapter 13) is a bond sinking fund, consisting of cash being accumulated by a corporation for the specific purpose of paying off bonded indebtedness at a future date and not available for any other use. A bank account located in a foreign country may also be restricted if monetary regulations prevent the transfer of funds between the two countries. Restricted bank accounts are not regarded as current assets because they are not available for use in paying current liabilities.

Management responsibilities relating to cash

Efficient management of cash includes measures that will:

1 Provide accurate accounting for cash receipts, cash payments, and cash balances
2 Prevent losses from fraud or theft
3 Maintain a sufficient amount of cash at all times to make necessary payments, plus a reasonable balance for emergencies
4 Prevent unnecessarily large amounts of cash from being held idle in bank accounts which produce no revenue

Internal control over cash is sometimes regarded merely as a means of preventing fraud or theft. A good system of internal control, however, will also aid in achieving management's other objectives of accurate accounting for cash transactions and the maintenance of adequate but not excessive cash balances.

Basic requirements for internal control over cash

Cash is more susceptible to theft than any other asset. Furthermore, a large portion of the total transactions of a business involve the receipt or disbursement of cash. For both these reasons, internal control over cash is of great importance to management and also to the employees of a business. If a cash shortage arises in a business in which internal controls are weak or nonexistent, every employee is under suspicion. Perhaps no one employee can be proved guilty of the theft, but neither can any employee prove his or her innocence.

On the other hand, if internal controls over cash are adequate, theft without detection is virtually impossible except through the collusion of two or more employees. To achieve internal control over cash or any other group of assets requires first of all that *the custody of assets be clearly separated from the recording of transactions.* Secondly, the recording function should be subdivided among employees, so that the work of one person is verified by that of another. This *subdivision of duties* discourages fraud, because collusion among employees would be necessary to conceal an irregularity. Internal control is more easily achieved in large companies than in small companies, because extensive subdivision of duties is more feasible in the larger business.

The major steps in establishing internal controls over cash include the following:

1 Separate the function of handling cash from the maintenance of accounting records. Employees who handle cash should not have access to the accounting records, and accounting personnel should not have access to cash.
2 Prepare an immediate listing of cash receipts at the time and place that the money is received. This initial listing may consist of a cash register tape or serially numbered sales tickets rather than formal entries in the accounting records.
3 Require that all cash receipts be deposited daily in the bank and that all significant cash payments be made by check. Cash payments should *not* be made directly from cash receipts on hand.
4 Require that the validity and amount of every expenditure be verified before payment is made.
5 Separate the function of approving expenditures from the function of signing checks.

The application of these principles in building an adequate system of internal control over cash can best be illustrated by considering separately the topics of cash receipts and cash disbursements.

Cash receipts

Cash receipts consist of two major types: cash received over the counter at the time of a sale and cash received through the mail as collections on accounts receivable.

Use of cash registers   Cash received over the counter at the time of a sale should be rung up on a cash register, *so located that the customer will see the amount recorded.* Since the customer presumably will not pay more than the amount shown on the register, the use of cash registers provides assurance that an immediate record is made of all cash sales. At the end of the day, the store manager or other supervisor should compare the cash register tape with the total cash collected.

ILLUSTRATIVE CASE   Many large supermarkets have achieved faster checkout lines and stronger internal control by using electronic scanning equipment to read and record the price of all groceries passing the checkout counters. All of the 12,000 or so grocery items on the shelves bear a product code, consisting of a pattern of thick and thin vertical bars. At the checkout counter, the code on each item is read by a scanning laser. The code is sent instantaneously to a computer which locates the price and description of the item and flashes that information on a display panel in view of the customer and the checkout clerk. After all of the items have been passed through the scanner, the display panel shows the total amount of the sale. The clerk then enters the amount of cash received from the customer, and the display panel shows the amount of change that the customer should receive.

This system has many advantages. Not only is an immediate record made of all cash receipts, but the risk of errors in pricing merchandise or in making change is greatly reduced. This system also improves inventory control by giving management continuous information on what is being sold moment by moment, classified by product and by manufacturer. Comparison of these sales records with records of purchases will direct attention to any losses from theft or shoplifting.

Use of prenumbered sales tickets   Another means of establishing internal control over cash sales is by writing out a prenumbered sales ticket in duplicate at the time of each sale. The original is given to the customer and the carbon copy is retained. Prenumbered sales tickets are widely used in businesses such as restaurants where one central cashier rings up the sales made by all salespeople.

At the end of the day, an employee computes the total sales figure from these sales tickets and also makes sure that no tickets are missing from the series. This total sales figure is then compared with the cash register tape and the total cash receipts.

Cash received through the mail   The procedures for handling checks and currency received through the mail are also based on the internal control principle that two or more employees should participate in every transaction.

The employee who opens the mail should prepare a list of the checks received. In order that this list shall represent the total receipts of the day, the totals recorded on the cash registers may be added to the list. One copy of the list is forwarded with the cash (currency and checks) to the cashier, who will deposit in the bank all the cash received for the day. Another copy of the list is sent to the accounting department, which will record the amount of cash received.

At the close of business each day, the manager should determine that the total cash receipts recorded that day in the accounting records agree with the amount of the cashier's deposit, and also with the list of total cash receipts for the day.

Cash over and short   In handling over-the-counter cash receipts, a few errors in making change will inevitably occur. These errors will cause a cash shortage or overage at the end of the day, when the cash is counted and compared with the reading on the cash register.

For example, assume that the total cash sales for the day amount to $500 as recorded by the cash register, but that the cash in the drawer when counted amounts to only $490. The following entry would be made to record the day's sales and the cash shortage of $10.

Recording cash shortage

Cash	*490*
Cash Over and Short	*10*
Sales	*500*

The account entitled Cash Over and Short is debited with shortages and credited with overages. If the cash shortages during an entire accounting period are in excess of the cash overages, the Cash Over and Short account will have a debit balance and will be shown as miscellaneous *expense* in the income statement. On the other hand, if the overages exceed the shortages, the Cash Over and Short account will show a credit balance at the end of the period and should be treated as an item of miscellaneous *revenue*.

Cash disbursements

An adequate system of internal control requires that each day's cash receipts be deposited intact in the bank and that *all disbursements be made by check*. Checks should be prenumbered. Any spoiled checks should be marked "Void" and filed in sequence so that all numbers in the series can be accounted for.

Every transaction requiring a cash disbursement should be verified and approved before payment is made. The official designated to sign checks should not be given authority to approve invoices for payment or to make entries in the accounting records. When a check is presented to a company official for signature, it should be accompanied by the approved invoice and voucher showing that the transaction has been fully verified and that payment is justified. When the check is signed, the supporting invoices and vouchers should be perforated or stamped "Paid" to eliminate any possibility of their being presented later in support of another check. If these rules are followed, it is almost impossible for a fraudulent cash disbursement to be concealed without the collusion of two or more persons.

In large companies which issue hundreds or thousands of checks daily, it is not practicable for a company official to sign each check manually. Instead, check-signing machines with various built-in control devices are used. This automation of the check-signing function does not weaken the system of internal control if attention is given to proper use of the machine and to control of the checks both before and after they pass through the check-signing machine.

ILLUSTRATIVE CASE   Manning Corporation issued a great many checks every day but paid little attention to internal controls over its cash payments. Stacks of unissued checks were kept in an unlocked supply closet along with Styrofoam coffee cups. Because the number of checks issued was too great for the treasurer to sign them manually, a check-signing machine was used. This machine, after signing the checks, ejected them into a box equipped with a lock. In spite of warnings from the company's CPA firm, company officials found that it was "too inconvenient" to keep the box locked. Manning Corporation also failed to make any use of the check-counting device built into the check-signing machine. Although the company maintained very large amounts on deposit in checking accounts, it did not bother to reconcile bank statements for weeks or months at a time.

These weaknesses in internal control led to a crisis when a new employee was given a three-week-old bank statement and a bundle of paid checks and told to prepare a bank reconciliation. The new employee found that the bundle of paid checks accompanying the bank statement was incomplete. No paid checks were on hand to support over $700,000 of charges deducted on the bank statement. Manning Corporation's CPA firm was asked to make a detailed investigation of cash transactions. This investigation revealed that over $1 million in unauthorized and unrecorded checks had been paid from the corporation's bank accounts. These checks had been issued out of serial number sequence and had been run through the company check-signing machine. It was not possible to determine who had carried out the theft and the money was not recovered.

The voucher system

One widely used method of establishing control over cash disbursements is the voucher system. This system provides that every transaction requiring a cash payment be verified and approved before a check is issued. A written authorization called a *voucher* is prepared for every expenditure, regardless of whether the expenditure is for payment of an expense, purchase of an asset, or payment of a liability.

A voucher is attached to each incoming invoice and given an identification number. The voucher (as illustrated on page 262) has spaces for listing the data from the invoice and specifying the ledger accounts to be debited and credited in recording the transaction. Space is also provided for approval signatures for each step in the verification and approval process. A completed voucher provides a description of the transaction and also of the work performed in verifying the liability and approving the cash disbursement.

Preparing a voucher   To illustrate the functioning of a voucher system, let us begin with the receipt of an invoice from a supplier. A voucher is prepared by filling in the appropriate blanks with information taken from the invoice, such as the invoice date, invoice number, amount, and the creditor's name and address. The voucher with the seller's invoice attached is then sent to the employees responsible for verifying the extensions and footings on the invoice and for comparing prices, quantities, and terms with those specified in the purchase order and receiving report. When completion of the verification process has been evidenced by approval signatures of the persons performing these steps, the voucher and supporting documents are sent to an employee of the accounting department, who indicates on the voucher the accounts to be debited and credited.

The voucher is now reviewed by an accounting official to provide assurance that the verification procedures have been satisfactorily completed and that the liability is a proper one. After receiving this supervisory approval, the voucher is entered in a journal called a *voucher register.*

Entries in the voucher register indicate the nature of the expenditure by debiting the appropriate asset, expense, or liability accounts. The credit portion of each entry is always to a short-term liability account entitled *Vouchers Payable.* Note that the entry in the voucher register is not made until the liability has been verified and approved.

In the voucher system, the ledger account, Vouchers Payable, replaces Accounts Payable. For purposes of balance sheet presentation, however, most companies continue to use the more widely understood term Accounts Payable.

Paying the voucher within the discount period   After the voucher has been entered in the voucher register, it is placed (with the supporting documents attached) in a tickler file according to the date of required payment. Cash discount periods generally run from the date of the invoice. Since a voucher is prepared for each

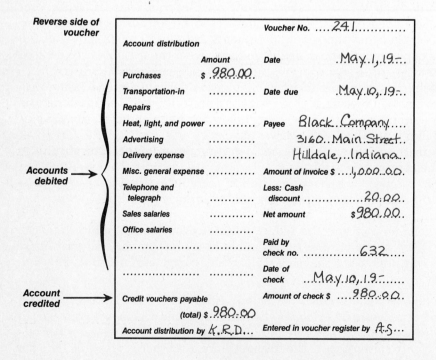

Use of voucher ensures verification of invoice

BROADHILL CORPORATION
Chicago, Illinois

Voucher No. ..241........ ← Serial number

Pay to ..Black..Company........   Date ..May.1,.19-.....

..3160..Main..Street......   Date due ..May.10,.19-...

..Hilldale,..Indiana......

Date of invoice ..April.30,.19-.   Gross amount $ .1,000.00..

Invoice number ......847........   Less: Cash discount ......20..00..

Net amount $ .980.00..

Approval

	Dates	Approved by
Extensions and footings verified	May.1,.19-	R.G......
Prices in agreement with purchase order	May.1,.19-	R.G......
Quantities in agreement with receiving report	May.1,.19-	R.G......
Credit terms in agreement with purchase order	May.1,.19-	R.G......
Account distribution & recording approved	William..Cross.....	
Approved for payment	Judith..Davis........	

} ← Verification procedures

Accounting Supervisor ← Approved for payment

Reverse side of voucher

Voucher No. ......241............

Account distribution

	Amount		Date	May.1,.19-.
Purchases	$ 980.00			
Transportation-in	....		Date due	May.10,.19-.
Repairs	....			
Heat, light, and power	....		Payee	Black..Company....
Advertising	....			3160..Main..Street..
Delivery expense	....			Hilldale,..Indiana..
Misc. general expense	....		Amount of invoice $ ....1,000..00..
Telephone and telegraph	....		Less: Cash discount ....20..00..
Sales salaries	....		Net amount $980.00..
Office salaries	....		
....	....		Paid by check no. ....632....
....	....		Date of check May.10,.19-......

Accounts debited →

Account credited →   Credit vouchers payable
   (total) $ .980.00

Amount of check $ ....980..00..

Account distribution by K..R.D...   Entered in voucher register by A.S...

invoice, the required date of payment is the last day on which a check can be prepared and mailed to the creditor in time to qualify for the discount.

When the payment date arrives, an employee in the accounting department removes the voucher from the unpaid file, draws a check for signature by the treasurer, and records payment of the voucher in a special journal called a *check register*. Since checks are issued only in payment of approved vouchers, every entry in the check register represents a debit to Vouchers Payable and a credit to Cash.

An important factor in achieving internal control is that the employee in the accounting department who prepares the check *is not authorized to sign it.* The unsigned check and the supporting voucher are now sent to the treasurer or other designated official in the finance department. The treasurer reviews the voucher, especially the approval signatures, and signs the check. Thus, the invoice is *approved for payment* in the accounting department, but the actual cash disbursement is made by the finance department. *No one person or department is in a position both to approve invoices for payment and to issue signed checks.*

Once the check has been signed, the treasurer should mail it directly to the creditor. The voucher and all supporting documents are then perforated with a PAID stamp and are forwarded to the accounting department, which will note payment of the voucher in the voucher register and file the paid voucher. The operation of a voucher system is illustrated in the flow chart on page 264. Notes have been made on the illustration identifying the most important internal control features in the system.

Petty cash

As previously emphasized, adequate internal control over cash requires that all receipts be deposited in the bank and all disbursements be made by check. However, every business finds it convenient to have a small amount of cash on hand with which to make some minor expenditures. Examples include payments for small purchases of office supplies, postage stamps, and taxi fares. Internal control over these small cash payments can best be achieved through a petty cash fund.

Establishing the petty cash fund   To create a petty cash fund, a check is written for a round amount such as $100 or $200, which will cover the small expenditures to be paid in cash for a period of two or three weeks. This check is cashed and the money kept on hand in a petty cash box or drawer in the office.

The entry for the issuance of the check is:

Creating the petty cash fund

Petty Cash	200	
Cash		200

To establish a petty cash fund.

Operation of a Voucher System

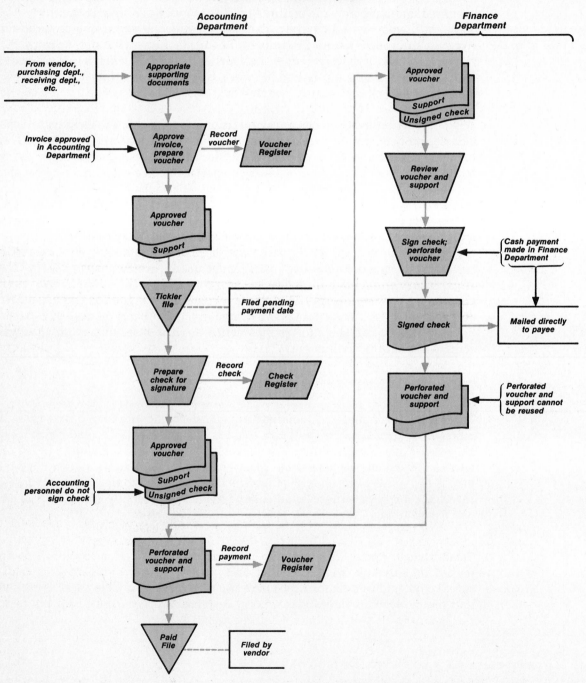

Making disbursements from the petty cash fund   As cash payments are made out of the petty cash box, the custodian of the fund is required to fill out a *petty cash voucher* for each expenditure. A petty cash voucher shows the amount paid, the purpose of the expenditure, the date, and the signature of the person receiving the money. A petty cash voucher should be prepared for every payment made from the fund. The petty cash box should, therefore, always contain cash and/or vouchers totaling the exact amount of the fund.

The petty cash custodian should be informed that occasional surprise counts of the fund will be made and that he or she is personally responsible for the fund being intact at all times. Careless handling of petty cash has often been a first step toward large thefts; consequently, misuse of petty cash funds should not be tolerated.

Replenishing the petty cash fund   Assume that a petty cash fund of $200 was established on June 1 and that payments totaling $174.95 were made from the fund during the next two weeks. Since the $200 originally placed in the fund is nearly exhausted, the fund should be replenished. To replenish a petty cash fund means to replace the amount of money that has been spent, thus restoring the fund to its original amount. A check is drawn payable to Petty Cash for the exact amount of the expenditures, $174.95. This check is cashed and the money placed in the petty cash box. The vouchers totaling that amount are perforated to prevent their reuse and filed in support of the replenishment check. The journal entry to record the issuance of the check will debit the expense accounts indicated by inspection of the vouchers, as follows:

Replenishment of petty cash fund	Office Supplies Expense	80.60	
	Freight-in	16.00	
	Postage Expense	45.25	
	Miscellaneous Expense	33.10	
	Cash		174.95

To replenish the petty cash fund.

Note that *expense accounts* are debited each time the fund is replenished. The Petty Cash account is debited only when the fund is first established. There ordinarily will be no further entries in the Petty Cash account after the fund is established, unless the fund is discontinued or a decision is made to change its size from the original $200 amount.

The petty cash fund is usually replenished at the end of an accounting period, even though the fund is not running low, so that all vouchers in the fund are charged to expense accounts before these accounts are closed and financial statements prepared.

Control features of bank checking accounts

We have already emphasized that all significant cash disbursements should be made by check. The use of checking accounts contributes to strong internal control in many ways. For example:

1 Checking accounts eliminate the need to keep large amounts of cash on hand.

2 The board of directors must notify the bank who is authorized to sign checks. Thus, access to cash is limited to those officers or employees designated by the board.

3 The person responsible for each cash disbursement is readily identified by the signature on the check.

4 The bank returns all checks which have been paid from the account. Thus, the depositor has documentary evidence showing the date and amount of each cash payment and the identity of the person who received the cash.

5 A comparison of the monthly *bank statement* with the depositor's accounting records will bring to light any errors made either by the bank or by the depositor in accounting for cash transactions.

Bank statements

Each month the bank will provide the depositor with a statement of the depositor's account, accompanied by the checks paid and charged to the account during the month.[1] As illustrated on page 267 a bank statement shows the balance on deposit at the beginning of the month, the deposits, the checks paid, any other debits and credits during the month, and the new balance at the end of the month. (To keep the illustration short, we have shown a limited number of deposits rather than one for each business day in the month.)

Certain items in the bank statement of Parkview Company need explanation and are discussed in the following paragraphs.

NSF checks Bank deposits made by a business include checks received from customers. Occasionally a customer's check may "bounce"; that is, the bank on which the check is drawn may refuse payment. The most common cause for such refusal is that the customer's bank balance is less than the amount of the check. For example, on July 24 Parkview Company received a check for $50.25 from J. B. Ball, and the check was included in the bank deposit made on that day. The Ball check was returned to Western National Bank by the bank on which it was drawn marked NSF (Not Sufficient Funds), indicating that Ball did not have a sufficient balance on deposit to cover the check. Western National Bank therefore charged the NSF check against Parkview Company's account as shown by the July 30 debit of $50.25. (The letter M alongside this entry stands for Miscellaneous Entry.)

After getting the NSF check back from the bank, Parkview Company should remove this check from the cash classification by a journal entry debiting an account receivable from J. B. Ball and crediting Cash. The NSF check is thus regarded as a receivable until it is collected directly from the maker and redeposited, or is determined to be worthless.

---

[1]Large businesses may receive bank statements on a weekly basis.

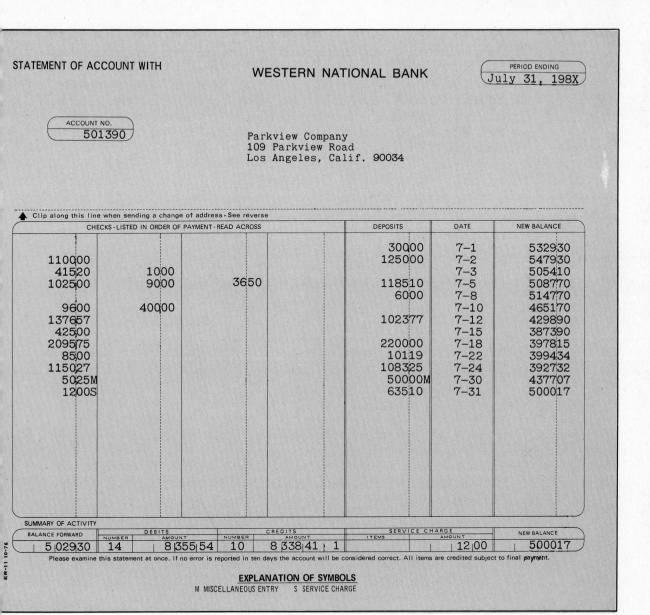

STATEMENT OF ACCOUNT WITH

WESTERN NATIONAL BANK

PERIOD ENDING
July 31, 198X

ACCOUNT NO.
501390

Parkview Company
109 Parkview Road
Los Angeles, Calif. 90034

Clip along this line when sending a change of address - See reverse

CHECKS - LISTED IN ORDER OF PAYMENT - READ ACROSS				DEPOSITS	DATE	NEW BALANCE
				300 00	7-1	5329 30
1100 00				1250 00	7-2	5479 30
415 20	10 00				7-3	5054 10
1025 00	90 00	36 50		1185 10	7-5	5087 70
				60 00	7-8	5147 70
96 00	400 00				7-10	4651 70
1376 57				1023 77	7-12	4298 90
425 00					7-15	3873 90
2095 75				2200 00	7-18	3978 15
85 00				101 19	7-22	3994 34
1150 27				1083 25	7-24	3927 32
50 25M				500 00M	7-30	4377 07
12 00S				635 10	7-31	5000 17

SUMMARY OF ACTIVITY								
BALANCE FORWARD	DEBITS		CREDITS		SERVICE CHARGE			NEW BALANCE
	NUMBER	AMOUNT	NUMBER	AMOUNT	ITEMS		AMOUNT	
5 029 30	14	8 355 54	10	8 338 41	1		12 00	500017

Please examine this statement at once. If no error is reported in ten days the account will be considered correct. All items are credited subject to final payment.

EXPLANATION OF SYMBOLS
M MISCELLANEOUS ENTRY   S SERVICE CHARGE

ER-11 10-76

Bank service charges   Under the date of July 31 on the illustrated bank statement is a debit for \$12 accompanied by the symbol S. This symbol means Service Charge, a charge made by the bank to cover the expense of handling the account. The amount of the service charge is based upon such considerations as the average balance of the account and the number of checks and deposits. Banks do not usually impose a service charge on large checking accounts. However, a service charge is shown here for illustrative purposes.

When the bank sends the monthly statement and paid checks to the depositor, it will include debit memoranda for service charges and any other charges not represented by checks.

Miscellaneous charges   Other charges which may appear on the bank statement include rental fees for safe deposit boxes, charges for printing checks, collection charges on notes left with the bank for collection, and interest charges on borrowing from the bank.

Reconciling the bank account

The purpose of reconciling the bank account is to assure that the bank and the depositor are in agreement on the amount of money on deposit. Remember that the bank and the depositor are maintaining independent records of the deposits, the checks, and the running balance of the bank account. Once a month an employee prepares a *bank reconciliation* to verify that these two independent sets of records are in agreement. For strong internal control, the employee who prepares the bank reconciliation should not have access to cash or be responsible for recording cash transactions in the accounting records.

The balance shown on the monthly statement received from the bank will usually not agree with the balance of cash shown by the depositor's accounting records. Certain transactions recorded by the depositor will not yet have been recorded by the bank. The most common examples are:

1 Outstanding checks. These are checks written by the depositor and deducted from the Cash account on the depositor's records but not yet presented to the bank for payment.
2 Deposits in transit. Deposits mailed to the bank are usually not received by the bank and not entered on the bank's records until a day or two later than the entry on the depositor's accounting records.

Transactions which may appear on the bank statement but which have not yet been recorded by the depositor include:

1 Service charges
2 Charges for NSF checks
3 Miscellaneous bank charges and credits

In some cases the bank reconciliation will be complete after such items as outstanding checks, deposits in transit, and miscellaneous bank charges have been taken into account. Other cases may require the correction of errors by the bank or errors in the depositor's accounting records to complete the reconciliation.

Preparing a bank reconciliation   Specific steps to be taken in preparing a bank reconciliation are:

1 Compare the deposits listed on the bank statement with the deposits shown in the company's records. Place check marks in the company's cash records and

on the bank statement beside the items which agree. Any unchecked item in the company's records of deposits will be deposits not yet recorded by the bank, and should be added to the balance reported by the bank. Determine that any deposits in transit listed in last month's bank reconciliation are included as deposits in the current month's bank statement.

2 Arrange the paid checks in sequence by serial numbers and compare each check with the corresponding entry in the cash payments journal. (In the case of personal bank accounts for which the only record maintained is the check-book, compare each paid check with the check stub.) Place a check mark in the depositor's cash payments journal opposite each entry for which a paid check has been returned by the bank. The unchecked entries should be listed in the bank reconciliation as *outstanding checks to be deducted from the balance reported by the bank.* Determine whether the checks listed as outstanding in the bank reconciliation for the preceding month have been returned by the bank this month. If not, such checks should be listed as outstanding in the current reconciliation.

3 Deduct from the balance per the depositor's records any debit memoranda issued by the bank which have not been recorded by the depositor. In the illustrated bank reconciliation on page 270, examples are the NSF check for $50.25 and the $12 service charge.

4 Add to the balance per the depositor's records any credit memoranda issued by the bank which have not been recorded by the depositor. An example in the illustrated bank reconciliation is the credit of $500 collected by the bank in behalf of Parkview Company.

5 Prepare a bank reconciliation, reflecting the preceding steps, similar to the illustration on page 270.

6 Prepare journal entries for any items on the bank statement which have not yet been recorded in the depositor's accounts.

Illustration of bank reconciliation The July bank statement prepared by the bank for Parkview Company was illustrated on page 267. This statement shows a balance of cash on deposit at July 31 of $5,000.17. We shall assume that Parkview Company's records at July 31 show a bank balance of $4,182.57. Our purpose in preparing the bank reconciliation is to identify the items that make up the difference of $817.60 and to determine the correct cash balance.

Assume that the specific steps to be taken in preparing a bank reconciliation have been carried out and that the following reconciling items have been discovered:

1 A deposit of $310.90 mailed to the bank on July 31 does not appear on the bank statement.

2 A credit memorandum issued by the bank on July 30 in the amount of $500 was returned with the July bank statement and appears in the Deposits column of that statement. This credit represents the proceeds of a note receivable left with the bank by Parkview Company for the purpose of collection. The collection of the note has not yet been recorded by Parkview Company.

I l0VE y0υrθθ¹¹

3 Four checks issued in July or prior months have not yet been paid by the bank. These checks are:

Check No.	Date	Amount
801	June 15	$100.00
888	July 24	10.25
890	July 27	402.50
891	July 30	205.00

4 A debit memorandum issued by the bank on July 31 for a $12 service charge was enclosed with the July bank statement.

5 Check no. 875 was issued July 20 in the amount of $85 but was erroneously listed on the check stub and in the cash payments journal as $58. The check, in payment of telephone service, was paid by the bank, returned with the July bank statement, and correctly listed on the bank statement as an $85 charge to the account. The Cash account is overstated because of this $27 error ($85 − $58).

6 No entry has as yet been made in Parkview Company's accounts to reflect the bank's action on July 30 of charging against the account the NSF check for $50.25 drawn by J. B. Ball.

The July 31 bank reconciliation for Parkview Company follows:

PARKVIEW COMPANY
Bank Reconciliation
July 31, 19___

Update and correct the balance per depositor's records	Balance per depositor's records, July 31, 19___	$4,182.57
	Add: Note receivable collected for us by bank	500.00
		$4,682.57
	Less: Service charge .... $ 12.00	
	NSF check of J. B. Ball 50.25	
	Error on check stub no. 875 .... 27.00	89.25
	Adjusted balance	$4,593.32
Update and correct the balance per bank statement	Balance per bank statement, July 31, 19___	$5,000.17
	Add: Deposit of July 31 not recorded by bank	310.90
		$5,311.07
	Less: Outstanding checks	
	No. 801 .... $100.00	
	No. 888 .... 10.25	
	No. 890 .... 402.50	
	No. 891 .... 205.00	717.75
	Adjusted balance (as above)	$4,593.32

The adjusted balance of $4,593.32 is the amount of cash owned by Parkview Company and is, therefore, the amount which should appear as cash in the July 31 balance sheet.

Note that the adjusted balance of cash differs from both the bank statement and the depositor's records. This difference is explained by the fact that neither set of records is up to date as of July 31, and also by the existence of an error on Parkview Company's records.

Adjusting the records after the reconciliation   To make Parkview Company's records up-to-date and accurate, four journal entries affecting the Cash account are necessary for the four items that make up the difference between the $4,182.57 balance per the depositor's records and the adjusted balance of $4,593.32. These four reconciling items call for the following entries:

Cash	500.00	
Notes Receivable		500.00
To record the note receivable collected for us by the bank.		

Miscellaneous Expense	12.00	
Cash		12.00
To record the service charge by the bank.		

Accounts Receivable, J. B. Ball	50.25	
Cash		50.25
To record as a receivable from J. B. Ball the amount of the NSF check returned to us by the bank.		

Telephone Expense	27.00	
Cash		27.00
To correct the error by which check no. 875 for an $85 payment for telephone service was recorded as $58 ($85 − $58 = $27).		

Instead of making four separate journal entries affecting the Cash account, one compound journal entry can be made to record all four of the above items.

INVESTMENTS IN MARKETABLE SECURITIES

The term *marketable securities* refers primarily to U.S. government bonds and the bonds and stocks of large corporations. Because marketable securities can be sold quickly on securities exchanges, an investment in these securities is almost as liquid an asset as cash itself. In fact, investments in marketable securities are often called "secondary cash resources." If cash is needed for any operating purpose, these securities may be converted quickly into cash; in the meantime, investments in marketable securities are preferable to cash because of the interest or dividend revenue which they produce. Most companies watch their cash balances very carefully and invest any cash not needed for current operations in high-grade marketable securities.

When an investor owns several different marketable securities, the group of securities is termed an investment *portfolio.* In deciding upon the securities to include in the portfolio, the investor seeks to maximize return while minimizing risk. Risk often can be reduced by *diversification,* that is, by including in the portfolio a variety of securities, especially securities of companies in different industries.

Some investors own enough of a company's capital stock to influence or control the company's activities through the voting rights of the shares owned. Such large holdings of capital stock create an important business relationship between the investor and the issuing corporation. Since investments of this type cannot be sold without disturbing this relationship, they are not considered marketable securities. *Investments for purposes of control* will be discussed in Appendix B, which follows Chapter 14.

Securities exchanges

The stocks and bonds of most large corporations are listed on organized securities exchanges, such as the *New York Stock Exchange.* An investor may either buy or sell these listed securities through any brokerage house which is a member of the exchange. The brokerage company represents the investor and negotiates with other exchange members either to buy or sell the securities on behalf of its customer. The price at which the broker negotiates the transaction represents the current market value of the security and is immediately printed on the stock exchange ticker tape for reference by other investors. The financial pages of many newspapers report on a daily basis the highest, lowest, and closing (last) prices at which each listed security is exchanged.

At the time of issuance of stocks or bonds, the transaction is between the investor and the issuing corporation. The great daily volume of transactions in securities, however, consists of the sale of stocks and bonds by investors to other investors. On the New York Stock Exchange alone, 80 million or more shares of stock may be exchanged on a single day. The stocks and bonds of many smaller companies are not listed on an organized securities exchange, but brokerage firms also arrange for the purchase and sale of these unlisted or *over-the-counter* securities.

Quoted market prices   The market prices of stocks are quoted in terms of dollars per share. Bond prices, however, are quoted as a *percentage* of their face value or *maturity* value, which is usually $1,000. The maturity value is the amount the issuing company must pay to redeem the bond at the date it matures (becomes due). A bond quoted at *102* would therefore have a market price of $1,020 (102% of $1,000). The following line from the financial page of a daily newspaper summarizes the previous day's trading in bonds of American Telephone & Telegraph (AT&T):

What is the market value of this bond?	Bonds	Sales	High	Low	Close	Net Change
	ATT 10⅜ 90	145	86	84	84½	−1

This line of condensed information indicates that 145 of AT&T's 10⅜, $1,000 bonds maturing in 1990 were traded. The highest price is reported as 86 or $860 for a bond of $1,000 face value. The lowest price was 84 or $840, for a $1,000 bond. The closing price (last sale of the day) was 84½ or $845. This was one point below the closing price of the previous day, a decrease of $10 in the price of a $1,000 bond.

The primary factors which determine the market value of a bond are (1) the relationship of the bond's interest rate to other investment opportunities and (2) investors' confidence that the issuing company will be able to meet its obligations for future interest and principal payments. A bond selling at a market price greater than its maturity value is said to be selling at a *premium;* a bond selling at a price below its maturity value is selling at a *discount.* As a bond nears its maturity date, the market price of the bond approaches its maturity value. At the maturity date the market price of the bond should be exactly equal to its maturity value, and the issuing corporation will redeem the bond for that amount.

Listed corporations report to a million owners   When a corporation invites the public to purchase its stocks and bonds, it accepts an obligation to keep the public informed on its financial condition and the profitability of operations. This obligation of disclosure includes public distribution of financial statements. The Securities and Exchange Commission is the government agency responsible for seeing that corporations make adequate disclosure of their affairs so that investors have a basis for intelligent investment decisions. The flow of corporate accounting data distributed through newspapers and financial advisory services to millions of investors is a vital force in the functioning of our economy; in fact, the successful working of a profit-motivated economy rests upon the quality and dependability of the accounting information being recorded.

Listed corporations are audited by certified public accountants   Corporations with securities listed on organized stock exchanges are required to have regular audits by independent public accouts. The financial statements distributed each year to stockholders are accompanied by a report by a firm of certified public accountants indicating that an audit has been made and expressing an opinion as to the fairness of the company's financial statements. It is the *independent status* of the auditing firm that enables investors to place confidence in audited financial statements.

Marketable securities as current assets

A recent balance sheet of International Business Machines Corporation (IBM) shows the following items listed first in the current assets section.

Current assets:

Cash	$ 208,607,210
Marketable securities, at lower of cost or market	5,947,653,848

The large investment by IBM in marketable securities is not surprising; many corporations have large holdings of marketable securities. In the balance sheet, marketable securities are usually listed immediately after the asset Cash, because they are so liquid as to be almost the equivalent of cash.

In *Statement No. 12,* the Financial Accounting Standards Board indicated that a company may choose to separate its marketable securities into two groups: (1) temporary investments classified as current assets, and (2) long-term investments classified as noncurrent assets.[2]

If management intends to hold certain marketable securities on a long-term basis, these securities should be listed in the balance sheet just below the current asset section under the caption Long-Term Investments. In most cases, however, management stands ready to sell marketable securities whenever company needs or stock market trends make such action advantageous. Consequently, marketable securities are generally viewed as current assets.

Accounting for investments in marketable securities

When securities are purchased, an account entitled Marketable Securities is debited for the entire purchase price, including any commissions to stockbrokers and any transfer taxes. A subsidiary ledger must also be maintained which shows for each security owned the acquisition date, total cost, number of shares (or bonds) owned, and cost per share (or bond). This subsidiary ledger provides the information necessary to determine the amount of gain or loss when an investment in a particular stock or bond is sold.

The principal distinction between the recording of an investment in bonds and an investment in stocks is that interest on bonds accrues from day to day. The interest accrued since the last semiannual interest payment date is paid for by the purchaser and should be recorded separately from the cost of the bond itself. Dividends on stock, however, *do not accrue* and the entire purchase price paid by the investor in stocks is recorded in the Marketable Securities account.

Bond interest payments The amount of interest paid to bondholders is equal to a stated percentage of the bond's maturity value. Thus, the owner of a 12% bond would receive $120 interest (12% of $1,000) every year. Since bond interest usually is paid semiannually, the bondholder would receive two semiannual interest payments of $60 each.

When bonds are purchased between interest dates, the purchaser pays the quoted market price for the bond *plus* the interest accrued since the last interest payment date. By this arrangement the new owner becomes entitled to receive in full the next semiannual interest payment. An account called Bond Interest Receivable should be debited for the amount of interest purchased.

---

[2]FASB Statement No. 12, "Accounting for Certain Marketable Securities" (Stamford, Conn.: 1975).

Income on investments in bonds   To illustrate the accounting entries for an investment in bonds, assume that on August 1 an investor purchases ten 9%, $1,000 bonds which pay interest on June 1 and December 1. The investor buys the bonds on August 1 at a price of 98, plus a brokerage commission of $50 and two months' accrued interest of $150 ($10,000 × 9% × $\frac{2}{12}$ = $150). The entry on August 1 to record this investment is:

Separate account for accrued bond interest purchased

Marketable Securities	9,850	
Bond Interest Receivable	150	
Cash		10,000

Purchased ten 9% bonds of Rider Co. at 98 plus a brokerage commission of $50 and two months' accrued interest.

On December 1, the semiannual interest payment date, the investor will receive an interest check for $450, which will be recorded as follows:

Note portion of interest check earned

Cash	450	
Bond Interest Receivable		150
Bond Interest Revenue		300

Received semiannual interest on Rider Co. bonds.

The $300 credit to Bond Interest Revenue represents the amount actually earned during the four months the bonds were owned by the investor (9% × $10,000 × $\frac{4}{12}$ = $300).

If the investor's accounting records are maintained on a calendar-year basis, the following adjusting entry is required at December 31 to record bond interest earned since December 1:

Bond Interest Receivable	75	
Bond Interest Revenue		75

To accrue one month's interest earned (Dec. 1–Dec. 31) on Rider Co. bonds ($10,000 × 9% × $\frac{1}{12}$ = $75).

The $75 in bond interest receivable recorded at December 31 will not be collected until the next semiannual interest payment date, which will be June 1 of the following year. The entry on June 1 will be:

Cash	450	
Bond Interest Receivable		75
Bond Interest Revenue		375

To record receipt of semiannual interest on Rider Co. bonds and recognize interest earned since December 31 ($10,000 × 9% × $\frac{5}{12}$ = $375).

Income on investments in stock   Since dividends do not accrue, they generally are not recognized by the stockholder as revenue until the dividend check arrives. The entry upon receipt of the dividend check consists of a debit to Cash and a credit to Dividend Revenue.

Gains and losses from sale of investments in securities

The sale of an investment in stocks is recorded by debiting Cash for the amount received and crediting the Marketable Securities account for the cost of the securities sold. Any difference between the proceeds of the sale and the cost of the investment is recorded by a debit to Loss on Sale of Marketable Securities or by a credit to Gain on Sale of Marketable Securities.

At the date of sale of an investment in bonds, any interest which has accrued since the last interest payment date (or year-end) should be recognized as interest revenue. For example, assume that 10 bonds of the Elk Corporation carried in the accounts of an investor at $9,600 are sold at a price of 94 and accrued interest of $90. The commission on the sale is $50. The following entry should be made:

Investment in bonds sold at a loss

Cash	9,440	
Loss on Sale of Marketable Securities	250	
Marketable Securities		9,600
Bond Interest Revenue		90
Sold 10 bonds of Elk Corporation at 94 and accrued interest of $90 less broker's commission of $50.		

Balance sheet valuation of marketable securities

Although the market price of a bond may fluctuate from day to day, we can be reasonably certain that when the maturity date arrives the market price will be equal to the bond's maturity value. Stocks, on the other hand, do not have maturity values. When the market price of a stock declines, there is no way we can be certain whether the decline will be temporary or permanent. For this reason, different valuation standards are applied in accounting for investments in marketable *debt* securities (bonds) and investments in marketable *equity* securities (stocks).

Valuation of marketable debt securities A short-term investment in bonds is generally carried in the accounting records at *cost* and a gain or loss is recognized when the investment is sold. If bonds are held as a long-term investment and the difference between the cost of the investment and its maturity value is substantial, the valuation of the investment becomes more complex. The valuation of long-term investments in bonds is discussed in Chapter 13.

Valuation of marketable equity securities The market values of stocks may rise or fall dramatically during an accounting period. An investor who sells an investment at a price above or below cost will recognize a gain or loss on the sale. But what if the investor continues to hold securities after a significant change in their market value? In this case, should any gain or loss be recognized in the financial statements?

In *Statement No. 12,* the FASB (Financial Accounting Standards Board) ruled that a portfolio of marketable equity securities should be shown in the balance sheet at the *lower* of aggregate cost or current market value. The effect of the *lower-of-cost-or-market (LCM)* rule is to recognize losses from drops in market value without recognizing gains from rising market prices.

Note that this rule does not accord the same treatment to market gains and losses. Accountants traditionally have applied different criteria in recognizing gains and losses. One of the basic principles in accounting is that increases in market value above original cost shall not be recognized until they are *realized,* and the usual test of realization is the sale of the asset in question. Losses, on the other hand, are recognized as soon as objective evidence indicates that a loss has been incurred.

Lower of cost or market (LCM)

In applying the lower-of-cost-or-market rule, the total cost of the portfolio of marketable equity securities is compared with its current market value, and the lower of these two amounts is used as the balance sheet valuation. If the market value of the portfolio is below cost, an entry is made to reduce the carrying value of the portfolio to current market value and to recognize an *unrealized loss* for the amount of the market decline. The write-down of an investment in marketable equity securities to a market value below cost is an end-of-period adjusting entry and should be based upon market prices at the balance sheet date.

To illustrate the lower-of-cost-or-market adjustment, assume the following facts for the investment portfolio of Eagle Corporation at December 31, Year 1:

	Cost	Market Value
Capital stock of Adams Corporation	$100,000	$106,000
Capital stock of Barnes Company	60,000	52,000
Capital stock of Parker Industries	200,000	182,000
Other marketable equity securities	25,000	25,000
Totals	$385,000	$365,000

Since the total market value of the securities in our example is less than their cost to Eagle Corporation, the balance sheet valuation would be the lower amount of $365,000. This downward adjustment of $20,000 means that an unrealized loss of $20,000 will be included in the determination of the year's net income. The accounting entry would be as follows:

Year 1			
Dec. 31	Unrealized Loss on Marketable Securities	20,000	
	Valuation Allowance for Marketable Securities		20,000
	To reduce the carrying value of the investment in marketable securities to the lower of cost or market.		

The loss from the decline in the market value of securities owned is termed an *unrealized loss* to distinguish it from a loss which is realized by an actual sale of securities.

The valuation account   The Valuation Allowance for Marketable Securities is a *contra-asset* account or *valuation* account. In the balance sheet, this valuation account is offset against the asset Marketable Securities in the same manner as the Accumulated Depreciation account is offset against the asset Building. The following partial balance sheet illustrates the use of the Valuation Allowance for Marketable Securities:

Current assets:

Cash		$ 80,000
Marketable securities	$385,000	
Less: Valuation allowance for marketable securities	20,000	365,000

The valuation account is adjusted every period   At the end of every period, the balance of the valuation account is adjusted to cause marketable equity securities to be shown in the balance sheet at the lower of cost or current market value. If the valuation allowance must be increased because of further declines in market value, the adjusting entry will recognize an additional unrealized loss. On the other hand, if market prices have gone up since the last balance sheet date, the adjusting entry will reduce or eliminate the valuation allowance and recognize an *unrealized gain*.

To illustrate the adjustment of the valuation account, let us assume that by the end of Year 2 the market value of Eagle Corporation's portfolio has increased to an amount greater than cost. Since market value is no longer below cost, the valuation allowance, which has a credit balance of $20,000, is no longer needed. Thus, the following entry would be made to eliminate the balance of the valuation allowance:

Year 2

Unrealized gain cannot exceed the former balance of the valuation account

Dec. 31 Valuation Allowance for Marketable Securities	20,000	
Unrealized Gain on Marketable Securities		20,000
To increase the carrying value of marketable securities to		
original cost following recovery of market value.		

Note that the amount of unrealized gain recognized is limited to the amount in the valuation account. *Increases in market value above cost are not recognized in the accounting records.* In brief, when marketable securities have been written down to the lower of cost or market, they can be written back up *to original cost* if the market prices recover. However, current rules of the FASB do not permit recognition of a market rise above the original cost of the portfolio.

Because the valuation allowance is based upon a comparison of *total* portfolio cost and market value, the allowance cannot be directly associated with individual investments. The valuation allowance reduces the carrying value of the total portfolio but does not affect the individual carrying values of the investments which comprise the portfolio. Lower-of-cost-or-market adjustments, therefore, have *no effect* upon the gain or loss recognized when an investment is sold. When specific securities are sold, the gain or loss realized from the sale is determined by comparing the *cost* of the securities (without regard to lower-of-cost-or-market adjustments) to their selling price.[3]

Income tax rules for marketable securities   The FASB rules described above are not acceptable in determining income subject to income tax. The only gains or losses recognized for income tax purposes are realized gains and losses resulting from sale of an investment.

The argument for valuation at market value

A weakness in the position taken by the FASB is that some increases in the market value of securities owned are recognized in the financial statements while others are ignored. For this reason, many accountants believe that investments in marketable securities should be valued in the balance sheet at current market price regardless of whether this price is above or below cost. Increases and decreases in market value would then be recognized as gains or losses as these changes occur.

Several strong arguments exist for valuing marketable securities at market value:

1 Market value is a better indicator of the current debt-paying ability represented by the securities than is their original cost.
2 Market values may be objectively determined from market price quotations.
3 The market price may be realized at any time without interfering with the normal operations of the business.
4 Changes in market price may constitute a major portion of the economic benefit resulting from investments in marketable securities.

At this point it is important to stress that valuation of marketable securities at current market values which exceed cost is not in accordance with the present accounting practices of most companies.[4] However, the valuation of marketable securities is a controversial issue in the accounting profession and may be an area of forthcoming change in generally accepted accounting principles.

Presentation of marketable securities in financial statements

Gains and losses on the sale of investments, as well as interest and dividend revenue, are nonoperating types of income. These items should be specifically identified in the income statement and shown after the determination of operating income.

---

[3]The reader may notice that a decline in the market value of securities owned could be reported in the income statement on two separate occasions: first, as an unrealized loss in the period in which the price decline occurs; and second, as a realized loss in the period in which the securities are sold. However, after securities with market values below cost have been sold, the valuation allowance may be reduced or eliminated. The entry to reduce the valuation allowance involves the recognition of an unrealized gain which offsets the unrealized losses reported in earlier periods.

[4]Companies whose principal business activity includes investing in marketable securities (such as mutual funds and brokerage houses) currently use market values in accounting for their investment portfolios.

Although marketable securities are usually classified as current assets in the balance sheet, they may alternatively be classified as long-term investments if management has a definite intention to hold the securities for more than one year. Regardless of how marketable equity securities are classified in the balance sheet, they are shown at the lower-of-cost-or-market value.

The unrealized gains and losses resulting from application of the lower-of-cost-or-market rule, however, are presented differently in the financial statements depending upon whether the securities portfolio is classified as a current asset or a long-term investment. When the portfolio is viewed as a current asset, the unrealized gains and losses are closed into the Income Summary account and shown in the income statement along with other types of investment income.

In *Statement No. 12,* the FASB ruled that holding gains and losses on *long-term* investments should *not* be included in the measurement of the current year's income because management does not intend to sell these securities in the near future. Therefore, any unrealized loss recognized on long-term investments is shown in the balance sheet as a *reduction in stockholders' equity* instead of being closed into the Income Summary account.

KEY TERMS INTRODUCED OR EMPHASIZED IN CHAPTER 7

Bank reconciliation   A schedule listing the items which make up the difference between the balance shown on the bank statement and the balance of cash according to the depositor's records.

Bond   A formal certificate (or debt instrument) issued by a corporation to borrow money on a long-term basis.

Check register   A simplified version of the cash payments journal (see Chapter 6) used for recording cash payments when a voucher system is in use.

Deposits in transit   Cash receipts which have been entered in the depositor's accounting records and mailed to the bank or left in the bank's night depository, but which reached the bank too late to be credited to the depositor's current monthly bank statement.

Lower of cost or market   The technique of valuing a portfolio of marketable equity securities in the balance sheet at the lower of cost or current market value. A write-down to a market value below cost involves recognition of an *unrealized loss.*

Marketable securities   A highly liquid type of investment which can be sold at any time without interfering with normal operation of the business. Usually classified as a current asset second only to cash in liquidity.

Maturity value   The amount (usually $1,000 per bond) which the issuing company must pay to redeem its bonds at the date they mature (become due). Bond prices and interest rates are stated as percentages of maturity value.

NSF check   A customer's check which was deposited but returned because of a lack of funds (Not Sufficient Funds) in the account on which the check was drawn.

Outstanding checks   Checks issued by a business to suppliers, employees, or other payees but not yet presented to the bank for payment.

Petty cash fund   A small amount of cash set aside for making minor cash payments for which writing of checks is not practicable.

Portfolio An investment in various marketable securities which is managed and accounted for as a single unit rather than as a number of separate investments. An investor may have both short-term and long-term investment portfolios.

Realization principle The principle of recognizing revenue and gains in the accounting records only when the earning process is virtually complete. The usual criterion for realization is a sales transaction.

Unrealized losses and gains An unrealized loss results from writing down marketable equity securities to a market value below cost. An unrealized gain results from restoring a former write-down because of a recovery in market price. Securities cannot be written up above aggregate cost. Unrealized losses and gains on marketable securities classified as current assets are included in the determination of the year's net income. The net unrealized loss on marketable securities classified as long-term investments is excluded from the determination of net income and is shown in the balance sheet as a reduction in stockholders' equity.

Valuation allowance for marketable securities The contra-asset account used to reduce the carrying value of marketable equity securities from cost to a market value below cost. Adjusted at each balance sheet date.

Voucher A document prepared to authorize and describe an expenditure.

Voucher register A special journal used to record all liabilities which have been approved for payment.

Voucher system A method of controlling expenditures and the payment of liabilities. Requires that every liability be recorded as soon as it is incurred, and that checks be issued only in payment of approved liabilities.

DEMONSTRATION PROBLEM FOR YOUR REVIEW

The information listed below is available in reconciling the bank statement for the White River Company on November 30, 19___.

(1) The ledger account for Cash showed a balance at November 30 of $12,761.94; the bank statement at November 30 indicated a balance of $9,734.70.

(2) The November 30 cash receipts of $5,846.20 had been mailed to the bank on that date and did not appear among the deposits on the November bank statement.

(3) The paid checks returned with the November bank statement disclosed two errors in the cash records. Check no. 936 for $504.00 had been erroneously recorded as $50.40 in the cash payments journal, and check no. 942 for $245.50 had been recorded as $254.50. Check no. 936 was issued in payment of advertising expense, and check no. 942 was for the acquisition of office equipment.

(4) Included with the November bank statement was an NSF check for $220 signed by a customer, J. Wilson. This amount had been charged against the bank account on November 30.

(5) Of the checks issued in November, the following were not included among the paid checks returned by the bank:

Check No.	Amount	Check No.	Amount
924	$136.25	944	$ 95.00
940	105.00	945	716.15
941	11.46	946	60.00
943	826.70		

(6) A service charge for $340 by the bank had been made in error against the White River Company account.

(7) A non-interest-bearing note receivable for $1,890 owned by the White River Company had been left with the bank for collection. On November 30 the company received a memorandum from the bank indicating that the note had been collected and credited to the company's account after deduction of a $5 collection charge. No entry has been made by the company to record collection of the note.

(8) A debit memorandum for $12 was enclosed with the paid checks at November 30. This charge covered the cost of printing checks bearing the White River Company name and address.

Instructions

a Prepare a bank reconciliation at November 30, 19___.

b Prepare journal entries required as of November 30, 19___, to bring the company's records up to date. Use one journal entry to record all increases in the cash account and another journal entry to record all decreases.

SOLUTION TO DEMONSTRATION PROBLEM

a

WHITE RIVER COMPANY
Bank Reconciliation
November 30, 19___

Balance per depositor's records, Nov. 30			$12,761.94
Add: Error in recording check no. 942			
for office equipment:			
Recorded as	$254.50		
Correct amount	245.50	$ 9.00	
Note receivable collected by bank, $1,890,			
less collection charge, $5		1,885.00	1,894.00
			$14,665.94
Less: Error in recording check no. 936			
for advertising expense:			
Correct amount	$504.00		
Recorded as	50.40	$ 453.60	
NSF check, J. Wilson		220.00	
Charge by bank for printing checks		12.00	685.60
Adjusted balance			$13,970.34
Balance per bank statement, Nov. 30			$ 9,734.70
Add: Deposit of Nov. 30 not recorded by bank		$5,846.20	
Service charge made by bank in error		340.00	6,186.20
Subtotal (carried forward to next page)			$15,920.90

Subtotal (carried forward from preceding page)		$15,920.90
Less: Outstanding checks on Nov. 30:		
No. 924	$ 136.25	
No. 940	105.00	
No. 941	.11.46	
No. 943	826.70	
No. 944	95.00	
No. 945	716.15	
No. 946	60.00	1,950.56
Adjusted balance (as above)		$13,970.34

b   ***General Journal***

19___		
Nov. 30 *Cash*	1,894.00	
Miscellaneous Expense	5.00	
Office Equipment		9.00
Notes Receivable		1,890.00
To record increase in Cash account as indicated by		
bank reconciliation.		
Nov. 30 *Advertising Expense*	453.60	
Miscellaneous Expense	12.00	
Accounts Receivable, J. Wilson	220.00	
Cash		685.60

REVIEW QUESTIONS

1 In bidding for some surplus property offered at auction by a government agency, the Argus Company on December 28 drew a check for $3,000 and mailed it with the bid. The government agency on January 3 rejected the bid and returned the check. Should the $3,000 be included as cash in the December 31 balance sheet, which was prepared by the Argus Company on January 5 after the check had been returned? Explain.

2 Does the expression "efficient management of cash" mean anything more than procedures to prevent losses from fraud or theft? Explain.

3 Mention some principles to be observed by a business in establishing strong internal control over cash receipts.

4 Explain how internal control over cash transactions is strengthened by compliance with the following rule: "Deposit each day's cash receipts intact in the bank, and make all disbursements by check."

5 Name three internal control practices relating to cash which would be practicable even in a small business having little opportunity for division of duties.

6 With respect to a *voucher system,* what is meant by the terms *voucher, voucher register,* and *check register?*

7 What is the greatest single advantage of the voucher system?

8 Randall Company uses a voucher system to control its cash disbursements. With respect to a purchase of merchandise, what three documents would need to be examined to verify that the voucher should be approved?

9 Suggest an internal control procedure to prevent the documents supporting a paid voucher from being resubmitted later in support of another cash disbursement.

10 Pico Stationery Shop has for years maintained a petty cash fund of $75, which is replenished twice a month.

    a How many debit entries would you expect to find in the Petty Cash account each year?

    b When would expenditures from the petty cash fund be entered in the ledger accounts?

11 Classify each of the numbered reconciling items listed below under one of the following headings: (a) an addition to the balance per depositor's records; (b) a deduction from the balance per depositor's records; (c) an addition to the balance per bank statement; (d) a deduction from the balance per bank statement.

    (1) Deposits in transit

    (2) Outstanding checks

    (3) Customer's check deposited but returned by bank marked NSF

    (4) Bank service charges

    (5) Collection by bank of note receivable left with bank for collection in behalf of depositor

12 A check for $455 issued in payment of an account payable was erroneously listed in the cash payments journal as $545. The error was discovered early in the following month when the paid check was returned by the bank. What corrective action is needed?

13 In the reconciliation of a bank account, what reconciling items necessitate a journal entry in the depositor's accounting records?

14 It is standard accounting practice to treat as cash all checks received from customers. When a customer's check is received, recorded, and deposited, but later returned by the bank marked NSF, what accounting entry or entries would be appropriate?

15 Why are investments in marketable securities usually regarded as current assets?

16 Why must an investor who owns numerous marketable securities maintain a marketable securities subsidiary ledger?

17 If an investor buys a bond between interest dates, he or she pays as a part of the purchase price the accrued interest since the last interest date. On the other hand, if the investor buys a share of common or preferred stock, no "accrued dividend" is added to the quoted price. Explain why this difference exists.

18 Because of a decline in market prices, National Corporation had to write down the carrying value of its investment in marketable securities by $70,000 in the current year. In the determination of net income for the current year, does it make any difference if National Corporation's investment portfolio is classified as a current asset or a long-term investment? Explain fully.

19 In the current asset section of its balance sheet, Delta Industries shows marketable securities at a market value $82,000 below cost. If the market value of these securities rises by $99,000 during the next accounting period, how large an unrealized gain (if any) should Delta Industries include in its next income statement? Explain fully.

20 How does the financial reporting requirement of valuing marketable securities at the lower-of-cost-or-market value compare with income tax rules concerning marketable securities?

21 "To substitute current market value for cost as a basis for valuing marketable securities would represent a departure from traditional accounting practice." Discuss the case for and against using market value consistently as the basis of valuation in accounting for marketable securities.

EXERCISES

Ex. 7-1 Solana Corporation maintains a petty cash fund of $300. At December 31, the end of the company's fiscal year, the fund contained the following:

Currency and coins	$ 78.82
Expense vouchers:	
Taxi fares (Debit Travel Expense)	34.98
Office supplies expense	146.20
Contributions to Boy Scouts and others	40.00
Total	$300.00

Prepare the entry (in general journal form) to replenish the petty cash fund.

Ex. 7-2 At July 31 the Cash account in the ledger of Art Mart, Inc., showed a balance of $36,500. The bank statement, however, showed a balance of $43,700 at the same date. If the only reconciling items consisted of a $2,400 deposit in transit, a bank service charge of $4, and 30 outstanding checks, what was the total amount of the outstanding checks?

Ex. 7-3 At the end of the month Matson Company received a bank statement showing a balance of $28,000 on deposit. Among the reconciling items were outstanding checks totaling $5,800, bank service charges of $6, a deposit in transit of $4,400, and a memorandum showing that a $2,400 note receivable owned by Matson Company and left with the bank for collection had been collected and credited to the company's account.

a What is the adjusted amount of cash which should appear on the Matson Company's balance sheet?

b What was the balance per the depositor's records before making adjusting entries for any of the reconciling items?

Ex. 7-4 Gray Rock Company uses a voucher system. You are to record the following transactions in *general journal form* (without explanations). Also indicate after each entry the book of original entry in which the transaction would in practice be recorded.

a Voucher no. 100 prepared to purchase office equipment at cost of $4,000 from Coast Furniture Co.

b Check no. 114 issued in payment of voucher no. 100.

c Voucher no. 101 prepared to establish a petty cash fund of $150.

d Check no. 115 issued in payment of voucher no. 101.

e Voucher no. 102 prepared to replenish the petty cash fund which contained $40 cash, and receipts for postage $38, miscellaneous expense $54, and delivery service $18.

f Check no. 116 issued in payment of voucher no. 102. Check cashed and proceeds placed in petty cash fund.

Ex. 7-5 The following information relates to the Truesdale Company's September 30 cash balance:

(1) As of September 30, cash per the accounting records was $5,815; per bank statement, $5,327.

(2) Cash receipts of $1,451 on September 30 were not deposited until October 1.

(3) The following memoranda accompanied the bank statement:

    (a) A debit memo for service charges for the month of September, $8.

    (b) A debit memo attached to a $200 check for Susan Scott, marked NSF.

(4) The following checks had been issued but were not included among the paid checks returned by the bank: No. 921 for $326, No. 924 for $684, and No. 925 for $161.

Instructions

a Prepare a bank reconciliation as of September 30.

b Prepare the necessary adjusting journal entries.

Ex. 7-6   Yamato Company purchased as a short-term investment $10,000 face value of the 9% bonds of Lorenzo, Inc., on March 31 of the current year, at a total cost of $10,125, including interest accrued since January 1. Interest is paid by Lorenzo, Inc., on June 30 and December 31. On July 31, four months after the purchase, Yamato Company sold the bonds and interest accrued since July 1 for a total price of $10,105.

    Prepare in general journal form all entries required in the accounting records of Yamato Company relating to the investment in Lorenzo, Inc., bonds. (Commissions are to be ignored.)

Ex. 7-7   Prepare general journal entries in the accounting records of Axel Masters, Inc., to record the following transactions.

Jan. 7 Purchased as a temporary investment 1,000 shares of Reed Company common stock at a price of $41.50 per share, plus a brokerage commission of $500.

Feb. 12 Received a cash dividend of $2.20 per share on the investment in Reed Company stock.

Aug. 14 Sold 500 shares of Reed Company common stock at a price of $46 per share, less a brokerage commission of $290.

Ex. 7-8   The cost and market value of Edgebrook Corporation's portfolio of marketable securities at the end of Years 1 and 2 are shown below. The marketable securities are viewed as a current asset.

	Cost	Market Value
Year 1	$79,000	$67,800
Year 2	91,000	97,600

    Show how the portfolio would appear in the balance sheet at the end of Year 1 and at the end of Year 2. If appropriate, use a valuation account in your presentation.

PROBLEMS

7-1   Robert Smith, a <u>trusted</u> employee of Bluestem Products, found himself in personal financial difficulties and carried out the following plan to steal $1,000 from the company and to conceal the fraud.

    Smith removed $1,000 in currency from the cash register. This amount represented the bulk of the cash received in over-the-counter sales during the three business days since the last bank deposit. Smith then removed a $1,000 check from the day's incoming mail; this check had been mailed in by a customer, Larry Jansen, in full payment of his account. Smith made no entry in the cash receipts journal for the $1,000 collection from Jansen but deposited the check in Bluestem Products' bank account in place of the $1,000 of over-the-counter cash receipts he had stolen. In order to keep Jansen from protesting when his month-end statement reached him, Smith made a general journal entry debiting Sales Returns and Allowances and crediting Accounts Receivable—Larry Jansen. Smith posted this entry to the two general ledger accounts affected and also to Jansen's account in the subsidiary ledger for accounts receivable.

Instructions

a Did these actions by Smith cause the general ledger to be out of balance or the subsidiary ledger to disagree with the control account? Explain.

b Several weaknesses in internal control apparently exist in Bluestem Products. Indicate the corrective actions needed.

7-2 Portside, Inc., reports the following information concerning cash balances and cash transaction for the month of September:

(1) The Cash account showed the following entries during September:

Cash

Sept	1	Balance			18,341.82	Sept	30			CD7	11,514.63
	30		CR5	14,411.58							

(2) Cash balance per bank statement as of September 30 was $20,793.25.

(3) Two debit memoranda accompanied the bank statement: one for $4 was for service charges for the month; the other for $64.60 was attached to an NSF check from A. Smith.

(4) The paid checks returned with the September bank statement disclosed two errors in the cash records. Check no. 832 for $456.30 had been erroneously recorded as $465.30 in the cash payments journal, and check no. 851 for $77.44 had been recorded as $44.77. Check no. 832 was issued in payment for a store display counter; check no. 851 was for telephone expense. Note that both these errors were made by the depositor.

(5) A collection charge for $126.00 (not applicable to Portside, Inc.) was erroneously deducted from the account by the bank. Notice that this error was made by the bank.

(6) Cash receipts of September 30 amounting to $585.25 were mailed to the bank too late to be included in the September bank statement.

(7) Checks outstanding as of September 30 were as follows: no. 860 for $151.93, no 867 for $82.46, and no. 869 for $123.61.

Instructions

a Prepare a bank reconciliation at September 30.

b Prepare the necessary adjusting entries in general journal form.

7-3 Information necessary for the preparation of a bank reconciliation and related journal entries for the Green Valley Motel at March 31 is listed below.

(1) The balance per records of the Green Valley Motel is $17,244.02.

(2) The bank statement shows a balance of $21,278.29 as of March 31.

(3) Accompanying the bank statement was a check of D. Jones for $186.00, which was marked NSF by the bank.

(4) Checks outstanding as of March 31 were as follows: no. 84 for $1,841.02; no. 88 for $1,323.00; no. 89 for $16.26.

(5) Also accompanying the bank statement was a debit memorandum for $44.80 for safe deposit box rent; the bank had erroneously charged this item to the account of the Green Valley Motel.

(6) On March 29, the bank collected a non-interest-bearing note for Green Valley Motel. The note was for $2,963; the bank charged a collection fee of $8.40.

(7) A deposit of $2,008.50 was in transit; it had been mailed to the bank on March 31.

(8) In recording a $160 check received on account from a customer, Ross Company, the accountant for the Green Valley Motel erroneously listed the collection in the cash receipts journal as $16. The check appeared correctly among the deposits on the March bank statement.

(9) The bank service charge for March amounted to $5.31; a debit memo in this amount was returned with the bank statement.

Instructions

a Prepare a bank reconciliation at March 31.

b Prepare the necessary journal entries.

7-4 Rancho Lumber Co. had never given much attention to internal control concepts and the internal conrols over cash transactions were not adequate. Donna Jones, the cashier-bookkeeper, handled cash receipts, made small disbursements from the cash receipts, maintained accounting records, and prepared the monthly reconciliations of the bank account.

At April 30, the statement received from the bank showed a balance on deposit of $30,510. The outstanding checks were as follows: no. 7062 for $371.16, no. 7183 for $306.00, no. 7284 for $470.61, no. 8621 for $315.34, no. 8623 for $613.80, and no. 8632 for $311.04. The balance of cash shown by the company's ledger account for Cash was $35,474.96, which included the cash on hand. The bank statement for April showed a credit of $360 arising from the collection of a note left with the bank; the company's accounts did not include an entry to record this collection.

Recognizing the weakness existing in internal control over cash transactions, Jones removed all the cash on hand in excess of $6,025.14, and then prepared the following reconciliation in an attempt to conceal this theft.

Balance per accounting records, Apr. 30		*$35,474.96*
Add: Outstanding checks:		
No. 8621	*$315.34*	
No. 8623	*613.80*	
No. 8632	*311.04*	*1,060.18*
		$36,535.14
Less: Cash on hand		*6,025.14*
Balance per bank statement, Apr. 30		*$30,510.00*
Less: Unrecorded credit		*360.00*
True cash, Apr. 30		*$30,150.00*

Instructions

a Determine how much cash Jones took. Prepare a bank reconciliation in a form which first shows the balance per the accounting records after adding the cash from collection of the note and, second, shows an adjusted bank balance after deducting the proper amount for all outstanding checks. The two adjusted balances will not agree; the difference is the amount of undeposited cash which should be on hand. Comparison of the undeposited cash which should be on hand with the actual amount on hand of $6,025.14 will indicate the amount of the cash shortage.

b Explain how Jones attempted to conceal her theft in the improper bank reconciliation shown on the preceding page. Your explanation may be in the form of a list of dollar amounts which add up to the total cash stolen by Jones.

c Suggest some specific internal control devices for the Rancho Lumber Co.

7-5 In order to handle small cash disbursements in an efficient manner, Capital Ventures, Inc., established a petty cash fund on December 1 of the current year. The company does not use a voucher system. The following transactions occurred relating to petty cash.

Dec. 1 A check for $100 was issued and cashed to establish a petty cash fund.

Dec. 15 The fund was replenished after a count which revealed the following cash and petty cash vouchers for disbursements:

Office supplies expense	$15.70
Postage expense	26.00
Travel expense	31.25
Miscellaneous expense	8.40
Business promotion expense	12.70
Currency and coin	5.95

Dec. 31 A count of the fund at year-end disclosed the following:

Office supplies expense	$23.76
Postage expense	24.00
Travel expense	23.75
Miscellaneous expense	16.25
Currency and coin	12.24

A check was issued on December 31 to replenish the petty cash fund. A second check for $50 was used to increase the amount of the fund to $150.

Instructions

a Prepare entries in general journal form to record the above transactions.

b Explain briefly why the petty cash fund should be replenished at the end of the accounting period even though the fund contains considerable cash.

7-6 On April 1, Year 7, Imperial Motors purchased $60,000 face value of the 12% bonds of Crest Theatres, Inc., at a price of 96 plus accrued interest. The bonds pay interest semiannually on March 1 and September 1.

Instructions

a In general journal form, prepare the entries required in Year 7 to record:
 (1) Purchase of the bonds on April 1
 (2) Receipt of the semiannual interest payment on September 1
 (3) Adjustment of the accounts at December 31 for bond interest earned since September 1. (Imperial Motors adjusts and closes its accounts annually, using the calendar year.)

b Assume that on January 31, Year 8, Imperial Motors sells the entire investment in Crest Theatre bonds for $57,850 plus accrued interest. Prepare the entries to:
  (1) Accrue bond interest earned from December 31, Year 7, through the date of sale
  (2) Record the sale of the bonds on January 31

7-7 In the current asset section of its most recent balance sheet, Mirage Corporation showed marketable securities as follows:

Marketable securities	*$72,400*	
Less: Valuation allowance for marketable securities	*5,250*	*$67,150*

Shortly after the above balance sheet date, Mirage Corporation sold for $44,000 marketable securities which had cost $42,600.

Instructions

a Prepare a journal entry to record the above sale for $44,000 of marketable securities which had cost $42,600.

b The following numbered items are ***independent*** assumptions as to the current market value of the equity securities which remain in Mirage Corporation's portfolio at the next balance sheet date after the sale recorded in part **a**. For each assumption, prepare the journal entry required to adjust the carrying value of the portfolio to the lower of cost or market as of the balance sheet date. Show computations supporting each entry.
  (1) Assume current market value is $22,100.
  (2) Assume current market value is $29,270.
  (3) Assume current market value is $31,800.

7-8 Target Corporation owns marketable equity securities which cost $100,000 and are classified in the balance sheet as a long-term investment. In the current year, the market value of the securities declined from an amount greater than cost to $90,000, and Target Corporation correctly made the following year-end adjusting entry:

Unrealized Loss on Long-Term Investments	*10,000*	
Valuation Allowance for Long-Term Investments		*10,000*
To adjust carrying value of long-term investment in equity securities		
to lower of cost or market.		

Instructions

For each of the financial statement items or relationships listed below, explain what change (if any) would result if the marketable securities were classified as a current asset instead of a long-term investment.

a Current assets

b Total assets

c Current ratio (With the portfolio classified as a long-term investment, current assets total $180,000 and current liabilities total $100,000.)

d Net income

e Retained earnings

f Total stockholders' equity
  The type of explanation desired is illustrated below, using item **a** as an example:

a Current assets would be increased by $90,000 if the securities were classified as a current asset.

7-9   The portfolio of marketable securities owned by Blue Marlin Corporation at January 1 of the current year consisted of the four securities listed below. All marketable securities are classified as current assets.

$100,000 maturity value Bay Resort Corporation 13% bonds due Dec. 31, 199X. Interest is payable on June 30 and Dec. 31 of each year. Cost basis $976 per bond	*$97,600*
$50,000 maturity value Copper Products Company 9% bonds due Apr. 30, 198X. Interest is payable on Apr. 30 and Oct. 31 of each year. Cost basis $910 per bond	*45,500*
1,200 shares of Aztec Corporation common stock. Cost basis $58.50 per share	*70,200*

Transactions relating to marketable securities during the current year were as follows:

Jan. 21   Received quarterly cash dividend of $1.20 per share on the 1,200 shares of Aztec Corporation capital stock.

Mar. 5   Sold 400 shares of Aztec Corporation capital stock at a price of $67 per share, less a brokerage commission of $280.

Apr. 20   Received quarterly cash dividend of $1.20 per share on the remaining 800 shares of Aztec Corporation capital stock.

Apr. 30   Received semiannual interest payment on Copper Products Company 9% bonds. Accrued interest of $750 had been recorded on December 31 of last year in the Bond Interest Receivable account.

May 1   Sold $25,000 face value of the Copper Products Company bonds at 84, less a commission of $125.

June 30   Received semiannual interest payment on Bay Resort Company bonds.

July 21   Received quarterly dividend on 800 shares of Aztec Corporation capital stock. Amount of the dividend has increased to $1.40 per share.

Aug. 19   Purchased 1,000 shares of Rhoades International capital stock at $76 per share, plus a brokerage commission of $500.

Oct. 20   Received $1.40 quarterly dividend on 800 shares of Aztec Corporation capital stock.

Oct. 31   Received semiannual interest payment on remaining $25,000 face value Copper Products Company 9% bonds.

Dec. 31   Received semiannual interest payment on Bay Resort Corporation 13% bonds.

At December 31 of the current year, the quoted market prices of the marketable equity securities owned by Blue Marlin Co. were as follows: Aztec Corporation, $63 per share; Rhoades Corporation, $65 per share.

Instructions

a Prepare journal entries to record the transactions listed above. Include an adjusting entry to record the accrued interest on the remaining Copper Products Company bonds through December 31. (Do not consider a lower-of-cost-or-market adjustment in part **a.**)

b Prepare a schedule showing the cost and market value of the marketable equity securities owned by Blue Marlin Corporation at December 31. Prepare the adjusting entry, if one is required, to reduce the portfolio to the lower of cost or market. (At January 1, the market value of the portfolio was above cost and the Valuation Allowance for Marketable Securities account had a zero balance.)

BUSINESS DECISION PROBLEM 7

June Davis inherited a highly successful business, Glacier Corporation, shortly after her twenty-second birthday and took over the active management of the business. A portion of the company's business consisted of over-the-counter sales for cash, but most sales were on credit and were shipped by truck. Davis had no knowledge of internal control practices and relied implicitly upon the bookkeeper-cashier, J. K. Wiley, in all matters relating to cash and accounting records. Wiley, who had been with the company for many years, maintained the accounting records and prepared all financial statements with the help of two assistants, made bank deposits, signed checks, and prepared bank reconciliations.

The monthly income statements submitted to Davis by Wiley showed a very satisfactory rate of net income; however, the amount of cash in the bank declined steadily during the first 18 months after Davis took over the business. To meet the company's weakening cash position, a bank loan was obtained and a few months later when the cash position again grew critical, the loan was increased.

On April 1, two years after Davis assumed the management of the company, Wiley suddenly left town, leaving no forwarding address. Davis was immediately deluged with claims of creditors who stated their accounts were several months past due and that Wiley had promised all debts would be paid by April 1. The bank telephoned to notify Davis that the company's account was overdrawn and that a number of checks had just been presented for payment.

In an effort to get together some cash to meet this emergency, Davis called on two of the largest customers of the company, to whom substantial sales on account had recently been made, and asked if they could pay their accounts at once. Both customers informed her that their accounts were paid in full. They produced paid checks to substantiate their payments and explained that Wiley had offered them reduced prices on merchandise if they would pay within 24 hours after delivery.

To keep the business from insolvency, Davis agreed to sell at a bargain price a half interest in the company. The sale was made to Helen Smith, who had had considerable experience in the industry. One condition for the sale was that Smith should become the general manager of the business. The cash investment by Smith for her half interest was sufficient for the company to meet the demands on it and continue operations.

Immediately after Smith entered the business, she launched an investigation of Wiley's activities. During the course of this investigation the following irregularities were disclosed:

(1) During the last few months of Wiley's employment with the company, bank deposits were much smaller than the cash receipts. Wiley had abstracted most of the receipts and substituted for them a number of worthless checks bearing fictitious signatures. These checks had been accumulated in an envelope marked "Cash Receipts—For Deposit Only."

(2) Numerous legitimate sales of merchandise on account had been charged to fictitious customers. When the actual customer later made payment for the goods, Wiley abstracted the check or cash and made no entry. The account receivable with the fictitious customer remained in the records.

(3) When checks were received from customers in payment of their accounts, Wiley had frequently recorded the transaction by debiting an expense account and crediting Accounts Receivable. In such cases Wiley had removed from the cash receipts an equivalent amount of currency, thus substituting the check for the currency and causing the bank deposit to agree with the recorded cash receipts.

(4) More than $3,000 a month had been stolen from petty cash. Fraudulent petty cash vouchers, mostly charged to the Purchases account, had been created to conceal these thefts and to support the checks cashed to replenish the petty cash fund.

(5) For many sales made over the counter, Wiley had recorded lesser amounts on the cash register or had not rung up any amount. He had abstracted the funds received but not recorded.

(6) To produce income statements that showed profitable operations, Wiley had recorded many fictitious sales. The recorded accounts receivable included many from nonexistent customers.

(7) In preparing bank reconciliations, Wiley had omitted many outstanding checks, thus concealing the fact that the cash in the bank was less than the amount shown by the ledger.

(8) Inventory had been recorded at inflated amounts in order to increase reported profits from the business.

Instructions

a For each of the numbered paragraphs, describe one or more internal control procedures you would recommend to prevent the occurrence of such fraud.

b Apart from specific internal controls over cash and other accounts, what general precaution could June Davis have taken to assure herself that the accounting records were properly maintained and the company's financial statements complete and dependable? Explain fully.

8

RECEIVABLES
AND PAYABLES

After studying this chapter you should be able to:

- Describe the allowance method and the direct charge-off method of accounting for uncollectible accounts.
- Apply the balance sheet approach and the income statement approach to estimating doubtful accounts.
- Account for the write-off and reinstatement of an account receivable.
- Account for credit card sales.
- Account for the receipt of notes, accrual of interest, collection or default, and the discounting of notes to banks.
- Explain the nature of a discount on a note receivable or note payable.
- Discuss the concept of present value.
- Account for notes with the interest charges included in the face amount.

One of the key factors underlying the tremendous expansion of the American economy has been the trend toward selling all types of goods and services on credit. The automobile industry has long been the classic example of the use of retail credit to achieve the efficiencies of large-scale output. Today, however, in nearly every field of retail trade it appears that sales and profits can be increased by granting customers the privilege of making payment a month or more after the date of sale. The sales of manufacturers and wholesalers are made on credit to an even greater extent than in retail trade.

ACCOUNTS RECEIVABLE

The credit department

No business concern wants to sell on credit to a customer who will prove unable or unwilling to pay his or her account. Consequently, most business organizations have a credit department which investigates the credit worthiness of each prospective customer. If the prospective customer is a business concern as, for example, a retail store, the financial statements of the store will be obtained and analyzed to determine its financial strength and the trend of operating results. The credit department naturally prefers to rely upon financial statements which have been audited by certified public accountants.

Regardless of whether the prospective customer is a business concern or an individual consumer, the investigation by the credit department will probably include the obtaining of a credit report from a local credit agency or from a national credit-rating institution such as Dun & Bradstreet, Inc. A credit agency compiles credit data on individuals and business concerns and distributes this information to its clients. Most companies that make numerous sales on credit find it worthwhile to subscribe to the services of one or more credit agencies.

Uncollectible accounts

A business that sells its goods or services on credit will inevitably find that some of its accounts receivable are uncollectible. Regardless of how thoroughly the credit department investigates prospective customers, some uncollectible accounts will arise as a result of errors in judgment or because of unexpected developments. In fact, a limited amount of uncollectible accounts is evidence of a sound credit policy. If the credit department should become too cautious and conservative in rating customers, it might avoid all credit losses but, in so doing, lose profitable business by rejecting many acceptable customers.

Reflecting uncollectible accounts in the financial statements

In measuring business income, one of the most fundamental principles of accounting is that *revenue must be matched with the expenses incurred in generating that revenue.*

Uncollectible accounts expense is caused by selling goods on credit to customers who fail to pay their bills; such expenses, therefore, are incurred in the year in which the sales are made, even though the accounts receivable are not determined to be uncollectible until the following year. An account receivable which originates from a sale on credit in the year 1984 and is determined to be uncollectible sometime during 1985 represents an expense of the year 1984. Unless each year's uncollectible accounts expense is *estimated* and reflected in the year-end balance sheet and income statement, both of these financial statements will be seriously deficient.

To illustrate, let us assume that Arlington Corporation began business on

January 1, Year 1, and made most of its sales on credit throughout the year. At December 31, Year 1, accounts receivable amounted to $200,000. On this date the management reviewed the status of the accounts receivable, giving particular study to accounts which were past due. This review indicated that the collectible portion of the $200,000 of accounts receivable amounted to approximately $190,000. In other words, management estimated that uncollectible accounts expense for the first year of operations amounted to $10,000. The following adjusting entry should be made at December 31, Year 1:

Provision for uncollectible accounts

Uncollectible Accounts Expense 10,000
    Allowance for Doubtful Accounts 10,000
To record the estimated uncollectible accounts expense for Year 1.

The Uncollectible Accounts Expense account created by the debit part of this entry is closed into the Income Summary account in the same manner as any other expense account. The allowance for Doubtful Accounts which was credited in the above journal entry will appear in the balance sheet as a deduction from the face amount of the accounts receivable. It serves to reduce the accounts receivable to their *net realizable value* in the balance sheet, as shown by the following illustration:

ARLINGTON CORPORATION
Partial Balance Sheet
December 31, Year 1

How much is the estimated realizable value of the accounts receivable?

Current assets:		
Cash		$ 75,000
Accounts receivable	$200,000	
Less: Allowance for doubtful accounts	10,000	190,000
Inventory		300,000
Total current assets		$565,000

The Allowance for Doubtful Accounts

There is no way of telling in advance which accounts receivable will be collected and which ones will prove to be worthless. It is therefore not possible to credit the account of any particular customer to reflect our overall estimate of the year's credit losses. Neither is it possible to credit the Accounts Receivable controlling account in the general ledger. If the Accounts Receivable controlling account were to be credited with the estimated amount of doubtful accounts, this controlling account would no longer be in balance with the total of the numerous customers' accounts in the subsidiary ledger. The only practicable alternative, therefore, is to credit a separate account called Allowance for Doubtful Accounts with the amount estimated to be uncollectible.

The Allowance for Doubtful Accounts often is described as a ***contra-asset*** account or a *valuation* account. Both of these terms indicate that the Allowance for Doubtful Accounts has a credit balance, which is offset against the asset Accounts Receivable to produce the proper balance sheet value for this asset.

Estimating uncollectible accounts expense

Before the accounts are closed and financial statements are prepared at the end of the accounting period, an estimate of uncollectible accounts expense must be made. This estimate will usually be based upon past experience, perhaps modified in accordance with current business conditions. Since the allowance for doubtful accounts is necessarily an estimate and not a precise calculation, the factor of personal judgment may play a considerable part in determining the size of this valuation account.

Conservatism as a factor in valuing accounts receivable   The larger the allowance established for doubtful accounts, the lower the net valuation of accounts receivable will be. Some accountants and some business executives tend to favor the most conservative valuation of assets that logically can be supported. Conservatism in the preparation of a balance sheet implies a tendency to resolve uncertainties in the valuation of assets by reporting assets at the lower end of the range of reasonable values rather than by establishing values in a purely objective manner.

The valuation of assets at conservative amounts is a long-standing tradition in accounting, stemming from the days when creditors were the major users of financial statements. From the viewpoint of bankers and others who use financial statements as a basis for granting loans, conservatism in valuing assets has long been regarded as a desirable policy.

Two methods of estimating uncollectible accounts expense

The provision for uncollectible accounts is an estimate of expense sustained in the current year. Two alternative approaches are widely used in making the annual estimate of uncollectible accounts. One method consists of adjusting the valuation account to a new balance equal to the estimated uncollectible portion of the existing accounts receivable. This method is referred to as the *balance sheet* approach and rests on an *aging of the accounts receivable*. The adjusting entry takes into consideration the existing balance in the Allowance for Doubtful Accounts.

The alternative method requires an adjusting entry computed as a percentage of the year's net sales. This method may be regarded as the *income statement* approach to estimating uncollectible accounts expense. This *percentage of sales* method emphasizes the expense side of the adjustment and leaves out of consideration any existing balance in the valuation allowance account. If any substantial balance should accumulate in the Allowance for Doubtful Accounts, however, a change in the percentage figure being applied to sales might be appropriate. These two methods are explained below.

Aging the accounts receivable   A past-due account receivable is always viewed with some suspicion. The fact that a receivable is past due suggests that the customer is either unable or unwilling to pay. The analysis of accounts receivable by age is known as aging the accounts, as illustrated by the schedule below.

Analysis of Accounts Receivable by Age
December 31, 19___

Customer	Total	Not Yet Due	1–30 Days Past Due	31–60 Days Past Due	61–90 Days Past Due	Over 90 Days Past Due
A. B. Adams	$ 500	$ 500				
B. L. Baker	150			$ 150		
R. D. Carl	800	800				
H. V. Davis	900				$ 800	$ 100
R. M. Evans	400	400				
Others	32,250	16,300	$10,000	4,200	200	1,550
Totals	$35,000	$18,000	$10,000	$4,350	$1,000	$1,650
Percentage	100	51	29	12	3	5

If you were credit manager . . .?

This analysis of accounts receivable gives management a useful picture of the status of collections and the probabilities of credit losses. Almost half the total accounts receivable are past due. The question "How long past due?" is pertinent, and is answered by the bottom line of the aging analysis. About 29% of the total receivables are past due from 1 to 30 days; another 12% are past due from 31 to 60 days; about 3% are past due from 61 to 90 days; and 5% of the total receivables consist of accounts past due more than three months. If an analysis of this type is prepared at the end of each month, management will be informed continuously on the trend of collections and can take appropriate action to ease or to tighten credit policy. Moreover, a yardstick is available to measure the performance of the persons responsible for collection activities.

The longer past due an account receivable becomes, the greater the likelihood that it will not be collected in full. In recognition of this fact, the analysis of receivables by age groups can be used as a stepping-stone in determining a reasonable amount to add to the Allowance for Doubtful Accounts. To determine this amount, we estimate the percentage of probable expense for each age group of accounts receivable. This percentage, when applied to the dollar amount in each age group, gives a probable expense for each group. By adding together the probable expense for all the age groups, the required balance in the Allowance for Doubtful Accounts is determined. The following schedule lists the group totals from the preceding illustration and shows how the total probable expense from uncollectible accounts is computed.

Accounts Receivable by Age Groups

	Amount	Percentage Considered Uncollectible	Allowance for Doubtful Accounts
Not yet due	$18,000	1	$ 180
1–30 days past due	10,000	3	300
31–60 days past due	4,350	10	435
61–90 days past due	1,000	20	200
Over 90 days past due	1,650	50	825
Totals	$35,000		$1,940

Estimate of probable uncollectible accounts expense

This summary indicates that an allowance for doubtful accounts of $1,940 is required. Before making the adjusting entry, it is necessary to consider the existing balance in the allowance account. If the Allowance for Doubtful Accounts has a credit balance of, say, $500, the adjusting entry should be for $1,440 in order to bring the account up to the required balance of $1,940. This entry is as follows:

Increasing allowance for doubtful accounts

Uncollectible Accounts Expense	1,440	
Allowance for Doubtful Accounts		1,440

To increase the valuation account to the estimated required total of $1,940, computed as follows:

Present credit balance of valuation account	$ 500
Current provision for doubtful accounts	1,440
New credit balance in valuation account	$1,940

On the other hand, if the Allowance for Doubtful Accounts contained a *debit* balance of $500 before adjustment, the adjusting entry would be made in the amount of $2,440 ($1,940 + $500) in order to create the desired credit balance of $1,940. (The circumstances which could lead to a temporary debit balance in the Allowance for Doubtful Accounts will be explained later in this chapter.)

Estimating uncollectible accounts as a percentage of net sales   An alternative approach preferred by some companies consists of computing the charge to uncollectible accounts expense as a percentage of the net sales for the year. The question to be answered is not "How large a valuation allowance is needed to reduce our receivables to realizable value?" Instead, the question is stated as "How much uncollectible accounts expense is associated with this year's volume of sales?" This method may be regarded as the *income statement* approach to estimating uncollectible accounts.

As an example, assume that for several years the expense of uncollectible accounts has averaged 1% of net sales (sales minus returns and allowances and sales discounts). At the end of the current year, before adjusting entries, the following account balances appear in the ledger:

	Dr	Cr
Sales		$1,260,000
Sales returns and allowances	$40,000	
Sales discounts	20,000	
Allowance for doubtful accounts		1,500

The *net sales* of the current year amount to $1,200,000; 1% of this amount is $12,000. The existing balance in the Allowance for Doubtful Accounts *should be ignored in computing the amount of the adjusting entry,* because the percentage of net sales method stresses the *relationship between uncollectible accounts expense and net sales* rather than the valuation of receivables at the balance sheet date. The entry is

<table>
<tr><td style="width:20%">

Provision for uncollectible accounts based on percentage of net sales

</td><td>

Uncollectible Accounts Expense 12,000
    Allowance for Doubtful Accounts 12,000
To record uncollectible accounts expense of 1% of the year's net sales (.01 × $1,200,000).

</td></tr>
</table>

If a company makes both cash sales and credit sales, it is better to exclude the cash sales from consideration and to compute the percentage relationship of uncollectible accounts expense to credit sales only.

This approach of estimating uncollectible accounts receivable as a percentage of credit sales is easier to apply than the method of aging accounts receivable. The aging of receivables, however, tends to give a more reliable estimate of uncollectible accounts because of the consideration given to the age and collectibility of the specific accounts receivable at the balance sheet date. Some companies use the income statement approach for preparing monthly financial statements and internal reports but use the balance sheet method for preparing annual financial statements.

Writing off an uncollectible account receivable

Whenever an account receivable from a specific customer is determined to be uncollectible, it no longer qualifies as an asset and should be written off. To *write off* an account receivable is to reduce the balance of the customer's account to zero. The journal entry to accomplish this consists of a credit to the Accounts Receivable controlling account in the general ledger (and to the customer's account in the subsidiary ledger), and an offsetting debit to the Allowance for Doubtful Accounts.

Referring again to the example of Arlington Corporation as shown on page 296, the ledger accounts were as follows after the adjusting entry for estimated uncollectible accounts had been made on December 31, Year 1:

Accounts receivable	$200,000
Less: Allowance for doubtful accounts	10,000

Next let us assume that on January 27, Year 2, customer William Brown became bankrupt and the account receivable from him in the amount of $1,000 was determined to be worthless. The following entry should be made by Arlington Corporation:

Writing off an uncollectible account

Allowance for Doubtful Accounts 1,000
    Accounts Receivable, William Brown 1,000
To write off the receivable from William Brown as uncollectible.

The important thing to note in this entry is that the debit is made to the Allowance for Doubtful Accounts and *not* to the Uncollectible Accounts Expense account. The estimated expense of customer credit losses is charged to the Uncollectible Accounts Expense account at the end of each accounting period. When a particular account receivable is later determined to be worthless and is written off, this action does not represent an additional expense but merely confirms our previous estimate of the expense. If the Uncollectible Accounts Expense account were first charged with *estimated* credit losses and then later charged with *proven* credit losses, we would be double counting the actual uncollectible accounts expense.

After the entry writing off William Brown's account has been posted, the Accounts Receivable controlling account and the Allowance for Doubtful Accounts appear as follows:

Accounts Receivable

Both accounts reduced by write-off of worthless receivable

Year 1		Year 2	
Dec. 31	200,000	Jan. 27 (Brown write-off)	1,000

Allowance for Doubtful Accounts

Year 2		Year 1	
Jan. 27 (Brown write-off)	1,000	Dec. 31	10,000

Note that the *net* amount of the accounts receivable was unchanged by writing off William Brown's account against the Allowance for Doubtful Accounts. The write-off reduced the asset account by the same amount.

Net value of receivables unchanged by write-off

Before the Write-Off		**After the Write-Off**	
Accounts receivable	$200,000	Accounts receivable	$199,000
Less: Allowance for		Less: Allowance for	
doubtful accounts	10,000	doubtful accounts	9,000
Net value of receivables	$190,000	Net value of receivables	$190,000

The fact that writing off a worthless receivable against the Allowance for Doubtful Accounts does not change the net carrying value of accounts receivable shows that no expense is entered in the accounting records when an account receivable is written off. This example bears out the point stressed earlier in the chapter: *Credit losses belong in the period in which the sale is made, not in a later period in which the account receivable is discovered to be uncollectible.*

Write-offs seldom agree with previous estimates The total amount of accounts receivable written off in a given year will seldom, if ever, be exactly equal to the estimated amount previously credited to the Allowance for Doubtful Accounts.

If the amounts written off as uncollectible turn out to be less than the estimated amount, the Allowance for Doubtful Accounts will continue to show a credit balance. If the amounts written off as uncollectible are greater than the estimated amount, the Allowance for Doubtful Accounts will acquire a *temporary debit balance*, which will be eliminated by the adjustment at the end of the period.

Recovery of an account receivable previously written off

Occasionally a receivable which has been written off as worthless will later be collected in full or in part. Such collections are often referred to as *recoveries* of bad debts. Collection of an account receivable previously written off is evidence that the write-off was an error; the receivable should therefore be reinstated as an asset.

Let us assume, for example, that a past-due account receivable in the amount of $400 from J. B. Barker was written off by the following entry:

Barker account considered uncollectible	*Allowance for Doubtful Accounts* 400	
	Accounts Receivable, J. B. Barker	400
	To write off the receivable from J. B. Barker as uncollectible.	

At some later date the customer, J. B. Barker, pays the account in full. The entry to restore Barker's account will be

Barker account reinstated	*Accounts Receivable, J. B. Barker* 400	
	Allowance for Doubtful Accounts	400
	To reverse the entry writing off J. B. Barker's account.	

A separate entry will be made in the cash receipts journal to record the collection from Barker. This entry will debit Cash and credit Accounts Receivable, J. B. Barker.

Direct charge-off method of recognizing uncollectible accounts expense

A few companies do not use a valuation allowance for accounts receivable. Instead of making adjusting entries to record uncollectible accounts expense on the basis of estimates, these companies recognize no uncollectible accounts expense until specific receivables are determined to be worthless. This method makes no attempt to match revenue and related expenses. Uncollectible accounts expense is recorded in the period in which individual accounts receivable are determined to be worthless rather than in the period in which the sales were made.

When the direct charge-off method is in use, the accounts receivable will be listed in the balance sheet at their gross amount, and *no valuation allowance* will be used. The receivables, therefore, are not stated at their probable realizable value.

In the determination of taxable income under present federal income tax regulations, both the direct charge-off method and the allowance method of estimating uncollectible accounts expense are acceptable. From the standpoint of accounting theory, the allowance method is much the better, for it enables expenses to be matched with related revenue and thus aids in making a logical measurement of net income.

Credit card sales

Many retailing businesses avoid the risk of uncollectible accounts by making credit sales to customers who use well-known credit cards, such as American Express, Visa, and MasterCard. A customer who makes a purchase using one of these cards must sign a multiple-copy form, which includes a *credit card draft*. A credit card draft is similar to a check which is drawn upon the funds of the credit card company rather than upon the personal bank account of the customer. The credit card company promptly pays cash to the merchant to redeem these drafts. At the end of each month, the credit card company bills the credit card holder for all the drafts it has redeemed during the month. If the credit card holder fails to pay the amount owed, it is the credit card company which sustains the loss.

By making sales through credit card companies, merchants receive cash more quickly from credit sales and avoid uncollectible accounts expense. Also, the merchant avoids the expenses of investigating customers' credit, maintaining an accounts receivable subsidiary ledger, and making collections from customers.

Bank credit cards   Some widely used credit cards (such as Visa and MasterCard) are issued by banks. When the credit card company is a bank, the retailing business may deposit the signed credit card drafts directly in its bank account, along with the currency and personal checks received from customers. Since banks accept these credit card drafts for immediate deposit, sales to customers using bank credit cards are recorded as cash sales.

In exchange for handling the credit card drafts, the bank makes a monthly service charge which usually runs between 1¼ and 3½% of the amount of the drafts deposited by the merchant during the month. This monthly service charge is automatically deducted from the merchant's bank account and appears with other bank service charges in the merchant's monthly bank statement.

Other credit cards   When customers use nonbank credit cards (such as American Express, Diners' Club, and Carte Blanche), the retailing business cannot deposit the credit card drafts directly in its bank account. Instead of debiting Cash, the merchant records an account receivable from the credit card company. Periodically, the credit card drafts are mailed to the credit card company, which then sends a check to the merchant. Credit card companies, however, do not redeem the drafts at the full sales price. The agreement between the credit card company and the merchant usually allows the credit card company to take a discount of between 31/2 and 5% when redeeming the drafts.

To illustrate the procedures in accounting for these credit card sales, assume that Bradshaw Camera Shop sells a camera for $200 to a customer who uses a Quick Charge credit card. The entry would be

Receivable is from the credit card company

Accounts Receivable, Quick Charge Co.	200	
Sales		200

To record sale to customer using Quick Charge credit card.

At the end of the week, Bradshaw Camera Shop mails credit card drafts totaling $1,200 to Quick Charge Co., which redeems the drafts less a 5% discount. When payment is received, the entry is

Cash	1,140	
Credit Card Discount Expense	60	
Accounts Receivable, Quick Charge Co.		1,200

To record collection of account receivable from Quick Charge Co., less 5% discount.

The expense account, Credit Card Discount Expense, should be included among the selling expenses in the income statement of Bradshaw Camera Shop.

From a theoretical viewpoint, one might argue that the credit card discount expense should be recorded at the date of sale rather than at the date of collection. In this case, the sale of the camera for $200 would have been recorded by debiting Credit Card Discount Expense for $10 and Accounts Receivable, Quick Charge Co. for $190. Although this procedure would be theoretically preferable in terms of matching revenue with related expenses, it requires computing the discount expense separately for each sales transaction. For this reason, it is common practice to record the discount expense at the date of collection. Since the discount expense is small and collection usually occurs shortly after the date of sale, the difference between the two methods does not have a material effect upon the financial statements.

Analysis of accounts receivable

What dollar amount of accounts receivable would be reasonable for a business making annual credit sales of $1,200,000? Comparison of the average amount of accounts receivable with the sales made on credit during the period indicates how long it takes to convert receivables into cash. For example, if annual credit sales of $1,200,000 are made at a uniform rate throughout the year and the accounts receivable at year-end amount to $200,000, we can see at a glance that the receivables represent one-sixth of the year's sales, or about 60 days of uncollected sales. Management naturally wants to make efficient use of the available capital in the business, and therefore is interested in a rapid "turnover" of accounts receivable. If the credit terms offered by the business in this example were, say, 30 days net, the existence of receivables equal to 60 days' sales would warrant investigation. The analysis of receivables is considered more fully in Chapter 16.

NOTES RECEIVABLE

Definition of a promissory note

A promissory note is an unconditional promise in writing to pay on demand or at a future date a definite sum of money.

The person who signs the note and thereby promises to pay is called the *maker* of the note. The person to whom payment is to be made is called the *payee* of the note. In the illustration below, G. L. Smith is the maker of the note and A. B. Davis is the payee.

Simplified form of promissory note

$1,000	Los Angeles, California July 10, 19—

One month *after date* I *promise to pay*

to the order of A. B. Davis

————One thousand and no/100———— *dollars*

payable at First National Bank of Los Angeles

for value received, with interest at 12% per annum.

G. L. Smith

From the viewpoint of the maker, G. L. Smith, the illustrated note is a liability and is recorded by crediting the Notes Payable account. However, from the viewpoint of the payee, A. B. Davis, this same note is an asset and is recorded by debiting the Notes Receivable account. The maker of a note expects to pay cash at the maturity date; the payee expects to receive cash at that date.

Nature of interest

Interest is a charge made for the use of money. To the borrower (maker of a note) interest is an expense; to the lender (payee of a note) interest is revenue.

Computing interest   A formula used in computing interest is as follows:

$$\text{Principal} \times \text{Rate of Interest} \times \text{Time} = \text{Interest}$$

(Often expressed as $P \times R \times T = I$)

10,000 × .09% × $5

Interest rates are usually stated on an annual basis. For example, the interest on a $1,000, one-year, 12% note is computed as follows:

$$\$1,000 \times 0.12 \times 1 = \$120$$

If the term of the note were only four months instead of a year, the interest charge would be $40, computed as follows:

$$\$1,000 \times 0.12 \times \tfrac{4}{12} = \$40$$

If the term of the note is expressed in days, the exact number of days must be used in computing the interest. *The day on which a note is dated is not included; the day on which a note falls due is included.* Thus, a note dated today and maturing tomorrow involves only one day's interest. As a matter of convenience in making calculations, it is customary to assume that a year contains 360 days. Suppose, for example, that a 60-day, 12% note for $1,000 is drawn on June 10. The interest charge could be computed as follows:

$$\$1,000 \times 0.12 \times \tfrac{60}{360} = \$20$$

The principal of the note ($1,000) plus the interest ($20) equals $1,020, and this amount (the *maturity value*) will be payable on August 9. The computation of days to maturity is as follows:

Days remaining in June (30 − 10; date of origin is not included)	20
Days in July	31
Days in August to maturity date (date of payment is included)	9
Total days called for by note	60

Prevailing interest rates   Interest rates, like the prices of goods and services, are always in a process of change. The Federal Reserve Board has a policy of deliberately causing interest rates to rise or fall in an effort to keep the economy running at a reasonable level of activity. Recently, emphasis has been placed on raising interest rates in the hope of limiting inflation.

The rate of interest you receive by depositing money in a savings account at a bank or a savings and loan association depends on the length of time you agree to leave the deposit untouched. The lowest interest rate (presently 5 or 6% a year) applies to a passbook account which gives you the right to withdraw all or part of your deposit at any time. However, you can earn a higher rate of interest (perhaps 10 to 15% a year) if you agree to leave your money on deposit for, say, six months or a year or more.

If you had obtained a long-term mortgage loan on a residence at the time this book was going to press, you would now be paying about 14 or 16% as an annual interest rate. A business obtaining a loan from a bank may pay between 14 and 25% a year. Early in the 1980s interest rates were roughly double the rates which prevailed a few years earlier. The interest rate which banks charge on loans to the largest and strongest corporations is called the *prime rate.* Smaller companies and those not in a strong financial position may have to pay several percentage points more than the prime rate in order to obtain a bank loan.

Many retail stores charge interest on installment accounts at 1½% a month, which is equivalent to 18% a year. Keep in mind that interest rates vary widely depending upon the nature of the loan and the financial strength of the borrower—and upon the fiscal policy of the federal government.

Accounting for notes receivable

In some lines of business, notes receivable are seldom encountered; in other fields they occur frequently and may constitute an important part of total assets. Business concerns that sell high-priced durable goods such as automobiles and farm machinery often accept notes receivable from their customers. Many companies obtain notes receivable in settlement of past-due accounts receivable.

All notes receivable are usually posted to a single account in the general ledger. A subsidiary ledger is not essential because the notes themselves, when filed by due dates, are the equivalent of a subsidiary ledger and provide any necessary information as to maturity, interest rates, collateral pledged, and other details. The amount debited to Notes Receivable is always the *face amount* of the note, regardless of whether or not the note bears interest. When an interest-bearing note is collected, the amount of cash received will be larger than the face amount of the note. The interest collected is credited to an Interest Revenue account, and only the face amount of the note is credited to the Notes Receivable account.

Illustrative entries   Assume that a 12%, 90-day note receivable is acquired from a customer, Marvin White, in settlement of an existing account receivable of $2,000. The entry for acquisition of the note is as follows:

Note received to replace account receivable	Notes Receivable 2,000	
	Accounts Receivable, Marvin White	2,000
	Accepted 12%, 90-day note in settlement of account receivable.	

The entry 90 days later to record collection of the note will be

Collection of principal and interest	Cash 2,060	
	Notes Receivable	2,000
	Interest Revenue	60
	Collected 12%, 90-day note from Marvin White.	

When a note is received from a customer at the time of making a sale of merchandise on account, two entries may be made, as follows:

Sale may be run through accounts receivable when note is received from customer	Accounts Receivable, Russ Company 7,500	
	Sales	7,500
	To record sale of merchandise on account.	

	Notes Receivable 7,500	
	Accounts Receivable, Russ Company	7,500
	To record receipt of note from customer.	

When this procedure is employed, the account with a particular customer in the subsidiary ledger for accounts receivable provides a complete record of all transactions with that customer, regardless of the fact that some sales may have been made on open account and others may have involved a note receivable. Having a complete history of all transactions with a customer on a single ledger card may be helpful in reaching decisions as to collection efforts or further extensions of credit.

If the maker of a note defaults   A note receivable which cannot be collected at maturity is said to have been *defaulted* by the maker. Immediately after the default of a note, an entry should be made by the holder to transfer the amount due from the Notes Receivable account to an account receivable from the debtor.

Assuming that a 60-day, 12% note receivable for $1,000 from Robert Jones is not collected at maturity, the following entry would be made:

Default of note
receivable

Accounts Receivable, Robert Jones	1,020	
Notes Receivable		1,000
Interest Revenue		20

To record default by Robert Jones of a 12%, 60-day note.

The interest earned on the note is recorded as a credit to Interest Revenue and is also included in the account receivable from the maker. The interest receivable on a defaulted note is just as valid a claim against the maker as is the principal of the note; if the principal is collectible, then presumably the interest too can be collected.

The transfer of past-due notes receivable into Accounts Receivable accomplishes two things. First, the Notes Receivable account is limited to current notes not yet matured and is, therefore, regarded as a highly liquid type of asset. Second, the account receivable ledger card will show that a note has been defaulted and will present a complete picture of all transactions with the customer.

Adjustments for interest at end of period   Notes receivable acquired in one accounting period often do not mature until a following period. Interest is being earned throughout the life of the note, and this revenue should be apportioned between accounting periods on a time basis. At the end of an accounting period, interest earned to date on notes receivable should be accrued by an adjusting entry debiting the asset account, Interest Receivable, and crediting Interest Revenue. When the note matures and the interest is received in cash in the following period, the entry to be made consists of a debit to Cash, a credit to Interest Receivable for the amount of the accrual, and a credit to Interest Revenue for the remainder of the interest collected.

Discounting notes receivable

Many business concerns which obtain notes receivable from their customers prefer to sell the notes to a bank for cash rather than to hold them until maturity. Selling a note receivable to a bank or finance company is often called *discounting* a note receivable. The holder of the note endorses the back of the note (as in endorsing a check) and delivers the note to the bank. The bank expects to collect the *maturity value* (principal plus interest) from the maker of the note at the maturity date, but if the maker fails to pay, the bank can demand payment from the endorser.

When a business endorses a note and turns it over to a bank for cash, it is promising to pay the note if the maker fails to do so. The endorser is therefore contingently liable to the bank. A *contingent liability* may be regarded as a potential liability which either will develop into a full-fledged liability or will be eliminated entirely by a future event. The future event in the case of a discounted note receivable is the payment (or default) of the note by the maker. If the maker pays, the contingent liability of the endorser is thereby ended. If the maker fails to pay, the contingent liability of the endorser becomes a real liability. In either case the period of contingent liability ends at the maturity date of the note.

The discounting of notes receivable with a bank may be regarded by a company as an alternative to borrowing by issuing its own note payable. To issue its own note payable to the bank would, of course, mean the creation of a liability; to obtain cash by discounting a note receivable creates only a contingent liability.

Computing the proceeds   The amount of cash obtained from the bank by discounting a note receivable is termed the *proceeds* of the note. The proceeds are computed by applying an interest rate (termed the *discount rate*) to the maturity value of the note for the time remaining before the note matures.

To illustrate, assume that on July 1 Retail Sales Company receives a 75-day, 12% note for $8,000 from Raymond Kelly. The note will mature on September 14 (30 days in July, 31 days in August, and 14 days in September). On July 16, Retail Sales Company discounts this note receivable with its bank, which charges a discount rate of 15% a year. How much cash will Retail Sales Company receive? The computation is as follows:

Face of the note	$8,000
Add: Interest from date of note to maturity ($8,000 × .12 × $75/360$)	200
Maturity value	$8,200
Less: Bank discount at 15% for the discount period of 60 days	
(July 16 to Sept. 14) ($8,200 × .15 × $60/360$)	205
Proceeds (cash received from bank)	$7,995

The entry made by Retail Sales Company to record the discounting of the Kelly note would be as follows:

Cash	7,995	
Interest Expense	5	
Note Receivable		8,000
Discounted Raymond Kelly note at bank at 15% annual interest rate.		
Maturity value $8,200 minus $205 discount equals proceeds of $7,995.		

In this illustration, the cash of $7,995 received from the bank was less than the $8,000 face amount of the note. The proceeds received from discounting a note may be *either more or less* than the face amount of the note, depending upon the interest rates and time periods involved. The difference between the face amount of the note being discounted and the cash proceeds is usually recorded as either Interest Expense or Interest Revenue. If the proceeds are less than the face value, the difference is debited to Interest Expense. However, if the proceeds exceed the face value of the note, the difference is credited to Interest Revenue.

Discounted note receivable paid by maker   Before the maturity date of the discounted note, the bank will notify the maker, Raymond Kelly, that it is holding the note. Kelly will therefore make payment directly to the bank.

Discounted note receivable defaulted by maker   If Kelly should be unable to pay the note at maturity, the bank will give notice of the default to the endorser, Retail Sales Company, which immediately becomes obligated to pay, and will make the following entry to record the payment:

Accounts Receivable, Raymond Kelly 8,200
    Cash 8,200
To record payment to bank of discounted Kelly note, defaulted by maker.

Under these assumptions Retail Sales Company's contingent liability to the bank has become a real liability and has been discharged by a cash payment. Retail Sales Company now has an account receivable from the maker of the defaulted note for the amount which it was compelled to pay to the bank.

Classification of receivables in the balance sheet

Accounts receivable from customers ordinarily will be collected within the operating cycle; they are therefore listed among the current assets on the balance sheet. Receivables may also arise from miscellaneous transactions other than the sale of goods and services. These miscellaneous receivables, such as advances to officers and employees, and claims against insurance companies for losses sustained, should be listed separately on the balance sheet and should not be merged with trade accounts receivable. If an account receivable from an officer or employee originates as a favor to the officer or employee, efforts at collection may await the convenience of the debtor. Consequently, it is customary to include such receivables in the balance sheet as noncurrent assets under the caption of Other Assets.

Notes receivable usually appear among the current assets; however, if the maturity date of a note is more than a year distant and beyond the operating cycle of the business, the note should be listed as noncurrent under a heading such as Long-Term Investments. Any accrued interest receivable at the balance sheet date is a current asset and may be combined on the balance sheet with other accrued items such as accrued rents receivable or royalties receivable.

Disclosure of contingent liabilities   Since contingent liabilities are potential liabilities rather than full-fledged liabilities, they are not included in the liability section of the balance sheet. However, these potential liabilities may affect the financial position of the business if future events cause them to become real liabilities. Therefore, contingent liabilities should be *disclosed in footnotes to the financial statements.* The contingent liability arising from the discounting of notes receivable could be disclosed by the following footnote:

Note 6: Contingencies and commitments
 At December 31, 19____, the Company was contingently liable for notes receivable discounted with maturity values in the amount of $250,000.

CURRENT LIABILITIES

Current liabilities are obligations that must be paid within the operating cycle or one year (whichever is longer). Comparison of the amount of current liabilities with the amount of current assets is one means of appraising the financial position of a business. In other words, a comparison of the amount of current liabilities with the amount of current assets available for paying these debts helps us in judging a company's short-run debt-paying ability.

In accounting for current liabilities, we are especially interested in making certain that all such obligations are included in the balance sheet. Fraud may be concealed by deliberate understatement of a liability. The omission or understatement of a liability will usually be accompanied by an overstatement of owners' equity or else by an understatement of assets. Depending on the nature of the error, the net income of the business may also be overstated.

Among the more common current liabilities are notes payable, accounts payable, accrued liabilities such as interest and wages, and estimated liabilities such as income taxes. An *estimated* liability is an obligation known to exist but for which the dollar amount is uncertain. In this chapter we shall consider the accounting problems relating to notes payable; the liabilities arising from payrolls will be considered in Chapter 13.

NOTES PAYABLE

Notes payable are issued whenever bank loans are obtained. Other transactions which may give rise to notes payable include the purchase of real estate or costly equipment, the purchase of merchandise, and the substitution of a note for a past-due account payable.

Notes payable issued to banks

Assume that on November 1 Porter Company borrows $10,000 from its bank for a period of six months at an annual interest rate of 12%. Six months later on May 1, Porter Company will have to pay the bank the *principal* amount of $10,000 plus

$600 interest ($10,000 × .12 × ⁶⁄₁₂). The owners of Porter Company have authorized John Caldwell, the company's treasurer, to sign notes payable issued by the company. The note issued by Porter Company could read as shown below (omitting a few minor details).

This note is for the principal amount with interest stated separately

Miami, Florida	November 1, Year 1

Six months .... **after this date**   Porter Company ....

promises to pay to Security National Bank the sum of $ .... 10,000 ....

with interest at the rate of ..... 12% ..... **per annum.**

Signed *John Caldwell*

Title Treasurer ....

The journal entry in Porter Company's accounting records for this borrowing is

Face amount of note

```
Cash ......................................................... 10,000
     Notes Payable ....................................................   10,000
Borrowed $10,000 for six months at 12% interest per year.
```

Notice that no liability is recorded for the interest charges when the note is issued. At the date that money is borrowed, the borrower has a liability *only for the principal amount of the loan;* the liability for interest charges comes into existence gradually over the life of the loan. At December 31, two months' interest expense has been incurred, and the following year-end adjusting entry is made:

A liability arises for accrued interest

```
Interest Expense .............................................. 200
     Interest Payable .......................................................   200
To record interest expense incurred through year-end on 12%, six-month note
dated Nov. 1 ($10,000 × .12 × ²⁄₁₂ = $200).
```

The entry on May 1 when the note is paid will be:

Payment of principal and interest

```
Notes Payable ............................................. 10,000
Interest Payable ...........................................    200
Interest Expense ..........................................    400
     Cash .............................................................   10,600
To record payment of 12%, six-month note on maturity date and to
recognize interest expense incurred since year-end
($10,000 × .12 × ⁴⁄₁₂ = $400).
```

Notes payable with interest charges included in the face amount

Instead of stating the interest rate separately as in the preceding illustration, the note payable issued by Porter Company could have been drawn so as to include the interest charge in the face amount of the note, as shown below:

This note shows interest included in face amount of note

Miami, Florida	November 1, Year 1

Six months .... *after this date* ...... Porter Company

promises to pay to Security National Bank the sum of $10,600

Signed *John Caldwell*

Title ...... Treasurer

Notice that the face amount of this note ($10,600) is greater than the amount borrowed ($10,000). Porter Company's liability at November 1 is only $10,000; the other $600 included in the face amount of the note represents *future interest charges.* As interest expense is incurred over the life of the note, Porter Company's liability will grow to $10,600, just as in the preceding illustration.

The entry to record Porter Company's $10,000 borrowing from the bank at November 1 will be as follows for this type of note payable:

Interest included in face of note

Cash	10,000	
Discount on Notes Payable	600	
Notes Payable		10,600

Issued to bank at 12%, six-month note payable with interest charge included in face amount of note.

The liability account, Notes Payable, was credited with the full face amount of the note ($10,600). It is therefore necessary to debit a *contra-liability* account, *Discount on Notes Payable,* for the future interest charges included in the face amount of the note. Discount on Notes Payable is shown in the balance sheet as a deduction from the Notes Payable account. In our illustration, the amounts in the balance sheet would be Notes Payable, $10,600, minus Discount on Notes Payable, $600, or a net liability of $10,000 at November 1.

Discount on notes payable The balance of the account Discount on Notes Payable represents *interest charges applicable to future periods.* As this interest expense is incurred, the balance of the discount account gradually is transferred into the Interest Expense account. Thus, at the maturity date of the note, Discount on Notes Payable will have a zero balance, and the net liability will have increased to $10,600. The process of transferring the amount in the Discount on Notes Payable account into the Interest Expense account is called *amortization* of the discount.

Amortization of the discount   The discount on *short-term* notes payable usually is amortized by the straight-line method, which allocates a proportionate amount of the discount to interest expense in each accounting period.[1] If the $600 discount on the Porter Company note payable is amortized by the straight-line method, the discount will be transferred from the Discount on Notes Payable account into Interest Expense at the rate of $100 per month ($600 discount ÷ 6 months). Alternatively, we can compute the monthly interest expense by applying the rate of interest included in the face amount of the note (12% in our example) to the principal amount of the note, as follows: $10,000 × 12% × $\frac{1}{12}$ = $100.

Entries should be made to amortize an appropriate portion of the discount at the end of each accounting period and at the date the note matures. At December 31, Year 1, Porter Company will make the following adjusting entry to recognize the two months' interest expense incurred since November 1.

Amortization of discount

Interest Expense	200	
Discount on Notes Payable		200

To record interest expense incurred to end of year on 12%, six-month note dated Nov. 1 ($600 discount × ⅔).

Notice that the liability for accrued interest is recorded by crediting Discount on Notes Payable rather than Accrued Interest Payable. The credit to Discount on Notes Payable reduces the debit balance in this contra-liability account from $600 to $400, thereby increasing the *net liability* for notes payable by $200.

At December 31, Porter Company's net liability for the bank loan will appear in the balance sheet as shown below:

Liability shown net of discount

Current liabilities:		
Notes payable	$10,600	
Less: Discount on notes payable	400	$10,200

The net liability of $10,200 consists of the $10,000 principal amount of the debt plus the $200 interest which has accrued since November 1.

When the note matures on May 1, Year 2, Porter Company will recognize the four months' interest expense incurred since year-end and will pay the bank $10,600. The entry is

Two-thirds of interest applicable to second year

Notes Payable	10,600	
Interest Expense	400	
Discount on Notes Payable		400
Cash		10,600

To record payment of six-month note due today and recognize interest expense incurred since year-end ($10,000 × 12% × ⁴⁄₁₂ = $400).

---

[1]When an interest charge is included in the face amount of a long-term note, the effective interest method of amortizing the discount is often used instead of the straight-line method. The effective interest method of amortization is discussed in Chapter 13.

Comparison of the two forms of notes payable

We have illustrated two alternative methods which Porter Company could use in accounting for its $10,000 bank loan, depending upon the form of the note payable. The journal entries for both methods, along with the resulting balance sheet presentations of the liability at November 1 and December 31, are summarized on page 316. Notice that both methods result in Porter Company recognizing the same amount of interest expense and the same total liability in its balance sheet. The form of the note does not change the economic substance of the transaction.

The concept of present value applied to long-term notes

When a note payable is issued in exchange for cash, it is easy to determine whether an interest charge is included in the face amount of the note. Any difference between the face amount of the note and the amount of cash borrowed should be viewed as an interest charge. However, when a note is issued in exchange for other kinds of assets, such as land or equipment, the amount of interest (if any) included in the face amount of the note may be less apparent.

If a realistic rate of interest is stated separately in a long-term note, we may assume that no interest charge is included in the face amount. If no interest charge is specified, however, or if the specified interest rate is unrealistically low (such as 2% a year), a portion of the face amount of the note must be assumed to represent an interest charge. When such a note is issued or received, the transaction should be recorded at the *present value* of the note rather than at the face amount.

The concept of present value is based upon the "time value" of money—the idea that an amount of money which will not be received until some future date is equivalent to a smaller amount of money received today. The present value of a future cash receipt is the amount of money which, if received today, would be considered equivalent to the future receipt. The present value is always less than the future amount, because money available today can be invested to earn interest and thereby become equivalent to a larger amount in the future.

When a note does not call for the payment of interest, the present value of the note is less than its face amount, because the face amount of the note will not be received until the maturity date. The difference between the present value of a note and its face amount should be viewed as an interest charge included in the face amount. Often we can determine the present value of a note by the fair market value of the asset acquired when the note is issued. Alternatively, the present value can be computed using mathematical techniques which are illustrated in Appendix A following Chapter 13.

The *effective rate of interest* associated with a note is that interest rate which will cause the note's present value to increase to the full maturity value of the note by the time the note matures.

Note written for $10,000 plus 12% interest

Entry to record borrowing on Nov. 1

Cash	10,000	
Notes Payable		10,000

Partial balance sheet at Nov. 1

Current liabilities:
Notes payable	$10,000

Adjusting entry at Dec. 31

Interest Expense	200	
Interest Payable		200

Partial balance sheet at Dec. 31

Current liabilities:
Notes payable	$10,000	
Interest payable	200	$10,200

Entry to record payment of note on May 1

Notes Payable	10,000	
Interest Payable	200	
Interest Expense	400	
Cash		10,600

Note written with interest included in face amount

Entry to record borrowing on Nov. 1

Cash	10,000	
Discount on Notes Payable	600	
Notes Payable		10,600

Partial balance sheet at Nov. 1

Current liabilities:
Notes payable	$10,600	
Less: Discount on notes payable	600	$10,000

Adjusting entry at Dec. 31

Interest Expense	200	
Discount on Notes Payable		200

Partial balance sheet at Dec. 31

Current liabilities:
Notes payable	$10,600	
Less: Discount on notes payable	400	$10,200

Entry to record payment of note on May 1

Notes Payable	10,600	
Interest Expense	400	
Discount on Notes Payable		400
Cash		10,600

An illustration of notes recorded at present value

To illustrate the use of present value in transactions involving long-term notes, let us assume that on September 1, Everts Company buys equipment from Tru-Tool, Inc., by issuing a one-year note payable in the face amount of $230,000 with no mention of an interest rate. It is not logical to assume that Tru-Tool, Inc., would extend credit for one year without charging any interest. Therefore, some portion of the $230,000 face amount of the note should be regarded as a charge for interest. In the accounting records of Everts Company, the amount of this interest charge should be debited to the contra-liability account Discount on Notes Payable, instead of being treated as part of the cost of the equipment.

If Everts Company were to debit Equipment and credit Notes Payable for the full $230,000 face amount of the note, the following errors would result: (1) the cost of the equipment and the amount of the related liability would be *overstated* by the amount of the interest charge included in the face amount of the note; (2) interest expense would be *understated* over the life of the note; and (3) depreciation expense would be *overstated* throughout the estimated service life of the equipment.

Let us assume that the regular sales price of this equipment is $200,000. In this case, the present value of the note is apparently $200,000, and the remaining $30,000 of the face amount represents a charge for interest. The rate of interest which will cause the $200,000 present value of the note to increase to the $230,000 maturity value in one year is 15%. Thus, the face amount of the note actually includes an interest charge computed at the effective interest rate of 15%.

Everts Company should use the present value of the note in determining the cost of the equipment and the amount of the related net liability, as shown by the following journal entry:

Equipment	200,000	
Discount on Notes Payable	30,000	
Notes Payable		230,000
Purchased equipment for $200,000 by issuing a one-year note payable with a 15% interest charge included in the face amount.		

Over the next 12 months, the $30,000 recorded as a discount on the note payable will be amortized into interest expense.

It is equally important for the selling company, Tru-Tool, Inc., to use the present value of the note in determining the amount of revenue to be recognized from the sale. The $30,000 interest charge included in the face amount of the note receivable from Everts Company represents *unearned interest* to Tru-Tool, Inc., and is *not part of the sales price of the equipment.* If Tru-Tool, Inc., were to treat the entire face amount of the note receivable as the sales price of the equipment, the result would be to overstate sales revenue and notes receivable by $30,000, and also to understate interest revenue by this amount over the life of the note. Tru-Tool, Inc., should record the sale at the present value of the note received, as shown on the next page.

Accounts Receivable, Everts Company	200,000	
Sales		200,000

To record sale of equipment to Everts Company.

Notes Receivable	230,000	
Discount on Notes Receivable		30,000
Accounts Receivable, Everts Company		200,000

Obtained from Everts Company a one-year note with a 15% interest charge included in the face amount.

Notice that the interest charge included in the face amount of the note receivable is credited to *Discount on Notes Receivable*. This account represents unearned interest and is a contra-asset account which appears in the balance sheet as a deduction from notes receivable. As the interest is earned, the balance of the discount account will gradually be transferred into Interest Revenue. At December 31, Tru-Tool, Inc., will have earned four months' interest revenue and will make the following entry:

Discount on Notes Receivable	10,000	
Interest Revenue		10,000

To record interest earned from Sept. 1 through Dec. 31 on Everts Company note ($200,000 × 15% × 4/12).

On September 1 of the following year, when the note receivable is collected from Everts Company, the required entry will be

Cash	230,000	
Discount on Notes Receivable	20,000	
Interest Revenue		20,000
Notes Receivable		230,000

To record collection of Everts Company note and to recognize interest earned since year-end.

In an earlier era of accounting practice, failure to use the concept of present value in recording transactions involving long-term notes sometimes resulted in large overstatements of assets and sales revenue, especially by real estate development companies. In recognition of this problem, the Financial Accounting Standards Board now requires the use of present value in recording transactions involving *long-term* notes receivable or payable which do not bear reasonable stated rates of interest.[2]

When a note is issued for a short period of time, any interest charge included in its face amount is likely to be relatively small. Therefore, the use of present value is not required in recording normal transactions with customers or suppliers involving notes due in less than one year. Notes given or received in such transactions which do not specify an interest rate may be considered non-interest-bearing.

---

[2]*APB Opinion No. 21,* "Interest on Receivables and Payable," AICPA (New York: 1971).

Installment receivables

Another application of present value is found in the recording of *installment sales*. Many retailing businesses sell merchandise on installment sales plans, which permit customers to pay for their credit purchases through a series of periodic payments. The importance of installment sales is emphasized by a recent balance sheet of Sears, Roebuck, and Co., which shows about $6 billion of customer accounts receivable, nearly all of which call for collection in periodic monthly installments.

When merchandise is sold on an installment plan, substantial interest charges are usually added to the "cash selling price" of the product in determining the total dollar amount to be collected in the series of installment payments. The amount of sales revenue recognized at the time of sale, however, is limited to the *present value* of these installment payments. In most cases, the present value of these future payments is equal to the regular sales price of the merchandise. The portion of the installment account receivable which represents unearned finance charges is credited to the contra-asset account, Discount on Installment Receivables. The balance of this contra-asset account is then amortized into Interest Revenue over the length of the collection period.

Although the collection period for an installment receivable often runs as long as 24 to 36 months, such receivables are regarded as current assets if they correspond to customary credit terms of the industry. In published balance sheets, the Discount on Installment Receivables is often called Deferred Interest Income or Unearned Finance Charges. A typical balance sheet presentation of installment accounts receivable is illustrated below:

Trade accounts receivable:

Accounts receivable	$ 75,040,000
Installment contracts receivable, including $31,000,000 due after one year . . .	52,640,000
	$127,680,000
Less: Deferred interest income ($8,070,000) and allowance for doubtful	
accounts ($1,872,000)	9,942,000
Total trade accounts and notes receivable	$117,738,000

Income tax aspects of installment sales Current provisions of the federal income tax law permit sellers to spread the recognition of the gross profit from installment sales over the years in which collections are received. The result of this treatment is to postpone the recognition of taxable income and the payment of income tax. For financial statement purposes, however, the entire gross profit from installment sales is recognized *in the period in which the sale occurs*. The method of recognizing gross profit from installment sales for income tax purposes will be illustrated in Chapter 14. There are a number of other more complex issues relating to installment sales; these are covered in advanced accounting courses.

KEY TERMS INTRODUCED OR EMPHASIZED IN CHAPTER 8

Aging the accounts receivable   The process of classifying accounts receivable by age groups such as current, past due 1–30 days, past due 31–60 days, etc. A step in estimating the uncollectible portion of the accounts receivable.

Allowance for Doubtful Accounts   A valuation account or contra account relating to accounts receivable and showing the portion of the receivables estimated to be uncollectible.

Contingent liability   A potential liability which either will develop into a full-fledged liability or will be eliminated entirely by a future event.

Contra account   A ledger account which is deducted from or offset against a related account in the financial statements, for example, Allowance for Doubtful Accounts, Discount on Notes Payable, and Discount on Notes Receivable.

Default   Failure to pay interest or principal of a promissory note at the due date.

Direct charge-off method   A method of accounting for uncollectible receivables in which no expense is recognized until individual accounts are determined to be worthless. At that point the account receivable is written off with an offsetting debit to uncollectible accounts expense. Fails to match revenue and related expenses.

Discount on Notes Payable   A contra-liability account representing any interest charges applicable to future periods included in the face amount of a note payable. Over the life of the note, the balance of the Discount on Notes Payable account is amortized into Interest Expense.

Discount on Notes Receivable   A contra-asset account representing any unearned interest included in the face amount of a note receivable. Over the life of the note, the balance of the Discount on Notes Receivable account is amortized into Interest Revenue.

Discounting notes receivable   Selling a note receivable prior to its maturity date.

Effective interest rate   The rate of interest which will cause the present value of a note to increase to the maturity value by the maturity date.

Installment sales   Sales on credit in which the customer agrees to make a series of installment payments, including substantial interest charges.

Interest   A charge made for the use of money. The formula for computing interest is Principal $\times$ Rate of interest $\times$ Time = Interest ($P \times R \times T = I$).

Maker (of a note)   A person or entity who issues a promissory note.

Maturity date   The date on which a note becomes due and payable.

Maturity value   The value of a note at its maturity date, consisting of principal plus interest.

Notes payable   A liability evidenced by issuance of a formal written promise to pay a certain amount of money, usually with interest, at a future date.

Notes receivable   A receivable (asset) evidenced by a formal written promise to pay a certain amount of money, usually with interest, at a future date.

Payee   The person named in a promissory note to whom payment is to be made (the lender).

Present value concept   Based upon the time value of money. The basic premise is that an amount of money which will not be received until a future date is equivalent to a smaller amount of money available today.

Present value of a future cash receipt   The amount of money which an informed investor would pay today for the right to receive that future cash receipt. The present value is always less than the future amount, because money available today can be invested to earn interest and thereby become equivalent to a larger amount in the future.

Principal amount   That portion of the maturity value of a note which is attributable to the amount borrowed or to the cost of the asset acquired when the note was issued, rather than being attributable to interest charges.

Proceeds   The amount received from selling a note receivable prior to its maturity. Maturity value minus discount equals proceeds.

DEMONSTRATION PROBLEM FOR YOUR REVIEW

The Monastery, Inc., sells custom wood furniture to decorators and the general public. Selected transactions relating to the company's receivables and payables for the month of August are shown below. The company uses the allowance method in accounting for uncollectible accounts.

Aug. 1 Borrowed $48,000 from Central Bank by issuing a 90-day note payable with a stated interest rate of 15%.

Aug. 5 Sold merchandise for $960 to R. Lucas on the installment plan. Lucas signed an installment contract requiring 12 monthly payments of $90 each, beginning September 5. (Record transaction by debiting Installment Contracts Receivable rather than Accounts Receivable.)

Aug. 8 A $420 account receivable from S. Wilson was determined to be worthless and was written off.

Aug. 10 Sold merchandise to Century Interiors on account, $15,200. It was agreed that Century Interiors would issue a 60-day, 8% note upon receipt of the merchandise and could deduct any freight it paid on the goods.

Aug. 11 Received a 60-day note from StyleCraft Co. in settlement of $3,600 open account. Interest computed at the effective rate of 8% was included in the face amount of the note.

Aug. 13 Received a letter from Century Interiors stating that it had paid $200 freight on the shipment of August 10. Enclosed was a 60-day, 8% note dated August 13 for $15,000.

Aug. 16 Purchased land for $92,000, making a cash down payment of $20,000 and issuing a one-year note payable for the balance. The face amount of the note was $78,480, which included interest computed at an effective rate of 9%.

Aug. 20 Received full payment from J. Porter of a $4,500, 60-day, 12% note dated June 21. Accrued interest receivable of $30 had been recorded in prior months.

Aug. 23 Discounted the Century Interiors note dated August 13 at the bank. The bank discount rate of 9% was applied to the maturity value of the note for the 50 days remaining to maturity.

Aug. 25 An account receivable of $325 from G. Davis had been written off in June; full payment was unexpectedly received from Davis.

Aug. 29 Sales to ExtraCash credit card customers during August amounted to $14,800. (Summarize all credit card sales in one entry. ExtraCash Co. is not a bank.)

Aug. 30 Collected cash from ExtraCash Co. for the August credit card sales, less a 5% discount charged by ExtraCash.

Aug. 31 The Discount on Installment Receivables account is amortized to reflect $3,960 of finance charges earned during August.

Aug. 31 As a result of substantial write-offs, the Allowance for Doubtful Accounts has a debit balance of $320. Aging of the accounts receivable indicates that the allowance account should have a $1,200 credit balance at the end of August.

Instructions   Prepare journal entries to record the transactions listed above and to make any adjusting entries necessary at August 31.

SOLUTION TO DEMONSTRATION PROBLEM

General Journal

19___

Aug. 1 Cash 48,000
        Notes Payable 48,000
        Borrowed $48,000 from Central Bank; issued a 90-day, 15%
        note payable.

5 Installment Contracts Receivable, R. Lucas 1,080
        Discount on Installment Receivables 120
        Sales 960
        Installment sale, due in 12 monthly installments of $90 each.

8 Allowance for Doubtful Accounts 420
        Accounts Receivable, S. Wilson 420
        Wrote off uncollectible account from S. Wilson.

10 Accounts Receivable, Century Interiors 15,200
        Sales 15,200
        Sale of merchandise on account.

11 Notes Receivable 3,648
        Discount on Notes Receivable 48
        Accounts Receivable, StyleCraft Co. 3,600
        Received 60-day note with interest at effective rate of 8%
        included in face amount in settlement of open account.

13 Notes Receivable 15,000
   Delivery Expense 200
        Accounts Receivable, Century Interiors 15,200
        To record credit to Century Interiors for freight paid by them
        and receipt of 60-day, 8% note for balance of amount owed.

16 Land 92,000
   Discount on Notes Payable 6,480
        Notes Payable 78,480
        Cash 20,000
        Purchased land for $92,000, paying $20,000 cash and issuing
        a one-year note payable with a 9% interest charge included in
        the face amount.

20 Cash 4,590
        Notes Receivable 4,500
        Accrued Interest Receivable 30
        Interest Revenue 60
        Collected note from J. Porter, including $90 interest.

Aug. 23	Cash	15,010	
	Notes Receivable		15,000
	Interest Revenue		10

Discounted Century Interiors' note at bank, proceeds computed as follows: Maturity value $15,200 − bank charge of $190 ($15,200 × .09 × 50/360) = $15,010.

25	Account Receivable, G. Davis	325	
	Allowance for Doubtful Accounts		325

To reinstate Davis receivable previously written off.

25	Cash	325	
	Accounts Receivable, G. Davis		325

To record collection of Davis account.

29	Accounts Receivable, ExtraCash Co.	14,800	
	Sales		14,800

To record credit card sales for August.

30	Cash	14,060	
	Credit Card Discount Expense	740	
	Accounts Receivable, ExtraCash Co.		14,800

Collected August credit card sales invoices, less 5%.

31	Discount on Installment Receivables	3,960	
	Interest Revenue		3,960

To record finance charges earned on installment contracts receivable during August.

31	Uncollectible Accounts Expense	1,520	
	Allowance for Doubtful Accounts		1,520

To provide for estimated uncollectibles as follows:

Balance required	*$1,200*
Present balance (debit)	*320*
Required increase in allowance	*$1,520*

31	Interest Expense	600	
	Interest Payable		600

To record interest expense on note payable to Central Bank ($48,000 × 15% × 30/360).

31	Discount on Notes Receivable	16	
	Interest Revenue		16

To record interest earned through Aug. 31 on StyleCraft note receivable ($48 discount × 20/60 = $16).

Aug. 31	*Interest Expense*	*270*	
	Discount on Notes Payable		*270*
	To amortize discount through Aug. 31 on one-year note payable		
	dated Aug. 16 ($6,480 × ¹⁄₁₂ × ½).		

REVIEW QUESTIONS

1 Adams Company determines at year-end that its Allowance for Doubtful Accounts should be increased by $6,500. Give the adjusting entry to carry out this decision.

2 In making the annual adjusting entry for uncollectible accounts, a company may utilize a **balance sheet approach** to make the estimate or it may use an **income statement approach.** Explain these two alternative approaches.

3 At the end of its first year in business, Baxter Laboratories had accounts receivable totaling $148,500. After careful analysis of the individual accounts, the credit manager estimated that $146,100 would ultimately be collected. Give the journal entry required to reflect this estimate in the accounts.

4 In February of its second year of operations, Baxter Laboratories (Question **3** above) learned of the failure of a customer, Sterling Corporation, which owed Baxter $800. Nothing could be collected. Give the journal entry to recognize the uncollectibility of the receivable from Sterling Corporation.

5 What is the **direct charge-off method** of handling credit losses as opposed to the **allowance method?** What is its principal shortcoming?

6 Morgan Corporation has decided to write off its account receivable from Brill Company because the latter has entered bankruptcy. What general ledger accounts should be debited and credited, assuming that the allowance method is in use? What general ledger accounts should be debited and credited if the direct charge-off method is in use?

7 Mill Company, which has accounts receivable of $309,600 and an allowance for doubtful accounts of $3,600, decides to write off as worthless a past-due account receivable for $1,500 from J. D. North. What effect will the write-off have upon total current assets? Upon net income for the period? Explain.

8 Describe a procedure by which management could be informed each month of the status of collections and the overall quality of the accounts receivable on hand.

9 What are the advantages to a retailer of making credit sales only to customers who use nationally recognized credit cards?

10 Alta Mine Co., a restaurant that had always made cash sales only, adopted a new policy of honoring several nationally known credit cards. Sales did not increase, but many of Alta Mine Co.'s regular customers began charging dinner bills on the credit cards. Has the new policy been beneficial to Alta Mine Co.? Explain.

11 Determine the maturity date of the following notes:
   a A three-month note dated March 10
   b A 30-day note dated August 15
   c A 90-day note dated July 2

12 X Company acquires a 9%, 60-day note receivable from a customer, Robert Waters, in settlement of an existing account receivable of $4,000. Give the journal entry to record acquisition of the note and the journal entry to record its collection at maturity.

13 Distinguish between
   a Current and long-term liabilities
   b Estimated and contingent liabilities

14 Does a contingent liability appear on a balance sheet? If so, in what part of the balance sheet?

15 Jonas Company issues a 90-day, 12% note payable to replace an account payable to Smith Supply Company in the amount of $8,000. Draft the journal entries (in general journal form) to record the issuance of the note payable and the payment of the note at the maturity date.

16 Howard Benson applied to the City Bank for a loan of $20,000 for a period of three months. The loan was granted at an annual interest rate of 12%. Write a sentence illustrating the wording of the note signed by Benson if
   a Interest is stated separately in the note.
   b Interest is included in the face amount of the note.

17 With reference to Question **16** above, give the journal entry required on the books of Howard Benson for issuance of each of the two types of notes.

18 Rager Products sold merchandise to Baron Company in exchange for a one-year note receivable. The note was made out in the face amount of $13,189, *including* a 9% interest charge. Compute the amount of sales revenue to be recognized by Rager Products. (Hint: $13,189 equals 109% of sales amount.)

19 Sylmar Industries buys a substantial amount of equipment having an estimated service life of five years by issuing a two-year note payable. The note includes no mention of an interest charge. Explain the errors which will result in the future financial statements of Sylmar Industries if the equipment and related liability are recorded at the face value, rather than the present value, of the note.

20 Maxline Stores sells merchandise with a sales price of $1,260 on an installment plan requiring 12 monthly payments of $120 each. How much revenue will this sale ultimately generate for Maxline Stores? Explain the nature of this revenue and when it should be recognized in the accounting records.

21 With reference to Question **20** above, make the journal entries required in the accounting records of Maxline Stores to record
   a Sale of the merchandise on the installment plan.
   b Collection of the first monthly installment payment. (Assume that an equal portion of the discount is amortized at the time that each installment payment is received.)

EXERCISES

Ex. 8-1 The general ledger control account for accounts receivable shows a balance of $98,000 at the end of the year. An aging analysis of the individual customers' accounts indicates doubtful accounts totaling $2,440. Draft the year-end adjusting entry for uncollectible accounts under each of the following independent assumptions:
   a The Allowance for Doubtful Accounts had a credit balance of $1,760.
   b The Allowance for Doubtful Accounts had a debit balance of $592.

Ex. 8-2 The unadjusted trial balance for Zane Corporation at the end of the current year includes the following accounts:

	Debit	Credit
Accounts receivable	$244,000	
Allowance for doubtful accounts		$ 1,092
Sales (25% represent cash sales)		576,000

Compute the uncollectible accounts expense for the current year, assuming that uncollectible accounts expense is determined as follows:

a 1% of total sales.

b 1½% of credit sales.

c Allowance for doubtful accounts is increased to $7,000, the portion of accounts receivable estimated to be uncollectible.

Ex. 8-3 Runners, Inc., reported the following amounts on its balance sheet at the end of last year:

Notes receivable from customers	$12,000
Accrued interest on notes receivable	240
Accounts receivable	50,400
Less: Allowance for doubtful accounts	1,200

You are to record the following events of the current year in general journal entries:

a Accounts receivable of $1,152 are written off as uncollectible.

b A customer's note for $330 on which interest of $18 has been accrued in the accounts is deemed uncollectible, and both balances are written off against the Allowance for Doubtful Accounts.

c An account receivable for $156 previously written off is collected.

d Aging of accounts receivable at the end of the current year indicates a need for an $1,800 allowance to cover possible failure to collect accounts currently outstanding. (Consider the effect of entries for **a, b,** and **c** on the amount of the Allowance for Doubtful Accounts.)

Ex. 8-4 Three notes receivable, each in the amount of $20,000, were discounted by Electro-Magnet at its bank on May 10. The bank charged a discount rate of 12% per year, applied to the maturity value.

Date of Note	Annual Interest Rate, %	Life of Note
Note A—Apr. 10	12	3 months
Note B—Mar. 31	9	60 days
Note C—Mar. 11	16	90 days

Instructions

From the above date, compute the proceeds of each note. Remember that all interest rates quoted are annual rates. In making interest calculations, assume a 360-day year. Answers should be rounded to the nearest cent wherever necessary.

Ex. 8-5 Mavis Corporation on November 1 borrowed $100,000 from a local bank, and agreed to repay that amount plus 12% interest (per year) at the end of six months. (Remember that interest is stated at an annual rate.) Show two different presentations of the liability to the bank on Mavis Corporation's December 31 balance sheet, assuming that the note payable to the bank was drawn as follows:

a For $100,000, with interest stated separately and payable at maturity.

b With the total interest charge included in the face amount of the note.

Ex. 8-6 Dale Motors, an automobile dealer, sold three trucks to Zorro Truck Lines on April 1, Year 1, for a total price of $68,000. Under the terms of the sale, Dale Motors received $20,000 cash and a promissory note due in full 18 months later. The face amount of the note was $53,760, which included interest on the note for the 18 months.

Prepare all entries (in general journal form) for Dale Motors relating to the sales transaction and to the note for the fiscal year ended September 30, Year 1. Include the adjusting entry needed to record interest earned to September 30.

Ex. 8-7 Based upon the information in Exercise 8-6 above, prepare all entries (in general journal form) for Zorro Truck Lines relating to the purchase of the trucks and the note for the fiscal year ended December 31, Year 1. Include the adjusting entries to record interest expense and depreciation expense to December 31. (The trucks are to be depreciated over an eight-year service life by the straight-line method. There is no estimated salvage value.)

PROBLEMS

8-1 Books, Etc., owned by Linda Snow, has for the past three years been engaged in selling paper novelty goods to retail stores. Sales are made on credit and the company has regularly estimated its uncollectible accounts expense as a percentage of net sales. The percentage used has been ½ of 1% of net sales. However, it appears that this provision has been inadequate because the Allowance for Doubtful Accounts has a debit balance of $2,700 at May 31 prior to making the annual provision. Snow has therefore decided to change the method of estimating uncollectible accounts expense and to rely upon an analysis of the age and character of the accounts receivable at the end of each accounting period.

At May 31, the end of the company's fiscal year, the accounts receivable totaled $180,000. This total amount included past-due accounts in the amount of $38,000. None of these past-due accounts was considered hopeless; all accounts regarded as worthless had been written off as rapidly as they were determined to be uncollectible. These write-offs had totaled $5,113.90 during the year. After careful investigation of the past-due accounts at May 31, Linda Snow decided that the probable loss contained therein was 10%, and that in addition she would anticipate a loss of 1% of the current accounts receivable.

Instructions

a Compute the probable uncollectible accounts expense applicable to the accounts receivable at May 31, based on the analysis by the owner.

b Prepare the journal entry necessary to carry out the change in company policy with respect to providing for uncollectible accounts expense.

8-2 The balance sheet of Mile-Hi Corporation at December 31 of last year showed $252,000 in accounts receivable and a credit balance of $13,200 in the allowance for doubtful accounts. The following summary shows the totals of certain types of transactions occurring during January of the current year.

(1) Sales on account	$180,000
(2) Sales returns & allowances	3,600
(3) Cash collections from customers (no cash discounts)	177,600
(4) Account receivable from Dan King written off as worthless following the failure of his business	3,840

At January 31, after a careful aging and analysis of all customers' accounts, the company decided that the allowance for doubtful accounts should be adjusted to the amount of $14,640 in order to reflect accounts receivable at net realizable value in the January 31 balance sheet.

Instructions

a Give the appropriate entry in general journal form for each of the four numbered items and also for the adjusting entry at January 31 to provide for uncollectible accounts.

b Show the amounts of accounts receivable and the allowance for doubtful accounts as they would appear in a partial balance sheet at January 31.

c Assume that six months after the receivable from Dan King had been written off as worthless, he won $120,000 in a lottery and immediately paid the $3,840 owed to Mile-Hi Corporation. Give the journal entry or entries to reflect this collection in Mile-Hi Corporation's accounts. (Use general journal form.)

8-3 Forecasts, Incorporated, has been in business for three yars and has used the direct charge-off method. In other words, the company has written off accounts receivable when they were determined to be worthless. It has not used an allowance for doubtful accounts.

At the end of Year 3, management decides to adopt the allowance method of accounting for uncollectible accounts and asks you to help them determine the proper balance in the Allowance for Doubtful Accounts. The following information is available for your consideration.

			Year of Origin of Accounts Written Off			
Year	Sales	Accounts Written Off	Year 1	Year 2	Year 3	Net Income
1	$300,000	$2,400	$2,400			$20,000
2	500,000	5,200	1,200	$4,000		40,000
3	880,000	9,000		3,600	$5,400	50,000

The accounts receivable at the end of Year 3 amount to $160,000. All of these receivables resulted from sales made in Years 2 or 3. The company's policy has been to write off any account receivable that became more than six months past due. In studying the above table, note that the write-offs of receivables originating in a given year occur in that year or in the following year.

Instructions

a Based on the average experience for Years 1 and 2, compute the amount of the total uncollectible accounts that can reasonably be anticipated on the sales for Year 3. (Hint: Compute the percentage of actual write-offs to the combined sales of Years 1 and 2. Apply this percentage to the sales of Year 3.)

b Since $5,400 of accounts receivable originating in Year 3 have already been written off, compute the amount of the allowance that should be established at the end of Year 3 to cover estimated uncollectible accounts.

c The direct charge-off method used by Forecasts, Incorporated, caused net income to be overstated each year. Compute the amount of the overstatement of net income for each of the three years and the total overstatement. Show computations supporting the figure for each year. (Example: The overstatement in Year 1 is the excess of the write-offs during Years 1 and 2 of receivables originating in Year 1, as compared with the write-offs in Year 1.)

8-4   The balance sheet prepared by Highland Products at December 31, Year 6, contained accounts receivable of $380,000 and an allowance for doubtful accounts of $10,000.

    During Year 7, the company's sales volume reached a new high of $2,600,000; all sales during the year were made on credit. The total cash collections from customers in Year 7 (collections of accounts receivable) amounted to $2,500,000. Included in this figure for total collections was $5,000 representing the recovery in full of a $5,000 account receivable from Anthony Walker, a customer whose account had been written off as worthless late in Year 6. During Year 7, it was necessary to write off as worthless various customers' accounts totaling $11,000.

    On December 1, Year 7, Highland Products sold for $216,000 a tract of land acquired as a possible building site several years earlier at a cost of $144,000. The land was now considered unsuitable as a building site. Terms of sale were $60,000 cash and a 12%, six-month note for $156,000. The buyer was a large corporation and the note was regarded as fully collectible. (Credit the profit on this transaction to Gain on Sale of Land.)

    At December 31, Year 7, the accounts receivable included $60,000 of past-due accounts. After careful study of all past-due accounts, the management estimated that the probable loss contained therein was 20%, and that, in addition, 2% of the current accounts receivable should be regarded as doubtful of collection.

Instructions

a Prepare journal entries in general journal form for all transactions in Year 7 relating to accounts and notes receivable. (Five journal entries are needed: one to record all sales for the year; one to reinstate the Walker receivable; one to record total cash collections for the year; one to write off worthless accounts; and one to record the sale of the land at a profit.)

b Prepare two ledger accounts in three-column, running balance form—one a controlling account for Accounts Receivable, and the other for Allowance for Doubtful Accounts. Enter in these accounts the beginning balances for Year 7; then post the debits and credits indicated by the transactions of Year 7.

c Prepare the necessary adjusting journal entries at December 31, Year 7. Use one entry to provide for uncollectible accounts expense based on management's estimates and another entry to accrue interest on the note receivable. Post this entry to the ledger account Allowance for Doubtful Accounts prepared in **b**.

d What amount should appear in the income statement for Year 7 as uncollectible accounts expense?

e Prepare a partial balance sheet at December 31, Year 7, showing under the heading of current assets the note receivable, the accounts receivable and the allowance for doubtful accounts, and the accrued interest receivable on the note.

8-5   Indio Farm Supply sells to retail stores on 30-day open account, but requires customers who fail to pay invoices within 30 days to substitute promissory notes for their past-due accounts. No sales discount is offered. Among recent transactions were the following:

Mar. 17 Sold merchandise to S. R. Davis on account, $72,000, terms n/30.

Apr. 16 Received a 60-day, 10% note from Davis dated today in settlement of the open account of $72,000.

May 26 Discounted the Davis note at the bank. The bank discount rate was 12% applied to the maturity value of the note for the 20 days remaining to maturity.

June 15 Received notice from the bank that the Davis note due today was in default. Paid the bank the maturity value of the note. Since Davis has extensive business interests, the management of Indio Farm Supply is confident that no loss will be incurred on the defaulted note.

June 25 Made a $48,000 loan to John Raymond on a 30-day, 15% note.

Instructions

a Prepare in general journal form the entries necessary to record the preceding transactions. (In making interest calculations, assume a 360-day year.)

b Prepare the adjusting journal entry needed at June 30, the end of the company's fiscal year, to record interest accrued on the two notes receivable. [Accrue interest at 10% per annum from date of default (June 15) on the maturity value of the Davis note.]

8-6 The following information concerning the receivables of the Bunker Corporation appeared in the accounts on December 1, Year 7. The company uses a 360-day year for all interest calculations. During December, the company made sales only for cash.

Accounts receivable:

C. L. Laurence	$ 2,425
E. D. Nemson	3,870
C. A. Shively	6,200
Total	$12,495

Notes receivable:

A. P. Marra, 16%, 45-day note, dated Nov. 4, Year 7	$ 6,000
C. M. Hines, 18%, 90-day note, dated Nov. 30, Year 7	4,000
Total	$10,000

Installment contracts receivable:

M. Moyers (monthly payment $150)	$ 2,850

Unearned interest on installment contracts:

Applicable to M. Moyers contract	$ 386

During the month of December, the following additional transactions took place:

Dec. 7 E. D. Nemson paid $870 on account and gave a 30-day, 16% note to cover the balance.

Dec. 12 Received a 60-day, 16% note from C. L. Laurence in full settlement of his account.

Dec. 19 A. P. Marra wrote that he would be unable to pay the note due today and included a check to cover the interest due and a new 30-day, 14% note renewing the old note. No accrued interest has been recorded in prior months.

Dec. 28 Discounted the C. L. Laurence note at the bank. The proceeds on the note amounted to $2,432.

Dec. 31 Received the monthly payment on the M. Moyers contract. The payment of $150 includes $20 of interest revenue earned during December. The interest charges included in the face amount of the installment contract had originally been credited to the contra-asset account, Unearned Interest on Installment Contracts.

Instructions

a Prepare five journal entries (in general journal form) for the five December transactions listed above.

b Prepare an adjusting entry at December 31 to accrue interest receivable on the three notes receivable on hand (the Nemson, Marra, and Hines notes). Include in the explanation portion of the adjusting entry the computations to determine the accrued interest on each of the three notes. Add these three accrued amounts to find the total amount for the adjusting entry.

c Prepare a partial balance sheet for Bunker Corporation at December 31 showing under the heading of current assets the notes receivable, accounts receivable, installment contracts receivable, unearned interest on installment contracts, and accrued interest receivable. Also add a footnote to disclose the amount of the contingent liability for the discounted note receivable.

8-7 During the year ended December 31, Holden & Sons had a number of transactions relating to accounts payable and notes payable. Among these transactions were the following:

Mar. 6 Purchased merchandise from A. B. Hayes on open account, $25,200.

Apr. 8 Informed A. B. Hayes that Holden & Sons was unable to make payment as agreed. Hayes accepted a 14%, eight-month note to replace the open account.

Apr. 20 Borrowed $48,000 from Third National Bank today and signed a six-month, 16% note as evidence of indebtedness. The interest was added to the $48,000 amount borrowed and included in the face amount of the note.

May 15 Purchased merchandise from Birmingham, Incorporated, on 30-day open account, $19,200.

Oct. 20 Paid note (principal and interest) due today at Third National Bank.

Dec. 8 Paid note (principal and interest) due today to A. B. Hayes.

Instructions Prepare all necessary journal entries (in general journal form) to record the above transactions in the accounts of Holden & Sons. Show all supporting computations as part of the explanations of the journal entries. Adjusting entries are not required.

8-8 On April 1, Year 8, Merrimack Corporation sold merchandise to West Supply Co. in exchange for a note receivable due in *one year*. The note was drawn in the face amount of $47,880, which included the principal amount and an interest charge. In its December 31, Year 8, balance sheet, Merrimack correctly presented the note receivable as follows:

Note receivable, due Mar. 31, Year 9	$47,880	
Less: Discount on note receivable	1,470	$46,410

Instructions

a Determine the monthly interest revenue earned by Merrimack Corporation from this note receivable. (Hint: The balance in the discount account represents unearned interest as of December 31, Year 8. This is a one-year note with three months remaining before it matures.)

b Compute the amount of interest revenue recognized by Merrimack Corporation from the note during Year 8.

c Compute the amount of sales revenue recognized by Merrimack Corporation on April 1, Year 8, when this note was received.

d Compute the effective annual rate of interest (stated as a percentage) represented by the interest charge originally included in the face amount of the note.

e Prepare all journal entries relating to this note receivable in the accounting records of

Merrimack Corporation for Years 8 and 9. Assume that adjusting entries are made only at December 31.

8-9   During the fiscal year ending June 30 and shortly thereafter, Malibu Lake had the following transactions relating to notes payable.

Feb.   6 Borrowed $10,000 from L. W. Smith and issued a 45-day, 16% note payable.

Mar. 12 Purchased delivery truck from E-Z Company. Issued a 12%, three-month note payable for $15,000, the full cost of the truck.

Mar. 23 Paid the note due today to L. W. Smith plus accrued interest.

May   1 Borrowed the amount of $200,000 for 90 days from First Bank at an interest rate of 14% per year; signed a note payable with the interest included in the face amount of the note.

May   31 Purchased merchandise for $7,500 from Patten Co. Issued a 90-day note bearing interest at 16% annually. (Use two entries: one to record the purchase with a credit to Accounts Payable, and the other to transfer the liability to Notes Payable.)

June 12 The $15,000 note payable to E-Z Company matured today. Paid in cash the interest accrued and issued a new 30-day note bearing interest at 14% per annum to replace the maturing note. (Use one compound journal entry for this transaction.)

June 30 End of fiscal year.

July 12 Paid principal and interest of the 30-day, 14% note to E-Z Company dated June 12 which matured today.

July 30 Paid in full the 90-day note to First Bank dated May 1 and maturing today.

Instructions

a Prepare journal entries (in general journal form) to record the six transactions dated prior to June 30. All interest rates quoted are annual rates. Use a 360-day year for interest computations.

b Prepare two adjusting entries at June 30 relating to interest expense. The first entry should accrue interest on the two notes with interest stated separately (the note to Patten Company and the note to E-Z Company). The explanation should include computations showing the amount of interest accrued on each note. The second adjusting entry should record interest on the First Bank note in which interest was included in the face amount.

c Prepare journal entries for the two transactions occurring in July.

8-10   During the month of August, Delux Office Supply Co. engaged in the following transactions involving receivables and payables:

Aug.   1 Sold merchandise to C. Reed for $4,500. Reed issued a 90-day, 16% note for the amount of the purchase.

Aug.   4 Received a 60-day, 18% note from Reno Corporation for $6,200 in settlement of open account.

Aug. 11 Issued a 60-day, 15% note payable to Magnum Company for $5,040 in settlement of open account.

Aug. 16 Borrowed $12,000 from First Charter Bank and signed a six-month, 18% note payable which included the interest in the face amount.

Aug. 17 Discounted the Reno Corporation note. The proceeds from the bank amounted to $6,221.

25.70

,12

Aug. 21 Sold merchandise to Howard Wright. As payment, Wright issued a 60-day note for a face amount of $5,814, which included an interest charge of $114.

Aug. 24 Received payment from W. Harned of a $4,000, 60-day, 12% note dated June 25. Accrued interest receivable of $48 had been recorded in prior months.

Aug. 26 A long overdue account receivable from J. Bartlett in the amount of $720 was written off as uncollectible against the allowance for doubtful accounts.

Aug. 28 Full payment of a $290 account receivable was unexpectedly received from J. Kievits. This account had been written off as uncollectible several months ago.

Aug. 30 Sales to HandyCharge credit card customers in August amounted to $9,500. (Summarize all credit card sales in one entry. HandyCharge Co. is not a bank.)

Aug. 31 Collected cash from HandyCharge for August credit card sales, less 3% discount charged by HandyCharge.

Aug. 31 An aging of accounts receivable on August 31 indicates the allowance for doubtful accounts should be increased to $1,950. On July 31, the balance in the allowance account had been $1,830. No entries other than those described above have been made in the allowance account during August.

Instructions

a Prepare in general journal form the entries necessary to record the preceding transactions.

b Prepare any adjusting entries needed at August 31. (*Hint:* Four notes require adjusting entries.)

c Draft the appropriate footnote to the financial statements to disclose the contingent liability relating to the discounted note receivable.

BUSINESS DECISION PROBLEM 8

Record House and Concert Sound are two companies engaged in selling stereo equipment to the public. Both companies sell equipment at a price 50% greater than cost. Customers may pay cash, purchase on 30-day accounts, or make installment payments over a 36-month period. The installment receivables include a three-year interest charge (which amounts to 30% of the sales price) in the face amount of the contract. Condensed income statements prepared by the companies for their first year of operations are shown below:

	Record House	Concert Sound
Sales	$387,000	$288,000
Cost of goods sold	210,000	192,000
Gross profit on sales	$177,000	$ 96,000
Operating expenses	63,000	60,000
Operating income	$114,000	$ 36,000
Interest earned	–0–	10,800
Net income	$114,000	$ 46,800

When Record House makes a sale of stereo equipment on the installment plan it immediately credits the Sales account with the face amount of the installment receivable. In other words, the interest charges are included in sales revenue at the time of the sale. The interest charges included in Record House's installment receivables originating in the first year amount to $72,000, of which $59,100 is unearned at the end of the first year. Record House uses the direct charge-off method to recognize uncollectible accounts expense. During the year, accounts receivable of $2,100 were written off as uncollectible, but no entry was made for $37,200 of accounts estimated to be uncollectible at year-end.

Concert Sound records sales revenue equal to the present value of its installment receivables and recognizes the interest *earned during the year* as interest revenue. Concert Sound provides for uncollectible accounts by the allowance method. The company recognized uncollectible accounts expense of $11,100 during the year and this amount appeared to be adequate.

Instructions

a Prepare a condensed income statement for Record House for the year, using the same methods of accounting for installment sales and uncollectible accounts as were used by Concert Sound. The income statement you prepare should contain the same seven items shown in the illustrated income statements. Provide footnotes showing the computations you made in revising the amount of sales and any other figures you decide to change.

b Compare the income statement you have prepared in part **a** to the one originally prepared by Record House. Which income statement do you believe better reflects the results of the company's operations during the year? Explain.

c What do you believe to be the key factor responsible for making one of these companies more profitable than the other? What corrective action would you recommend be taken by the less profitable company to improve future performance?

9

INVENTORIES

After studying this chapter you should be able to:

- Explain what goods should be included in inventory.
- Describe the effects of an inventory error in the income statements of the current and succeeding years.
- Determine the cost of inventory by using *(a)* specific identification, *(b)* average cost, *(c)* fifo, and *(d)* lifo. Discuss the relative merits and shortcomings of these methods.
- Define inventory profits and explain why some accountants consider these profits fictitious.
- Explain the lower-of-cost-or-market rule.
- Estimate ending inventory by the gross profit method and by the retail method.
- Explain how a perpetual inventory system operates.

In the previous chapters we have illustrated how the amount of inventory on hand at year-end is recorded in the accounts. Remember that the inventory figure appears in both the balance sheet and the income statement. In the balance sheet, inventory is often the largest current asset. In the income statement, inventory is subtracted from the cost of goods *available* for sale to determine the *cost of goods sold* during the period.

In our previous discussions, the dollar amount of the ending inventory was given with only a brief explanation as to how this amount was determined. The basis for the valuation of inventory, as for most other types of assets, is cost. We are now ready to explore the concept of *cost* as applied to inventories of merchandise.

Inventory defined

One of the largest assets in a retail store or in a wholesale business is the inventory of merchandise, and the sale of this merchandise at prices in excess of cost is the major source of revenue. For a merchandising company, *the inventory consists of all goods owned and held for sale in the regular course of business.* Merchandise held for sale will normally be converted into cash within less than a year's time and is therefore regarded as a current asset. In the balance sheet, inventory is listed immediately after accounts receivable, because it is just one step further removed from conversion into cash than are the accounts receivable.

In manufacturing businesses there are three major types of inventories: *raw materials, goods in process of manufacture,* and *finished goods.* All three classes of inventories are included in the current asset section of the balance sheet.

To expand our definition of inventory to fit manufacturing companies as well as merchandising companies, we can say that inventory means "the aggregate of those items of tangible personal property which (1) are held for sale in the ordinary course of business, (2) are in process of production for such sale, or (3) are to be currently consumed in the production of goods or services to be available for sale."[1]

Periodic inventory system versus perpetual inventory system

The distinction between a periodic inventory system and a perpetual inventory system was explained earlier in Chapter 5. To summarize briefly, a periodic system of inventory accounting requires that acquisitions of merchandise be recorded by debits to a Purchases account. At the date of a sales transaction, no entry is made to record the cost of the goods sold. Under the periodic inventory system, the Inventory account is brought up to date only at the end of the accounting period when all the goods on hand are counted and priced.

The periodic inventory system is likely to be used by a business that sells a variety of merchandise with low unit prices, such as a drugstore or hardware store. To maintain perpetual inventory records in such a business would ordinarily be too time-consuming and expensive.

Companies that sell products of high unit value such as automobiles and television sets usually maintain a perpetual inventory system that shows at all times the amount of inventory on hand. As merchandise is acquired, it is added to an inventory account; as goods are sold, their cost is transferred out of inventory and into a cost of goods sold account. This continuous updating of the inventory account explains the name *perpetual* inventory system.

In the early part of this chapter we will use the periodic inventory system as a point of reference; in the latter part we will emphasize perpetual inventories.

Inventory valuation and the measurement of income

In measuring the gross profit on sales earned during an accounting period, we subtract the *cost of goods sold* from the total *sales* of the period. The figure for sales

---

[1]AICPA, *Accounting Research and Terminology Bulletins,* Final Edition (New York: 1961), p. 28.

is easily accumulated from the daily record of sales transactions, but in many businesses no day-to-day record is maintained showing the cost of goods sold.[2] The figure representing the cost of goods sold during an entire accounting period is computed at the end of the period by separating the *cost of goods available for sale* into two elements:

1 The cost of the goods sold
2 The cost of the goods not sold, which therefore comprise the ending inventory

This idea, with which you are already quite familiar, may be concisely stated in the form of an equation as follows:

Finding cost of goods sold

$$\frac{\textit{Cost of Goods}}{\textit{Available for Sale}} - \frac{\textit{Ending}}{\textit{Inventory}} = \frac{\textit{Cost of}}{\textit{Goods Sold}}$$

Determining the amount of the ending inventory is the key step in establishing the cost of goods sold. In separating the *cost of goods available for sale* into its components of *goods sold* and *goods not sold,* we are just as much interested in establishing the proper amount for cost of goods sold as in determining a proper figure for inventory. Throughout this chapter you should bear in mind that the procedures for determining the amount of the ending inventory are also the means for determining the cost of goods sold. The valuation of inventory and the determination of the cost of goods sold are in effect the two sides of a single coin.

The American Institute of Certified Public Accountants has summarized this relationship between inventory valuation and the measurement of income in the following words: "A major objective of accounting for inventories is the proper determination of income through the process of matching appropriate costs against revenues."[3] The expression "matching costs against revenues" means determining what portion of the cost of goods available for sale should be deducted from the revenue of the current period and what portion should be carried forward (as inventory) to be matched against the revenue of the following period.

Importance of an accurate valuation of inventory

The most important current assets in the balance sheets of most companies are cash, accounts receivable, and inventory. Of these three, the inventory of merchandise is usually much the largest. Because of the relatively large size of this asset, an error in the valuation of inventory may cause a material misstatement of financial position and of net income. An error of 20% in valuing the inventory may have as much effect on the financial statements as would the complete omission of the asset cash.

An error in inventory will of course lead to other erroneous figures in the balance sheet, such as the total current assets, total assets, owners' equity, and the total liabilities and owners' equity. The error will also affect key figures in the income

---

[2]As explained in Chap. 5, a company that maintains perpetual inventory records will have a day-to-day record of the cost of goods sold and of goods in inventory. Our present discussion, however, is based on the assumption that the periodic system of inventory is being used.
[3]AICPA, op. cit.

statement, such as the cost of goods sold, the gross profit on sales, and the net income for the period. Finally, it is important to recognize that *the ending inventory of one year is also the beginning inventory of the following year.* Consequently, the income statement of the second year will also be in error by the full amount of the original error in inventory valuation.

Effects of an error in valuing inventory: illustration   Assume that on December 31, Year 1, the inventory of the Hillside Company is actually $100,000 but, through an accidental error, it is recorded as $90,000. The effects of this $10,000 error on the income statement for Year 1 are indicated in the first illustration shown below, showing two income statements side by side. The left-hand set of figures shows the inventory of December 31, Year 1, at the *proper value of $100,000* and represents a correct income statement for Year 1. The right-hand set of figures represents an incorrect income statement, because the ending inventory is *erroneously listed as $90,000.* Note the differences between the two income statements with respect to net income, gross profit on sales, and cost of goods sold. (Income taxes have purposely been omitted in this illustration.)

HILLSIDE COMPANY
Income Statement
For the Year Ended December 31, Year 1

		With Correct Ending Inventory	With Incorrect Ending Inventory
Effect of error in inventory	Sales	$240,000	$240,000
	Cost of goods sold:		
	Beginning inventory, Jan. 1, Year 1 .... $ 75,000		$ 75,000
	Purchases 210,000		210,000
	Cost of goods available for sale $285,000		$285,000
	Less: Ending inventory, Dec. 31, Year 1 100,000		90,000
	Cost of goods sold	185,000	195,000
	Gross profit on sales	$ 55,000	$ 45,000
	Operating expenses	30,000	30,000
	Net income	$ 25,000	$ 15,000

This illustration shows that an understatement of $10,000 in the ending inventory for Year 1 caused an understatement of $10,000 in the net income for Year 1. Next, consider the effect of this error on the income statement of the following year. The ending inventory of Year 1 is, of course, the beginning inventory of Year 2. The preceding illustration is now continued to show side by side a correct income statement and an incorrect statement for Year 2. The *ending* inventory of $120,000 for Year 2 is the same in both statements and is to be considered correct. Note that the $10,000 error in the beginning inventory of the right-hand statement causes an error in the cost of goods sold, in gross profit, and in net income for Year 2.

HILLSIDE COMPANY
Income Statement
For the Year Ended December 31, Year 2

	With Correct Beginning Inventory		With Incorrect Beginning Inventory	
Sales		$265,000		$265,000
Cost of goods sold:				
Beginning inventory, Jan. 1, Year 2	$100,000		$ 90,000	
Purchases	230,000		230,000	
Cost of goods available for sale	$330,000		$320,000	
Less: Ending inventory, Dec. 31, Year 2	120,000		120,000	
Cost of goods sold		210,000		200,000
Gross profit on sales		$ 55,000		$ 65,000
Operating expenses		33,000		33,000
Net income		$ 22,000		$ 32,000

Effect on succeeding year (left margin)

Counterbalancing errors   The illustrated income statements for Years 1 and 2 show that an understatement of the ending inventory in Year 1 caused an understatement of net income in that year and an offsetting overstatement of net income for Year 2. Over a period of two years the effects of an inventory error on net income will *counterbalance,* and the total net income for the two years together is the same as if the error had not occurred. Since the error in reported net income for the first year is exactly offset by the error in reported net income for the second year, it might be argued that an inventory error has no serious consequences. Such an argument is not sound, for it disregards the fact that accurate yearly figures for net income are a primary objective of the accounting process. Moreover, many actions by management and many decisions by creditors and owners are based upon *trends* indicated in the financial statements for two or more years. Note that the inventory error has made the Year 2 net income appear to be more than twice as large as the Year 1 net income, when in fact *less* net income was earned in Year 2 than in Year 1. Anyone relying on the erroneous financial statements would be greatly misled as to the trend of Hillside Company's earnings.

To produce dependable financial statements, inventory must be accurately determined at the end of each accounting period. The counterbalancing effect of the inventory error by the Hillside Company is illustrated below:

		With Inventory at Dec. 31, Year 1, Understated	
	With Inventory Correctly Stated	Reported Net Income Will Be	Reported Net Income Will Be Overstated (Understated)
Net income for Year 1	$25,000	$15,000	$(10,000)
Net income for Year 2	22,000	32,000	10,000
Total net income for two years	$47,000	$47,000	$ –0–

Counterbalancing effect on net income (left margin)

Relation of inventory errors to net income   The effects of errors in inventory upon net income may be summarized as follows:

1 When the *ending* inventory is understated, the net income for the period will be understated.
2 When the *ending* inventory is overstated, the net income for the period will be overstated.
3 When the *beginning* inventory is understated, the net income for the period will be overstated.
4 When the *beginning* inventory is overstated, the net income for the period will be understated.

Taking a physical inventory

At the end of each accounting period the ledger accounts will show up-to-date balances for most of the assets. For inventory, however, the balance in the ledger account represents the *beginning* inventory, because no entry has been made in the Inventory account since the end of the preceding period. All purchases of merchandise during the present period have been recorded in the Purchases account. The ending inventory does not appear anywhere in the ledger accounts; it must be determined by a physical count of merchandise on hand at the end of the accounting period.

Establishing a balance sheet valuation for the ending inventory requires two steps: (1) determining the quantity of each kind of merchandise on hand, and (2) multiplying the quantity by the cost per unit. The first step is called *taking the inventory;* the second is called *pricing the inventory.* Taking inventory, or more precisely, taking a physical inventory, means making a systematic count of all merchandise on hand.

In most merchandising businesses the taking of a physical inventory is a year-end event. In some lines of business an inventory may be taken at the close of each month. It is common practice to take inventory after regular business hours or on Sunday. By taking the inventory while business operations are suspended, a more accurate count is possible than if goods were being sold or received while the count was in process.

Planning the physical inventory   Unless the taking of a physical inventory is carefully planned and supervised, serious errors are apt to occur which will invalidate the results of the count. To prevent such errors as the double counting of items, the omission of goods from the count, and other quantitative errors, it is desirable to plan the inventory so that the work of one person serves as a check on the accuracy of another.

There are various methods of counting merchandise. One of the simplest procedures is carried out by the use of two-member teams. One member of the team counts and calls the description and quantity of each item. The other person lists the descriptions and quantities on an inventory sheet. (In some situations, a tape recorder is useful in recording quantities counted.) When all goods have been counted and listed, the items on the inventory sheet are priced at cost, and the unit prices are multiplied by the quantities to determine the valuation of the inventory.

Goods in transit   Do goods in transit belong in the inventory of the seller or of the buyer? If the selling company makes delivery of the merchandise in its own trucks, the merchandise remains its property while in transit. If the goods are shipped by rail, air, or other public carrier, the question of ownership of the goods while in transit depends upon whether the public carrier is acting as the agent of the seller or of the buyer. If the terms of the shipment are *F.O.B.* (free on board) *shipping point,* title passes at the point of shipment and the goods are the property of the buyer while in transit. If the terms of the shipment are *F.O.B. destination,* title does not pass until the shipment reaches the destination, and the goods belong to the seller while in transit. In deciding whether goods in transit at year-end should be included in inventory, it is therefore necessary to refer to the terms of the agreement with vendors (suppliers) and customers.

At the end of the year a company may have received numerous orders from customers, for which goods have been segregated and packed but not yet shipped. These goods generally should be included in inventory. An exception to this rule is found occasionally when the goods have been prepared for shipment but are being held for later delivery at the request of the customer.

Passage of title to merchandise   The debit to Accounts Receivable and the offsetting credit to the Sales account should be made *when title to the goods passes to the customer.* It would obviously be improper to set up an account receivable and at the same time to include the goods in question in inventory. Great care is necessary at year-end to ensure that all last-minute shipments to customers are recorded as sales of the current year and, on the other hand, that no customer's order is recorded as a sale until the date when the goods are shipped. Sometimes, in an effort to meet sales quotas, companies have recorded sales on the last day of the accounting period, when in fact the merchandise was not shipped until early in the next period. Such practices lead to an overstatement of the year's earnings and are not in accordance with generally accepted principles of accounting.

Merchandise in inventory is valued at *cost,* whereas accounts receivable are stated at the *sales price* of the merchandise sold. Consequently, the recording of a sale prior to delivery of the goods results in an unjustified increase in the total assets of the company. The increase will equal the difference between the cost and the selling price of the goods in question. The amount of the increase will also be reflected in the income statement, where it will show up as additional earnings. An unscrupulous company, which wanted to make its financial statements present a more favorable picture than actually existed, might do so by treating year-end orders from customers as sales even though the goods were not yet shipped.

Pricing the inventory

One of the most interesting and widely discussed problems in accounting is the pricing of inventory. Even those business executives who have little knowledge of accounting are usually interested in the various methods of pricing inventory, because inventory valuation may have a significant effect upon reported net income.

Inventory, as well as most other assets, is valued in the accounting records at cost. However, several interesting questions arise in determining the "cost" of inventory. For example, should any expenditures other than the invoice price of purchased goods be considered as part of "cost"? Also, if similar items of merchandise are purchased at different prices during the year, which of these purchase prices represent the "cost" of the items remaining in inventory at year-end? We shall now address the problems involved in determining the cost of inventory.

Inclusion of indirect expenditures in inventory cost—a question of materiality   The starting point in determining the cost of inventory is the *net invoice price* of the goods in inventory. From a conceptual point of view, all indirect expenditures incurred in the acquisition of these goods should be added to the invoice prices in determining the cost of inventory. For example, part of the expenditure during the period for transportation-in is applicable to ending inventory and should be included in the inventory cost. In determining the cost of the ending inventory, many businesses add to the net invoice price of the goods a reasonable portion of the transportation charges incurred during the period.

In some lines of business, however, it is customary to price the year-end inventory without giving any consideration to transportation charges, because these charges are *not material in amount*. Although this practice results in a slight understatement of inventory cost, the understatement is so small that it does not affect the usefulness or reliability of the financial statements. Thus, the omission of transportation charges from the cost of inventory often may be justified by the factors of convenience and economy. Accounting textbooks stress theoretical concepts of cost and income determination. The student of accounting should be aware, however, that in many business situations a close *approximation* of cost will serve the purpose at hand. The extra work involved in developing more precise accounting data must be weighed against the benefits that will result.

Inventory valuation methods

The prices of many kinds of merchandise are subject to frequent change. When identical lots of merchandise are purchased at various dates during the year, each lot may be acquired at a different cost price.

To illustrate the several alternative methods in common use for determining which purchase prices apply to the units remaining in inventory at the end of the period, assume the data shown at the top of the next page.

This schedule shows that 180 units were sold during the year and that 120 units are on hand at year-end to make up the ending inventory. In order to

	Number of Units	Cost per Unit	Total Cost
Beginning inventory	100	$ 80	$ 8,000
First purchase (Mar. 1)	50	90	4,500
Second purchase (July 1)	50	100	5,000
Third purchase (Oct. 1)	50	120	6,000
Fourth purchase (Dec. 1)	50	130	6,500
Available for sale	300		$30,000
Units sold	180		
Units in ending inventory	120		

establish a dollar amount for cost of goods sold and for the ending inventory, we must make an assumption as to which units were sold and which units remain on hand at the end of the year. There are several acceptable assumptions on this point; four of the most common will be considered. Each assumption made as to the cost of the units in the ending inventory leads to a different method of pricing inventory and to different amounts in the financial statements. The four assumptions (and inventory valuation methods) to be considered are known as (1) specific identification, (2) average cost, (3) first-in, first-out, and (4) last-in, first-out.

Although each of these four methods will produce a different answer as to the cost of goods sold and the cost of the ending inventory, the valuation of inventory in each case is said to be at "cost." In other words, *these methods represent alternative definitions of inventory cost.*

Specific identification method If the units in the ending inventory can be identified as coming from specific purchases, they *may* be priced at the amounts listed on the purchase invoices. Continuing the example already presented, if the ending inventory of 120 units can be identified as, say, 50 units from the purchase of March 1, 40 units from the purchase of July 1, and 30 units from the purchase of December 1, the cost of the ending inventory may be computed as follows:

Specific identification method and . . .

50 units from the purchase of Mar. 1 @ $90	$ 4,500
40 units from the purchase of July 1 @ $100	4,000
30 units from the purchase of Dec. 1 @ $130	3,900
Ending inventory (specific identification)	$12,400

The cost of goods sold during the period is determined by subtracting the ending inventory from the cost of goods available for sale.

. . . cost of goods sold computation

Cost of goods available for sale	$30,000
Less: Ending inventory	12,400
Cost of goods sold (specific identification method)	$17,600

The specific identification method has an intuitive appeal because it assigns actual purchase costs to the specific units purchased. For decision-making purposes, however, this approach does not always provide the most useful accounting information.

As a simple example, assume that a coal dealer purchased 100 tons of coal at $60 a ton and a short time later made a second purchase of 100 tons of the same grade of coal at $80 a ton. The two purchases are in separate piles and it is a matter of indifference as to which pile is used in making sales to customers. Assume that the dealer makes a retail sale of one ton of coal at a price of $100. In measuring the gross profit on the sale, which cost figure should be used, $60 or $80? To insist that the cost depended on which of the two identical piles of coal was used in filling the delivery truck is an argument of questionable logic.

A situation in which the specific identification method is more likely to give meaningful results is in the purchase and sale of such high-priced articles as boats, automobiles, and jewelry.

Average-cost method   Average cost is computed by dividing the total cost of goods available for sale by the number of units available for sale. This computation gives a *weighted-average unit cost,* which is then applied to the units in the ending inventory.

Average-cost method and . . .

Cost of goods available for sale	$30,000
Number of units available for sale	300
Average unit cost	$ 100
Ending inventory (at average cost, 120 units @ $100)	$12,000

Note that this method, when compared with the specific identification method, leads to a different amount for cost of goods sold as well as a different amount for the ending inventory.

. . . cost of goods sold computation

Cost of goods available for sale	$30,000
Less: Ending inventory	12,000
Cost of goods sold (average-cost method)	$18,000

When the average-cost method is used, the cost figure of $12,000 determined for the ending inventory is influenced by all the various prices paid during the year. The price paid early in the year may carry as much weight in pricing the ending inventory as a price paid at the end of the year. A common criticism of the average-cost method of pricing inventory is that it attaches no more significance to current prices than to prices which prevailed several months earlier.

First-in, first-out method   The first-in, first-out method, which is often referred to as *fifo,* is based on the assumption that the first merchandise acquired is the first merchandise sold. In other words, each sale is made out of the *oldest* goods in stock; *the ending inventory therefore consists of the most recently acquired goods.* The fifo method of determining inventory cost may be adopted by any business, regardless of whether or not the physical flow of merchandise actually corresponds to this assumption of selling the oldest units in stock. Using the same data as in the preceding illustrations, the 120 units in the ending inventory would be regarded as consisting of the most recently acquired goods, as follows:

First-in, first-out method and . . .	50 units from the Dec. 1 purchase @ $130	$ 6,500
	50 units from the Oct. 1 purchase @ $120	6,000
	20 units from the July 1 purchase @ $100	2,000
	Ending inventory, 120 units (at fifo cost)	$14,500

During a period of *rising prices* the first-in, first-out method will result in a larger amount ($14,500) being assigned as the cost of the ending inventory than would be assigned under the average-cost method. When a relatively large amount is allocated as cost of the ending inventory, a relatively small amount will remain as cost of goods sold, as indicated by the following calculation:

. . . cost of goods sold computation	Cost of goods available for sale	$30,000
	Less: Ending inventory	14,500
	Cost of goods sold (first-in, first-out method)	$15,500

It may be argued in support of the first-in, first-out method that the inventory valuation reflects recent costs and is therefore a realistic value in the light of conditions prevailing at the balance sheet date.

Last-in, first-out method   The last-in, first-out method, commonly known as *lifo*, is one of the most interesting methods of pricing inventories. The title of this method suggests that the most recently acquired goods are sold first, and that *the ending inventory consists of "old" goods acquired in the earliest purchases.* Although this assumption is not in accord with the physical movement of merchandise in most businesses, there is a strong logical argument to support the lifo method.

For the purpose of measuring income, the *flow of costs* may be more significant than the physical flow of merchandise. Supporters of the lifo method contend that the measurement of income should be based upon *current* market conditions. Therefore, current sales revenue should be offset by the *current* cost of the merchandise sold. Under the lifo method, the costs assigned to the cost of goods sold are relatively current, because they stem from the most recent purchases. Under the *fifo* method, on the other hand, the cost of goods sold is based on "older" costs.

Using the same data as in the preceding illustrations, the 120 units in the ending inventory would be priced as if they were the oldest goods available for sale during the period, as follows:

Last-in, first-out method and . . .	100 units from the beginning inventory @ $80	$8,000
	20 units from the purchase of Mar. 1 @ $90	1,800
	Ending inventory, 120 units (at lifo cost)	$9,800

Note that the lifo cost of the ending inventory ($9,800) is very much lower than the fifo cost ($14,500) of ending inventory in the preceding example. Since a relatively small part of the cost of goods available for sale is assigned to ending inventory, it follows that a relatively large portion must have been assigned to cost of goods sold, as shown by the following computation:

. . . cost of goods sold computation	Cost of goods available for sale	$30,000
	Less: Ending inventory	9,800
	Cost of goods sold (last-in, first-out method)	$20,200

Comparison of the alternative methods of pricing inventory   We have now illustrated four common methods of pricing inventory at cost; the specific identification method, the average-cost method, the first-in, first-out method, and the last-in, first-out method. By way of contrasting the results obtained from the four methods illustrated, especially during a period of rapid price increases, let us summarize the amounts computed for ending inventory, cost of goods sold, and gross profit on sales under each of the four methods. Assume that sales for the period amounted to $27,500.

Fours methods of determining inventory cost compared

	Specific Identification Method	Average-Cost Method	First-In, First-Out Method	Last-In, First-Out Method
Sales	$27,500	$27,500	$27,500	$27,500
Cost of goods sold:				
Beginning inventory	$ 8,000	$ 8,000	$ 8,000	$ 8,000
Purchases	22,000	22,000	22,000	22,000
Cost of goods available for sale	$30,000	$30,000	$30,000	$30,000
Less: Ending inventory	12,400	12,000	14,500	9,800
Cost of goods sold	$17,600	$18,000	$15,500	$20,200
Gross profit on sales	$ 9,900	$ 9,500	$12,000	$ 7,300

This comparison of the four methods makes it apparent that during periods of *rising prices,* the use of lifo will result in lower reported profits and lower income taxes than would be the case under the other methods of inventory valuation. Perhaps for this reason many businesses have adopted lifo. Current income tax regulations permit virtually any business to use the last-in, first-out method in determining taxable income.[4]

During a period of *declining prices,* the use of lifo will cause the reporting of relatively large profits as compared with fifo, which will hold reported profits to a minimum. Therefore, the choice of an inventory pricing method may significantly affect the amount of income reported during prolonged periods of changing price levels.

Which method of inventory valuation is best?   All four of the inventory methods described are regarded as acceptable accounting practices and all four are acceptable in the determination of taxable income. No one method of inventory valuation can be considered as the "correct" or the "best" method. In the selection of a method, consideration should be given to the probable effect upon the balance sheet, upon the income statement, upon the amount of taxable income, and upon such business decisions as the establishment of selling prices for goods.

The specific identification method has the advantage of portraying the actual physical flow of merchandise. However, this method permits manipulation of income by selecting which items to deliver in filling a sales order. Also, the

---

[4]Income tax laws require the use of lifo for financial reporting if it is used for tax purposes.

specific identification method may lead to faulty pricing decisions by implying that identical items of merchandise have different economic values.

Identical items will have the same accounting values only under the average-cost method. Assume for example that a hardware store sells a given size nail for 65 cents per pound. The hardware store buys the nails in 100-pound quantities at different times at prices ranging from 40 to 50 cents per pound. Several hundred pounds of nails are always on hand, stored in a large bin. The average-cost method properly recognizes that when a customer buys a pound of nails it is not necessary to know exactly which nails the customer happened to select from the bin in order to measure the gross profit on the sale.

A shortcoming in the average-cost method is that changes in current replacement costs of inventory are concealed because these costs are averaged with older costs. As a result of this averaging, the reported gross profit may not reflect current market conditions. This problem is illustrated in the discussion of *inventory profits* later in this chapter.

The inflation of recent years is a strong argument for the use of the lifo method. When prices are rising drastically, the most significant cost data to use as a guide to sales policies are probably the *current replacement costs* of the goods being sold. The lifo method of inventory valuation comes closer than any of the other methods described to measuring net income in the light of current selling prices and replacement costs.

On the other hand, the use of lifo during a period of rising prices is apt to produce a balance sheet figure for inventory which is far below the current replacement cost of the goods on hand. The fifo method of inventory valuation will lead to a balance sheet valuation of inventory more in line with current replacement costs.

Some business concerns which adopted lifo more than 30 years ago now show a balance sheet figure for inventory which is less than half the present replacement cost of the goods in stock. An inventory valuation method which gives significant figures for the income statement may thus produce misleading amounts for the balance sheet, whereas a method which produces a realistic figure for inventory on the balance sheet may provide less realistic data for the income statement.

The search for the "best" method of inventory valuation is rendered difficult because the inventory figure is used in both the balance sheet and the income statement, and these two financial statements are intended for different purposes. In the income statement the function of the inventory figure is to permit a matching of costs and revenue. In the balance sheet the inventory and the other current assets are regarded as a measure of the company's ability to meet its current debts. For this purpose a valuation of inventory in line with current replacement cost would appear to be more significant.

Consistency in the valuation of inventory

The *principle of consistency* is one of the basic concepts underlying reliable financial statements. This principle means that once a company has adopted a particular accounting method, that company should follow that method consistently rather than switch methods from one year to the next. Consider the consequences if we were to ignore the principle of consistency in accounting for inventories. A company could cause its net income for any given year to increase or decrease merely by changing its method of inventory valuation. The principle of consistency does not mean that every company in an industry must use the same accounting method; it does mean that a given company should not switch year after year from one accounting method to another.

Bear in mind that a company has considerable latitude in selecting a method of inventory valuation best suited to its needs. The principle of consistency comes into play after a given method has been selected. We have already illustrated in the example on page 346 how different methods can produce differences in reported income. Consequently, a change from one inventory method to another will usually cause reported income to change significantly in the year in which the change is made. Frequent switching of methods would make the income statements undependable as a means of portraying trends in operating results. Because of the principle of consistency, the user of financial statements is able to assume that the company has followed the same accounting methods it used in the preceding year. Thus, the value of financial statements is increased because they enable the user to make reliable comparisons of the results achieved from year to year.

The principle of consistency does not mean that a business can *never* change its method of inventory valuation. However, when a change is made, the effects of the change upon reported net income should be *disclosed fully* in the footnotes accompanying the financial statements.[5] *Adequate disclosure* of all information necessary for the proper interpretation of financial statements is another basic principle of accounting. Even when the same method of inventory pricing is being followed consistently, the financial statements should include a disclosure of the pricing method in use.

The environment of inflation

We have previously discussed the relationship between the valuation of assets in the balance sheet and the recognition of costs and expenses in the income statement. As assets are sold or used up, their cost is removed from the balance sheet and recognized in the income statement as a cost or expense. In the case of inventory, the cost of units sold is transferred from the balance sheet to the income statement as cost of goods sold. In the case of depreciable assets, such as a building, the cost is gradually transferred to the income statement as depreciation expense. This flow of costs is illustrated at the top of the next page.

A period of sustained inflation causes some distortion in financial statements which are based upon historical costs. Rising price levels may cause assets to be valued in the balance sheets at amounts substantially below their current replacement cost. Similarly, the cost assigned to the income statement as these

---

[5]A change in the method of inventory valuation also requires the approval of the Internal Revenue Service.

Historical costs appear in both balance sheet and income statement

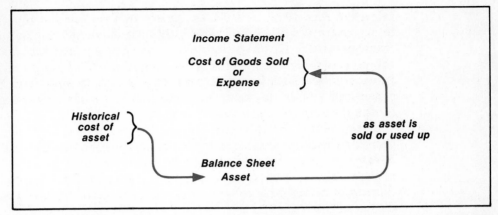

assets are sold or used up tends to understate the cost to the business of replacing these assets.

The inflationary policies and high income tax rates of recent years have stimulated the interest of business management in the choice of inventory methods. Most business executives and government officials expect the trend of rising prices to continue; in other words, an environment of inflation has come to be considered as normal. The lifo method of inventory valuation causes reported net income to reflect the increasing cost of replacing the merchandise sold during the year and also tends to avoid basing income tax payments on an exaggerated measurement of taxable income. Therefore, the existence of inflation is an argument for the lifo method of inventory.

Inventory profits

Many accountants believe that the use of fifo or of average cost during a period of inflation results in the reporting of overstated profits and consequently in the payment of excessive income taxes. Profits are overstated under both the fifo and average-cost methods because the gross profit is computed by subtracting "old" inventory costs rather than current replacement costs from sales revenue. These old costs are relatively low, resulting in a high reported gross profit. However, the company must pay the higher current cost in order to replenish its inventory.

To illustrate this concept, assume that TV Sales Shop has an inventory of 20 television sets which were acquired at an average cost of $270. During the current month, 10 television sets are sold for cash at a sales price of $350 each. Using the average-cost method to value inventory, the company will report the following gross profit for the month:

Sales (10 × $350)	$3,500
Cost of goods sold (10 × $270)	2,700
Gross profit on sales	$ 800

However, TV Sales Shop must replace its inventory of television sets to continue in business. Because of inflation, TV Sales Shop can no longer buy 10 television sets for $2,700. Let us assume that the current replacement cost of television sets is $325 each; TV Sales Shop must pay $3,250 to replenish its inventory. Thus, TV Sales Shop is able to keep only $250 ($3,500 − $3,250) of the reported $800 gross profit; the remaining $550 has to be reinvested in inventory because of the increasing cost of television sets. This $550 would be considered a fictitious profit, or an *inventory profit*, by many accountants and business executives.

The inventory profit included in the reported net income of a business may be computed by deducting the cost of goods shown in the income statement from the *replacement cost* (computed at the date of sale) of these goods.

In periods of rapid inflation, a significant portion of the reported net income of companies using fifo or average cost actually may be inventory profits. The net income of companies using lifo will include much less inventory profit because lifo causes more current costs to be included in the cost of goods sold.

FASB Statement No. 33—Disclosing the effects of inflation

In an effort to compensate for the distortions in financial statements caused by inflation, the Financial Accounting Standards Board adopted *Statement No. 33*, "Financial Reporting and Changing Prices."[6] This Statement requires large corporations to disclose the extent to which historical costs in both the balance sheet and the income statement understate current price levels. These disclosures can be in a footnote to the historical cost-based financial statements, or in a special set of supplementary financial statements. This information thus *supplements* rather than replaces the use of historical cost as a basis of accounting.

One requirement of Statement No. 33 is that large corporations disclose what it would cost to *replace* their inventories at year-end and what their cost of goods sold would be if computed by using the *current replacement cost* at the date of sale. The disclosure of the cost of goods sold computed on the basis of replacement cost has revealed that a substantial portion of the net income reported by many large corporations *is actually inventory profit*. In other words, net income tends to be *overstated* when companies rely solely on historical cost values during a period of inflation.

The FASB's action to require disclosure of replacement cost information may prove to be one of the most significant changes in accounting practice in many years. Some accountants view it as a major step away from cost-based accounting toward current-value accounting. At present, only very large corporations are required to make the disclosures called for in Statement No. 33, but the FASB encourages smaller companies to comply on a voluntary basis. Statement No. 33 calls for many disclosures in addition to the replacement cost of inventories and the cost of goods sold. These other disclosure requirements, including general price level adjustments and replacement costs of plant assets, are discussed in later chapters of this text.

---

[6]FASB, *Statement No. 33*, "Financial Reporting and Changing Prices" (Stamford, Conn.: 1979).

The lower-of-cost-or-market rule (LCM)

Although cost is the primary basis for valuation of inventories, circumstances may arise under which inventory may properly be valued at less than its cost. If the *utility* of the inventory has fallen below cost because of a decline in the price level, a loss has occurred. This loss may appropriately be recognized as a loss of the current period by reducing the accounting value of the inventory from cost to a lower level designated as *market*. The word market as used in this context means *current replacement cost.* For a merchandising company, market is the amount which the concern would have to pay at the present time for the goods in question, purchased in the customary quantities through the usual sources of supply and including transportation-in. To avoid misunderstanding, the rule might better read "lower of actual cost or replacement cost."

In the early days of accounting when the principal users of financial statements were creditors and attention was concentrated upon the balance sheet, *conservatism* was a dominant consideration in asset valuation. The lower-of-cost-or-market rule was then considered justifiable because it tended to produce a "safe" or minimum value for inventory. The rule was widely applied for a time without regard for the possibility that although replacement costs had declined, there might be no corresponding and immediate decline in selling prices.

As the significance of the income statement has increased, considerable dissatisfaction with the lower-of-cost-or-market rule has developed. If ending inventory is written down from cost to a lower market figure but the merchandise is sold during the next period at the usual selling prices, the effect of the writedown will have been to reflect a fictitious loss in the first period and an exaggerated profit in the second period. Selling prices do not always drop when replacement prices decline. Even if selling prices do follow replacement prices downward, they may not decline by a proportionate amount.

Because of these objections, the lower-of-cost-or-market rule has undergone some modification and is now qualified in the following respects. If the inventory can probably be sold at prices which will yield a *normal profit,* the inventory should be carried at cost even though current replacement cost is lower. Assume, for example, that merchandise is purchased for $1,000 with the intention of reselling it to customers for $1,500. The replacement cost then declines from $1,000 to $800, but it is believed that the merchandise can still be sold to customers for $1,450. In other words, the normal anticipated profit has shrunk by $50. The carrying value of the inventory could then be written down from $1,000 to $950. There is no justification for reducing the inventory to the replacement cost of $800 under these circumstances.

Another qualification of the lower-of-cost-or-market rule is that inventory should never be carried at an amount greater than *net realizable value,* which may be defined as prospective selling price minus anticipated selling expenses. Assume, for example, that because of unstable market conditions, it is believed that goods acquired at a cost of $500 and having a current replacement cost of $450 will probably have to be sold for no more than $520 and that the selling expenses involved will amount to $120. The inventory should then be reduced to a carrying value (net realizable value) of $400, which is less than current replacement cost.

Application of the lower-of-cost-or-market rule The lower of cost or market for inventory is often computed by determining the cost and the market figures for each item in inventory and using the lower of the two amounts in every case. If, for example, item A cost $100 and replacement cost is $90, the item should be priced at $90. If item B cost $200 and replacement cost is $225, this item should be priced at $200. The total cost of the two items is $300 and total replacement cost is $315, but the total inventory value determined by applying the lower-of-cost-or-market rule to each item in inventory is only $290. This application of the lower-of-cost-or-market rule is illustrated by the tabulation shown below:

Application of Lower-of-Cost-or-Market Rule, Item-by-Item Method

| | | Unit Cost | | Total Cost | | Lower of Cost or Market |
Item	Quantity	Cost	Market	Cost	Market	
A	10	$100	$ 90	$ 1,000	$ 900	$ 900
B	8	200	225	1,600	1,800	1,600
C	50	50	60	2,500	3,000	2,500
D	80	90	70	7,200	5,600	5,600
Totals				$12,300	$11,300	$10,600

Pricing inventory at lower of cost or market

If the lower-of-cost-or-market rule is applied item by item, the carrying value of the above inventory would be $10,600. However, an alternative and less rigorous version of the lower-of-cost-or-market rule calls for applying it to the total of the entire inventory rather than to the individual items. If the above inventory is to be valued by applying the lower-of-cost-or-market rule to the total of the inventory, the balance sheet amount for inventory is determined merely by comparing the total cost of $12,300 with the total replacement cost of $11,300 and using the lower of the two figures. Still another alternative method of using the lower-of-cost-or-market concept is to apply it to categories of the inventory rather than item by item. Each of these alternative methods of applying the lower-of-cost-or-market rule is acceptable in current accounting practice, although once a method has been selected it should be followed consistently from year to year.

Gross profit method of estimating inventories

The taking of a physical inventory is a time-consuming and costly job in many lines of business; consequently, a physical inventory may be taken only once a year. Monthly financial statements are needed, however, for intelligent administration of the business, and the preparation of monthly statements requires a determination of the amount of inventory at the end of each month. In many cases this dilemma may be solved satisfactorily by estimating the inventory each month by using the *gross profit method*.

The gross profit method of estimating inventory is based on the assumption that the rate of gross profit remains about the same from one accounting period to the next. This assumption is a realistic one for many fields of business. When the gross profit rate is known, the ending inventory can be estimated by the following procedures:

1 Determine the cost of goods available for sale from the general ledger records of beginning inventory and net purchases.
2 Estimate the cost of goods sold by reducing the net sales figure by the usual gross profit rate.
3 Subtract the estimated cost of goods sold from the cost of goods available for sale to find the estimated ending inventory.

To illustrate, assume that Metro Hardware Co. has a beginning inventory of $50,000 on January 1. During the month of January, net purchases amount to $8,000 and net sales total $20,000. Assuming that the company's normal gross profit rate is 40% of net sales, the inventory on hand at January 31 may be estimated as follows:

	Beginning inventory (Jan. 1)	*$50,000*
	Net purchases	*8,000*
Step 1...	*Cost of goods available for sale*	*$58,000*
Step 2...	*Less: Estimated cost of goods sold (60%* of $20,000 net sales)*	*12,000*
Step 3...	*Estimated ending inventory (Jan. 31)*	*$46,000*

*Since the gross profit rate is 40%, the cost of goods sold must equal 60% of net sales.

The gross profit method of estimating inventory has several uses apart from the preparation of monthly financial statements. This technique may be used after the taking of a physical inventory to confirm the overall reasonableness of the amount determined by the counting and pricing process. In the event of a fire which destroys the inventory, the approximate amount of goods on hand at the date of the fire also may be computed by the gross profit method.

The retail method of inventory valuation

The retail method of estimating ending inventory is somewhat similar to the gross profit method. It is widely used by chain stores, department stores, and other types of retail business. Goods on sale in retail stores are marked at the retail prices; it is therefore more convenient to take inventory at current retail prices than to look up invoices to find the unit cost of each item in stock. After first determining the value of the inventory at retail price, the next step is to convert the inventory to cost price by applying the ratio prevailing between cost and selling price during the current period. This method of approximating an inventory may also be carried out by using data from the accounts without taking any physical count of the goods on hand. The underlying basis for the *retail method* of inventory valuation is the ratio of cost to selling price for the *current period,* whereas the *gross profit method* of estimating inventory rests on the rate of gross profit experienced in *preceding periods.*

When the retail method of inventory is to be used, it is necessary to maintain records of the beginning inventory and of all purchases during the period in terms of selling price as well as at cost. Goods available for sale during the period can then be stated both at cost and at selling price. By deducting the sales for the period from the sales value of the goods available for sale, the ending inventory at selling price may be determined without the need for a physical count. The ending inventory at selling price is then converted to a cost basis by using the percentage ratio of cost to selling price for the current period.

In practice, the application of this method may be complicated because the originally established sales prices are modified by frequent price markups and markdowns. These frequent changes in retail price present some difficulties in determining the correct rate to use in reducing the inventory from selling price to cost. The following illustration shows the calculation of inventory by the retail method, without going into the complications which would arise from markups and markdowns in the original retail selling price.

	Cost Price	Selling Price
Used by many department stores — *Beginning inventory*	$20,000	$30,000
Net purchases during the month	11,950	15,000
Goods available for sale	$31,950	$45,000
Less: Net sales for the month		20,000
Ending inventory at selling price		$25,000
Cost ratio ($31,950 ÷ $45,000)		71%
Ending inventory at cost (71% × $25,000)	$17,750	

Perpetual inventory system

Companies which deal in merchandise of high unit cost, such as television sets or outboard motors, find a perpetual inventory system worthwhile and efficient. Since inventory may be one of the largest assets in a business and has a rapid rate of turnover, strong internal control is especially important. A perpetual inventory system, if properly designed and operated, can provide the strongest possible internal control over the inventory of merchandise. The key feature of a perpetual inventory system is that the records show continuously the amount of inventory on hand and the cost of goods sold. Large companies that maintain their accounting records electronically are in a good position to carry on continuous updating of inventory records.

Internal control and perpetual inventory systems

A perpetual inventory system has the potential of providing excellent internal control. However, the fact that perpetual inventory records are in use does not automatically guarantee strong internal control. Such basic internal control concepts as the subdivision of duties, the control of documents by serial numbers, and separation of the accounting function from the custody of assets are essential elements with either the perpetual or periodic inventory systems.

ILLUSTRATIVE CASE   Par-Flite, a manufacturer of golf equipment, maintained an inventory of several thousand sets of golf clubs. The clubs were kept in a storeroom with barred windows and doors under the supervision of John Adams. Adams was also responsible for maintaining detailed perpetual inventory records of the golf clubs in the storeroom. Another employee acquired an unauthorized key to the storeroom and began stealing large numbers of clubs. Adams discovered that the quantities on hand did not agree with the perpetual records he maintained. Afraid that his records would be criticized as highly inaccurate, he made numerous changes in the records so they would agree with quantities of golf clubs on hand. The theft of clubs continued and large losses were sustained before the inventory shortage came to the attention of management.

If the person maintaining inventory records had not also been responsible for physical custody of the merchandise, there would have been no incentive or opportunity to conceal a shortage by falsifying the records. Satisfactory internal control over inventories requires that the accounting function be separate from the custody of assets. Frequent comparison of quantities of merchandise on hand with the quantities shown by the perpetual inventory records should be made by employees who do not have responsibility either for custody of assets or for maintenance of records.

Perpetual inventory records

The information required for a perpetual inventory system can be processed electronically or manually. In a manual system a subsidiary record card, as shown below, is used for each type of merchandise on hand. If the company has 100 different kinds of products in stock, then 100 inventory record cards will make up the subsidiary inventory record. Shown below is an inventory record card for item XL-2000.

Perpetual inventory record card

Item XL-2000						Maximum 20		
Location Storeroom 2						Minimum 8		
	PURCHASED			SOLD			BALANCE		
Date	Units	Unit Cost	Total	Units	Unit Cost	Total	Units	Unit Cost	Balance
Jan. 1							12	$50.00	$600.00
7				2	$50.00	$100.00	10	50.00	500.00
9	10	$55.00	$550.00				10	50.00	
							10	55.00	1,050.00
12				8	50.00	400.00	2	50.00	
							10	55.00	650.00
31				2	50.00	100.00			
				1	55.00	55.00	9	55.00	495.00

On this card, the quantity and cost of units received will be listed at the date of receipt; the quantity and cost of units sold will be recorded at the date of sale; and after each purchase or sales transaction, the balance remaining on hand will be shown. This running balance will be shown in number of units, cost per unit, and total dollar amount.

The information on the illustrated inventory record shows that the first-in, first-out basis of pricing the inventory is being used. After the sale of two units on January 7, the remaining inventory consisted of 10 units at a cost of $50 each. The purchase on January 9 of 10 units carried a unit cost of $55, rather than $50, hence must be accounted for separately. The balance on hand after the January 9 purchase appears on two lines: 10 units at $50 and 10 units at $55. When eight units were sold on January 12, they were treated as coming from the oldest stock on hand and therefore had a cost of $50 each. The balance remaining on hand then consisted of two units at $50 and 10 units at $55. When three units were sold on January 31, the cost consisted of two units at $50 and one unit at $55. The ending inventory of nine units consists of the most recently acquired units with a cost of $55 each.

Perpetual inventory records may also be maintained on a last-in, first-out basis or on an average-cost basis, but these systems involve some complexities which are considered in advanced accounting courses.

Control over the amount invested in inventory can be strengthened by listing on each inventory card the maximum and minimum quantities that should be kept in stock. By maintaining quantities within these limits, overstocking and out-of-stock situations can be avoided.

General ledger entries for a perpetual inventory system   The general ledger controlling account entitled *Inventory* is continuously (perpetually) updated when a perpetual inventory system is in use. This Inventory account controls the many subsidiary record cards discussed above. A continuously updated Cost of Goods Sold account is also maintained in the general ledger.

The purchase of merchandise by a company using a perpetual inventory system requires a journal entry affecting general ledger controlling accounts as follows:

Inventory	*1,500*	
Accounts Payable, Lake Company		*1,500*
To record purchase of merchandise on credit.		

This purchase transaction would also be recorded in the subsidiary ledger (the perpetual inventory cards) showing the quantity of each kind of merchandise purchased. The $1,500 purchase from Lake Company might affect only one or perhaps a dozen of the subsidiary records, depending on how many types of merchandise were included in this purchase transaction.

For every sales transaction, we can determine the cost of the goods sold by referring to the appropriate perpetual inventory card record. Therefore, at the time of a sale, we can record both the amount of the selling price and the *cost* of the goods sold, as illustrated in the following pair of related entries.

Accounts Receivable, J. Williams 140

    Sales 140

To record the sales of merchandise on credit.

Cost of Goods Sold 100

    Inventory 100

To record the cost of goods sold and the related decrease in inventory.

To avoid making a large number of entries in the general journal, a special column can be entered in the sales journal to show the cost of the goods involved in each sales transaction. At the end of the month the total of this "Cost" column can be posted as a debit to Cost of Goods Sold and a credit to Inventory.

A company maintaining perpetual inventory records will also conduct a physical count of all merchandise once a year and compare the amount of the physical inventory with the perpetual inventory records. An adjusting entry can be made to bring the inventory records into agreement with the physical inventory. For example, if shoplifting or other factors have caused an inventory shortage, the adjusting entry will consist of a debit to the loss account, Inventory Shortage, and a credit to Inventory.

When a perpetual inventory system is in use, the Inventory account is increased by purchases of merchandise. It is decreased by the cost of goods sold, by purchase returns and allowances, and by purchase discounts. At the end of the year the dollar balances of all the subsidiary inventory record cards should be added to see that the total is in agreement with the general ledger controlling account. The only adjustment necessary at year-end will be to correct the Inventory controlling account and the subsidiary records for any discrepancies indicated by the taking of a physical inventory.

The advantages of a perpetual inventory system as indicated in the preceding discussion include:

1 Stronger internal control. By comparing the physical inventory with the perpetual records, management will be made aware of any shortages or errors and can take corrective action.
2 A physical inventory can be taken at dates other than year-end, or it can be taken for different products or different departments at various dates during the year, since the perpetual records always show the amounts which *should* be on hand.
3 Quarterly or monthly financial statements can be prepared more readily because of the availability of dollar amounts for inventory and cost of goods sold in the accounting records.

KEY TERMS INTRODUCED OR EMPHASIZED IN CHAPTER 9

Average-cost method   A method of inventory valuation. Weighted-average unit cost is computed by dividing the total cost of goods available for sale by the number of units available for sale.

Consistency in inventory valuation   An accounting standard that calls for the use of the same method of inventory pricing from year to year, with full disclosure of the effects of any change in method. Intended to make financial statements comparable.

First-in, first-out (fifo)   A method of computing the cost of inventory and the cost of goods sold based on the assumption that the first merchandise acquired is the first merchandise sold, and that the ending inventory consists of the most recently acquired goods.

F.O.B. destination   A term meaning the seller bears the cost of shipping goods to the buyer's location. Title to the goods remains with the seller while the goods are in transit.

F.O.B. shipping point   The buyer of goods bears the cost of transportation from the seller's location to the buyer's location. Title to the goods passes at the point of shipment and the goods are the property of the buyer while in transit.

Gross profit method   A method of estimating the cost of the ending inventory based on the assumption that the rate of gross profit remains approximately the same from year to year.

Inventory profits   The amount by which the cost of replacing goods sold (computed at the date of sale) **exceeds** the reported cost of goods sold. Many accountants consider inventory profits to be a "fictitious" profit, because this amount usually must be reinvested in inventories and therefore is not available for distribution to stockholders.

Last-in, first-out (lifo) method   A method of computing the cost of goods sold by use of the prices paid for the most recently acquired units. Ending inventory is valued on the basis of prices paid for the units first acquired.

Lower-of-cost-or-market method   A method of inventory pricing in which goods are valued at original cost or replacement cost (market), whichever is lower.

Manufacturing costs   The costs incurred by a manufacturing business in manufacturing its products. Manufacturing costs consist of the costs of raw materials used, direct labor, and factory overhead.

Net realizable value   The prospective selling price minus anticipated selling expenses. Inventory should not be carried at more than net realizable value.

Perpetual inventory system   Provides a continuous (perpetual) running record of the goods on hand. As goods are sold their cost is transferred to a Cost of Goods Sold account.

Physical inventory   A systematic count of all goods on hand, followed by the application of unit prices to the quantities counted and development of a dollar value for ending inventory.

Retail method   A method of estimating inventory in a retail store based on the assumption that the cost of goods on hand bears the same percentage relationship to retail prices as does the cost of all goods available for sale to the original retail prices. Inventory is first priced at retail and then converted to cost by application of a cost-to-retail percentage.

Specific identification method   A method of pricing inventory by identifying the units in the ending inventory as coming from specific purchases.

DEMONSTRATION PROBLEM FOR YOUR REVIEW

Information relating to the inventory quantities, purchases, and sales of a certain type of capacitor by Morton Electronics during Year 4 is shown at the top of the next page.

	Number of Units	Cost per Unit	Total Cost
Inventory, Jan. 1, Year 4	8,000	$5.89	$ 47,120
First purchase (Mar. 15)	10,300	6.20	63,860
Second purchase (June 6)	12,400	6.60	81,840
Third purchase (Sept. 20)	9,600	6.80	65,280
Fourth purchase (Dec. 31)	7,700	7.00	53,900
Goods available for sale	48,000		$312,000
Units sold during Year 4	37,200		
Inventory, Dec. 31, Year 4	10,800		

Instructions Compute the cost of the December 31, Year 4, inventory and the cost of goods sold for the capacitors in Year 4 using:

a The first-in, first-out method
b The last-in, first-out method
c The average-cost method

SOLUTION TO DEMONSTRATION PROBLEM

a Fifo method

Inventory:

7,700 units from the Dec. 31 purchase @ $7.00	$ 53,900
3,100 units from the Sept. 20 purchase @ $6.80	21,080
Ending inventory, 10,800 units (at fifo cost)	$ 74,980

Cost of goods sold:

Cost of goods available for sale	$312,000
Less: Ending inventory (fifo)	74,980
Cost of goods sold (fifo)	$237,020

b Lifo method

Inventory:

8,000 units from beginning inventory @ $5.89	$ 47,120
2,800 units from the Mar. 15 purchase @ $6.20	17,360
Ending inventory, 10,800 units (at lifo cost)	$ 64,480

Cost of goods sold:

Cost of goods available for sale	$312,000
Less: Ending inventory (lifo)	64,480
Cost of goods sold (lifo)	$247,520

c Average-cost method

Inventory:

Cost of goods available for sale	$312,000
Number of units available for sale	48,000
Average cost per unit ($312,000 ÷ 48,000 units)	$ 6.50
Ending inventory (at average cost, 10,800 units × $6.50)	$ 70,200

Cost of goods sold:

Cost of goods available for sale	$312,000
Less: Ending inventory (average cost)	70,200
Cost of goods sold (average cost)	$241,800

Alternative computation of cost of goods sold:

Cost of goods sold (37,200 units at $6.50)	$241,800

REVIEW QUESTIONS

1 Which of the seven items listed below are used in computing the *cost of goods available for sale?*

   a Ending inventory   **e** Transportation-in

   b Sales   **f** Purchase returns and allowances

   c Beginning inventory   **g** Delivery expense

   d Purchases

2 Through an error in counting of merchandise at December 31, Year 4, the Trophy Company overstated the amount of goods on hand by $8,000. Assuming that the error was not discovered, what was the effect upon net income for Year 4? Upon owners' equity at December 31, Year 4? Upon net income for Year 5? Upon owners' equity at December 31, Year 5?

3 Is the establishment of an appropriate valuation for the merchandise inventory at the end of the year more important in producing a dependable income statement, or in producing a dependable balance sheet?

4 Explain the meaning of the term *physical inventory.*

5 Near the end of December, Hadley Company received a large order from a major customer. The work of packing the goods for shipment was begun at once but could not be completed before the close of business on December 31. Since a written order from the customer was on hand and the goods were nearly all packed and ready for shipment, Hadley felt that this merchandise should not be included in the physical inventory taken on December 31. Do you agree? What is probably the reason behind Hadley's opinion?

6 During a prolonged period of rising prices, will the fifo or lifo method of inventory valuation result in higher reported profits?

7 Throughout several years of strongly rising prices, Company A used the lifo method of inventory valuation and Company B used the fifo method. In which company would the balance sheet figure for inventory be closer to current replacement cost of the merchandise on hand? Why?

8 You are making a detailed analysis of the financial statements and accounting records of two companies in the same industry, Adams Company and Bar Company. Price levels have been rising steadily for several years. In the course of your investigation, you observe that the inventory value shown on the Adams Company balance sheet is quite close to the current replacement cost of the merchandise on hand. However, for Bar Company, the carrying value of the inventory is far below current replacement cost. What method of inventory valuation is probably used by Adams Company? By Bar Company? If we assume that the two companies are identical except for the inventory valuation method used, which company has probably been reporting higher net income in recent years?

9 Why do some accountants consider the net income reported by businesses during a period of rising prices to be overstated?

10 Assume that a business uses the first-in, first-out method of accounting for inventories during a prolonged period of inflation and that the business pays dividends equal to the amount of reported net income. Suggest a problem that may arise in continued successful operation of the business. What does this situation have to do with "inventory profits"?

11 The Financial Accounting Standards Board requires large corporations to disclose the cost of replacing their inventories and to disclose what their cost of goods sold would be if computed by using replacement costs. Do you think this policy indicates that corporate profits have tended to be overstated or understated in recent years? Explain.

12 Explain the meaning of the term *market* as used in the expression "lower of cost or market."

13 One of the items in the inventory of Grayline Stores is marked for sale at $125. The purchase invoice shows the item cost $95, but a newly issued price list from the manufacturer shows the present replacement cost to be $90. What inventory valuation should be assigned to this item if Grayline Stores follows the lower-of-cost-or-market rule?

14 Explain the usefulness of the *gross profit method* of estimating inventories.

15 A store using the *retail inventory method* takes its physical inventory by applying current retail prices as marked on the merchandise to the quantities counted. Does this procedure indicate that the inventory will appear in the financial statements at retail selling price? Explain.

16 Estimate the ending inventory by the gross profit method, given the following data: beginning inventory $40,000, net purchases $100,000, net sales $106,667, average gross profit rate 25% of net sales.

17 Summarize the difference between the *periodic system* and the *perpetual system* of accounting for inventory. Which system would usually cost more to maintain? Which system would be most practicable for a restaurant, a retail drugstore, a new car dealer?

18 Identify each of the four statements shown below as true or false. In the accounting records of a company using a perpetual inventory system:
   a The Inventory account will ordinarily remain unchanged until the end of an accounting period.
   b The Cost of Goods Sold account is debited with the sales price of merchandise sold.
   c The Inventory account and the Cost of Goods Sold account will both normally have debit balances.
   d The Inventory account and the Cost of Goods Sold account will normally have equal but offsetting balances.

EXERCISES

Ex. 9-1   The condensed income statements prepared by Blaze Company for two years are shown below:

	Year 2	Year 1
Sales	$500,000	$480,000
Cost of goods sold	293,200	304,800
Gross profit on sales	$206,800	$175,200
Operating expenses	153,500	149,000
Net income	$ 53,300	$ 26,200

The inventory at the end of Year 1 was understated by $16,800, but the error was not discovered until after the accounts had been closed and financial statements prepared at the end of Year 2. The balance sheets for the two years showed owners' equity of $71,400 at the end of Year 1 and $86,800 at the end of Year 2.

Compute the correct net income figures for Year 1 and Year 2 and the gross profit percentage for each year based on corrected data. What correction, if any, should be made in owners' equity at the end of Year 1 and at the end of Year 2?

Ex. 9-2   Information relating to the inventory quantities, purchases, and sales of gate valves by National Plumbing Supply during the current year is as follows:

	Number of Units	Cost per Unit	Total Cost
Beginning inventory (Jan. 1)	9,100	$4.00	$ 36,400
First purchase (Feb. 20)	20,000	4.10	82,000
Second purchase (May 10)	30,000	4.25	127,500
Third purchase (Aug. 24)	50,000	4.60	230,000
Fourth purchase (Nov. 30)	10,900	5.00	54,500
Goods available for sale	120,000		$530,400
Units sold during the year	106,000		
Ending inventory (Dec. 31)	14,000		

Compute the cost of the ending inventory of gate valves, using the following inventory valuation methods:

a First-in, first-out

b Last-in, first-out

c Average cost

Ex. 9-3   The beginning inventory balance of item X on January 1 and the purchases of this item during the current year were as follows:

Jan.	1	Beginning inventory	500 units @ $10.00	$ 5,000
Feb.	23	Purchase	1,600 units @ $11.00	17,600
Apr.	20	Purchase	1,000 units @ $11.20	11,200
May	4	Purchase	1,000 units @ $11.60	11,600
Nov.	30	Purchase	400 units @ $12.50	5,000
		Totals	4,500 units	$50,400

At December 31 the ending inventory consisted of 650 units.

Determine the cost of the ending inventory, based on each of the following methods of inventory valuation:

a Average cost

b First-in, first-out

c Last-in, first-out

Ex. 9-4   Marantz Corporation sells only one product; sales and purchases occur at a uniform rate throughout the year. The following items appear in the company's financial statements for Year 4:

Purchases	$2,000,000
Cost of goods sold	1,900,000
Inventory, Jan. 1, Year 4 (fifo basis)	520,000
Inventory, Dec. 31, Year 4 (fifo basis)	620,000

A footnote to the financial statements disclosed that the replacement cost of inventory at December 31, Year 4, was $650,000 and that the cost of goods sold computed using replacement costs at the date of sale amounted to $2,150,000.

a Compute the amount of inventory profit included in Marantz Corporation's reported operating results for Year 4.

b Did the number of units in Marantz Corporation's inventory increase or decrease during Year 4? Explain your reasoning. (Hint: Was the company's spending for merchandise purchases sufficient to replace the units sold?)

Ex. 9-5 Ruger Company has compiled the following information concerning items in its inventory at December 31:

		Unit Cost	
Item	Quantity	Cost (fifo)	Market
A	120	$ 46	$ 50
B	70	160	136
C	62	100	110
D	81	280	290

Determine the total inventory value to appear on Ruger Company's balance sheet under the lower-of-cost-or-market rule, assuming (**a**) that the rule is applied to inventory as a whole and (**b**) that the rule is applied on an item-by-item basis.

Ex. 9-6 When Ellen Sharp arrived at her store on the morning of May 29, she found empty shelves and display racks; thieves had broken in during the night and stolen the entire inventory. Sharp's accounting records showed that she had $48,000 inventory on May 1 (cost value). From May 1 to May 29, she had made sales of $196,000 and purchases of $141,800. The gross profit during the past several years had consistently averaged 30% of sales. Sharp wishes to file an insurance claim for the theft loss. What is the estimated cost of her inventory at the time of the theft? Show computations.

Ex. 9-7 Vagabond Shop wishes to determine the approximate month-end inventory using data from the accounting records without taking a physical count of merchandise on hand. From the following information, estimate the cost of the September 30 inventory by the retail method of inventory valuation.

	Cost Price	Selling Price
Inventory of merchandise, Aug. 31	$264,800	$400,000
Purchases (net) during September	170,400	240,000
Sales (net) during September		275,200

Ex. 9-8   Santa Cruz Wholesale Company uses a ***perpetual inventory system.*** On January 1, the Inventory account had a balance of $87,500. During the first few days of January the following transactions occurred.
Jan. 2 Purchased merchandise on credit from Bell Company for $12,500.
Jan. 3 Sold merchandise for cash, $9,000. The cost of this merchandise was $6,300.
a Prepare entries in general journal form to record the above transactions.
b What was the balance of the Inventory account at the close of business January 3?

Ex. 9-9   Stream Bicycle Shop uses the first-in, first-out method of inventory valuation. At the end of the current year the shop had exactly the same number of bicycles in stock as at the beginning of the year, and the same proportion of each model. However, the year had been one of severe inflation and the cost of the ending inventory was shown in the accounts at $24,000 whereas the cost of the beginning inventory had been only $16,000. The net income reported by the shop for the year was $27,000. Comment on the validity of the reported net income and indicate what adjustment might be reasonable to give the owner of this business a realistic picture of the results of the year's operations.

PROBLEMS

9-1   Hollywood Costume Co. is being offered for sale as a going concern. Its income statements for the last three years include the following key figures:

	Year 3	Year 2	Year 1
Net sales	$540,000	$520,000	$500,000
Cost of goods sold	356,400	348,800	345,000
Gross profit on sales	$183,600	$171,200	$155,000
Gross profit percentage	34%	33%*	31%

*Rounded to the nearest full percentage point.

In discussions with prospective buyers, the owners are emphasizing the rising trends of gross profit and gross profit percentage as very favorable factors.

Assume that you are retained by a prospective purchaser of the business to make an investigation of the fairness and reliability of Hollywood Costume Co.'s accounting records and financial statements. You find everything in order except for the following: (1) An arithmetical error in the computation of inventory at the end of Year 1 had caused a $10,000 understatement in that inventory; and (2) a duplication of figures in the computation of inventory at the end of Year 3 had caused an overstatement of $27,000 in that inventory. The company uses the periodic inventory system and these errors had not been brought to light prior to your investigation.

Instructions
a Prepare a revised three-year schedule along the lines of the one illustrated above.
b Comment on the trend of gross profit and gross profit percentage before and after the revision.

9-2   Information relating to the inventory quantities, purchases, and sales of an 8-inch speaker unit by The Audio Shop during the current year is shown on the next page.

	Number of Units	Cost per Unit	Total Cost
Inventory, Jan. 1	900	$10.00	$ 9,000
First purchase (Apr. 3)	1,180	10.20	12,036
Second purchase (July 7)	800	10.35	8,280
Third purchase (Oct. 22)	620	10.70	6,634
Fourth purchase (Dec. 15)	1,000	10.85	10,850
Goods available for sale	4,500		$46,800
Units sold during the year	3,200		
Inventory, Dec. 31	1,300		

Instructions

a Compute the cost of the December 31 inventory and the cost of goods sold for the 8-inch speaker units in the current year using:
  (1) The first-in, first-out method
  (2) The last-in, first-out method
  (3) The average-cost method

b Which of the three inventory pricing methods provides the most realistic balance sheet valuation of inventory in light of the current replacement cost of the speaker units? Does this same method also produce the most realistic measure of income in light of the costs being incurred by The Audio Shop to replace the speakers when they are sold? Explain.

9-3 Water Massage, Inc., sells only one product. During the current year, 77,500 units were sold for total sales revenue of $930,000. The beginning inventory at January 1 consisted of 15,000 units valued at cost of $112,500. Purchases during the year were as follows: 20,000 units at $7.75; 28,500 units at $8.00; 21,000 units at $8.30; and 15,500 units at $8.40.

Instructions

a Compute the year-end (December 31) inventory using:
  (1) The first-in, first-out method
  (2) The last-in, first-out method
  (3) The average-cost method

b Prepare partial income statements for each of the above three methods of pricing inventory. The income statements are to be carried only to the determination of gross profit on sales.

c Which of the three methods of pricing inventory would be most advantageous from an income tax standpoint during a period of rising prices? Comment on the significance of the inventory figure under the method you recommend with respect to current replacement cost.

9-4 The entire inventory of Airbrush Shirt Company was destroyed by fire on April 19, Year 5. The company does not maintain perpetual inventory records, and the last physical inventory had been taken on December 31, Year 4. Therefore, an estimate of the inventory value at April 19 must be prepared in order to file an insurance claim. The following partial income statement for Year 4 is available to aid you in estimating the amount of inventory at the date of the fire:

AIRBRUSH SHIRT COMPANY
Income Statement
For the Year Ended, December 31, Year 4

Net Sales		$397,000
Cost of goods sold:		
Inventory, Jan. 1, Year 4	$122,500	
Purchases	315,000	
Cost of goods available for sale	$437,500	
Less: Inventory, Dec. 31, Year 4	140,000	297,500
Gross profit on sales		$ 99,500

Other data   The sales figure in the above income statement does not include $13,000 sales value of merchandise sold to a customer late in the day on December 31. This sale was erroneously recorded as occurring on the following business day, which was January 2, Year 5. Also, the $10,000 cost of this merchandise was erroneously included in the figure for inventory at December 31, Year 4.

Records salvaged from the fire revealed the merchandise transactions after December 31, Year 4, to the date of the fire to be: net sales, $181,500 (including the $13,000 sale erroneously recorded on January 2); and net purchases, $108,000.

Instructions

a Prepare a report directed to the insurance adjuster summarizing your findings. Include an estimate of the inventory value as of the date of the fire and a computation of the applicable gross profit rate.

b Explain how the gross profit method of estimating inventories may be used other than in case of a fire loss.

9-5   Toy Castle, a retail business, had net sales during January of $32,600. Purchases of merchandise from suppliers during January amounted to $20,620. Of these January purchases, invoices totaling $13,620 were paid during the month; the remaining January invoices totaling $7,000 were still unpaid at January 31. The merchandise purchased during January had a retail sales value of $29,500.

On January 1 the merchandise on hand represented a cost of $21,200 as determined by the year-end physical inventory. The retail sales value of this inventory was $32,000. The retail selling price was plainly marked on every item of merchandise in the store.

At January 31 the manager of Toy Castle wished to estimate the cost of inventory on hand without taking time to count the merchandise and look up the cost prices as shown on purchase invoices.

Instructions

a Use the retail inventory method to estimate the cost of the inventory at January 31.

b What effect, if any, does the fact that January purchase invoices in the amount of $7,000 were unpaid at January 31 have upon the determination of the amount of inventory at January 31?

9-6 Porterfield's, a retail store, carries a wide range of merchandise consisting mostly of articles of low unit price. The selling price of each item is plainly marked on the merchandise. At each year-end, the company has taken a physical count of goods on hand and has priced these goods at cost by looking up individual purchase invoices to determine the unit cost of each item in stock. Stevens, the store manager, is anxious to find a more economical method of assigning dollar values to the year-end inventory, explaining that it takes much more time to price the inventory than to count the merchandise on hand.

By analyzing the accounting records you are able to determine that net purchases of merchandise in Year 4 totaled $1,330,000; the retail selling price of this merchandise was $1,750,000. At the end of Year 4, a physical inventory showed goods on hand priced to sell at $375,000. This represented a considerable increase over the inventory of a year earlier. At December 31, Year 3, the inventory on hand had appeared in the balance sheet at cost of $170,000, although it had a retail value of $250,000.

Instructions

a Outline a plan whereby the inventory can be computed without the necessity of looking up individual purchase invoices. List step by step the procedures to be followed. Ignore the possibility of markups and markdowns in the original retail price of merchandise.

b Compute the cost of the inventory at December 31, Year 4, using the method described in a.

c Explain how the inventory method you have described can be modified for the preparation of monthly financial statements when no physical count of inventory is taken.

9-7 Oaktree Wholesale Company uses a perpetual inventory system, including a perpetual inventory record card for each of the 60 types of products it keeps in stock. The following transactions show the purchases and sales of one of these products (XK3) during September.

Sept.	1 Balance on hand, 50 units, cost $60 each	$3,000
	4 Purchase, 20 units, cost $65 each	1,300
	8 Sale, 35 units, sales price $100 each	3,500
	9 Purchase, 40 units, cost $65 each	2,600
	20 Sale, 60 units, sales price $100 each	6,000
	25 Purchase, 40 units, cost $70 each	2,800
	30 Sale, 5 units, sales price $110 each	550

Instructions

a Record the beginning inventory, the purchases, the cost of goods sold, and the running balance on an inventory record card like the one illustrated on page 355. Use the first-in, first-out method.

b Assume that all sales were made on credit. Compute the total sales and total cost of goods sold of product XK3 for September. Prepare an entry in general journal form to record these sales and a second entry to record the cost of goods sold for September.

c Compute the gross profit on sales of product XK3 for the month of September.

9-8   Income statements prepared by Sunflower Paints for Year 4 and Year 5 are shown below. The periodic inventory system is being used.

	Year 5	Year 4
Net sales	$700,000	$660,000
Cost of goods sold:		
Beginning inventory	$240,400	$240,000
Net purchases	444,740	409,160
Cost of goods available for sale	$685,140	$649,160
Ending inventory	241,000	240,400
Cost of goods sold	$444,140	$408,760
Gross profit on sales	$255,860	$251,240
Expenses	180,000	170,100
Net income	$ 75,860	$ 81,140

The owners' equity as shown in the company's balance sheet was as follows: December 31, Year 3, $350,000; December 31, Year 4, $431,140; and December 31, Year 5, $507,000.

Early in Year 6, Alan Frank, accountant for Sunflower Paints, made a review of the documents and procedures used in taking the physical inventory at December 31 for both Year 4 and Year 5. His investigation disclosed the two questionable items listed below:

(1) Merchandise shipped to a customer on December 31, Year 4, F.O.B. shipping point, was included in the physical inventory taken that date. The cost of the merchandise was $2,900 and the sales price was $3,600. Because of the press of year-end work, the sales invoice was not prepared until January 6, Year 5. On that date the sale was recorded as a January transaction by entry in the sales journal, and the sales invoice mailed to the customer.

(2) Merchandise costing $6,840 which had been received on December 31, Year 4, had been included in the inventory taken on that date, although the purchase was not recorded until January 8 when the vendor's invoice arrived. The invoice was then recorded in the purchases journal as a January transaction.

Instructions

a Prepare corrected income statements for the years ended December 31, Year 4 and Year 5. (You may find it helpful to set up T accounts for Sales, Year 4, and Sales, Year 5; Purchases, Year 4, and Purchases, Year 5; and Inventory, December 31, Year 4.)

b Compute corrected amounts for owners' equity at December 31, Year 4 and Year 5. Assume no dividends were declared in Year 4 or Year 5.

BUSINESS DECISION PROBLEM 9

You are the sales manager of Import Motors, an automobile dealership specializing in European imports. Among the automobiles in Import Motors' showroom are two Italian sports cars, which are identical in every respect except for color; one is red and the other white. The red car had been ordered last February, at a cost of $13,300 American dollars. The white car had been ordered early last March, but because of a revaluation of the Italian lira relative to the dollar, the white car had cost only $12,000 American dollars. Both cars arrived in the United States on the same boat and had just been delivered to your showroom. Since the cars were identical except for color and both colors were equally popular, you had listed both cars at the same suggested retail price, $18,000.

Smiley Miles, one of your best salesmen, comes into your office with a proposal. He has a customer in the showroom who wants to buy the red car for $18,000. However, when Miles pulled the inventory card on the red car to see what options were included, he happened to notice the inventory card of the white car. Import Motors, like most automobile dealerships, uses the specific identification method to value inventory. Consequently, Miles noticed that the red car had cost $13,300, while the white one had cost Import Motors only $12,000. This gave Miles the idea for the following proposal.

"If I sell the red car for $18,000, Import Motors makes a gross profit of $4,700. But if you'll let me discount that white car $500, I think I can get my customer to buy that one instead. If I sell the white car for $17,500, the gross profit will be $5,500, so Import Motors is $800 better off than if I sell the red car for $18,000. Since I came up with this plan, I feel I should get part of the benefit, so Import Motors should split the extra $800 with me. That way, I'll get an extra $400 commission, and the company still makes $400 more than if I sell the red car."

Instructions

a Prepare a schedule which shows the total revenue, cost of goods sold, and gross profit to Import Motors if *both* cars are sold for $18,000 each.

b Prepare a schedule showing the revenue, cost of goods sold, and gross profit to Import Motors if both cars are sold but Miles's plan is adopted and the white car is sold for $17,500. Assume the red car is still sold for $18,000. To simplify comparison of this schedule to the one prepared in part **a,** include the extra $400 commission to Miles in the cost of goods sold of the part **b** schedule.

c Write out your decision whether or not to accept Miles's proposal, and explain to Miles why the proposal either would or would not be to the advantage of Import Motors. (Hint: Refer to your schedules prepared in parts **a** and **b** in your explanation.)

10

PLANT AND EQUIPMENT, DEPRECIATION, NATURAL RESOURCES, AND INTANGIBLE ASSETS

After studying this chapter you should be able to:

- Determine the cost of plant assets.
- Distinguish between capital expenditures and revenue expenditures.
- Explain the relationship between depreciation and the matching principle.
- Compute depreciation by the straight-line, units-of-output, declining-balance, sum-of-the-years'-digits, and ACRS methods.
- Explain why depreciation based upon historical costs may cause an overstatement of profits.
- Record disposals of plant assets.
- Account for the depletion of natural resources and the amortization of intangibles.
- Explain the nature of goodwill.

PLANT AND EQUIPMENT

The term *plant and equipment* is used to describe long-lived assets acquired for use in the operation of the business and not intended for resale to customers. Among the more common examples are land, buildings, machinery, furniture and fixtures, office equipment, and automobiles. A delivery truck in the showroom of an automobile dealer is inventory; when this same truck is sold to a drugstore for use in making deliveries to customers, it becomes a unit of plant and equipment.

The term *fixed assets* has long been used in accounting literature to describe all types of plant and equipment. This term, however, has virtually disappeared from the published financial statements of large corporations. *Plant and equipment* appears to be a more descriptive term. Another alternative title used on many corporation balance sheets is *property, plant, and equipment*.

370

Plant and equipment represent a stream of services to be received

It is convenient to think of a plant asset as a stream of services to be received by the owner over a period of years. Ownership of a delivery truck, for example, may provide about 100,000 miles of transportation. The cost of the delivery truck is customarily entered in a plant and equipment account entitled Delivery Truck, which in essence represents payment in advance for several years of transportation service. Similarly, a building may be regarded as payment in advance for several years' supply of housing services. As the years go by, these services are utilized by the business and the cost of the plant asset is gradually transferred into depreciation expense.

An awareness of the similarity between plant assets and prepaid expenses is essential to an understanding of the accounting process by which the cost of plant assets is allocated to the years in which the benefits of ownership are received.

Major categories of plant and equipment

Plant and equipment items are often classified into the following groups:

1 Tangible plant assets. The term *tangible* denotes physical substance, as exemplified by land, a building, or a machine. This category may be subdivided into two distinct classifications:
   a Plant property subject to depreciation; included are plant assets of limited useful life such as buildings and office equipment.
   b Land. The only plant asset not subject to depreciation is land, which has an unlimited term of existence.
2 Intangible assets. The term *intangible assets* is used to describe assets which are used in the operation of the business but have no physical substance, and are noncurrent. Examples include patents, copyrights, trademarks, franchises, and goodwill. Current assets such as accounts receivable or prepaid rent are not included in the intangible classification, even though they are lacking in physical substance.

Determining the cost of plant and equipment

The cost of plant and equipment includes all expenditures reasonable and necessary in acquiring the asset and placing it in a position and condition for use in the operations of the business. Only *reasonable* and *necessary* expenditures should be included. For example, if the company's truck driver receives a traffic ticket while hauling a new machine to the plant, the traffic fine is *not* part of the cost of the new machine. If the machine is dropped and damaged while being unloaded, the cost of repairing the damage should be recognized as expense in the current period and should *not* be added to the cost of the machine.

Cost is most easily determined when an asset is purchased for cash. The cost of the asset is then equal to the cash outlay necessary in acquiring the asset plus any expenditures for freight, insurance while in transit, installation, trial runs, and any other costs necessary to make *the asset ready for use.* If plant assets are *purchased* on the installment plan or by issuance of notes payable, the interest element or carrying charge should be recorded as interest expense and *not* as part of the cost of the plant assets. However, if a company *constructs* a plant asset for its own use, interest costs incurred *during the construction period* are viewed as part of the cost of the asset.[1]

This principle of including in the cost of a plant asset all the incidental charges necessary to put the asset in use is illustrated by the following example. A factory in Minneapolis orders a machine from a San Francisco tool manufacturer at a list price of $10,000, with terms of 2/10, n/30. Sales tax of $588 must be paid, also freight charges of $1,250. Transportation from the railroad station to the factory costs $150, and installation labor amounts to $400. The cost of the machine to be entered in the Machinery account is computed as follows:

Items included in cost of machine

List price of machine	$10,000
Less: Cash discount (2% × $10,000)	200
Net cash price	$ 9,800
Sales tax	588
Freight	1,250
Transportation from railroad station to factory	150
Installation labor	400
Cost of machine	$12,188

Why should all the incidental charges relating to the acquisition of a machine be included in its cost? Why not treat these incidental charges as expenses of the period in which the machine is acquired?

The answer is to be found in the basic accounting principle of *matching costs and revenue.* The benefits of owning the machine will be received over a span of years, 10 years, for example. During those 10 years the operation of the machine will contribute to revenue. Consequently, the total costs of the machine should be recorded in the accounts as an asset and allocated against the revenue of the 10 years. All costs incurred in acquiring the machine are costs of the services to be received from using the machine.

Land   When land is purchased, various incidental costs are generally incurred, in addition to the purchase price. These additional costs may include commissions to real estate brokers, escrow fees, legal fees for examining and insuring the title, delinquent taxes paid by the purchaser, and fees for surveying, draining, clearing, and grading the property. All these expenditures are part of the cost of the land.

Apportionment of a lump-sum purchase   Separate ledger accounts are necessary for land and buildings, because buildings are subject to depreciation and land is not. The treatment of land as a nondepreciable asset is based on the premise that

---

[1]*FASB Statement No. 34,* "Capitalization of Interest Costs" (Stamford, Conn.: 1979).

land used as a building site has an unlimited life. When land and building are purchased for a lump sum, the purchase price must be apportioned between the land and the building. An appraisal may be necessary for this purpose. Assume, for example, that land and a building are purchased for a bargain price of $400,000. The apportionment of this cost on the basis of an appraisal may be made as follows:

	Value per Appraisal	Percentage of Total	Apportionment of Cost
Apportioning cost between land and building Land	$200,000	40%	$160,000
Building	300,000	60%	240,000
Total	$500,000	100%	$400,000

Sometimes a tract of land purchased as a building site has on it an old building which is not suitable for the buyer's use. The Land account should be charged with the entire purchase price *plus any costs incurred in tearing down or removing the building.* Proceeds received from sale of the materials salvaged from the old building are recorded as a credit in the Land account.

Land improvements Improvements to real estate such as driveways, fences, parking lots, and sprinkler systems have a limited life and are therefore subject to depreciation. For this reason they should be recorded not in the Land account but in a separate account entitled Land Improvements.

Buildings Old buildings are sometimes purchased with the intention of repairing them prior to placing them in use. Repairs made under these circumstances are charged to the Buildings account. After the building has been placed in use, ordinary repairs are considered as maintenance expense when incurred.

Capital expenditures and revenue expenditures

Expenditures for the purchase or expansion of plant assets are called *capital expenditures* and are recorded in asset accounts. Expenditures for ordinary repairs, maintenance, fuel, and other items necessary to the ownership and use of plant and equipment are called *revenue expenditures* and are recorded by debits to expense accounts. The charge to an expense account is based on the assumption that the benefits from the expenditure will be used up in the current period, and the cost should therefore be deducted from the revenue of the current period in determining the net income.

A business may purchase many items which will benefit several accounting periods, but which have a relatively low cost. Examples of such items include auto batteries, wastebaskets, and pencil sharpeners. Such items are theoretically capital expenditures, but if they are recorded as assets in the accounting records it will be necessary to compute and record the related depreciation expense in future periods. We have previously mentioned the idea that the extra work involved in developing more precise accounting information should be weighed against the benefits that result. Thus, for reasons of convenience and economy, expenditures which are *not material* in dollar amount are treated in the accounting records as expenses of the current period. In brief, *any material expenditure that will benefit several accounting periods is considered a capital expenditure. Any expenditure that will benefit only the current period or that is not material in amount is treated as a revenue expenditure.*

Many companies develop formal policy statements defining capital and revenue expenditures as a guide toward consistent accounting practice from year to year. These policy statements often set a minimum dollar limit for a capital expenditure (such as $100 or $200).

Effect of errors in distinguishing between capital and revenue expenditures   Because a capital expenditure is recorded by debiting an asset account, the transaction has no immediate effect upon net income. However, the depreciation of the amount entered in the asset account will be reflected as an expense in future periods. A revenue expenditure, on the other hand, is recorded by debiting an expense account and therefore represents an immediate deduction from earnings in the current period.

Assume that the cost of a new delivery truck is erroneously debited to the Repairs Expense account. The result will be to overstate repairs expense, thereby understating the current year's net income. If the error is not corrected, the net income of subsequent years will be overstated because no depreciation expense will be recognized during the years in which the truck is used.

On the other hand, assume that ordinary truck repairs are erroneously debited to the asset account, Delivery Truck. The result will be to understate repairs expense, thereby overstating the current year's net income. If the error is not corrected, the net income of future years will be understated because of excessive depreciation charges based upon the inflated balance of the Delivery Truck account.

These examples indicate that a careful distinction between capital and revenue expenditures is essential to attainment of one of the most fundamental objectives of accounting—the determination of net income for each year of operation of a business.

ILLUSTRATIVE CASE   During an annual audit of Bowden Company, a CPA firm was reviewing entries in the general journal. An entry that caught the attention of Carol Jones, CPA, consisted of a debit to Office Furniture and a credit to Notes Payable for $52,000. Upon investigation, Jones learned that the transaction involved a hand-carved clock acquired from James Burns, the former president of Bowden Company. Burns's hobby for many years had been the building of hand-carved clocks. At a retirement banquet honoring Burns, Bowden Company had awarded him a $52,000 bonus, represented by the company's 12%, five-year note payable. At the same banquet, Burns had presented Bowden Company with one of his clocks.

Further investigation by Jones indicated that the commercial value of the clock was about $400. Jones therefore advised the company to transfer the $52,000 expenditure out of the Office Furniture account and into Executive Compensation Expense.

DEPRECIATION

Allocating the cost of plant and equipment over the years of use

Plant assets, with the exception of land, are of use to a company for only a limited number of years, and the cost of each plant asset is allocated as expense among the years in which it is used. Accountants use the term *depreciation* to describe this gradual conversion of the cost of a plant asset into expense. Depreciation, as the term is used in accounting, does not mean the decrease in market value of a plant asset over a period of time. *Depreciation means the allocation of the cost of a plant asset to expense in the periods in which services are received from the asset.*

When a delivery truck is purchased, its cost is first recorded as an asset. This cost becomes expense over a period of years through the accounting process of depreciation. On the other hand, when gasoline is purchased for the truck, the price paid for each tankful is immediately recorded as expense. In theory, both outlays (for the truck and for a tank of gas) represent the acquisition of assets. However, since it is reasonable to assume that a tankful of gasoline will be consumed in the accounting period in which it is purchased, we record the outlay for gasoline as an expense immediately. It is important to recognize, however, that *both the outlay for the truck and the payment for the gasoline become expense in the period or periods in which each renders services.*

Depreciation differs from most expenses in that it does not require a cash payment at or near the time it is recorded. The entry to record depreciation (a debit to Depreciation Expense and a credit to Accumulated Depreciation) has no effect on current assets or current liabilities. However, when depreciable assets wear out, a large cash payment must be made in order to replace them.

A separate Depreciation Expense account and a separate Accumulated Depreciation account are generally maintained for each group of depreciable assets such as factory buildings, delivery equipment, and office equipment so that a proper allocation of depreciation expense can be made between functional areas of activity such as sales and manufacturing.

Depreciation not a process of valuation

Accounting records do not purport to show the constantly fluctuating market values of plant and equipment. Occasionally the market value of a building may rise substantially over a period of years because of a change in the price level, or for other reasons. Depreciation is continued, however, regardless of the increase in market value. The accountant recognizes that the building will render useful services for only a limited number of years, and that its full cost must be allocated as expense of those years regardless of fluctuations in market value.

The *book value* or *carrying value* of a plant asset is its cost minus the related accumulated depreciation. Plant assets are shown in the balance sheet at their book values, representing the portion of their cost which will be allocated to expense in future periods. Accumulated depreciation represents the portion of the assets' cost which has already been recognized as expense.

Accumulated depreciation does not consist of cash

Many readers of financial statements who have not studied accounting mistakenly believe that accumulated depreciation accounts represent money accumulated for the purpose of buying new equipment when the present equipment wears out. Perhaps the best way to combat such mistaken notions is to emphasize that a credit balance in an accumulated depreciation account represents the *expired cost* of assets acquired in the past. The amounts credited to the accumulated depreciation account could, as an alternative, have been credited directly to the plant and equipment account. An accumulated depreciation account has a *credit* balance; it does not represent an asset; and it cannot be used in any way to pay for new equipment. To buy a new plant asset requires cash; the total amount of cash owned by a company is shown by the asset account for cash.

Causes of depreciation

The two major causes of depreciation are physical deterioration and obsolescence.

Physical deterioration   Physical deterioration of a plant asset results from use, and also from exposure to sun, wind, and other climatic factors. When a plant asset has been carefully maintained, it is not uncommon for the owner to claim that the asset is as "good as new." Such statements are not literally true. Although a good repair policy may greatly lengthen the useful life of a machine, every machine eventually reaches the point at which it must be discarded. In brief, the making of repairs does not lessen the need for recognition of depreciation.

Obsolescence   The term *obsolescence* means the process of becoming out of date or obsolete. An airplane, for example, may become obsolete even though it is in excellent physical condition; it becomes obsolete because better planes of superior design and performance have become available.

   The usefulness of plant assets may also be reduced because the rapid growth of a company renders such assets inadequate. *Inadequacy* of a plant asset may necessitate replacement with a larger unit even though the asset is in good physical condition and is not obsolete. Obsolescence and inadequacy are often closely associated; both relate to the opportunity for economical and efficient use of an asset rather than to its physical condition.

Methods of computing depreciation

There are several alternative methods of computing depreciation. A business need not use the same method of depreciation for all its various assets. For example, a company may use straight-line depreciation on some assets and a declining-balance method for other assets. Furthermore, the methods used for computing depreciation expense in financial statements *may differ* from the methods used in the preparation of the company's income tax return.

Straight-line method   The simplest and most widely used method of computing depreciation is the straight-line method. This method was described in Chapter 3 and has been used repeatedly in problems throughout this book. Under the straight-line method, an equal portion of the cost of the asset is allocated to each period of use; consequently, this method is most appropriate when usage of an asset is fairly uniform from year to year.

The computation of the periodic charge for depreciation is made by deducting the estimated *residual* or *salvage value* from the cost of the asset and dividing the remaining *depreciable cost* by the years of estimated useful life. For example, if a delivery truck has a cost of $20,000, a residual value of $2,000, and an estimated useful life of four years, the annual computation of depreciation expense will be as follows:

$$\frac{\text{Cost} - \text{Residual Value}}{\text{Years of Useful Life}} = \frac{\$20,000 - \$2,000}{4} = \$4,500$$

This same depreciation computation is shown below in tabular form.

Computing depreciation by straight-line method

Cost of the depreciable asset	$20,000
Less: Estimated residual value (amount to be realized by sale of asset when it is retired from use)	2,000
Total amount to be depreciated (depreciable cost)	$18,000
Estimated useful life	4 years
Depreciation expense each year ($18,000 ÷ 4)	$ 4,500

The following schedule summarizes the accumulation of depreciation over the useful life of the asset. The amount to be depreciated is $18,000 (cost of $20,000 minus estimated residual value of $2,000).

Depreciation Schedule: Straight-Line Method

Year	Computation	Depreciation Expense	Accumulated Depreciation	Book Value
				$20,000
First	(¼ × $18,000)	$ 4,500	$ 4,500	15,500
Second	(¼ × $18,000)	4,500	9,000	11,000
Third	(¼ × $18,000)	4,500	13,500	6,500
Fourth	(¼ × $18,000)	4,500	18,000	2,000
		$18,000		

Constant annual depreciation expense

Depreciation rates for various types of assets can conveniently be stated as percentages. In the above example the asset had an estimated life of four years, so the depreciation expense each year was ¼ of the depreciable amount. The fraction "¼" is of course equivalent to an annual rate of 25%. Similarly, a 10-year life indicates a depreciation rate of $\frac{1}{10}$, or 10% and an 8-year life a depreciation rate of $\frac{1}{8}$, or $12\frac{1}{2}\%$.

In the preceding illustration we assumed that the company maintained its accounts on a calendar-year basis and that the asset was acquired on January 1, the beginning of the accounting period. If the asset had been acquired sometime during the year, on October 1 for example, it would have been in use for only three months, or $\frac{3}{12}$ of a year. Consequently, the depreciation to be recorded at December 31 would be only $\frac{3}{12}$ of $4,500, or $1,125. Stated more precisely, the depreciation expense in this situation is computed as follows: $25\% \times \$18,000 \times \frac{3}{12} = \$1,125$.

In practice, the possibility of residual value is sometimes ignored and the annual depreciation charge computed by dividing the total cost of the asset by the number of years of estimated useful life. This practice may be justified in those cases in which residual value is not material and is difficult to estimate accurately.

Units-of-output method   For certain kinds of assets, more equitable allocation of the cost can be obtained by dividing the cost (minus salvage value, if significant) by the estimated units of output rather than by the estimated years of useful life. A truck line or bus company, for example, might compute depreciation on its vehicles by a mileage basis. If we assume that the delivery truck in our example has an estimated useful life of 200,000 miles, the depreciation rate per mile of operation is 9 cents ($18,000 ÷ 200,000). This calculation of the depreciation rate may be stated as follows:

$$\frac{\text{Cost} - \text{Residual Value}}{\text{Estimated Units of Output (Miles)}} = \frac{\text{Depreciation per}}{\text{Unit of Output (Mile)}}$$

or

$$\frac{\$20,000 - \$2,000}{200,000 \text{ miles}} = \$0.09 \text{ depreciation per mile}$$

At the end of each year, the amount of depreciation to be recorded would be determined by multiplying the 9-cent rate by the number of miles the truck had operated during the year. This method is suitable only when the total units of output of the asset over its entire useful life can be estimated with reasonable accuracy.

Accelerated depreciation methods   The term *accelerated depreciation* means recognition of relatively large amounts of depreciation in the early years of use and reduced amounts in the later years. Many types of plant and equipment are most efficient when new and therefore provide more and better services in the early years of useful life. If we assume that the benefits derived from owning an asset are greatest in the early years when the asset is relatively new, then the amount of the asset's cost which we allocate as depreciation expense should be greatest in these same early years. This is consistent with the basic accounting concept of matching costs with related revenue. Accelerated depreciation methods are widely used in income tax returns because they reduce the current year's tax burden by recognizing a relatively large amount of depreciation expense.

Declining-balance method   The accelerated depreciation method which allocates the largest portion of the cost of an asset to the early years of its useful life is called *double declining balance*. This method consists of doubling the straight-line depreciation rate and applying this doubled rate to the undepreciated cost (book value) of the asset.

To illustrate, consider our example of the $20,000 delivery truck. The estimated useful life of the truck is four years; therefore, the depreciation rate under the straight-line method would be 25%. To depreciate the automobile by the double-declining-balance method, we double the straight-line rate of 25% and apply the doubled rate of 50% to the book value. Depreciation expense in the first year would then amount to $10,000. In the second year the depreciation expense would drop to $5,000, computed at 50% of the remaining book value of $10,000. In the third year depreciation would be $2,500, and in the fourth year only $1,250. The following table shows the computation of each year's depreciation expense by the declining-balance method:

Depreciation Schedule: Declining-Balance Method

Year	Computation	Depreciation Expense	Accumulated Depreciation	Book Value
				$20,000
First	(50% × $20,000)	$10,000	$10,000	10,000
Second	(50% × $10,000)	5,000	15,000	5,000
Third	(50% × $ 5,000)	2,500	17,500	2,500
Fourth	(50% × $ 2,500)	1,250	18,750	1,250

Accelerated depreciation: declining-balance

Notice that the estimated residual value of the delivery truck did not enter into the computation of depreciation expense by the declining-balance method. This is because the declining-balance method provides an "automatic" residual value. As long as each year's depreciation expense is equal to only a portion of the undepreciated cost of the asset, the asset will never be entirely written off. However, if the asset has a significant residual value, depreciation should stop at this point. Since our delivery truck has an estimated residual value of $2,000, the depreciation expense for the fourth year should be limited to $500 rather than the $1,250 computed in the table. By limiting the last year's depreciation expense in this manner, the book value of the truck at the end of the fourth year will be equal to its $2,000 estimated residual value.

If the asset in the above illustration had been acquired on October 1 rather than on January 1, depreciation for only three months would be recorded in the first year. The computation would be 50% × $20,000 × 3⁄12, or $2,500. For the next calendar year the calculation would be 50% × ($20,000 − $2,500), or $8,750.

Sum-of-the-years'-digits method This is another method of allocating a large portion of the cost of an asset to the early years of its use. The depreciation rate to be used is a fraction, of which the numerator is the remaining years of useful life (as of the beginning of the year) and the denominator is the sum of the years of useful life. Consider again the example of the delivery truck costing $20,000 having an estimated life of four years and an estimated residual value of $2,000. Since the asset has an estimated life of four years, the denominator of the fraction will be 10, computed as follows:[2] $1 + 2 + 3 + 4 = 10$. For the first year, the depreciation will be $\frac{4}{10}$ × ($20,000 − $2,000), or $7,200. (Notice that we reduced the cost of the truck by the estimated residual value in determining the amount to be depreciated.) For the second year, the depreciation will be $\frac{3}{10}$ × $18,000, or $5,400; in the third year $\frac{2}{10}$ × $18,000, or $3,600; and in the fourth year, $\frac{1}{10}$ × $18,000, or $1,800. In tabular form, this depreciation program will appear as follows:

Depreciation Schedule: Sum-of-the-Years'-Digits Method

Year	Computation	Depreciation Expense	Accumulated Depreciation	Book Value
				$20,000
First	($\frac{4}{10}$ × $18,000)	$ 7,200	$ 7,200	12,800
Second	($\frac{3}{10}$ × $18,000)	5,400	12,600	7,400
Third	($\frac{2}{10}$ × $18,000)	3,600	16,200	3,800
Fourth	($\frac{1}{10}$ × $18,000)	1,800	18,000	2,000
		$18,000		

Accelerated depreciation: sum of the years' digits

Assume that the asset being depreciated by the sum-of-the-years'-digits method was acquired on October 1 and the company maintains its accounts on a calendar-year basis. Since the asset was in use for only three months during the first accounting period, the depreciation to be recorded in this first period will be for only $\frac{3}{12}$ of a full year, that is, $\frac{3}{12}$ × $7,200, or $1,800. For the second accounting period the depreciation computation will be:

$\frac{9}{12}$ × ($\frac{4}{10}$ × $18,000) $5,400
$\frac{3}{12}$ × ($\frac{3}{10}$ × $18,000) 1,350
Depreciation expense, second period $6,750

A similar pattern of allocation will be followed for each accounting period of the asset's life.

---

[2]Alternatively, the denominator may be computed by using the formula $n\left(\dfrac{n+1}{2}\right)$, where n is the useful life of the asset. According to this formula, the sum of the years' digits for an asset with a four-year life is computed as follows: $4\left(\dfrac{4+1}{2}\right) = 4(2.5) = 10$. Similarly, the sum of the years' digits for an asset with a 10-year life would be computed as follows: $10\left(\dfrac{10+1}{2}\right) = 10(5.5) = 55$.

Depreciation for fractional periods   When an asset is acquired in the middle of an accounting period, it is not necessary to compute depreciation expense to the nearest day or week. In fact, such a computation would give a misleading impression of great precision. Since depreciation is based upon an estimated useful life of many years, the depreciation applicable to any one year is only an approximation at best.

One widely used method of computing depreciation for part of a year is to round the calculation to the nearest whole month. Thus, if an asset is acquired on July 12, depreciation is computed for the six months beginning July 1. If an asset is acquired on July 16 (or any date in the latter half of July), depreciation is recorded for only five months (August through December) in the current calendar year.

Another acceptable approach, called the *half-year convention,* is to record six months' depreciation on all assets acquired during the year. This approach is based upon the assumption that the actual purchase dates will "average out" to approximately midyear. The half-year convention is widely used for assets such as office equipment, automobiles, and machinery. For buildings, however, income tax rules require that depreciation be computed for the actual number of months that the building is owned.

The half-year convention enables us to treat similar assets acquired at different dates during the year as a single group. For example, assume that an insurance company purchases hundreds of typewriters throughout the current year at a total cost of $600,000. The company depreciates typewriters by the straight-line method, assuming a five-year life and no residual value. Using the half-year convention, the depreciation expense on all of the typewriters purchased during the year may be computed as follows: $600,000 \div 5$ years $\times \frac{6}{12} =$ $60,000. If we did not use the half-year convention, depreciation would have to be computed separately for typewriters which had been purchased in different months.

Revision of depreciation rates

Depreciation rates are based on estimates of the useful life of assets. These estimates of useful life are seldom precise and sometimes are grossly in error. Consequently, the annual depreciation expense based on the estimated useful life may be either excessive or inadequate. What action should be taken when, after a few years of using a plant asset, it is decided that the asset actually is going to last for a considerably longer or shorter period than was originally estimated? When either of these situation arises, a revised estimate of useful life should be made and the periodic depreciation expense decreased or increased accordingly.

The procedure for correcting the depreciation program is to *spread the remaining undepreciated cost of the asset over the years of remaining useful life.* This correction affects only the amount of depreciation expense that will be recorded in the *current and future periods.* The financial statements of past periods are *not* revised to reflect changes in the estimated useful lives of depreciable assets.

To illustrate, assume that a company acquires a $10,000 asset which is estimated to have a 10-year useful life and no residual value. Under the straight-line method, the annual depreciation expense is $1,000. At the end of the sixth year, accumulated depreciation amounts to $6,000, and the asset has an undepreciated cost (or book value) of $4,000.

At the beginning of the seventh year, it is decided that the asset will last for eight more years. The revised estimate of useful life is, therefore, a total of 14 years. The depreciation expense to be recognized for the seventh year and for each of the remaining years is $500, computed as follows:

Revision of depreciation program

Undepreciated cost at end of sixth year ($10,000 − $6,000)	$4,000
Revised estimate of remaining years of useful life	8 years
Revised amount of annual depreciation expense ($4,000 ÷ 8)	$ 500

Depreciation and income taxes

Different methods of depreciation may be used for the purpose of preparing financial statements and the purpose of preparing income tax returns. Many large corporations use straight-line depreciation in their financial statements, because this permits reporting higher earnings which in turn suggests that management is doing an efficient job. For income tax purposes, however, many businesses use an accelerated depreciation method.

For assets acquired prior to 1981, taxpayers may use such accelerated depreciation methods as double declining balance and sum of the years' digits. For assets acquired after January 1, 1981, federal income tax rules require taxpayers to use either straight-line depreciation or a special accelerated method called the accelerated cost recovery system.

Accelerated Cost Recovery System (ACRS)

ACRS is a depreciation method which allows businesses to depreciate assets in an extremely rapid manner for income tax purposes. By claiming large deductions for depreciation expense in the early years of an asset's life, the business is able to reduce its current income tax burden. Thus, ACRS is intended to create a powerful incentive for businesses to invest in new plant and equipment. This investment, in turn, should create new jobs and stimulate the entire economy through higher levels of production.

ACRS speeds up the write-off of the cost of an asset in two ways. First, ACRS designates four "recovery periods" over which the costs of various types of assets are written off. In most cases, these recovery periods are substantially shorter than the useful life of the assets. For example, buildings and land improvements are considered "15-year property," which means that they may be fully depreciated over 15 years. Pipelines, nuclear plants, and amusement parks may be written off over 10 years. Most machinery and equipment is written off over a five-year period. Automobiles, trucks, and some special tools qualify for write-off over only three years.

ACRS also requires the use of an accelerated depreciation rate, similar to the declining-balance rate. The table that follows shows the percentages of an asset's total cost that may be written off in each year of the recovery period.

ACRS Depreciation Rates

Depreciation rates for federal income tax purposes; applicable only to assets purchased after January 1, 1981

Year	3-year Property	5-year Property	10-year Property	15-year Property*
1	25%	15%	8%	12%
2	38	22	14	10
3	37	21	12	9
4		21	10	8
5		21	10	7
6			10	6
7			9	6
8			9	6
9			9	6
10			9	5
11				5
12				5
13				5
14				5
15				5
	100%	100%	100%	100%

*Our percentages for 15-year property assume that the asset was purchased in January of the first year. Other tables must be used if the asset was purchased in another month. These tables are scheduled for revision in 1985 and may be revised sooner. A complete set of tables is published each year by the Internal Revenue Service.

To demonstrate the use of the ACRS depreciation table, consider again our example of the delivery truck costing $20,000. We may disregard the estimated four-year useful life; for income tax purposes, trucks are considered three-year property. The depreciation expense that may be reported on the federal income tax return each year is determined as follows:

Truck Depreciation Schedule: ACRS Income Tax Method

Year	Computation	Depreciation Expense	Accumulated Depreciation	Book Value
				$20,000
First	(25% × $20,000)	$ 5,000	$ 5,000	15,000
Second	(38% × $20,000)	7,600	12,600	7,400
Third	(37% × $20,000)	7,400	20,000	–0–
		$20,000		

Notice that under ACRS, the truck is depreciated to a book value of zero. ACRS ignores residual values. Also, no fractional-period computations are made in the year of acquisition; the full percentage rate shown in the table is applied regardless of when during the year the asset was acquired.[3] ACRS is used for *income tax purposes only.* If the estimated residual value is material in dollar amount, or if the ACRS recovery period differs substantially from the asset's estimated useful life, the ACRS method is *not acceptable* in financial statements.[4]

Inflation and depreciation

The valuation of plant and equipment on a cost basis and the computation of depreciation in terms of cost will work very well during periods of stable price levels. However, the substantial rise in the price level in recent years has led many government officials and business executives to suggest that a more realistic measurement of net income could be achieved by basing depreciation on the *estimated replacement cost* of plant assets rather than on the original cost of the assets presently in use.

As a specific illustration, assume that a manufacturing company purchased machinery in 1970 at a cost of $1,000,000. Estimated useful life was 10 years and straight-line depreciation was used. Throughout this 10-year period the price level rose sharply. By 1980 the machinery purchased in 1970 was fully depreciated; it was scrapped and replaced by new machinery in 1980. Although the new machines were not significantly different from the old, they cost $3,000,000, or three times as much as the old machinery. Many accountants would argue that the depreciation expense for the 10 years was in reality $3,000,000, because this was the outlay required for new machinery if the company was merely to "stay even" in its productive facilities. It also may be argued that reported profits are *overstated* during a period of rising prices if depreciation is based on the lower plant costs of some years ago.

Historical cost versus replacement cost

The above criticism of depreciation accounting based on the historical cost of assets is a convincing one. (*Historical cost* means the cost actually incurred by a company in acquiring an asset, as evidenced by paid checks and other documents.) However, this criticism does not mean that American business is on the verge of abandoning the cost principle in accounting for assets and computing depreciation. To substitute estimated current replacement cost for the historical cost of plant and equipment would create many new difficulties and a great deal of confusion. For many assets, current replacement cost cannot be determined easily or with precision. For example, the current cost of replacing a steel mill with its great variety of complex, made-to-order machinery would involve mak-

---

[3]The depreciation rates shown for the first year in the 3-, 5-, and 10-year property columns of the previous table are based upon the half-year convention. For 15-year property, separate tables are used depending upon the month in which the asset is acquired. Here we illustrate only the table for depreciation of 15-year property acquired in January.

[4]As a matter of convenience, some small businesses use ACRS depreciation in both their income tax returns and their financial statements. In such cases, the financial statements are *not* in conformity with generally accepted accounting principles.

ing many assumptions and unprovable estimates. Or, as another example, consider the difficulty of estimating the replacement cost of a large tract of timber or of a gold mine.

Another difficulty in substituting replacement cost for historical cost of plant assets would be that the whole process of establishing estimated cost data would presumably need to be repeated each year. In contrast, historical cost (which we presently use as the basis of accounting for plant and equipment) is determined at the time of acquiring an asset and remains unchanged throughout the useful life of the asset.

These difficulties connected with the possible adoption of replacement cost as a basis of accounting for assets do not mean that such a change cannot or should not be attempted. However, these difficulties do explain why American business has continued to use historical cost as a primary basis of accounting for assets even during continued inflation.

FASB Statement No. 33—Disclosure of replacement cost

Persistent inflation has led to criticism that traditional financial statements do not portray adequately the effects of rising prices on earnings or on certain assets. In response, the Financial Accounting Standards Board in *Statement No. 33,* "Financial Reporting and Changing Prices," recently required large corporations to *disclose* the estimated current replacement cost of plant and equipment.[5] Also required to be disclosed is depreciation expense based on the replacement cost of the assets. *This rule does not mean that replacement cost is to be used instead of historical cost, but rather that additional supplementary information is to be disclosed.* The disclosure can be made in a footnote to the financial statements or as a supplementary section accompanying the financial statements. The disclosure requirements of *Statement No. 33* will be considered further in Chapter 14, including the use of a general price-level index to adjust historical cost data.

DISPOSAL OF PLANT AND EQUIPMENT

When depreciable assets are disposed of at any date other than the end of the year, an entry should be made to record depreciation for the *fraction of the year* ending with the date of disposal. If the half-year convention is in use, six months' depreciation should be recorded on all assets disposed of during the year. In the following illustrations of the disposal of items of plant and equipment, it is assumed that any necessary entries for fractional-period depreciation have been recorded.

As units of plant and equipment wear out or become obsolete, they must be scrapped, sold, or traded in on new equipment. Upon the disposal or retirement of a depreciable asset, the cost of the property is removed from the asset account, and the accumulated depreciation is removed from the related valuation

---

[5]*FASB Statement No. 33,* "Financial Reporting and Changing Prices" (Stamford, Conn.: 1979).

account. Assume, for example, that office equipment purchased 10 years ago at a cost of $5,000 has been fully depreciated and is no longer useful. The entry to record the scrapping of the worthless equipment is as follows:

Scrapping fully depreciated asset

Accumulated Depreciation: Office Equipment	5,000	
Office Equipment		5,000

To remove from the accounts the cost and the accumulated depreciation on fully depreciated office equipment now being scrapped. No salvage value.

Once an asset has been fully depreciated, no more depreciation should be recorded on it, even though the property is in good condition and is continued in use. The objective of depreciation is to spread the *cost* of an asset over the periods of its usefulness; in no case can depreciation expense be greater than the amount paid for the asset. When a fully depreciated asset is continued in use beyond the original estimate of useful life, the asset account and the Accumulated Depreciation account should remain in the accounting records without further entries until the asset is retired.

Gains and losses on disposal of plant and equipment

Since the residual value and useful life of plant assets are only estimates, it is not uncommon for plant assets to be sold at a price which differs from their book value at the date of disposal. When plant assets are sold, any gain or loss on the disposal is computed by comparing the ***book value with the amount received from the sale***. A sales price in excess of the book value produces a gain; a sales price below the book value produces a loss. These gains or losses, if material in amount, should be shown separately in the income statement in computing the income from operations.

Disposal at a price above book value Assume that a machine which cost $10,000 and has a book value of $2,000 is sold for $3,000. The journal entry to record this disposal is as follows:

Gain on disposal of plant asset

Cash	3,000	
Accumulated Depreciation: Machinery	8,000	
Machinery		10,000
Gain on Disposal of Plant Assets		1,000

To record sale of machinery at a price above book value.

Disposal at a price below book value Now assume that the same machine is sold for $500. The journal entry in this case would be as follows:

Loss on disposal of plant asset

Cash	500	
Accumulated Depreciation: Machinery	8,000	
Loss on Disposal of Plant Assets	1,500	
Machinery		10,000

To record sale of machinery at a price below book value.

The disposal of a depreciable asset at a price equal to book value would result in neither a gain nor a loss. The entry for such a transaction would consist of a debit to Cash for the amount received, a debit to Accumulated Depreciation for the balance accumulated, and a credit to the asset account for the original cost.

Trading in used assets on new

Certain types of depreciable assets, such as automobiles and office equipment, are customarily traded in on new assets of the same kind. The trade-in allowance granted by the dealer may differ materially from the book value of the old asset. If the dealer grants a trade-in allowance in excess of the book value of the asset being traded in, there is the suggestion of a gain being realized on the exchange. The evidence of a gain is not conclusive, however, because the list price of the new asset may purposely have been set higher than a realistic cash price to permit the offering of inflated trade-in allowances.

For the purpose of determining taxable income, no gain or loss is recognized when a depreciable asset is traded in on another similar asset. The tax regulations provide that *the cost of the new asset shall be the sum of the book value of the old asset traded in plus the additional amount paid or to be paid in acquiring the new asset.*

To illustrate the handling of an exchange transaction in this manner, assume that a delivery truck is acquired at a cost of $8,000. The truck is depreciated on the straight-line basis with the assumption of a five-year life and no salvage value. Annual depreciation expense is ($8,000 ÷ 5), or $1,600. After four years of use, the truck is traded in on a new model having a list price of $10,000. The truck dealer grants a trade-in allowance of $2,400 for the old truck; the additional amount to be paid to acquire the new truck is, therefore, $7,600 ($10,000 list price minus $2,400 trade-in allowance). The *cost basis* of the new truck is computed as follows:

Trade-in: cost of new equipment	
Cost of old truck	$8,000
Less: Accumulated depreciation ($1,600 × 4)	6,400
Book value of old truck	$1,600
Add: Cash payment for new truck (list price, $10,000 − $2,400 trade-in allowance)	7,600
Cost basis of new truck	$9,200

The trade-in allowance and the list price of the new truck are not recorded in the accounts; their only function lies in determining the amount which the purchaser must pay in addition to turning in the old truck. The journal entry for this exchange transaction is as follows:

Entry for trade-in		
Delivery Truck (new)	9,200	
Accumulated Depreciation: Delivery Truck (old)	6,400	
Delivery Truck (old)		8,000
Cash		7,600

To remove from the accounts the cost of old truck and accumulated depreciation thereon, and to record new truck at cost equal to book value of old truck traded in plus cash paid.

Note that the method used above to record the trade-in of an old productive asset for a new one is different from the usual assumption that the cost of a newly acquired asset is equal to its implied cash price. The reason for not recognizing a gain on a trade-in is that revenue is not realized merely by the act of substituting a new productive asset for an old one. Revenue flows from the production and sale of the goods or services which the productive asset makes possible.[6]

Financial accounting principles and income tax regulations are alike in not recognizing a *gain* on a trade-in, they differ in the case of a trade-in which involves a material *loss*. Tax regulations do not permit recognition of the loss, but for financial statements **the loss should be recognized.** For example, assume that a company received a trade-in allowance of only $10,000 for old machinery which has a book value of $100,000. A journal entry illustrating this situation follows:

Machinery (new)	600,000	
Accumulated Depreciation: Machinery (old)	300,000	
Loss on Trade-in of Plant Assets	90,000	
Machinery (old)		400,000
Cash		590,000

To recognize for financial reporting purposes a material loss on trade-in of machinery. Loss not recognized in determining taxable income.

If a trade-in transaction involved only a very small loss, most companies would probably follow the income tax rules and not recognize the loss. This treatment would eliminate the need for a double record of depreciable assets and depreciation expense; the departure from financial accounting rules would be permissible if the amount of the loss was not material.

NATURAL RESOURCES

Accounting for natural resources

Mining properties, oil and gas reserves, and tracts of standing timber are leading examples of natural resources or "wasting assets." The distinguishing characteristics of these assets are that they are physically consumed and converted into inventory. Theoretically, a coal mine might be regarded as an underground "inventory" of coal; however, such an "inventory" is certainly not a current asset. In the balance sheet, mining property and other natural resources are classified as property, plant, and equipment.

We have explained that plant assets such as buildings and equipment depreciate because of physical deterioration or obsolescence. A mine or an oil reserve does not "depreciate" for these reasons, but it is gradually *depleted* as the natural resource is removed from the ground. Once all of the coal has been removed from a coal mine, for example, the mine is "fully depleted" and will be abandoned or sold for its residual value.

---

[6]*APB Opinion No. 29*, "Accounting for Nonmonetary Transactions, AICPA (New York: 1973).

To illustrate the depletion of a natural resource, assume that Rainbow Minerals pays $10,500,000 to acquire the Red Valley Mine, which is believed to contain 10 million tons of coal. The residual value of the mine after all of the coal is removed is estimated to be $500,000. The depletion that will occur over the life of the mine is the original cost minus the residual value, or $10,000,000. This depletion will occur at the rate of $1 per ton ($10,000,000 ÷ 10 million tons) as the coal is removed from the mine. If we assume that 2 million tons are mined during the first year of operations, the entry to record the depletion of the mine would be as follows:

Recording
depletion

Depletion of Coal Deposits	*2,000,000*	
Accumulated Depletion: Red Valley Mine		*2,000,000*

To record depletion of the Red Valley Mine for the year; 2,000,000 tons mined @ $1 per ton.

Accumulated Depletion is a contra-asset account similar to the Accumulated Depreciation account; it represents the portion of the mine which has been used up (depleted) to date. In Rainbow Mineral's balance sheet, the Red Valley Mine now appears as follows:

Property, Plant, & Equipment:		
Mining properties: Red Valley Mine	*$10,500,000*	
Less: Accumulated depletion	*2,000,000*	*$8,500,000*

The Depletion of Coal Deposits account may be viewed as similar to the Purchases account of a merchandising business. This account is added to any other mining costs and any beginning inventory of coal to arrive at the cost of goods (coal) available for sale. If all of the coal has been sold by year-end, these costs are deducted from revenue as the cost of goods sold. If some of the coal is still on hand at year-end, a portion of these costs should be assigned to the ending inventory of coal, which is a current asset.

Percentage depletion versus cost depletion For the determination of taxable income, the Internal Revenue Code permits a deduction for depletion expense equal to a specified *percentage of the revenue* from production from a few mineral deposits such as gold, silver, lead, and zinc ore. Depletion computed as a percentage of revenue *is used only for income tax purposes, not for financial statements.* In terms of generally accepted accounting principles, depletion is always based on the *cost* of the mine or other natural resource.

Depreciation of buildings and equipment closely related to natural resources Buildings and equipment installed at a mine or drilling site may be useful only at that particular location. Consequently, such assets should be depreciated over their normal useful lives, or over the life of the natural resource, *whichever is shorter.* Often depreciation on such assets is computed using the units-of-output method, thus relating the depreciation expense to the rate at which units of the natural resource are removed.

INTANGIBLE ASSETS

Characteristics

As the word *intangible* suggests, assets in this classification have no physical substance. Leading examples are goodwill, patents, and trademarks. Intangible assets are classified in the balance sheet as a subgroup of plant assets. However, not all assets which lack physical substance are regarded as intangible assets. An account receivable, for example, or a short-term prepayment is of nonphysical nature but is classified as a current asset and is not regarded as an intangible. In brief, *intangible assets are assets which are used in the operation of the business but which have no physical substance and are noncurrent.*

The basis of valuation for intangible assets is cost. In some companies, certain intangible assets such as trademarks may be of great importance but may have been acquired without the incurring of any cost. An intangible asset should appear in the balance sheet *only* if a cost of acquisition or development has been incurred.

Operating expenses versus intangible assets

Many types of expenditures offer at least a half promise of yielding benefits in subsequent years, but the evidence is so doubtful and the period of usefulness so hard to define that most companies treat these expenditures as expense when incurred. Another reason for charging these outlays to expense is the practical difficulty of separating them from the recurring expenses of current operations.

Examples are the expenditures for intensive advertising campaigns to introduce new products, and the expense of training employees to work with new types of machinery or office equipment. There is little doubt that some benefits from these outlays continue beyond the current period, but because of the uncertain duration of the benefits, it is almost universal practice to treat expenditures of this nature as expense of the current period.

Amortization

The term *amortization* is used to describe the write-off to expense of the cost of an intangible asset over its useful life. The usual accounting entry for amortization consists of a debit to Amortization Expense and a credit to the intangible asset account. There is no theoretical objection to crediting an accumulated amortization account rather than the intangible asset account, but this method is seldom encountered in practice.

Although it is difficult to estimate the useful life of an intangible such as a trademark, it is highly probable that such an asset will not contribute to future earnings on a permanent basis. The cost of the intangible asset should, therefore, be deducted from revenue during the years in which it may be expected to aid in producing revenue. Under the current rules of the Financial Accounting

Standards Board, the maximum period for amortization of an intangible asset cannot exceed 40 years.[7] The straight-line method of amortization is generally used for intangible assets.

Goodwill

Business executives used the term *goodwill* in a variety of meanings before it became part of accounting terminology. One of the most common meanings of goodwill in a nonaccounting sense concerns the benefits derived from a favorable reputation among customers. To accountants, however, goodwill has a very specific meaning not necessarily limited to customer relations. It means the *present value of future earnings in excess of the normal return on net identifiable assets.* Above-average earnings may arise not only from favorable customer relations but also from such factors as superior management, manufacturing efficiency, and weak competition.

The phrase *normal return on net identifiable assets* requires explanation. Net assets means the owners' equity in a business, or assets minus liabilities. Goodwill, however, is not an *identifiable* asset. The existence of goodwill is implied by the ability of a business to earn an above-average return; however, the cause and precise dollar value of goodwill are largely matters of personal opinion. Therefore, *net identifiable assets* means all assets except goodwill, minus liabilities. A *normal return* on net identifiable assets is the rate of return which investors demand in a particular industry to justify their buying a business at the *fair market value* of its net identifiable assets. A business has goodwill when investors will pay a higher price because the business earns more than the normal rate of return.

Assume that two businesses in the same line of trade are offered for sale and that the normal return on the fair market value of net identifiable assets in this industry is 15% a year. The relative earning power of the two companies during the past five years is shown below:

	Company X	Company Y
Fair market value of net identifiable assets	$1,000,000	$1,000,000
Normal rate of return on net assets	15%	15%
Average net income for past five years	$ 150,000	$ 190,000
Normal earnings, computed as 15% of net identifiable assets ...	150,000	150,000
Earnings in excess of normal	$ –0–	$ 40,000

An investor would be willing to pay $1,000,000 to buy Company X, because Company X earns the normal 15% return which justifies the fair market value of its net identifiable assets. Although Company Y has the same amount of net identifiable assets, an investor would be willing to pay *more* for Company Y than for Company X because Company Y has a record of superior earnings which will

---

[7]*APB Opinion No. 17,* "Intangible Assets," AICPA (New York: 1970), par. 29.

presumably continue for some time in the future. The extra amount that a buyer would pay to purchase Company Y represents the value of Company Y's goodwill.

Estimating goodwill How much will an investor pay for goodwill? Above-average earnings in past years are of significance to prospective purchasers only if they believe that these earnings will continue after they acquire the business. Investors' appraisals of goodwill, therefore, will vary with their estimates of the future earning power of the business. Very few businesses, however, are able to maintain above-average earnings for more than a few years. Consequently, the purchaser of a business will usually limit any amount paid for goodwill to not more than four or five times the amount by which annual earnings exceed normal earnings.

Arriving at a fair value for the goodwill of a going business is a difficult and subjective process. Any estimate of goodwill is in large part a matter of personal opinion. The following are several methods which a prospective purchaser might use in estimating a value for goodwill:

1 Negotiated agreement between buyer and seller of the business may be reached on the amount of goodwill. For example, it might be agreed that the fair market value of net identifiable assets is $1,000,000 and that the total purchase price for the business will be $1,180,000, thus providing a $180,000 payment for goodwill.

2 Goodwill may be determined as a multiple of the amount by which average annual earnings exceed normal earnings. Referring to our example involving Company Y, a prospective buyer may be willing to pay four times the amount by which average earnings exceed normal earnings, indicating a value of $160,000 (4 × $40,000) for goodwill. The purchase price of the business, therefore, would be $1,160,000.

The multiple applied to the excess annual earnings will vary widely from perhaps 1 to 10. An investor who pays four times the excess earnings for goodwill must, of course, expect these earnings to continue for at least four years.

3 Goodwill may be estimated by *capitalizing* the amount by which average earnings exceed normal earnings. Capitalizing an earnings stream means dividing those earnings by the investor's required rate of return. The result is the maximum amount which the investor could pay for the earnings and have them represent the required rate of return on the investment. To illustrate, assume that the prospective buyer decides to capitalize the $40,000 annual excess earnings of Company Y at a rate of 20%. This approach results in a $200,000 estimate ($40,000 ÷ .20 = $200,000) for the value of goodwill. (Note that $40,000 per year represents a 20% return on a $200,000 investment.)

A weakness in the capitalization method is that *no provision is made for the recovery* of the investment. If the prospective buyer is to earn a 20% return on the $200,000 investment in goodwill, either the excess earnings must continue *forever* (an unlikely assumption) or the buyer must be able to recover the

$200,000 investment at a later date by selling the business at a price above the fair market value of net identifiable assets.

Recording goodwill in the accounting records Goodwill is recorded in the accounting records *only when it is purchased;* this situation usually occurs only when a going business is purchased in its entirety. After the fair market values of all identifiable assets have been recorded in the accounting records of the new owners, any additional amount paid for the business may properly be debited to an asset account entitled Goodwill. This intangible asset must then be amortized over a period not to exceed 40 years, although a much shorter amortization period usually is appropriate.

Many businesses have never purchased goodwill but have generated it internally through developing good customer relations, superior management, or other factors which result in above-average earnings. Because there is no objective means of determining the dollar value of goodwill unless the business is sold, internally developed goodwill is *not recorded* in the accounting records. Thus, goodwill may be a very important asset of a successful business but may not even appear in the company's balance sheet.

Patents

A patent is an exclusive right granted by the federal government for manufacture, use, and sale of a particular product. The purpose of this exclusive grant is to encourage the invention of new machines and processes. When a company acquires a patent by purchase from the inventor or other holder, the purchase price should be recorded by debiting the intangible asset account Patents.

Patents are granted for a period of 17 years, and the period of amortization must not exceed that period. However, if the patent is likely to lose its usefulness in less than 17 years, amortization should be based on the shorter period of estimated useful life. Assume that a patent is purchased from the inventor at a cost of $100,000, after five years of the legal life have expired. The remaining *legal* life is, therefore, 12 years, but if the estimated *useful* life is only four years, amortization should be based on this shorter period. The entry to be made to record the annual amortization expense would be:

Entry for amortization of patent

Amortization Expense: Patents	25,000	
Patents		25,000

To amortize cost of patent on a straight-line basis and estimated life of four years.

Trademarks and trade names

Coca Cola's distinctive bottle is an example of a trademark known around the world. A trademark is a word, symbol, or design that identifies a product or group of products. A permanent exclusive right to the use of a trademark, brand name, or commercial symbol may be obtained by registering it with the federal government. The costs of developing a trademark or brand name often consists of advertising compaigns which should be treated as expense when incurred. If a trademark or trade name is purchased, however, the cost may be substantial. Such cost should be capitalized and amortized to expense over a period of not more than 40 years. If the use of the trademark is discontinued or its contribution to earnings becomes doubtful, any unamortized cost should be written off immediately.

Franchises

A franchise is a right granted by a company or a governmental unit to conduct a certain type of business in a specific geographical area. An example of a franchise is the right to operate a McDonald's restaurant in a specific neighborhood. The cost of franchises varies greatly and often may be quite substantial. When the cost of a franchise is small, it may be charged immediately to expense or amortized over a short period such as five years. When the cost is substantial, amortization should be based upon the life of the franchise (if limited); the amortization period, however, may not exceed 40 years.

Copyrights

A copyright is an exclusive right granted by the federal government to protect the production and sale of literary or artistic materials for the life of the creator plus 50 years. The cost of obtaining a copyright in some cases is minor and therefore is chargeable to expense when paid. Only when a copyright is purchased will the expenditure be material enough to warrant its being capitalized and spread over the useful life. The revenue from copyrights is usually limited to only a few years, and the purchase cost should, of course, be amortized over the years in which the revenue is expected.

Other intangibles and deferred charges

Many other types of intangible assets are found in the published balance sheets of large corporations. Some examples are formulas, processes, name lists, and film rights.

Intangibles, particularly those with limited lives, are sometimes classified as "deferred charges" in the balance sheet. A *deferred charge* is an expenditure that is expected to yield benefits for several accounting periods, and should be amortized over its estimated useful life. Included in this category are such items as bond issuance costs, plant rearrangement and moving costs, start-up costs, and organization costs. The distinction between intangibles and deferred charges is not an important one; both represent a "stream of services" in the form of long-term prepayments awaiting allocation to those accounting periods in which the services will be consumed.

Research and development (R&D) costs

The spending of billions of dollars a year on research and development leading to all kinds of new products is a striking characteristic of American industry. In the past, some companies treated all research and development costs as expense in the year incurred; other companies in the same industry recorded these costs as intangible assets to be amortized over future years. This diversity of practice prevented the financial statements of different companies from being comparable.

The lack of uniformity in accounting for R&D was ended when the Financial Accounting Standards Board ruled that all research and development expenditures should be charged to expense when incurred.[8] This action by the FASB had the beneficial effect of reducing the number of alternative accounting practices and helping to make financial statements of different companies more comparable. However, the FASB's decision was very controversial. Critics argued that a policy of reducing current earnings for all R&D expenditures might discourage companies from undertaking large R&D programs.

The controversy over the FASB's position on R&D expenditures raises an interesting question about the formulation of accounting standards: Is it possible for accounting standards to *describe* economic activity without also *influencing* that activity?

KEY TERMS INTRODUCED OR EMPHASIZED IN CHAPTER 10

Accelerated cost recovery system (ACRS)   An accelerated depreciation method for depreciating assets acquired after January 1, 1981, for federal income tax reporting. All assets are fully depreciated over a period of 3, 5, 10, or 15 years. The method is *not* used in financial statements prepared in accordance with generally accepted accounting principles.

Accelerated depreciation   Methods of depreciation that call for recognition of relatively large amounts of depreciation in the early years of an asset's useful life and relatively small amounts in the later years.

Amortization   The systematic write-off to expense of the cost of an intangible asset over the periods of its economic usefulness.

Book value   The cost of a plant asset minus the total recorded depreciation, as shown by the Accumulated Depreciation account. The remaining undepreciated cost is also known as *carrying value.*

Capital expenditure   A cost incurred to acquire a long-lived asset. An expenditure that will benefit several accounting periods.

Declining-balance depreciation   An accelerated method of depreciation in which the rate is a multiple of the straight-line rate, which is applied each year to the *undepreciated cost* of the asset. Most commonly used is double the straight-line rate.

Deferred charge   An expenditure expected to yield benfits for several accounting periods and therefore capitalized and written off during the periods benefited.

---

[8]*FASB Statement No. 2*, "Accounting for Research and Development Costs" (Stamford, Conn.: 1974), par. 12.

Depletion   Allocating the cost of a natural resource to the units removed as the resource is mined, pumped, cut, or otherwise consumed.

Depreciation   The systematic allocation of the cost of an asset to expense over the years of its estimated useful life.

Goodwill   The present value of expected future earnings of a business in excess of the earnings normally realized in the industry. Recorded when a business entity is purchased at a price in excess of the fair value of its net identifiable assets (excluding goodwill) less liabilities.

Half-year convention   The practice of taking six months' depreciation in the year of acquisition and the year of disposition, rather than computing depreciation for partial periods to the nearest month. This method is widely used and is acceptable for both income tax reporting and financial reports, as long as it is applied to **all** assets of a particular type acquired during the year. The half-year convention generally is **not** used for buildings.

Intangible assets   Those assets which are used in the operation of a business but which have no physical substance and are noncurrent.

Natural resources   Mines, oil fields, standing timber, and similar assets which are physically consumed and converted into inventory.

Net identifiable assets   Total of all assets **except goodwill** minus liabilities.

Percentage depletion   For income tax purposes only, a deduction for depletion expense equal to a specified percentage of the revenue from a natural resource. Eliminated or reduced by recent legislation.

Replacement cost   The estimated cost of replacing an asset at the current balance sheet date. Disclosure of such data is required of large companies.

Residual (salvage) value   The portion of an asset's cost expected to be recovered through sale or trade-in of the asset at the end of its useful life.

Revenue expenditure   Any expenditure that will benefit only the current accounting period.

Straight-line depreciation   A method of depreciation which allocates the cost of an asset (minus any residual value) equally to each year of its useful life.

Sum-of-the-years'-digits depreciation   An accelerated method of depreciation. The depreciable cost is multiplied each year by a fraction of which the numerator is the remaining years of useful life (as of the beginning of the current year) and the denominator is the sum of the years of useful life.

Units-of-output depreciation   A depreciation method is which cost (minus residual value) is divided by the estimated units of lifetime output. The unit depreciation cost is multiplied by the actual units of output each year to compute the annual depreciation expense.

DEMONSTRATION PROBLEM FOR YOUR REVIEW

The ledger of Cypress Company contained an account entitled Property, which had been used to record a variety of expenditures. At the end of Year 6, the Property account contained the following entries:

Debit entries:

1/10	Purchase for cash of building site	$200,000
2/4	Cost of removing old building from site	8,000
8/15	Paid contract price for new building completed today	560,000
8/30	Insurance, inspection fees, and other costs directly related to construction	
	of new building	18,000
	Total debits	$786,000

Credit entries:

2/4	Proceeds from sale of salvaged material from demolition of old	
	building	$ 3,000
12/31	Depreciation for Year 6, computed at 4% of balance in	
	Property account ($783,000). Debit was to Depreciation	
	Expense	31,320
	Total credits	34,320
12/31	Balance in Property account at year-end	$751,680

Instructions

a List the errors made in the application of accounting principles or practices by Cypress Company.

b Prepare a compound correcting journal entry at December 31, Year 6, assuming that the estimated life of the new building is 25 years and that depreciation is to be recognized for three months of Year 6 using the straight-line method. The accounts have not been closed for Year 6.

SOLUTION TO DEMONSTRATION PROBLEM

a Errors in accounting principles or practices were:

(1) Including land (a nondepreciable asset) in the same account with building (a depreciable asset)

(2) Using the total of land and building as a base for applying the depreciation rate on building

(3) Recording a full year's depreciation on a new building that was in use only the last three months of the year

(4) Crediting the depreciation for the period directly to the asset account (Property) rather than to a valuation account (Accumulated Depreciation: Building)

b   *Correcting Journal Entry*

Year 6

Dec. 31 Land 205,000

       Building 578,000

              Property 751,680

              Accumulated Depreciation: Building 5,780

              Depreciation Expense 25,540

    To correct the accounts reflecting land, building, and
    depreciation in accordance with the computations shown in
    the following schedule:

	Land	Building
Amount paid to acquire building site	$200,000	
Cost of removing old building from site	8,000	
Less: Proceeds from salvaged materials	(3,000)	
Contract price for new building		$560,000
Insurance, inspection fees, and other costs directly related to construction of new building		18,000
Totals	$205,000	$578,000

Depreciation: $578,000 × 4% × ³/₁₂ = $5,780

Correction of depreciation expense: $31,320 − $5,780 = $25,540

REVIEW QUESTIONS

1 Which of the following characteristics would prevent an item from being included in the classification of plant and equipment? (**a**) intangible, (**b**) limited life, (**c**) unlimited life, (**d**) held for sale in the regular course of business, (**e**) not capable of rendering benefits to the business in the future.

2 The following expenditures were incurred in connection with a large new machine acquired by a metals manufacturing company. Identify those which should be included in the cost of the asset. (**a**) Freight charges, (**b**) sales tax on the machine, (**c**) payment to a passing motorist whose car was damaged by the equipment used in unloading the machine, (**d**) wages of employees for time spent in installing and testing the machine before it was placed in service, (**e**) wages of employees assigned to lubrication and minor adjustments of machine one year after it was placed in service.

3 What is the distinction between a *capital expenditure* and a *revenue expenditure?*

4 Identify the following expenditures as capital expenditures or revenue expenditures:
  a Purchased new spark plugs at a cost of $9.20 for two-year-old delivery truck.
  b Installed an escalator at a cost of $14,800 in a three-store building which had previously been used for some years without elevators or escalators.
  c Purchased an electric pencil sharpener at a cost of $19.95.
  d Immediately after acquiring new delivery truck at a cost of $5,800, paid $75 to have the name of the store and other advertising material painted on the truck.
  e Painted delivery truck at a cost of $140 after two years of use.

5 Which of the following statements best describes the nature of depreciation?
  a Regular reduction of asset value to correspond to the decline in market value as the asset ages.
  b A process of correlating the carrying value of an asset with its gradual decline in physical efficiency.
  c Allocation of cost in a manner that will ensure that plant and equipment items are not carried on the balance sheet at amounts in excess of net realizable value.
  d Allocation of the cost of a plant asset to the periods in which services are received from the asset.

6 Should depreciation continue to be recorded on a building when ample evidence exists that the current market value is greater than original cost and that the rising trend of market values is continuing? Explain.

7 What connection exists between the choice of a depreciation method used to depreciate expensive new machinery for income tax reporting and the amount of income taxes payable in the near future?

8 Criticize the following quotation:
  "We shall have no difficulty in paying for new plant assets needed during the coming year because our estimated outlays for new equipment amount to only $80,000, and we have more than twice that amount in our depreciation reserves at present."

9 A factory machine acquired at a cost of $94,200 was to be depreciated by the sum-of-the-years'-digits method over an estimated life of eight years. Residual salvage value was estimated to be $15,000. State the amount of depreciation during the first year and during the eighth year.

10 After four years of using a machine acquired at a cost of $15,000, Ohio Construction Company determined that the original estimated life of 10 years had been too short and that a total useful life of 12 years was a more reasonable estimate. Explain briefly the method that should be used to revise the depreciation program, assuming that straight-line depreciation has been used.

11 a Give some reasons why a company may change its depreciation policy for financial reporting purposes from an accelerated depreciation method to the straight-line method.
  b Is it possible for a corporation to use accelerated depreciation for income tax purposes and straight-line depreciation for financial reporting purposes?

12 What is *ACRS?* Can it be applied to all assets? Why is ACRS not generally considered acceptable for use in financial statements? Are there any circumstances under which ACRS would conform to generally accepted accounting principles?

13 Explain two approaches to computing depreciation for the fractional period in the year in which an asset is purchased. (Neither of your approaches should require the computation of depreciation to the nearest day or week.)

14 Explain what is meant by the following quotation: "In periods of rising prices companies do not recognize adequate depreciation expense, and reported corporate profits are substantially overstated."

15 Century Company traded in its old computer on a new model. The trade-in allowance for the old computer is greater than its book value. Should Century Company recognize a gain on the exchange in computing its taxable income or in determining its net income for financial reporting? Explain.

16 Dell Company traded in an old machine on a similar new one. The original cost of the old machine was $30,000 and the accumulated depreciation was $24,000. The list price of the new machine was $40,000 and the trade-in allowance was $8,000. How much cash must Dell pay to acquire the new machine? Compute the indicated gain or loss (regardless of whether it should be recorded in the accounts). Compute the cost basis of the new machine to be used in figuring depreciation for determination of income subject to federal income tax.

17 Lead Hill Corporation recognizes $1 depletion for each ton of ore mined. During the current year the company mined 600,000 tons but sold only 500,000 tons, as it was attempting to build up inventories in anticipation of a possible strike by employees. How much depletion should be deducted from revenue of the current year?

18 Define *intangible assets*. Would an account receivable arising from a sale of merchandise under terms of 2/10, n/30 qualify as an intangible asset under your definition?

19 Over what period of time should the cost of various types of intangible assets be amortized by regular charges against revenue? (Your answer should be in the form of a principle or guideline rather than a specific number of years.) What method of amortization is generally used?

20 Several years ago March Metals purchased for $120,000 a well-known trademark for padlocks and other security products. After using the trademark for three years, March Metals discontinued it altogether when the company withdrew from the lock business and concentrated on the manufacture of aircraft parts. Amortization of the trademark at the rate of $3,000 a year is being continued on the basis of a 40-year life, which the owner of March Metals says is required by accounting standards. Do you agree? Explain.

21 Under what circumstances should *goodwill* be recorded in the accounts?

22 In reviewing the financial statements of Digital Products Co. with a view to investing in the company's stock, you notice that net tangible assets total $1 million, that goodwill is listed at $400,000, and that average earnings for the past five years have been $50,000 a year. How would these relationships influence your thinking about the company?

EXERCISES

Ex. 10-1 New office equipment was purchased by the Barker Company at a list price of $36,000 with credit terms of 2/10, n/30. Payment of the invoice was made within the discount period; it included 5% sales tax on the net price. Transportation charges of $430 on the new equipment were paid by Barker Company as well as labor cost of $760 for installing the equipment in the appropriate locations. During the unloading and installation work, some of the equipment fell from a loading platform and was damaged. Repair of the damaged parts cost $2,180. After the equipment had been in use for three months, it was thoroughly cleaned and lubricated at a cost of $260. Prepare a list of the items which should be capitalized by debit to the Office Equipment account and state the total cost of the new equipment.

Ex. 10-2 Machinery with a useful life of five years was acquired by Gulf Converters at a cost of $50,000. The estimated residual salvage value was $5,000. You are to compute the annual depreciation charges applicable to the machinery under each of the following methods of depreciation:

a Straight line

b Sum of the years' digits

c Double declining balance

Ex. 10-3 Henry Morgan, general manager of Catalog Printers, attended an auction of used machinery and was the successful bidder on a lot consisting of three machines for a total price of $17,100. Freight charges of $900 were incurred to have the three machines delivered to Catalog Printers plant. In anticipation of this auction the company had borrowed $15,000 in order to be able to make cash bids for the equipment being auctioned. The interest charge on the borrowing amounted to $500.

The estimated fair market values of the machines and the costs of installations and trial runs necessary to prepare them for regular operations were as follows:

	Machine No. 1	Machine No. 2	Machine No. 3
Fair market value	$10,000	$6,000	$4,000
Installation cost	400	800	300
Cost of trial runs	100	150	None

Determine the cost of each machine for accounting purposes, assuming that the auction and delivery costs were apportioned to the three machines on the basis of relative market value.

Ex. 10-4 On June 3, Year 1, Standard Tire Company purchased equipment at a cost of $300,000. The useful life of the equipment was estimated at six years and the residual value at $30,000. Compute the depreciation expense to be recognized in each calendar year during the life of the equipment under each of the following methods:

a Straight line (round computations for a partial year to the nearest full month)

b Straight line (use the half-year convention)

c Accelerated cost recovery system (use the table on page 383; assume the equipment qualifies as three-year property)

Ex. 10-5 An airplane with a book value of $30,000 was traded in on a new airplane with a list price of $300,000. The trade-in allowance (not necessarily the fair market value) for the old airplane was $48,000. Cash was paid for the balance.

a How much cash must be paid for the new airplane?

b What is the cost basis of the new airplane for income tax purposes?

c How much depreciation should be recorded on the new airplane for the first year of use, assuming a four-year life, a residual value of $42,000, and the use of straight-line depreciation?

Ex. 10-6 A tractor which cost $25,000 had an estimated useful life of five years and an estimated salvage value of $5,000. Straight-line depreciation was used. Give the entry (in general journal form) required by each of the following alternative assumptions:

a The tractor was sold for cash of $15,000 after two years' use.

b The tractor was traded in after three years on another tractor with a list price of $36,000. Trade-in allowance was $14,600. The trade-in was recorded in a manner acceptable for income tax purposes.

c The tractor was scrapped after four years' use. Since scrap dealers were unwilling to pay anything for the tractor, it was given to a scrap dealer for his services in removing it.

Ex. 10-7   In 198X, Midwest Mining Company purchased the Black Hills Mine for $3,800,000 cash. The mine was estimated to contain 2 million tons of ore and have a residual value of $800,000.

During the first year of mining operations at the Black Hills Mine, 400,000 tons of ore were mined, of which 300,000 tons were sold.

a Prepare a journal entry to record depletion of the Black Hills Mine during the year.

b Show how the mine and accumulated depletion would appear in Midwest Mining Company's balance sheet after the first year of operations.

c Will the entire balance of the account debited in part **a** be deducted from revenue in determining the income for the year? Explain.

Ex. 10-8   During the past several years the annual net income of Goldtone Appliance Company has averaged $270,000. At the present time the company is being offered for sale. Its accounting records show net assets (total assets minus all liabilities) to be $1,500,000.

An investor negotiating to buy the company offers to pay an amount equal to the book value for the net assets and to assume all liabilities. In addition, the investor is willing to pay for goodwill an amount equal to net earnings in excess of 15% on net assets, capitalized at a rate of 25%.

On the basis of this agreement, what price should the investor offer for Goldtone Appliance?

Ex. 10-9   Edison Company acquired its plant and equipment 20 years ago at a cost of $200,000 paid in cash. After paying for the plant and equipment, the company had about $15,000 cash for use in operations. The company has consistently used straight-line depreciation based on historical cost and an estimated useful life of 20 years. Residual or salvage value was estimated to be virtually zero. The company has reported a net income each year. However, each year Edison Company paid cash dividends equal to the reported net income.

The plant and equipment are now worn out and must be replaced. Replacement cost is approximately four times the cost of the original plant and equipment.

a Based solely on the above information, about how much cash would you expect Edison Company to have today? Explain the basis for your answer. (Assume that the cash balance increases each year by an amount equal to revenue minus the outlays for cash expenses and dividends. Remember that depreciation is a noncash expense.)

b What is the prospect for Edison Company being able to pay for the new plant and equipment it needs?

c On what grounds might the accounting measurement of net income by Edison Company be criticized in the light of 20 years of operation in an inflationary environment?

PROBLEMS

10-1   New machinery was acquired by Del Mar Electronics at a cost of $200,000. Useful life of the machinery was estimated to be five years, with residual salvage value of $5,000.

Instructions   Compute the annual depreciation expense throughout the five-year life of the machinery under each of the following methods of depreciation:

a Straight line

b Sum of the years' digits

c Double declining balance

10-2　Soft-Lens Optical acquired new equipment with an estimated useful life of five years. Cost of the equipment was $300,000 and the residual salvage value was estimated to be $6,000.

Instructions　Compute the annual depreciation expense throughout the five-year life of the equipment under each of the following methods of depreciation:

a Straight line

b Sum of the years' digits

c Double declining balance

d ACRS—the income tax method. Use the rate table on page 383; assume that the equipment qualifies as three-year property for income tax purposes.)

10-3　Sunrise Corporation early in the current year purchased some hilly land with old abandoned buildings. The old buildings were removed, the land was leveled, and a new building was constructed. The company moved from its former rented quarters into the new building on October 1. Transactions relating to these events were recorded in an account entitled Property, which contained the following entries at the end of the current year.

Debit entries:

3/9	Purchase for cash of building site	$ 68,750
4/28	Payment for demolition of old building	7,500
5/15	Payment for leveling of land	25,000
9/28	Payment for insurance on building during construction	15,000
9/28	Payment for new building completed today	300,000
10/7	Payment to caterer for office party for employees, customers, and friends to celebrate the move to new building	3,750
	Total debits	$420,000

Credit entries:

4/28	Cash received from sale of materials from demolished building	$11,250	
12/31	Depreciation for the current year, computed at 4% of balance in Property account ($408,750). Debit was to Depreciation Expense	16,350	
	Total credits		27,600
12/31	Balance in Property account at year-end		$392,400

Instructions

a List the errors made in the application of accounting principles or practices by Sunrise Corporation.

b Prepare a three-column schedule with column headings of Entertainment Expense, Land, and Buildings. Use this schedule to classify properly the debits and credits (other than depreciation) which Sunrise Corporation entered in its account entitled Property. For example, use the first line of your schedule to show in which account the debit of March 9 should be recorded.

c Prepare a compound journal entry to correct the accounts according to the classification developed in **b.** This correcting entry should include a credit for $392,400 to close the Property account and replace it with more descriptive accounts. The entry will also include adjustment of the incorrect treatment of depreciation. Estimated life of the new building was 25 years; depreciation should be recognized for the three months the building was in use during the current year, using the straight-line method. The revenue and expense accounts have not been closed for the current year.

10-4 In the last few years Jayhawk Corporation has acquired four machines. At the time of acquiring each machine, different personnel were employed in the accounting department; consequently, various methods of depreciation have been adopted for the several machines. Information concerning the four machines may be summarized as follows:

Machine	Date Acquired	Cost	Estimated Useful Life, Years	Estimated Residual Value	Method of Depreciation
A	Jan. 1, Year 8	$ 97,200	6	None	Declining balance
B	June 30, Year 8	151,200	8	10%	Straight line
C	Jan. 1, Year 9	100,800	10	$1,800	Sum of the years' digits
D	Jan. 1, Year 10	118,800	12	None	Declining balance

Instructions

a Compute the amount of accumulated depreciation, if any, on each machine owned at December 31, Year 9. For machines A and D, assume that the depreciation rate was double the rate which would be applicable under the straight-line method.

b Prepare a depreciation schedule for use in the computation of the Year 10 depreciation expense. Use the following column headings:

Machine	Method of Depreciation	Date of Acquisition	Cost	Estimated Residual Value	Amount to Be Depreciated	Useful Life, Years	Accumulated Depreciation, Dec. 31, Year 9	Depreciation Expense, Year 10

c Prepare a journal entry to record the Year 10 depreciation expense.

d Using the ACRS rate table on page 383, compute the amount of depreciation (cost recovery) that would be allowed on each machine for income tax reporting in Year 10. Assume that all of the machines qualify as five-year property.

10-5 Wright Manufacturing Company acquired equipment for cash on January 5, Year 1, at a cost of $108,800. Useful life was estimated to be 10 years; the residual value, $10,000. The company depreciates its plant assets by the straight-line method and closes its accounts annually at December 31. Depreciation for partial years is recorded to the nearest full month.

In Year 3, after almost three years of experience with the equipment, management decided that, in view of technological changes, the estimated life of the equipment should be revised from 10 years to 7 years. The revised estimate of the useful life was made prior to recording depreciation expense for Year 3.

On September 25, Year 4, the equipment was sold for $63,000 cash.

Instructions   Prepare general journal entries in chronological order to record the above events, beginning with the purchase of the equipment on January 5, Year 1. Show separately the depreciation for Years 1, 2, and 3. Also make separate entries dated September 25, Year 4, to record depreciation for the portion of Year 4 that the equipment was owned and the sale of the equipment.

10-6 Wind River Ranch maintains its accounts on a calendar-year basis. On May 1, the company purchased machinery priced at $290,000, but received a trade-in allowance of $24,000 for used machinery. Cash of $60,000 was paid and a 12%, one-year note payable given for the balance. The machinery traded in had an original cost of $180,000 and had been depreciated at the rate of $18,000 a year. Residual value had been ignored on the grounds of not being material. Accumulated depreciation amounted to $144,000 at December 31 prior to the year of the exchange. No depreciation had been recorded between the closing of the accounts on December 31 and the exchange for the new machinery on May 1.

Instructions In general journal form, give the entries to record:
a Depreciation for the fraction of a year prior to the May 1 transaction.
b The acquisition of the new machinery on May 1 under the rules acceptable for income tax purposes.
c The acquisition of the new machinery on May 1 under the assumption that gain or loss is to be recognized and that the trade-in allowance represents the fair market value of the old machinery being traded in.

10-7 On March 17, Year 4, Wildcat Oil Company began operations at its Southfork Oil Field. The oil field had been acquired several years earlier at a cost of $11,600,000. The field is estimated to contain 4 million barrels of oil and to have a residual value of $2,000,000 after all of the oil has been pumped out. Equipment costing $480,000 was purchased for use at the Southfork Field. This equipment will have no economic usefulness once Southfork is depleted; therefore, it is depreciated on a units-of-output basis.

Wildcat Oil also built a pipeline at a cost of $2,880,000 to serve the Southfork Field. Although this pipeline is physically capable of being used for many years, its economic usefulness is limited to the productive life of the Southfork Field and there is no residual value. Therefore, depreciation of the pipeline also is based upon the estimated number of barrels of oil to be produced.

Production at the Southfork Field amounted to 420,000 barrels in Year 4 and 510,000 barrels in Year 5.

Instructions
a Compute the per-barrel depletion rate of the oil field and the per-barrel depreciation rates of the equipment and the pipeline.
b Make the year-end adjusting entries required at December 31, Year 4, and December 31, Year 5, to record depletion of the oil field and the related depreciation. (Make separate entries to record depletion of the oil field, depreciation of the equipment, and depreciation of the pipeline.)
c Show how the Southfork Field should appear in Wildcat Oil's balance sheet at the end of Year 5. (Use "Oil Reserves: Southfork Field" as the title of the asset account; show accumulated depletion, but do not include the equipment or pipeline.)

10-8 Classic Furniture is considering purchasing the net assets of Antique Reproductions on January 2, Year 7. Antique Reproductions, a single proprietorship owned by Francis

Taylor, has been in business for six years and has reported an average annual net income of $61,300 during this period.

After any necessary adjustments have been made to the accounting records of Antique Reproductions, Classic Furniture will pay a price equal to the book value of net assets plus an amount for goodwill. Classic Furniture will assume all liabilities of Antique Reproductions. The goodwill is to be determined by capitalizing at a rate of 30% the amount by which the adjusted average earnings exceed a 20% return on the adjusted net identifiable assets (owners' equity exclusive of goodwill). The purchase plan calls for Classic Furniture to make a cash down payment of $100,000 and issue a promissory note for the balance of the purchase price.

The balance sheet for Antique Reproductions on December 31, Year 6, follows:

Assets

Cash			$ 5,000
Accounts receivable			71,000
Inventory			80,000
Plant and equipment:			
Land		$ 63,600	
Buildings	$146,400		
Less: Accumulated depreciation	38,400	108,000	
Equipment	$186,000		
Less: Accumulated depreciation	117,000	69,000	240,600
Patent			54,000
Goodwill			15,000
Total assets			$465,600

Liabilities & Owners' Equity

Accounts payable	$ 74,000
Long-term liabilities:	
Mortgage note payable	110,000
Francis Taylor, capital	281,600
Total liabilities & owners' equity	$465,600

Other data

(1) The $15,000 of goodwill was recorded in the accounts three years ago when Taylor decided that the increasing profitability of the business should be recognized. Since profitability continued to increase, the goodwill was not amortized.

(2) The patent appears at original cost. It was acquired by purchase six years ago from a competitor who had owned the patent for two years of its legal life. The patent is considered very valuable to the business and should have a useful life equal to its legal life (15 years from the date Antique Reproductions acquired it).

Instructions

a Prepare any adjusting entries needed in the accounts of Antique Reproductions to bring the amounts shown in the balance sheet into accord with generally accepted accounting principles. (Two corrections are required.)

b Compute the amount to be paid for goodwill by Classic Furniture after considering the effects of the adjustments in part **a**. (The reported average net income should be adjusted to reflect amortization of the patent.) Also compute the total purchase price Classic Furniture will pay for the net assets of Antique Reproductions.

c Prepare a compound journal entry in the accounting records of Antique Reproductions to record the sale to Classic Furniture. The entry should record:
(1) The closing of the asset and liability accounts to reflect the transfer of these items to Classic Furniture.
(2) The receipt of the cash and the note receivable from Classic Furniture.
(3) The gain on the sale of the business.

d Prepare a compound journal entry in the accounting records of Classic Furniture to record the purchase of the assets (including goodwill as determined in **b**) and the assumption of the liabilities of Antique Reproductions. Classic Furniture records the assets acquired net of accumulated depreciation.

BUSINESS DECISION PROBLEM 10

Samuel Slater is interested in buying a manufacturing business and has located two similar companies being offered for sale. Both companies are single proprietorships which began operations three years ago, each with invested capital of $400,000. A considerable part of the assets in each company is represented by a building with an original cost of $100,000 and an estimated life of 40 years, and by machinery with an original cost of $200,000 and an estimated life of 20 years. Residual value is negligible.

Bay Company uses straight-line depreciation and Cove Company uses fixed-percentage-on-declining-balance depreciation (double the straight-line rate). In all other respects the accounting policies of the two companies are quite similar. Neither company has borrowed from banks or incurred any indebtedness other than normal trade payables. The nature of products and other characteristics of operations are much the same for the two companies.

Audited financial statements for the three years show net income as follows:

Year	Bay Company	Cove Company
1	$ 62,000	$ 59,000
2	65,200	63,200
3	68,400	66,900
Totals	$195,600	$189,100

Slater asks your advice as to which company to buy. They are offered for sale at approximately the same price, and Slater is inclined to choose Bay Company because of its consistently higher earnings. On the other hand, the fact that Cove Company has more cash and a stronger working capital position is impressive. The audited financial statements show that withdrawals by the two owners have been approximately equal during the three-year life of the two companies.

Instructions

a Compute the depreciation recorded by each company in the first three years. Round off depreciation expense for each year to the nearest dollar.

b Write a memorandum to Slater advising which company in your judgment represents the more promising purchase. Give specific reasons to support your recommendation. Include a recomputation of the earnings of Cove Company by using straight-line depreciation in order to make its income statements comparable with those of Bay Company. Compare the earnings of the two companies year by year after such revision to a uniform basis.

FORMS OF BUSINESS ORGANIZATION

After studying this chapter you should be able to:

- Explain the basic characteristics of a single proprietorship, a partnership, and a corporation.
- Account for investments and withdrawals by the owners of an unincorporated business.
- Prepare a statement of owner's (or partners') capital.
- Prepare a schedule distributing partnership income among the partners.
- Explain the rights of stockholders and the roles of corporate directors and officers.
- Discuss the features of preferred stock and of common stock.
- Account for the issuance of stock in exchange for cash or other assets.
- Account for subscriptions to capital stock and for donated capital.

Three types of business organization are common to American business: the single proprietorship, the partnership, and the corporation. When these forms of organization were introduced in Chapter 1, we stressed that most accounting principles apply to all three forms and that the main area of difference lies in accounting for owners' equity. In this chapter, we shall describe briefly the unique characteristics and accounting practices of single proprietorships and partnerships, and then move to a discussion of corporations. Our discussion of the accounting practices of corporations will continue into the following chapter.

SINGLE PROPRIETORSHIPS

Any unincorporated business owned by one person is called a single proprietorship. This form of organization is common among small retail stores, farms, service businesses, and professional practices. In fact, the single proprietorship is the most common form of business organization in our economy. Most of these businesses, however, tend to be relatively small.

An important characteristic of the single proprietorship is that, from a legal viewpoint, the business and its owner are not regarded as separate entities. Thus, the owner is *personally liable* for the debts of the business. If the business becomes insolvent, creditors can force the owner to sell his or her personal assets to pay the business debts.

From an accounting viewpoint, however, a single proprietorship is regarded as an entity *separate from the other affairs of its owner*. For example, assume that Jill Green owns two single proprietorships—a gas station and a shoe store. The assets, liabilities, revenue, and expenses relating to the gas station would not appear in the financial statements of the shoe store. Also, Green's personal assets, such as her house, furniture, and savings account, would not appear in the financial statements of either business entity.

Accounting for the owner's equity in a single proprietorship

A balance sheet for a single proprietorship shows the entire ownership equity as a single dollar amount without any effort to distinguish between the amount originally invested by the owner and the later increase or decrease in owner's equity as a result of profitable or unprofitable operations. A corporation must maintain separate accounts for capital stock and retained earnings, because distributions to owners in the form of dividends cannot legally exceed the earnings of the corporation. In an unincorporated business, however, the owner is free to withdraw assets from the business at any time and in any amount.

The accounting records for a single proprietorship do not include accounts for capital stock, retained earnings, or dividends. Instead of these accounts, a *capital* account and a *drawing* account are maintained for the owner.

The owner's capital account   In a single proprietorship, the title of the capital account includes the name of the owner, as, for example, *John Jones, Capital.* The capital account is credited with the amount of the proprietor's original investment in the business and also with any subsequent investments. When the accounts are closed at the end of each accounting period, the Income Summary account is closed into the owner's capital account. Thus the capital account is credited with the net income earned (or debited with the net loss incurred). Withdrawals by the proprietor during the period are debited to a drawing account, which later is closed into the capital account.

The owner's drawing account   A withdrawal of cash or other assets by the owner reduces the owner's equity in the business and could be recorded by debiting the owner's capital account. However, a clearer record is created if a separate Drawing account is maintained. This drawing account (entitled, for example, *John Jones, Drawing*) replaces the Dividends account used by a corporation.

The drawing account is debited for any of the following transactions:

1 Withdrawals of cash or other assets. If the proprietor of a clothing store, for example, withdraws merchandise for personal use, the Drawing account is debited for the cost of the goods withdrawn. The offsetting credit is to the Purchases account (or to Inventory if a perpetual inventory system is maintained).

2 Payment of the proprietor's personal bills out of the business bank account.

3 Collection of an account receivable of the business, with the cash collected being retained personally by the proprietor.

Withdrawals by the proprietor (like dividends to stockholders) are not an expense of the business. Expenses are incurred for the purpose of generating revenue, and a withdrawal of cash or other assets by the proprietor does not have this purpose.

Closing the accounts

The revenue and expense accounts of a single proprietorship are closed into the Income Summary account in the same way as for a corporation. The Income Summary account is then closed to the proprietor's Capital account, rather than to a Retained Earnings account. To complete the closing of the accounts, the balance sheet of a proprietorship and of a corporation was illustrated in Chapter 1 on pages 18 and 19.

Financial statements for a single proprietorship

The balance sheet of a single proprietorship differs from that of a corporation only in the owner's equity section. The presentation of ownership equity in the balance sheet of a proprietorship and of a corporation was illustrated in Chapter 1 on pages 18 and 19.

A *statement of owner's equity* may be prepared in a form similar to the statement of retained earnings used by a corporation. The statement of owner's equity, however, shows additional investments made by the owner as well as the earnings retained in the business. An illustration follows:

JONES INSURANCE AGENCY
Statement of Owner's Equity
For the Year Ended December 31, 19__

Note that withdrawals may exceed net income John Jones, capital, Jan. 1, 19__	$ 80,400
Add: Additional investments	10,000
Net income for year	30,500
Subtotal	$120,900
Less: Withdrawals	34,000
John Jones, capital, Dec. 31, 19__	$ 86,900

The *income statement* of a proprietorship differs from that of a corporation in two significant respects. First, the income statement for a single proprietorship does not include any salary expense representing managerial services rendered by the owner. One reason for not including a salary to the owner-manager is the fact that individuals in such a position are able to set their own salaries at any amount they choose. The use of an unrealistic salary to the proprietor would tend to destroy the significance of the income statement as a device for measuring the earning power of the business. It is more logical to regard the owner-manager as working to earn the entire net income of the business than as working for a salary.

The second distinctive feature of the income statement of a single proprietorship is the absence of any income taxes expense. Since a proprietorship is not recognized as a legal entity separate from its owner, the business does not file its own income tax return or pay any income taxes. However, the proprietor must include the income of the business on his or her individual income tax return, along with any taxable income from other sources. (Notice that the proprietor must pay income taxes upon the entire net income of the business, not merely upon the amount withdrawn during the year.) In contrast, a corporation does pay income taxes on its earnings, and income taxes expense will appear in its income statement.

PARTNERSHIPS

A partnership is an unincorporated business that is jointly owned by two or more people. In the professions and in businesses which stress the factor of personal service, the partnership form of organization is widely used. In the fields of manufacturing, wholesaling, and retail trade, partnerships are also popular, because they afford a means of combining the capital and abilities of two or more persons. A partnership is often referred to as a *firm;* the name of the firm often includes the word "company" as, for example, "Adams, Myers, and Company."

Significant features of a partnership

Before taking up the accounting problems peculiar to partnerships, it will be helpful to consider briefly some of the distinctive characteristics of the partnership form of organization. These characteristics (such as limited life and unlimited liability) all stem from the basic point that a partnership is not a separate legal entity in itself but merely a voluntary association of individuals.

Ease of formation   A partnership can be created without any legal formalities. When two or more persons agree to become partners, such agreement constitutes a contract and a partnership is automatically created. The contract should be in writing in order to lessen the chances for misunderstanding and future disagreement.

Limited life   A partnership may be ended at any time by the death or withdrawal of any member of the firm. Other factors which may bring an end to a partnership include the bankruptcy or incapacity of a partner, or the completion of the project for which the partnership was formed. The admission of a new partner or the retirement of an existing member means an end to the old partnership, although the business may be continued by the formation of a new partnership.

Mutual agency   Each partner acts as an agent of the partnership, with authority to enter into contracts. The partnership is bound by the acts of any partner as long as these acts are within the scope of normal operations. The factor of mutual agency suggests the need for exercising great caution in the selection of a partner. To be in partnership with an irresponsible person or one lacking in integrity is an intolerable situation.

Unlimited liability   Each partner in a *general partnership* is personally responsible for the debts of the partnership. The lack of any ceiling on the liability of a general partner may deter a wealthy person from entering a general partnership. In a *limited partnership* one (or more) of the partners has no personal liability for the debts of the partnership.

Co-ownership of partnership property and profits   When a partner invests a building, inventory, or other property in a partnership, he or she does not retain any personal right to the assets contributed. The property becomes jointly owned by all partners. Each member of a partnership also has an ownership right in the profits.

Advantages and disadvantages of a partnership

Perhaps the most important advantage of most partnerships is the opportunity to bring together sufficient capital to carry on a business. The opportunity to combine special skills, as, for example, the specialized talents of engineers, accountants, or lawyers may also induce individuals to join forces in a partnership. Members of a partnership enjoy more freedom from government regulation and more flexibility of action than do the owners of a corporation; the partners may withdraw funds and make business decisions of all types without the necessity of formal meetings or legalistic procedures. Finally, operating as a partnership may, in certain instances, result in significant income tax advantages.

Offsetting these advantages of a partnership are such serious disadvantages as limited life, unlimited liability, and mutual agency. Furthermore, if a business is to require a large amount of capital, the partnership is a less effective device for raising funds than is a corporation. Many persons who invest freely in the capital stocks of corporations are unwilling to enter a partnership because of the unlimited liability imposed on partners.

Although a partnership can be formed by an oral agreement, it is highly desirable that a written partnership agreement be prepared, summarizing the partners' mutual understanding on such points as:

1 Names of the partners, and the duties and rights of each.
2 Amount to be invested by each partner. Procedure for valuing any noncash assets invested or withdrawn by partners.
3 Method of sharing profits and losses.
4 Withdrawals to be allowed each partner.

Partnership accounting

Partnership accounting is similar to that in a single proprietorship, except that separate capital and drawing accounts must be maintained for each partner. A distinctive feature of partnership accounting is that the net income of the business must be divided among the partners in the manner specified by the partnership agreement.

Opening the accounts of a new partnership   When a partner contributes assets other than cash, a question always arises as to the value of such assets. The valuations assigned to noncash assets should be their *fair market values* at the date of transfer to the partnership. The valuations assigned must be agreed to by all the partners.

To illustrate the opening entries for a newly formed partnership, assume that on January 1 John Blair and Melinda Cross, who operate competing retail stores, decide to form a partnership by consolidating their two businesses. A capital account will be opened for each partner and credited with the agreed valuation of the *net assets* (total assets less total liabilities) that partner contributes. The journal entries to open the accounts of the partnership of Blair and Cross are as follows:

Entries for formation of partnership	Cash	40,000	
	Accounts Receivable	60,000	
	Inventory	90,000	
	Accounts Payable		30,000
	John Blair, Capital		160,000

To record the investment by John Blair in the partnership of Blair and Cross.

Cash	10,000	
Land	60,000	
Building	100,000	
Inventory	60,000	
Accounts Payable		70,000
Melinda Cross, Capital		160,000

To record the investment by Melinda Cross in the partnership of Blair and Cross.

The values assigned to assets in the accounts of the new partnership may be quite different from the amounts at which these assets were carried in the accounts of their previous owners. For example, the land contributed by Cross and valued at $60,000 might have appeared in her accounting records at a cost of $20,000. The building which she contributed was valued at $100,000 by the partnership, but it might have cost Cross only $80,000 some years ago and might have been depreciated on her records to a net value of $60,000. Assuming that market values of land and buildings had risen sharply while Cross owned this property, it is only fair to recognize the *current market value* of these assets at the time she transfers them to the partnership and to credit her capital account accordingly. Depreciation of the building in the partnership accounts will be based on the assigned value of $100,000 at the date of acquisition by the partnership.

Withdrawals and additional investments   Partners may make withdrawals of cash or other partnership assets at any time; there is no need for a formal "declaration" as with dividends paid by a corporation. The amounts withdrawn need not be the same for all partners. The withdrawal of cash or other assets by a partner is recorded by debiting that partner's drawing account. If a partner invests additional assets in the business, the investment is recorded by crediting the partner's capital account.

Closing the accounts at year-end   The revenue and expense accounts of a partnership are closed into the Income Summary account in the same way as for a corporation. The balance of the Income Summary account is then closed into the partners' capital accounts, in accordance with the profit-sharing provisions of the partnership agreement. If the partnership agreement does not specify how profits are to be divided, the law requires that any profits or losses be divided equally among the partners.

Let us assume that Blair and Cross have agreed to share profits equally and that the partnership earns net income of $60,000 during its first year of operations. The entry to close the Income Summary account would be as follows:

Closing Income Summary: profits shared equally

Income Summary	60,000	
John Blair, Capital		30,000
Melinda Cross, Capital		30,000

To divide net income for 19___ in accordance with partnership agreement to share profits equally.

The next step in closing the accounts is to transfer the balance of each partner's drawing account to his or her capital account. Assuming that withdrawals during the year amounted to $12,000 for Blair and $8,000 for Cross, the entry at December 31 to close the drawing accounts is as follows:

Closing the drawing accounts to capital accounts

John Blair, Capital	12,000	
Melinda Cross, Capital	8,000	
John Blair, Drawing		12,000
Melinda Cross, Drawing		8,000

To transfer debit balances in partners' accounts to their respective capital accounts.

Income statement for a partnership   The income statement for a partnership differs from that of a single proprietorship in only one respect: a final section may be added to show the division of the net income between the partners, as illustrated below for the firm of Blair and Cross. The income statement of a partnership is consistent with that of a single proprietorship in showing no income taxes expense and no salaries expense relating to services rendered by partners.

BLAIR AND CROSS
Income Statement
For the Year Ended December 31, 19___

Note distribution of net income

Sales			$600,000
Cost of goods sold:			
Inventory, Jan. 1		$150,000	
Purchases		460,000	
Cost of goods available for sale		$610,000	
Less: Inventory, Dec. 31		210,000	
Cost of goods sold			400,000
Gross profit on sales			$200,000
Operating expenses:			
Selling expenses		$100,000	
General & administrative expenses		40,000	140,000
Net income			$ 60,000
Distribution of net income:			
To John Blair (50%)		$ 30,000	
To Melinda Cross (50%)		30,000	$ 60,000

Statement of partners' capitals   The partners will usually want an explanation of the change in their capital accounts from one year-end to the next. A financial statement called a *statement of partners' capitals* is prepared to show this information and is illustrated below for the partnership of Blair and Cross:

BLAIR AND CROSS
Statement of Partners' Capitals
For the Year Ended December 31, 19___

Changes in capital accounts during the year

	Blair	Cross	Total
Investment, Jan. 1, 19___	$160,000	$160,000	$320,000
Add: Additional investment	10,000	10,000	20,000
Net income for the year	30,000	30,000	60,000
Subtotals	$200,000	$200,000	$400,000
Less: Drawings	12,000	8,000	20,000
Balances, Dec. 31, 19___	$188,000	$192,000	$380,000

The balance sheet of Blair and Cross would show the capital balance for each partner, as well as the total capital of $380,000.

Partnership profits and income taxes

Partnerships are not required to pay income taxes. However, a partnership is required to file an information tax return showing the amount of the partnership net income, and the share of each partner in the net income. Each partner must include his share of the partnership profit (after certain technical adjustments) on his individual income tax return. Partnership net income is thus taxable to the partners individually in the year in which it is earned. The income tax rules applicable to investment in a partnership are quite complex; those complexities are appropriate to advanced accounting courses.

Note that partners report and pay tax on their respective shares of the profits earned by the partnership during the year and not on the amounts which they have drawn out of the business during the year. *The net income of the partnership is taxable to the partners each year,* even though there may have been no withdrawals. This treatment is consistent with that accorded a single proprietorship.

Alternative methods of dividing partnership income

In the preceding illustration, the partners divided net income equally. Partners can, however, share net income in any way they wish. Factors that partners might consider in arriving at an equitable plan to divide net income include (1) the amount of time each partner devotes to the business, (2) the amount of capital invested by each partner, and (3) any other contribution by each partner to the success of the partnership. Net income, for example, may be shared in any agreed ratio such as in the ratio of beginning capitals, or in a fixed ratio after an allowance is made to each partner for salary and interest on capital invested.

To illustrate, assume that the partnership of Adams and Barnes earned $97,000 (before interest and salary allowances to partners) in Year 1 and that they had agreed to share net income as follows:

1 Salary allowances of $24,000 per year to Adams and $48,000 per year to Barnes. (Partners' salaries are merely a device for sharing net income and are not necessarily withdrawn from the business.)
2 Interest at 15% on average capitals to be allowed to each partner. Average capital balances for Adams and Barnes amounted to $100,000 and $40,000, respectively.
3 Any amount in excess of the foregoing salary and interest allowances to be divided equally.

In accordance with the terms of this agreement, the net income of $97,000 would be divided between Adams and Barnes as follows:

Distribution of Net Income

	Adams	Barnes	Net Income
Net income to be divided			$97,000
Salaries to partners	$24,000	$48,000	72,000
Income after salaries			$25,000
Interest on beginning capitals:			
Adams ($100,000 × 15%)	15,000		
Barnes ($40,000 × 15%)		6,000	
Total allocated as interest			21,000
Remaining income after salaries and interest			$ 4,000
Allocated in a fixed ratio:			
Adams (50%)	2,000		
Barnes (50%)		2,000	4,000
Total share to each partner	$41,000	$56,000	$ –0–

Profit sharing; salaries, interest, and fixed ratio as basis

The journal entry to close the Income Summary account in this case will be:

Income Summary	97,000	
Lynn Adams, Capital		41,000
Dale Barnes, Capital		56,000

To close the Income Summary account by crediting each partner with authorized salary, interest at 15% on beginning capital, and dividing the remaining profits equally.

Authorized salaries and interest in excess of net income   In the preceding example the total of the authorized salaries and interest was $93,000 and the net income to be divided was $97,000. Suppose that the net income had been only $75,000; how should the division have been made?

If the partnership contract provides for salaries and interest on invested capital, these provisions are to be followed even though the net income for the year is less than the total of the authorized salaries and interest. If the net income of the firm of Adams and Barnes amounted to only $75,000, this amount would be distributed as shown below.

Distribution of Net Income

	Adams	Barnes	Net Income
Net income to be divided			$ 75,000
Salaries to partners	$24,000	$48,000	72,000
Income after salaries			$ 3,000
Interest on beginning capitals:			
Adams ($100,000 × 15%)	15,000		
Barnes ($40,000 × 15%)		6,000	
Total allocated as interest			21,000
Residual loss after salaries and interest			$(18,000)
Allocated in a fixed ratio:			
Adams (50%)	(9,000)		
Barnes (50%)		(9,000)	18,000
Total share to each partner	$30,000	$45,000	$ –0–

Authorized salaries and interest may exceed net income

The residual loss of $18,000 is divided equally because the partnership contract states that profits and losses are to be divided equally after providing for salaries and interest.

Other aspects of partnership accounting

The foregoing discussion of partnership accounting is by no means exhaustive. The admission of a new partner to the partnership, the withdrawal of a partner, and the liquidation of a partnership, for example, may raise some very complex accounting issues. These issues are primarily of interest to advanced accounting students and for that reason are not included in this introductory text.

CORPORATIONS

Nearly all large businesses and many small ones are organized as corporations. There are still more single proprietorships and partnerships than corporations, but in dollar volume of business activity, corporations hold an impressive lead. Why is the corporation the most common form of organization for large businesses? One reason is that corporations obtain their equity capital by issuing shares of capital stock. Since a corporation may issue a vast number of these shares, it may amass the combined savings of a great number of investors. Thus, the corporation is an ideal means of obtaining the capital necessary to finance large-scale operations. Because of the prominent role of corporations in our economy, it is important for everyone with an interest in business, economics, or politics to have an understanding of corporations and their accounting practices.

What is a corporation?

A corporation is a legal entity having an existence separate and distinct from that of its owners. In the eyes of the law, a corporation is an artificial person having many of the rights and responsibilities of a real person.

A corporation, as a separate legal entity, may own property in its own name. Thus, the assets of a corporation belong to the corporation itself, not to the stockholders. A corporation has legal status in court, that is, it may sue and be sued as if it were a person. As a legal entity, a corporation enters into contracts, is responsible for its own debts, and pays income taxes on its earnings.

A corporation is owned by its stockholders. To administer the affairs of the corporation, the stockholders elect a *board of directors*. The directors in turn select a president and other corporate officers to carry on active management of the business.

Advantages of the corporate form of organization

The corporation offers a number of advantages not available in other forms of organization. Among these advantages are the following:

1 No personal liability for stockholders Creditors of a corporation have a claim against the assets of the corporation, not against the personal property of the stockholders. Thus, the amount of money which stockholders risk by investing in a corporation is *limited to the amount of their investment.* To many investors, this is the most important advantage of the corporate form.

2 **Ease of accumulating capital**   Ownership of a corporation is evidenced by transferable *shares of stock.* The sale of corporate ownership in units of one or more shares permits both large and small investors to participate in ownership of the business. Some corporations actually have more than a million individual stockholders. For this reason, large corporations are often said to be *publicly owned.* Of course not all corporations are large. Many small businesses are organized as corporations and are owned by a limited number of stockholders. Such corporations are said to be *closely held.*

3 **Ownership shares are readily transferable**   Shares of stock may be sold by one investor to another without dissolving or disrupting the business organization. The shares of most large corporations may be bought or sold by investors in organized markets, such as the *New York Stock Exchange.* Investments in these shares have the advantage of *liquidity,* because investors may easily convert their corporate ownership into cash by selling their stock.

4 **Continuous existence**   A corporation is a separate legal entity with a perpetual existence. The continuous life of the corporation despite changes in ownership is made possible by the issuance of transferable shares of stock. By way of contrast, a partnership is a relatively unstable form of organization which is dissolved by the death or retirement of any of its members. The continuity of the corporate entity is essential to most large-scale business activities.

5 **Professional management**   The stockholders own the corporation, but they do not manage it on a daily basis. To administer the affairs of the corporation, the stockholders elect a *board of directors.* The directors, in turn, hire a president and other corporate officers to manage the business. There is no mutual agency in a corporation; thus, an individual stockholder has no right to participate in the management of the business unless he or she has been hired as a corporate officer.

Disadvantages of the corporate form of organization

Among the disadvantages of the corporation are:

1 **Heavy taxation**   The income of a partnership or a single proprietorship is taxable only as personal income to the owners of the business. The income of a corporation, on the other hand, is subject to income taxes which must be paid by the corporation. The combination of federal and state corporate income taxes often takes about 50% of a corporation's before-tax income. If a corporation distributes its earnings to stockholders, the stockholders must pay personal income taxes on the amounts they receive. This practice of first taxing corporate income to the corporation and then taxing distributions of that income to the stockholders is sometimes called *double taxation.*

2 **Greater regulation**   A corporation comes into existence under the terms of state laws and these same laws may provide for considerable regulation of the corporation's activities. For example, the withdrawal of funds from a corporation is subject to certain limits set by law. Federal laws administered by the Securities and Exchange Commission require large corporations to make extensive public disclosure of their affairs.

3 **Separation of ownership and control**   The separation of the functions of ownership and management may be an advantage in some cases but a disadvantage in others. On the whole, the excellent record of growth and earnings in most large corporations indicates that the separation of ownership and control has benefited rather than injured stockholders. In a few instances, however, a management group has chosen to operate a corporation for the benefit of insiders. The stockholders may find it difficult in such cases to take the concerted action necessary to oust the officers.

Formation of a corporation

A corporation is created by obtaining a corporate *charter* from the state in which the company is to be incorporated. To obtain a corporate charter, an application called the *articles of incorporation* is submitted to the state corporations commissioner or other designated official. Once the charter is obtained, the stockholders in the new corporation hold a meeting to elect *directors* and to pass *bylaws* as a guide to the company's affairs. The directors in turn hold a meeting at which officers of the corporation are appointed.

Organization costs   The formation of a corporation is a much more costly step than the organization of a partnership. The necessary costs include the payment of an incorporation fee to the state, the payment of fees to attorneys for their services in drawing up the articles of incorporation, payments to promoters, and a variety of other outlays necessary to bring the corporation into existence. These costs are charged to an asset account called Organization Costs. In the balance sheet, organization costs appear under the "Other assets" caption, as illustrated on page 43.

   The incurring of these organization costs leads to the existence of the corporate entity; consequently, the benefits derived from these costs may be regarded as extending over the entire life of the corporation. Since the life of a corporation may continue indefinitely, one might argue that organization costs are an asset with an unlimited life. However, present income tax rules permit organization costs to be written off over a period of five years or more; consequently, most companies elect to write off organization costs over a five-year period. Accountants have been willing to accept this practice, because organization costs are not material in amount. The accounting principle of *materiality* permits departures from theoretical concepts on the grounds of convenience if the practice in question will not cause any material distortion of net income.

Rights of stockholders   The ownership of stock in a corporation usually carries the following basic rights:

1 To vote for directors, and thereby to be represented in the management of the business. The approval of a majority of stockholders may also be required for such important corporate actions as mergers and acquisitions, the selection of independent auditors, the incurring of long-term debts, the establishment of stock option plans, or the splitting of capital stock into a larger number of shares.

When a corporation issues both common stock and preferred stock, voting rights generally are granted only to the holders of common stock. These two different types of capital stock will be discussed in detail later in this chapter.

2 To share in profits by receiving *dividends* declared by the board of directors. Stockholders in a corporation may not make withdrawals of company assets, as may an owner of an unincorporated business.

3 To share in the distribution of assets if the corporation is liquidated. When a corporation ends its existence, the creditors of the corporation must first be paid in full; any remaining assets are divided among stockholders in proportion to the number of shares owned.

4 To subscribe for additional shares in the event that the corporation decides to increase the amount of stock outstanding. This *preemptive right* entitles stockholders to maintain their percentages of ownership in the company by subscribing, in proportion to their present stockholdings, to any additional shares issued. In many cases stockholders agree to waive their preemptive rights in order to grant more flexibility to management in issuing stock.

Stockholders' meetings are usually held once a year. Each share of stock is entitled to one vote. In large corporations, these annual meetings are usually attended by relatively few persons, often by less than 1% of the stockholders. Prior to the meeting, the management group will request stockholders who do not plan to attend in person to send in *proxy statements* assigning their votes to the existing management. Through this use of the proxy system, management may secure the right to vote as much as, perhaps, 90% or more of the total outstanding shares.

Functions of the board of directors   The primary functions of the board of directors are to manage the corporation and to protect the interests of the stockholders. At this level, management may consist principally of formulating policies and reviewing acts of the officers. Specific duties of the directors include declaring dividends, setting the salaries of officers, reviewing the system of internal control with the internal auditors and with the company's independent auditors, authorizing officers to arrange loans from banks, and authorizing important contracts of various kinds.

The extent of participation in management by the board of directors varies widely from one company to another. In recent years increased importance has been attached to the inclusion on the boards of large corporations of individuals who were not officers of the company and who could thus have a view independent of that of corporate officers.

The official actions of the board are recorded in minutes of their meetings. The *minutes book* is the source of many of the accounting entries affecting the stockholders' equity accounts.

Functions of corporate officers Corporate officers usually include a president, one or more vice-presidents, a controller, a treasurer, and a secretary. A vice-president is often made responsible for the sales function; other vice-presidents may be given responsibility for such important functions as personnel, finance, and production.

The responsibilities of the controller, treasurer, and secretary are most directly related to the accounting phase of business operation. The *controller,* or chief accounting officer, is responsible for the maintenance of adequate internal control and for the preparation of accounting records and financial statements. Such specialized activities as budgeting, tax planning, and preparation of tax returns are usually placed under the controller's jurisdiction. The *treasurer* has custody of the company's funds and is generally responsible for planning and controlling the company's cash position. The *secretary* represents the corporation in many contractual and legal matters and maintains minutes of the meetings of directors and stockholders. Another responsibility of the secretary is to coordinate the preparation of the annual report, which includes the financial statements and other information relating to corporate activities. In small corporations, one officer frequently acts as both secretary and treasurer. The following organization chart indicates lines of authority extending from stockholders to the directors to the president and other officers.

Typical corporate organization

STOCKHOLDERS

Board of Directors

President

| Secretary Treasurer | Controller | Vice-Pres. (sales) | Vice-Pres. (production) | Vice-Pres. (personnel) |

Authorization and issuance of capital stock

In previous chapters we have seen that corporations use separate owners' equity accounts (Capital Stock and Retained Earnings) to represent (1) the capital invested by the stockholders (called *paid-in capital*) and (2) the capital acquired and retained through profitable operations *(earned capital)*. Up to this point we have assumed that all paid-in capital may be recorded in a single ledger account entitled Capital Stock. In this chapter we will see that a corporation may issue several different types of capital stock. In addition, state laws may affect the manner in which the issuance of capital stock is recorded in the accounts. In these situations, additional ledger accounts are necessary to indicate the nature of the capital invested by the stockholders.

The articles of incorporation specify the number of shares of each type of capital stock which a corporation is authorized to issue and the *par value,* if any, per share. Large issues of capital stock to be offered for sale to the general public must be approved by the SEC as well as by state officials. The corporation may choose not to issue immediately all the authorized shares; in fact, it is customary to secure authorization for a larger number of shares than presently needed. In future years, if more capital is needed, the previously authorized shares will be readily available for issue; otherwise, the corporation would be forced to apply to the state for permission to increase the number of authorized shares.

Par value

The chief significance of par value is that it represents the *legal capital* per share, that is, the amount below which stockholders' equity cannot be reduced except by (1) losses from business operations or (2) legal action taken by a majority vote of stockholders. A dividend cannot be declared by a corporation if such action would cause the stockholders' equity to fall below the par value of the outstanding shares. Par value, therefore, may be regarded as a minimum cushion of equity capital existing for the protection of creditors.

Par value may be $1 per share, $5, $100, or any other amount decided upon by the corporation. The par value of the stock is *no indication of its market value;* the par value merely indicates the amount per share to be entered in the Capital Stock account. The par value of most common stocks is relatively low. Polaroid Corporation common stock, for example has a par value of $1; Sears, Roebuck & Co. common stock has a par value of 75 cents, Avon Products stock has a par value of 50 cent per share. The market value of all these securities is far above their par value.

Issuance of par value stock   Mere authorization of a stock issue does not bring an asset into existence, nor does it give the corporation any capital. The obtaining of authorization from the state for a stock issue merely affords a legal opportunity to obtain assets through the sale of stock.

When par value stock is *issued,* the Capital Stock account is credited with the par value of the shares issued, regardless of whether the issuance price is more or less than par. Assuming that 10,000 shares of $10 par value stock have been authorized and that 6,000 of these authorized shares are issued at a price of $10 each, Cash would be debited and Capital Stock would be credited for $60,000. When stock is sold for more than par value, the Capital Stock account is credited with the par value of the shares issued, and a separate account, Paid-in Capital in Excess of Par Value, is credited for the excess of selling price over par. If, for example, the issuance price is $15, the entry is as follows:

Stockholders' investment in excess of par value

Cash	*90,000*	
Capital Stock		*60,000*
Paid-in Capital in Excess of Par Value		*30,000*
Issued 6,000 shares of $10 par value stock at a price of $15 a share.		

The amount received in excess of par value *does not represent a profit* to the corporation. It is part of the invested capital and it will be added to the capital stock on the balance sheet to show the total paid-in capital. The stockholders' equity section of the balance sheet is illustrated below. (The existence of $10,000 in retained earnings is assumed in order to have a complete illustration.)

Corporation's capital classified by source

Stockholders' equity:	
Capital stock, $10 par value, authorized 10,000 shares, issued and	
outstanding 6,000 shares	*$ 60,000*
Paid-in capital in excess of par value	*30,000*
Total paid-in capital	*$ 90,000*
Retained earnings	*10,000*
Total stockholders' equity	*$100,000*

If stock is issued by a corporation for less than par, the account Discount on Capital Stock should be debited for the difference between the issuance price and the par value. The issuance of stock at a discount is seldom encountered; it is illegal in many states.

No-par stock

In an earlier period of the history of American corporations, all capital stock had par value, but in more recent years state laws have permitted corporations to choose between par value stock and no-par value stock. However, most companies which issue no-par capital stock establish a stated value per share. From an accounting viewpoint, stated value and par value mean the same thing— both terms designate the legal capital per share and the amount to be credited to the Capital Stock account.

Assume that a corporation is organized in a state which permits the board of directors to establish a *stated value* on no-par stock, and that the board passed a resolution setting the stated value per share at $5. If a total of 40,000 shares were issued at $20 per share, the journal entry to record the issuance would be:

Note stated value per share

Cash	*800,000*	
Capital Stock		*200,000*
Paid-in Capital in Excess of Stated Value		*600,000*
Issued 40,000 shares of no-par value capital stock at $20 each.		
Stated value set by directors at $5 per share.		

In the absence of a stated value, the entire proceeds on the sale of stock ($800,000) would be credited to the Capital Stock account and would be viewed as legal capital not subject to withdrawal.

Preferred stock and common stock

In order to appeal to as many investors as possible, a corporation may issue more than one kind of capital stock. The basic type of capital stock issued by every corporation is called *common stock*. Common stock has the four basic rights previously mentioned. Whenever these rights are modified, the term *preferred stock* (or sometimes Class B Common) is used to describe this second type of capital stock. A few corporations issue two or more classes of preferred stock, each class having certain distinctive features designed to interest a particular type of investor. In summary, we may say that every business corporation has common stock; a good many corporations also issue preferred stock; and some companies have two or more types of preferred stock.

Common stock may be regarded as the basic, residual element of ownership. It carries voting rights and, therefore, is the means of exercising control over the business. Common stock has unlimited possibilities of increase in value; during periods of business expansion the market prices of common stocks of some leading corporations may rise to many times their former values. On the other hand, common stocks lose value more rapidly than other types of securities when corporations encounter periods of unprofitable business.

The following stockholders' equity section illustrates the balance sheet presentation for a corporation having both preferred and common stock; note that the item of retained earnings is not apportioned between the two groups of stockholders.

Balance sheet presentation

Stockholders' equity:	
12% cumulative preferred stock, $100 par value, authorized 100,000 shares, issued 50,000 shares	$ 5,000,000
Common stock, $5 par value, authorized 3 million shares, issued 2 million shares	10,000,000
Retained earnings	3.500.000
Total stockholders' equity	$18.500.000

Characteristics of preferred stock

Most preferred stocks have the following distinctive features:

1 Preferred as to dividends
2 Preferred as to assets in event of the liquidation of the company
3 Callable at the option of the corporation
4 No voting power

Another very important but less common feature is a clause permitting the *conversion* of preferred stock into common at the option of the holder. Preferred stocks vary widely with respect to the special rights and privileges granted. Careful study of the terms of the individual preferred stock contract is a necessary step in the evaluation of any preferred stock.

Stock preferred as to dividends   Stock preferred as to dividends is entitled to receive each year a dividend of specified amount before any dividend is paid on the common stock. The dividend is usually stated as a dollar amount per share. For example, the balance sheet of General Motors Corporation shows two types of preferred stock outstanding, one paying $5.00 a year and the other $3.75 a year, as shown below:

Dividend stated as dollar amount

Capital stock:

  Preferred, without par value (authorized 6 million shares):

    $5.00 series; stated value $100 per share, redeemable at $120 per share, outstanding 1,835,644 shares $183,564,400

    $3.75 series; stated value $100 per share, redeemable at $101 per share, outstanding 1,000,000 shares 100,000,000

Some preferred stocks state the dividend preference as a percentage of par value. For example, a 9% preferred stock with a par value of $100 per share would mean that $9 must be paid yearly on each share of preferred stock before any dividends are paid on the common. An example of the percentage method of stating the dividend on a preferred stock is found in the balance sheet of UAL, Inc. (United Airlines).

Dividend stated as percentage of par

Shareholders' equity:

  5½% cumulative prior preferred stock, $100 par value; authorized and outstanding 71,702 shares $7,170,200

The holders of preferred stock have no assurance that they will always receive the indicated dividend. A corporation is obligated to pay dividends to stockholders only when the board of directors declares a dividend. Dividends must be paid on preferred stock before anything is paid to the common stockholders, but if the corporation is not prospering, it may decide not to pay dividends on either preferred or common stock. For a corporation to pay dividends, profits must be earned and cash must be available. However, preferred stocks in general offer more assurance of regular dividend payments than do common stocks.

Cumulative preferred stock   The dividend preference carried by most preferred stocks is a *cumulative* one. If all or any part of the regular dividend on the preferred stock is omitted in a given year, the amount omitted is said to be *in arrears* and must be paid in a subsequent year before any dividend can be paid on the common stock. Assume that a corporation was organized January 1, Year 1, with 10,000 shares of $4 cumulative preferred stock and 50,000 shares of common stock. Dividends paid in Year 1 were at the rate of $4 per share of preferred stock and $2 per share of common. In Year 2, earnings declined sharply and the only dividend paid was $1 per share on the preferred stock. No dividends were paid in Year 3. What is the status of the preferred stock at December 31, Year 3?

Dividends are in arrears in the amount of $7 a share ($3 omitted during Year 2 and $4 omitted in Year 3). On the entire issue of 10,000 shares of preferred stock, the dividends in arrears amount to $70,000.

Dividends in arrears *are not listed among the liabilities of a corporation,* because no liability exists until a dividend is declared by the board of directors. Nevertheless, the amount of any dividends in arrears on preferred stock is an important factor to investors and should always be disclosed. This disclosure is usually made by a note accompanying the balance sheet such as the following:

Footnote disclosure of dividends in arrears

Note 6: Dividends in arrears

> *As of December 31, Year 3, dividends on the $4 cumulative preferred stock were in arrears to the extent of $7 per share and amounted in total to $70,000.*

In Year 4, we shall assume that the company earned large profits and wished to pay dividends on both the preferred and common stocks. Before paying a dividend on the common, the corporation must pay the $70,000 in arrears on the cumulative preferred stock plus the regular $4 a share applicable to the current year. The preferred stockholders would, therefore, receive a total of $110,000 in dividends in Year 4; the board of directors would then be free to declare dividends on the common stock.

For a *noncumulative preferred stock,* any unpaid or omitted dividend is lost forever. Because of this factor, investors view the noncumulative feature as an unfavorable element, and very few noncumulative preferred stocks are issued.

Stock preferred as to assets   Most preferred stocks carry a preference as to assets in the event of liquidation of the corporation. If the business is terminated, the preferred stock is entitled to payment in full of its par value or a higher stated liquidation value before any payment is made on the common stock. This priority also includes any dividends in arrears.

Callable preferred stock   Most preferred stocks include a *call provision.* This provision grants the issuing corporation the right to repurchase the stock from the stockholders at a stipulated *call price.* The call price is usually slightly higher than the par value of the stock. For example, $100 par value preferred stock may be callable at $105 or $110 per share. In addition to paying the call price, a corporation which redeems its preferred stock must pay any dividends in arrears. A call provision gives a corporation flexibility in adjusting its financial structure, for example, by eliminating a preferred stock and replacing it with other securities if future growth of the company makes such change advantageous.

Convertible preferred stock   In order to add to the attractiveness of preferred stock as an investment, corporations sometimes offer a conversion privilege which entitles the preferred stockholders to exchange their shares for common stock in a stipulated ratio. If the corporation prospers, its common stock will probably rise in market value, and dividends on the common stock will probably be increased. The investor who buys a convertible preferred stock rather than common stock has greater assurance of regular dividends. In addition, through the conversion privilege, the investor is assured of sharing in any substantial increase in value of the company's common stock.

As an example, assume that Remington Corporation issued a 10%, $100 par, convertible preferred stock on January 1, at a price of $100 a share. Each share was convertible into four shares of the company's $10 par value common stock at any time. The common stock had a market price of $20 a share on January 1, and an annual dividend of $1 a share was being paid. During the next few years, Remington Corporation's earnings increased, the dividend on the common stock was raised to an annual rate of $4, and the market price of the common stock rose to $40 a share. At this point the preferred stock would have a market value of at least $160, since it could be converted at any time into four shares of common stock with a market value of $40 each. In other words, the market value of a convertible preferred stock will tend to move in accordance with the price of the common.

When the dividend rate is increased on the common stock, some holders of the preferred stock may convert their holdings into common stock in order to obtain a higher cash return on their investments. If the holder of 100 shares of the preferred stock presented these shares for conversion, Remington Corporation would make the following journal entry:

Conversion of preferred stock into common

$10 Convertible Preferred Stock	10,000	
Common Stock		4,000
Paid-in Capital in Excess of Par Value		6,000

To record the conversion of 100 shares of preferred stock, par $100, into 400 shares of $10 par value common stock.

Note that the issue price recorded for the 400 shares of common stock is based upon the carrying value of the preferred stock in the accounting records, not upon market prices at the date of conversion.

Participating clauses in preferred stock   Since participating preferred stocks are very seldom issued, discussion of them will be brief. A fully participating preferred stock is one which, in addition to the regular specified dividend, is entitled to participate in some manner with the common stock in any additional dividends paid. For example, a $5 participating preferred stock would be entitled to receive $5 a share before the common stock received anything. After $5 a share had been paid to the preferred stockholders, a $5 dividend could be paid on the common stock. If the company desired to pay an additional dividend to the common, say, an extra $3 per share, the preferred stock would also be entitled to receive an extra $3 dividend. In brief, a fully participating preferred stock participates dollar for dollar with the common stock in any dividends paid in excess of the stated rate on the preferred stock.

It is important to remember that most preferred stocks are *not* participating. Although common stock dividends may increase year after year if the corporation prospers, the dividends on most preferred stocks are fixed in amount. A $6 preferred stock, unless it is participating, will never pay an annual dividend in excess of $6.

The underwriting of stock issues

When a large amount of stock is to be issued, the corporation will probably utilize the services of an investment banking firm, frequently referred to as an *underwriter.* The underwriter guarantees the issuing corporation a specific price for the stock and makes a profit by selling the stock to the investing public at a higher price. The corporation records the issuance of the stock at the net amount received from the underwriter. The use of an underwriter assures the corporation that the entire stock issue will be sold without delay, and the entire amount of funds to be raised will be available on a specific date.

Market price of common stock

The preceding sections concerning the issuance of stock at prices above and below par value raise a question as to how the market price of stock is determined. The price which the corporation sets on a new issue of stock is based on several factors including (1) an appraisal of the company's expected future earnings, (2) the probable dividend rate per share, (3) the present financial position of the company, and (4) the current state of the investment market.

After the stock has been issued, the price at which it will be traded among investors will rise and fall in response to all the forces of the marketplace. The market price per share will tend to reflect the progress of the company, with primary emphasis being placed on earnings and dividends. At this point in our discussion, the significant fact to emphasize is that market price is not related to par value, and that it tends to reflect investors' expectations of future earnings and dividends.

Stock issued for assets other than cash

Corporations generally sell their capital stock for cash and use the cash to buy the various types of assets needed in the business. Sometimes, however, a corporation may issue shares of its capital stock in a direct exchange for land, buildings, or other assets. Stock may also be issued in payment for services rendered by attorneys and promoters in the formation of the corporation.

When a corporation issues capital stock in exchange for services or for assets other than cash, the transaction should be recorded at the current *market value* of the goods or services received. Often, the best evidence as to the market value of these goods or services is the market value of the shares issued in exchange. For example, assume that a company issues 1,000 shares of its $1 par value common stock in exchange for land. Competent appraisers may have differing opinions as to the market value of the land. But let us assume that the company's stock is currently selling on a stock exchange for $90 per share. It is logical to say that the cost of the land to the company is $90,000, the market value of the shares issued in exchange.

Once the valuation has been decided, the entry to record the issuance of the stock in exchange for the land is as follows:

<table>
<tbody>
<tr><td>*How were dollar amounts determined?*</td><td>Land .... 900,000</td><td></td></tr>
<tr><td></td><td>Common Stock ....</td><td>10,000</td></tr>
<tr><td></td><td>Paid-in Capital in Excess of Par Value ....</td><td>890,000</td></tr>
</tbody>
</table>

To record the issuance of 10,000 shares of $1 par value common stock in exchange for land. Current market value of stock ($90 per share) used as basis for valuing the land.

Subscriptions to capital stock

Small corporations sometimes sell stock on a subscription plan, in which the investor agrees to pay the subscription price at a future date or in a series of installments. When the subscription contract is signed, Subscriptions Receivable: Common is debited and Common Stock Subscribed is credited. Later, as installments are collected, the entry is a debit to Cash and a credit to Subscriptions Receivable: Common. When the entire subscription price has been collected, the stock certificates are issued. The issuance of the stock is recorded by debiting Common Stock Subscribed and crediting Common stock. The following illustration demonstrates the accounting procedures for stock subscriptions.

In this example, 10,000 shares of $10 par value stock are subscribed at a price of $15. Subscriptions for 6,000 of these shares are then collected in full. A partial payment is received on the other 4,000 shares.

<table>
<tbody>
<tr><td>*Subscription price above par*</td><td>Subscriptions Receivable: Common .... 150,000</td><td></td></tr>
<tr><td></td><td>Common Stock Subscribed ....</td><td>100,000</td></tr>
<tr><td></td><td>Paid-in Capital in Excess of Par Value ....</td><td>50,000</td></tr>
</tbody>
</table>

Received subscriptions for 10,000 shares of $10 par value stock at price of $15 a share.

When the subscriptions for 6,000 shares are collected in full, certificates for 6,000 shares will be issued. The following entries are made:

<table>
<tbody>
<tr><td>*Certificates issued for fully paid shares*</td><td>Cash .... 90,000</td><td></td></tr>
<tr><td></td><td>Subscriptions Receivable: Common ....</td><td>90,000</td></tr>
</tbody>
</table>

Collected subscriptions in full for 6,000 shares at $15 each.

<table>
<tbody>
<tr><td>Common Stock Subscribed .... 60,000</td><td></td></tr>
<tr><td>Common Stock ....</td><td>60,000</td></tr>
</tbody>
</table>

Issued certificates for 6,000 fully paid $10 par value shares.

The subscriber to the remaining 4,000 shares paid only half of the amount of the subscription but promised to pay the remainder within a month. Stock certificates will not be issued until the subscription is collected in full, but the partial collection is recorded by the following entry:

<table>
<tbody>
<tr><td>*Partial collection of subscription*</td><td>Cash .... 30,000</td><td></td></tr>
<tr><td></td><td>Subscriptions Receivable: Common ....</td><td>30,000</td></tr>
</tbody>
</table>

Collected partial payment on subscription for 4,000 shares.

From the corporation's point of view, Subscriptions Receivable is a current asset, which ordinarily will be collected within a short time. If financial statements are prepared between the date of obtaining subscriptions and the date of issuing the stock, the Common Stock Subscribed account is regarded as legal capital and will appear in the stockholders' equity section of the balance sheet.

Stockholder records in a corporation

A large corporation with shares listed on the New York Stock Exchange usually has millions of shares outstanding and several hundred thousand stockholders. Each day many stockholders sell their shares; the buyers of these shares become new members of the company's family of stockholders. An investor purchasing stock in a corporation receives a *stock certificate* from the company indicating the number of shares acquired. If the investor later sells these shares, this stock certificate must be surrendered to the corporation for cancellation before a new certificate is issued to the new owner of the shares.

A corporation must have an up-to-date record of the names and addresses of this constantly changing army of stockholders so that it can send dividend checks, financial statements, and voting forms to the right people. Also, the corporation must make sure that old stock certificates are canceled as new ones are issued so that no excess certificates become outstanding.

Stockholders' ledger When there are numerous stockholders, it is not practical to include a separate account for each stockholder in the general ledger. Instead, a single controlling account entitled Capital Stock appears in the general ledger, and a subsidiary stockholders' ledger is maintained. This ledger contains a page for each individual stockholder. Entries in the stockholders' ledger are made in number of shares rather than in dollars. Thus, each stockholder's account shows the number of shares owned, and the dates of acquisitions and sales. This record enables the corporation to send each stockholder a single dividend check, even though the stockholder may have acquired several stock certificates at different dates.

Stock transfer agent and stock registrar Companies with shares traded on organized stock exchanges must engage an independent stock transfer agent and stock registrar to maintain their stockholder records and to control the issuance of stock certificates. These transfer agents and registrars usually are large banks or trust companies.[1] When stock certificates are to be transferred from one owner to another, the old certificates are sent to the transfer agent, who cancels them, makes the necessary entries in the stockholders' ledger, and prepares a new certificate for the new owner of the shares. This new certificate then must be registered with the stock registrar before it represents valid and transferable ownership of stock in the corporation.

---

[1]Regulations of the New York Stock Exchange now allow a single bank or trust company to act as both stock transfer agent and stock registrar for the same corporation. Traditionally, these functions were performed by two separate institutions.

Small, closely-held corporations generally do not use the services of independent registrars and transfer agents. In these companies, the stockholder records usually are maintained by the corporate secretary. To prevent the accidental or fraudulent issuance of an excessive number of stock certificates, even a small corporation should require that each certificate be signed by at least two designated corporate officers.

Retained earnings or deficit

Capital provided to a corporation by stockholders in exchange for shares of either preferred or common stock is called paid-in capital, or contributed capital. The second major type of stockholders' equity is retained earnings. The amount of the Retained Earnings account at any balance sheet date represents the accumulated earnings of the company since the date of incorporation, minus any losses and minus all dividends distributed to stockholders.

For a corporation with $1,000,000 of paid-in capital and $600,000 of retained earnings, the stockholders' equity section of the balance sheet may appear as follows:

Paid-in capital and earned capital

Stockholders' equity:

Capital stock, $10 par value, 100,000 shares authorized, 20,000 shares issued	$ 200,000
Paid-in capital in excess of par value	800,000
Total paid-in capital	$1,000,000
Retained earnings	600,000
Total stockholders' equity	$1,600,000

If this same company had been unprofitable and incurred losses of $300,000 since its organization, the stockholders' equity section of the balance would be as follows:

Paid-in capital reduced by losses incurred

Stockholders' equity:

Capital stock, $10 par value, 100,000 shares authorized, 20,000 shares issued	$ 200,000
Paid-in capital in excess of par value	800,000
Total paid-in capital	$1,000,000
Less: Deficit	300,000
Total stockholders' equity	$ 700,000

This second illustration tells us that $300,000 of the original $1,000,000 invested by stockholders has been lost. Note that the presentation of total paid-in capital in both illustrations remains at the fixed amount of $1,000,000, the stockholders' original investment. The accumulated profits or losses since the organization of the corporation are shown as *retained earnings* or as a *deficit* and are not intermingled with the paid-in capital. The term *deficit* indicates a negative amount of retained earnings.

DEL MAR CORPORATION
Balance Sheet
December 31, Year 10

Assets

Current assets:

Cash			$ 305,600
Accounts receivable (net of allowance for doubtful accounts)			1,105,200
Subscriptions receivable: Common stock			110,000
Inventories (lower of fifo cost or market)			1,300,800
Short-term prepayments			125,900
Total current assets			$2,947,500
Plant and equipment:			
Land		$ 900,000	
Buildings and equipment	$5,283,000		
Less: Accumulated depreciation	1,250,000	4,033,000	4,933,000
Other assets: Organization costs			14,000
Total assets			$7,894,500

Liabilities & Stockholders' Equity

Current liabilities:

Accounts payable			$ 998,100
Income taxes payable			324,300
Dividends payable			109,700
Interest payable			20,000
Total current liabilities			$1,452,100
Long-term liabilities: Bonds payable, 12%, due Oct. 1, Year 20			1,000,000
Total liabilities			$2,452,100

Stockholders' equity:

Cumulative 8% preferred stock, $100 par, callable at $104, authorized and issued 10,000 shares	$1,000,000	
Common stock, $1 par, authorized 1,000,000 shares, issued 600,000 shares	600,000	
Common stock subscribed, 20,000 shares	20,000	
Paid-in capital in excess of par: common	2,070,000	
Donated capital	210,000	
Total paid-in capital	$3,900,000	
Retained earnings	1,542,400	
Total stockholders' equity		5,442,400
Total liabilities & stockholders' equity		$7,894,500

Donated capital

On occasion, a corporation may receive assets as a gift. To increase local employment, for example, some cities have given corporations the land upon which to build factories. A corporation's total assets and total stockholders' equity are both increased by the market value of the assets received. *No profit is recognized when a gift is received;* the increase in stockholders' equity is regarded as paid-in capital. The receipt of a gift is recorded by debiting asset accounts and crediting an account entitled *Donated Capital.* Donated capital appears in the stockholders' equity section of the balance sheet.

Balance sheet for a corporation illustrated

A fairly complete balance sheet for a corporation is illustrated on page 434. Note the inclusion in this balance sheet of liabilities for income taxes payable and dividends payable. These liabilities do not appear in the balance sheets of unincorporated businesses. Note also that the caption for each capital stock account indicates the type of stock, the par value per share, and the number of shares authorized and issued. The caption for preferred stock also indicates the dividend rate, call price, and other important features.

Bear in mind that current practice includes many alternatives in the choice of terminology and the arrangement of items in financial statements. Some of these alternatives are illustrated in the appendix following Chapter 17.

KEY TERMS INTRODUCED OR EMPHASIZED IN CHAPTER 11

Board of directors   Persons elected by common stockholders to direct the affairs of a corporation.

Call price   The price to be paid by a corporation for each share of callable preferred stock if the corporation decides to call (redeem) the preferred stock.

Capital stock   Transferable units of ownership in a corporation. A broad term which may refer to common stock, preferred stock, or both.

Closely held corporation   A corporation owned by a small group of stockholders. The stock of closely held corporations is not traded on stock exchanges.

Common stock   A type of capital stock which possesses the basic rights of ownership including the right to vote. Represents the residual element of ownership in a corporation.

Convertible preferred stock   Preferred stock which entitles the owner to exchange his or her shares for common stock in a specified ratio.

Corporation   A business organized as a legal entity separate from its owners. Chartered by the state with ownership divided into shares of transferable stock. Stockholders are not liable for debts of the corporation.

Cumulative preferred stock   A class of stock with a provision that if dividends are reduced or omitted in any year, this amount accumulates and must be paid prior to payment of dividends on the common stock.

Deficit   Accumulated losses incurred by a corporation. A negative amount of retained earnings.

Dividend   A distribution of cash by a corporation to its stockholders.

Drawing account   The account used to record the withdrawals of cash or other assets by the owner (or owners) of an unincorporated business. Closed at the end of the period by transferring its balance to the owner's capital account.

Limited liability   An important characteristic of the corporate form of organization. The corporation as a separate legal entity is responsible for its own debts; the stockholders are not personally liable for the corporation's debts.

Minutes book   Formal record of official actions taken in meetings of stockholders and of the board of directors.

Mutual agency   Authority of each partner to act as agent for the partnership within its normal scope of operations and to enter into contracts which bind the partnership.

No-par stock   Stock without par value. Usually has a stated value which is similar to par value.

Organization costs   Costs incurred to form a corporation.

Paid-in capital   The amounts invested in a corporation by its stockholders.

Partnership   An association of two or more persons to carry on as co-owners a business for profit.

Par value   The legal capital of a corporation. Also the face amount of a share of capital stock. Represents the minimum amount per share to be invested in the corporation when shares are originally issued.

Preferred stock   A class of capital stock usually having preferences as to dividends and in the distribution of assets in event of liquidation.

Retained earnings   That portion of stockholders' equity resulting from profits earned and retained in the business. Retained earnings is increased by the earning of net income and is decreased by the incurring of net losses and by the declaration of dividends.

Single proprietorship   An unincorporated business owned by one person.

Stated capital   That portion of capital invested by stockholders which cannot be withdrawn. Provides protection for creditors. Also called *legal capital.*

Statement of partners' capitals   An annual financial statement which shows for each partner and for the firm the amounts of beginning capitals, additional investments, net income, drawings, and ending capitals.

Stock certificate   A document issued by a corporation (or its transfer agent) as evidence of the ownership of the number of shares stated on the certificate.

Stock registrar   An independent fiscal agent, usually a large bank, retained by a corporation to provide assurance against overissuance of stock certificates.

Stock transfer agent   A bank or trust company retained by a corporation to maintain its records of capital stock ownership and make transfers from one investor to another.

Stockholders' ledger   A subsidiary record showing the number of shares owned by each stockholder.

Subscriptions to capital stock   Formal promises to buy shares of stock from a corporation with payment at a later date. Stock certificates delivered when full payment received.

Underwriter   An investment banking firm which handles the sale of a corporation's stock to the public.

DEMONSTRATION PROBLEM FOR YOUR REVIEW

At the close of the current year, the stockholders' equity section of the Rockhurst Corporation's balance sheet appeared as follows:

Stockholders' equity:

$1.50 preferred stock, $25 par value, authorized 1,500,000 shares:		
Issued	*$10,800,000*	
Subscribed	*5,400,000*	*$16,200,000*
Common stock, no par, $5 stated value, authorized		
6,000,000 shares		*12,300,000*
Paid-in capital in excess of par or stated value:		
On preferred stock	*$ 810,000*	
On common stock	*7,626,000*	*8,436,000*
Retained earnings (deficit)		*(600,000)*
Total stockholders' equity		*$36,336,000*

Among the assets of the corporation appears the following item: Subscriptions Receivable: Preferred, $1,123,200.

Instructions On the basis of this information, write a brief answer to the following questions, showing any necessary supporting computations.

a How many shares of preferred and common stock have been issued?

b How many shares of preferred stock have been subscribed?

c What was the average price per share received (including stock subscribed) by the corporation on its preferred stock?

d What was the average price per share received by the corporation on its common stock?

e What is the average amount per share that subscribers of preferred stock have yet to pay on their subscriptions?

f What is the total paid-in capital including stock subscribed?

g What is the total legal or stated value of the capital stock including stock subscribed?

SOLUTION TO DEMONSTRATION PROBLEM

a *Preferred stock issued <u>432,000 shares</u> ($10,800,000 ÷ $25)*

  Common stock issued <u>2,460,000 shares</u> ($12,300,000 ÷ $5)

b *Preferred stock subscribed <u>216,000 shares</u> ($5,400,000 ÷ $25)*

c

Preferred stock par value ($10,800,000 + $5,400,000)	*$16,200,000*
Paid-in capital in excess of par	*810,000*
Total paid-in and subscribed	*$17,010,000*
Total shares (432,000 + 216,000)	*648,000*
Average price per share ($17,010,000 ÷ 648,000 as	
computed in a and b)	*$26.25*

d Common stock stated value	$12,300,000	
Paid-in capital in excess of par	7,626,000	
Total paid-in	$19,926,000	
Total shares (see a)	2,460,000	
Average price per share ($19,926,000 ÷ 2,460,000)		$8.10
e Subscriptions receivable, preferred	$ 1,123,200	
Shares subscribed	216,000	
Average price per share ($1,123,200 ÷ 216,000)		$5.20

f $36,936,000 (preferred $16,200,000 + common $12,300,000 +

paid-in capital in excess of par or stated value $8,436,000)

g $28,500,000 (preferred $16,200,000 + common $12,300,000)

REVIEW QUESTIONS

1 Three types of business organization are common to American business: the single proprietorship, the partnership, and the corporation. Which of these three forms accounts for the largest number of business organization? Which form accounts for the largest dollar volume of business activity?

2 Compare the right of partners to withdraw assets from a partnership with the right of stockholders to receive dividends from a corporation. Explain any significant differences in these rights.

3 What is meant by the term *mutual agency?*

4 Allen and Baker are considering forming a partnership. What do you think are the two most important factors for them to include in their partnership agreement?

5 Is it possible that a partnership agreement containing interest and salary allowances as a step toward distributing income could cause a partnership net loss to be distributed so that one partner's capital account would be decreased by more than the amount of the partnership net loss? Explain.

6 Scott has land having a book value of $50,000 and a fair market value of $80,000 and a building having a book value of $70,000 and a fair market value of $60,000. The land and building become Scott's sole capital contribution to a partnership. What is Scott's capital balance in the new partnership? Why?

7 Partner Susan Reed withdraws $35,000 from a partnership during the year. When the financial statements are prepared at the end of the year, Reed's share of the partnership income is $25,000. Which amount must Reed report on her individual income tax return?

8 Partner John Young has a choice to make. He has been offered by his partners a choice between no salary allowance with a one-third share in the partnership income or a salary of $16,000 per year with a one-quarter share of residual profits. Write a brief memorandum explaining the factors he should consider in reaching a decision.

9 What factors should be considered in drawing up an agreement as to the way in which income shall be shared by two or more partners?

10 Why are large corporations often said to be *publicly owned?*

11 Distinguish between corporations and partnerships in terms of the following characteristics:

a Owners' liability

b Transferability of ownership interest

c Continuity of existence

d Federal taxation on income

12 What are the basic rights of the owner of a share of corporate stock? In what way are these basic rights commonly modified with respect to the owner of a share of preferred stock?

13 Explain the meaning of the term *double taxation* as it applies to corporate profits.

14 In theory, a corporation may sell its stock for an amount greater or less than par value; in practice, stock is seldom if ever issued for less than par. Explain the significance of par value and why shares are seldom issued for less than par.

15 Describe the usual nature of the following features as they apply to a share of preferred stock: (**a**) cumulative, (**b**) convertible, and (**c**) callable.

16 When stock is issued by a corporation in exchange for assets other than cash, accountants face the problem of determining the dollar amount at which to record the transaction. Discuss the factors they should consider and explain their significance.

17 State the classification (asset, liability, stockholders' equity, revenue, or expense) of each of the following accounts:

a Subscriptions receivable   **f** Paid-in capital in

b Organization costs   excess of par value

c Preferred stock   **g** Discount on preferred stock

d Retained earnings   **h** Income taxes payable

e Capital stock subscribed

18 If the Retained Earnings account has a debit balance, how is it presented in the balance sheet and what is it called?

19 A professional baseball team received as a gift from the city the land upon which to build a stadium. What effect, if any, will the receipt of this gift have upon the baseball team's balance sheet and income statement? Explain.

20 Explain the following terms:

a Stock transfer agent   **d** Minutes book

b Stockholders' ledger   **e** Stock registrar

c Underwriter

EXERCISES

Ex. 11-1   A business owned by John Rogers was short of cash and Rogers therefore decided to form a partnership with Steve Wilson, who was able to contribute cash to the new partnership. The assets contributed by Rogers appeared as follows in the balance sheet of his business: cash, $900; accounts receivable, $18,900; inventory, $42,000; and store equipment, $15,000. Rogers had recorded depreciation of $1,500 during his use of the store equipment in his single proprietorship.

Rogers and Wilson agreed that a fair value for the inventory was its replacement cost of $46,000 and that the fair value of the store equipment was $12,000. You are to open the partnership accounts by making a general journal entry to record the investment by Rogers.

Ex. 11-2 Marsh and Nelson form a partnership by investing $40,000 and $60,000, respectively. Determine how the first year's net income of $55,000 would be divided under each of the following assumptions:

a The partnership agreement does not mention profit sharing.

b Net income to be divided in the ratio of the original investments.

c Interest at 12% to be allowed on original capital investments and balance to be divided equally.

d Salaries of $28,000 to Marsh and $25,000 to Nelson, balance to be divided equally.

e Interest at 9% to be allowed on original capital investments, salaries of $28,000 to Marsh and $25,000 to Nelson, balance to be divided equally.

Ex. 11-3 Redmond and Adams, both of whom are CPAs, form a partnership, with Redmond investing $40,000 and Adams $30,000. They agree to share net income as follows:

(1) Interest at 10% on beginning capital balances.

(2) Salary allowances of $45,000 to Redmond and $25,000 to Adams.

(3) Any partnership earnings in excess of the amount required to cover the interest and salary allowances to be divided 45% to Redmond and 55% to Adams.

The partnership net income for the first year of operations amounted to $97,000 before interest and salary allowances. Show how this $97,000 should be divided between the two partners. Use a three-column schedule with a separate column for each partner and a total column. List on separate lines the amounts of interest, salaries, and the residual amount divided.

Ex. 11-4 Heritage Corporation was organized on July 1, 19___. The corporation was authorized to issue 10,000 shares of $100 par value, 8% cumulative preferred stock, and 200,000 shares of no-par common stock with a stated value of $5 per share.

All the preferred stock was issued at par and 120,000 shares of the common stock were sold for $24 per share. Prepare the stockholders' equity section immediately after the issuance of the securities but prior to any operation of the company.

Ex. 11-5 Wolfe Company has outstanding two classes of $100 par value stock: 5,000 shares of 7% cumulative preferred and 25,000 shares of common. The company had a $50,000 deficit at the beginning of the current year, and preferred dividends had not been paid for two years. During the current year, the company earned $250,000. What will be the balance in retained earnings at the end of the current year, if the company pays a dividend of $1.10 per share on the common stock?

Ex. 11-6 A portion of the stockholders' equity section from the balance sheet of Palermo Corporation appears below:

Stockholders' equity:

Preferred stock, 6% cumulative, $50 par, 40,000 shares authorized and issued ..	$2,000,000
Preferred stock, 9% noncumulative, $100 par, 8,000 shares authorized and issued	800,000
Common stock, $5 par, 400,000 shares authorized and issued	2,000,000
Total paid-in capital	$4,800,000

Instructions Assume that all the stock was issued on January 1, 19___, and that no dividends were paid during the first two years of operations. During the third year, Palermo Corporation paid total cash dividends of $532,000.

a Compute the amount of cash dividends paid during the third year to each of the three classes of stock.

b Compute the dividends paid *per share* during the third year for each of the three classes of stock.

Ex. 11-7 The stockholders' equity section of the balance sheet appeared as follows in a recent annual report of Samoa Corporation:

Stockholders' equity:
  Capital stock:
    $5.50 dividend cumulative preferred stock; no-par value, 300,000
      shares authorized, 180,000 shares outstanding, stated at .... $ 18,000,000
    Common stock; no-par value, 5,000,000 shares authorized,
      4,300,000 shares issued, stated at 32,250,000
  Retained earnings 75,800,000
    Total stockholders' equity $126,050,000

Instructions   From this information compute answers to the following questions:
a What is the stated value per share of the preferred stock?
b What was the average issuance price of a share of common stock?
c What is the amount of the total legal capital and the amount of the total paid in capital?
d What is the total amount of the annual dividend requirement on the preferred stock issue?
e Total dividends of $5,200,000 were declared on the preferred and common stock during the year, and the balance in retained earnings at the beginning of the year amounted to $67,800,000. What was the amount of net income for the year?

PROBLEMS

11-1 Dean Engineering is a single proprietorship owned by Sharon Dean. During the month of April, Dean's ownership equity was affected by the following events:
Apr. 7 Dean invested an additional $20,000 cash in the business.
Apr. 15 Dean withdrew $6,500 in cash and used the money to pay her personal income taxes.
Apr. 22 Dean collected from J. Barker an $1,800 account receivable of the business and deposited the money in her personal checking account.
Apr. 30 Dean drew a check payable to herself on the business bank account in the amount of $4,000. She had stipulated this amount as her monthly salary as owner-manager of the business.
Apr. 30 The Income Summary account shows a credit balance of $7,200; the accounts of Dean Engineering are closed monthly.

Instructions
a Prepare journal entries for each of the above events in the accounts of Dean Engineering. Include the entries necessary to close the Income Summary account and Dean's drawing account at April 30.

b Prepare a statement of owner's capital for the month ended April 30. Assume that the balance of Dean's capital account on April 1 was $57,800.

11-2 The partnership of Avery and Kirk was formed on July 1, when George Avery and Dinah Kirk agreed to invest equal amounts and to share profits and losses equally. The investment by Avery consists of $40,000 cash and an inventory of merchandise valued at $56,000.

Kirk also is to contribute a total of $96,000. However, it is agreed that her contribution will consist of the following assets of her business along with the transfer to the partnership of her business liabilities. The agreed values of the various items as well as their carrying values on Kirk's records are listed below. Kirk also contributes enough cash to bring her capital account to $96,000.

	Investment by Kirk	
	Balances on Kirk's Records	Agreed Value
Accounts receivable (net)	$81,600	$81,600
Inventory	9,600	12,800
Office equipment (net)	12,800	9,000
Accounts payable	28,800	28,800

Instructions

a Draft entries (in general journal form) to record the investments of Avery and Kirk in the new partnership.

b Prepare the beginning balance sheet of the partnership (in report form) at the close of business July 1, reflecting the above transfers to the firm.

c On the following June 30 after one year of operation, the Income Summary account showed a credit balance of $78,000 and the Drawing account for each partner showed a debit balance of $32,000. Prepare journal entries to close the Income Summary account and the drawing accounts at June 30.

11-3 Rob King owns and operates a small business called London Shop. The business is in need of additional working capital and King is personally in need of $21,000 in cash. To meet these needs, King agreed on August 31 to join in partnership with John Hill in a business to be known as King-Hill. Hill will invest $56,000 cash in the business. King will contribute all assets of his business (except cash) to the partnership and the liabilities of King's business will be assumed by the partnership. It is also agreed that on August 31 King will withdraw (from funds invested by Hill) the sum of $21,000 in cash. The partnership contract provides that income will be divided 60% to King and 40% to Hill.

Information as to the assets and liabilities of King's business on August 31, 19___, and their agreed valuation is shown below.

	Per King's Accounts	Agreed Valuation
Accounts receivable	$39,760	$39,760
Merchandise inventory	82,910	75,600
Store equipment	17,360	
Accumulated depreciation	5,880	12,600
Note payable	33,600	33,600
Interest payable	588	588
Accounts payable	19,600	19,600

Instructions

a Make the necessary journal entries to record the formation of the King-Hill partnership at August 31. (Debit Store Equipment $12,600; do not record accumulated depreciation. Debit Rob King, Capital for the $21,000 withdrawal.)

b At the end of September, after all adjusting entries, the Income Summary account of King-Hill shows a credit balance of $7,000. The partners' drawing accounts have debit balances as follows: King, $2,800; Hill, $1,400. Make the journal entries necessary to complete the closing of the partnership accounts at the end of September.

c Prepare a statement of partners' capitals for the month of September.

11-4 River Train has three partners—A, B, and C. During the current year their capital balances were: A, $140,000; B, $100,000; and C, $60,000. The partnership agreement provides that partners shall receive salary allowances as follows: A, none; B, $48,000; and C, $40,000. The partners shall also be allowed interest at 12% annually on their capital balances. Residual profits or loss are to be divided: A, ½; B, ⅓; and C, ⅙.

Instructions Prepare separate schedules showing how income will be divided among the three partners in each of the following cases. The figure given in each case is the annual income available for distribution among the partners.

a Loss of $23,000

b Income of $37,000

c Income of $200,000 (round amounts to the nearest even dollar.)

11-5 Presented below are two separate cases requiring preparation of the stockholders' equity section of a corporate balance sheet.

(1) Early in Year 3 Marine Corporation was formed with authorization to issue 320,000 shares of $5 par value common. The stock was issued at par, and the corporation reported a net loss of $96,000 for Year 3 and a net loss of $224,000 in Year 4. In Year 5 net income was $844,000.

(2) Pacific Corporation was organized early in Year 1 and authorized to issue 200,000 shares of $10 par value common and 32,000 shares of cumulative preferred stock. All the preferred and 192,000 shares of common were issued at par. The preferred stock was callable at 105% of its $100 par value and was entitled to dividends of 6% before any dividends were paid to common. During the first five years of its existence, the corporation earned a total of $2,304,000 and paid dividends of 50 cents per share each year on the common stock.

Instructions For each of the independent situations described, prepare in good form the stockholders' equity section of the balance sheet as of December 31, Year 5. Include a supporting schedule for each case showing your determination of the balance of retained earnings that should appear in the balance sheet.

11-6 The following information provides the basis for preparing journal entries and the stockholders' equity section of a corporate balance sheet.

Early in Year 10, Roger Gordon and several friends organized a corporation called Racquetball Courts, Inc. The corporation was authorized to issue 50,000 shares of $100 par value, 8% cumulative preferred stock and 400,000 shares of $1 par value common stock. The following transactions (among others) occurred during Year 10:

Jan. **6** Issued for cash 25,000 shares of common stock at $12 per share. The shares were issued to Gordon and 14 other investors.

Jan. 7 Issued an additional 500 shares of common stock to Gordon in exchange for his services in organizing the corporation. The stockholders agreed that these services were worth $6,000.

Jan. 12 Issued 2,500 shares of preferred stock for cash of $250,000.

June 4 Acquired land as a building site in exchange for 15,000 shares of common stock. In view of the appraised value of the land and the progress of the company, the directors of Racquetball Courts, Inc., agreed that the common stock was to be valued for purposes of this transaction at $15 per share.

Nov. 15 The first annual dividend of $8 per share was declared on the preferred stock to be paid December 20 of Year 10. (Debit Retained Earnings.)

Dec. 20 Paid the cash dividend declared on November 15.

Dec. 31 After the revenue and expense accounts were closed into the Income Summary account, that account indicated a net income for the year of $72,000.

Instructions

a Prepare journal entries for Year 10 in general journal form to record the above transactions. Include entry at December 31 to close the Income Summary account.

b Prepare the stockholders' equity section of the balance sheet at December 31, Year 10.

11-7 Cedar Products, Inc., was authorized to issue 500,000 shares of $5 par value common stock and 20,000 shares of $6 convertible and cumulative, no-par value, preferred stock. Each share of preferred stock is convertible, at the option of the shareholder, into four shares of common stock. All the preferred stock was issued at $103 per share, and 300,000 shares of common stock were issued at $15 per share. The balance in Retained Earnings at January 1, Year 10, is $670,000, and there are no dividends in arrears.

Instructions

a Prepare the stockholders' equity section of the balance sheet at January 1, Year 10.

b Assume that on January 1, Year 10, all the preferred stock is converted into shares of common stock. Prepare a journal entry to record the conversion.

c Prepare a revised stockholders' equity section of the balance sheet at January 1, Year 10, after the conversion of the preferred stock.

11-8 For several years, Linda Green has operated a successful business organized as a single proprietorship. In order to raise the capital to operate on a larger scale, she decided to organize a new corporation to continue in the same line of business. In January of Year 1, Green organized Far West Corporation, which was authorized to issue capital stock as follows:

50,000 shares of 8% cumulative preferred stock with a $50 par value per share
250,000 shares of $1 par value common stock

During January Far West Corporation completed the following transactions:

Jan. 10 Issued 20,000 shares of common stock to various investors for cash at $11 per share.

Jan. 10 Issued 40,000 shares of common stock to Green in exchange for assets with a current market value as follows:

Inventory	$ 90,000
Equipment	50,000
Building	160,000
Land	140,000

Jan. 15 Received an invoice from an attorney for $7,000 for services relating to the formation of Far West Corporation. The invoice will be paid in 30 days.

Jan. 17 Received subscriptions for 10,000 shares of preferred stock at $50 per share; 1,000 of the shares were subscribed by Green and 9,000 were subscribed by other investors.

Jan. 31 Collected from Green the full amount of her subscription to 1,000 shares of preferred stock and issued a stock certificate for these shares. (No collection has yet been made from the subscribers to the other 9,000 shares of preferred stock.)

The corporation will begin operations in February; no revenue was earned and no expenses were incurred during January. No depreciation of plant assets and no amortization of organization cost will be recognized until February when operations get under way.

Instructions

a Prepare journal entries to record the transactions for January in the accounting records of Far West Corporation.

b Prepare a classified balance sheet for the corporation at January 31, Year 1.

11-9 Shown below is the stockholders' equity section of the balance sheet of Reno Corporation at the end of the current year.

RENO CORPORATION
Stockholders' Equity
December 31, Current Year

$2.75 preferred stock, $50 par value, authorized 40,000 shares:		
Issued	$720,000	
Subscribed	360,000	$1,080,000
Common stock, no par, $5 stated value, authorized 320,000 shares:		
Issued	$680,000	
Subscribed	140,000	820,000
Paid-in capital in excess of par or stated value:		
On preferred	$108,000	
On common	164,000	272,000
Retained earnings (deficit)		(300,000)
Total stockholders' equity		$1,872,000

Among the assets of the corporation appear the following items: Subscriptions Receivable: Preferred, $180,000; Subscriptions Receivable: Common, $91,000.

Instructions On the basis of this information, write a brief answer to the following questions, showing any necessary supporting computations.

a How many shares of preferred and common have been issued?

b How many shares of preferred and common have been subscribed?

c What was the average price per share received by the corporation on its preferred stock, including preferred stock subscribed?

d What was the average price per share received by the corporation on its common stock, including common stock subscribed?

e What is the average amount per share that subscribers of preferred stock have yet to pay on their subscriptions?

f What is the total paid-in capital of the Reno Corporation?

g What is the total legal or stated value of all capital stock of Reno Corporation?

h What is the average amount per share that common stock subscribers have already paid on their subscriptions? (Assume common subscribed at $6.)

11-10 The two independent cases presented below require preparation of the stockholders' equity section of a corporate balance sheet.

Case A In Year 1, Barbara Sterns organized Flowerland, Inc., a chain of retail nurseries. The corporation was authorized to issue 100,000 shares of $2 par value common stock and 10,000 shares of $5 cumulative, no-par value, preferred stock. All the preferred stock was issued for a total of $511,000, and 35,000 shares of common stock were issued at $20 per share. During the first three years of its existence, Flowerland, Inc., earned a total of $347,500 and paid yearly dividends of 90 cents per share on the common stock, in addition to the regular dividends on the preferred stock. During Year 4, however, the corporation incurred a loss of $204,000 and paid no dividends.

Case B Tom Martinez organized Urban Transport Company in January, Year 1. The corporation issued at $15 per share one-half of its 100,000 authorized shares of $5 par common stock. On January 1, Year 2, the corporation sold at par the entire 5,000 authorized shares of 8%, $100 par value, cumulative preferred stock. On January 1, Year 3, the company again needed money and issued 5,000 shares of an authorized 10,000 shares of $9, no-par, cumulative preferred stock for a total of $494,000. The company suffered losses in Years 1 and 2, reporting a deficit of $270,000 at the end of Year 2. During Years 3 and 4 combined, the company earned a total of $950,000. Dividends of $1 per share were paid on common stock in Year 3 and $3.50 per share in Year 4.

Instructions For each of the independent cases described, prepare in good form the stockholders' equity section of the balance sheet at December 31, Year 4. Include a supporting schedule for each case showing your determination of the balance of retained earnings at that date.

BUSINESS DECISION PROBLEM 11

City Electric and Metropolitan Power are two utility companies with very stable earnings. City Electric consistently has a net income of approximately $96 million per year, and Metropolitan Power's net income consistently approximates $84 million per year. City Electric has 5,400,000 share of 6% preferred stock, $50 par value, and 13,300,000 shares of $50 par value common stock outstanding. Metropolitan Power has 2,400,000 shares of 6% preferred stock, $100 par value, and 8,700,000 shares of $10 par value common stock outstanding. Assume that both companies distribute all net income as dividends every year, and will continue to do so. Neither company plans to issue additional shares of capital stock.

Instructions

a Compute the annual dividend which would be paid on the common stock of each company, assuming that City Electric has a net income of $96 million and Metropolitan Power has a net income of $84 million.

b Which company's common stock would you expect to have the higher *market price per share?* Support your answer with information provided in the problem.

12

CORPORATIONS: A CLOSER LOOK

After studying this chapter you should be able to:

- Describe how discontinued operations and extraordinary items are presented in the income statement.
- Compute earnings per share.
- Distinguish between primary and fully diluted earnings per share.
- Account for stock dividends and stock splits, and explain the probable effect of these transactions upon market price.
- Define prior period adjustments and explain how they are presented in financial statements.
- Account for treasury stock transactions.
- Compute book value per share.

The most important aspect of corporate financial reporting, in the view of most stockholders, is the determination of periodic net income. Both the market price of common stock and the amount of cash dividends per share depend to a considerable extent on the current level of earnings (net income). Even more important than the absolute amount of net income is the *trend* of earnings over time. Is net income increasing or decreasing from one year to the next? The common stocks of those companies which regularly achieve higher earnings year after year become the favorite securities of the investment community. Such stature helps greatly in raising new capital, in attracting and retaining highly competent management, and in many other ways.

In this chapter, we will see that the corporate income statement is organized to help investors to evaluate the trend of earnings and to associate total earnings with their ownership shares. In addition, we will discuss transactions that may affect the amount of stockholders' equity and the market price of common stock, but that do not affect net income. Transactions of this nature include cash and stock dividends, stock splits, prior period adjustments, and treasury stock transactions.

Public misconceptions of the rate of corporate earnings

Numerous public opinion surveys indicate that most people mistakenly believe that corporate earnings generally amount to somewhere between 20 and 50% of sales. College and university students should be better informed, but the authors have found, from questioning students in classes at the beginning of the first course in accounting, that college students in guessing at the average rate of corporate earnings usually suggest far higher rates than actually exist. If you will look at the published annual reports of leading corporations, you will find that net income usually falls somewhere between 2 and 10% of sales. Remember that these financial statements have been audited by independent CPA firms, and also reviewed by the SEC. For all manufacturing companies a representative rate of earnings in recent years has been around 4 to 5%. Of course, there are exceptions. In the airline industry, for example, American Airlines, TWA, and Pan American each operated at a net loss for several years during the last decade. This question of the rate of corporate earnings will be considered more fully in Chapter 16.

Developing predictive information

An income statement tells us a great deal about the performance of a company over the past year. For example, study of the income statement makes clear the rate of gross profit on sales, the net income for the year, the percentage of profit per dollar of sales, and the net income earned on each share of common stock. Can we expect the income statement for *next year* to indicate about the same level of performance? If the transactions summarized in the income statement for the year just completed were of a normal recurring nature, such as selling merchandise, paying employees, and incurring other normal expenses, we can reasonably assume that the operating results were typical and that somewhat similar results can be expected in the following year. However, in any business, unusual and nonrecurring events may occur which cause the current year's net income to be quite different from the income we should expect the company to earn in the future. For example, the company may have sustained large losses in the current year from an earthquake or some other event which is not likely to recur in the near future.

Ideally, the results of unusual and nonrecurring transactions should be shown in a separate section of the income statement *after* the income or loss from normal business activities has been determined. Income from *normal and recurring* activities presumably should be a more useful figure for predicting future earnings than is a net income figure which includes the results of nonrecurring events. The problem in creating such an income statement, however, is in determining which events are so unlikely to recur that they should be excluded from the results of "normal" operations.

The question of how unusual an event should be to require separate presentation has long been debated by accountants and other interested parties. Two categories of events that currently require special treatment in the income statement are (1) the results of discontinued operations and (2) extraordinary items. The criteria which define these categories and the related income statement presentation are still being debated and may well change in future years.

Discontinued operations

Virtually all large corporations are engaged in several different types of business activity. For example, Exxon, the oil company, has a division which manufactures office equipment. PepsiCo, known primarily as a soft drink manufacturer, owns and operates the Pizza Hut restaurant chain. Sears Roebuck & Co., in addition to its retail stores, has a variety of business lines, including an insurance company, a real estate firm, and a chain of savings and loan companies. Accountants use the term *segment of a business* to describe each distinct type of business activity. Some corporations may have a dozen or more segments.

Sometimes a corporation may sell a segment of its operations to another company. A problem then arises in using past income statements to forecast future earnings because the size and scope of the company's operations change whenever a segment of the business is discontinued. The FASB has accepted the position that the results of a company's *continuing operations* should be reported in the income statement separately from the operating results of any segments discontinued during the year.[1] The income of a discontinued segment (including any gain or loss on the disposal of the segment) is listed separately in the income statement *after* determining the income from continuing operations. The purpose of such separate disclosure is to enable users of financial statements to make better predictive judgments as to the future performance of the company.

For example, assume that Commuter Airways operates both an airline service and a small chain of motels. Near the end of the current year, the company sells all of the motels to a national motel chain. The operating results of Commuter Airways' two business segments for the current year are as follows:

	Airline Operations	Motel Operations*
Net revenue	$12,000,000	$5,000,000
Costs and expenses (including applicable income tax effects)	11,200,000	6,100,000
Gain on sale of motels (net of income taxes)		500,000

*Revenue and expenses of motel operations are prior to date of sale.

---

[1]*APB Opinion No. 30,* "Reporting the Results of Operations—Reporting the Effects of Disposal of a Segment of a Business, and Extraordinary, Unusual and Infrequently Occurring Events and Transactions," AICPA (New York: 1973).

The following condensed income statement illustrates the proper presentation of the discontinued motel operations:

COMMUTER AIRWAYS
Condensed Income Statement
For the Current Year

Net revenue		$12,000,000
Cost and expenses (including applicable income taxes)		11.200.000
Income from continuing operations		$ 800,000
Discontinued operations:		
Operating loss from motels, net of income taxes	$(1,100,000)	
Gain on sale of motels, net of income taxes	500,000	(600,000)
Net income		$ 200,000

Income from continuing operations Notice that the top section of this income statement includes only the revenue and expenses of the continuing airline operations. This enables us to develop a subtotal, Income from Continuing Operations, which measures the profitability of the ongoing business activities. This subtotal should be helpful in making predictions of the company's future earnings. For example, if we predict no significant changes in the profitability of airline operations, we should expect Commuter Airways to earn a net income of approximately $800,000 next year.

In their annual reports to stockholders, many companies include the income statements from one or more prior years to assist investors in evaluating the trend in earnings. If Commuter Airways includes prior years' income statements in its annual report, these statements should be reorganized to show separately the operating results of the airlines and of the motels. This will further assist investors in evaluating the earnings prospects for the company's ongoing operations.

Presentation of the discontinued operations After determination of the income from continuing operations, the operating results of the discontinued motel segment are shown in two parts. The first of these parts is the $1,100,000 net operating loss ($5,000,000 revenue, minus $6,100,000 in costs and expenses) incurred during the portion of the year that the motels were owned by Commuter Airways. The second item is the gain or loss resulting from the sale of the motels. Since the motels are no longer owned by Commuter Airways, it is not considered necessary to itemize the revenue and expense items which contributed to the net operating loss for this segment of the business. However, the total revenue earned by the discontinued segment ($5,000,000) should be disclosed in a footnote to the financial statements.

Notice the phrase *net of income taxes* in the discontinued operations section of the income statement. This phrase means that the operating loss on the discontinued segment and the gain on its sale have been adjusted for any applicable income tax effects. For example, Commuter Airways may have realized a

$700,000 gain on the sale of the motels, but if this $700,000 gain results in an additional $200,000 in income taxes being owed, the after-tax gain is only $500,000. Similarly, before considering income taxes, the operating loss on the motels may have amounted to $2,000,000 for the year. If this loss results in a $900,000 reduction in income taxes, however, the loss *net of related income tax effects* is only $1,100,000.

Income taxes applicable to the airline segment of the business are included among the $11,200,000 in costs and expenses deducted in arriving at the Income from Continuing Operations. Corporate income taxes are discussed further in Chapter 17.

Extraordinary items

The second category of events requiring disclosure in a separate section of the income statements is extraordinary items. An extraordinary item is a gain or loss that is material in amount, *unusual in nature, and not expected to recur in the foreseeable future.* By definition, extraordinary items are extremely rare; hence, they seldom appear in financial statements. Examples of extraordinary items include the effects of unusual casualties (such as earthquakes or tornadoes), expropriation of assets by a foreign government, and gains or losses that may result from a newly enacted law. Gains or losses from such transactions as sales of plant assets, strikes, or settlements of litigation are recurring events in the business environment and do *not* qualify as extraordinary items.

When a gain or loss qualifies as an extraordinary item, it appears at the bottom of the income statement following the subtotal, *Income before Extraordinary Items.* Since the extraordinary item is so unusual, this subtotal is considered necessary to show investors what the net income *would have been* if the unusual event had not occurred. Extraordinary items are shown net of any related income tax effects. The presentation of an extraordinary item is illustrated in the following income statement:

SEAPORT MALL
Income Statement
For the Year Ended December 31, 19___

Net sales		$10,000,000
Costs and expenses:		
Cost of goods sold	$6,000,000	
Selling expenses	1,100,000	
General and administrative expenses	700,000	
Loss from settlement of litigation	200,000	
Income taxes (excluding tax effects of the extraordinary loss) ...	800,000	8,800,000
Income before extraordinary items		$ 1,200,000
Extraordinary item: Loss from earthquake damage,		
net of related tax effects		300,000
Net income		$ 900,000

Other nonoperating gains and losses   Some transactions are not typical of normal operations but also do not meet the criteria for separate presentation as extraordinary items. Among such events are losses incurred because of strikes and the gains or losses resulting from sales of plant assets. Such items, if material, should be individually listed as items of revenue or expense, rather than being combined with other items in broad categories such as sales revenue or general and administrative expenses.

In the income statement illustrated, the nonoperating loss of $200,000 resulting from the settlement of a lawsuit was disclosed separately in the income statement but was *not* listed as an extraordinary item. This loss was important enough to bring to the attention of readers of the financial statements, but lawsuits are not so unusual or infrequent as to be considered extraordinary items.

The income or loss from a discontinued segment of the business (including any gain or loss on disposal of the segment) is *not* an extraordinary item. When discontinued operations and an extraordinary item appear in the same income statement, the income or loss from the discontinued operations is presented *before* the extraordinary item. Thus, the subtotal Income before Extraordinary Items *includes* the operating results of any segments of the business which have been discontinued during the year.

Earnings per share (EPS)

Perhaps the most widely used of all accounting statistics is *earnings per share* of common stock. Everyone who buys or sells stock in a corporation needs to know the annual earnings per share. Stock market prices are quoted on a per-share basis. If you are considering investing in IBM stock at a price of, say, $70 per share, you need to know the earnings per share and the annual dividend per share in order to decide whether this price is reasonable. In other words, how much earning power and how much dividend income would you be getting for each share you buy?

To compute earnings per share, the annual net income available to the common stockholders is divided by the average number of common shares outstanding. The concept of earnings per share applies *only to common stock;* preferred stock has no claim to earnings beyond the stipulated preferred stock dividends.

Many financial analysts express the relationship between earnings per share and market price per share as a *price-earnings ratio* (p/e ratio). This ratio is computed by dividing the market price per share of common stock by the annual earnings per share.

Weighted-average number of shares outstanding   The simplest example of computing earnings per share is found when a company has issued only common stock and the number of shares outstanding has not changed during the year. In this situation, the net income for the year divided by the number of shares outstanding at year-end equals earnings per share.

In many companies, however, the number of shares of stock outstanding is changed one or more times during the year. When additional shares are issued in exchange for assets during the year, the computation of earnings per share is based upon the *weighted-average* number of shares outstanding.[2]

The weighted-average number of shares for the year is determined by multiplying the number of shares outstanding by the fraction of the year that said number of shares outstanding remained unchanged. For example, assume that 100,000 shares of common stock were outstanding during the first nine months of Year 1 and 140,000 shares during the last three months. Assume also that the increase in shares outstanding resulted from the sale of 40,000 shares for cash. The weighted-average number of shares outstanding during Year 1 would be 110,000, determined as follows:

100,000 shares × ¾ *of a year*	*75,000*
140,000 shares × ¼ *of a year*	*35,000*
Weighted-average number of common shares outstanding	*110,000*

This procedure gives more meaningful earnings per share data than if the total number of shares outstanding at the end of the year were used in the calculations. By using the weighted-average number of shares, we recognize that the proceeds from the sale of the 40,000 shares were available to generate earnings only during the last three months of the year. The contribution to earnings made by 40,000 shares outstanding during one-fourth of the year is equivalent to that of 10,000 shares outstanding for a full year. In other words, the weighted-average number of shares outstanding consists of 100,000 shares outstanding during the entire year plus the 10,000-share full-year equivalent of the shares issued during the year.

Preferred dividends and earnings per share   When a company has preferred stock outstanding, the preferred stockholders participate in net income to the extent of the preferred stock dividends. To determine the earnings *applicable to the common stock,* we must first deduct from net income the amount of any preferred stock dividends. To illustrate, let us assume that Tanner Corporation has 200,000 shares of common stock and 10,000 shares of $4 preferred stock outstanding throughout the year. Net income for the year totals $480,000. Earnings per share of common stock would be computed as follows:

Net income	*$480,000*
Less: Dividends on preferred stock (10,000 shares × $4)	*40,000*
Income applicable to common stock	*$440,000*
Weighted-average number of common shares outstanding	*200,000*
Earnings per share of common stock ($440,000 ÷ 200,000 shares)	*$2.20*

---

[2]When the number of shares outstanding changes as a result of a stock split or a stock dividend (discussed later in this chapter), the computation of the weighted-average number of shares outstanding should be adjusted **retroactively** rather than weighted for the period the new shares were outstanding. Earnings per share data for prior years thus will be consistently stated in terms of the current capital structure.

Primary and fully diluted earnings per share

Let us now assume that each share of Tanner Corporation's $4 preferred stock is *convertible* into 4 shares of common stock. The conversion of this preferred stock would increase the number of common shares outstanding and might dilute (reduce) earnings per share. Any common stockholder interested in the trend of earnings per share will want to know what effect the conversion of the preferred stock would have had upon this statistic.

To inform investors of the potential dilution which might occur, two amounts are computed for earnings per share. The first figure, called *primary* earnings per share, is based upon the weighted-average number of common shares actually outstanding during the year. Thus, this figure ignores the potential dilution represented by the convertible preferred stock.[3] The second figure, called *fully diluted* earnings per share, shows the impact that conversion of the preferred stock would have upon primary earnings per share.

Primary earnings per share are computed in the same manner illustrated in our preceding calculation. In computing fully diluted earnings per share, *we assume that the preferred stock was converted into common stock at the beginning of the current year.*[4] Under this assumption, there would have been no preferred stock dividends; however, there would have been an additional 40,000 shares of common stock outstanding throughout the year. The computation of primary earnings per share and fully diluted earnings per share is shown below:

	Primary	Fully Diluted
Net income	$480,000	$480,000
Less: Dividends on preferred stock, 10,000 × $4	40,000	–0–
Earnings available for common stock	$440,000	$480,000
Number of shares of common stock outstanding:		
In computing primary earnings per share	200,000	
In computing fully diluted earnings per share, 200,000 +		
(10,000 × 4)		240,000
Earnings per share of common stock	$2.20	$2.00

Primary and fully diluted earnings per share

It is important to remember that fully diluted earnings per share represent a *hypothetical case.* The preferred stock actually was not converted during the year. The presentation of fully diluted earnings per share merely warns common stockholders what *could* have happened. When the difference between primary and fully diluted earnings per share is significant, investors should recognize the *risk* that future earnings per share may be diluted by conversions of other securities into common stock.

---

[3]If certain criteria are met, convertible securities qualify as **common stock equivalents** and enter into the computation of primary earnings per share. Common stock equivalents and other complex issues relating to earnings per share are discussed in *APB Opinion No. 15,* "Earnings per Share," AICPA (New York, 1969).

[4]If the preferred stock had been issued during the current year, we would assume that it was converted into common stock on the date it was issued.

Presentation of earnings per share in the income statement

All publicly owned corporations are required to present earnings per share data in their income statements.[5] If an income statement includes subtotals for income from continuing operations, or income before extraordinary items, per-share figures are shown for these amounts as well as for net income. These additional per-share amounts are computed by substituting the amount of the appropriate subtotal for the net income figure in the preceding calculation.

To illustrate all of the potential per-share computations, we will expand our Tanner Corporation example to include income from continuing operations and income before extraordinary items. In this case, we will actually need to compute six per-share amounts. We should point out, however, that all of these figures seldom appear in the same income statement. Very few companies have both discontinued operations and an extraordinary item to report in the same year. The following condensed income statement is intended to illustrate the proper format for presenting earnings per share figures and to provide a review of the calculations.

TANNER CORPORATION
Condensed Income Statement
For the Year Ended December 31, 19___

Net sales	$8,000,000
Cost and expenses (detail omitted for illustrative purposes)	7,340,000
Income from continuing operations	$ 660,000
Loss from discontinued operations, net of related tax effects	(60,000)
Income before extraordinary items	$ 600,000
Less: Extraordinary loss from tornado damage, net of related tax effects	(120,000)
Net income	$ 480,000

Earnings per share of common stock:

	Primary	Fully Diluted
Earnings from continuing operations	$3.10[a]	$2.75[d]
Loss from discontinued operations	(.30)	(.25)
Earnings before extraordinary items	$2.80[b]	$2.50[e]
Extraordinary loss	(.60)	(.50)
Net earnings	$2.20[c]	$2.00[f]

[a]($660,000 − $40,000 preferred dividends) ÷ 200,000 shares
[b]($600,000 − $40,000) ÷ 200,000 shares
[c]($480,000 − $40,000) ÷ 200,000 shares
[d]$660,000 ÷ [200,000 shares + (10,000 × 4)]
[e]$600,000 ÷ 240,000 shares
[f]$480,000 ÷ 240,000 shares

---

[5]The FASB has exempted closely held corporations (those not publicly owned) from the requirement of computing and reporting earnings per share. See *FASB Statement No. 23,* "Suspension of the Reporting of Earnings per Share and Segment Information by Nonpublic Enterprises" (Stamford, Conn.: 1978).

For emphasis the six required figures for earnings per share are printed in black. We have shown in red the per-share amounts for the loss from discontinued operations and the extraordinary loss, but these are merely reconciling amounts and sometimes are omitted in a formal income statement. For illustration, we have also shown how the various amounts for earnings per share were computed. These explanatory computations would not be included in an actual income statement.

Interpreting the different per-share amounts   To informed users of financial statements, each of these figures has a different significance. Earnings per share from continuing operations represents the results of continuing and ordinary business activity. This figure is the most useful one for predicting future operating results. *Net earnings* per share, on the other hand, shows the overall operating results of the current year, including any discontinued operations or extraordinary items. The fully diluted per-share figures indicate the extent to which primary earnings per share could be diluted by the conversion of other securities into common stock.

Unfortunately the term *earnings per share* often is used without qualification in referring to various types of per-share data. When using per-share information, it is important to know exactly which per-share statistic is being presented. For example, the price-earnings ratios (market price divided by earnings per share) for common stocks listed on major stock exchanges are reported daily in the *Wall Street Journal* and many other newspapers. Which earnings per share figures are used in computing these ratios? Generally, these price-earnings ratios are based upon *net earnings* per share. If a company reports an extraordinary gain or loss, however, the ratio is computed using the per-share earnings *before the extraordinary item.* When a company reports both primary and full diluted earnings per share, the price-earnings ratio is based upon the primary figure.

Cash dividends

The prospect of receiving cash dividends is a principal reason for investing in the stocks of corporations. An increase or decrease in the established rate of dividends will usually cause an immediate rise or fall in the market price of the company's stock. Stockholders are keenly interested in prospects for future dividends and as a group are strongly in favor of more generous dividend payments. The board of directors, on the other hand, is primarily concerned with the long-run growth and financial strength of the corporation; it may prefer to restrict dividends to a minimum in order to conserve cash for purchase of plant and equipment or for other needs of the company. Many of the so-called "growth companies" plow back into the business most of their earnings and pay only very small cash dividends.

The preceding discussion suggests three requirements for the payment of a cash dividend. These are:

1 **Retained earnings**   Since dividends represent a distribution of earnings to stockholders, the theoretical maximum for dividends is the total undistributed net income of the company, represented by the credit balance of the Retained Earnings account. As a practical matter, many corporations limit dividends to somewhere near 40% of annual net income, in the belief that a major portion of the net income must be retained in the business if the company is to grow and to keep pace with its competitors.

2 **An adequate cash position**   The fact that the company reports large earnings does not mean that it has a large amount of cash on hand. Earnings may have been invested in new plant and equipment, or in paying off debts, or in acquiring a larger inventory. There is no necessary relationship between the balance in the Retained Earnings account and the balance in the Cash account. The traditional expression of "paying dividends out of retained earnings" is misleading. Cash dividends can be paid only "out of" cash.

3 **Dividend action by the board of directors**   Even though the company's net income is substantial and its cash position seemingly satisfactory, dividends are not paid automatically. A formal action by the board of directors is necessary to declare a dividend.

Dividend dates

Four significant dates are involved in the distribution of a dividend. These dates are:

1 **Date of declaration**   On the day on which the dividend is declared by the board of directors, a liability to make the payment comes into existence.

2 **Date of record**   The date of record always follows the date of declaration, usually by a period or two or three weeks, and is always stated in the dividend declaration. In order to be eligible to receive the dividend, a person must be listed as the owner of the stock on the date of record.

3 **Ex-dividend date**   The ex-dividend date is significant for investors in companies with stocks traded on the stock exchanges. To permit the compilation of the list of stockholders as of the record date, it is customary for the stock to go "ex-dividend" three business days before the date of record. A stock is said to be selling ex-dividend on the day that it loses the right to receive the latest declared dividend. A person who buys the stock before the ex-dividend date is entitled to receive the dividend; conversely, a stockholder who sells shares before the ex-dividend date does not receive the dividend.

4 **Date of payment**   The declaration of a dividend always includes announcement of the date of payment as well as the date of record. Usually the date of payment comes from two to four weeks after the date of record.

The journal entries to record the declaration and payment of a cash dividend were illustrated in Chapter 3 but are repeated here with emphasis on the date of declaration and date of payment.

Entries made on declaration date and . . .

| June 1 | Dividends .... | 100,000 | |
| | Dividends Payable .... | | 100,000 |

To record declaration of a cash dividend of $1 per share on the 100,000 shares of common stock outstanding. Payable July 10 to stockholders of record on June 20.

. . . on payment date

| July 10 | Dividends Payable .... | 100,000 | |
| | Cash .... | | 100,000 |

To record payment of $1 per share dividend declared June 1 to stockholders of record on June 20.

At the end of the accounting period, a closing entry is required to transfer the debit balance of the Dividends account into the Retained Earnings account. Some companies follow the alternative practice of debiting Retained Earnings when the dividend is declared instead of using a Dividends account. Under either method, the balance of the Retained Earnings account ultimately is reduced by all dividends declared during the period.

Most dividends are paid in cash, but occasionally a dividend declaration calls for payment in assets other than cash. A large distillery once paid a dividend consisting of a bottle of whiskey for each share of stock. When a corporation goes out of existence (particularly a small corporation with only a few stockholders), it may choose to distribute noncash assets to its owners rather than to convert all its assets into cash.

Liquidating dividends

A *liquidating* dividend occurs when a corporation returns to stockholders all or part of their paid-in capital investment. Liquidating dividends are usually paid only when a corporation is going out of existence or is making a permanent reduction in the size of its operations. Normally dividends are paid as a result of profitable operations, and the recipients of a dividend are entitled to assume that the dividend represents a distribution of income unless they are specifically notified that the dividend is a return of invested capital.

Stock dividends

Stock dividend is a term used to describe a distribution of additional shares of stock to a company's stockholders in proportion to their present holdings. In brief, the dividend is payable in *additional shares of stock* rather than in cash. Most stock dividends consist of additional shares of common stock distributed to holders of common stock, and our discussion will be limited to this type of stock dividend.

A cash dividend reduces the assets of a corporation and reduces the stockholders' equity by the same amount. A stock dividend, on the other hand, causes no change in assets and no change in the *total* amount of the stockholders' equity. The only effect of a stock dividend on the accounts is to transfer a portion of the retained earnings into the Common Stock account and the Paid-in Capital from Stock Dividends account. In other words, a stock dividend merely "reshuffles" the stockholders' equity accounts, increasing the permanent capital accounts and decreasing the Retained Earnings account. A stockholder who receives a stock dividend will own an increased number of shares, but his or her total ownership equity in the company will be *no larger than before.*

To illustrate this point, assume that a corporation with 2,000 shares of stock is owned equally by James Davis and Susan Miller, each owning 1,000 shares of stock. The corporation declares a stock dividend of 10% and distributes 200 additional shares (10% of 2,000 shares), with 100 shares going to each of the two stockholders. Davis and Miller now hold 1,100 shares apiece, but each still owns one-half of the business. The corporation has not changed; its assets and liabilities and its total stockholders' equity are exactly the same as before the dividend. From the stockholders' viewpoint, the ownership of 1,100 shares out of a total of 2,200 outstanding shares represents no more than did the ownership of 1,000 shares out of a total of 2,000 shares previously outstanding.

Assume that the market price of this stock was $110 per share prior to the stock dividend. Total market value of all the outstanding shares was, therefore, 2,000 times $110, or $220,000. What would be the market value per share and in total after the additional 200 dividend shares were issued? The 2,200 shares now outstanding should have the same total market value as the previously outstanding 2,000 shares, because the "pie" has merely been divided into more but smaller pieces. The price per share should have dropped from $110 to $100, and the aggregate market value of outstanding shares would consequently be computed as 2,200 shares times $100, or $220,000. Whether the market price per share will, in all cases, decrease in proportion to the change in number of outstanding shares is another matter. The market prices of stocks listed on a stock exchange are influenced daily by many different factors.

Reasons for distribution of stock dividends Many reasons have been given for the popularity of stock dividends; for example:

1 To conserve cash. When the trend of earnings is favorable but cash is needed for expansion, a stock dividend may be an appropriate device for "passing along the earnings" to stockholders without weakening the corporation's cash position.[6]
2 To reduce the market price of a corporation's stock to a more convenient trading range by increasing the number of shares outstanding. This objective is usually present in large stock dividends (25 to 100% or more).
3 To avoid income tax on stockholders. For income tax purposes, stock dividends are not considered as income to the recipient; therefore, no income tax is payable.

---

[6]For example, the Standard Oil Company of California, in a letter to its stockholders, gave the following reason for the "payment" of a 5% stock dividend: "Payment of this stock dividend recognizes the continuing increase in your stockholders' equity in the Company's assets, resulting from reinvestment of part of the Company's earnings. Reinvestment of earnings has helped to sustain the Company's long-range program of capital and exploratory expenditures and investments aimed to increase future income and enhance further the value of your shareholding."

Entries to record stock dividends   Assume that a corporation had the following stockholders' equity accounts on December 15, Year 1, just prior to declaring a 10% stock dividend:

Stockholders' equity before stock dividend

Stockholders' equity:

Common stock, $10 par value, 300,000 shares authorized, 100,000 shares issued and outstanding	$1,000,000
Paid-in capital in excess of par	500,000
Retained earnings	2,000,000
Total stockholders' equity	$3,500,000

Assume also that the closing market price of the stock on December 15, Year 1, was $30 a share. The company declares a 10% stock dividend, consisting of 10,000 common shares (10% × 100,000 = 10,000). The entry to record the *declaration* of the dividend is as follows:

Stock dividend declared; note use of market price of stock

Year 1

Dec. 15 Retained Earnings	300,000	
Stock Dividend to Be Distributed		100,000
Paid-in Capital from Stock Dividends		200,000

To record declaration of a 10% stock dividend consisting of 10,000 shares of $10 par value common stock. To be distributed on Feb. 9, Year 2, to stockholders of record on Jan. 15, Year 2. Amount of retained earnings transferred to permanent capital is based on market price of $30 a share on Dec. 15, Year 1.

The Stock Dividend to Be Distributed account is *not a liability,* because there is no obligation to distribute cash or any other asset. If a balance sheet is prepared between the date of declaration of a stock dividend and the date of distribution of the shares, this account, as well as Paid-in Capital from Stock Dividends, should be presented in the stockholders' equity section of the balance sheet.

The entry to record *distribution* of the dividend shares is as follows:

Stock dividend distributed

Year 2

Feb. 9 Stock Dividend to Be Distributed	100,000	
Common Stock		100,000

To record distribution of stock dividend of 10,000 shares.

Note that the amount of retained earnings transferred to permanent capital accounts by the above entries is not the par value of the new shares, but the *market value,* as indicated by the market price prevailing at the date of declaration. The reasoning behind this practice is simple: Since stockholders tend to measure the "worth" of a small stock dividend (say, 20 to 25% or less) in terms of the market value of the additional shares issued, then Retained Earnings should be reduced by this amount.

Large stock dividends (for example, those in excess of 20 to 25%) should be recorded by transferring only the par or stated value of the dividend shares from the Retained Earnings account to the Common Stock account. Large stock dividends generally have the effect of proportionately reducing the market price of the stock. For example, a 100% stock dividend would reduce the market price by about 50%, because twice as many shares would be outstanding. A 100% stock dividend is very similar to the 2 for 1 *stock split* discussed in the following section of this chapter.

Stock splits

Most large corporations are interested in as wide as possible a distribution of their securities among the investing public. If the market price reaches very high levels as, for example, $150 per share, the corporation may feel that, by splitting the stock 5 for 1 and thereby reducing the price to $30 per share, the number of shareholders may be increased. The bulk of trading in securities occurs in 100-share lots and an extra commission is charged on smaller transactions. Many investors with limited funds prefer to make their investments in 100-share lots of lower-priced stocks. The majority of leading American corporations have split their stock; some have done so several times. Generally the number of shareholders has increased noticeably after the stock has been split.

A stock split consists of increasing the number of outstanding shares and reducing the par or stated value per share in proportion. For example, assume that a corporation has outstanding 1 million shares of $10 par value stock. The market price is $90 per share. The corporation now reduces the par value from $10 to $5 per share and increases the number of shares from 1 million to 2 million. This action would be called a 2 for 1 stock split. A stockholder who owned 100 shares of the stock before the split would own 200 shares after the split. Since the number of outstanding shares has been doubled without any change in the affairs of the corporation, the market price will probably drop from $90 to approximately $45 a share.

A stock split does not change the balance of any ledger account; consequently, the transaction may be recorded merely by a memorandum notation in the general journal and in the Common Stock account.

Distinction between stock splits and large stock dividends　What is the difference between a 2 for 1 stock split and a 100% stock dividend? There is very little difference; both will double the number of outstanding shares without changing total stockholders' equity, and both will serve to cut the market price of the stock in half. The stock dividend, however, will cause a transfer from the Retained Earnings account to the Common Stock account equal to the par or stated value of the dividend shares, whereas the stock split does not change the dollar balance of any account.

After an increase in the number of shares as a result of a stock split or stock dividend, earnings per share are computed in terms of the increased number of shares. In presenting five- or ten-year summaries, the earnings per share for earlier years are *retroactively revised* to reflect the increased number of shares currently outstanding and thus make the trend of earnings per share from year to year a valid comparison.

Stock splits and stock dividends from the investor's viewpoint How should an investor account for the additional shares received in a stock split or a stock dividend? These additional shares are *not income* to the investor. Rather, the new shares reduce the investor's cost basis per share, because the original investment is now represented by an increased number of shares. The reduction in the cost basis per share is recorded by a *memorandum entry* in the investor's general journal.

To illustrate, assume that Pat Smith buys 100 shares of Delta Company common stock for $72 per share, a total investment of $7,200. Later Smith receives an additional 20 shares in a 20% stock dividend. Smith's $7,200 investment now consists of 120 shares, indicating a new cost per share of $60. The memorandum entry to be made in Smith's general journal is:

July 10 Memorandum: Received 20 additional shares of Delta Co. common stock as a result of 20% stock dividend. Now own 120 shares with a cost basis of $7,200, or $60 per share.

If Smith later sells any of these investment shares, she will measure her gain or loss by comparing the sales price to the adjusted cost basis per share. For example, if Smith sells 50 shares at a price of $68 per share, the gain on the sale should be computed as follows:

Sales price ($68 × 50 shares)	$3,400
Cost of shares sold ($60 × 50 shares)	3,000
Gain on sale of marketable securities	$ 400

Retained earnings

Throughout this book the term *retained earnings* is used to describe that portion of stockholders' equity derived from profitable operations. Retained earnings is a historical concept, representing the accumulated earnings (including prior period adjustments) minus dividends declared from the date of incorporation to the present. If we assume that there are no *prior period adjustments,* the major sources of entries in the Retained Earnings account will be (1) the periodic transfer of net income (or loss) from the Income Summary account and (2) the debits resulting from the declaration of dividends.

Prior period adjustments to the Retained Earnings account

On occasion, a company may discover that a material error was made in the measurement of net income in a prior year. Since net income is the source of retained earnings, an error in reported net income will cause an error in the amount of retained earnings shown in all subsequent balance sheets. When such an error comes to light, it should be corrected. However, if the error in measuring the net income of a prior year is corrected in the current period's income statement, net income for the current period will be distorted. Therefore, material errors in the amount of net income reported in prior periods are corrected by adjusting the balance of the Retained Earnings account. Such adjustments are called *prior period adjustments.*

Material errors in the financial statements of prior years may arise as a result of mathematical errors, failure to interpret properly the accounting effects of transactions, or the use of inappropriate accounting principles and concepts. Assume, for example, that in Year 10 Vista Corporation is audited for the first time by a firm of certified public accountants. During the audit, the CPAs discover that in Year 6 land costing $220,000 had been written up in Vista Corporation's accounting records to an appraised value of $280,000 and a $60,000 gain had been included in net income. Since land should be valued in accounting records at cost rather than appraised value, the recognition of this $60,000 gain constitutes a material error in Vista Corporation's Year 6 financial statements.

What effect does this error have upon the Vista Corporation's financial statements in Year 10? Since the net income of Year 6 has been closed into the Retained Earnings account, both land and retained earnings are overstated in Year 10 by $60,000. The entry to correct this error is shown below:

Retained Earnings 60,000
    Land 60,000
Prior period adjustment to correct error made in the valuation of land and recognition of income in Year 6.

Presentation of prior period adjustments in financial statements   Corrections of the operating results of prior years are *not* included in the income statement of the current year. Prior period adjustments are shown in the *statement of retained earnings* as an adjustment to the balance of retained earnings at the beginning of the current year.[7] The amount of the prior period adjustment should be shown net of any related tax effects. The presentation of the prior period adjustment in the statement of retained earnings of Vista Corporation is illustrated on page 464.

Most companies present comparative financial statements; that is, financial statements of the preceding year are presented along with those of the current year. If the financial statements for the year in which the error occurred are being presented for comparative purposes, these statements should be *revised to eliminate the error.* A footnote to the comparative statements should explain that the financial statements for the earlier year have been revised to reflect correction of the error.

Prior period adjustments rarely appear in the financial statements of large, publicly owned corporations. The financial statements of these corporations are audited annually by certified public accountants and are not likely to contain material errors which subsequently will require correction by prior period adjustments. Such adjustments are much more likely to appear in the financial statements of closely held corporations that are not audited on an annual basis.

---

[7]*FASB Statement No. 16,* "Prior Period Adjustments" (Stamford, Conn.: 1977).

Statement of retained earnings

In addition to the balance sheet and the income statement, most corporations include a statement of retained earnings and a statement of changes in financial position in their annual reports to stockholders. (The latter statement will be illustrated in Chapter 15.) If a company is audited by a CPA firm, all four of these basic financial statements are covered by the audit report. A simple example of a statement of retained earnings follows:

SHORE LINE CORPORATION
Statement of Retained Earnings
For the Year Ended December 31, 19___

Retained earnings at beginning of year	$620,000
Net income for the year	280,000
Subtotal	$900,000
Less: Dividends	100,000
Retained earnings at end of year	$800,000

In the published annual reports of publicly owned corporations, the statement of retained earnings is usually presented in *comparative* form covering two years. This format and the treatment of a prior period adjustment are illustrated below for Vista Corporation.

VISTA CORPORATION
Statement of Retained Earnings
For Years Ended December 31

	Year 10	Year 9
Retained earnings at beginning of year:		
As originally reported	$ 810,000	$780,000
Prior period adjustment—to correct error in valuation of land recorded in Year 6	(60,000)	(60,000)
As restated	$ 750,000	$720,000
Net income	360,000	210,000
Subtotal	$1,110,000	$930,000
Less: Cash dividends on common stock:		
$2.40 per share in Year 10	240,000	
$1.80 per share in Year 9		180,000
Retained earnings at end of year	$ 870,000	$750,000

Statement of retained earnings shows prior period adjustments, net income, and dividends

The error in the Year 6 financial statements was discovered in Year 10 and is shown as a correction to the beginning balance of retained earnings for both Year 10 and Year 9, since both beginning amounts were overstated. The statement of retained earnings thus provides a useful vehicle for the disclosure of prior period adjustments and for the explanation of all changes in retained earnings during the accounting period.

An alternative presentation of net income and retained earnings is used by some companies. The reconciliation of retained earnings may be shown in the body of a *combined statement of income and retained earnings,* as illustrated below for Lacey Corporation.

LACEY CORPORATION
Combined Statement of Income and Retained Earnings
For Years Ended December 31

	Year 5	Year 4
Net sales	$2,900,000	$2,700,000
Cost of goods sold	1,730,000	1,650,000
Gross profit on sales	$1,170,000	$1,050,000
Operating expenses	620,000	590,000
Income before income taxes	$ 550,000	$ 460,000
Income taxes	260,000	215,000
Net income	290,000	245,000
Retained earnings at beginning of year	730,000	665,000
Subtotal	$1,020,000	$ 910,000
Dividends: $1 per share in Year 5 and $0.90 per share in Year 4	210,000	180,000
Retained earnings at end of year	$ 810,000	$ 730,000
Earnings per share of common stock	$1.38	$1.22

The statement for Lacey Corporation emphasizes the close relationship of operating results and retained earnings. Some readers of financial statements, however, object to the fact that net income (or loss) is "buried" in the body of a combined statement of income and retained earnings rather than being prominently displayed as the final figure before reporting earnings per share.

Appropriations and restrictions of retained earnings

A few corporations transfer a portion of their retained earnings into separate accounts called *appropriations.* The purpose of such appropriations is to indicate to users of financial statements that a portion of retained earnings is not available for the declaration of cash dividends. The limitation on cash dividends may be established voluntarily by the board of directors or it may be required by law or contract. An appropriation of retained earnings is recorded by a debit to Retained Earnings and a credit to the appropriation account such as Retained Earnings Appropriated for Contingencies. Appropriation accounts are still a part of total retained earnings, as indicated by the following partial stockholders' equity section which appeared in a recent balance sheet of Wm. Wrigley Jr. Company:

Appropriations in the balance sheet

Stockholders' equity:

Capital stock, no-par value—authorized and issued—2,000,000 shares	$ 19,200,000
Accumulated earnings retained for use in the business	109,130,000
Accumulated earnings appropriated for guarantees under employment assurance contracts	2,000,000

When the restriction on retained earnings is no longer needed, the appropriation account is eliminated by transferring its balance back to the Retained Earnings account.

Instead of establishing appropriations of retained earnings, most corporations disclose restrictions on the declaration of cash dividends in notes accompanying the financial statements.[8] An example of such disclosure is shown below.

Alternative disclosure of restrictions placed on retained earnings

Rockwell International Corporation:

Among other covenants, certain of the long-term debt agreements contain limitations on creation of additional long-term debt and restrictions on payment of dividends and acquisition of treasury stock. Retained earnings . . . not so restricted amounted to approximately $117,000,000.

Since the only purpose of appropriating retained earnings is to inform readers of the financial statements that a portion of the retained earnings is "reserved" for a specific purpose and is not available for declaration of cash dividends, this information can be conveyed more directly, with less danger of misunderstanding, by a note accompanying the financial statements.

Treasury stock

Corporations frequently reacquire shares of their own capital stock by purchase in the open market. Paying out cash to reacquire shares will reduce the assets of the corporation and reduce the stockholders' equity by the same amount. One reason for such purchases is to have stock available to reissue to officers and employees under bonus plans. Other reasons may include a desire to increase the reported earnings per share or to support the current market price of the stock.

Treasury stock may be defined as shares of a corporation's own capital stock that have been issued and later *reacquired by the issuing company,* but that have not been canceled or permanently retired. Treasury shares may be held indefinitely or may be issued again at any time. Shares of capital stock held in the treasury are not entitled to receive dividends, to vote, or to share in assets upon dissolution of the company. In the computation of earnings per share, shares held in the treasury are not regarded as outstanding shares.

Recording purchases of treasury stock

Purchases of treasury stock should be recorded by debiting the Treasury Stock account with the cost of the stock.[9] For example, if Torrey Corporation reacquires 150 shares of its own $5 par stock at a price of $100 per share, the entry is as follows:

---

[8]According to a recent issue of *Accounting Trends & Techniques* published by the AICPA, very few of the 600 annual reports surveyed showed appropriated retained earnings while a large majority of the annual reports referred to restrictions on retained earnings.

[9]State laws may prescribe different methods of accounting for treasury stock transactions. In this text, we illustrate only the widely used "cost method." Alternative methods are presented in intermediate accounting courses.

<table>
<tr><td>*Treasury stock recorded at cost*</td><td>Treasury Stock ....</td><td>15,000</td><td></td></tr>
<tr><td></td><td>Cash ....</td><td></td><td>15,000</td></tr>
</table>

Purchased 150 shares of $5 par treasury stock at $100 per share.

Note that the Treasury Stock account is debited for the *cost* of the shares purchased, not their par value.

Treasury stock not an asset   When treasury stock is purchased, the corporation is eliminating part of its stockholders' equity by paying off one or more stockholders. The purchase of treasury stock should be regarded as a *reduction of stockholders' equity,* not as the acquisition of an asset. For this reason, the Treasury Stock account should appear in the balance sheet *as a deduction in the stockholders' equity section.*[10] The presentation of treasury stock in a corporate balance sheet is illustrated on page 470.

Reissuance of treasury stock

When treasury shares are reissued, the Treasury Stock account is credited for the cost of the shares reissued and Paid-in Capital from Treasury Stock Transactions is debited or credited for any difference between *cost* and the reissue price. To illustrate, assume that 100 of the treasury shares acquired by Torrey Corporation at a cost of $100 per share are now reissued at a price of $115 per share. The entry to record the reissuance of these shares at a price above cost would be:

<table>
<tr><td>*Reissued at a price above cost*</td><td>Cash ....</td><td>11,500</td><td></td></tr>
<tr><td></td><td>Treasury Stock ....</td><td></td><td>10,000</td></tr>
<tr><td></td><td>Paid-in Capital from Treasury Stock Transactions ....</td><td></td><td>1,500</td></tr>
</table>

Sold 100 shares of treasury stock, which cost $10,000, at a price of $115 per share.

If treasury stock is reissued at a price below cost, paid-in capital from previous treasury stock transactions is reduced (debited) by the excess of cost over the reissue price. To illustrate, assume that Torrey Corporation reissues its remaining 50 shares of treasury stock (cost $100 per share) at a price of $90 per share. The entry would be:

<table>
<tr><td>*Reissued at a price below cost*</td><td>Cash ....</td><td>4,500</td><td></td></tr>
<tr><td></td><td>Paid-in Capital from Treasury Stock Transactions ....</td><td>500</td><td></td></tr>
<tr><td></td><td>Treasury Stock ....</td><td></td><td>5,000</td></tr>
</table>

Sold 50 shares of treasury stock, which cost $5,000, at a price of $90 each.

If there is no paid-in capital from previous treasury stock transactions, the excess of the cost of the treasury shares over the reissue price may be recorded as a debit in any other paid-in capital account. If the company had no paid-in capital in excess of par from any source, the debit would be entered in the Retained Earnings account.

---

[10]Despite a lack of theoretical support, a few corporations do classify treasury stock as an asset, on the grounds that the shares could be sold for cash just as readily as shares owned in another corporation. The same argument could be made for treating unissued shares as assets. Treasury shares are basically the same as unissued shares, and an unissued share of stock is definitely not an asset.

No profit or loss on treasury stock transactions   Note that *no gain or loss is recognized on treasury stock transactions,* even when the shares are reissued at a price above or below cost. A corporation earns profits by selling goods and services to outsiders, not by issuing or reissuing shares of its own capital stock. When treasury shares are reissued at a price above cost, the corporation receives from the new stockholder a larger amount of paid-in capital than was eliminated when the corporation acquired the treasury shares. Conversely, if treasury shares are reissued at a price below cost, the corporation ends up with less paid-in capital as a result of the purchase and reissuance of the shares. Thus, any changes in stockholders' equity resulting from treasury stock transactions are regarded as changes in *paid-in capital* and are *not* included in the measurement of net income.

Restriction of retained earnings when treasury stock is acquired

If a corporation is to maintain its paid-in capital intact, it must not pay out to its stockholders any more than it earns. As previously stated in the section dealing with dividends, the amount of dividends to be paid must not exceed the corporation's accumulated earnings, or the corporation will be returning a portion of the stockholders' original investment to them.

The payment of cash dividends and the acquisition of treasury stock have a good deal in common. In both transactions, the corporation is disbursing cash to its stockholders. Of course, the dividend payment is spread out among all the stockholders, whereas the payment to purchase treasury stock may go to only a few stockholders, but this does not alter the fact that the corporation is turning over some of its assets to its owners. The total amount which a corporation may pay to its stockholders without reducing paid-in capital is shown by the balance in the Retained Earnings account. Consequently, it is important that a corporation keep track of the total amount disbursed in payment for treasury stock and make sure that this amount plus any dividends paid does not exceed the company's accumulated earnings. This objective is conveniently accomplished by *restricting* the availability of retained earnings for dividends to the extent of the cost of treasury stock purchased. The restriction should be disclosed in a note accompanying the financial statements.

Book value per share of common stock

Since each stockholders' equity in a corporation is determined by the number of shares he or she owns, an accounting measurement of interest to many stockholders is book value per share of common stock. Book value per share is equal to the *net assets* represented by one share of stock. The term *net assets* means total assets minus total liabilities; in other words, net assets are equal to total stockholders' equity. Thus in a corporation which has issued common stock only, the book value per share is computed by dividing total stockholders' equity by the number of shares outstanding.

For example, assume that a corporation has 4,000 shares of capital stock outstanding and the stockholders' equity section of the balance sheet is as follows:

How much is book value per share?

Capital stock, $1 par value	$ 4,000
Paid-in capital in excess of par value	40,000
Retained earnings	76,000
Total stockholders' equity	$120,000

The book value per share is $30; it is computed by dividing the stockholders' equity of $120,000 by the 4,000 shares of outstanding stock. In computing book value, we are not concerned with the number of authorized shares but merely with the outstanding shares, because the total of the outstanding shares represents 100% of the stockholders' equity.

Book value when a company has both preferred and common stock   Book value is usually computed only for common stock. If a company has both preferred and common stock outstanding, the computation of book value per share of common stock requires two steps. First, the redemption value or call price of the entire preferred stock issue and any dividends in arrears are deducted from total stockholders' equity. Second, the remaining amount of stockholders' equity is divided by the number of common shares outstanding to determine book value per common share. This procedure reflects the fact that the common stockholders are the residual owners of the corporate entity.

To illustrate, assume that the stockholders' equity of Video Company at December 31 is as follows:

Two classes of stock

8% preferred stock, $100 par, callable at $110	$1,000,000
Common stock, no-par; $10 stated value; authorized 100,000 shares, issued and outstanding 50,000 shares	500,000
Paid-in capital in excess of par value	750,000
Retained earnings	130,000
Total stockholders' equity	$2,380,000

Because of a weak cash position, Video Company has paid no dividends during the current year. As of December 31, dividends in arrears on the cumulative preferred stock total $80,000.

All the capital belongs to the common stockholders, except the $1.1 million call price ($110 × 10,000 shares) applicable to the preferred stock and the $80,000 of dividends in arrears on preferred stock. The calculation of book value per share of common stock can therefore be made as follows:

Total stockholders' equity		$2,380,000
Less: Equity of preferred stockholders:		
Call price of preferred stock	$1,100,000	
Dividends in arrears	80,000	1,180,000
Equity of common stockholders		$1,200,000
Number of common shares outstanding		50,000
Book value per share of common stock ($1,200,000 ÷ 50,000)		$24

The concept of book value is of vital importance in many contracts. For example, a majority stockholder might obtain an option to purchase the shares of the minority stockholders at book value at a specified future date. Many court cases have hinged on definitions of book value.

Book value is also used in judging the reasonableness of the market price of a stock. However, it must be used with great caution; the fact that a stock is selling at less than its book value does not necessarily indicate a bargain. The disparity between book value and market price per share is indicated by the following data currently available for three well-known corporations: International Paper, book value $64, market price $36; United Airlines, book value $37, market price $17; Johnson & Johnson, book value $14, market price $39. Current earnings, dividends per share, and prospects for future earnings are usually more important factors affecting market price than is book value.

Book value does *not* indicate the amount which the holder of a share of stock would receive if the corporation were to be dissolved. In liquidation, the assets would probably be sold at prices quite different from their carrying values in the accounts, and the stockholders' equity would go up or down accordingly.

Illustration of stockholders' equity section

The following illustration of a stockholders' equity section of a balance sheet shows a fairly detailed classification by source of the various elements of corporate capital:

Stockholders' Equity

Compare with published financial statements

Capital stock:		
9% preferred stock, $100 par value, authorized and issued		
1,000 shares	$100,000	
Common stock, $5 stated value, authorized 100,000 shares,		
issued 60,000 shares, of which 1,000 are held in treasury	300,000	
Common stock subscribed, 6,000 shares	30,000	$430,000
Additional paid-in capital:		
Paid-in capital from stock dividends	$ 50,000	
Paid-in capital in excess of stated value: common stock	290,000	
Paid-in capital from treasury stock transactions	5,000	345,000
Total paid-in capital		$775,000
Retained earnings (of which $12,000, an amount equal to the cost		
of treasury stock purchased, is unavailable for dividends)		162,000
		$937,000
Less: Treasury stock, common, 1,000 shares at cost		12,000
Total stockholders' equity		$925,000

The published financial statements of leading corporations indicate that there is no one standard arrangement for the various items making up the stockholders' equity section. Variations occur in the selection of titles, in the sequence of items, and in the extent of detailed classification. Many companies, in an effort to avoid excessive detail in the balance sheet, will combine several related ledger accounts into a single balance sheet item. An example of published financial statements appears in the appendix at the end of this book.

KEY TERMS INTRODUCED OR EMPHASIZED IN CHAPTER 12

Book value per share   The stockholders' equity represented by each share of common stock, computed by dividing common stockholders' equity by the number of common shares outstanding.

Comparative financial statements   Financial statements of current year and the preceding year which are presented together to facilitate comparison.

Date of record   The date on which a person must be listed as a shareholder in order to be eligible to receive a dividend. Follows the date of declaration of a dividend by two or three weeks.

Discontinued operations   The net operating results (revenue and expenses) of a segment of a company which has been or is being sold.

Earnings per share (EPS)   Net income available to the common stock divided by the weighted-average number of common shares outstanding during the year.

Ex-dividend date   A date three days prior to the date of record specified in a dividend declaration. A person buying a stock prior to the ex-dividend date also acquires the right to receive the dividend. The three-day interval permits the compilation of a list of stockholders as of the date of record.

Extraordinary items   Transactions and events that are both unusual in nature and occur infrequently; for example, a large earthquake loss.

Fully diluted earnings per share   Net income available to the common stock divided by the weighted-average number of common shares outstanding during the year plus any other securities convertible into common shares (if conversion would decrease EPS).

Price-earnings ratio   Market price of a share of common stock divided by annual earnings per share.

Primary earnings per share   Net income available to the common stock divided by weighted-average number of common shares outstanding.

Prior period adjustment   A correction of a material error in the earnings reported in the financial statements of a prior year. Prior period adjustments are recorded directly in the Retained Earnings account and are not included in the income statement of the current period.

Restrictions of retained earnings   Action by the board of directors to classify a portion of retained earnings as unavailable for dividends.

Segment of a business   A component of a business. The activities of the component represent a major line of business or class of customer.

Statement of retained earnings   A basic financial statement showing the change in retained earnings during the year.

Stock dividend   A distribution of additional shares to common stockholders in proportion to their holdings.

Stock split   An increase in the number of shares outstanding with a corresponding decrease in par value per share. The additional shares are distributed proportionately to all common shareholders. Purpose is to reduce market price per share and encourage wider public ownership of the company's stock. A 2 for 1 stock split will give each stockholder twice as many shares as previously owned.

Treasury stock   Shares of a corporation's own stock which have been issued and then reacquired, but not canceled.

DEMONSTRATION PROBLEM FOR YOUR REVIEW

The stockholders' equity of Sutton Corporation at December 31, Year 9, is shown below:

Stockholders' equity:
Common stock, $10 par, 100,000 shares authorized,

40,000 shares issued	$ 400,000
Paid-in capital in excess of par: common stock	200,000
Total paid-in capital	$ 600,000
Retained earnings	1,500,000
Total stockholders' equity	$2,100,000

Transactions affecting stockholders' equity during Year 10 are as follows:

Mar.   1   A 5 for 4 stock split proposed by the board of directors was approved by vote of the stockholders.

Mar. 31   Additional shares were distributed to stockholders pursuant to the 5 for 4 split.

Apr.   1   The company purchased 2,000 shares of its common stock on the open market at $37 per share.

July   1   The company reissued 1,000 shares of treasury stock at $45 per share.

July   1   Issued for cash 20,000 shares of previously unissued $8 par value common stock at a price of $45 per share.

Dec.   1   A cash dividend of $1 per share was declared, payable on December 30, to stockholders of record at December 14.

Dec. 22   A 10% stock dividend was declared; the dividend shares to be distributed on January 24, Year 11. The market price of the stock on December 22 was $48 per share.

The net income for the year ended December 31, Year 10, amounted to $177,000, after an extraordinary loss of $35,400 (net of related tax effects).

Instructions

a Prepare journal entries to record the transactions relating to stockholders' equity that took place during Year 10.

b Prepare the lower section of the income statement for the year ended December 31, Year 10, beginning with the income before extraordinary items and showing the extraordinary loss and the net income. Also illustrate the presentation of earnings per share in the income statement, assuming that earnings per share is determined on the basis of the weighted-average number of shares outstanding during the year.

c Prepare a statement of retained earnings for the year ended December 31, Year 10.

SOLUTION TO DEMONSTRATION PROBLEM

a   *General Journal*

Mar. 1 *Memorandum: Stockholders approved a 5 for 4 stock split.*
         This action increased the number of shares of common stock
         outstanding from 40,000 to 50,000 and reduced the par value
         from $10 to $8 per share.

     31 *Common Stock, $10 par*   400,000
                Common Stock, $8 par   400,000
         Distributed 10,000 additional shares of stock pursuant to 5
         for 4 stock split, and reduced par value.

Apr. 1 *Treasury Stock*   74,000
                Cash   74,000
         Acquired 2,000 shares of treasury stock at $37 per share.

July 1 *Cash*   45,000
                Treasury Stock   37,000
                Paid-in Capital from Treasury Stock Transactions   8,000
         Sold 1,000 shares of treasury stock at $45 per share.

      1 *Cash*   900,000
                Common Stock, $8 par   160,000
                Paid-in Capital in Excess of Par: Common Stock   740,000
         Issued 20,000 shares of previously unissued $8 par value
         stock for cash.

Dec. 1 *Dividends*   69,000
                Dividends Payable   69,000
         To record declaration of cash dividend of $1 per share on
         69,000 shares of common stock outstanding (1,000 shares
         in treasury are not entitled to receive dividends).

Note: Entry to record the payment of the cash dividend is not shown here since
the action does not affect the stockholders' equity.

Dec. 22 *Retained Earnings*   331,200
                Stock Dividends to be Distributed   55,200
                Paid-in Capital from Stock Dividends   276,000
         To record declaration of 10% stock dividend consisting of
         6,900 shares of $8 par value common stock to be distributed
         on Jan. 24, Year 11. Excess of fair market value of stock
         over par value, $40 ($48 − $8), is credited to Paid-in Capital
         from Stock Dividends.

31	Income Summary	177,000	
	Retained Earnings		177,000
	To close Income Summary account.		

31	Retained Earnings	69,000	
	Dividends		69,000
	To close Dividends account.		

b

SUTTON CORPORATION
Partial Income Statement
For Year Ended December 31, Year 10

Income before extraordinary items	$212,400
Extraordinary loss, net of tax effects	(35,400)
Net income	$177,000

Earnings per share:*

Income before extraordinary items	$3.60
Extraordinary loss, net of tax effects	(0.60)
Net income	$3.00

*On 59,000 weighted-average number of shares of common stock outstanding during Year 10: determined as follows:

Jan. 1–Mar. 31: (40,000 + 10,000 shares issued pursuant to a 5 for 4 split) × ¼ of year	12,500
Apr. 1–June 30: (50,000 − 2,000 shares of treasury stock) × ¼ of year	12,000
July 1–Dec. 31: (50,000 + 20,000 shares of new stock − 1,000 shares of treasury stock) × ½ of year	34,500
Weighted-average number of shares outstanding	59,000

c

SUTTON CORPORATION
Statement of Retained Earnings
For the Year Ended December 31, Year 10

Retained earnings, Jan. 1, Year 10		$1,500,000
Net income		177,000
Subtotal		$1,677,000
Dividends:		
Cash, $1 per share	$ 69,000	
Stock, 10% (to be distributed Jan. 24, Year 11)	331,200	400,200
Retained earnings, Dec. 31, Year 10		$1,276,800

REVIEW QUESTIONS

1 What is the purpose of arranging an income statement to show subtotals for Income from Continuing Operations and for Income before Extraordinary Items?

2 Define a *segment* of a business and give three examples.

3 Define *extraordinary items.* Give three examples of losses which qualify as extraordinary items and three examples of losses which would not be classified as extraordinary.

4 Briefly describe how each of the following should be reported in the income statement for the current year:

a Write-off of a large account receivable from a bankrupt customer

b Large loss from sale of a major segment of a business

c Large gain from sale of one of many investments in common stock

d Large write-off of obsolete inventory

e Large uninsured loss from earthquake

f Correction of a material error in the reported net income of an earlier year

5 Briefly define each of the following:

a Price-earnings ratio

b Primary earnings per share

c Fully diluted earnings per share

6 A financial analyst notes that Baxter Corporation's earnings per share have been rising steadily for the last five years. The analyst expects the company's net income to continue to increase at the same rate as in the past. In forecasting future primary earnings per share, what special risk should the analyst consider if Baxter's primary earnings are significantly larger than its fully diluted earnings?

7 Explain the significance of the following dates relating to dividends: date of declaration, date of record, date of payment, ex-dividend date.

8 Should stock dividends received be considered revenue to an investor? Explain.

9 Distinguish between a *stock split* and a *stock dividend.* Is there any reason for the difference in accounting treatment of these two events?

10 What are *prior period adjustments?* How are they presented in financial statements?

11 What is the purpose of an appropriation of retained earnings? What are the arguments for and against the use of such appropriations?

12 If a statement of retained earnings consisted of only four items, what would these four items most probably be?

13 What is the most effective method of disclosing in financial statements the fact that a portion of the retained earnings is restricted by the terms of a long-term debt agreement and therefore not available for payment of dividends or acquisition of treasury stock?

14 "In a long-established, successful corporation the Cash account would normally have a dollar balance equal to or larger than the Retained Earnings account." Do you agree with this quotation? Explain.

15 What is *treasury stock?* Why do corporations purchase their own shares? Is treasury stock an asset? How should it be reported in the balance sheet?

16 In many states, the corporation law requires that retained earnings be restricted for dividend purposes to the extent of the cost of treasury shares. What is the reason for this legal rule?

17 What does *book value per share* of common stock represent? Does it represent the amount common stockholders would receive in the event that the corporation were liquidated? Explain briefly.

18 How is book value per share of common stock computed when a company has both preferred and common stock outstanding?

19 What would be the effect, if any, on book value per share of common stock as a result of each of the following independent events: **(a)** a corporation obtains a bank loan; **(b)** a dividend is declared (to be paid in the next accounting period); and **(c)** a corporation issues additional shares of common stock as a stock dividend.

EXERCISES

Ex. 12-1 In Year 5, Salarno Company had net sales of $1,200,000, costs and other expenses (including income taxes) of $720,000, and an extraordinary loss (net of income tax) of $200,000. Prepare a condensed income statement (including earnings per share) for Year 5, assuming that 100,000 shares of common stock were outstanding throughout Year 5.

Ex. 12-2 The operations for National Glass, Inc., are summarized below for Year 10:

	From Continuing Operations	From Discontinued Operations
Net sales	$14,000,000	$3,000,000
Cost and expenses (including applicable income taxes)	12,200,000	2,850,000
Loss on disposal of discontinued segment, net of income taxes		450,000

National Glass, Inc., had 200,000 shares of capital stock outstanding throughout Year 10. Prepare a condensed income statement for the year, including the appropriate earnings per share.

Ex. 12-3 San Lorenzo Corporation has been in existence for three years and at the end of Year 3 intends to report earnings per share for each of the three years on a *comparable basis.* During Years 1 and 2 the common stock outstanding remained unchanged at 2,000,000 shares. In Year 3, the stock was split 3 for 1 on March 1, and 1,200,000 new shares were sold for cash on July 1. (Note that the company had the use of additional funds paid in by stockholders for the last half of Year 3.) The corporation had 7,200,000 shares outstanding at the end of Year 3.

a Compute the *weighted-average number* of shares outstanding for each year that should be used in reporting *comparative earnings per share data* in the financial statements at the end of Year 3. (Hint: For earnings per share to be comparable for all three years, the number of shares outstanding in Years 1 and 2 must be retroactively revised to reflect the stock split.)

b Assuming that net earnings were $22,500,000 in Year 1, $23,400,000 in Year 2, and $27,720,000 in Year 3, compute the earnings per share for each year to be reported on a comparable basis at the end of Year 3.

Ex. 12-4 Lee Company had 180,000 shares of $10 par common stock and 10,000 shares of $6.60 cumulative preferred stock outstanding throughout the current year. Each share of preferred stock is convertible into four shares of common stock. Net income for the current year is $660,000. Show how the primary and fully diluted earnings per share should appear in the income statement for the current year.

Ex. 12-5 Martin Corporation has a total of 20,000 shares of common stock outstanding and no preferred stock. The net assets of the Martin Corporation at the end of the current year are $750,000 and the market value of the stock is $48 per share. At year-end, the company declares a stock dividend of one share for each five shares held. If all parties concerned clearly recognized the nature of the stock dividend, what would you expect the market price per share of Martin's common stock to be on the ex-dividend date?

Ex. 12-6   Brass Corporation has 1 million shares of $5 par value capital stock outstanding. You are to prepare the journal entries to record the following transactions:

June 1 Declared a cash dividend of 80 cents per share. (Debit Dividends.)

July 1 Paid the 80-cent cash dividend to stockholders.

Aug. 1 Declared a 5% stock dividend. Market price of stock was $18 per share.

Sept. 10 Issued 50,000 shares pursuant to the 5% stock dividend.

Dec. 1 Declared a 50% stock dividend. Market price of stock was $20 per share.

Ex. 12-7   Sharon Reed owns 1,000 out of a total of 20,000 outstanding common shares of McNerney Corporation. McNerney Corporation reports assets of $1,360,000 and total liabilities of $480,000 at the end of the current year, and at that time the board declares a stock dividend of one share for each 10 shares held. Compute the book value *per share* of Reed's stock and the total book value of Reed's investment in the corporation: **(a)** before the stock dividend; **(b)** after the stock dividend.

Ex. 12-8   Presented below is the information necessary to compute the net assets (stockholders' equity) and book value per share of common stock for Ringside Corporation:

9% cumulative preferred stock, $100 par (callable at $110)	$200,000
Common stock, $5 par, authorized 100,000 shares, issued 60,000 shares	300,000
Paid-in capital in excess of par	470,800
Deficit	126,800
Dividends in arrears on preferred stock, 2 full years	36,000

Instructions

a Compute the amount of net assets (stockholders' equity).

b Compute the book value per share of common stock.

PROBLEMS

12-1   Summarized below are the operations of Multi-Media, Inc., for Year 6:

	From Continuing Operations	From Discontinued Operations
Net sales	$9,640,000	$1,940,000
Cost and expenses (including applicable income tax effects) ..	8,650,000	2,100,000
Loss on disposal of discontinued segment, net of income taxes		290,000
Extraordinary loss, net of income tax effects	310,000	

Instructions   Assuming that the company had an average of 200,000 shares of a single class of capital stock outstanding during Year 10, prepare a condensed income statement (including earnings per share).

12-2 Katherine McCall, accountant for Alternative Energy Systems, Inc., was injured in a skiing accident at year-end, and a temporary employee was assigned responsibility for preparing the financial statements. The temporary employee had a limited knowledge of accounting and improperly prepared the following income statement:

ALTERNATIVE ENERGY SYSTEMS, INC.
Income Statement
For Year 5

Net sales		$4,400,000
Gain on sale of treasury stock in Year 5 (cost $650,000;		
proceeds, $800,000)		150,000
Excess of proceeds over par value of capital stock		
issued in Year 5		960,000
Elimination of restriction of retained earnings		
(for treasury stock owned)		650,000
Total revenue		$6,160,000
Less:		
Prior period adjustment to correct valuation of land	$ 250,000	
Cost of goods sold	2,480,000	
Operating expenses	1,020,000	
Loss from tornado (net of related income tax effects)	130,000	
Dividends declared on capital stock	150,000	
Income taxes expense (other than tax effects of		
tornado loss)	420,000	4,450,000
Net income		$1,710,000

The prior period adjustment is to correct the carrying value of land which was erroneously written up to its appraised value in Year 4. At the beginning of Year 5, the company's financial statements showed retained earnings of $2,300,000, of which $650,000 was unavailable for dividends because of treasury stock owned. However, this retained earnings figure was overstated by $250,000 because of the gain erroneously recorded in Year 4 from the write-up of the land to appraised value.

The tornado loss should be reported in the income statement as an extraordinary item. An income tax advisor has correctly reduced this loss for the related tax effects. In addition, the advisor has correctly computed the income tax expense ($420,000) to be deducted in arriving at Income before Extraordinary Items.

Instructions

a Prepare a corrected income statement for Year 5. Show appropriate earnings per share figures in the income statement. Assume that the company had a weighted average of 200,000 shares of a single class of capital stock outstanding during the year.

b Prepare a statement of retained earnings for Year 5. The starting point for your statement should be retained earnings at the beginning of Year 5 as originally reported ($2,300,000).

12-3 Sea Quest Corporation operated both a fleet of commercial vessels and a chain of six seafood restaurants. The restaurants continuously lost money and were discontinued during Year 6. The company's operating results for Year 6, before incomes taxes, were as follows:

Cont   Div.

	Fishing Fleet	Seafood Restaurants
Net sales	$24,000,000	$5,200,000
Costs and expenses (including applicable income taxes)	20,100,000	6,740,000
Gain on sale of restaurant properties, net of income taxes		460,000
Extraordinary loss, net of income taxes	720,000	

The extraordinary loss resulted from the expropriation of a fishing vessel by a foreign government.

Sea Quest Corporation had 500,000 shares of common stock and 50,000 shares of 6%, $100 par value, convertible preferred stock outstanding throughout Year 6. Each share of the preferred stock is convertible into two shares of common stock.

Instructions Prepare a condensed income statement for Year 6, including proper presentation of the discontinued restaurant operations and the extraordinary loss. Include all appropriate earnings-per-share figures.

12-4 At the beginning of Year 5, Hydro-Spa Co. has total stockholders' equity of $660,000 and 20,000 outstanding shares of a single class of capital stock. During Year 5, the corporation completes the following transactions affecting its stockholders' equity accounts:

Jan. 10 A 10% stock dividend is declared and distributed. (Market price, $40 per share.)

Mar. 15 The corporation acquires 1,000 shares of its own capital stock at a cost of $40.50 per share.

May 30 All 1,000 shares of the treasury stock are reissued at a price of $44.90 per share.

July 31 The capital stock is split, two shares for one.

Dec. 15 The board of directors declares a cash dividend of $1.10 per share, payable on January 15 of Year 6.

Dec. 31 Net income of $127,600 (equal to $2.90 per share) is reported for Year 5.

Instructions Compute the amount of total stockholders' equity, the number of shares of capital stock outstanding, and the book value per share following each successive transaction. Organize your solution as a three-column schedule with separate column headings for (1) Total Stockholders' Equity, (2) Number of Shares Outstanding, and (3) Book Value per Share.

12-5 When Greg Martin was hired at the end of Year 12 as the new controller of Loma Vista Corporation, he was shown the following comparative statement of retained earnings which had been prepared by the corporation's part-time accountant:

	Year 12	Year 11
Retained earnings, Jan. 1	$754,000	$621,000
Net income	214,000	228,000
Subtotal	$968,000	$849,000
Less: Dividends	95,000	95,000
Retained earnings, Dec. 31	$873,000	$754,000

Because Loma Vista Corporation had never been audited by a firm of CPAs, Martin decided to make a careful investigation of the company's accounting records. His investigation disclosed the following errors made in prior years:

(1) In Year 6, land costing $220,000 had been written up to an appraised value of $425,000, and an "appraisal gain" of $205,000 had been included in net income of that year.

(2) In year 11, the company had recorded no depreciation expense on machinery acquired in April of that year. The unrecorded depreciation expense for Year 11 amounted to $38,000. Depreciation expense for Year 12, however, had been computed and recorded correctly.

Neither of these errors had entered into the computation of the company's income taxes. Thus, income taxes expense had been correctly computed and recorded each year.

Instructions

a Prepare the journal entries necessary at December 31, Year 12, to correct the two errors made in Years 6 and 11. Prepare a separate entry to correct each error.

b Prepare a revised comparative statement of retained earnings for Years 11 and 12. Your statement should begin with the balance of retained earnings at the beginning of Years 11 and 12 *as originally reported* and should then show any necessary prior period adjustments to these balances. The net income for Year 11 should be shown at the corrected amount. (Hint: The error made in Year 11 does not cause an error in the amount of retained earnings at the beginning of Year 11.)

12-6 Frost Corporation builds an excellent product, but the company is poorly managed. Maria Soto wants to acquire enough of the company's voting stock to elect a new board of directors which will hire new management. Soto has entered into contracts with several of Frost Corporation's stockholders to buy their common stock at a price equal to its book value at the end of Year 5. Because Frost Corporation has issued both preferred and common stock, Soto is not certain how the book value per share of common stock should be computed. She has come to you for assistance and has provided you with the following information.

At the end of Year 5, the total stockholders' equity of Frost Corporation is $1,230,000. The company was organized early in Year 1 and immediately issued 5,000 shares of 8%, $100 par, preferred stock and 30,000 shares of $5 par common stock. Except as explained below, there have been no changes in the number of shares outstanding.

Instructions Compute for Soto the book value per share of common stock at the end of Year 5 under each of the following independent assumptions:

a The preferred stock was redeemed by Frost Corporation in Year 4 and only the common stock remains outstanding.

b All shares of preferred and common stock are still outstanding. The preferred stock is callable at $105 and there are no dividends in arrears.

c The preferred stock is cumulative and callable at $108. The company paid the full preferred dividend in Years 1 and 2, but has paid no dividends in Years 3, 4, or 5.

d The preferred stock was convertible into common stock at a rate of four shares of common stock for each share of preferred. By the end of Year 5, all 5,000 shares of preferred stock had been converted into common stock.

12-7   The stockholders' equity of Geothermal Resources, Inc., at January 1, Year 5, is as follows:

Stockholders' equity:

Common stock, $5 par value, 500,000 shares authorized, 240,000 issued	$1,200,000
Paid-in capital in excess of par: common stock	4,065,000
Total paid-in capital	$5,265,000
Retained earnings	1,610,000
Total stockholders' equity	$6,875,000

During Year 5, the following transactions relating to stockholders' equity occurred:

Jan. 15 Paid a $2 per share cash dividend declared in December of Year 4. This dividend was properly recorded at the declaration date and was the only dividend declared during Year 4.

June 10 Declared a 10% stock dividend to stockholders of record on June 30, to be distributed on July 15. At June 10, the market price of the stock was $35 per share. (Debit Retained Earnings.)

July 15 Distributed the stock dividend declared on June 10.

Aug. 4 Purchased 5,200 shares of treasury stock at a price of $30 per share.

Oct. 15 Reissued 2,200 shares of treasury stock at a price of $34 per share.

Dec. 10 Reissued 1,000 shares of treasury stock at a price of $28.50 per share.

Dec. 15 Declared a cash dividend of $2 per share to be paid on January 15 of Year 6 to stockholders of record on December 31. (Debit Retained Earnings.)

Dec. 31 The Income Summary account, showing net income of $890,000, was closed into the Retained Earnings account.

Instructions

a Prepare in general journal form the entries necessary to record these transactions.

b Prepare the stockholders' equity section of the balance sheet at December 31, Year 5. Include a note following your stockholders' equity section indicating any portion of retained earnings which is not available for dividends. Also include a supporting schedule showing your computation of the balance of retained earnings at year-end.

c Comment on whether Geothermal Resources, Inc., increased or decreased the total amount of cash dividends declared during Year 5 in comparison with dividends declared in the preceding year.

12-8   The Ramirez family decided early in Year 1 to incorporate their family-owned vineyards under the name Ramirez Corporation. The corporation was authorized to issue 200,000 shares of a single class of $10 par value capital stock. Presented below is the information necessary to prepare the stockholders' equity section of the company's balance sheet at the end of Years 1 and 2.

Year 1 In January the corporation issued to members of the Ramirez family 84,000 shares of capital stock in exchange for cash and other assets used in the operation of the vineyards. The fair market value of these assets indicated an issue price of $30 per share. In December, Juan Ramirez died, and the corporation purchased 4,000 shares of its own capital stock from his estate at $35 per share. Because of the large cash outlay to acquire this treasury stock, the directors decided not to declare cash dividends in Year 1 and instead declared a 10% stock dividend to be distributed in January of Year 2. The stock price at the declaration date was $35 per share. (The treasury shares do not participate in the stock dividend.) Net income for Year 1 was $475,000.

Year 2   In January the corporation distributed the stock dividend declared in Year 1, and in February, the 4,000 treasury shares were sold to Maria Ramirez at $39 per share. In June, the capital stock was split, two shares for one. (Approval was obtained to increase the authorized number of shares to 400,000.) On December 15, the directors declared a cash dividend of $2 per share, payable in January of Year 3. Net income for Year 2 was $542,000.

Instructions   Prepare the stockholders' equity section of the balance sheet at
a December 31, Year 1
b December 31, Year 2
Show any necessary computations.

BUSINESS DECISION PROBLEM 12

Near the end of the current year, the board of directors of the Shadetree Corporation is presented with the following statement of stockholders' equity:

Capital stock (120,000 shares issued)	$2,400,000
Paid-in capital in excess of par	1,440,000
Retained earnings	1,920,000
Total stockholders' equity	$5,760,000

Shadetree Corporation has paid dividends of $3.60 per share in each of the last five years. After careful consideration of the company's cash needs, the board of directors declared a stock dividend of 24,000 shares. Shortly after the stock dividend had been distributed and before the end of the year, the company declared a cash dividend of $3 per share.

John Joseph owned 10,000 shares of Shadetree Corporation's stock, acquired several years ago. The market price of this stock before any dividend action in the current year was $60 per share.

Instructions   Based on the information given above, answer each of the following questions, showing all relevant computations.
a What is Joseph's share (in dollars) of the net assets as reported in the balance sheet of the Shadetree Corporation before the stock dividend action? What is his share after the stock dividend action? Explain why there is or is not any change as a result of the 20% stock dividend.
b What are the probable reasons why the market value of Joseph's stock differs from the amount of net assets per share shown in the accounting records?
c How does the amount of cash dividends that Joseph received in the current year compare with dividends received in prior years?
d On the day the stock went ex-dividend (with respect to the 20% stock dividend), its quoted market price fell from $60 to $50 per share. Did this represent a loss to Joseph? Explain.
e If the Shadetree Corporation had announced that it would continue its regular cash dividend of $3.60 per share on the increased number of shares outstanding after the 20% stock dividend, would you expect the market price of the stock to react in any way different from the change described in **d**? Why?

13

BONDS PAYABLE, LEASES, AND OTHER LIABILITIES

After studying this chapter you should be able to:

- Describe the typical characteristics of bonds.
- Explain the advantages of raising capital by issuing bonds instead of stock.
- Discuss the relationship between interest rates and bond prices.
- Explain how bond discount or premium affects the cost of borrowing.
- Account for bond interest payments and year-end adjustments. Amortize discount or premium by the straight-line and effective interest methods.
- Explain the accounting treatment of operating leases and of capital leases.
- Account for payrolls.
- Define loss contingencies and explain how they are presented in financial statements.

BONDS PAYABLE

Financially sound corporations may arrange some long-term loans by issuing a note payable to a bank or an insurance company. But to finance a large project, such as building a refinery or acquiring a new fleet of jumbo jets, a corporation may need more long-term financing than any single lender can supply. When a corporation needs to raise a large amount of long-term capital—perhaps 10, 50, or 100 million dollars or more—it generally sells additional shares of capital stock or issues *bonds payable*.[1]

---

[1]Bonds payable also are issued by the federal government and by many other governmental units such as states, cities, and school districts. In this chapter, our discussion is limited to corporate bonds, although many of the concepts also apply to the bond issues of governmental agencies.

The issuance of bonds payable is the equivalent of splitting a large loan into a great many units, called *bonds.* Each bond is, in essence, a long-term interest-bearing note payable, usually in the face amount of $1,000. The bonds are sold to the investing public, thus allowing many different investors to participate in the loan. An example of a corporate bond issue is the 8% sinking fund debentures of The Singer Company, due January 15, 1999. With this bond issue, The Singer Company borrowed $100 million by issuing 100,000 bonds of $1,000 each.

Issuance of bonds payable

From the viewpoint of the issuing corporation, bonds payable constitute a long-term liability. Throughout the life of this liability, the corporation makes semi-annual interest payments to the bondholders for the use of their money. A bondholder is a creditor of the corporation, not an owner. Therefore, bondholders generally do not have voting rights and do not participate in the earnings of the corporation beyond receiving the contractual, semiannual interest payments.

Authorization of a bond issue Formal approval of the board of directors and the stockholders is usually required before bonds can be issued. If the bonds are to be sold to the general public, approval must also be obtained from the SEC, just as for an issue of capital stock which is offered to the public.

The issuing corporation also selects a *trustee* to represent the interests of the bondholders. This trustee generally is a large bank or trust company. A contract is drawn up indicating the terms of the bond issue and the assets (if any) which are pledged as collateral for the bonds. Sometimes this contract places limitations on the payment of dividends to stockholders during the life of the bonds. For example, dividends may be permitted only when working capital is above specified amounts. If the issuing corporation defaults on any of the terms of this contract, the trustee may foreclose upon the assets which secure the bonds or may take other legal action on behalf of the bondholders.

The role of the underwriter in marketing a bond issue An investment banker or underwriter is usually employed to market a bond issue, just as in the case of capital stock. The corporation turns the entire bond issue over to the underwriter at a specified price; the underwriter sells the bonds to the public at a slightly higher price. By this arrangement the corporation is assured of receiving the entire proceeds on a specified date.

Transferability of bonds Corporation bonds, like capital stocks, are traded daily on organized securities exchanges. The holders of a 25-year bond issue need not wait 25 years to convert their investment into cash. By placing a telephone call to a broker, an investor may sell bonds within a matter of minutes at the going market price. This quality of liquidity is one of the most attractive features of an investment in corporation bonds.

Quoted market prices As illustrated on page 272 in Chapter 7, corporate bond prices are quoted as a *percentage* of the bond's face value or *maturity* value, which is usually $1,000. The maturity value is the amount the issuing company must pay to redeem the bond at the date it matures (becomes due). A bond quoted in the financial section of today's newspaper at *96* would therefore have a market price of $960 (96% of $1,000). Bond prices are quoted at the nearest one-eighth of a percentage point.

Types of bonds   Bonds secured by the pledge of specific assets are called *mortgage bonds.* An unsecured bond is called a *debenture bond;* its value rests upon the general credit of the corporation. A debenture bond issued by a very large and strong corporation may have a higher investment rating than a secured bond issued by a corporation in less satisfactory financial condition. For example, the $500 million of debenture bonds recently issued by IBM are rated AAA, the highest possible rating.

Some bonds have a single fixed maturity date for the entire issue. Other bond issues, called *serial bonds,* provide for varying maturity dates to lessen the problem of accumulating cash for payment. For example, serial bonds in the amount of $20 million issued in 1980 might call for $2 million of bonds to mature in 1990, and an additional $2 million to become due in each of the succeeding nine years. Almost all bonds are *callable,* which means that the corporation has the right to pay off the bonds in advance of the scheduled maturity date. To compensate the bondholders for being forced to give up their investments, the call price is usually somewhat higher than the face value of the bonds.

Most corporation bonds issued in recent years have been *registered bonds;* that is, the name of the owner is registered with the issuing corporation. Payment of interest is made by semiannual checks mailed to the registered owners. *Coupon bonds* were more popular some years ago and many are still outstanding. Coupon bonds have interest coupons attached; each six months during the life of the bond one of these coupons becomes due. The bondholder detaches the coupon and deposits it with a bank for collection. The names of the bondholders are not registered with the corporation.

As an additional attraction to investors, corporations sometimes include a conversion privilege in the bond indenture. A *convertible bond* is one which may be exchanged for common stock at the option of the bondholder. The advantages to the investor of the conversion feature in the event of increased earnings for the company were described in Chapter 11 with regard to convertible preferred stock.

Effect of bond financing on holders of capital stock

Interest payments on bonds payable are deductible as an expense by the issuing company in determining the income subject to corporation income tax, but dividends paid on capital stock are not. High tax rates on corporate earnings thus encourage the use of bonds rather than capital stock to obtain long-term capital.

Assume that a growing and profitable corporation with 100,000 shares of capital stock outstanding is in need of $10 million cash to finance the construction of a new plant. Management is considering whether to issue an additional

100,000 shares of stock or to issue 10% bonds. Assume also that after acquisition of the new plant, the annual earnings of the corporation, before deducting interest expense or income taxes, will amount to $4 million. From the viewpoint of the stockholders, which financing plan is preferable? The following schedule shows the earnings per share of capital stock under the two alternative methods of financing:

Which financing plan is better?

	If Capital Stock Is Issued	If 10% Bonds Are Issued
Annual earnings before bond interest and income taxes	$4,000,000	$4,000,000
Less: Interest on bonds (10% of $10,000,000)		1,000,000
Earnings before income taxes	$4,000,000	$3,000,000
Less: Income taxes (assume 50% rate)	2,000,000	1,500,000
Net income	$2,000,000	$1,500,000
Number of shares of capital stock outstanding	200,000	100,000
Earnings per share of capital stock	$10.00	$15.00

Financing through issuance of additional capital stock rather than issuance of bonds saves $500,000 (after taxes) but results in *lower earnings per share* because of the *dilution* caused by doubling the number of shares outstanding. Under these circumstances, stockholders should prefer financing the plant expansion through issuance of bonds, which results in higher earnings per share and possibly in higher dividends and higher market prices for the stock.

The use of borrowed capital by business firms is referred to as *leverage* or *trading on the equity;* this concept is discussed further in Chapter 16.

Accounting entries for a bond issue

Assume that Wells Corporation on January 1, Year 5, after proper authorization by the board of directors and approval by the stockholders, issues $1,000,000 of 20-year, 12% bonds payable. All the bonds bear the January 1, Year 5, date, and interest is computed from this date. Interest on the bonds is payable semiannually, each July 1 and January 1. If all the bonds are sold at par value (face value), the sale will be recorded by the following entry:

Jan. 1 Cash	1,000,000	
Bonds Payable		1,000,000
To record issuance of 12%, 20-year bonds at 100 on the		
interest date.		

The first semiannual interest payment of $60,000 would be due on July 1. The computation is ($1,000,000 × .12) ÷ 2 = $60,000. The interest payment would be recorded by the following entry:

July 1 Bond Interest Expense	60,000	
Cash		60,000
Paid semiannual interest on 12%, 20-year bonds with face amount		
of $1,000,000.		

When the bonds mature 20 years later on January 1, Year 25, the entry to record payment of the principal amount will be:

Jan. 1 Bonds Payable	1,000,000	
Cash		1,000,000
Paid face amount of bonds at maturity.		

Recording the issuance of bonds between interest dates The semiannual interest dates (such as January 1 and July 1, or April 1 and October 1) are printed on the bond certificates. However, bonds are often issued between the specified interest dates. The investor is then required to pay the interest accrued to date of issuance in addition to the stated price of the bond. This practice enables the corporation to pay a full six months' interest on all bonds outstanding at the semiannual interest payment date. The accrued interest collected from investors purchasing bonds between interest payment dates is thus returned to them on the next interest payment date. To illustrate, let us modify our present example for Wells Corporation and assume that the $1,000,000 face value of 12% bonds were issued at 100 and accrued interest, *two months after the interest date printed on the bonds*. The entry will be:

<table>
<tr><td>Bonds issued
between interest
dates</td><td>Cash ....</td><td>1,020,000</td><td></td></tr>
<tr><td></td><td>   Bonds Payable ....</td><td></td><td>1,000,000</td></tr>
<tr><td></td><td>   Bond Interest Payable ....</td><td></td><td>20,000</td></tr>
<tr><td></td><td colspan="3">Issued $1,000,000 face value of 12%, 20-year bonds at 100 plus
accrued interest for two months.</td></tr>
</table>

Four months later on the regular semiannual interest payment date, a full six months' interest ($60 per each $1,000 bond) will be paid to all bondholders, regardless of when they purchased their bonds. The entry for the semiannual interest payment is illustrated below:

<table>
<tr><td>What is the net
interest expense?</td><td>Bond Interest Payable ....</td><td>20,000</td><td></td></tr>
<tr><td></td><td>Bond Interest Expense ....</td><td>40,000</td><td></td></tr>
<tr><td></td><td>   Cash ....</td><td></td><td>60,000</td></tr>
<tr><td></td><td colspan="3">Paid semiannual interest on $1,000,000 face value of 12% bonds.</td></tr>
</table>

Now consider these interest transactions from the standpoint of the investors. They paid for two months' accrued interest at the time of purchasing the bonds, and they received checks for six months' interest after holding the bonds for only four months. They have, therefore, been reimbursed properly for the use of their money for four months.

When bonds are subsequently sold by one investor to another, they sell at the quoted market price *plus accrued interest* since the last interest payment date. This practice enables the issuing corporation to pay all the interest for an interest period to the investor owning the bond at the interest date. Otherwise, the corporation would have to make partial payments to every investor who bought or sold the bond during the interest period.

The amount which investors will pay for bonds is the *present value* of the principal and interest payments they will receive. Before going further in our discussion of bonds payable, it will be helpful to review the concepts of present value and effective yield.

The concept of present value

The concept of present value is based upon the "time value" of money—the idea that receiving money today is preferable to receiving money at some later date. Assume, for example, that a bond will have a maturity value of $1,000 five years from today but will pay no interest in the meantime. Investors would not pay $1,000 for this bond today, because they would receive no return on their investment over the next five years. There are prices less than $1,000, however, at which investors would buy the bond. For example, if the bond could be purchased for $600, the investor could expect a return (interest) of $400 from the investment over the five-year period.

The *present value* of a future cash receipt is the amount that a knowledgeable investor will pay *today* for the right to receive that future payment. The exact amount of the present value depends upon (1) the amount of the future payment, (2) the length of time until the payment will be received, and (3) the rate of return required by the investor. However, the present value will always be *less* than the future amount. This is because money received today can be invested to earn interest and thereby becomes equivalent to a larger amount in the future.

The rate of interest which will cause a given present value to grow to a given future amount is called the discount rate or *effective interest rate.* The effective interest rate required by investors at any given time is regarded as the going *market rate* of interest. The procedures for computing the present value of a future amount are illustrated in an appendix following this chapter.

The present value concept and bond prices

The price at which bonds will sell is the present value to investors of the future principal and interest payments.[2] If the bonds sell at par, the effective interest rate is equal to the *contract interest rate* (or nominal rate) printed on the bonds. The higher the effective interest rate investors require, the less they will pay for bonds with a given contract rate of interest. For example, if investors insist upon a 10% return, they will pay less than $1,000 for a 9%, $1,000 bond. Thus, if investors require an effective interest rate *greater* than the contract rate of

---

[2] The mechanics of determining the market price of a bond issue using present value techniques are illustrated in the appendix following this chapter.

interest for the bonds, the bonds will sell at a *discount* (price less than face value). On the other hand, if investors require an effective interest rate of *less* than the contract rate, the bonds will sell at a *premium* (price above face value).

A corporation wishing to borrow money by issuing bonds must pay the going market rate of interest. Since market rates of interest are fluctuating constantly, it must be expected that the contract rate of interest may vary somewhat from the market rate at the date the bonds are issued. Thus, bonds often are issued at either a discount or a premium.

Bond prices after issuance   As stated earlier, many corporate bonds are traded daily on organized securities exchanges at quoted market prices. After bonds are issued, their market prices vary *inversely* with changes in market interest rates. As interest rates rise, investors will be willing to pay less money to own a bond that pays a given contract rate of interest. Conversely, as interest rates decline, the market prices of bonds rise.

Bonds sold at a discount

To illustrate the sale of bonds at a discount, assume that a corporation plans to issue $1,000,000 face value of 9%, 10-year bonds. At the issuance date, however, the going market rate of interest is slightly above 9% and the bonds sell at a price of only 98 ($980 for each $1,000 bond). The issuance of the bonds will be recorded by the following entry:

Issuing bonds at discount

Cash	980,000	
Discount on Bonds Payable	20,000	
Bonds Payable		1,000,000
Issued $1,000,000 face value of 9%, 10-year bonds at 98.		

If a balance sheet is prepared immediately after the issuance of the bonds, the liability for bonds payable will be shown as follows:

Liability shown net of discount

Long-term liabilities:		
9% bonds payable, due Dec. 31, Year 10	*$1,000,000*	
Less: Discount on bonds payable	*20,000*	*$980,000*

The amount of the discount is deducted from the face value of the bonds payable to show the present value or *carrying value* of the liability. At the date of issuance, the carrying value of bonds payable is equal to the amount for which the bonds were sold. In other words, the amount of the company's liability at the date of issuing the bonds is equal to the amount of money borrowed. Over the life of the bonds, however, we shall see that this carrying value gradually increases until it reaches the face value of the bonds at the maturity date.

Bond discount as part of the cost of borrowing   In Chapter 8, we illustrated two ways in which interest charges can be specified in a note payable: the interest may be stated as an annual percentage rate of the face amount of the note, or it may be included in the face amount. Bonds issued at a discount include *both* types of interest charge. The $1,000,000 bond issue in our example calls for cash interest payments of $90,000 per year ($1,000,000 × 9% contract interest rate), payable semiannually. In addition to making the semiannual interest payments, the corporation must redeem the bond issue for $1 million on December 31, Year 10. This maturity value is $20,000 greater than the $980,000 received when the bonds were issued. Thus, the $20,000 discount in the issue price may be regarded as an *interest charge included in the maturity value of the bonds.*

Although the interest charge represented by the discount will not be paid to bondholders until the bonds mature, the corporation benefits from this cost during the entire period that it has the use of the bondholders' money. Therefore, the cost represented by the discount should be allocated over the life of the bond issue. The process of allocating bond discount to interest expense is termed *amortization* of the discount.

In short, whenever bonds are issued at a discount, the total interest cost over the life of the bonds is equal to the total regular cash interest payments *plus the amount of the discount.* For the $1 million bond issue in our example, the total interest cost over the 10-year life of the bonds is $920,000, of which $900,000 represents the 20 semiannual cash interest payments and $20,000 represents the discount. The average annual interest expense, therefore, is $92,000 ($920,000 ÷ 10 years), consisting of $90,000 paid in cash and $2,000 amortization of the bond discount. This analysis is illustrated below:

Total cash interest payments to bondholders		
($1,000,000 × 9% × 10 years)		$900,000
Add: Interest charge included in face amount of bonds:		
Maturity value of bonds	$1,000,000	
Amount borrowed	980,000	20,000
Total cost of borrowing over life of bond issue		$920,000
Average annual interest expense ($920,000 ÷ 10 years)		$ 92,000

Amortization of bond discount

The simplest method of amortizing bond discount is the *straight-line method,* which allocates an equal portion of the discount to Bond Interest Expense in each period.[3] In our example, the Discount on Bonds Payable account has an initial debit balance of $20,000; each year one-tenth of this amount, or $2,000, will be amortized into Bond Interest Expense. Assuming that the interest payment dates are June 30 and December 31, the entries to be made each six months to record bond interest expense are as follows:

Payment of bond interest and straight-line amortization of bond discount

Bond Interest Expense	45,000	
Cash		45,000
Paid semiannual interest on $1,000,000 of 9%, 10-year bonds.		
Bond Interest Expense	1,000	
Discount on Bonds Payable		1,000
Amortized discount for six months on 10-year bond issue ($20,000 discount × 1/20).		

---

[3]An alternative method of amortization, called the *effective interest method,* is illustrated later in this chapter. Although the effective interest method is theoretically preferable to the straight-line method, the resulting differences generally are not material in dollar amount.

The two entries shown above to record the cash payment of bond interest and to record the amortization of bond discount can conveniently by combined into one compound entry, as follows:

Bond Interest Expense	*46,000*	
Cash		*45,000*
Discount on Bonds Payable		*1,000*

To record payment of semiannual interest on $1,000,000 of 9%, 10-year bonds ($1,000,000 × 9% × ½) and to amortize ¹⁄₂₀ of the discount on the 10-year bond issue.

Regardless of whether the cash payment of interest and the amortization of bond discount are recorded in separate entries or combined in one entry, the amount recognized as Bond Interest Expense is the same—$46,000 each six months, or a total of $92,000 a year. An alternative accounting procedure that will produce the same results is to amortize the bond discount only at year-end rather than at each interest-payment date.

Note that the additional interest expense resulting from amortization of the discount does not require any additional cash payment. The credit portion of the entry is to the contra-liability account, Discount on Bonds Payable, rather than to the Cash account. Crediting this contra-liability account *increases the carrying value of bonds payable.* The original $20,000 discount will be completely written off by the end of the tenth year, and the net liability (carrying value) will be the full face value of the bonds.

Bonds sold at a premium

Bonds will sell above par if the contract rate of interest specified on the bonds is higher than the current market rate for bonds of this grade. Let us now change our basic illustration by assuming that the $1 million issue of 9%, 10-year bonds is sold at a price of 102 ($1,020 for each $1,000 bond). The entry is shown below:

Issuing bonds at premium

Cash	*1,020,000*	
Bonds Payable		*1,000,000*
Premium on Bonds Payable		*20,000*

Issued $1,000,000 face value of 9%, 10-year bonds at price of 102.

If a balance sheet is prepared immediately following the sale of the bonds, the liability will be shown as follows:

Carrying value increased by premium

Long-term liabilities:		
9% bonds payable, due Dec. 31, Year 10	*$1,000,000*	
Add: Premium on bonds payable	*20,000*	*$1,020,000*

The amount of any unamortized premium is *added* to the maturity value of the bonds payable to show the current carrying value of the liability. Over the life of the bond issue, this carrying value will be reduced toward the maturity value of $1,000,000.

Bond premium as reduction in the cost of borrowing We have illustrated how issuing bonds at a discount increases the cost of borrowing above the amount of the regular cash interest payments. Issuing bonds at a premium, on the other hand, *reduces the cost of borrowing below the amount of the regular cash interest payments.*

The amount received from issuance of the bonds is $20,000 greater than the amount which must be repaid at maturity. This $20,000 premium is not a gain but is to be offset against the periodic interest payments in determining the net cost of borrowing. Whenever bonds are issued at a premium, the total interest cost over the life of the bonds is equal to the regular cash interest payments *minus the amount of the premium.* In our example, the total interest cost over the life of the bonds is computed as $900,000 of cash interest payments minus $20,000 of premium amortized, or a net borrowing cost of $880,000. The annual interest expense will be $88,000, consisting of $90,000 paid in cash less an offsetting $2,000 transferred from the Premium on Bonds Payable account to the credit side of the Bond Interest Expense account.

The semiannual entries on June 30 and December 31 to record the payment of bond interest and amortization of bond premium are as follows:

Payment of bond interest and straight-line amortization of bond premium

Bond Interest Expense	45,000	
Cash		45,000
Paid semiannual interest on $1,000,000 of 9%, 10-year bonds.		
Premium on Bonds Payable	1,000	
Bond Interest Expense		1,000
Amortized premium for six months on 10-year bond issue ($20,000 × ¹⁄₂₀).		

Year-end adjustments for bond interest expense

In the preceding illustration, it was assumed that one of the semiannual dates for payment of bond interest coincided with the end of the company's accounting year. In most cases, however, the semiannual interest payment dates will fall during an accounting period rather than on the last day of the year.

For purposes of illustration, assume that $1 million of 12%, 10-year bonds are issued at a price of 97 on October 1, Year 1. Interest payment dates are April 1 and October 1. The total discount to be amortized amounts to $30,000, or $1,500 in each six-month interest period. The company keeps its accounts on a calendar-year basis; consequently, the adjusting entries shown below will be necessary at December 31 for the accrued interest and the amortization of discount applicable to the three-month period since the bonds were issued.

Bond Interest Expense	30,750	
Bond Interest Payable		30,000
Discount on Bonds Payable		750
To adjust for accrued interest on bonds and to amortize discount for		
period from Oct. 1 to Dec. 31. Accrued interest: $1,000,000 × .12 × ³⁄₁₂ =		
$30,000. Amortization: $30,000 × ³⁄₁₂₀ = $750.		

If the above bonds had been issued at a premium, similar entries would be made at the end of the period for any accrued interest and for amortization of premium for the fractional period from October 1 to December 31.

In the December 31, Year 1, balance sheet, the $30,000 of accrued bond interest payable will appear as a current liability; the long-term liability for bonds payable will appear as follows:

Long-term liabilities:
12% Bonds payable, due Oct. 1, Year 11	$1,000,000	
Less: Discount on bonds payable	29,250	$970,750

When the bonds were issued on October 1, the net liability for bonds payable was $970,000. Notice that the carrying value of the bonds has *increased* over the three months by the amount of discount amortized. When the entire discount has been amortized, the carrying value of the bonds will be $1,000,000, which is equal to their maturity value.

At April 1, Year 2, it is necessary to record interest expense and discount amortization only for the three-month period since year-end. Of the semiannual $60,000 cash payment to bondholders, one-half, or $30,000, represents payment of the liability for bond interest payable recorded on December 31, Year 1. The entry on April 1 is:

Bond Interest Expense	*30,750*	
Bond Interest Payable	*30,000*	
Discount on Bonds Payable		*750*
Cash		*60,000*

To record bond interest expense and amortization of discount for three-month period since year-end and to record semiannual payment to bondholders.

Straight-line amortization: a theoretical shortcoming

Although the straight-line method of amortizing bond discount or premium recognizes the full cost of borrowing over the life of a bond issue, the method has one conceptual weakness: the same dollar amount of interest expense is recognized each year. Amortizing a discount, however, causes a gradual increase in the liability for bonds payable; amortizing a premium causes a gradual decrease in the liability. If the uniform annual interest expense is expressed as a *percentage* of either an increasing or a decreasing liability, it appears that the borrower's cost of capital is changing over the life of the bonds.

This problem can be avoided by using the *effective interest method* of amortizing bond discount or premium. The effective interest method recognizes annual interest expense equal to a *constant percentage of the carrying value of the related liability.* This percentage is the effective rate of interest incurred by the borrower. For this reason, the effective interest method of amortization is considered theoretically preferable to the straight-line method. Whenever the two methods would produce *materially different* annual results, the Financial Accounting Standards Board requires the use of the effective interest method.

Over the life of the bonds, both amortization methods recognize the same total amount of interest expense. Even on an annual basis, the results produced by the two methods usually are very similar. Consequently, either method generally would meet the requirements of the FASB. Because of its simplicity, the straight-line method is widely used despite the theoretical arguments favoring the effective interest method.

Effective interest method of amortization

When bonds are sold at a discount, the effective interest rate incurred by the issuing corporation is *higher* than the contract rate printed on the bonds. Conversely, when bonds are sold at a premium, the effective rate of interest is *lower* than the contract rate.

When the effective interest method is used, bond interest expense is determined by multiplying the *carrying value of the bonds* at the beginning of the period by the *effective rate of interest* for the bond issue. The amount of discount or premium to be amortized is the *difference* between the interest expense computed in this manner and the amount of interest paid (or payable) to bondholders for the period. The computation of effective interest expense and the amount of discount or premium amortization for the life of the bond issue is made in advance on a schedule called an *amortization table.*

Sale of bonds at a discount   To illustrate the effective interest method, assume that on May 1, Year 1, a corporation issues $1,000,000 face value, 9%, 10-year bonds with interest dates of November 1 and May 1. The bonds sell for $937,689, a price resulting in an effective interest rate of 10%.[4] An amortization table for this bond issue is shown on the next page. (Amounts of interest expense have been rounded to the nearest dollar.)

This amortization table can be used to illustrate the concepts underlying the effective interest method of determining interest expense and discount amortization. Note that the "interest periods" in the table are the *semiannual* (six-month) interest periods. Thus, the interest payments (column A), interest expense (column B), and discount amortization (column C) are for six-month periods. Similarly, the balance of the Discount on Bonds Payable account (column D) and the carrying value of the liability (column E) are shown as of each semiannual interest payment date.

The original issuance price of the bonds ($937,689) is entered at the top of column E. This represents the carrying value of the liability throughout the first six-month interest period. The semiannual interest payment, shown in column A, is 4½% (one-half of the annual contract rate) of the $1,000,000 face value of

---

[4]Computation of the exact effective interest rate involves mathematical techniques beyond the scope of this course. A very close estimate of the effective interest rate can be obtained by dividing the **average** annual interest expense by the **average** carrying value of the bonds. Computation of average annual interest expense was illustrated on page 490. The average carrying value of the bonds is found by adding the issue price and the maturity value of the bond issue and dividing this sum by 2. Applying these procedures to the bond issue in our example provides an estimated effective interest rate of 9.93%, computed [($900,000 interest + $62,311 discount) ÷ 10 years] divided by [($937,689 + $1,000,000) ÷ 2].

Amortization Table for Bonds Sold at a Discount

**($1,000,000, 10-year bonds, 9% interest payable semiannually,
sold at $937,689 to yield 10% compounded semiannually)**

Six-Month Interest Period	(A) Interest Paid Semiannually (4½% of Face Value)	(B) Effective Semiannual Interest Expense (5% of Bond Carrying Value)	(C) Discount Amortiz-ation (B − A)	(D) Bond Discount Balance	(E) Carrying Value of Bonds, End of Period ($1,000,000 − D)
Issue date				$62,311	$ 937,689
1	$45,000	$46,884	$1,884	60,427	939,573
2	45,000	46,979	1,979	58,448	941,552
3	45,000	47,078	2,078	56,370	943,630
4	45,000	47,182	2,182	54,188	945,812
5	45,000	47,291	2,291	51,897	948,103
6	45,000	47,405	2,405	49,492	950,508
7	45,000	47,525	2,525	46,967	953,033
8	45,000	47,652	2,652	44,315	955,685
9	45,000	47,784	2,784	41,531	958,469
10	45,000	47,923	2,923	38,608	961,392
11	45,000	48,070	3,070	35,538	964,462
12	45,000	48,223	3,223	32,315	967,685
13	45,000	48,384	3,384	28,931	971,069
14	45,000	48,553	3,553	25,378	974,622
15	45,000	48,731	3,731	21,647	978,353
16	45,000	48,918	3,918	17,729	982,271
17	45,000	49,114	4,114	13,615	986,385
18	45,000	49,319	4,319	9,296	990,704
19	45,000	49,535	4,535	4,761	995,239
20	45,000	49,761*	4,761	−0−	1,000,000

*In the last period, interest expense is equal to interest paid to bondholders plus the remaining balance on the bond discount. This compensates for the accumulated effects of rounding amounts.

the bond issue. The semiannual cash interest payment does not change over the life of the bonds. The interest expense shown in column B, however, *changes every period.* This expense is always a *constant percentage* of the carrying value of the liability as of the end of the preceding period. The "constant percentage" is the effective interest rate of the bond issue. The bonds have an effective annual interest rate of 10%, indicating a semiannual rate of 5%. Thus, the effective interest expense for the first six-month period is $46,884 (5% of $937,689). The discount amortization for period 1 is the difference between this effective interest expense and the contract rate of interest paid to bondholders.

After the discount is reduced by $1,884 at the end of period 1, the carrying value of the bonds in column E *increases* by $1,884 (from $937,689 to $939,573). In period 2, the effective interest expense is determined by multiplying the effective semiannual interest rate of 5% by this new carrying value of $939,573 (5% × $939,573 = $46,979).

Semiannual interest expense may be recorded every period directly from the data in the amortization table. For example, the entry to record bond interest expense at the end of the first six-month period is:

Bond Interest Expense	46,884	
Discount on Bonds Payable		1,884
Cash		45,000

To record semiannual interest payment and amortize discount for six months.

Similarly, interest expense at the end of the fifteenth six-month period would be recorded by:

Bond Interest Expense	48,731	
Discount on Bonds Payable		3,731
Cash		45,000

To record semiannual interest payment and amortize discount for six months.

When bond discount is amortized, the carrying value of the liability for bonds payable *increases* every period toward the maturity value. Since the effective interest expense in each period is a constant percentage of this increasing carrying value, the interest expense also increases from one period to the next. This is the basic difference between the effective interest method and straight-line amortization.

Sale of bonds at a premium   Let us now change our basic illustration by assuming that the $1,000,000 issue of 9%, 10-year bonds is sold on May 1, Year 1, at a price of $1,067,952, resulting in an effective interest rate of 8% annually (4% per six-month interest period). (See the amortization table on the next page.)

In this amortization table, the interest expense for each six-month period is equal to 4% of the carrying value at the beginning of that period. This amount of interest expense is less than the amount of cash being paid to bondholders, illustrating that the effective interest rate is less than the contract rate.

Based upon this amortization table, the entry to record the interest payment and amortization of the premium for the first six months of the bond issue is:

Amortization of premium decreases interest expense

Bond Interest Expense	42,718	
Premium on Bonds Payable	2,282	
Cash		45,000

To record semiannual interest payment and amortization of premium.

As the carrying value of the liability declines, so does the amount recognized as bond interest expense.

Year-end adjusting entries   Since the amounts recognized as interest expense change from one period to the next, we must refer to the appropriate interest

Amortization Table for Bonds Sold at a Premium

**($1,000,000, 10-year bonds, 9% interest payable semiannually,
sold at $1,067,952 to yield 8% compounded semiannually)**

Six-Month Interest Period	(A) Interest Paid Semiannually (4½% of Face Value)	(B) Effective Semiannual Interest Expense (4% of Bond Carrying Value)	(C) Premium Amortiz- ation (A − B)	(D) Bond Premium Balance	(E) Carrying Value of Bonds, End of Period ($1,000,000 + D)
Issue date				$67,952	$1,067,952
1	$45,000	$42,718	$2,282	65,670	1,065,670
2	45,000	42,627	2,373	63,297	1,063,297
3	45,000	42,532	2,468	60,829	1,060,829
4	45,000	42,433	2,567	58,262	1,058,262
5	45,000	42,330	2,670	55,592	1,055,592
6	45,000	42,224	2,776	52,816	1,052,816
7	45,000	42,113	2,887	49,929	1,049,929
8	45,000	41,997	3,003	46,926	1,046,926
9	45,000	41,877	3,123	43,803	1,043,803
10	45,000	41,752	3,248	40,555	1,040,555
11	45,000	41,622	3,378	37,177	1,037,177
12	45,000	41,487	3,513	33,664	1,033,664
13	45,000	41,347	3,653	30,011	1,030,011
14	45,000	41,200	3,800	26,211	1,026,211
15	45,000	41,048	3,952	22,259	1,022,259
16	45,000	40,890	4,110	18,149	1,018,149
17	45,000	40,726	4,274	13,875	1,013,875
18	45,000	40,555	4,445	9,430	1,009,430
19	45,000	40,377	4,623	4,807	1,004,807
20	45,000	40,193*	4,807	–0–	1,000,000

*In the last period, interest expense is equal to interest paid to bondholders minus the remaining balance of the bond premium. This compensates for the accumulated effects of rounding amounts.

period in the amortization table to obtain the dollar amounts for use in year-end adjusting entries. To illustrate, consider our example of the bonds sold at a premium on May 1, Year 1. The entry shown above records interest and amortization of the premium through November 1, Year 1. If the company keeps its accounts on a calendar-year basis, two months' interest has accrued as of December 31, Year 1, and the following adjusting entry is made at year-end:

Year-end adjustment	Bond Interest Expense	14,209	
	Premium on Bonds Payable	791	
	Bond Interest Payable		15,000

To record two months' accrued interest and amortize one-third of the premium for the interest period.

This adjusting entry covers one-third (two months) of the second interest period. Consequently, the amounts shown as bond interest expense and amortization of premium are one-third of the amounts shown in the amortization table for the second interest period. Similar adjusting entries must be made at the end of every accounting period while the bonds are outstanding. The dollar amounts of these adjusting entries will vary, however, because the amounts of interest expense and premium amortization change in every interest period. The amounts applicable to any given adjusting entry will be the appropriate fraction of the amounts for the interest period then in progress.

Following the year-end adjusting entry illustrated above, the interest expense and premium amortization on May 1, Year 2, are recorded as follows:

Interest payment following year-end adjustment

Bond Interest Expense	*28,418*	
Bond Interest Payable	*15,000*	
Premium on Bonds Payable	*1,582*	
Cash		*45,000*

To record semiannual interest payment, a portion of which had been accrued, and amortize remainder of premium applicable to interest period.

Amortization of bond discount or premium from the investor's viewpoint

We have discussed the need for the corporation issuing bonds payable to amortize any bond discount or premium to measure correctly the bond interest expense. But what about the *purchaser* of the bonds? Should an investor in bonds amortize any difference between the cost of the investment and its future maturity value in order to measure investment income correctly? The answer to this question depends upon whether the investor considers the bonds to be a *short-term* or a *long-term* investment.

A short-term investment in bonds generally is carried in the investor's accounting records at *cost,* and a gain or a loss is recognized when the investment is sold. Short-term investments in bonds usually will be sold before the bonds mature and the sales price will be determined by the current state of the bond market. Under these conditions, there is no assurance that amortization of premium or discount would give any more accurate measurement of investment income than would be obtained by carrying the bonds at cost.

When bonds are owned for the long term, however, it becomes more probable that the market price of the investment will move toward the maturity value of the bonds. At the maturity date the market value equals the maturity value of the bonds. Thus, companies making long-term investments in bonds *should* amortize over the life of the bonds any difference between the cost of the investment and its maturity value. If the effective interest method of amortization would produce results materially different from those obtained by the straight-line method, the effective interest method should be used.[5]

---

[5]*APB Opinion No. 21,* "Interest on Receivables and Payables," AICPA (New York: 1971), p. 423.

Retirement of bonds payable

Bonds are sometimes retired before the maturity date. The principal reason for retiring bonds early is to relieve the issuing corporation of the obligation to make future interest payments. If interest rates decline to the point that a corporation can borrow at an interest rate below that being paid on a particular bond issue, the corporation may benefit from retiring those bonds and issuing new bonds at a lower interest rate.

Most bond issues contain a call provision, permitting the corporation to redeem the bonds by paying a specified price, usually a few points above par. Even without a call provision, the corporation may retire its bonds before maturity by purchasing them in the open market. If the bonds can be purchased by the issuing corporation at less than their *carrying value,* a gain is realized on the retirement of the debt. If the bonds are reacquired by the issuing corporation at a price in excess of their carrying value, a loss must be recognized. The FASB has ruled that these gains and losses, if *material* in amount, should be shown separately in the income statement as extraordinary items.[6]

For example, assume that the Briggs Corporation has outstanding a $1 million bond issue with unamortized premium in the amount of $20,000. The bonds are callable at 105 and the company exercises the call provision on 100 of the bonds, or 10% of the issue. The entry would be as follows:

Bonds called at price above carrying value

Bonds Payable 100,000	
Premium on Bonds Payable 2,000	
Loss on Retirement of Bonds 3,000	
Cash	105,000

To record retirement of $100,000 face value of bonds called at 105.

The carrying value of each of the 100 called bonds was $1,020, whereas the call price was $1,050. For each bond called the company incurred a loss of $30, or a total loss of $3,000. Note that when 10% of the total issue was called, 10% of the unamortized premium was written off.

If bonds remain outstanding until the maturity date, the discount or premium will have been completely amortized and the accounting entry to retire the bonds (assuming that interest is paid separately) will consist of a debit to Bonds Payable and a credit to Cash.

One year before the maturity date, the bonds payable may be reclassified from long-term debt to a current liability in the balance sheet if payment is to be made from current assets rather than from a *bond sinking fund.*

Bond sinking fund

To make a bond issue attractive to investors, corporations may agree to create a sinking fund, exclusively for use in paying the bonds at maturity. A bond sinking fund is created by setting aside a specified amount of cash at regular intervals.

---

[6]Financial Accounting Standards Board, *Statement No. 4,* "Reporting Gains and Losses from Extinguishment of Debt," FASB (Stamford, Conn.: 1975).

The cash is usually deposited with a trustee, who invests it and adds the earnings to the amount of the sinking fund. The periodic deposits of cash plus the earnings on the sinking fund investments should cause the fund to equal approximately the amount of the bond issue by the maturity date. When the bond issue approaches maturity, the trustee sells all the securities in the fund and uses the cash proceeds to pay the holders of the bonds. Any excess cash remaining in the fund will be returned to the corporation by the trustee.

A bond sinking fund is not included in current assets because it is not available for payment of current liabilities. The cash and securities comprising the fund are usually shown as a single amount under a caption such as Long-Term Investments, which is placed just below the current asset section. Interest earned on sinking fund securities constitutes revenue to the corporation.

Conversion of bonds payable into common stock

Convertible bonds represent a popular form of financing, particularly during periods when common stock prices are rising. The conversion feature gives bondholders an opportunity to profit from a rise in the market price of the issuing company's common stock while still maintaining their status of creditors rather than stockholders. Because of this potential gain, convertible bonds generally carry lower interest rates than nonconvertible bonds.

The conversion ratio is typically set at a price above the current market price of the common stock at the date the bonds are authorized. For example, if common stock with a par value of $10 a share has a current market price of $42 a share, the *conversion price* might be set at $50 per share, thus enabling a holder of a $1,000 par value convertible bond to exchange the bond for 20 shares of common stock.[7] Let us assume that $5 million of such bonds are issued at par, and that some time later when the common stock has risen in price to $60 per share, the holders of 100 bonds decide to convert their bonds into common stock. The conversion transaction would be recorded as follows:

Conversion of bonds into common stock

Convertible Bonds Payable	100,000	
Common Stock, $10 par		20,000
Paid-in Capital in Excess of Par		80,000

To record the conversion of 100 bonds into 2,000 shares of common stock.

No gain or loss is recognized by the issuing corporation upon conversion of bonds; the carrying value of the bonds is simply assigned to the common stock issued in exchange. If the bonds had been issued at a price above or below face value, the unamortized premium or discount relating to the bonds would be written off at the time of conversion in order to assign the carrying value of the bonds to the common stock.

---

[7]$1,000 ÷ $50 conversion price = 20 shares of common stock.

LEASES

A company may purchase the assets needed for use in its business or it may choose to lease them. Examples of assets often acquired by lease include buildings, office equipment, automobiles, and factory machinery. A *lease* is a contract in which the *lessor* gives the *lessee* the right to use an asset in return for periodic rental payments. The lessor is the owner of the property; the lessee is the tenant or renter. Accounting for the many forms of lease transactions and the disclosure of lease obligations by lessees are among the more important issues facing accountants today.

Operating lease

When the lessor gives the lessee the right to use the leased property for a limited period of time but retains the usual risks and rewards of ownership, the contract is known as an *operating lease*. In accounting for an operating lease, the lessor accounts for the monthly lease payments received as rental revenue. The lessee accounts for the lease payments as rental expense; no asset or liability (other than a short-term liability for accrued rent payable) relating to the lease is recorded in the lessee's accounts.

Capital lease

When the objectives of the lease contract are to provide financing to the lessee for the eventual purchase of the property, or for use of the property over most of its useful life, the contract is referred to as a *capital lease* (or a *financing lease*). Even though title to the leased property has not been transferred, capital leases are regarded as *essentially equivalent to a sale* of the property by the lessor to the lessee. Thus, a capital lease should be recorded by the lessor as a *sale* of property and by the lessee as a *purchase*. In such lease agreements, an appropriate interest charge usually is added to the regular sales price of the property in determining the total amount of the lease payments.

Some manufacturing companies frequently use capital lease agreements as a means of financing the sale of their products to customers. In accounting for merchandise "sold" through a capital lease, the lessor debits Lease Payments Receivable and credits Sales for an amount equal to the *present value of the future lease payments.*[8] In most cases, the present value of these future payments is equal to the regular sales price of the merchandise. In addition, the lessor transfers the cost of the leased merchandise from the Inventory account to the Cost of Goods Sold account (assuming a perpetual inventory system is in use). When lease payments are received, the lessor should recognize an appropriate portion of the payment as representing interest revenue and the remainder as a reduction in Lease Payments Receivable.

---

[8]We have elected to record the present value of the future lease payments by a single debit entry to Lease Payments Receivable. An alternative is to debit Lease Payments Receivable for the total amount of the future payments and to credit Discount on Lease Payments Receivable, a contra-asset account, for the unearned finance charges included in the contractual amount. Either approach results in the lessor recording a net receivable equal to the present value of the future lease payments.

When equipment is acquired through a capital lease, the lessee should debit an asset account, Leased Equipment, and credit a liability account, Lease Payment Obligation, for the present value of the future lease payments. Lease payments made by the lessee are allocated between Interest Expense and a reduction in the liability, Lease Payment Obligation. No rent expense is involved. The asset account, Leased Equipment, is depreciated over the life of the equipment rather than the life of the lease. (The journal entries used in accounting for a capital lease are illustrated on page 529 of the appendix to this chapter.)

Distinguishing between capital leases and operating leases   In *Statement No. 13,* the FASB required that a lease which meets at least one of the following criteria be accounted for as a capital lease:[9]

1 The lease transfers ownership of the property to the lessee at the end of the lease term.
2 The lease contains a "bargain purchase option."
3 The lease term is equal to 75% or more of the estimated economic life of the property.
4 The present value of the minimum lease payments is at least 90% of the fair value of the lease property.

Only those leases which meet none of the above criteria may be accounted for as operating leases.

New standards reduce off-balance-sheet financing   Prior to the issuance of *FASB Statement No. 13,* the criteria defining capital leases were much narrower. As a result, a great number of long-term leases were accounted for as operating leases by the lessees. Operating leases often are called *off-balance-sheet financing,* because the obligation for future lease payments does not appear as a liability in the balance sheet of the lessee. As a result of the criteria set forth in *Statement No. 13,* the number of lease contracts qualifying as operating leases has been greatly reduced. In the opinion of the authors, accounting for long-term lease contracts as capital leases significantly improves the usefulness of the balance sheet in evaluating the resources and obligations of companies which lease substantial portions of their productive assets.

A number of more complex issues and special situations are involved in accounting for leases; these are covered in intermediate accounting.

OTHER LIABILITIES
Mortgage notes payable

Purchases of real estate and certain types of equipment often are financed by the issuance of mortgage notes payable. When a mortgage note is issued, the borrower pledges title to specific assets as collateral for the loan. If the borrower defaults on the note, the lender may foreclose upon these assets. Mortgage notes usually are payable in equal monthly installments. These monthly installments

---

[9]*FASB Statement No. 13,* "Accounting for Leases" (Stamford, Conn.: 1976), pp. 9–10.

may continue until the loan is completely repaid, or the note may contain a "due date" at which the remaining unpaid balance of the loan must be repaid in a single, lump-sum payment.

A portion of each monthly payment represents interest on the unpaid balance of the loan and the remainder of the monthly payment reduces the amount of the unpaid balance (principal). Since the principal is being reduced each month, the portion of each successive payment representing interest will *decrease*, and the portion of the payment going toward repayment of the principal will *increase*. To illustrate, assume that on June 30 a company issues a $100,000 mortgage note to finance the purchase of a warehouse. The note requires monthly payments in the amount of $1,250 and bears interest at the annual rate of 12% (equal to 1% per month). The following partial amortization table shows the allocation of the first three monthly payments between interest and principal:

		(A)	(B) Monthly Interest Expense (1% of Unpaid Balance)	(C) Reduction in Principal (A − B)	(D) Unpaid Principal Balance
	Payment Date	Monthly Payment			
Monthly payments on a mortgage note	June 30—Issuance date				$100,000.00
	July 31	$1,250.00	$1,000.00	$250.00	99,750.00
	Aug. 31	1,250.00	997.50	252.50	99,497.50
	Sept. 30	1,250.00	994.98	255.02	99,242.48

The entry to record the first monthly mortgage payment on July 31 would be:

Payment is allocated between interest and principal

Interest Expense	1,000	
Mortgage Payable	250	
Cash		1,250

To record interest expense and reduction in principal included in July 31 mortgage payment.

Pension plans

A *pension plan* is a contract between a company and its employees under which the company agrees to pay retirement benefits to eligible employees. An employer company generally meets its obligations under a pension plan by making regular payments to an insurance company or other outside agency. As pension obligations accrue, the employer company records them by a debit to Pension Expense and a credit to Cash. If all required payments are made promptly to the pension fund trustee, no liability need appear on the employer company's financial statements. When employees retire, their retirement benefits are paid by the insurance company. This type of arrangement is called a *funded pension plan.*

The Employee Retirement Income Security Act of 1974 (ERISA) was a most complex piece of legislation requiring extensive reporting of pension plans to the federal government. The objectives included assuring that the enormous amounts of money in pension plans were properly accounted for, audited regularly, and available to meet obligations to retiring employees. The FASB is currently studying the need for new accounting standards to meet the requirements imposed by ERISA. Pension plans are considered in some detail in more advanced accounting courses.

Payroll Accounting

Labor costs and related payroll taxes constitute a large and constantly increasing portion of the total costs of operating most business organizations. In the commercial airlines, for example, labor costs traditionally have represented 40 to 50% of total operation costs.

The task of accounting for payroll costs would be an important one simply because of the large amounts involved; however, it is further complicated by the many federal and state laws which require employers to maintain certain specific information in their payroll records not only for the business as a whole but also for each individual employee. Frequent reports of total wages and amounts withheld must be filed with government agencies. These reports are prepared by every employer and must be accompanied by payment to the government of the amounts withheld from employees and of the payroll taxes levied on the employer.

Deductions from earnings of employees

The take-home pay of most employees is much less than the gross earnings. Major factors explaining this difference between the amount earned and the amount received are social security taxes, federal income taxes withheld, and other deductions discussed in the following pages.

Social security taxes (FICA)

Under the terms of the Social Security Act, qualified workers who retire after reaching a specified age receive monthly retirement payments and Medicare benefits. Benefits are also provided for the family of a worker who dies before or after reaching this retirement age. Funds for the operation of this program are obtained through taxes levied under the Federal Insurance Contributions Act, often referred to as FICA taxes, or simply as *social security taxes.*

Employers are required by the Federal Insurance Contributions Act to withhold a portion of each employee's earnings as a contribution to the social security program. A tax at the same rate is levied against the employer. For example, assume that an employee earns $20,000 subject to FICA taxes of 7%. The employer will withhold $1,400 ($20,000 × .07) from the employee's earnings. The employer will then pay to the government the amount of $2,800, consisting of the $1,400 withheld from the employee plus an additional $1,400 of FICA tax on the employer.

Two factors are involved in computing the FICA tax: the *base* or amount of earnings subject to the tax, and the *rate* which is applied to the base. Both the *base* and the *rate* have been increased many times in recent years and probably will continue to be changed in future years. The following table indicates that individuals were required to pay approximately 72 times as much in 1982 as they were in 1937 when the social security plan was started.

Year	Base (Earnings Subject to FICA Tax)	Tax Rate	Amount of Tax
1937	$ 3,000	1.0%	$ 30
1951	3,600	1.5%	54
1966	6,600	4.2%	277
1972	9,000	5.2%	468
1977	16,500	5.85%	965
1982	32,400	6.70%	2,171
1990	?	?	?

These changes in rates and in the base do not affect the accounting principles or procedures involved. For illustrative purposes in this book, we shall assume the rate of tax to be 7% on both the employee and the employer, applicable to a base of $35,000 (the first $35,000 of wages received by each employee in each calendar year). This assumption of round amounts for both the tax and the base is a convenient one for the purpose of illustrations and for the solution of problems by the student, regardless of frequent changes in the rate and base.

Federal income taxes

Our pay-as-you-go system of federal income tax requires employers to withhold a portion of the earnings of their employees. The amount withheld depends upon the amount of the earnings and upon the number of income tax exemptions claimed by the employee. For each income tax exemption, the employee is entitled to a withholding allowance currently amounting to $1,000. Each withholding allowance thus causes $1,000 of yearly earnings to be exempt from income tax. On a federal income tax return, one exemption is allowed for oneself, one for a spouse, and one for each dependent. Thus a married couple with three dependent children would be entitled to five exemptions and would qualify for five withholding allowances.

Present regulations provide a graduated system of withholding, designed to make the amount of income tax withheld approximate the individual's tax liability at the end of the year. Because persons in higher income brackets are subject to higher rates of taxation, the withholding rates are correspondingly higher for them. There is no ceiling with respect to the amount of salary subject to income tax.

Most states and cities which levy income taxes also require the employer to withhold the tax from employees' earnings. Because such situations involve a variety of rates, they will not be discussed here.

Other deductions from employees' earnings

In addition to the compulsory deductions for taxes, many other deductions are voluntarily authorized by employees. Union dues and insurance premiums already have been mentioned as examples of payroll deductions. Others include charitable contributions, retirement programs, savings bond purchases, and pension plans.

Employer's responsibility for amounts withheld

In withholding amounts from an employee's earnings for either voluntary or involuntary deductions, the employer acts merely as a collection agent. The amounts withheld are paid to the designated organization, such as a government agency or labor union. The employer is also responsible for maintaining accounting records which will enable it to file required reports and make timely payments of the amounts withheld. From the employer's viewpoint, the amounts withheld from employees' earnings represent current liabilities.

Payroll records and procedures

Although payroll records and procedures vary greatly according to the number of employees and the extent of automation in processing payroll data, there are a few fundamental steps common to payroll work in most organizations. One of these steps taken at the end of each pay period is the preparation of a *payroll register* showing for each employee the gross earnings, amounts withheld, and net pay. When the computation of the payroll register has been completed, the next step is to reflect the expense and the related liabilities in the ledger accounts. A general journal entry such as shown below may be made to bring into the accounts the information summarized in the payroll register. (This entry does not include payroll taxes on the employer.)

Journal entry to record payroll

Sales Salaries Expense	4,800	
Office Salaries Expense	3,200	
FICA Tax Payable (7% of $8,000)		560
Liability for Income Tax Withheld		1,370
Liability for Group Insurance Withheld		150
Accrued Payroll		5,920

To record the payroll for the period Jan. 1–Jan. 15.

The two debits to expense accounts indicate that the business has incurred salaries expense of $8,000; however, only $5,920 of this amount will be paid to the employees on payday. The payment will be recorded by a debit to Accrued Payroll and a credit to Cash. The remaining $2,080 (consisting of deductions for taxes and insurance premiums withheld) is lodged in liability accounts. Payment of these liabilities must be made at frequent intervals.

Wage and tax statement   By January 31 each year, employers are required to furnish every employee with a Wage and Tax Statement (Form W-2). This form shows gross earnings for the preceding calendar year and the amounts withheld for FICA tax and income taxes. The employer send one copy of this form to the Director of Internal Revenue and gives three copies to the employee. When the employee files a federal income tax return, he or she must attach a copy of the withholding statement. A copy also must be attached to the employee's state income tax return.

Payroll taxes on the employer

The discussion of payroll taxes up to this point has dealt with taxes levied on employees and withheld from their pay. From the viewpoint of the employing company, such withheld taxes are significant because they must be accounted for and remitted in a timely manner to the appropriate government agencies. However, *payroll taxes are also levied on the employer.* These taxes on the employer are expenses of the business and *are recorded by debits to expense accounts,* just as in the case of property taxes or license fees for doing business.

Social security (FICA) tax   The employer is taxed to help finance the social security program. The tax is figured at the same rate and on the same amount of earnings used to compute FICA tax on employees. (In all problems and illustrations in this book, the tax is assumed to be 7% on the first $35,000 of gross earnings by each employee in each calendar year.)

Federal unemployment insurance tax   Unemployment insurance is another part of the national social security program designed to offer temporary relief to unemployed persons. The FUTA tax (Federal Unemployment Tax Act) is levied on *employers only* and is not deducted from the wages of employees. The FUTA tax (also known as "unemployment compensation" or UC) applies to approximately the same classes of employment as the FICA tax. The rates of tax and the wage base subject to the tax are changed from time to time. For purposes of illustration in this book, we shall assume that employers are subject to federal unemployment tax at the rate of 3.4% on the first $6,000 of *each employee's earnings* in each calendar year. However, the employer may take a credit against this tax (not in excess of 2.7% of the first $6,000 of each employee's wages) for amounts that are paid into state unemployment funds. As a result, an employer may be subject to a *federal* tax of only 0.7% on wages up to $6,000 per employee.

State unemployment compensation tax   All the states participate in the federal-state unemployment insurance program. Although the state laws vary somewhat as to types of covered employment, the usual rate of tax is 2.7% of the first $6,000 of earnings by each employee during the calendar year. Under this provision, the employer actually makes payment of the larger part of the FUTA tax directly to state governments which carry out the federal-state unemployment insurance program.

This arrangement means that the FUTA tax is divided into two parts: the larger part, or 2.7%, of the first $6,000 of wages paid going to the state and the remainder to the federal government. Some states use a merit-rating plan enabling those employers who maintain stable work forces to pay a reduced rate of state unemployment tax. Under the merit-rating plans of some states, an employer whose employees have applied for little or no unemployment compensation may be rewarded with a rate of perhaps 1 to 2% rather than the standard 2.7%. In computing the federal unemployment compensation tax, the employer company will still receive credit for the full 2.7% it would have been required to pay the state if it had not qualified as a superior risk.

Accounting entry for employer's payroll taxes   The entry to record the employer's payroll taxes is usually made at the same time the payroll is recorded. To illustrate, let us use again the $8,000 payroll first used on page 506 in the discussion of amounts withheld from employees; this time, however, we are illustrating taxes levied on the *employer*. (None of the employees has earned over $6,000 since this is the first pay period of the current year.)

Journal entry to record payroll taxes on employer

Payroll Taxes Expense	832	
FICA Tax Payable (7% of $8,000)		560
State Unemployment Tax Payable (2.7% of $8,000)		216
Federal Unemployment Tax Payable (0.7% of $8,000)		56
To record payroll taxes on employer for period ended Jan. 15.		

Thus the total payroll expense for the employer is $8,832, which consists of wages of $8,000 and payroll taxes of $832.

Estimated liabilities

An estimated liability is one known to exist, but for which the dollar amount is uncertain. A common example is the liability of a manufacturer to honor any warranty on products sold. For example, assume that a company manufactures and sells television sets which carry a two-year warranty. To achieve the objective of offsetting current revenue with all related expenses, the liability for future warranty repairs on television sets sold during the current period should be estimated and recorded at the balance sheet date. This estimate will be based upon the company's past experience.

Loss contingencies

In Chapter 8, we discussed the *contingent liability* which arises when notes receivable are discounted at a bank. A contingent liability may be regarded as a *possible* liability, which may develop into a full-fledged liability or may be eliminated entirely by a future event. Contingent liabilities are also called *loss contingencies.* "Loss contingencies," however, is a broader term, encompassing the possible impairment of assets as well as the possible existence of liabilities.

A common loss contingency is the possibility of loss which arises when a lawsuit is filed against a company. Until the lawsuit is resolved, uncertainty exists as to the amount, if any, of the company's liability. Central to the definition of a loss contingency is the element of *uncertainty*—uncertainty both as to the amount of loss and whether, in fact, a loss actually has occurred.

Loss contingencies are recorded in the accounting records at estimated amounts only when both of the following criteria are met: (1) it is *probable* that a loss has been incurred, and (2) the amount of loss can be *reasonably estimated.*[10] An example of a loss contingency which meets these criteria and is recorded in the accounts is the estimated loss from doubtful accounts receivable. Loss contingencies which do not meet both of these criteria should be *disclosed in footnotes* to the financial statements whenever there is at least a *reasonable possibility* that a loss has been incurred. Pending lawsuits, for example, almost always are disclosed in footnotes, but the loss, if any, is not recorded in the accounting records until the lawsuit is settled.

When loss contingencies are disclosed in footnotes to the financial statements, the footnote should describe the nature of the contingency and, if possible, provide an estimate of the amount of possible loss. If a reasonable estimate of the amount of possible loss cannot be made, the footnote should include the range of possible loss or a statement that an estimate cannot be made. The following footnote is typical of the disclosure of the loss contingency arising from pending litigation:

Footnote disclosure of a loss contingency

Note 8: Contingencies

In October of the current year, the Company was named as defendant in a lawsuit alleging patent infringement and claiming damages of $408 million. The Company denies all charges in this case and is preparing its defenses against them. The Company is advised by legal counsel that it is not possible at this time to determine the ultimate legal and financial responsibility with respect to this litigation.

Users of financial statements should pay close attention to the footnote disclosure of loss contingencies. Even though no loss has been recorded in the accounting records, some loss contingencies may be so material in amount as to threaten the continued existence of the company.

KEY TERMS INTRODUCED OR EMPHASIZED IN CHAPTER 13

Amortization of discount or premium on bonds payable The process of systematically writing off a portion of bond discount to increase interest expense or writing off a portion of bond premium to decrease interest expense each period the bonds are outstanding.

Bond sinking fund Cash set aside by the corporation at regular intervals (usually with a trustee) to be used to pay the bonds at maturity.

Capital lease A lease contract which, in essence, finances the eventual purchase by the lessee of leased property. The lessor accounts for a capital lease as a sale of property; the lessee records an asset and a liability equal to the present value of the future lease payments. Also called a *financing lease.*

---

[10]*FASB Statement No. 5, "Accounting for Contingencies" (Stamford, Conn.: 1975).*

Carrying value of bonds   The face amount of the bonds plus any unamortized premium or minus any unamortized discount.

Contract interest rate   The contractual rate of interest printed on bonds. The contract interest rate, applied to the face value of the bonds, determines the amount of the annual cash interest payments to bondholders. Also called the *nominal interest rate.*

Debenture bond   An unsecured bond, the value of which rests on the general credit of the corporation. Not secured by pledge of specific assets.

Discount on bonds payable   Amount by which the face amount of the bond exceeds the price received by the corporation at the date of issuance. Indicates that the contractual rate of interest is lower than the market rate of interest.

Effective interest method of amortization   Discount or premium on bonds is amortized by the difference between the contractual cash interest payment each period and the amount of interest computed by applying the effective interest rate to the carrying value of the bonds at the beginning of the current interest period. Causes bond interest expense to be a constant percentage of the carrying value of the liability.

Effective interest rate   The actual rate of interest expense to the borrowing corporation, taking into account the contractual cash interest payments and the discount or premium to be amortized.

Federal unemployment compensation tax (FUTA)   A tax imposed on the employer by the Federal Unemployment Tax Act based on amount of payrolls. Designed to provide temporary payments to unemployed persons.

FICA tax   A tax imposed by the Federal Insurance Contributions Act on both employer and employees. Used to finance the social security program.

Lessee   The tenant, user, or renter of leased property.

Lessor   The owner of property leased to a lessee.

Loss contingency   A situation involving uncertainty as to whether or not a loss has occurred. The uncertainty will be resolved by a future event. An example of a loss contingency is the possible loss related to a lawsuit pending against a company. Although loss contingencies are sometimes recorded in the accounts, they are more frequently disclosed only in footnotes in the financial statements.

Off-balance-sheet financing   An arrangement in which the use of resources is financed without the obligation for future payments appearing as a liability in the balance sheet. An operating lease is a common example of off-balance-sheet financing.

Operating lease   A lease contract which is in essence a rental agreement. The lessee has the use of the leased property, but the lessor retains the usual risks and rewards of ownership. The periodic lease payments are accounted for as rent expense by the lessee and as rental revenue by the lessor.

Payroll register   A payroll record showing for each pay period all payroll information for employees individually and in total.

Premium on bonds payable   Amount by which the issuance price of a bond exceeds the face value. Indicates that the contractual rate of interest is higher than the market rate.

Present value of a future amount   The amount of money that an informed investor would pay today for the right to receive the future amount, based upon a specific rate of return required by the investor. Bond prices are the present value to investors of the future principal and interest payments. Capital leases are recorded as an asset and a related liability in the accounting records of the lessee at the present value of the future lease payments.

DEMONSTRATION PROBLEM FOR YOUR REVIEW

A partial list of the liabilities appearing in the December 31, Year 6, balance sheet of Denver Industries is shown below:

Current liabilities:		
Bond interest payable		$ 375,000
Accrued liabilities relating to payroll:		
FICA tax payable	$ 7,200	
Liability for income tax withheld	4,850	
State unemployment tax payable	405	
Federal unemployment tax payable	105	12,560
Long-term liabilities:		
15% bonds payable, due Jan. 1, Year 15	$5,000,000	
Less: Discount on bonds payable	72,000	4,928,000

During January of Year 7, the corporation completed the following transactions relating to liabilities:

Jan. 1 Issued $10,000,000 of 12%, 20-year bonds payable to an underwriter for cash. The issuance price was 101½. The bonds are dated January 1, Year 7, with semiannual interest payments to be made on July 1 and January 1.

Jan. 1 Paid the $375,000 semiannual interest payment on the outstanding 15% bonds, and retired this entire bond issue at its call price of 106.

Jan. 4 Paid in cash the liabilities at December 31, Year 6, relating to payroll taxes and amounts withheld from employees.

Jan. 31 The payroll register shows the following totals for the month of January:

Wages Expense	FICA Tax Withheld	Income Tax Withheld	Take-Home Pay	Payroll Taxes on Employer
$65,000	$4,550	$5,050	$55,400	$6,760

Payroll taxes on the employer consist of FICA tax, 7%; state unemployment tax, 2.7%; federal unemployment tax, 0.7%. Employees were paid on January 31; however, none of the taxes relating to the January payroll has been remitted to governmental agencies.

Instructions

a Prepare entries in general journal form to record these January transactions. In recording the January payroll, use separate journal entries to record the amounts withheld from employees and the payroll taxes on Denver Industries.

b Prepare the adjusting entry required at January 31, Year 7, to accrue interest and amortize the premium on the 12% bond issue for the month. Use the straight-line method of amortization.

SOLUTION TO DEMONSTRATION PROBLEM

a   *General Journal*

Year 7

Jan. 1	Cash	10,150,000	
	12% Bonds Payable		10,000,000
	Premium on Bonds Payable		150,000
	To record issuance of $10,000,000, 12%,		
	20-year bonds payable at 1011/2.		
1	Bond Interest Payable	375,000	
	Cash		375,000
	Paid semiannual interest on 15% bonds payable.		
1	15% Bonds Payable	5,000,000	
	Loss on Retirement of Bonds	372,000	
	Discount on Bonds Payable		72,000
	Cash		5,300,000
	To record the retirement of bonds payable		
	at call price of 106.		
4	FICA Tax Payable	7,200	
	Liability for Income Tax Withheld	4,850	
	State Unemployment Tax Payable	405	
	Federal Unemployment Tax Payable	105	
	Cash		12,560
	To record payment of liabilities for payroll		
	taxes and amounts withheld from employees.		
31	Wages Expense	65,000	
	FICA Tax Payable		4,550
	Liability for Income Tax Withheld		5,050
	Cash		55,400
	To record payroll for January.		
31	Payroll Taxes Expense	6,760	
	FICA Tax Payable		4,550
	State Unemployment Tax Payable		1,755
	Federal Unemployment Tax Payable		455
	To record payroll taxes on employer for January.		

b   *Adjusting Entry*

Jan. 31 *Bond Interest Expense* 99,375
       Premium on Bonds Payable ($150,000 × ¹/₂₄₀) 625
          Bond Interest Payable   100,000
       To record accrued interest and amortization of premium
       on 12% bond issue for January.
       ($10,000,000 × 12% × ¹/₁₂ = $100,000)

REVIEW QUESTIONS

1 Distinguish between the two terms in each of the following pairs:
  a Mortgage bond; debenture bond
  b Contract (or nominal) interest rate; effective interest rate
  c Fixed-maturity bond; serial bond
  d Coupon bond; registered bond
  e Operating lease; capital lease
  f Estimated liability; contingent liability

2 K Company has decided to finance expansion by issuing $10 million of 20-year debenture bonds and will ask a number of underwriters to bid on the bond issue. Discuss the factors that will determine the amount bid by the underwriters for these bonds.

3 What is a *convertible bond?* Discuss the advantages and disadvantages of convertible bonds from the standpoint of **(a)** the investor and **(b)** the issuing corporation.

4 The Computer Sharing Co. has paid-in capital of $10 million and retained earnings of $3 million. The company has just issued $1 million in 20-year, 8% bonds. It is proposed that a policy be established of appropriating $50,000 of retained earnings each year to enable the company to retire the bonds at maturity. Evaluate the merits of this proposal in accomplishing the desired result.

5 The following excerpt is taken from an article in a leading business periodical: "In the bond market high interest rates mean low prices. Bonds pay out a fixed percentage of their face value, usually $1,000; an 8% bond, for instance, will pay $80 a year. In order for its yield to rise to 10%, its price would have to drop to $800." Give a critical evaluation of this quotation.

6 Discuss the advantages and disadvantages of a *call provision* in a bond contract from the viewpoint of **(a)** the bondholder and **(b)** the issuing corporation.

7 Many bonds now being bought and sold by investors on organized securities exchanges were issued when interest rates were much lower than they are today. Would you expect these bonds to be trading at prices above or below their face values? Explain.

8 Explain why the effective rate of interest differs from the contract rate when bonds are issued **(a)** at a discount and **(b)** at a premium.

9 When the effective interest method is used to amortize bond discount or premium, the amount of bond interest expense will differ in each period from that of the preceding period. Explain how the amount of bond interest expense changes from one period to another when the bonds are issued **(a)** at a discount and **(b)** at a premium.

10 Explain why the effective interest method of amortizing bond discount or premium is considered to be theoretically preferable to the straight-line method.

11 John Lee buys a $1,000, 16% bond for 106, five years from the maturity date. After holding the bond for four years, he sells it for 102. Lee claims that he has a loss of $40 on the sale. A friend argues that Lee has made a gain on the sale. Explain the difference in viewpoint. With whom do you agree? Why?

12 Explain how the lessee accounts for an operating lease and a capital lease. Why is an operating lease sometimes called *off-balance-sheet-financing?*

13 A friend of yours has just purchased a house and has incurred a $50,000, 11% mortgage, payable at $476.17 per month. After making the first monthly payment, he received a receipt from the bank stating that only $17.84 of the $476.17 had been applied to reducing the principal amount of the loan. Your friend computes that at the rate of $17.84 per month, it will take over 233 years to pay off the $50,000 mortgage. Do you agree with your friend's analysis?

14 Name the federal taxes that most employers are required to withhold from employees. What account or accounts would be credited with the amounts withheld?

15 Explain which of the following taxes relating to an employee's wages are borne by the employee and which by the employer:
a FICA taxes
b Federal unemployment compensation taxes
c State unemployment compensation taxes
d Federal income taxes

16 Explain two methods which have been used repeatedly by the federal government in increasing the amount of FICA taxes over the years.

17 Under what conditions are *loss contingencies* recorded at estimated amounts in the accounting records?

18 A lawsuit has been filed against Telmar Corporation alleging violations of federal antitrust laws and claiming damages which, when trebled, total $1.2 billion. Telmar Corporation denies the charges and intends to contest the suit vigorously. Legal counsel advises the company that the litigation will last for several years and that a reasonable estimate of the final outcome cannot be made at this time.

Should Telmar Corporation include in its current balance sheet a liability for the damages claimed in this lawsuit? Explain fully.

19 With reference to question **18** above, illustrate the disclosure of the pending lawsuit which should be included in the current financial statements of Telmar Corporation.

EXERCISES

Ex. 13-1 On December 31, Year 10, Wayne Corporation received authorization to issue $15,000,000 of 10%, 30-year debenture bonds. Interest payment dates were June 30 and December 31. The bonds were all issued at par on January 31, Year 11, one month after the interest date printed on the bonds.

Instructions
a Prepare the journal entry at January 31, Year 11, to record the sale of the bonds.
b Prepare the journal entry at June 30, Year 11, to record the semiannual bond interest payment.

Ex. 13-2 Companies A and B have the same amount of operating income (earnings before bond interest and income taxes) and the same number of outstanding shares of common stock. However, the two companies have different capital structures. Determine the amount earned per share of common stock for each of the two companies and explain the source of any difference.

	Company A	Company B
12% debenture bonds payable	$5,000,000	$ –0–
12% cumulative preferred stock, $100 par	–0–	5,000,000
Common stock, $20 par, 200,000 shares outstanding	4,000,000	4,000,000
Operating income, before interest and income taxes		
(assume a 40% tax rate)	3,500,000	3,500,000

Ex. 13-3 Crest Company issued $10,000,000 par value $9\frac{1}{2}$% bonds on July 1, Year 5, at $97\frac{1}{2}$. Interest is due on June 30 and December 31 of each year, and the bonds mature on June 30, Year 15. The fiscal year ends on December 31; bond discount is amortized by the straight-line method. Prepare the following journal entries:

a July 1, Year 5, to record the issuance of the bonds

b December 31, Year 5, to pay interest and amortize the bond discount (two entries)

c June 30, Year 15, to pay interest, amortize the bond discount, and retire the bonds at maturity (three entries)

Ex. 13-4 North Company issued $20 million of 11%, 10-year bonds on January 1, Year 1. Interest is payable semiannually on June 30 and December 31. The bonds were sold to an underwriting group at 105.

South Company issued $20 million of 10%, 10-year bonds on January 1, Year 1. Interest is payable semiannually on June 30 and December 31. The bonds were sold to an underwriting group at 95.

Prepare journal entries to record all transactions during Year 1 for **(a)** the North Company bond issue and **(b)** the South Company bond issue. Assume that both companies amortize bond discount or premium by the straight-line method at each interest payment date.

Ex. 13-5 The following liability appears on the balance sheet of the Sunrise Company on December 31, Year 1:

Long-term liabilities:

| Bonds payable, $9\frac{3}{4}$%, due Dec. 31, Year 15 . . . . | $1,000,000 | |
| Premium on bonds payable . . . . | 42,000 | $1,042,000 |

On January 1, Year 2, 20% of the bonds are retired at 98. Interest was paid on December 31, Year 1.

a Record the retirement of $200,000 of bonds on January 1, Year 2.

b Record the interest payment for the six months ending December 31, Year 2, and the amortization of the premium on December 31, Year 2, assuming that amortization is recorded by the straight-line method only at the end of each year.

Ex. 13-6 On April 1, Year 1, Basin Corporation issued $1,000,000 of 10-year, 9% bonds payable and received proceeds of $937,689, resulting in an effective interest rate of 10%. Interest is payable on September 30 and March 31. The effective interest method is used to amortize bond discount; an amortization table for this bond issue is illustrated on page 495.

Instructions   Prepare the necessary journal entries (rounding all amounts to the nearest dollar) on:

a April 1, Year 1, to record the issuance of the bonds

b September 30, Year 1, to record the payment of interest and amortization of discount at the first semiannual interest payment date

c December 31, Year 1, to accrue bond interest expense through year-end

d March 31, Year 2, to record the payment of interest and amortization of bond discount at the second semiannual interest payment date

Ex. 13-7   Crown Point Corporation issued on the authorization date $1,000,000 of 10-year, 9% bonds payable and received proceeds of $1,067,952, resulting in an effective interest rate of 8%. The premium is amortized by the effective interest method; the amortization table for this bond issue is illustrated on page 497. Interest is payable semiannually.

Instructions

a Show how the liability for the bonds would appear on a balance sheet prepared immediately after issuance of the bonds.

b Show how the liability for the bonds would appear on a balance sheet prepared after 16 semiannual interest periods (two years prior to maturity).

c Show the necessary calculations to determine for this bond issue interest expense by the effective interest method for the first six-month period, the premium amortized at the end of that first period, and the cash interest payment. Your calculations should include use of the effective interest rate and also the contractual rate. Round all amounts to the nearest dollar.

Ex. 13-8   Brand Corporation issued $1,000,000 of 7%, 10-year convertible bonds dated December 31, Year 8, at a price of 98. Semiannual interest payment dates were June 30 and December 31. The conversion rate was 20 shares of $10 par common stock for each $1,000 bond. Four years later on December 31, Year 12, bondholders converted $250,000 face value of bonds into common stock. Assume that unamortized discount on this date amounted to $12,000 for the entire bond issue. Prepare a journal entry to record the conversion of the bonds.

Ex. 13-9   Martin earns a salary of $28,000 a year from Rand Corporation. FICA taxes are 7% of wages up to $35,000. Federal unemployment taxes are 3.4% of wages up to $6,000 a year, but a credit against this FUTA tax is permitted for payment to the state of 2.7% of wages up to $6,000 a year. Federal income tax of $5,800 was withheld from Martin's paychecks during the year.

a Prepare entries (in general journal form) to summarize for the entire year (1) the amounts paid to and withheld from Martin, and (2) the payroll taxes on the employer relating to employee Martin. (In drafting these summary entries, ignore any payments of tax during the year and let the liability accounts show the totals for the year. Credit Cash for the amount paid to Martin.)

b What is the total yearly cost (including taxes) to Rand Corporation of having Martin on the payroll at an annual salary of $28,000?

Ex. 13-10   The payroll record of Miller Company for the week ended January 7 showed the following amounts for total earnings: sales employees $8,800; office employees $7,200. Amounts withheld consisted of FICA taxes at a 7% rate on all earnings for this period, federal income taxes $1,920, and medical insurance $600.

a After computing the amount of FICA taxes withheld, prepare a general journal entry to record the payroll. Do not include taxes on the employer.

b Prepare a general journal entry to record the payroll taxes expense to Miller Company relating to this payroll. Assume that the federal unemployment tax rate is 3.4% of the first $6,000 paid each employee, and that 2.7% of this tax is payable to the state. No employee received more than $6,000 in this first pay period of the year.

PROBLEMS

13-1 Texas Bus & Tractor Co. obtained all necessary approvals to issue $10,000,000 face value of 9%, 20-year bonds dated March 31, Year 4. Interest payment dates were September 30 and March 31. The bonds were not issued, however, until four months later, August 1, Year 4. On this date the entire bond issue was sold to an underwriter at a price of 100 plus accrued interest.

Instructions   Prepare the required entries in general journal form on:
a August 1, Year 4, to record the issuance of the bonds
b September 30, Year 4, to record the first semiannual interest payment on the bonds
c December 31, Year 4, to accrue bond interest expense through year-end and to close the Bond Interest Expense account for the year
d March 31, Year 5, to record the second semiannual interest payment

13-2 On October 31, Year 1, Perfect Racquet Mfg. Co. issued $12,000,000 face value of 11% debenture bonds, with interest payable on April 30 and October 31. The bonds mature 10 years from the date of issuance. Company policy is to amortize bond discount or premium by the straight-line method at each interest payment date; the company's fiscal year ends at December 31.

Instructions
a Make the necessary adjusting entries at December 31, Year 1, and the journal entry to record the payment of bond interest on April 30, Year 2, under each of the following assumptions:
   (1) The bonds were issued at 97.
   (2) The bonds were issued at 102.
b Compute the net bond liability at December 31, Year 1, under assumptions (1) and (2) above.

13-3 The items shown below appear in the balance sheet of Pilsner Breweries at December 31, Year 10:

Current liabilities:		
Bond interest payable (for three months from Sept. 30 to Dec. 31)		$ 180,000
Long term-debt:		
Bonds payable, 9%, due Sept. 30, Year 15	$8,000,000	
Less: Discount on bonds payable	68,400	7,931,600

The bonds are callable on any interest date. On September 30, Year 11, Pilsner Breweries called $2 million of the bonds at 105.

Instructions

a Prepare journal entries to record the semiannual interest payment on March 31, Year 11. Discount is amortized by the straight-line method at each interest payment date and was amortized to December 31, Year 10. Base the amortization on the 57-month period from December 31, Year 10; to September 30, Year 15.

b Prepare journal entries to record the amortization of bond discount and payment of bond interest at September 30, Year 11, and also to record the calling of $2 million of the bonds at this date.

c Prepare a journal entry to record the accrual of interest at December 31, Year 11. Include the amortization of bond discount to the year-end.

13-4 Country Recording Studios obtained the necessary approvals to issue $3 million of 10%, 10-year bonds, dated March 1, Year 1. Interest payment dates were September 1 and March 1. Issuance of the bonds did not occur until June 1, Year 1. On this date, the entire bond issue was sold to an underwriter at a price which included three months' accrued interest. Country Recording Studios follows the policy of amortizing bond discount or premium by the straight-line method at each interest date as well as for year-end adjusting entries at December 31.

Instructions

a Prepare all journal entries necessary to record the issuance of the bonds and bond interest expense during Year 1, assuming that the sales price of the bonds on June 1 was $3,309,000, including accrued interest. (Note that the bonds will be outstanding for a period of only nine years and nine months.)

b Assume that the sales price of the bonds on June 1 had been $2,899,500, including accrued interest. Prepare journal entries for Year 1 parallel to those in part **a** above.

c Show the proper balance sheet presentation of the liability for bonds payable (including accrued interest) in the balance sheet prepared at December 31, *Year 5,* assuming that the original sales price of the bonds (including accrued interest) had been:
   (1) $3,309,000, as described in part **a**
   (2) $2,899,500, as described in part **b**

13-5 On June 30, Year 4, King Cotton Company issued $4,000,000 face value of 10-year, 9½% bonds payable at a price of 103¼, resulting in an effective annual rate of interest of 9%. The semiannual interest payment dates are June 30 and December 31, and the bonds mature on June 30, Year 14. The company maintains its accounts on a calendar-year basis and amortizes bond premium by the effective interest method.

Instructions

a Prepare the required journal entries (with explanations) on:
   (1) June 30, Year 4, to record the sale of the bonds.
   (2) December 31, Year 4, for payment of interest and amortization of premium on bonds. (Use one compound entry.)
   (3) June 30, Year 14, for payment of interest, amortization of the remaining premium, and to retire the bonds. Assume that the carrying value of the bonds at the beginning of this last six-month interest period is $4,009,569.

b Show how the accounts, Bonds Payable and Premium on Bonds Payable, would appear on the balance sheet at December 31, Year 4.

13-6 On December 31, Year 10, Apache Corporation sold a $6,000,000 face value, 10%, 10-year bond issue to an underwriter at a price of 94. This price results in an effective annual interest rate of 11%. Interest is payable semiannually on June 30 and December 31. Apache Corporation amortizes bond discount by the effective interest method.

Instructions

a Prepare an amortization table for the first two years (four interest periods) of this bond issue. Round all amounts to the nearest dollar and use the following column headings for your table:

Six-Month Interest Period	(A) Interest Paid Semi-annually ($6,000,000 × 5%)	(B) Effective Semi-annual Interest Expense (Carrying Value × 5½%)	(C) Discount Amortiz-ation (B − A)	(D) Bond Discount Balance	(E) Carrying Value of Bonds, End of Period ($6,000,000 − D)

b Using the information from your amortization table, prepare all journal entries necessary to record issuance of the bonds and bond interest for Year 11. (Use a compound entry for interest payment and amortization of bond discount at each semiannual interest payment date.)

c Show the proper balance sheet presentation of Bonds Payable and Discount on Bonds Payable at December 31, Year 12.

13-7 Roan Antelope, Inc., on September 1, Year 1, issued $9,000,000 par value, 8½%, 10-year bonds payable with interest dates of March 1 and September 1. The company maintains its accounts on a calendar-year basis and follows the policy of amortizing bond discount and bond premium by the effective interest method at the semiannual interest payment dates as well as at the year-end adjusting of the accounts.

Instructions

a Prepare the necessary journal entries to record the following transactions, assuming that the bonds were sold for $8,700,000, a price resulting in an effective annual interest rate of 9%.

(1) Sale of the bonds on September 1, Year 1

(2) Adjustment of the accounts at December 31, Year 1, for accrued interest and amortization of a discount

(3) Payment of bond interest and amortization of discount on March 1, Year 2

b Assume that the sales price of the bonds on September 1, Year 1, had been $9,300,000, resulting in an effective annual interest rate of 8%. Prepare journal entries parallel to those called for in **a** above at the dates of September 1, Year 1; December 31, Year 1; and March 1, Year 2.

c State the amounts of bond interest expense for Year 1 and the *net* amount of the liability for the bonds payable at December 31, Year 1, under the independent assumptions set forth in both **a** and **b** above. Show your computations.

13-8 Maria Mandella invested in $420,000 face value of 9%, 10-year bonds at a price of 95. The investment was made at the date of original issuance of the bonds and consequently there was no accrued interest and no broker's commission. Shortly after this transaction, the market price of the bonds dropped to 90. After holding the bonds exactly six years,

Mandella sold them at a price of 102. The broker's commission charged was $1,500. There was no accrued interest at the date of sale because the sale occurred immediately after receipt of the semiannual interest payment.

Instructions

a Assume that Mandella at the date of purchase had no intention of holding the bonds to maturity and did not amortize the discount. Determine the total interest earned during the six-year period and the gain or loss on disposal.

b Assume that Mandella did intend to hold the bonds until maturity and did amortize the discount. When Mandella sold the bonds six years later, her carrying value for the investment was $411,600. Determine the total interest earned during the six-year period and the gain or loss on disposal.

c What is the most probable reason for the price of the bonds being above their face value at the date Mandella disposed of them? Would amortization of discount on the bonds have produced a more realistic measurement of yearly income in this case? Explain.

13-9 Custom Truck Builders frequently uses long-term lease contracts to finance the sale of its trucks. On November 1, Year 1, Custom Truck Builders leased to Interstate Van Lines a truck carried in the perpetual inventory records at $33,520. The terms of the lease call for Interstate Van Lines to make 36 monthly payments of $1,400 each, beginning on November 30, Year 1. The present value of these payments, after considering a built-in interest charge of 1% per month, is equal to the regular $42,150 sales price of the truck. At the end of the 36-month lease, title to the truck will transfer to Interstate Van Lines.

Instructions

a Prepare journal entries in the accounts of Custom Truck Builders on:
   (1) November 1 to record the sale financed by the lease and the related cost of goods sold. (Debit Lease Payments Receivable for the $42,150 present value of the future lease payments.)
   (2) November 30, to record receipt of the first $1,400 monthly payment. (Prepare a compound journal entry which allocates the cash receipt between interest revenue and reduction of Lease Payments Receivable. The portion of each monthly payment recognized as interest revenue is equal to 1% of the balance of the account Lease Payments Receivable, at the beginning of that month. Round all interest computations to the nearest dollar.)
   (3) December 31, to record receipt of the second monthly payment.

b Prepare journal entries for Year 1 in the accounts of Interstate Van Lines on:
   (1) November 1, to record acquisition of the leased truck.
   (2) November 30, to record the first monthly lease payment. (Determine the portion of the payment representing interest expense in a manner parallel to that described in part **a**.)
   (3) December 31, to record the second monthly lease payment.
   (4) December 31, to recognize depreciation on the leased truck through year-end. Compute depreciation expense by the straight-line method, using a 10-year service life and an estimaed salvage value of $6,150.

c Compute the net carrying value of the leased truck in the balance sheet of Interstate Van Lines at December 31, Year 1.

d Compute the amount of Interstate Van Lines' lease payment obligation at December 31, Year 1.

13-10 The payroll records of Copper Kettle for the first week in January showed total salaries earned by employees of $12,000. This total included $7,000 of salaries to sales employees and $5,000 to office employees. No employee earned more than $6,000 in this first pay period of the year.

 The amounts withheld from employees' pay consisted of FICA taxes computed at an assumed rate of 7%, federal income taxes of $1,150, and group insurance premiums of $140.

Instructions

a Prepare a general journal entry to summarize the above payroll and the deductions from the earnings of employees. Payroll taxes on the employer are not to be included in this entry.

b Prepare a general journal entry to summarize the payroll taxes on the *employer* associated with the above payroll. Assumed tax rates are as follows: FICA tax of 7%, state unemployment tax of 2.7%, and a federal unemployment tax of .7%.

c What is the amount of the total payroll expense of Copper Kettle for the first week in January? Show computations.

13-11 Two of the employees of Window Craft receive monthly salaries; the remaining three employees are paid an hourly rate with provision for time and one-half for overtime. The basic data for the May 31 payroll are given below:

	Hours			Com-pensation to April 30	Gross Pay Due for May	Federal Income Tax Withheld
Employee	Reg	OT	Pay Rate			
Allen	160	15	$ 8.00/hr	$ 6,000	$1,460	$ 275
Benson	160		7.00/hr	4,000	1,120	230
Cramer	160	12	5.00/hr	3,560	890	125
Dodson .... Salary			1,440.00/mo	5,760	1,440	300
Eller .... Salary			3,000.00/mo	12,000	3,000	505
Total					$7,910	$1,435

Other data Compensation of Dodson and Eller is considered an administrative expense; the balance of the earnings is chargeable to Shop Wages. Payroll taxes apply as follows: FICA, 7% up to maximum of $35,000; state unemployment, 2.7% up to maximum of $6,000; federal unemployment, .7% up to maximum of $6,000. Window Craft has group insurance and a retirement plan under which all employees contribute 5% of their gross pay and the company matches this contribution. Both employees' and employer's contributions are deposited with the Reliable Insurance Company at the end of each month.

Instructions

a Prepare a payroll register for May using the following columns:

		Amount Subject to		Federal Income Tax Withheld	FICA Tax Withheld	Retire-ment Deduc-tion	Net Pay Due
Employee	Gross Pay	Unemploy-ment Taxes	FICA Tax				

b Explain why the federal income taxes withheld for Allen are less than those withheld for Dodson despite the fact that Allen received a higher gross compensation.

c Prepare in general journal form the entry to record the payroll for the month of May and the amounts withheld from employees. (Do not include payroll taxes on employer in this entry.)

d Prepare in general journal form the entry to record the employer's payroll taxes and insurance plan contributions for the month of May. (The account to be debited for the expense to the employer of contributions for group insurance and retirement may be entitled Group Insurance and Retirement Expense.)

BUSINESS DECISION PROBLEM 13

Marvelous Mattress Co. currently earns $2 million a year before income taxes and has 400,000 shares of capital stock outstanding. The company is planning to expand its plant facilities at a cost of $6 million. Management estimates that this expansion will increase annual income before income taxes by 24% of the cost of the new facilities. The company pays income taxes equal to 40% of its income before income taxes.

Two proposals are under consideration for raising the $6 million for the new plant facilities:

Stock Financing   Issue 200,000 shares of capital stock at a price of $30 per share.
Bond Financing   Borrow $6 million on a 20-year bond issue, with interest at 14%.

Instructions

a Prepare a schedule showing the expected earnings per share of capital stock during the first year of operations following the completion of the $6 million expansion, under each of the two proposed means of financing.

b Evaluate the two proposed means of financing from the viewpoint of a major stockholder of Marvelous Mattress Co.

APPLICATIONS OF PRESENT VALUE

After studying this appendix you should be able to:

- Explain the concept of present value.
- Identify the three factors that affect the present value of a future amount.
- Compute the present value of a future amount and of an annuity using present value tables.
- Discuss various accounting applications of the present value concept.

The concept of present value has many applications in accounting, but it is most easily explained in the context of evaluating investment opportunities. In this context, the present value of an expected future cash receipt is the amount that a knowledgeable investor would pay *today* for the right to receive that future amount. The present value is always *less* than the future amount, because the investor will expect to earn a return on the investment. The amount by which the future cash receipt exceeds its present value represents the investor's profit; in short, this difference may be regarded as *interest revenue* included in the future amount.

The present value of a particular investment opportunity depends upon three factors: (1) the expected dollar amount to be received in the future, (2) the length of time until the future amount will be received, and (3) the rate of return (called the *discount rate*) required by the investor. The process of determining the present value of a future cash receipt or payment is called *discounting* the future amount.

To illustrate the present value concept, assume that a specific investment is expected to result in a $1,000 cash receipt at the end of one year. An investor

523

requiring a 10% annual rate of return would be willing to pay $909 today (computed as $1,000 ÷ 1.10) for the right to receive this future amount. This computation may be verified as follows (amounts rounded to the nearest dollar):

Amount to be invested (present value)	$ 909
Required return on investment ($909 × 10%)	91
Amount to be received in one year (future value)	$1,000

If the $1,000 is to be received **two years** in the future, the investor would pay only $826 for the investment today [($1,000 ÷ 1.10) ÷ 1.10]. This computation may be verified as follows (amounts rounded to the nearest dollar):

Amount to be invested (present value)	$ 826
Required return on investment in first year ($826 × 10%)	83
Amount invested after one year	$ 909
Required return on investment in second year ($909 × 10%)	91
Amount to be received in two years (future value)	$1,000

The amount that our investor would pay today, $826, is the *present value* of $1,000 to be received two years later, discounted at an annual rate of 10%. The $174 difference between the $826 present value and the $1,000 future amount may be regarded as the return (interest revenue) to be earned by the investor over the two-year period.

Present value tables

Although we can compute the present value of future amounts by a series of divisions as illustrated above, a more convenient method is available. We can use a *table of present values* to find the present value of $1 at a specified discount rate and then multiply that value by the future amount. For example, in the table shown at the top of the next page, the present value of $1 to be received in two years, discounted at an annual rate of 10%, is $0.826. If we multiply .826 by the expected future cash receipt of $1,000, we get an answer of $826, the same amount produced by the series of divisions in our previous illustration.

Selecting an appropriate discount rate

The *discount rate* may be viewed as the investor's required rate of return. All investments involve some degree of risk that actual future cash flows may turn out to be less than expected. Investors usually will expect a rate of return which justifies taking this risk. Under today's market conditions, investors require annual returns of between 8% and 15% on low-risk investments, such as government bonds and certificates of deposit. For relatively high-risk investments, such as the introduction of a new product line, investors may expect to earn an annual return of perhaps 20% or more.

In addition to the amount of risk involved, the "appropriate" discount rate for determining the present value of a specific investment depends upon the investor's cost of capital and the returns available from other investment oppor-

Table 1   ***Present Value of $1 Due in n Periods****

Number of Periods (n)	Discount Rate							
	1%	**1½%**	**5%**	**6%**	**10%**	**12%**	**15%**	**20%**
1	.990	.985	.952	.943	.909	.893	.870	.833
2	.980	.971	.907	.890	.826	.797	.756	.694
3	.971	.956	.864	.840	.751	.712	.658	.579
4	.961	.942	.823	.792	.683	.636	.572	.482
5	.951	.928	.784	.747	.621	.567	.497	.402
6	.942	.915	.746	.705	.564	.507	.432	.335
7	.933	.901	.711	.665	.513	.452	.376	.279
8	.923	.888	.677	.627	.467	.404	.327	.233
9	.914	.875	.645	.592	.424	.361	.284	.194
10	.905	.862	.614	.558	.386	.322	.247	.162
20	.820	.742	.377	.312	.149	.104	.061	.026
24	.788	.700	.310	.247	.102	.066	.035	.013

*The present value of $1 is computed by the formula $p = 1/(1 + i)^n$, where p is the present value of $1, i is the discount rate, and n is the number of periods until the future cash flow will occur. Amounts in this table have been rounded to three decimal places and are shown for a limited number of periods and discount rates.

tunities. When a higher discount rate is used, the resulting present value will be lower and the investor, therefore, will be interested in the investment only at a lower price.

Discounting annual cash flows

Let us now assume that an investment is expected to produce an annual net cash flow of $10,000 for each of the next three years. If Camino Company expects a 12% return on this type of investment, it may compute the present value of these cash flows as follows:

Year	Expected Net Cash Flow	×	Present Value of $1 Discounted at 12%	=	Present Value of Net Cash Flows
1	$10,000		.893		$ 8,930
2	10,000		.797		7,970
3	10,000		.712		7,120
Total present value of the investment					$24,020

This analysis indicates that the present value of the expected net cash flows from the investment, discounted at an annual rate of 12%, amounts to $24,020. This is the maximum amount that Camino Company could afford to pay for this investment and still expect to earn the 12% required rate of return.

In the preceding schedule, we multiplied each of the expected annual cash flows by the present value of $1 in the appropriate future period, discounted at 12% per year. The present values of the annual cash flows were then added to determine the total present value of the investment. Separately discounting each annual cash flow to its present value is necessary only when the cash flows vary in amount from one year to the next. Since the annual cash flows in our example are *uniform in amount,* there are two easier ways to compute the total present value.

One way is to add the three decimal figures representing the present value of $1 in the successive years (.893 + .797 + .712) and then to multiply this total (2.402) by the $10,000 annual cash flow. This approach produces the same result ($10,000 × 2.402 = $24,020) we obtained by determining the present value of each year's cash flow separately and adding the results.

An even easier approach to determining the present value of uniform annual cash flows is to refer to an *annuity table,* which shows the present value of $1 to be received periodically for a given number of periods. An annuity table is shown below:

Table 2 **Present Value of $1 to Be Received Periodically for n Periods**

Number of Periods (n)	Discount Rate							
	1%	**1½%**	**5%**	**6%**	**10%**	**12%**	**15%**	**20%**
1	0.990	0.985	0.952	0.943	0.909	0.893	0.870	0.833
2	1.970	1.956	1.859	1.833	1.736	1.690	1.626	1.528
3	2.941	2.912	2.723	2.673	2.487	2.402	2.283	2.106
4	3.902	3.854	3.546	3.465	3.170	3.037	2.855	2.589
5	4.853	4.783	4.329	4.212	3.791	3.605	3.352	2.991
6	5.795	5.697	5.076	4.917	4.355	4.111	3.784	3.326
7	6.728	6.598	5.786	5.582	4.868	4.564	4.160	3.605
8	7.652	7.486	6.463	6.210	5.335	4.968	4.487	3.837
9	8.566	8.361	7.108	6.802	5.759	5.328	4.772	4.031
10	9.471	9.222	7.722	7.360	6.145	5.650	5.019	4.192
20	18.046	17.169	12.462	11.470	8.514	7.469	6.259	4.870
24	21.243	20.030	13.799	12.550	8.985	7.784	6.434	4.937

Note that the present value of $1 to be received periodically (annually) for three years, discounted at 12% per year, is 2.402. Thus, $10,000 received annually for three years, discounted at 12%, is $24,020 ($10,000 × 2.402).

Discount periods of less than one year

The interval between regular periodic cash flows is termed the *discount period.* In our preceding examples we have assumed annual cash flows and, therefore, discount periods of one year. Often a note or a contract may call for cash payments on a more frequent basis, such as monthly, quarterly, or semiannually. The illustrated present value tables can be used with discount periods of any length, *but the discount rate must relate to the time interval of the discount period.* Thus, if we use the annuity table to find the present value of a series of monthly cash payments, the discount rate must be expressed as a monthly interest rate.

To illustrate, assume that StyleMart purchases merchandise from Western Fashions, issuing in exchange a $9,600 note payable to be paid in 24 monthly installments of $400 each. As discussed in Chapter 8, both companies should record this transaction at the present value of the note. If a reasonable *annual* interest rate for this type of note is 12%, we should discount the monthly cash payments at the *monthly* rate of 1%. The annuity table shows the present value of $1 to be received (or paid) for 24 monthly periods, discounted at 1% per month, is 21.243. Thus, the present value of the installment note issued by StyleMart is $8,497 ($400 × 21.243, rounded to the nearest dollar).

Accounting applications of the present value concept

Accounting applications of the concept of present value have been discussed at appropriate points throughout this textbook. We will now demonstrate these applications with examples which make use of our present value tables.

Valuation of long-term notes receivable and payable (Chapter 8)   When a long-term note receivable or payable does not bear a realistic stated rate of interest, a portion of the face amount of the note should be regarded as representing an interest charge. The amount of this interest charge can be determined by discounting the note to its present value using as a discount rate a realistic rate of interest.

To illustrate, consider our preceding example in which StyleMart purchases merchandise from Western Fashions by issuing an installment note payable with a face amount of $9,600 and no stated rate of interest. The present value of this note, discounted at the realistic market interest rate of 1% per month, was $8,497. The difference between the $9,600 face amount of the note and its present value of $8,497 is $1,103, which represents the interest charge included in the face amount. StyleMart should use the present value of the note in determining the cost of the merchandise and the amount of the related net liability, as shown by the following entry:

Purchases	8,497	
Discount on Notes Payable	1,103	
Notes Payable		9,600

Purchased merchandise by issuing a 24-month installment note payable
with a 1% monthly interest charge included in the face amount.

Assuming that StyleMart uses the effective interest method to amortize the discount on the note, the entry to record the first monthly payment and the related interest expense is as follows:

Notes Payable	*400*	
Interest Expense	*85*	
Discount on Notes Payable		*85*
Cash		*400*

To record first monthly payment on installment note payable and recognize one month's interest expense ($8,497 × 1%, rounded to nearest dollar).

Estimating the value of goodwill (Chapter 10)   The asset goodwill may be defined as the present value of expected future earnings in excess of the normal return on net identifiable assets. One method of estimating goodwill is to estimate the annual amounts by which earnings are expected to exceed a normal return and then to discount these amounts to their present value.

For example, assume that John Reed is negotiating to purchase a small but very successful business. In addition to paying the fair market value of the company's net identifiable assets, Reed is willing to pay an appropriate amount for goodwill. He believes that the business will probably earn at least $40,000 in excess of "normal earnings" in each of the next five years. If Reed requires a 20% annual return on purchased goodwill, he would be willing to pay $119,640 for this expected five-year $40,000 annuity, computed as follows: $40,000 × 2.991 (from Table 2) = $119,640.

Market prices of bonds (Chapter 13)   The market price of bonds may be regarded as the *present value* to bondholders of the future principal and interest payments. To illustrate, assume that a corporation issues $1,000,000 face value of 9%, 10-year bonds when the going market rate of interest is 10%. Since bond interest is paid semiannually, we must use 20 *semiannual* periods as the life of the bond issue and a 5% *semiannual* market rate of interest in our present value calculations. The expected issuance price of this bond issue may be computed as follows:

Present value of future principal payments:
  $1,000,000 due after 20 semiannual periods, discounted at 5% per period:
    $1,000,000 × .377 (from Table 1, page 525) $377,000
Present value of future interest payments:
  $45,000 per period ($1,000,000 × 9% × ½) for 20 semiannual periods,
    discounted at 5%: $45,000 × 12.462 (from Table 2, page 526) 560,790
Expected issuance price of bond issue* $937,790

*The terms of this bond issue correspond with those of the bond issue illustrated in the amortization table on page 495 in Chapter 13. In the amortization table, however, the issuance price of the bonds is $937,689, or $101 less than indicated by our computations above. The difference results from our rounding the present value of $1 to only three decimal places. Rounding to three decimal places may cause an error of up to $500 per $1 million.

Capital leases (Chapter 13)   A capital lease is regarded as a sale of the leased asset by the lessor to the lessee. At the date of this sale, the lessor recognizes sales revenue equal to the *present value* of the future lease payments receivable, discounted at a realistic rate of interest. The lessee also uses the present value of the future payments to determine the cost of the leased asset and the valuation of the related liability.

To illustrate, assume that on December 1, Kelly Grading Co. enters into a capital lease contract to finance the purchase of a bulldozer from Midwest Tractor Sales. The terms of the lease call for 24 monthly payments of $7,000 each, beginning on December 31. These lease payments include an interest charge of 1½% per month. At the end of the 24-month lease, title to the bulldozer will pass to Kelly Grading Co.

The annuity table on page 526 shows that the present value of $1 to be received monthly for 24 months, discounted at 1½% per month, is 20.030. Therefore, the present value of the 24 future lease payments is $7,000 × 20.030, or $140,210. Kelly Grading Co. (the lessee) should use this present value in determining the cost of the bulldozer and the amount of the related liability, as shown in the following entry:

Entry by lessee

Leased Equipment	140,210	
Lease Payment Obligation		140,210

To record acquisition of bulldozer from Midwest Tractor Sales on a capital lease. Lease terms call for 24 monthly payments of $7,000, which include a 1½% monthly interest charge.

Note that the cost assigned to the leased equipment is only $140,210, even though Kelly Grading Co. must actually pay $168,000 ($7,000 × 24 payments) over the life of the lease. The difference between these two amounts, $27,790, will be recognized by Kelly Grading Co. as interest expense over the next 24 months.

Midwest Tractor Sales (the lessor) should also use the present value of the future lease payments in determining the sales price of the bulldozer and the amount of the related receivable. Assuming that the bulldozer was carried in the perpetual inventory records at a cost of $110,000, the entry to record the sale is:

Entry by lessor

Lease Payments Receivable (net)	140,210	
Cost of Goods Sold	110,000	
Inventory		110,000
Sales		140,210

Financed sale of bulldozer to Kelly Grading Co. using a capital lease. Terms call for 24 monthly payments of $7,000, including a 1½% monthly interest charge. Gross amount of the receivable is $168,000, of which $27,790 is unearned interest.

PROBLEMS

A-1   Use the tables on pages 525 and 526 to determine the present value of the following cash flows:

a $10,000 to be paid annually for seven years, discounted at an annual rate of 15%.

b $4,250 to be received today, assuming that money can be invested to earn 20% annually.

c $350 to be paid monthly for 24 months, with an additional "balloon payment" of $15,000 due at the end of the twenty-fourth month, discounted at a monthly interest rate of 1½%.

d $30,000 to be received annually for the first three years, followed by $20,000 to be received annually for the next two years (total of five years in which payments are made), discounted at an annual rate of 12%.

A-2 On June 30 of the current year, Rural Gas & Electric Co. issued $10,000,000 par value, 11%, 10-year bonds payable, with interest dates of December 31 and June 30. The bonds were issued at a discount, resulting in an effective semiannual interest rate of 6%. The company maintains its accounts on a calendar-year basis and amortizes the bond discount by the effective interest method.

Instructions

a Compute the issuance price for the bond issue which results in an effective semiannual interest rate of 6%. (Hint: Discount both the interest payments and the maturity value over 20 semiannual periods.)

b Prepare all journal entries necessary to record the issuance of the bonds and bond interest expense during Year 1, assuming that the sales price of the bonds on June 30 was the amount you computed in part **a**.

A-3 On December 1, Showcase Interiors purchased a shipment of furniture from Colonial House by paying $10,500 cash and issuing an installment note payable in the face amount of $28,800. The note is to be paid in 24 monthly installments of $1,200 each. Although the note makes no mention of an interest charge, the rate of interest usually charged to Showcase Interiors in such transactions is 1½% per month.

Instructions

a Compute the present value of the note payable, using a discount rate of 1½% per month.

b Prepare the journal entries in the accounts of Showcase Interiors on:
   (1) December 1, to record the purchase of the furniture (debit Purchases).
   (2) December 31, to record the first $1,200 monthly payment on the note and to recognize interest expense for one month by the effective interest method. (Round interest expense to the nearest dollar.)

c Show how the liability for this note would appear in the balance sheet at December 31. (Assume that the note is classified as a current liability.)

A-4 Metropolitan Transit District plans to acquire a large computer system by entering into a long-term lease agreement with the computer manufacturer. The manufacturer will provide the computer system under either of the following lease agreements:

Five-year lease   MTD is to pay $2,500,000 at the beginning of the lease (delivery date) and $1,000,000 annually at the end of each of the next five years. At the end of the fifth year, MTD may take title to the system for an additional payment of $3,000,000.

Ten-year lease   MTD is to pay $2,000,000 at the beginning of the lease and $900,000 annually at the end of each of the next 10 years. At the end of the tenth year, MTD may take title for an additional payment of $1,300,000.

Under either proposal, MTD will buy the computer at the end of the lease. MTD is a governmental agency which does not seek to earn a profit and is not evaluating alternative investment opportunities. However, MTD does attempt to minimize its cost and it must borrow the money to finance either lease agreement at an annual interest rate of 12%.

Instructions

a Determine which lease proposal results in the lower cost for the computer system when the future cash outlays are discounted at an annual interest rate of 12%.

b Prepare a journal entry to record the acquisition of the computer system under the lease agreement selected in part **a.** This journal entry will include the initial cash payment to the computer manufacturer required at the beginning of the lease.

A-5   On December 31, Year 5, Richland Farms sold a tract of land, which had cost $300,000, to Skyline Developers in exchange for $50,000 cash and a four-year, 4%, note receivable for $400,000. Interest on the note is payable annually, and the principal amount is due on December 31, Year 9. The accountant for Richland Farms did not notice the unrealistically low interest rate on the note and made the following entry on December 31 to record the sale:

Cash	50,000	
Notes Receivable	400,000	
Land		300,000
Gain on Sale of Land		150,000
Sold land to Skyline Developers in exchange for cash and a four-		
year note with interest due annually.		

Instructions

a Compute the present value of the note receivable from Skyline Developers, assuming that a realistic rate of interest for this transaction is 20%. (Hint: Consider both the annual interest payments and the principal amount of the note.)

b Prepare the journal entry on December 31, Year 5, to record the sale of the land correctly. Show supporting computations for (1) the gain or loss on the sale, and (2) the discount on the note receivable.

c Explain what effects the error made by Richland Farms' accountant will have upon (1) the net income for Year 5, and (2) the combined net income for Years 6 through 9. Ignore income taxes.

14

ACCOUNTING PRINCIPLES AND CONCEPTS; EFFECTS OF INFLATION

After studying this chapter you should be able to:

- Identify the major sources of generally accepted accounting principles.
- Discuss the accounting principles, assumptions, and conventions presented on pages 535–544.
- Define an audit and discuss the nature of the auditors' report.
- Explain why using historical costs overstates profits during periods of inflation.
- Use a price index to restate historical costs to an equivalent number of current dollars.
- Distinguish between the constant dollar and current cost approaches to measuring net income. Prepare an income statement using either approach.
- Explain why holding monetary items causes gains or losses in purchasing power.

Throughout this book we try to explain the theoretical roots of each new accounting principle or standard as it comes under consideration. When you travel through new territory, however, you may find it useful to pause at some intermediate stage in your trip to consider what you have seen and to sort out your observations into some meaningful overall impression. This seems an appropriate point in our discussion of accounting for such a pause. You now have an overview of the accounting process and should be better prepared to understand how accounting procedures are shaped by theoretical concepts.

Need for recognized accounting standards

The basic objective of financial statements is to provide information about a business enterprise; information that will be useful in making economic decisions. Investors, managers, economists, bankers, labor leaders, and government administrators all rely upon financial statements and other accounting reports in making the decisions which shape our economy. Therefore, it is of vital importance that the information contained in financial statements be highly reliable and clearly understood. Also, it is important for financial statements to be prepared in a manner which permits them to be compared fairly with prior years' statements and with financial statements of other companies. In short, we need a well-defined body of accounting principles or standards to guide accountants in preparing financial statements with the characteristics of *reliability, understandability,* and *comparability.*

Generally accepted accounting principles

The principles which constitute the "ground rules" for financial reporting are termed *generally accepted accounting principles.* Accounting principles are also referred to as *standards, assumptions, postulates, and concepts.* The various terms used to describe accounting principles indicate the many efforts which have been made to develop a satisfactory framework of accounting theory.[1] For example, the word *standards* was chosen rather than *principles* when the Financial Accounting Standards Board replaced the Accounting Principles Board as the top rule-making body of the accounting profession. The efforts to construct a satisfactory body of accounting theory are still in process, because accounting theory must continually change with changes in the business environment and changes in the needs of financial statement users.

Accounting principles are not rooted in laws of nature, as are the laws of the physical sciences. Rather, accounting principles are developed in relation to what we consider to be the most important objectives of financial reporting. For example, in recent years accountants as well as business executives have recognized that part of the "cost" to society of conducting certain types of economic activity includes the pollution of air and water and other damage to the environment. Research is currently being undertaken to develop accounting principles for the identification and measurement of these "social costs."

The conceptual framework project

The most recent effort to develop a comprehensive framework for financial accounting and reporting is the conceptual framework project currently being carried on by the Financial Accounting Standards Board. The FASB has described the framework which it hopes to develop as ". . . a *constitution,* a coherent system of interrelated objectives and fundamentals that can lead to consistent standards and that prescribe the nature, function, and limits of financial accounting and financial statements."[2]

---

[1]See, for example, *Accounting Research Study No. 1,* "The Basic Postulates of Accounting," AICPA (New York: 1961); *Accounting Research Study No. 3,* "A Tentative Set of Broad Accounting Principles for Business Enterprises," AICPA (New York: 1962); and the series of *Statements of Financial Accounting Concepts* issued by the FASB.

[2]*FASB Discussion Memorandum,* "Conceptual Framework for Financial Accounting and Reporting: Elements of Financial Statements and Their Measurement," FASB (Stamford, Conn.: 1976).

It is difficult to predict the extent to which the conceptual framework project may affect the basic concepts and principles currently used in developing accounting information. Perhaps the changes will be few; on the other hand, the proposed changes could be as major a departure from historical cost as the basis for asset valuation and income determination. In any case, the conceptual framework project is indicative of the continuing effort within the accounting profession to improve the relevance and reliability of accounting information.

Authoritative support for accounting principles

To qualify as "generally accepted," an accounting principle must usually receive "substantial authoritative support." The most influential authoritative groups in this country include (1) the American Institute of Certified Public Accountants (AICPA), the professional association of licensed CPAs; (2) the Financial Accounting Standards Board which includes representatives from public accounting, industry, education, and government; and (3) the Securities and Exchange Commission (SEC), an agency of the federal government established to administer laws and regulations relating to the publication of financial information by corporations whose stock is publicly owned.[3] Also important in the development of accounting theory has been the American Accounting Association, an organization of accounting educators.

American Institute of Certified Public Accountants (AICPA)   The AICPA has long been concerned with stating and defining accounting principles because its members daily face the problem of making decisions about generally accepted principles as they perform audits and other professional work. Some years ago, the AICPA established the Accounting Principles Board (APB), which issued 31 formal *Opinions* on specific accounting practices and also issued broad *Statements* designed to improve the quality of financial reporting. In 1973, the Accounting Principles Board was replaced by the Financial Accounting Standards Board. However, the Opinions and Statements of the APB *remain in effect.*

Financial Accounting Standards Board (FASB)   The FASB was established by the AICPA as an independent body to assume the responsibilities of the former Accounting Principles Board. The FASB consists of seven full-time members, including representatives from public accounting, industry, government, and accounting education.

Lending support to the FASB are an advisory council and a large research staff. The FASB is authorized to issue *Statements of Financial Accounting Standards,* which represent expressions of generally accepted accounting principles. As discussed earlier in this chapter, the FASB also is attempting to develop a broad conceptual framework for financial accounting and reporting.

---

[3]Other professional organizations which have influenced the development of accounting principles are the National Association of Accountants and the Financial Executives Institute. In addition to the SEC, the following government regulatory agencies influence financial reporting of business units falling under their jurisdiction: Federal Power Commission, Interstate Commerce Commission, Civil Aeronautics Board, and Federal Communications Commission.

Securities and Exchange Commission (SEC) The SEC has legal authority to establish accounting principles and disclosure requirements for all large, publicly owned corporations. The views of the Commission on various accounting issues are published in the SEC's *Accounting Series Releases,* or *ASRs.* In the past, the SEC has tended to adopt or to modify the recommendations of the FASB, rather than to develop its own independent set of accounting principles.

American Accounting Association (AAA) The AAA has sponsored a number of research studies and monographs in which individual authors and Association committees attempt to summarize accounting principles. These statements have had considerable influence on the thinking of accounting theorists and practitioners. However, the AAA lacks the power of the FASB to impose its collective view on accounting practice; it therefore exercises its influence through the prestige of its authors and the persuasiveness of their views.

In addition to the above sources, "substantial authoritative support" may include widespread use of an accounting practice within a particular industry, or general recognition of a practice in the accounting literature.

Because accounting principles must evolve with changes in the business environment, there is no complete list of generally accepted accounting principles. There is, however, a consensus among accountants and informed users of financial statements as to what these principles are. Most accounting principles are applicable to profit-making organizations of any size and form. We shall now discuss briefly the major principles that govern the accounting process and comment on some areas of controversy.

The accounting entity concept

One of the basic principles of accounting is that information is compiled for a clearly defined accounting entity. An accounting entity is any *economic unit* which controls resources and engages in economic activities. An individual is an accounting entity. So is a business enterprise, whether organized as a proprietorship, partnership, or corporation. Governmental agencies are accounting entities, as are all nonprofit clubs and organizations. An accounting entity also may be defined as an identifiable economic unit *within a larger accounting entity.* For example, the Chevrolet Division of General Motors Corporation may be viewed as an accounting entity separate from GM's other activities.

The economic unit for which accounting information is compiled also may be larger than a single corporation. *Consolidated financial statements* show the financial position and operating results of a group of affiliated corporations as though the affiliated companies were a single business organization. Consolidated financial statements are discussed in the appendix following this chapter.

The basic accounting equation, Assets = Liabilities + Owners' Equity, reflects the accounting entity concept since the elements of the equation relate *to the particular entity whose economic activity is being reported in the financial statements.* Although we have considerable flexibility in defining our accounting entity, we must be careful to use the *same definition* in the measurement of assets, liabilities, owners' equity, revenue, and expense. An income statement would not make sense, for example, if it included all the revenue of General Motors Corporation but listed only the expenses of the Chevrolet Division.

The going-concern assumption

An underlying assumption in accounting is that an accounting entity will continue in operation for a period of time sufficient to carry out its existing commitments. The assumption of continuity, especially in the case of corporations, is in accord with experience in our economic system. This assumption leads to the concept of the *going concern.* In general, the going-concern assumption justifies ignoring immediate liquidating values in presenting assets and liabilities in the balance sheet.

For example, suppose that a company has just purchased a three-year insurance policy for $5,000. If we assume that the business will continue in operation for three years or more, we will consider the $5,000 cost of the insurance as an asset which provides services (freedom from risk) to the business over a three-year period. On the other hand, if we assume that the business is likely to terminate in the near future, the insurance policy should be recorded at its cancellation value—the amount of cash which can be obtained from the insurance company as a refund on immediate cancellation of the policy, which may be, say, $4,500.

Although the assumption of a going concern is justified in most normal situations, it should be dropped when it is not in accord with the facts. Accountants are sometimes asked to prepare a statement of financial position for an enterprise that is about to liquidate. In this case the assumption of continuity is no longer valid and the accountant drops the going-concern assumption and reports assets at their current liquidating value and liabilities at the amount required to settle the debts immediately.

The time period principle

We assume an indefinite life for most accounting entities. But accountants are asked to measure operating progress and changes in economic position at relatively short time intervals during this indefinite life. Users of financial statements need periodic measurements for decision making.

The need for frequent measurements creates many of the accountant's most challenging problems. Dividing the life of an enterprise into time segments, such as a year or a quarter of a year, requires numerous estimates and assumptions. For example, estimates must be made of the useful lives of depreciable assets and assumptions must be made as to appropriate depreciation methods. Thus periodic measurements of net income and financial position are at best only informed estimates. The tentative nature of periodic measurements should be understood by those who rely on periodic accounting information.

The monetary principle

The monetary principle means that money is used as the basic measuring unit for financial reporting. Money is the common denominator in which accounting measurements are made and summarized. The dollar, or any other monetary unit, represents a unit of value; that is, it reflects ability to command goods and services. Implicit in the use of money as a measuring unit is the *assumption that the dollar is a stable unit of value*, just as the mile is a stable unit of distance and an acre is a stable unit of area.

Having accepted money as a measuring unit, accountants freely combine dollar measures of economic transactions that occur at various times during the life of an accounting entity. They combine, for example, a $20,000 cost of equipment purchased in 1975 and the $40,000 cost of similar equipment purchased in 1980 and report the total as a $60,000 investment in equipment.

Unlike the mile and the acre, which are stable units of distance and area, the dollar *is not a stable unit of value.* The prices of goods and services in our economy change over time. When the *general price level* (a phrase used to describe the average of all prices) increases, the value of money (that is, its ability to command goods and services) decreases.

Despite the steady erosion in the purchasing power of the dollar in the United States during the last 40 years, accountants have continued to prepare financial statements in which the value of the dollar is assumed to be stable. This unrealistic assumption is one of the reasons why financial statements are viewed by some critics as misleading. Accounting principles are currently evolving toward restatement of accounting information for the changing value of the dollar and toward the preparation of supplementary statements showing current replacement costs. The adjustment of accounting information to reflect the effects of inflation will be discussed in a subsequent section of this chapter.

The objectivity principle

The term *objective* refers to measurements that are unbiased and subject to verification by independent experts. For example, the price established in an arm's-length transaction is an objective measure of exchange value at the time of the transaction. Exchange prices established in business transactions constitute much of the raw material from which accounting information is generated. Accountants rely on various kinds of evidence to support their financial measurements, but they seek always the most objective evidence available. Invoices, contracts, paid checks, and physical counts of inventory are examples of objective evidence.

If a measurement is objective, 10 competent investigators who make the same measurement will come up with substantially identical results. However, 10 competent accountants who set out independently to measure the net income of a given business would *not* arrive at an identical result. Despite the goal of objectivity, it is not possible to insulate accounting information from opinion and personal judgment. The cost of a depreciable asset can be determined objectively but not the periodic depreciation expense. To measure the cost of the asset services that have been used up during a given period requires estimates of the residual value and service life of the asset and judgment as to the depreciation method that should be used. Such estimates and judgments can produce significant variations in net income.

Objectivity in accounting has its roots in the quest for reliability. Accountants want to make their economic measurements reliable and, at the same time, as relevant to decision makers as possible. Where to draw the line in the trade-off between *reliability* and *relevance* is one of the crucial issues in accounting theory. Thus, accountants are constantly faced with the necessity of compromising between what users of financial information would like to know and what it is possible to measure with a reasonable degree of reliability.

Asset valuation: the cost principle

Both the balance sheet and the income statement are affected by the cost principle. Assets are initially recorded in the accounts at cost, and no adjustment is made to this valuation in later periods, except to allocate a portion of the original cost to expense as the assets expire. At the time an asset is originally acquired, cost represents the "fair market value" of the goods or services exchanged, as evidenced by an arm's-length transaction. With the passage of time, however, the fair market value of such assets as land and buildings may change greatly from their historical cost. These later changes in fair market value generally have been ignored in the accounts, and the assets have continued to be valued in the balance sheet at historical cost (less the portion of that cost which has been allocated to expense).

Increasing numbers of professional accountants believe that current market values should be used as the basis for asset valuation rather than historical cost. These accountants argue that current values would result in a more meaningful balance sheet. Also, they claim that current values should be allocated to expense to represent fairly the cost to the entity of the goods or services consumed in the effort to generate revenue.

The cost principle is derived from the principle of *objectivity.* Those who support the cost principle argue that it is important that users have confidence in financial statements, and this confidence can best be maintained if accountants recognize changes in assets and liabilities only on the basis of completed transactions. Objective evidence generally exists to support cost, but evidence supporting current values may be less readily available.

Measuring revenue: the realization principle

When should revenue be recognized? Under the assumptions of accrual accounting, revenue should be recognized "when it is earned." However, the "earning" of revenue usually is an extended *economic process* and does not actually take place at a single point in time.

Some revenue, such as interest earned, is directly related to time periods. For this type of revenue, it is easy to determine how much revenue has been earned by computing how much of the earning process is complete. However, the earning process for sales revenue relates to *economic activity* rather than to a specific period of time. In a manufacturing business, for example, the earning process involves (1) acquisition of raw materials, (2) production of finished goods, (3) sale of the finished goods, and (4) collection of cash from credit customers.

In the manufacturing example, there is little objective evidence to indicate how much revenue has been earned during the first two stages of the earning process. Accountants therefore usually do not recognize revenue until the revenue has been *realized*. Revenue is realized when both of the following conditions are met: (1) the earning process is *essentially complete* and (2) *objective evidence* exists as to the amount of revenue earned.

In most cases, the realization principle indicates that revenue should be recognized *at the time of the sale of goods or the rendering of services.* Recognizing revenue at this point is logical because the firm has essentially completed the earning process and the realized value of the goods or services sold can be measured objectively in terms of the price billed to customers. At any time prior to sale, the ultimate realizable value of the goods or services sold can only be estimated. After the sale, the only step that remains is to collect from the customer, and this is usually a relatively certain event.

In Chapter 3, we described a *cash basis* of income measurement whereby revenue is recognized only when cash is collected from customers and expenses are recorded only when cash is actually paid out. Cash basis accounting *does not conform* to generally accepted accounting principles, but it is widely used by individuals in determining their *taxable* income. (Remember that the accounting methods used in income tax returns often differ from those used in financial statements.)

The installment method   Companies selling goods on the installment plan sometimes use the installment method of accounting for income tax purposes. Under the installment method, the seller recognizes the gross profit on sales gradually over an extended time span as the cash is actually collected from customers. If the gross profit rate on installment sales is 30%, then out of every dollar collected on installment receivables, the sum of 30 cents represents gross profit.

To illustrate, assume that on December 15, Year 1, a retailer sells for $400 a television set which cost $280, or 70% of the sales price. The terms of the sale call for a $100 cash down payment with the balance payable in 15 monthly installments of $20 each, beginning on January 1, Year 2. (Interest charges are ignored in this illustration.) The collections of cash and recognition of profit under the installment method are summarized below:

	Year	Cash Collected	−	Cost Recovery. 70%	=	Profit Earned, 30%
Installment method illustrated	1	$100		$ 70		$ 30
	2	240		168		72
	3	60		42		18
	Totals	$400		$280		$120

This method of profit recognition exists largely because it is allowed for income tax purposes; it postpones the payment of income taxes until cash is collected from customers. From an accounting viewpoint, there is little theoretical justification for delaying the recognition of profit beyond the point of sale. Therefore, the installment method is seldom used in financial statements.[4]

Percentage-of-completion: an exception to the realization principle   Under certain circumstances, accountants may depart from the realization principle and recognize income during the production process. An example arises in the case of long-term construction contracts, such as the building of a dam over a period of five years. Clearly the income statements of a company engaged in such a project would not be useful to managers or investors if no profit or loss were reported until the dam was finally completed. The accountant therefore estimates the portion of the dam completed during each accounting period, and recognizes the gross profit on the project *in proportion* to the work completed. This is known as the percentage-of-completion method of accounting for long-term contracts.

The percentage-of-completion method works as follows:

1 An estimate is made of the total costs to be incurred and the total profit to be earned over the life of the project.
2 Each period, an estimate is made of the portion of the total project completed during the period. This estimate is usually made by expressing the costs incurred during the period as a percentage of the estimated total cost of the project.
3 The percentage figure determined in step **2** is applied to the estimated total profit on the contract to compute the amount of profit applicable to the current accounting period.
4 No estimate is made of the percentage of work during the final period. In the period in which the project is completed, any remaining profit is recognized.

To illustrate, assume that Reed Construction Company enters into a contract to build an irrigation canal at a price of $5,000,000. The canal will be built over a three-year period at an estimated total cost of $4,000,000. Therefore, the estimated total profit on the project is $1,000,000. The following schedule shows the actual costs incurred and the amount of profit to be recognized in each of the three years using the percentage-of-completion method:

	Year	**(A)** **Actual Costs** **Incurred**	**(B)** **Percentage of Work** **Done in Year** **(Column A ÷ $4,000,000)**	**(C)** **Profit Considered** **Earned** **($1,000,000 × Column B)**
Profit recognized as work progresses	1	$ 600,000	15	$150,000
	2	2,000,000	50	500,000
	3	1,452,000	*	298,000 *balance*
	Totals	$4,052,000		$948,000

*Balance required to complete the contract.

[4]Under generally accepted accounting principles, use of the installment method is permissible only when the amounts likely to be collected on installment sales are so uncertain that no reasonable basis exists for estimating an allowance for doubtful accounts.

The percentage of the work completed during Year 1 was estimated by dividing the actual cost incurred in the year by the estimated total cost of the project ($600,000 ÷ $4,000,000 = 15%). Because 15% of the work was done in Year 1, 15% of the estimated total profit of $1,000,000 was considered earned in that year ($1,000,000 × 15% = $150,000). Costs incurred in Year 2 amounted to 50% of the estimated total costs ($2,000,000 ÷ $4,000,000 = 50%); thus, 50% of the estimated total profit was recognized in Year 2 ($1,000,000 × 50% = $500,000). Note that no percentage of work completed figure was computed for Year 3. In Year 3, the total actual cost is known ($4,052,000), and the actual total profit on the contract is determined to be $948,000 ($5,000,000 − $4,052,000). Since profits of $650,000 were previously recognized in Years 1 and 2, the *remaining* profit ($948,000 − $650,000 = $298,000) must be recognized in Year 3.

Although an expected *profit* on a long-term construction contract is recognized in proportion to the work completed, a different treatment is accorded to an expected *loss*. If at the end of any accounting period it appears that a loss will be incurred on a contract in progress, the *entire loss should be recognized at once*.

The percentage-of-completion method should be used only when the total profit expected to be earned can be *reasonably estimated in advance*. If there are substantial uncertainties in the amount of profit which will ultimately be earned, no profit should be recognized until *production is completed*. This approach is often referred to as the *completed-contract method*. If the completed-contract method had been used in the preceding example, no profit would have been recognized in Years 1 and 2; the entire profit of $948,000 would be recorded in Year 3 when the contract was completed and actual costs known.

Measuring expenses: the matching principle

Revenue, the gross increase in net assets resulting from the production or sale of goods and services, if offset by expenses incurred in bringing the firm's output to the point of sale. Examples of expenses relating to revenue are the cost of merchandise sold, the expiration of asset services, and out-of-pocket expenditures for operating costs. The measurement of expenses occurs in two stages: (1) measuring the *cost* of goods and services that will be consumed or expire in generating revenue and (2) determining *when* the goods and services acquired have contributed to revenue and their cost thus *becomes an expense*. The second aspect of the measurement process is often referred to as *matching costs and revenue* and is fundamental to the *accrual basis* of accounting.

Costs are matched with revenue in two major ways:

1 In relation to the product sold or service rendered If goods or services can be related to the product or service which constitutes the output of the enterprise, its cost becomes an expense when the product is sold or the service rendered to customers. The cost of goods sold in a merchandising firm is a good example of this type of expense. Similarly, a commission paid to a real estate salesperson by a real estate brokerage office is an expense directly related to the revenue generated by the salesperson.

2 In relation to the time period during which revenue is earned Some costs incurred by businesses cannot be directly related to the product or service output of the firm. Expired fire insurance, property taxes, depreciation on a building, the salary of the president of the company—all are examples of costs incurred in generating revenue which cannot be related to specific transactions. The accountant refers to this class of costs as *period costs,* and charges them to expense by associating them with the *period of time* during which they are incurred and presumably contribute to revenue, rather than by associating them with specific revenue-producing transactions.

The consistency principle

The principle of *consistency* implies that a particular accounting method, once adopted, will not be changed from period to period. This assumption is important because it assists users of financial statements in interpreting changes in financial position and changes in net income.

Consider the confusion which would result if a company ignored the principle of consistency and changed its method of depreciation every year. The company could cause its net income for any given year to increase or decrease merely by changing its depreciation method.

The principle of consistency does not mean that a company should *never* make a change in its accounting methods. In fact, a company *should* make a change if the new accounting method will provide more useful information than does the method currently in use. But when a significant change in accounting methods does occur, the fact that a change has been made and the dollar effects of the change should be *fully disclosed* in the financial statements. In audited financial statements, the disclosure of a change in accounting method is also incorporated in the CPA's opinion on the financial statements. A typical disclosure might read as follows: "During the current year the company changed from the declining-balance method of computing depreciation to the straight-line method. This change in method had the effect of increasing net income by $210,000."

Consistency applies to a single accounting entity and increases the comparability of financial statements from period to period. Different companies, even those in the same industry, may follow different accounting methods. For this reason, it is important to determine the accounting methods used by companies whose financial statements are being compared.

The disclosure principle

Adequate disclosure means that all *material* and *relevant facts* concerning financial position and the results of operations *are communicated to users.* This can be accomplished either in the financial statements or in the notes accompanying the statements. Such disclosure should make the financial statements more useful and less subject to misinterpretation.

Adequate disclosure does not require that information be presented in great detail; it does require, however, that no important facts be withheld. For example, if a company has been named as defendant in a large lawsuit, this information must be disclosed. Other examples of information which should be disclosed in financial statements include:

1 A summary of the accounting methods used in the preparation of the statements
2 Dollar effects of any changes in these accounting methods during the current period
3 Other significant events affecting financial position, including major new contracts for sale of goods or services, labor strikes, shortages of raw materials, and pending legislation which may significantly affect operations
4 Identification of assets which have been pledged as collateral to secure loans
5 Terms of major borrowing arrangements and existence of large contingent liabilities
6 Contractual provisions relating to leasing arrangements, employee pension and bonus plans, and major proposed asset acquisitions

Even significant events which occur *after* the end of the accounting period but before the financial statements are issued may need to be disclosed.

Naturally, there are practical limits to the amount of disclosure that can be made in financial statements and the accompanying notes. The key point to bear in mind is that the supplementary information should be *relevant to the users* of the financial statements.

Materiality

The term *materiality* refers to the *relative importance* of an item or event. Accountants are primarily concerned with significant information and are not overly concerned with those items which have little effect on financial statements. For example, should the cost of a pencil sharpener, a wastepaper basket, or a stapler be recorded in asset accounts and depreciated over their useful lives? Even though more than one period will benefit from the use of these assets, the concept of materiality permits the immediate recognition of the cost of these items as an expense on grounds that it would be too expensive to undertake depreciation accounting for such low-cost assets and that the results would not differ significantly.

We must recognize that the materiality of an item is a relative matter; what is material for one business unit may not be material for another. Materiality of an item may depend not only on its *amount* but also on its *nature*. In summary, we can state the following rule: *An item is material if there is a reasonable expectation that knowledge of it would influence the decisions of prudent users of financial statements.*

Conservatism as a guide in resolving uncertainties

We have previously referred to the use of *conservatism* in connection with the measurement of net income and the reporting of accounts receivable and inventories in the balance sheet. Although the concept of conservatism may not qualify as an accounting principle, it has long been a powerful influence upon asset valuation and income determination. Conservatism is most useful when matters of judgment or estimates are involved. Ideally, accountants should base their estimates on sound logic and select those accounting methods which neither overstate nor understate the facts. When some doubt exists about the valuation of an asset or the realization of a gain, however, accountants traditionally select the accounting option which produces a lower net income for the current period and a less favorable financial position.

An example of conservatism is the traditional practice of pricing inventory at the lower of cost or market (replacement cost). Decreases in the market value of the inventory are recognized as a part of the cost of goods sold in the current period, but increases in market value of inventory are ignored. Failure to apply conservatism when valuations are especially uncertain may produce misleading information and result in losses to creditors and stockholders.

CPAs' opinion on published financial statements

The annual financial statements of large corporations are used by great numbers of stockholders, creditors, government regulators, and members of the general public. What assurance do these people have that the information in these statements is reliable and is presented in conformity with generally accepted accounting principles? The answer is that the annual financial statements of large corporations are *audited* by independent certified public accountants (CPAs).

An audit is a thorough investigation of every item, dollar amount, and disclosure which appears in the financial statements. After completing the audit, the CPAs express their opinion as to the *fairness* of the financial statements. This opinion, called the *auditors' report,* is published with the statements in the company's annual report to its stockholders.

Considering the extensive investigation that precedes it, the audit opinion is surprisingly short. It usually consists of two brief paragraphs, unless the CPAs comment on unusual features of the financial statements. The first paragraph describes the *scope* of the auditors' examination; the second states their *opinion* of the financial statements. A report by a CPA firm might read as follows:

Independent auditors' report

We have examined the balance sheet of American Oil Corporation as of December 31, 19___, and the related statements of income, retained earnings, and changes in financial position for the year then ended. Our examination was made in accordance with generally accepted auditing standards, and accordingly included such tests of the accounting records and such other auditing procedures as we considered necessary in the circumstances.

In our opinion, the financial statements referred to above *present fairly* the financial position of American Oil Corporation at December 31, 19___, and the results of its operations and the changes in its financial position for the year then ended, *in conformity with generally accepted accounting principles* applied on a basis *consistent with that of the preceding year.* [Emphasis supplied.]

Over many decades, audited financial statements have developed an excellent track record of reliability. Note, however, that the CPAs *do not guarantee* the accuracy of financial statements; rather, they render their *professional opinion* as to the overall *fairness* of the statements. "Fairness," in this context, means that the financial statements are *not misleading.* However, just as a physician may make an error in the diagnosis of a particular patient, there is always a possibility that an auditor's opinion may be in error. The primary responsibility for the reliability of financial statements rests with the management of the issuing company, not with the independent CPAs.

INFLATION—THE GREATEST CHALLENGE TO ACCOUNTING

Inflation may be defined as either an increase in the general price level or a decrease in the purchasing power of the dollar. The *general price level* is the weighted average of the prices of all goods and services in the economy. Changes in the general price level are measured by a *general price index* with a base year assigned a value of 100. The index compares the level of current prices with that of the base year. Assume, for example, that Year 1 is the base year. If prices rise by 10% during Year 2, the price index at the end of Year 2 will be 110. At the end of Year 9 the price index might be 200, indicating that the general price level had doubled since Year 1.

The most widely recognized measure of the general price level in the United States is the Consumer Price Index (CPI), published monthly by the Bureau of Labor Statistics. The base year of the Consumer Price Index is 1967. In October 1978, the CPI passed the 200 level, indicating that prices (on the average) had doubled since 1967.

We often hear statements such as "Today's dollar is worth only 50 cents." The "worth" or "value" of a dollar lies in its ability to buy goods or services. This "value" is called *purchasing power.* The reciprocal of the general price index (100 divided by the current level of the index) represents the purchasing power of the dollar in the current year relative to that in the base year. For example, the reciprocal of the CPI in October 1978 was 100 ÷ 200, or .5. Therefore, we might say that $1 in 1978 was equivalent in purchasing power to 50 cents in 1967.

What effect do material changes in general price levels, and thus changes in the value of money, have on accounting measures? By combining transactions measured in dollars of various years, the accountant in effect ignores changes in the size of the measuring unit. For example, suppose that a company purchased land early in Year 1 for $200,000 and sold this land for $400,000 late in Year 10. Using the dollar as a measuring unit, we would recognize a gain of $200,000 ($400,000 sales price − $200,000 cost) on the sale of the land. But if prices doubled during that 10-year period and the value of money was cut in half, we might say that the company was *no better off* as a result of buying and selling this land. The $400,000 received for the land in Year 10 represents the same command over goods and services as $200,000 did when invested in the land in Year 1.

We have experienced persistent inflation in the United States for almost 40 years; more important, the forces which have been built into our economic and political institutions almost guarantee that inflation will continue. The only question is how severe the inflationary trend will be. Our traditional accounting process is based upon the assumption of a stable dollar. This cost-based system works extremely well in periods of stable prices; it works reasonably well during prolonged but mild inflation; but it loses virtually all meaning if inflation becomes extreme. The greatest single challenge to the accounting profession today is to develop new accounting methods that will bring financial statements into accord with the economic reality of an inflationary environment.

Profits—fact or illusion?

Corporate profits are watched closely by business managers, investors, and government officials. The trend of these profits plays a significant role in the allocation of the nation's investment resources, in levels of employment, and in national economic policy. As a result of the *stable monetary assumption*, however, a strong argument may be made that much of the corporate profit reported today is an illusion.

In the measurement of business income, a distinction must be drawn between profit and the recovery of costs. A business earns a profit only when the value of goods sold and services rendered (revenue) *exceeds* the value of resources consumed in the earning process (costs and expenses). Accountants have traditionally assigned "values" to resources consumed in the earning process by using historical dollar amounts. Depreciation expense, for example, may be based upon prices paid to acquire assets 10 or 20 years ago.

When the general price level is rising rapidly, such historical costs may significantly understate the current economic value of the resources being consumed. If costs and expenses are understated, it follows that reported profits are overstated. In other words, the stable monetary assumption may lead to reporting *illusory* profits; much of the net income reported by business enterprises actually may be a return of costs.

When reported profit is actually a return of costs, what we label as income taxes is in reality a tax upon invested capital. Moreover, dividends labeled as distributions of earnings are in fact being paid from capital. The reporting of large, but fictitious, profits also leads to demands for higher wages consistent with the reported profits.

In summary, the real world is one of inflation. If we continue to measure profits on the assumption that price levels do not change, financial statements will be misleading and out of touch with reality. Several broad social consequences appear to follow. For one, corporate liquidity (debt-paying ability) may fall so low as to bring an economic crisis. Secondly, since we allocate economic resources in large part on the basis of financial statements, poor allocation of resources may be the end consequence of ignoring inflation in our financial reporting. Finally, the overstatement of profits may lead to an unrecognized failure to maintain reasonable rates of capital formation. A nation with a declining rate of capital formation will find it difficult to hold its relative position in a competitive world economy or to achieve a rising standard of living.

Two approaches to "inflation accounting"

Two alternative approaches to modifying our accounting process to cope with inflation have received much attention. These two approaches are:

1 **Constant dollar accounting**   Under this approach, historical costs in the financial statements are adjusted to the *number of current dollars representing an equivalent amount of purchasing power.* Thus, all amounts are expressed in units (current dollars) of equal purchasing power. Since a general price index is used in restating the historical costs, constant dollar accounting shows the effects of changes in the *general* price level. Constant dollar accounting is also called *general price level* accounting.

2 **Current cost accounting**   This method differs from constant dollar accounting in that assets and expenses are shown in the financial statements at the current cost to *replace* those specific resources. The *current replacement cost* of a specific asset may rise or fall at a different rate from the general price level. Thus, current cost accounting shows the effects of *specific price changes,* rather than changes in the general price level.

To illustrate these approaches to "inflation accounting," assume that in Year 1 you purchased 500 pounds of sugar for $100 when the general price index was at 100. Early in Year 2, you sold the sugar for $108 when the general price index was at 110 and the replacement cost of 500 pounds of sugar was $104. What is the amount of your profit or loss on this transaction? The amount of profit or loss determined under current accounting standards (unadjusted historical cost) and the two "inflation accounting" alternatives is shown below.

	Unadjusted Historical Cost	Adjusted for General Inflation (Constant Dollars)	Adjusted for Changes in Specific Prices (Current Costs)
Revenue	$108	$108	$108
Cost of goods sold	100	110	104
Profit (loss)	$ 8	$ (2)	$ 4

Which "cost" of goods sold is most realistic?

Under each method, an amount is deducted from revenue to provide for recovery of cost. However, the value assigned to the "cost" of goods sold differs under each of the three approaches.

Unadjusted historical cost   This method is used in current accounting practice. The use of unadjusted historical cost is based upon the assumption that the dollar is a stable unit of measure. Profit is determined by comparing sales revenue with the *historical costs* of the asset sold. In using this approach to income determination, accountants assume that a business is as well off when it has recovered its *original dollar investment,* and that it is better off whenever it recovers more than the original number of dollars invested in any given asset.

In our example of buying and selling sugar, the profit figure of $8 shows *how many dollars* you came out ahead. However, this approach ignores the fact that

Year 1 dollars and Year 2 dollars are *not equivalent in terms of purchasing power.* It also ignores the fact that the $100 deduction intended to provide for the recovery of cost is not sufficient to allow you to *replace* the 500 pounds of sugar.

Constant dollar accounting   When financial statements are adjusted for changes in the general price level, historical amounts are restated as the number of current dollars *equivalent in purchasing power* to the historical cost. Profit is determined by comparing revenue with the *amount of purchasing power* (stated in current dollars) originally invested.

The general price index tells us that $110 in Year 2 is equivalent in purchasing power to the $100 invested in sugar in Year 1. But you do not have $110 in Year 2; you received only $108 dollars from the sale of the sugar. Thus, you have sustained a *$2 loss in purchasing power.*

Current cost accounting   In current cost accounting, profit is measured by comparing revenue with the *current replacement cost* of the assets consumed in the earning process. The logic of this approach lies in the concept of the going concern. What will you do with the $108 received from the sale of the sugar? If you are going to continue in the sugar business, you will have to buy more sugar. At current market prices, it will cost you $104 to replace 500 pounds of sugar; the remaining $4, therefore, is designated as profit.

Current cost accounting recognizes in the income statement the costs which a going concern actually has to pay to replace its expiring assets. The resulting profit figure, therefore, closely parallels the maximum amount which a business could distribute to its owners and still be able to maintain the present size and scale of its operations.

Which approach measures income?   Each of these three approaches utilizes a different definition of cost and of income. The question confronting the accounting profession is which of these alternative measures of income is the *most useful to decision makers.* This question is being considered very carefully by the FASB, the SEC, and other interested parties. However, there is not yet widespread agreement as to the answer.

FASB Statement No. 33—Is a big change coming?

Perhaps the day is coming when constant dollar or current cost information will replace the use of historical costs in financial statements. However, a change of this magnitude cannot be made without extensive planning and consideration of the possible consequences. Accounting information is used on a daily basis by millions of economic decision makers. A major change in the nature of this information is sure to affect the allocation of resources within our economy. Decision makers would have to learn to interpret the new information; capital would move out of some industries and into others; income tax laws and other government economic policies might change. In light of these considerations, careful experimentation with constant dollar and current cost information is needed before we abandon the use of historical costs as our basis for financial statements.

As an experimental step, the FASB issued *Statement No. 33,* which requires large corporations to include with their cost-based financial statements *supple-*

mentary schedules showing certain constant dollar and current cost information. Note that this information is supplementary to the conventional financial statements and is not a substitute for them. This action by the FASB will introduce decision makers to constant dollar and current cost information on an experimental basis. If this experimentation leads to widespread use of constant dollar or current cost information, *Statement No. 33* will become a major milestone in the evolution of accounting principles.

FASB requirements for disclosure of constant dollar and current cost information

Statement No. 33 applies only to large corporations—those with total assets of $1 billion or total inventories and plant assets (before deducting accumulated depreciation) of more than $125 million. However, the FASB also encourages (but does not require) all business organizations of every size to comply with the provisions of the *Statement*.[5]

The supplementary disclosures required by *Statement No. 33* include:[6]

1 Net income measured in constant dollars[7]
2 The gain or loss in purchasing power which results from holding monetary assets or having monetary liabilities
3 Net income on a current cost basis

The format which many companies use for making these disclosures is illustrated below. (The three required disclosures are identified by the numbered arrows.)

Which income figure do you think is most realistic?

Supplement to financial statements:

FLATION COMPANY
Income Statement Adjusted for Changing Prices
For Year 10

	As Reported in the Primary Statements	Adjusted for General Inflation (Constant Dollars)*	Adjusted for Changes in Specific Prices (Current Costs)
Net sales	$600,000	$600,000	$600,000
Costs and expenses:			
Cost of goods sold	$360,000	$370,000	$391,500
Depreciation expense	60,000	80,000	90,000
Other expenses	130,000	130,000	130,000
Total	$550,000	$580,000	$611,500
Net income	$ 50,000	① → $ 20,000	③ → $ (11,500)
Net gain from decline in purchasing power of net amounts owed		② ↘ $ 8,000	

*Stated in dollars of average purchasing power during Year 10.

---

[5]*FASB Statement No. 33*, "Financial Reporting and Changing Prices," FASB (Stamford, Conn.: 1979), par. 23–25.
[6]Other disclosure requirements of *Statement No. 33,* including changes in current costs and five-year summaries, will be discussed in an intermediate level accounting course.
[7]When a company discontinues a segment of its operations or reports an extraordinary item in its income statement, the subtotal, Income from Continuing Operations, is disclosed instead of the net income figure.

We shall now use the information in this illustration to demonstrate further the concepts of constant dollar and current cost accounting and to interpret these disclosures from the viewpoint of the financial statement user.

Net income measured in constant dollars

A basic problem with the use of historical costs for measuring income is that revenue and expenses may be stated in dollars having different amounts of purchasing power. Sales revenue, for example, is recorded in current-year dollars. Depreciation expense, on the other hand, is based upon dollars spent to acquire assets in past years. As previously emphasized, dollars in the current year and dollars of past years are not equivalent in terms of purchasing power.

In a constant dollar income statement, expenses based on "old" dollars are *restated* at the number of current dollars representing the equivalent amount of purchasing power. When all revenue and expenses are stated in units of similar purchasing power, we can see whether the business is gaining or losing in terms of the amount of purchasing power it controls.

To restate a historical amount in terms of an equivalent number of current dollars, we multiply the historical amount by the ratio of the current price level to the historical price level, as illustrated below:

Converting to current dollars

$$\text{Historical cost} \times \frac{\text{Average price index for current period}}{\text{Index at date of historical cost}} = \frac{\text{Equivalent number}}{\text{of current dollars}}$$

For example, assume that land was purchased for $100,000 when the price index stood at 100. If the price index is now 170, we may find the number of current dollars equivalent to the purchasing power originally invested in the land by multiplying the $100,000 historical cost by *170/100*. The result, $170,000 represents the number of current dollars equivalent in purchasing power to the 100,000 historical dollars.

Price index levels for our illustration   The following changes in the general price index are assumed in our Flation Company illustration:

Date	Price Index
Beginning of Year 8 (acquisition date for depreciable assets)	*150*
End of Year 9	*180*
Average price level for Year 10*	*200*
End of Year 10	*216*
Rate of inflation for Year 10†	*20%*

*The "average" price level for the year is computed as a monthly average and need not lie exactly halfway between the price levels at the beginning and end of the year.
†The inflation rate is computed by dividing the increase in the price index over the year by the price index at the beginning of the year: (216 − 180) ÷ 180 = 20%.

In restating historical dollars to current dollars, we shall use the *average price level* for Year 10 (200) to represent the purchasing power of current dollars.[8]

---

[8]An acceptable alternative is to use the year-end price level to represent the purchasing power of current dollars. However, use of the year-end price level means that all income statement amounts, including revenue and expense transactions conducted during the current year, must be restated. For this reason, the vast majority of companies presenting constant dollar information use the average price level for the current year.

Not all amounts are restated Compare the constant dollar and historical cost income statements of the Flation Company for Year 10 (page 549). Note that only two items—depreciation expense and the cost of goods sold—have been restated in the constant dollar statement. Sales revenue and expenses other than depreciation consist of transactions occurring during the current year. Therefore, these amounts are *already* stated in current dollars. We need to adjust to current dollars only those expenses which are based on costs incurred in past years.

Restating depreciation expense Assume that Flation Company's depreciation expense all relates to equipment purchased early in Year 8 when the price level was 150. The equipment cost $600,000 and is being depreciated over 10 years by the straight-line method. Since the average price level in Year 10 is 200, the purchasing power originally invested in this equipment is equivalent to $800,000 current dollars ($600,000 × 200/150 = $800,000). Thus, the amount of purchasing power expiring in Year 10, stated in current dollars, is $80,000 ($800,000 ÷ 10 years).

A shortcut approach is simply to restate the historical depreciation expense, as follows:

Historical Dollars		Conversion Ratio		Equivalent Current Dollars
$60,000	×	200/150	=	$80,000

Since depreciable assets are long-lived, the price level prevailing when the assets were acquired may be substantially different from the current price level. In such cases, the amount of depreciation expense recognized becomes one of the most significant differences between historical dollar and current dollar financial statements.

Restating the cost of goods sold During Year 10, Flation Company sold merchandise with a historical cost of $360,000. Assume that $90,000 of these goods came from the beginning inventory, acquired at the end of Year 9 when the price level was 180; the remaining $270,000 of these goods were purchased during Year 10. The restatement of the cost of goods sold to average Year 10 dollars is shown below:

	Historical Dollars		Conversion Ratio		Equivalent Current Dollars
Beginning inventory	$ 90,000	×	200/180	=	100,000
Purchased in Year 10	270,000		*		270,000
Cost of goods sold	$360,000				$370,000

*No adjustment necessary—amount already is stated in current dollars.

Interpreting the constant dollar income statement

The basic difference between historical dollar and constant dollar income statements is the unit of measure. Historical dollar income statements use the dollar as a basic unit of measure. The unit of measure in constant dollar income statements is the *purchasing power of the current dollar.*

A conventional income statement shows how many dollars were added to owners' equity from the operation of the business. Identifying a dollar increase in owners' equity as "income" implies that owners are better off when they recover more than the original number of dollars they invested. No attention is given to the fact that a greater number of dollars may still have less purchasing power than was originally invested.

A *constant dollar* income statement shows whether the *inflow of purchasing power* from current operations is larger or smaller than the *purchasing power consumed* in the effort to generate revenue. In short, the net income figure tells us whether the amount of purchasing power controlled by the business has increased or decreased as a result of operations.

Gains and losses in purchasing power

Constant dollar accounting introduces a new consideration in measuring the effects of inflation upon a business: gains and losses in purchasing power from holding monetary items. *Monetary items* are those assets and liabilities representing claims to a *fixed number of dollars.* Examples of monetary assets are cash, notes receivable, and accounts receivable; most liabilities are monetary, including notes payable and accounts payable.

Holding monetary assets during a period of rising prices results in a loss of purchasing power because the value of the money is falling. In contrast, owing money during a period of rising prices give rise to a gain in purchasing power because debts may be repaid using dollars of less purchasing power than those originally borrowed.

To illustrate, assume that Flation Company held $30,000 in cash throughout Year 10, while the price level rose 20% (from 180 to 216). By the end of the year, this $30,000 cash balance will have lost 20% of its purchasing power, as demonstrated by the following analysis:

Number of dollars needed at year-end to represent the same purchasing power as
$30,000 at the beginning of the year ($30,000 × 216/180) $36,000
Number of dollars actually held at year-end 30,000

Loss in purchasing power as a result of holding monetary assets .... $ 6,000

(We can also compute this loss simply by multiplying the amount of the monetary assets held throughout the year by the 20% inflation rate: $30,000 × 20% = $6,000.)

A similar analysis is applied to any monetary liabilities. Assume, for example, that Flation Company has a $70,000 note payable outstanding throughout Year 10. The resulting gain in purchasing power is computed as follows:

Number of dollars at year-end representing the same purchasing power as $70,000
  owed at beginning of year ($70,000 × 216/180) $84,000
Number of dollars actually owed at year-end 70,000

Gain in purchasing power as a result of owing a fixed number of dollars $14,000

FASB Statement No. 33 requires disclosure of the *net gain or loss* from holding monetary assets and owing monetary liabilities. Flation Company has experienced a $8,000 net gain in purchasing power ($14,000 gain − $6,000 loss), because its monetary liabilities were greater than its monetary assets.[9] The disclosure of this net gain is illustrated in the supplementary schedule on page 549.

Interpreting the net gain or loss in purchasing power

In determining the change in the purchasing power represented by owners' equity, we must consider *both* the amount of constant dollar net income *and* the amount of any gain or loss resulting from monetary items. Thus, the purchasing power of the owners' equity in Flation Company increased by $28,000 during Year 10 ($20,000 net income + $8,000 gain in purchasing power from monetary items).

The purchasing power gain from monetary items is shown separately from the determination of net income to emphasize the special nature of this gain. The income statement shows the purchasing power created or lost *as a result of business operations.* The $8,000 net gain in purchasing power, however, is caused entirely by the *effect of inflation* upon the purchasing power of monetary assets and liabilities. A business that owns monetary assets or owes money may have a purchasing power gain or loss even if it earns no revenue and incurs no expenses.

In evaluating the effect of inflation upon a particular business, we must consider the effect of inflation upon operations and its effects upon the monetary assets and liabilities of the business. If a business must maintain high levels of cash or accounts receivable from customers, we should recognize that inflation will continually erode the purchasing power of these assets. On the other hand, if a business is able to finance its operations with borrowed capital, inflation will benefit the company by allowing it to repay smaller amounts of purchasing power than it originally borrowed.

Net income on a current cost basis

Constant dollar accounting does not abandon historical costs as the basis for measurement but simply expresses these costs in terms of the current value of money. Current cost accounting, on the other hand, does represent a departure

---

[9]Some readers may notice that our net gain is stated in end-of-Year-10 dollars. To be technically consistent with the other constant dollar data on page 549, this net gain should be restated in dollars of average purchasing power for Year 10. The gain can be restated as follows: $8,000 × 209/216 = $7,408. We have ignored this restatement because it is not material in dollar amount and is an unnecessary refinement for an introductory discussion.

from the historical cost concept. The term "current cost" usually refers to the *current replacement cost* of assets. In a current cost income statement, expenses are stated at the estimated cost to *replace the specific assets* sold or used up. Thus, current cost accounting involves estimates of current market values, rather than adjustments to historical costs for changes in the general price level.

Of course, the replacement cost of an asset may fluctuate during the year. Since a cost such as depreciation expense occurs continually *throughout* the year, current cost measurements are based on the *average* replacement cost during the year, not on the replacement cost at year-end.

To illustrate, assume that the replacement cost of Flation Company's equipment was estimated to be $850,000 at the beginning of Year 10 and $950,000 at year-end. Current cost depreciation expense should be based upon the $900,000 average replacement cost of the equipment during the year. Since the equipment has a 10-year life, the depreciation expense appearing in the current cost income statement (page 549) is $90,000 ($900,000 ÷ 10 years).

Now let us consider the determination of the cost of goods sold on a current cost basis. All we need to know is (1) how many units of inventory were sold during the year, and (2) the average replacement cost of these units during Year 10. If Flation Company sold 145,000 units during the year, and the average replacement cost was $2.70 per unit, the cost of goods sold would be $391,500 on a current cost basis (145,000 units × $2.70). Note that the historical cost of units in the company's beginning inventory does not enter into the current cost computation.

Interpreting a current cost income statement

A current cost income statement does *not* measure the flow of general purchasing power in and out of the business. Rather, it shows whether a company earns enough revenue to replace the goods and services used up in the effort to generate that revenue. The resulting net income figure closely parallels *distributable profit*—the maximum amount that the business can distribute to its owners and still maintain the present size and scale of its operations.

Unfortunately, the financial statements of large corporations show that many companies in industries vital to our economy are reporting profits measured on a historical cost basis but are incurring large *losses* according to their supplementary current cost disclosures. Companies in the steel industry and utilities industry provide excellent examples. What does this mean to an informed reader of financial statements? In short, it means that these companies do not earn sufficient revenue to maintain their productive capacity. In the long run, they must either obtain capital from other sources or scale down the size of their operations.

What direction will inflation accounting take?

The techniques for restating financial statements for changes in the general price level have been known for many years. Yet despite support from both the

FASB and the APB, the preparation of constant dollar financial statements has not become a widespread practice.

Current cost accounting is a much newer idea and appears to be gaining acceptance in many countries. The British government has given approval to a System of Current Cost Accounting and has arranged for development of methods to implement it. In the Netherlands, large corporations are basing depreciation on replacement cost and determining cost of goods sold in terms of replacement values. In Australia, the Institute of Chartered Accountants has gone on record as favoring the valuation of assets at current cost and the measurement of profit by stating both revenue and expenses at current values.

One factor contributing to support for current cost accounting is that constant dollar financial statements are based upon the *general* price level and not upon the prices of *specific* goods and services. Any given company has inventories of specific commodities for which prices may be changing in quite a different manner from the general price level.

ILLUSTRATIVE CASE.   In a recent year the wholesale price of sugar declined from over 60 cents a pound to approximately 12 cents a pound although the general price level was rising strongly. A company in the sugar industry would have presented a more realistic picture of the sugar business in that year by reducing its cost of goods sold to reflect the falling price of sugar than by increasing this cost upward for the change in the general price level.

On the other hand, a significant advantage of constant dollar accounting is its high degree of *objectivity*. Since all adjustments employ the same general price index, valuations are not based on estimates or personal opinion. The principal problem to be solved in the use of current cost accounting is the development of standards for measuring the replacement cost of various types of assets. It appears likely that *specific* price indexes will be the most objective and satisfactory means of developing replacement cost data. However, these will be specialized indexes measuring *specific types of commodities* rather than a single index of the general price level.

It is important to remember, however, that constant dollar accounting and current cost accounting each convey different types of useful information. The two approaches are not mutually exclusive; that is, the use of one does not preclude use of the other. Both approaches may be used within a single set of financial statements. In all probability, the gradual modification of the accounting process to disclose more clearly the effects of inflation will involve continuing experimentation with both constant dollar and current cost accounting.

KEY TERMS INTRODUCED OR EMPHASIZED IN CHAPTER 14

Audit opinion   The report issued by a firm of certified public accountants after auditing the financial statements of a business. Expresses an opinion on the fairness of the financial statements and indicates the nature and limits of the responsibility being assumed by the independent auditors

Conservatism   A traditional practice of resolving uncertainties by choosing an asset valuation at the lower point of the range of reasonableness. Also refers to the policy of postponing recognition of revenue to a later date when a range of reasonable choice exists. Designed to avoid overstatement of financial strength and earnings.

Consistency   An assumption that once a particular accounting method is adopted, it will not be changed from period to period. Intended to make financial statements of a given company comparable from year to year.

Consolidated financial statements   Financial statements which present the financial position and operating results of a group of affiliated corporations as though the group represented a single unified business.

Constant dollar accounting   The technique of expressing all financial statement amounts in dollars of equal purchasing power. This is accomplished by restating historical costs for subsequent changes in the general price level. Also called *general price level accounting.*

Cost principle   The traditional, widely used policy of accounting for assets at their historical cost determined through arm's-length bargaining. Justified by the need for objective evidence to support the valuation of assets.

Current cost accounting   The valuation of assets and measurement of income in terms of current replacement costs rather than historical costs. This approach to inflation accounting indicates the ability of a business to replace its physical capital (specific inventory and plant assets) as it is sold or used up.

Disclosure principle   Financial statements should disclose all material and relevant information about the financial position and operating results of a business. The notes accompanying financial statements are an important means of disclosure.

Entity concept   Any legal or economic unit which controls economic resources and is accountable for these resources may be considered an accounting entity. The resources and the transactions of the entity are not to be intermingled with those of its owner or owners.

General price level   The weighted-average price of all goods and services in the economy. Inflation may be defined as an increase in the general price level.

Generally accepted accounting principles   Those accounting principles which have received substantial authoritative support, such as the approval of the FASB, the AICPA, or the SEC. Often referred to by the acronym GAAP.

Going-concern assumption   An assumption that a business entity will continue in operation indefinitely and thus will carry out its existing commitments. If evidence to the contrary exists, then the assumption of liquidation would prevail and assets would be valued at their estimated liquidation values.

Installment method   An accounting method used principally in the determination of taxable income. It provides for recognition of realized profit on installment contracts in proportion to cash collected.

Matching principle   The revenue earned during an accounting period is compared or matched with the expenses incurred in generating this revenue in order to measure income. Fundamental to the accrual basis of accounting.

Materiality   The relative importance of an amount or item. An item which is not important or significant enough to influence the decisions of prudent users of financial statements is considered as *not* material. The accounting treatment of immaterial items may be guided by convenience rather than by theoretical principles. For example, purchase of 10 gallons of gasoline is treated as the incurring of an expense rather than the acquisition of an asset.

Monetary items With respect to changes in price levels, monetary items include assets representing claims to a fixed number of dollars (such as cash and receivables) and most liabilities. Holding monetary assets during a period of rising prices results in a loss in purchasing power; conversely, owing monetary liabilities results in a gain in purchasing power.

Monetary (stable-dollar) assumption In using money as a measuring unit and preparing financial statements expressed in dollars, accountants make the assumption that the dollar is a stable unit of measurement. This assumption is obviously faulty as a result of continued inflation, and strenuous efforts are being made to change to current cost accounting or general price-level-adjusted measurements.

Objectivity (objective evidence) The valuation of assets and the measurement of income are to be based as much as possible on objective evidence, such as exchange prices in arm's-length transactions. Objective evidence is subject to verification by independent experts.

Percentage-of-completion method A method of accounting for long-term construction projects which recognizes revenue and profits in proportion to the work completed, based on an estimate of the portion of the project completed each accounting period.

Purchasing power The ability of money to buy goods and services. As the general price level rises, the purchasing power of the dollar declines. Thus, in periods of inflation, an ever-increasing number of dollars is necessary to represent a given amount of purchasing power.

Realization principle The principle of recognizing revenue in the accounts only when earned. Revenue is realized when the earning process is virtually complete, which is usually at the time of sale of goods or rendering service to customers.

DEMONSTRATION PROBLEM FOR YOUR REVIEW

The accounting staff of Prescott Company has provided the following data to assist you in preparing constant dollar and current cost information to supplement the company's financial statements for the current year:

Income Statement—Historical Cost
For the Current Year

Net sales		$620,000
Cost and expenses:		
Cost of goods sold	$310,000	
Depreciation expense	50,000	
Other expenses	200,000	
Total costs and expenses		560,000
Net income		$ 60,000

Other data
(1) Changes in the general price level during the current year were as follows:

	Price Index
Beginning of year	140
Average for year	150
End of year	161
Rate of inflation [(161 − 140) ÷ 140]	15%

Amounts in the constant dollar income statement are to be stated in current-year dollars of average purchasing power.

(2) The company sells a single product and uses the first-in, first-out method to compute the cost of goods sold. The historical cost of goods sold included the following unit sales at the following costs:

	Units	×	Average Unit Costs	=	Total
From beginning inventory	14,000		$5.00		$ 70,000
From current-year purchases	40,000		6.00		240,000
Cost of goods sold	54,000		5.74		$310,000

The $70,000 beginning inventory was purchased when the general price index stood at 140. (It is not necessary to know total purchases or ending inventory for the current year.)

(3) The company's depreciable assets consist of equipment acquired four years ago when the general price index stood at 80. The equipment cost $500,000 and is being depreciated over a 10-year life by the straight-line method with no estimated salvage value.

The estimated replacement cost of the equipment was $980,000 at the beginning of the current year and $1,070,000 at year-end.

(4) Throughout the current year, the company owned monetary assets of $110,000 and owed monetary liabilities of $200,000.

Instructions   Prepare a supplementary schedule in the format illustrated on page 549. Include comparative income statements prepared on the basis of historical cost, constant dollars, and current costs. Also show the net gain or loss resulting from monetary items. Show supporting computations for the (1) cost of goods sold stated in constant dollars, (2) depreciation expense stated in constant dollars, (3) net gain or loss in purchasing power from monetary items, (4) cost of goods sold measured in current costs, and (5) depreciation expense measured in current costs.

SOLUTION TO DEMONSTRATION PROBLEM

PRESCOTT COMPANY
Income Statement Adjusted for Changing Prices
For the Current Year

	As Reported in The Primary Statements	Adjusted for General Inflation	Adjusted for Changes in Specific Prices
Net sales	$620,000	$620,000	$620,000
Cost and expenses:			
Cost of goods sold	$310,000	$315,000(1)	$324,000(4)
Depreciation expense	50,000	93,750(2)	102,500(5)
Other expenses	200,000	200,000	200,000
Total costs and expenses	$560,000	$608,750	$626,500
Net income (net loss)	$ 60,000	$ 11,250	$ (6,500)
Net gain from decline in purchasing power of net amounts owed		$ 13,500(3)	

Supporting Computations: Constant Dollar Amounts

	Historical Dollars	× Conversion Ratio	= Constant Dollars
(1) Cost of goods sold:			
From beginning inventory	$ 70,000	150/140	$ 75,000
From current year purchases	240,000	None	240,000
Cost of goods sold	$310,000		$315,000
(2) Depreciation expense	$ 50,000	150/80	$ 93,750
Alternative computation:			
Equipment	$500,000	150/80	$937,500
Depreciation expense ($937,500			
÷ 10 years)			$ 93,750

(3) Net gain or loss in purchasing power:

	Monetary Items	× Inflation Rate	= Gain or Loss in Purchasing Power
Average monetary assets	$110,000	15%	$16,500 L
Average monetary liabilities	200,000	15%	30,000 G
Net amount owed and net gain			
in purchasing power	$ 90,000		$13,500 G

Current Cost Amounts

(4) Cost of goods sold:	
Number of units sold	54,000
Average replacement cost per unit	$6
Current cost of goods sold ($54,000 × $6)	$324,000
(5) Depreciation expense:	
Average replacement cost of equipment	
($1,070,000 + $980,000) ÷ 2	$1,025,000
Estimated useful life	10 years
Depreciation expense ($1,025,000 ÷ 10)	$ 102,500

REVIEW QUESTIONS

1 What is the basic objective of financial statements?

2 To qualify as "generally accepted," accounting principles must receive substantial authoritative support. Name three groups or organizations in the United States which have been most influential in giving substantial authoritative support to accounting principles.

3 Explain what is meant by the expression "trade-off between *reliability* and *relevance*" in connection with the preparation of financial statements.

4 Barker Company has at the end of the current period an inventory of merchandise which cost $500,000. It would cost $600,000 to replace this inventory, and it is estimated that the goods will probably be sold for a total of $700,000. If the firm were

to terminate operations immediately, the inventory could probably be sold for $480,000. Discuss the relative reliability and relevance of each of these dollar measurements of the ending inventory.

5 Why is it necessary for accountants to assume the existence of a clearly defined accounting entity?

6 "The matching of costs and revenue is the natural extension of the time period principle." Evaluate this statement.

7 Define *objectivity, consistency, materiality,* and *conservatism.*

8 Is the assumption that the dollar is a stable unit of measure realistic? What alternatives can you suggest for financial reporting?

9 **a** Why is it important that any change in accounting methods from one period to the next be disclosed?

   b Does the concept of consistency mean that all companies in a given industry follow similar accounting methods?

10 Briefly define the principle of *disclosure.* List several examples of information that should be disclosed in financial statements or in notes accompanying the statements.

11 Publicly owned corporations are required to include in their annual reports a description of the accounting principles followed in the preparation of their financial statements. What advantages do you see in this practice?

12 List four stages of the productive process which might become the accountant's basis for recognizing changes in the value of a firm's output. Which stage is most commonly used as a basis for revenue recognition? Why?

13 A CPA firm's standard audit opinion consists of two major paragraphs. Describe the essential content of each paragraph.

14 Define *monetary assets* and indicate whether a gain or loss results from the holding of such assets during a period of rising prices.

15 Why is it advantageous to be in debt during an inflationary period?

16 Evaluate the following statement: "During a period of rising prices, the conventional income statements overstates net income because the amount of depreciation recorded is less than the value of the service potential of assets consumed."

17 List the three supplementary disclosures required of large corporations by *FASB Statement No. 33* which were discussed in this chapter.

18 How does constant dollar accounting differ from current cost accounting? For which one would the Consumer Price Index be used?

19 Alpha Company sells pocket calculators which have been decreasing in cost while the general price level has been rising. Explain why Alpha Company's cost of goods sold on a constant dollar basis and on a current cost basis would be higher or lower than on a historical cost basis.

20 The latest financial statements of Boston Manufacturing Co. indicate that income measured in terms of constant dollars is much lower than income measured in historical dollars. What is the most probable explanation for this large difference?

21 What conclusion would you draw about a company that consistently shows large net losses when its income is measured on a current cost basis?

EXERCISES

Ex. 14-1 For each situation described below, indicate the concept (or concepts) of accounting that is violated, if any. You may choose among the following concepts: conservatism, consistency, disclosure, entity, going concern, matching, materiality, objectivity.

Situations

a A pencil sharpener acquired by a small business at a cost of $5 is estimated to have a useful life of 10 years and is recorded by a debit to the Office Equipment account.

b The owner of a small business used the business bank account in writing a check to a department store in payment for personal expenditures.

c The machinery used by a car wash business was shown in the balance sheet at its estimated scrap value which was far below the book value.

d The assets of a partnership are combined with the separate assets of the partners in preparing a balance sheet.

e The cost of merchandise purchased is recognized as expense before it is sold in order to report a less favorable financial position.

f Plans to dispose of a major segment of the business are not communicated to readers of the balance sheet.

g A portion of the cost of a major television promotional campaign in the month of May is deferred and arbitrarily allocated to expense over a five-year period.

h The method of depreciation is changed every two years and the change is disclosed in financial statements.

Ex. 14-2 The Clinton Corporation recognizes the profit on a long-term construction project as work progresses. From the information given below, compute the profit that should be recognized each year, assuming that the original cost estimate on the contract was $6,000,000 and that the contract price is $7,500,000.

Year	Costs Incurred	Profit Considered Realized
1	$1,200,000	$?
2	3,000,000	?
3	1,762,000	?
Total	$5,962,000	$1,538,000

Ex. 14-3 On September 15, Year 1, Susan Moore sold a piece of property which cost her $48,000 for $80,000, net of commissions and other selling expenses. The terms of sale were as follows: down payment, $8,000; balance, $3,000 on the fifteenth day of each month for 24 months, starting October 15, Year 1. Compute the gross profit to be recognized by Moore in Year 1. Year 2, and Year 3 **(a)** on the *accrual basis* of accounting and **(b)** on the *installment basis* of accounting.

Ex. 14-4 Three companies started business with $500,000 at the beginning of the current year when the general price index stood at 125. First Company invested the money in a note receivable due in four years; Second Company invested its cash in land; and Third Company purchased a building for $2,000,000, assuming a liability for the unpaid balance of $1,500,000. The price level stood at 140 at the end of the year. Compute the purchasing power gain or loss on monetary items for each company during the year.

Ex. 14-5   Empire Company paid $400,000 cash in Year 1 to acquire land as a long-term investment. At this time, the general price level stood at 100. In Year 5, the general price index stands at 140, but the price of the land in the area in which Empire Company invested has doubled in value. Rental receipts for grazing and farming during the five-year period were sufficient to pay all carrying charges on the land.

Empire Company prepares a constant dollar income statement and discloses purchasing power gains and losses as supplementary information to its cost-based financial statements.

a How much of a purchasing power gain or loss relating to the land will be included in the supplementary disclosures over the five-year period? (Assume the land is still owned at the end of Year 5.)

b Assume the land is sold in Year 5 for $785,000. Compute the gain or loss on the sale on a basis of (1) historical cost and (2) constant dollars.

Ex. 14-6   For Year 9, PhotoMart computed the cost of goods sold for the Presto, its biggest-selling camera, as follows (historical cost, fifo basis):

	Units ×	Average Unit Cost =	Total
From beginning inventory	420	$30.00	$12,600
From Year 9 purchases	1.600	36.00	57,600
Cost of goods sold	2,020		$70,200

The beginning inventory of Presto cameras had been acquired when the general price index stood at 210. During Year 9, the average level of the price index was 230, and the average replacement cost of Prestos was $36.

Compute the cost of goods sold for Presto cameras during Year 9 on:
a A constant dollar basis
b A current cost basis

Ex. 14-7   Western Showcase purchased equipment for $240,000 in Year 3 when the general price index stood at 120. The company depreciates the equipment over 15 years by the straight-line method, with no estimated salvage value. In Year 7, the general price level is 180 and the estimated replacement cost of the equipment is $387,000.

Compute the amount of depreciation expense for Year 7 on:
a A historical dollar basis
b A constant dollar basis
c A current cost basis

PROBLEMS

14-1   In each of the situations described below, the question is whether generally accepted accounting principles have been properly observed. In each case state the accounting principle or concept, if any, that has been violated and explain briefly the nature of the violation. If you believe the treatment *is in accord with generally accepted accounting principles,* state this as your position and defend it.

a For a number of years the Waterman Company used the declining-balance method of depreciation both in its financial accounting records and in its income tax returns. During the current year the company decided to employ the straight-line method of depreciation in its accounting records but to continue to use the declining-balance method for income tax purposes.

b During the current year the Louis Company adopted a policy of charging purchases of small tools (unit cost less than $200) to expense as soon as they were acquired. In prior years the company had carried an asset account Small Tools which it had depreciated at the rate of 10% of the book value at the beginning of each year. The balance in the Small Tools account represented about 1% of the company's total plant and equipment, and depreciation on small tools was 0.4% of sales revenue. It is expected that purchases of small tools each year will run about the same as the depreciation that would be taken on these small tools.

c Ace Company printed a large mail-order catalog in July of each year, at a cost of $1.8 million. Customers ordered from this catalog throughout the year and the company agreed to maintain the catalog prices for 12 months after the date of the issue. The controller charged the entire cost of the catalog to Advertising Expense in August when it was issued. The Ace Company's fiscal year ends on January 31 of each year. In defending this policy, the controller stated, "Once those catalogs are mailed they are gone. We could never get a nickel out of them."

14-2 In each of the situations described below, the question is whether generally accepted accounting principles have been violated. In each case state the accounting principle or concept, if any, that has been violated and explain briefly the nature of the violation. If you believe the treatment *is in accord with generally accepted accounting principles,* state this as your position and briefly defend it.

a The Lynn Company has purchased a computer for $1.5 million. The company expects to use the computer for five years, at which time it will acquire a larger and faster computer. The new computer is expected to cost $3.5 million. During the current year the company debited $700,000 to the Depreciation Expense account to "provide for one-fifth of the estimated cost of the new computer."

b Bob Standish is president of Dutchman Mines. During the current year, geologists and engineers revised upward the estimated value of ore deposits on the company's property. Standish instructed the accountant for Dutchman Mines to record goodwill of $2 million, the estimated value of unmined ore in excess of previous estimates. The offsetting credit was made to revenue.

c Merchandise inventory which cost $2 million is reported in the balance sheet at $3 million, the expected sales price less estimated direct selling expenses.

d Jefferson Company reports net income for the current year of $1,300,010. In the audit report the auditors stated: "We certify that the results of operations shown in the income statement are a true and accurate portrayal of the company's operations for the current year."

e The Lee Oil Company reported on its balance sheet as an intangible asset the total of all wages, supplies, depreciation on equipment, and other costs related to the drilling of a producing oil well and then amortized this asset as oil was produced from the well.

14-3 Nantucket Boat Works builds custom sailboats. During the first year of operations, the company built four boats for Island Charter Company. The four boats had a total cost of $252,000 and were sold for a total price of $360,000, due on an installment basis. Island Charter Company paid $120,000 of this sales price during the first year, plus an additional amount for interest charges.

At year-end, work is in progress on two other boats which are 60% complete. The contract price for these two boats totals $220,000 and costs incurred on these boats during the year total $96,000 (60% of estimated total costs of $160,000).

Instructions Compute the gross profit for Nantucket Boat Works during its first year of operations under each of the following assumptions. (Interest earned from Island Charter Company does not enter into the computation of gross profit.)

a The entire profit is recognized on the four boats completed and profit on the two boats under construction is recognized on a percentage-of-completion basis.

b Profit on the four boats completed is recognized on the installment basis and no portion of the profit on the two boats under construction will be recognized until the boats are completed, delivered to customers, and cash is collected.

14-4   Early in Year 1, Roadbuilders, Inc., was notified that it was the successful bidder on the construction of a section of state highway. The bid price for the project was $20 million. Construction is to begin in Year 1 and will take about 15 months to complete; the deadline for completion is in April of Year 2.

    The contract calls for payments of $5 million per year to Roadbuilders, Inc., for four years, beginning in Year 1. (After the project is complete, the state will also pay a reasonable interest charge on the unpaid balance of the contract.) The company estimates that construction costs will total $16 million, of which $12 million will be incurred in Year 1 and $4 million in Year 2.

    The controller of the company, Joe Morgan, recognizes that there are a number of ways he might account for this contract. He might recognize income at the time the contract is completed (sales method), in April of Year 2. Alternatively, he might recognize income during construction (percentage-of-completion method), in proportion to the percentage of the total cost incurred in each of Years 1 and 2. Finally, he might recognize income in proportion to the percentage of the total contract price collected in installment receipts during the four-year period (installment method).

Instructions

a Prepare a schedule (in millions of dollars) showing the profit that would be recognized on this project in each of the next four years under each of the three accounting methods being considered by the controller. Assume that the timing and construction costs go according to plan. (Ignore the interest revenue relating to the unpaid balance of the contract.)

b Explain which accounting method you consider to be most appropriate in this situation. Also explain why you consider the other two methods less appropriate.

14-5   Edward Lopez received large amounts of income from investments in mining properties and consequently was subject to a very high income tax rate. At the beginning of the current year he organized Lopez Engineering Company, a single proprietorship which carried on construction work and also engaged in the purchase and sale of building materials.

    Because Lopez was concerned about the large amount of income taxes he expected to pay on income from mining investments, he gave the following instructions to the accountant: "In preparing the income statement for the first year of operations of Lopez Engineering Company, I want you to be as conservative as possible. Wherever alternative methods are available, you should choose the method which will lead to the minimum income tax this year."

    The accountant followed these instructions and prepared the following income statement.

LOPEZ ENGINEERING COMPANY
Income Statement
First Year of Operation

Revenue:

Sales—regular	$137,000
Collections on installment sales	180,000
Construction work completed	53,000
Total revenue	$370,000

Costs and expenses:

Cost of goods sold—regular	$ 95,800	
Cost of goods sold—installment basis, 70% of collections	126,000	
Cost of construction work completed	43,800	
Operating expenses	110,000	
Interest expense	29,400	
Total costs and expenses		405,000
Loss for first year of operations		$ (35,000)

Lopez was pleased to know that he will be able to reduce his other taxable income as a result of the loss from his business. He was, however, concerned because his banker refused to lend him $60,000 for use in his business because, as the banker put it, "You've lost too much money in your first year of operations and I have a policy against lending money to unprofitable businesses." At this point, Lopez comes to you for advice and gives you additional information relating to the items appearing in the income statement. After reviewing this information, you suggest that the following changes be made:

(1) Installment sales amounted to $390,000; the cost of goods sold was $273,000, or 70% of sales. The accountant reported only the cash collections as revenue and deducted a proportional amount as the cost of the goods sold on the installment basis. You recommend that the entire income on installment sales be included in the income statement.

(2) The revenue and cost of construction work include three contracts started and completed in the first year. In addition, the following data relate to the six contracts started in the first year which will be completed in the following year.

Total contract price	$645,000
Total estimated cost of contracts	540,000
Actual costs incurred in first year	180,000

You suggest that profit on these contracts be recognized on the percentage-of-completion basis.

(3) The ending inventory of goods to be sold on the regular basis was valued on the lifo basis at $30,600; this inventory on a fifo basis would have been $33,600. You propose that the first-in, first-out method be used in preparing the income statement to be resubmitted to the banker.

(4) Included in operating expense is depreciation of $9,600, computed by using an accelerated method. You recommend the use of the straight-line depreciation method, which would result in depreciation of only $7,200.

(5) Also included in operating expenses is $9,000 of expenditures which are applicable to future periods. You suggest that these items be deferred and reported in the balance sheet as assets.

Instructions

a Prepare a revised income statement for Lopez Engineering Company, giving effect to the changes in accounting you suggested to Lopez. (Ignore income taxes.) Certain key figures to appear in the revised income statement should be computed in supporting schedules. Reference to these supporting schedules should appear in the revised income statement. The appropriate supporting schedules are indicated in **b** below. (The first item of revenue, Sales—regular, means sales made on 30-day open account as opposed to sales on the installment plan.)

b Prepare the following separate schedules to support the revised income statement:
(1) A schedule showing the revenue from construction work measured on the percentage-of-completion basis
(2) A schedule showing the cost of goods sold—regular (30-day open account sales)
(3) A schedule showing the cost of construction work
(4) A schedule showing operating expenses

14-6 The following supplementary schedule appears with the financial statements of Navigational Instruments for 19___:

Income Statement Adjusted for Changing Prices
(in thousands of dollars)

	As Reported in the Primary Statements	Adjusted for General Inflation (Constant Dollars)	Adjusted for Changes in Specific Prices (Current Costs)
Net sales	$600,000	$600,000	$600,000
Costs and expenses:			
Cost of goods sold	$400,000	$415,000	$410,000
Depreciation expense	50,000	65,000	95,000
Other expenses	110,000	110,000	110,000
Total	$560,000	$590,000	$615,000
Net income	$ 40,000	$ 10,000	$ (15,000)
Loss from decline in purchasing power of net monetary assets owned		$ 18,000	

Instructions Explain the reasoning behind your answer to each of the following questions:

a Has the replacement cost of the company's inventory increased faster or more slowly than the general price level during the year?

b Has the replacement cost of the company's depreciable assets increased faster or more slowly than the general price level since these assets were acquired?

c Were the average monetary assets held by the company during the year greater or smaller than the average monetary liabilities owed?

d What was the total change in the purchasing power of the owners' equity in this business during the year?

e Assuming that this is a typical year, are the company's earnings sufficient to maintain the present size and scope of its operations on a long-term basis?

14-7 Sandy Malone, the president of Sandstone Art Company, has asked you to prepare constant dollar and current cost income statements to supplement the company's financial statements. The company's accountant has provided you with the following data:

Income Statement—Historical Cost
For the Current Year

Net sales		$420,000
Cost and expenses:		
Cost of goods sold	$210,000	
Depreciation expense	30,000	
Other expenses	160,000	
Total costs and expenses		400,000
Net income		$ 20,000

Other Data

(1) Changes in the general price index during the current year were as follows:

	Price Index
Beginning of current year	120
Average for current year	130
End of current year	138
Rate of inflation [(138 − 120) ÷ 120]	15%

Amounts in the constant dollar income statement are to be expressed in current-year dollars of average purchasing power.

(2) The company sells a single product and uses the first-in, first-out method to compute the cost of goods sold. The historical cost of goods sold includes the following unit sales at the following costs:

	Units ×	Average Unit Costs =	Total
From beginning inventory	10,000	$3.00	$ 30,000
From current-year purchases	56,250	3.20	180,000
Cost of goods sold	66,250	3.17	$210,000

The $30,000 beginning inventory was purchased when the general price index stood at 120. (It is not necessary to know total purchases or ending inventory for the current year.)

(3) The company's depreciable assets consist of equipment acquired five years ago when the price index stood at 75. The equipment cost $450,000 and is being depreciated over a 15-year life by the straight-line method with no estimated salvage value.

The estimated replacement cost of the equipment was $600,000 at the beginning of the current year and $630,000 at year-end.

(4) Throughout the current year, the company has owned monetary assets of $90,000 and has owed monetary liabilities of $160,000.

Instructions Prepare a supplementary schedule in the format illustrated on page 549. Include comparative income statements prepared on the bases of historical costs, constant dollars, and current costs. Also show the net gain or loss from holding monetary items. Include supporting computations for the (1) cost of goods sold—constant dollar basis, (2) depreciation expense—constant dollar basis, (3) net gain or loss in purchasing power from holding monetary items, (4) cost of goods sold—current cost basis, and (5) depreciation expense—current dollar basis.

BUSINESS DECISION PROBLEM 14

For many years, Festival Films used the lifo method of inventory valuation and the declining-balance method of depreciation in measuring the net income of its mail-order business. In addition, the company charged off all costs of catalogs as incurred. In Year 10, the company changed its inventory pricing method to fifo, adopted the straight-line method of depreciation, and decided to charge off catalog costs only as catalogs are distributed to potential customers.

The following information for the last three years is taken from the company's accounting records:

	Year 10	Year 9	Year 8
Sales (net)	$500,000	$400,000	$350,000
Purchases (net)	300,000	220,000	200,000
Ending inventory—fifo	50,000	45,000	40,000
Ending inventory—lifo	30,000	28,000	25,000
Depreciation—declining-balance method	27,500	30,000	35,000
Depreciation—straight-line method	20,000	20,000	20,000
Operating expenses other than depreciation	120,500	93,000	80,000
Catalog costs included in operating expenses but considered applicable to future revenue	18,500	8,000	5,000
Net income as computed by Festival Films	100,000	60,000	37,000

At the end of Year 10, Festival Films prepared the following comparative income statement and presented it to a banker in connection with an application for a substantial long-term loan:

FESTIVAL FILMS
Comparative Income Statement
For Years Ended December 31

	Year 10	Year 9
Sales (net)	$500,000	$400,000
Cost of goods sold*	278,000	217,000
Gross profit on sales	$222,000	$183,000
Operating expenses	122,000	123,000
Net income	$100,000	$ 60,000

*Based on lifo inventory method in Year 9; inventory at end of Year 10 was valued on fifo basis.

The loan officer for the Pacific National Bank, where Festival Films has applied for the loan, asks you to help decide whether to lend the money to Festival Films.

Instructions

a Prepare a more detailed comparative income statement for Years 9 and 10. For the cost of goods sold section, you should use the figures listed in the three-column schedule at the beginning of this problem to show as individual items the beginning inventory, net purchases, cost of goods available for sale, ending inventory, and cost of goods sold. In the section for operating expenses, show the depreciation expense separately from other operating expenses. Summary figures should be the same as those compiled by Festival Films.

Criticize the detailed comparative income statement in terms of generally accepted accounting principles. Indicate the dollar effect on net income of any violations of accounting principles.

b Prepare two comparative income statements for Years 9 and 10. First, prepare a comparative statement on the same accounting basis as in prior years. Second, prepare a comparative income statement on the revised basis of accounting decided upon by the company.

c What good feature is common to both of the comparative income statements called for in **b** above? Comment on the *trend* of net income shown in each income statement in **b** above, and also in the comparative income statement prepared by Festival Films.

APPENDIX

B

INVESTMENTS FOR PURPOSES OF CONTROL

After studying this appendix you should be able to:

- Account for an investment in common stock by the equity method.
- Describe how a parent company controls its subsidiaries.
- Explain why intercompany transactions must be eliminated as a step in preparing consolidated financial statements.
- Prepare a consolidated balance sheet.
- Differentiate between the purchase method and the pooling method of accounting for business combinations.
- Explain when consolidated statements should be prepared.

As discussed in Chapter 7, a portfolio of marketable securities may include investments in common stock. Marketable securities generally are classified as current assets, and the investor recognizes cash dividends received as investment income. Some investors, however, may own enough of a company's common stock to *influence or control* that company's activities through the voting rights of the shares owned. Such large holdings of common stock create an important business relationship between the investor and the issuing company (called the *investee*). Since investments of this type cannot be sold without disrupting this relationship, they are not included in the portfolio of marketable securities. Such investments are shown in the balance sheet under the caption Long-Term Investments, which follows the current asset section.

If an investor is able to exercise significant control over the investee's management, dividends paid by the investee may no longer be a good measure of the investor's income from the investment. This is because the investor may control the investee's dividend policy. In such cases, dividends paid by the investee are likely to reflect the *investor's* cash needs and income tax considerations, rather than the profitability of the investment.

For example, assume that Sigma Company owns all the common stock of Davis Company. For three years Davis Company is very profitable but pays no dividends, because Sigma Company has no need for additional cash. In the fourth year, Davis Company pays a large cash dividend to Sigma Company despite operating at a loss for that year. Clearly, it would be misleading for Sigma Company to report no investment income while the company it owns is operating profitably, and then to show large investment income in a year when Davis Company incurred a net loss.

The investor does not have to own 100% of the common stock of the investee to exercise a significant degree of control. An investor with much less than 50% of the voting stock may have effective control, since the remaining shares are not likely to vote as an organized block. In the absence of other evidence (such as another large stockholder), ownership of 20% or more of the investee's common stock is considered an investment for purposes of control. In such cases, the investor should account for the investment by using the *equity method.*[1]

The equity method

When the equity method is used, an investment in common stock is first recorded at cost but later is adjusted each year for changes in the stockholders' equity of the investee. As the investee earns net income, the stockholders' equity in the company increases. An investor using the equity method recognizes his *proportionate share of the investee's net income* as an increase in the carrying value of his investment. A proportionate share of a net loss reported by the investee is recognized as a decrease in the investment.

When the investee pays dividends, the stockholders' equity in the company is reduced. The investor, therefore, treats dividends received from the investee as a conversion of the investment into cash, thus reducing the carrying value of the investment. Investments accounted for by the equity method are *not* adjusted to the lower of cost or market value. In effect, the equity method causes the carrying value of the investment to rise and fall with changes in the book value of the shares.

Illustration of the equity method   Assume that Cove Corporation purchases 25% of the common stock of Bay Company for $200,000, which corresponds to the underlying book value. During the following year, Bay Company earns net income of $120,000 and pays dividends of $80,000. Cove Corporation would account for its investment as follows:

---

[1]*APB Opinion No. 18,* "The Equity Method of Accounting for Investments in Common Stock," AICPA (New York: 1971).

Investment in Bay Company	200,000	
Cash		200,000

To record acquisition of 25% of the common stock of Bay Company.

Investment in Bay Company	30,000	
Investment Income		30,000

To increase the investment for 25% share of net income earned by Bay
Company (25% × $120,000).

Cash	20,000	
Investment in Bay Company		20,000

To reduce investment for dividends received from Bay Company
(25% × $80,000).

The net result of these entries by Cove Corporation is to increase the carrying value of the investment in Bay Company account by $10,000. This corresponds to 25% of the increase reported in Bay Company's retained earnings during the period [25% × ($120,000 − $80,000) = $10,000].

In this illustration of the equity method, we have made several simplifying assumptions: (1) Cove Corporation purchased the stock of Bay Company at a price equal to the underlying book value; (2) Bay company had issued common stock only and the number of shares outstanding did not change during the year; and (3) there were no intercompany transactions between Cove Corporation and Bay Company. If we were to change any of these assumptions, the computations in applying the equity method would become more complicated. Application of the equity method in more complex situations is discussed in advanced accounting courses.

CONSOLIDATED FINANCIAL STATEMENTS

Parent and subsidiary companies

A corporation which owns *all or a majority* of another corporation's capital stock is called a *parent* company, and the corporation which is wholly owned or majority-held is called a *subsidiary*.[2] Through the voting rights of the owned shares, the parent company can elect the board of directors of the subsidiary company and thereby control the subsidiary's resources and activities. In effect, the *affiliated companies* (the parent and its subsidiaries) function as a *single economic unit* controlled by the directors of the parent company. This relationship is illustrated in the diagram at the top of the next page.

There are a number of economic, legal, and income tax advantages which encourage large business organizations to operate through subsidiaries rather than through a single legal entity. Although we think of Sears, General Electric, or IBM as single companies, each of these organizations is really a group of affiliated corporations. Since the parent company in each case controls the resources and activities of its subsidiaries, it is logical for us to consider an affiliated group such as IBM as one *economic* entity.

---

[2]Ownership of a majority of a company's voting stock means holding at least 50% plus one share.

Financial statements for a consolidated economic entity

Because the parent company and its subsidiaries are separate legal entities, separate financial statements are prepared for each company. In the *separate* financial statements of the parent company, the subsidiaries appear only as investments accounted for by the *equity method.* Since the affiliated companies function as a single economic unit, the parent company also prepares financial statements which show the financial position and operating results of the entire group of companies. Such statements are called *consolidated financial statements.*

The distinctive feature of consolidated financial statements is that the assets, liabilities, revenue, and expenses of *two or more separate corporations are combined in a single set of financial statements.* In a *consolidated balance sheet,* the assets of the entire group of affiliated companies are combined and reported as though only a single entity existed. For example, the amount shown as Cash on a consolidated balance sheet is the total of the cash owned by all of the affiliated companies. Liabilities of the various companies also are combined. Similarly, in a *consolidated income statement,* the revenue and expenses of the affiliated companies are combined to show the operating results of the consolidated economic entity.

Stockholders in the parent corporation have a vital interest in the financial results of all operations under the parent company's control, including those conducted through subsidiaries. Therefore, the parent company includes consolidated financial statements in its annual and quarterly reports to stockholders. Most of the companies listed on major stock exchanges are actually parent companies with one or more subsidiaries. Thus anyone using published financial statements will find it useful to understand the basic principles used in preparing consolidated financial statements.

Principles of consolidation

Consolidated financial statements are prepared by combining the amounts that appear in the separate financial statements of the parent and subsidiary companies. In the combining process, however, certain adjustments are made to *eliminate the effects of intercompany transactions* and thus to reflect the assets, liabilities, and stockholders' equity from the viewpoint of a single economic entity.

Intercompany transactions The term *intercompany transactions* refers to transactions between affiliated companies. These transactions may include, for example, the sale of merchandise, the leasing of property, and the making of loans. When the affiliated companies are viewed separately, these transactions may create assets and liabilities for the individual companies. However, when the affiliated companies are viewed as a single business entity, these assets and liabilities are merely the result of internal transfers within the business organization and should not appear in the consolidated financial statements.

For example, if a subsidiary borrows money from the parent company, a note payable will appear as a liability in the balance sheet of the subsidiary company and a note receivable will appear as an asset in the separate balance sheet of the parent. When the two companies are viewed as a single consolidated entity, however, this "loan" is nothing more than a transfer of cash from one part of the business to another. Transferring assets between two parts of a single business entity does not create either a receivable or a payable for that entity. Therefore, the parent company's note receivable and the subsidiary's note payable should not appear in the consolidated financial statements.

Preparing consolidated financial statements Separate accounting records are maintained for each company in an affiliated group, but no accounting records are maintained for the consolidated entity. The amounts shown in consolidated financial statements *do not come from a ledger;* they are determined on a *working paper* by combining the amounts of like items on the financial statements of the affiliated companies. For example, the inventories of all the affiliated companies are combined into one amount for inventories. Entries to eliminate the effects of intercompany transactions are made *only* on this working paper. These elimination entries are *not recorded in the accounting records* of either the parent company or its subsidiaries.

Consolidation at the date of acquisition

To illustrate the basic principles of consolidation, we will now prepare a consolidated balance sheet. Assume that on January 1, Year 10, Post Corporation purchases for cash 100% of the capital stock of Sun Company at its book value of $300,000. (The shares are purchased from Sun Company's former stockholders.) Also on this date, Post Corporation lends $40,000 cash to Sun Company, receiving a note as evidence of the loan. Immediately after these two transactions, the separate balance sheet accounts of Post Corporation and Sun Company are as shown in the working paper at the top of the next page.

Intercompany eliminations

Before the balance sheet amounts of Post Corporation and Sun Company are combined, entries are made in the working paper to eliminate the effects of intercompany transactions. Intercompany eliminations may be classified into three basic types:

1 Elimination of intercompany stock ownership
2 Elimination of intercompany debt
3 Elimination of intercompany revenue and expenses

POST CORPORATION AND SUBSIDIARY
Working Paper—Consolidated Balance Sheet
January 1, Year 10 (Date of Acquisition)

	Post Corporation	Sun Company	Intercompany Eliminations		Consolidated Balance Sheet
			Debit	Credit	
Cash	60,000	45,000			105,000
Notes receivable	40,000			(b) 40,000	
Accounts receivable (net)	70,000	50,000			120,000
Inventories	110,000	95,000			205,000
Investment in Sun Company	300,000			(a) 300,000	
Plant & equipment (net)	210,000	180,000			390,000
Totals	790,000	370,000			820,000
Notes payable		40,000	(b) 40,000		
Accounts payable	125,000	30,000			155,000
Capital stock—Post Corporation	400,000				400,000
Capital stock—Sun Company		200,000	(a) 200,000		
Retained earnings—Post Corporation ...	265,000				265,000
Retained earnings—Sun Company		100,000	(a) 100,000		
Totals	790,000	370,000	340,000	340,000	820,000

Explanation of elimination:
(a) To eliminate the investment in Sun Company against Sun Company's stockholders' equity.
(b) To eliminate intercompany note receivable against related note payable.

The first two types of eliminations are illustrated in our example of Post Corporation and Sun Company. The elimination of intercompany revenue and expenses will be discussed later in this appendix.

To understand the need for elimination entries, we must adopt the viewpoint of the consolidated entity, in which Post Corporation and Sun Company are regarded as two departments within a single company.

Entry *(a)*: Elimination of intercompany stock ownership The purpose of entry *(a)* in the illustrated working paper is to eliminate from the consolidated balance sheet both the asset account and the stockholders' equity accounts representing the parent company's ownership of the subsidiary.

Post Corporation's ownership interest in Sun Company appears in the *separate* balance sheets of both corporations. In the parent's balance sheet, this ownership interest is shown as the asset, Investment in Sun Company. In the separate balance sheet of the subsidiary, the parent company's ownership interest is represented by the stockholders' equity accounts, Capital Stock and Retained Earnings. In the *consolidated* balance sheet, however, this "ownership interest" is neither an asset nor a part of stockholders' equity.

From the viewpoint of the single consolidated entity, *there are no stockholders in Sun Company.* "Stockholders" are outside investors who have an ownership interest in the business. All of Sun Company's capital stock is "internally owned" by another part of the consolidated entity. A company's "ownership" of its own stock does not create either an asset or stockholders' equity. Therefore the asset account, Investment in Sun Company, and Sun Company's related stockholders' equity accounts must be eliminated from the consolidated balance sheet.

Entry (b): Elimination of intercompany debt When Post Corporation loaned $40,000 to Sun Company, the parent company recorded a note receivable and the subsidiary recorded a note payable. This "receivable" and "payable" exist only when Post Corporation and Sun Company are viewed as two separate entities. When both corporations are viewed as a single company, this "loan" is merely a transfer of cash from one part of the business to another. Such internal transfers of assets do not create either a receivable or a payable for the consolidated entity. Therefore, entry (b) is made to eliminate Post Corporation's note receivable and Sun Company's note payable from the consolidated balance sheet.

After the necessary eliminations have been entered in the working paper, the remaining balance sheet amounts of Post Corporation and Sun Company are combined to determine the assets, liabilities, and stockholders' equity of the consolidated entity. The following consolidated balance sheet is then prepared from the working paper.

POST CORPORATION AND SUBSIDIARY
Consolidated Balance Sheet
January 1, Year 10

Assets

Current assets:

Cash	$105,000
Accounts receivable (net)	120,000
Inventories	205,000
Total current assets	$430,000
Plant & equipment (net)	390,000
Total assets	$820,000

Note stockholders' equity is that of parent company

Liabilities & Stockholders' Equity

Current liabilities:

Accounts payable		$155,000
Stockholders' equity:		
Capital stock	$400,000	
Retained earnings	265,000	
Total stockholders' equity		665,000
Total liabilities & stockholders' equity		$820,000

Acquisition of subsidiary's stock at a price above book value

When a parent company purchases a controlling interest in a subsidiary, it often pays a price for the shares in excess of their book value.[3] We cannot ignore a difference between the cost of the parent company's investment and the underlying book value of these shares. In consolidation, the parent's investment is offset against the stockholders' equity accounts of the subsidiary, and if the two amounts are not equal, we must determine what the difference between them represents.

To illustrate, assume that C Company purchases all of the outstanding shares of D Company for $980,000. At the date of acquisition, D Company's balance sheet shows total stockholders' equity of $700,000, consisting of capital stock of $300,000 and retained earnings of $400,000. In preparing the elimination entry on the working papers for a consolidated balance sheet, we must determine what to do with the $280,000 difference between the price paid, $980,000, and the stockholders' equity of D Company, $700,000.

Why would C Company pay a price in excess of book value for D Company's stock? C Company's management must believe that either (1) the fair market value of certain specific assets of D Company (such as land or buildings) is in excess of book value, or (2) D Company's future earnings prospects are so favorable as to justify paying $280,000 for D Company's unrecorded *goodwill*.

If we assume that the $280,000 represents unrecorded goodwill, the entry in the working papers to eliminate C Company's investment account against the stockholders' equity accounts of D Company would be:

Elimination entry when price paid for shares of subsidiary exceeds their book value

Capital Stock—D Company	300,000	
Retained Earnings—D Company	400,000	
Goodwill	280,000	
Investment in D Company (C Company's asset account)		280,000

To eliminate the cost of C Company's 100% interest in D Company against D's stockholders' equity accounts and to recognize D Company's unrecorded goodwill.

(Although we have shown this entry in general journal form, it actually would be made only in the Intercompany Eliminations columns of the working paper for a consolidated balance sheet.)

The $280,000 of goodwill will appear as an asset in the consolidated balance sheet.[4] This asset will be amortized to expense over its useful life.

---

[3]The parent company also might acquire the shares of the subsidiary at a price below book value. This situation will be discussed in an advanced accounting course.

[4]If specific assets of D Company had been undervalued, the $280,000 would be allocated to increase the valuation of those assets in the consolidated working papers. The revaluation of specific assets is beyond the scope of our introductory discussion.

Less than 100% ownership in subsidiary

If a parent company owns a majority interest in a subsidiary but less than 100% of the outstanding shares, a new kind of ownership equity known as the *minority interest* will appear in the consolidated balance sheet. This minority interest represents the ownership interest in the subsidiary held by stockholders other than the parent company.

When there are minority stockholders, only the portion of the subsidiary's stockholders' equity owned by the parent company is eliminated. The remainder of the stockholders' equity of the subsidiary is included in the consolidated balance sheet under the caption Minority Interest.

To illustrate, assume that at the end of Year 4, Park Company purchases 75% of the outstanding capital stock of Sims Company for $150,000 cash, an amount equal to the book value of the stock acquired. The working paper to prepare a consolidated balance sheet on the date that control of Sims Company is acquired appears below:

PARK AND SUBSIDIARY
Working Paper—Consolidated Balance Sheet
December 31, Year 4 (Date of Acquisition)

	Park Company	Sims Company	Intercompany Eliminations		Consolidated Balance Sheet
			Debit	Credit	
Cash	200,000	50,000			250,000
Other assets	500,000	210,000			710,000
Investment in Sims Company	150,000			(a) 150,000	
Totals	850,000	260,000			960,000
Liabilities	250,000	60,000			310,000
Capital stock—Park Company	500,000				500,000
Capital stock—Sims Company		120,000	(a) 90,000		
			(b) 30,000		
Retained earnings—Park Company	100,000				100,000
Retained earnings—Sims Company		80,000	(a) 60,000		
			(b) 20,000		
Minority interest (25% of $200,000)				(b) 50,000	50,000
Totals	850,000	260,000	200,000	(b) 200,000	960,000

Explanation of elimination:
(a) To eliminate Park Company's investment in 75% of Sims Company's stockholders' equity.
(b) To classify the remaining 25% of Sims Company's stockholders' equity as a minority interest.

Entry *(a)* in this working paper offsets Park Company's asset, Investment in Sims Company, against 75% of Sims Company's capital stock and retained earnings. The purpose of this entry is to eliminate intercompany stock ownership from the assets and stockholders' equity shown in the consolidated balance sheet. Entry *(b)* reclassifies the remaining 25% of Sims Company's capital stock and retained earnings into a special stockholders' equity account entitled Minority Interest. In the consolidated balance sheet, the minority interest appears in the stockholders' equity section as shown below:

Stockholders' equity:	
Minority interest	$ 50,000
Capital stock	500,000
Retained earnings	100,000
Total stockholders' equity	$650,000

Minority interest   Why is the minority interest shown separately in the consolidated balance sheet instead of being included in the amounts shown for capital stock and retained earnings? The reason for this separate presentation is to distinguish between the ownership equity of the controlling stockholders and the equity of the minority stockholders.

The stockholders in the parent company own the controlling interest in the consolidated entity. Because these stockholders elect the directors of the parent company, they control the entire group of affiliated companies. The minority interest, however, has *no control* over any of the affiliated companies. Because they own shares only in a subsidiary, they cannot vote for the directors of the parent company. Also, they can never outvote the majority stockholder (the parent company) in electing the directors or establishing the policies of the subsidiary.[5]

The minority stockholders receive 25% of the dividends declared by Sims Company but do not participate in dividends declared by the parent company. The controlling stockholders, on the other hand, receive all the dividends declared by Park Company but do not receive dividends declared by the subsidiary.

Consolidated income statement

A consolidated income statement is prepared by combining the revenue and expense accounts of the parent and subsidiary. Revenue and expenses arising from *intercompany transactions* are eliminated because they reflect transfers of assets from one affiliated company to another and do not change the net assets from a consolidated viewpoint.

Elimination of intercompany revenue and expenses   Some of the more common examples of intercompany items that should be eliminated in preparing a consolidated income statement are:

1 Sales to affiliated companies
2 Cost of goods sold resulting from sales to affiliated companies

---

[5]Some companies emphasize the limited ownership role of the minority stockholders by showing the minority interest between the liabilities section and the stockholders' equity section of the consolidated balance sheet.

3 Interest expense on loans from affiliated companies
4 Interest revenue on loans made to affiliated companies
5 Rent or other revenue received for services rendered to affiliated companies
6 Rent or other expenses paid for services received from affiliated companies

In its separate accounting records, the parent company uses the *equity method* to account for its investment in a subsidiary. Under the equity method, the parent company recognizes as Investment Income its share of the subsidiary's earnings. Because the individual revenue and expenses of the subsidiary are included in a consolidated income statement, the parent company's Investment Income (from subsidiary) account must be eliminated to avoid double counting this portion of the subsidiary's earnings.

Because of the complexity of the intercompany eliminations, the preparation of a consolidated income statement and a consolidated statement of retained earnings are topics appropriately deferred to an advanced accounting course.

Purchase method and pooling-of-interests method: Two types of business combination

The transaction in which two corporations become affiliated is called a *business combination.* In our discussion of business combinations up to this point, we have assumed that the parent acquired a subsidiary company by paying cash for its shares. This kind of acquisition is accounted for by the *purchase method.* The purchase method is also used for cases in which the parent issues its own bonds payable or capital stock in payment for the subsidiary's shares. The term *purchase method* implies that the parent has acquired the subsidiary by purchase and that the former stockholders in the subsidiary have sold out. In addition to the purchase method which we have been discussing, there is an alternative called the *pooling-of-interests method.* We will now consider the type of business combination for which the pooling-of-interests method may be used.

If the stock of a subsidiary is acquired *in exchange for shares of the parent company's common stock* and if certain other criteria are met, a business combination may be treated as a pooling of interest.[6] A key aspect of such acquisitions is that the stockholders of the subsidiary company *become stockholders of the parent corporation.* The stockholders of the two companies are said to have *pooled their interests,* rather than one ownership group having sold its equity to the other.

When a subsidiary is acquired by a pooling of interests, no ownership interest is severed—in other words, no "purchase" or "sale" of the subsidiary's net assets occurs. Therefore, the net assets of the subsidiary are *not revalued* in the consolidated balance sheet, regardless of the market value of the securities issued in

---

[6]In addition to the parent company issuing only common stock in exchange for the subsidiary's shares, other specific criteria must be met for the affiliation to qualify as a pooling of interests. For example, at least 90% of the subsidiary's stock must be acquired within one year following the beginning of negotiations. For a more complete discussion of the differences between a purchase and a pooling of interests, see *APB Opinion No. 16,* "Business Combinations," AICPA (New York: 1970).

exchange. In the consolidated balance sheet, the assets of the subsidiary appear at their book values and *no goodwill is recorded.* Therefore, no amortization expense relating to goodwill appears in the consolidated income statement.

Another significant difference between the purchase and the pooling-of-interests methods is the treatment in the consolidated income statement of the subsidiary's earnings (revenue and expenses) in the year of affiliation. Under the purchase method, only the subsidiary's earnings *after the date of acquisition* are included in the consolidated income statement. Under the pooling-of-interests method, the consolidated income statement includes the earnings of the subsidiary *for the entire year.*

To illustrate, let us assume that X Company acquired 100% of Y Company's stock on November 1, Year 1, and that each company earned $600,000 during Year 1. Assuming the $600,000 net income of Y Company was earned at a uniform rate during Year 1, the consolidated net income for the two companies under the purchase method would be $700,000 (X Company's $600,000 + 2/12 of Y Company's $600,000). However, consolidated net income on a pooling basis would be $1,200,000 even though $500,000 ($10/12$ of $600,000) of the earnings of Y Company were earned before the two companies became affiliated on November 1.

The following brief summary emphasizes some of the points of contrast between treating a corporate acquisition as a *purchase* or as a *pooling of interests.*

Purchase Method	Pooling-of-Interests Method
1 If the price paid by the parent for the subsidary's stock exceeds book value, goodwill is recorded (or the subsidiary's assets are revalued).	No goodwill is recorded and the subsidiary's assets are not revalued, regardless of the market value of the shares issued by the parent company.
2 If goodwill appears in the consolidated balance sheet, consolidated net income in future periods is reduced by amortization expense relating to this asset.	Since no goodwill appears in the consolidated balance sheet, consolidated net income is not reduced by any related amortization expense.
3 Earnings of subsidiary are combined with the earnings of the parent only from the date of the affiliation.	Earnings of subsidiary for the entire year in which the affiliation occurs are included in the consolidated income statement.

In the opinion of the authors, the failure to record goodwill based upon the market value of the shares issued by the parent company is a serious weakness in the pooling-of-interests method. In many cases, the failure to record goodwill results in significant understatement of consolidated assets and an overstatement of consolidated net income.

To illustrate, assume that S Company has total assets and stockholders' equity with a book value of $6 million. (For simplicity, we will assume that S Company has no liabilities.) The *market value* of S Company's assets and stockholders' equity, however, is $10 million, due to the existence of $4 million in unrecorded goodwill.

Now assume that P Company issues $10 million (market value) of its own shares in exchange for 100% of S Company's capital stock. If this acquisition is treated as a purchase, S Company's assets will appear in the consolidated balance sheet at $10 million, including the $4 million in goodwill. As discussed in Chapter 10, goodwill must be amortized over a period of not more than 40 years. Therefore, consolidated net income will be reduced by at least $100,000 per year ($4 million ÷ 40 years) as the goodwill is amortized to expense.

If this affiliation is treated as a pooling of interests, the $4 million in unrecorded goodwill will *not appear* in the consolidated balance sheet, and the assets of S Company will be shown at their book values of $6 million. Also, there will be no amortization of goodwill in the consolidated income statement, thus causing net income to appear at a higher amount.

When should consolidated statements be prepared?

As a general rule, consolidated financial statements are prepared when one corporation owns a *controlling interest* (more than 50% of the voting stock) in one or more subsidiaries. However, the accounts of some subsidiary companies may not be included in consolidated statements. Consolidation of accounts is appropriate only when control over the subsidiary is a continuing situation and when the consolidated statements *give a meaningful picture of financial position*. For example, a subsidiary's accounts should not be consolidated with those of the parent if control is likely to be temporary or if the subsidiary is facing bankruptcy. Similarly, if the assets of a foreign subsidiary cannot be withdrawn by the parent because of restrictions placed on such assets by foreign governments, the accounts should not be consolidated.

In other instances, consolidation may not be appropriate because the activities of the subsidiary are *significantly different* from those of the parent. For example, Sears, Roebuck and Co. does not consolidate its wholly owned subsidiary, Allstate Insurance Company. When the parent company controls a subsidiary but consolidation is not considered appropriate, the *unconsolidated subsidiary* appears in the financial statements as a long-term investment, accounted for by the equity method.

REVIEW QUESTIONS

1 When should investors use the equity method to account for an investment in common stock?

2 Dividends on stock owned are usually recognized as income when they are received. Does an investor using the *equity method* to account for an investment in common stock follow this policy? Explain fully.

3 Alexander Corporation owns 80% of the outstanding common stock of Benton Company. Explain the basis for the assumption that these two companies constitute a single economic entity operating under unified control.

4 What are consolidated financial statements? Explain briefly how these statements are prepared.

5 List the three basic types of intercompany eliminations which should be made as a step in the preparation of consolidated financial statements.

6 Explain why the price paid to acquire a controlling interest in a subsidiary company may be different from the book value of the equity acquired.

7 The following item appears on a consolidated balance sheet: "Minority interest in subsidiary . . . $620,000." Explain the nature of this item, and where you would expect to find it on the consolidated balance sheet.

8 Briefly explain the differences found in consolidated financial statements when a business combination is viewed as a *pooling of interests* rather than as a *purchase.*

9 As a general rule, when should consolidated financial statements be prepared?

10 The annual report of Superior Manufacturing Company and Subsidiaries included the following note: "Accounts of all subsidiaries in which the Company owns more than 50% of the voting stock are shown on a consolidated basis, with three exceptions: Western Casualty and Indemnity Company, Consumer Credit Corporation, and Superior Manufacturing of Argentina, which are accounted for by the equity method."

Explain the probable reasons for not consolidating these three subsidiaries. Also explain how the investments in these unconsolidated subsidiaries will be shown in the consolidated balance sheet.

PROBLEMS

B-1 On January 1, Year 4, Travis Corporation purchases 40% of the common stock of Comoy, Inc. for $300,000, which corresponds to the underlying book value. Comoy, Inc., has issued common stock only. At December 31, Year 4, Comoy, Inc., reported net income for the year of $130,000 and paid cash dividends of $70,000. Travis Corporation uses the equity method to account for this investment.

Instructions

a Prepare all journal entries in the accounting records of Travis Corporation relating to the investment during Year 4.

b During Year 5, Comoy, Inc., reports a net loss of $90,000 and pays no dividends. Compute the carrying value of Travis Corporation's investment in Comoy, Inc., at the end of Year 5.

B-2 On June 30 of Year 1, P Company *purchased* 80% of the stock of S Company for $480,000 in cash. The separate condensed balance sheets immediately after the purchase are shown below:

	P Company	S Company
Cash	$ 140,000	$ 90,000
Investment in S Company	480,000	
Other assets	2,180,000	710,000
	$2,800,000	$800,000
Liabilities	$ 600,000	$200,000
Capital stock	1,200,000	400,000
Retained earnings	1,000,000	200,000
	$2,800,000	$800,000

Instructions Prepare a consolidated balance sheet immediately after P Company acquired control of S Company.

B-3 Condensed balance sheets of Wheat and Pine Companies at the end of Year 1 are shown below:

Assets	Wheat Company	Pine Company
Current assets	$1,680,000	$240,000
Other assets	1,920,000	660,000
Total assets	$3,600,000	$900,000

Liabilities & Stockholders' Equity		
Current liabilities	$ 840,000	$120,000
Long-term debt	600,000	84,000
Capital stock	1,200,000	360,000
Retained earnings	960,000	336,000
Total liabilities & stockholders' equity	$3,600,000	$900,000

Instructions Assume that, at the end of Year 1, Wheat Company purchased (using current assets) all the outstanding capital stock of Pine Company for $768,000. The excess of this purchase price over the book value of Pine Company's shares is regarded as payment for Pine Company's unrecorded goodwill. Prepare a consolidated balance sheet for Wheat and Pine Companies at the date of acquisition.

B-4 The following information relates to Major Company and its subsidiary, the Minor Company.

Assets	Major Company	Minor Company	Consolidated
Cash	$ 120,000	$ 75,000	$ 195,000
Accounts receivable	180,000	100,000	160,000
Merchandise inventory	360,000	230,000	590,000
Investment in Minor Company	900,000		
Other assets	1,200,000	530,000	1,730,000
Goodwill			220,000
Total assets	$2,760,000	$935,000	$2,895,000

Liabilities & Stockholders' Equity			
Accounts payable	$ 165,000	$ 90,000	$ 135,000
Accrued liabilities	30,000	45,000	75,000
Notes payable (long-term)	450,000		450,000
Capital stock	1,000,000	300,000	1,000,000
Paid-in capital in excess of par	365,000	160,000	365,000
Retained earnings	750,000	340,000	750,000
Minority interest			120,000
Total liabilities & stockholders' equity	$2,760,000	$935,000	$2,895,000

Major Company acquired its controlling interest in Minor Company by issuing a combination of notes payable and additional shares of capital stock.

Instructions

a Was the acquisition of Minor Company viewed as a purchase or a pooling of interests? Why?

b What percentage of the outstanding stock of Minor Company is owned by Major Company? (Hint: First determine the percentage of Minor Company's stockholders' equity owned by the minority stockholders.)

c If Minor Company's accounts payable include $85,000 owed to Major Company, how much of Major Company's accounts payable are apparently owed to Minor Company?

d Explain why $220,000 of goodwill appears in the consolidated balance sheet.

B-5 Osborne Electronics purchased 80% of the stock of Technical Instruments for cash. Shown below are the separate balance sheets of the two companies at the end of Year 10:

Assets	Osborne Electronics	Technical Instruments
Cash	$ 35,000	$ 18,000
Note receivable from Technical Instruments	50,000	
Accounts receivable	90,000	50,000
Inventories	100,000	145,000
Investment in Technical Instruments (equity method)	475,000	
Plant and equipment	350,000	450,000
Accumulated depreciation	(140,000)	(83,000)
Total assets	$960,000	$580,000

Liabilities & Stockholders' Equity		
Notes payable	$100,000	$ 50,000
Accounts payable	120,000	60,000
Accrued liabilities	30,000	20,000
Common stock, no par value	400,000	200,000
Retained earnings	310,000	250,000
Total liabilities & stockholders' equity	$960,000	$580,000

Other information

(1) Osborne Electronics' asset account, Investment in Technical Instruments, represents ownership of 80% of Technical Instruments stockholders' equity, which has a book value of $360,000 [80% × ($200,000 + $250,000) = $360,000]. The remainder of the Investment account balance represents the purchase of Technical Instruments' unrecorded goodwill. Amortization of this goodwill has already been recorded through December 31, Year 10.

(2) During Year 10, Technical Instruments borrowed $50,000 from Osborne Electronics by issuing a one-year note payable. Interest on this note has been paid through December 31.

(3) The accounts payable of Osborne Electronics include $9,000 owed to Technical Instruments for services rendered during Year 10. This amount also is included in the accounts receivable of Technical Instruments.

Instructions Prepare a working paper for a consolidated balance sheet at the end of Year 10. Use the form illustrated on page 578. Include at the bottom of the working paper explanations of the elimination entries.

15

STATEMENT OF CHANGES IN FINANCIAL POSITION: CASH FLOWS

After studying this chapter you should be able to:

- Differentiate between an income statement, a statement of changes in financial position, and a cash flow statement.
- Explain why working capital may be viewed as a "fund" of liquid resources.
- Identify the principal sources and uses of working capital.
- Determine the amount of working capital provided by operations.
- Prepare a statement of changes in financial position.
- Convert an income statement from accrual basis to cash basis.
- Prepare a cash flow statement.

The business activities of a going concern may be viewed as cycles of investment, recovery of investment, and reinvestment. During the operating cycle, for example, the business acquires merchandise inventories on credit, thus creating accounts payable. These merchandise inventories are in turn sold to customers on credit. When the accounts receivable are collected from the customers, the company again has cash to apply against its debts and to begin the operating cycle anew. Thus, the current assets circulate through the business during an operating cycle. Investments in plant and equipment also must be recovered through revenue at a rate fast enough to permit replacement of these assets as they wear out or become obsolete. If a business cannot recover the cash it has invested quickly enough to pay its debts as they become due, it must borrow or obtain cash from other sources in order to survive.

The balance sheet portrays the overall financial position of the business at a specific date during these recurring cycles of investment, recovery of investment, and reinvestment. The income statement shows the dollar amount of resources generated and consumed in business operations. In a sense, the fate of any given business enterprise is read in the income statement, since it tells whether revenue is larger or smaller during any period than the cost of the resources used up in generating this revenue. In this chapter we introduce a third major financial statement, the *statement of changes in financial position*[1] and a related summary of cash movements, the *cash flow statement.*

STATEMENT OF CHANGES IN FINANCIAL POSITION

A statement of changes in financial position helps us to understand how and why the financial position of a business has changed during the period. This statement summarizes the long-term *financing and investing activities* of the business; it shows where the financial resources (funds) have come from and where they have gone. With this understanding of how funds have flowed into the business and how these funds have been used, we can begin to answer such important questions as: Do the normal operations of the business generate sufficient funds to enable the company to continue paying dividends? Did the company have to borrow to finance the acquisition of new plant assets, or was it able to generate the funds from current operations? Is the business becoming more or less solvent? And perhaps the most puzzling question: How can a *profitable* business be running low on cash and working capital? Even though a business operates profitably, its working capital may decline and the business may even become insolvent.

The statement of changes in financial position gives us answers to these questions, because it shows in detail the amount of funds received from each source and the amount of funds used for each purpose throughout the year. In fact, this financial statement used to be called a Statement of Sources and Applications of Funds. Many people still call it simply a *Funds Statement.* However, the name officially recommended by the FASB is the *Statement of Changes in Financial Position.*

"Funds" defined as working capital

In ordinary usage, the term *funds* usually means cash. Accountants and financial executives, however, think of "funds" in a broader sense. They view the funds available to a company as its *working capital*—the excess of current assets over current liabilities.

---

[1] In *Opinion No. 19,* "Reporting Changes in Financial Position," the Accounting Principles Board of the AICPA concluded (p. 373) that "information concerning the financing and investing activities of a business enterprise and the changes in its financial position for a period is essential for financial statement users, particularly owners and creditors, in making economic decisions. When financial statements purporting to present both financial position (balance sheet) and results of operations (statement of income and retained earnings) are issued, a statement summarizing changes in financial position should also be presented as a basic financial statement for each period for which an income statement is presented."

During each operating cycle, the current assets are constantly being converted into cash, a portion of which is used to pay current liabilities. That portion of the current assets not needed to pay current liabilities is viewed as liquid resources or available funds. A portion of these funds may be used to buy plant assets, to pay long-term debt, and to pay dividends. However, only a part of the liquid resources can be used for these purposes, because a major portion must be retained in circulation to meet the day-to-day needs of the next operating cycle.

If the amount of working capital increased during a given fiscal period, this means that more working capital was generated than was used for various business purposes; if a decrease in working capital occurred, the reverse is true. One of the key purposes of the statement of changes in financial position is to explain fully the increase or decrease in working capital during a fiscal period.[2] This is done by showing where working capital originated and how it was used.

Sources and uses of working capital

Any transaction that increases the amount of working capital is a *source of working capital*. For example, the sale of merchandise at a price greater than its cost is a source of working capital, because the increase in cash or receivables from the sale is greater than the decrease in inventory. Any transaction that decreases working capital is a *use of working capital*. For example, either incurring a current liability to acquire a noncurrent asset or using cash to pay expenses represents a decrease in working capital.

On the other hand, some transactions affect current assets or current liabilites but do *not* change the amount of working capital. For example, the collection of an account receivable (which increases cash and decreases an account receivable by an equal amount) is not a source of working capital. Similarly, the payment of an account payable (which decreases cash and decreases an account payable by an equal amount) does not change the amount of working capital.

The principal sources and uses of working capital are listed below:

Sources of working capital:

1 **Current operations** If the inflow of funds from sales exceeds the outflow of funds to cover the cost of merchandise purchases and expenses of doing business, current operations will provide a net source of funds. If the inflow of funds from sales is less than these outflows, operations will result in a net use of funds. Not all expenses require the use of funds in the current period; therefore, the amount of funds provided by operations is *not* the same as the

---

[2]In the preparation of a statement of changes in financial position, some companies define "funds" as cash, rather than as working capital. In these cases, the statement of changes in financial position becomes similar to the cash flow statement discussed later in this chapter. The majority of publicly owned corporations, however, use the working capital definition of "funds."

amount of net income earned during the period. Differences between the amount of *working capital provided by operations* and the amount of net income will be discussed later in the chapter.

In the long run, operations must result in a net source of funds if the business is to survive. A business cannot obtain funds through other sources indefinitely if those funds will only be consumed by business operations.

2 Sale of noncurrent assets A business may obtain working capital by selling noncurrent assets, such as plant and equipment or long-term investments, in exchange for current assets. As long as current assets are received, the sale is a source of funds *regardless of whether the noncurrent assets are sold at a gain or a loss.* For example, assume that a company sells land which cost $80,000 for $60,000 in cash. Although the land was sold at a loss, the company has increased its current assets by $60,000. Thus, the transaction is a source of working capital.

3 Long-term borrowing Long-term borrowing, such as issuing bonds payable, results in an increase in current assets, thereby increasing working capital. *Short-term borrowing,* however, does *not* increase working capital. When a company borrows cash by signing a short-term note payable, working capital is unchanged because the increase in current assets is offset by an increase in current liabilities of the same amount.

4 Sale of additional shares of stock The sale of capital stock results in an inflow of current assets, thereby increasing working capital. In a similar manner, additional investments of current assets by owners represent sources of funds to single proprietorships and partnerships. The issuance of capital stock in conjunction with a stock dividend or a stock split, however, does not bring any new resources into the company and is not a source of funds.

Uses of working capital:

1 Declaration of cash dividends The declaration of a cash dividend results in a current liability (dividend payable) and is therefore a use of funds. Notice that it is the *declaration* of the dividend, rather than the payment of the dividend, which is the use of funds. Actual payment of the dividend reduces current assets and current liabilities by the same amount and thus has no effect upon the amount of working capital. (Stock dividends do not involve any distribution of assets and, therefore, are not a use of funds.)

2 Purchase of noncurrent assets Purchases of noncurrent assets, such as plant and equipment, reduce current assets or increase current liabilities. In either case, working capital is reduced. Special situations in which noncurrent assets are acquired in exchange for other noncurrent assets or long-term liabilities are discussed later in this chapter.

3 Repayment of long-term debt Working capital is decreased when current assets are used to repay long-term debt. However, repayment of short-term debt is not a use of funds, since current assets and current liabilities decrease by the same amount.

4 Repurchase of outstanding stock When cash is paid out to repurchase outstanding shares of stock, working capital is reduced.

Funds flow: a simple illustration

Assume that John Claire started a business, Claire Company, as a single proprietorship on April 30 by investing $40,000 cash; the company rented a building on May 1 and completed the transactions shown below during the month of May.

(1) Claire invested an additional $20,000 cash in the business.
(2) Purchased merchandise costing $40,000 on credit and sold three-fourths of this, also on credit, for $58,000.
(3) Collected $45,000 on receivables; paid $32,000 on accounts payable.
(4) Paid $20,500 cash for operating expenses.
(5) Purchased land for the construction of a store. Gave $30,000 cash and a six-month note for $17,000 in payment for the land.
(6) Withdrew $2,000 from the business for personal use.

The company's income statement and balance sheet at May 31 are shown below:

CLAIRE COMPANY
Income Statement
For the Month Ended May 31

Financial statements covering one month's operations of single proprietorship

Sales		$58,000
Cost of goods sold:		
Purchases	$40,000	
Less: Ending inventory (one-fourth of purchases)	10,000	30,000
Gross profit on sales		$28,000
Operating expenses		20,500
Net income for month of May		$ 7,500

CLAIRE COMPANY
Comparative Balance Sheet

Assets	May 31	Apr. 1
Cash	$20,500	$40,000
Accounts receivable	13,000	
Inventory	10,000	
Land	47,000	
Total assets	$90,500	$40,000

Liabilities & Owner's Equity		
Note payable	$17,000	
Accounts payable	8,000	
John Claire, capital	65,500	$40,000
Total liabilities & owner's equity	$90,500	$40,000

The working capital amounted to $40,000 (consisting entirely of cash) on April 30 but was only $18,500 ($43,500 − $25,000) on May 31, a decrease of $21,500. In analyzing the six transactions completed during the month of May, we see that working capital was increased and decreased as follows:

Transactions increasing working capital:

Additional investment by owner	$20,000
Sale of merchandise for more than cost ($58,000 − $30,000)	28,000
Total increases in working capital	$48,000

Transactions decreasing working capital:

Payment of operating expenses	$20,500	
Payment of cash for purchase of land	30,000	
Issuance of short-term note payable for purchase of land	17,000	
Withdrawal by owner	2,000	
Total decreases in working capital		69,500
Decrease in working capital during May		$21,500

A complete list of transactions for a fiscal period may not be readily available, and even if it were, analysis of such a list would be a laborious process. In practice, a statement of changes in financial position is prepared by analyzing the changes that occurred *in the noncurrent assets* during the fiscal period. An analysis of the comparative balance sheet for Claire Company indicates that the Land account increased by $47,000. This increase indicates that land, a noncurrent asset, was purchased during the period. Purchase of a noncurrent asset is a use of funds. Claire's capital account increased by $25,500 as a result of (1) additional investment of $20,000 (a source of funds), (2) net income of $7,500 (a source of funds), and (3) a withdrawal of $2,000 (a use of funds). We can therefore prepare the following statement of changes in financial position for the month of May, including a supporting schedule showing the changes in each element of working capital:

CLAIRE COMPANY
Statement of Changes in Financial Position
For Month of May

A simple statement of changes in financial position	*Sources of working capital:*		
	Operations (net income)		$ 7,500
	Additional investment by owner		20,000
	Total sources of working capital		$27,500
	Uses of working capital:		
	Purchase of land	$47,000	
	Withdrawal by owner	2,000	
	Total uses of working capital		49,000
	Decrease in working capital		$21,500

Changes in Composition of Working Capital

	End of May	End of April	Increase or (Decrease) in Working Capital
Current assets:			
Cash	$20,500	$40,000	$(19,500)
Accounts receivable	13,000	–0–	13,000
Inventory	10,000	–0–	10,000
Total current assets	$43,500	$40,000	
Current liabilities:			
Note payable	$17,000	$ –0–	(17,000)
Accounts payable	8,000	–0–	(8,000)
Total current liabilities	$25,000	$ –0–	
Working capital	$18,500	$40,000	
Decrease in working capital			$(21,500)

The differences between net income, net cash flow, and the change in working capital should be carefully noted in the foregoing example. Although Claire Company's net income for May was $7,500, its cash account *decreased* by $19,500 and its working capital *decreased* by $21,500.

Effect of transactions on working capital

In preparing a statement of changes in financial position, it is convenient to view all business transactions as falling into three categories:

1 Transactions which affect *only current asset or current liability accounts.* These transactions produce changes in working capital accounts but do not change the amount of working capital. For example, the purchase of merchandise increases inventory and accounts payable but has no effect on working capital; it may therefore be ignored in preparing a statement of changes in financial position.

2 Transactions which affect a *current asset or current liability account and a non-working capital account.* These transactions bring about either an increase or a decrease in the amount of working capital. The issuance of long-term bonds, for example, increases current assets and increases bonds payable, a non-working capital account; therefore, the issuance of bonds payable is a source of working capital. Similarly, when the bonds approach maturity they are transferred to the current liability classification in the balance sheet. This causes a reduction (a use) of working capital. If changes in non-working capital accounts are analyzed, these events are brought to light, and their effect on working capital will be reported in the statement of changes in financial position.

3 Transactions which affect *only noncurrent accounts* and therefore have no direct effect on the amount of working capital. The entry to record depreciation is an example of such a transaction. Other transactions in this category, such as the issuance of capital stock in exchange for plant assets, are called *exchange transactions* and are viewed as *both a source and use of working capital,* but do not change the amount of working capital.

Exchange transactions Suppose that equipment worth $200,000 is acquired in exchange for 10,000 shares of $5 par value capital stock. The entry to record this transaction would be:

An exchange transaction

Equipment	*200,000*	
Capital stock		*50,000*
Paid-in Capital in Excess of Par		*150,000*
Exchange of 10,000 shares of $5 par value capital stock for equipment worth $200,000.		

This exchange transaction does not involve any current asset or current liability accounts and therefore has no *direct* effect upon working capital. However, the transaction may be viewed as consisting of two parts: (1) the sale of capital stock for $200,000 and (2) the use of this $200,000 to purchase equipment. Instead of being omitted from the statement of changes in financial position, an exchange transaction of this type is shown as *both a source of funds* (sale of capital stock) *and a use of funds* (purchase of equipment). This treatment is consistent with the objective of explaining in the statement of changes in financial position all the long-term financing activities of the business.

The acquisition of plant assets by issuing long-term debt and the conversion of bonds payable or preferred stock into common stock are other examples of exchange transactions which have no direct effect upon working capital. In the statement of changes in financial position, however, these transactions are shown as both a source and a use of working capital.

Most transactions affecting only long-term accounts are exchange transactions. Two exceptions, however, are stock splits and stock dividends. Stock splits and stock dividends do not involve an exchange and *do not* affect the financial position of the business. For this reason, stock splits and dividends *are not shown* in a statement of changes in financial position.

Working capital provided by operations

Working capital provided by operations is the net increase or decrease in working capital resulting from the normal business activities of earning revenue and paying expenses. There are many similarities between the providing of working capital by operations and the earning of net income. For example, earning revenue increases net income and the related inflow of cash and receivables increases working capital. However, there also are significant differences between net income and the amount of working capital provided by operations.

Some expenses do not reduce working capital Some expenses, such as depreciation, amortization of intangible assets, and amortization of discount on bonds payable, reduce net income but have no immediate effect on the amount of working capital provided by normal operations.

To illustrate, assume that on December 31, Year 1, City Delivery Service buys two trucks at a cost of $30,000. As of January 1, Year 2, the company has no assets other than the trucks and has no liabilities. During Year 2 the company does business on a cash basis, collecting revenue of $40,000 and paying expenses of $22,000, thus showing an $18,000 increase in cash, which is its only working capital account. The company then records depreciation expense of $6,000 on its trucks, resulting in a $12,000 net income for Year 2. What is the amount of working capital provided by operations in Year 2? The recording of depreciation expense reduced net income, *but it did not reduce working capital;* working capital provided by operations remains at $18,000. The $12,000 net income figure therefore *understates* the amount of working capital provided by operations by the amount of depreciation expense recorded during the period.

One objective of the statement of changes in financial position is to explain any differences between net income and the amount of working capital provided by operations. If we are to convert the $12,000 net income of City Delivery Service to the amount of working capital provided by operations, we must *add back* the depreciation expense of $6,000. The computation of working capital provided by operations in the statement of changes in financial position of City Delivery Service for Year 2 is shown below:

Sources of working capital:
  Operations:
    Net income *$12,000*
    Add: Depreciation expense *6,000*
    Working capital provided by operations *$18,000*

Depreciation is not a source of funds   The addition of depreciation expense to the net income figure has led some people to view depreciation expense as a source of funds. It is important for the user of financial statements to understand that depreciation is neither a source nor a use of working capital. *No funds flow into a business as a result of recording depreciation expense.* It is shown in the statement of changes in financial position merely to explain one of the differences between the concept of net income and the concept of working capital provided by operations.

Some items which increase income do not increase working capital   We have seen that some expenses do not reduce working capital. Similarly, some items in the income statement increase net income without increasing working capital; such items must be *deducted* from net income in arriving at working capital provided by operations. An example of such an item is the amortization of premium on bonds payable, which causes annual interest expense to be less than the cash payments of interest to bondholders.[3]

Nonoperating gains and losses   Nonoperating gains and losses, if material in amount, should be eliminated from net income in order to show the working

---

[3]The treatment of this item in the working paper and in the statement of changes in financial position is illustrated in the Demonstration Problem on pages 607–610.

capital provided by "normal" operations.[4] For example, assume that land cost-ing $100,000 is sold at a net gain of $50,000. In the statement of changes in financial position, the entire $150,000 in proceeds from the sale should be reported as "working capital provided by the sale of land." The $50,000 non-operating gain, however, is included in the net income for the period. In deter-mining the amount of working capital provided by operations, this $50,000 nonoperating gain must be *deducted* from the net income figure because the entire proceeds from the sale of the land are reported elsewhere in the statement of changes in financial position.

As a separate example, assume that the same land is sold for $70,000; then the nonoperationg loss of $30,000 should be *added back* to net income to arrive at working capital provided by operations, and the working capital provided through sale of land should be reported at $70,000.

Computation of working capital provided by operations: a summary   The foregoing discussion relating to the measurement of working capital provided by opera-tions can be summarized as follows:

Computation of Working Capital Provided by Operations

Impact of operations on working capital

$$\text{Working capital provided by operations} = \text{Net income} + \left\{ \begin{array}{l} \text{Depreciation} \\ \text{Amortization of intangibles} \\ \text{Amortization of discount on bond payable} \\ \text{Nonoperating losses} \end{array} \right\} - \left\{ \begin{array}{l} \text{Amortization of premium on bonds payable} \\ \text{Nonoperating gains} \end{array} \right\}$$

Funds flow: a comprehensive illustration

To illustrate the points just discussed, we shall prepare a statement of changes in financial position for the Allison Corporation from the comparative balance sheet and the condensed income statement shown on page 596. A summary of the transactions completed by Allison Corporation which resulted in changes in *noncurrent accounts* during Year 4 follows these financial statements.

[4]Nonoperating gains and losses include extraordinary items, gains or losses on sales of plant assets, and other gains or losses not directly related to the company's principal business activities.

ALLISON CORPORATION
Comparative Balance Sheet
At December 31

Assets	Year 4	Year 3
Current assets:		
Cash	$ 15,000	$ 35,000
Accounts receivable (net)	105,000	85,000
Inventory	200,000	120,000
Short-term prepayments	25,000	12,000
Total current assets	$345,000	$252,000
Land	300,000	200,000
Equipment	470,000	380,000
Less: Accumulated depreciation	(192,500)	(125,000)
Total assets	$922,500	$707,000

Analysis of these financial statements will explain the sources and uses of working capital

Liabilities & Stockholders' Equity

	Year 4	Year 3
Current liabilities:		
Accounts payable	$145,000	$ 90,000
Accrued liabilities	22,500	42,000
Total current liabilities	$167,500	$132,000
Notes payable, long term	170,000	20,000
Bonds payable, due June 30, Year 20	110,000	185,000
Capital stock, $5 par	100,000	60,000
Paid-in capital in excess of par	155,000	100,000
Retained earnings	220,000	210,000
Total liabilities & stockholders' equity	$922,500	$707,000

ALLISON CORPORATION
Condensed Income Statement
For Year Ended December 31, Year 4

Sales (net)	$900,000
Cost of goods sold	500,000
Gross profit on sales	$400,000
Operating expenses and income taxes	340,000
Income before gain on sale of land	$ 60,000
Gain on sale of land	20,000
Net income	$ 80,000

1 Changes in noncurrent assets:

   a Land costing $50,000 was sold for $70,000 cash. Another parcel of land was acquired for $150,000 by issuing a long-term note payable for the entire purchase price.

   b Equipment was purchased for $90,000; the invoice was paid within 10 days.

   c Depreciation of $67,500 was recorded.

2 Changes in noncurrent liabilities:

a As stated in transaction **1a,** a $150,000 long-term note payable was issued in exchange for land.

b Bonds payable of $75,000 were retired at a price equal to par value.

3 Changes in stockholders' equity accounts:

a A 50% stock dividend was declared in January, requiring a transfer of $30,000 from the Retained Earnings account to the Capital Stock account.

b In February, 2,000 shares of $5 par value stock were issued for $65,000 cash, thus increasing Capital Stock by $10,000 and Paid-in Capital in Excess of Par by $55,000.

c Cash dividends of $40,000 were declared and paid, causing a reduction in retained earnings.

d The net income for the year, $80,000 (including the $20,000 nonoperating gain on sale of land), was transferred to the Retained Earnings account.

From the comparative balance sheets, the income statement, and the summary of transactions affecting noncurrent accounts, we can prepare a statement of changes in financial position by completing the following three steps:

1 Compute the change in working capital during the period.

2 Prepare a working paper for analysis of changes in noncurrent accounts.

3 Prepare the statement of changes in financial position.

Computation of increase in working capital during the period   The first step in preparing a statement of changes in financial position is to determine the net increase or decrease in working capital during the period covered by the statement.

The working capital of the Allison Corporation increased by $57,500 during Year 4, determined as follows:

Allison Corporation

Computation of Increase in Working Capital during Year 4

	Dec. 31, Year 4	Dec. 31, Year 3
Current assets	$345,000	$252,000
Less: Current liabilities	167,500	132,000
Working capital	$177,500	$120,000
Increase in working capital during Year 4 ($177,500 − $120,000)		57,500
	$177,500	$177,500

Sources of working capital exceed uses by $57,500

The purpose of the statement of changes in financial position is to explain the *reasons* for the change in working capital. This is accomplished by listing the specific sources and uses of working capital during the period. Since the working capital for the Allison Corporation increased by $57,500, the sources of working capital during Year 4 exceeded the uses by this amount. But before a statement of changes in financial position can be prepared, we must analyze the changes which took place during the year in the noncurrent accounts.

Preparation of working paper for analysis of changes in noncurrent accounts A working paper showing the analysis of changes in noncurrent accounts for the Allison Corporation is illustrated on page 599. The amount of working capital and the balances in noncurrent accounts at the beginning of the period are listed in the first column of the working paper; balances at the end of the year are listed in the last (right-hand) column. The two middle columns are used to *explain the changes* in each *noncurrent* account during the year and to indicate whether each change represents a source or a use of funds. Transactions for the year (in summary form) are recorded in these middle columns and an offsetting entry is made in the lower section of the working paper indicating the effect of each transaction upon working capital.

Explanation of entries in the middle columns By studying the changes in the noncurrent accounts during Year 4, we are able to find the specific reasons for the $57,500 increase in working capital. The noncurrent accounts may be analyzed in any sequence; however, we recommend the following approach:

1 Explain all transactions affecting the Retained Earnings account.
2 Complete the computation of working capital provided by operations.
3 Beginning at the top of the working paper, explain any remaining changes in noncurrent accounts.
4 Make an entry explaining the net change in working capital. This entry should bring both the upper and lower sets of middle columns into balance.

Using this approach, the entries in our illustrated working paper are explained below.

Step 1: Explain the changes in Retained Earnings

Entry

(1) Allison Corporation's net income explains an $80,000 credit change in the Retained Earnings account. In the bottom portion of the working papers, an offsetting entry is made identifying net income as a source of working capital.

(2) Cash dividends of $40,000 declared during Year 4 caused a debit change in the Retained Earnings account and were a use of funds.

(3) The 50% stock dividend caused a $30,000 debit change in the Retained Earnings account and a $30,000 credit change in the Capital Stock account. Notice that both the debit and credit portions of this entry appear in the top portion of the working papers. As previously stated, stock dividends (and stock splits) are an exception to the general rule that changes in noncurrent accounts represent either sources or uses of working capital. Stock dividends have no effect upon working capital.

With these first three entries, we have explained how the Retained Earnings account increased during Year 4 from $210,000 to its ending balance of $220,000.

Working Paper for Statement of Changes in Financial Position

For Year Ended December 31, Year 4

Debits	Account Balances, Jan. 1, Year 4	Analysis of Transactions for Year 4		Account Balances, Dec. 31, Year 4
		Debit	Credit	
Working capital	120,000	(x) 57,500		177,500
Land	200,000	(6) 150,000	(5) 50,000	300,000
Equipment	380,000	(7) 90,000		470,000
Total	700,000			947,500
Credits				
Accumulated depreciation	125,000		(4) 67,500	192,500
Notes payable, long-term	20,000		(6) 150,000	170,000
Bonds payable, due June 30, Year 20	185,000	(8) 75,000		110,000
Capital stock, $5 par	60,000		(3) 30,000 ⎱	100,000
			(9) 10,000 ⎰	
Paid-in capital in excess of par	100,000		(9) 55,000	155,000
Retained earnings	210,000	(2) 40,000	(1) 80,000 ⎱	220,000
		(3) 30,000		
Total	700,000	442,500	442,500	947,500

		Sources	Uses	
Sources of working capital:				
Operations—net income		(1) 80,000		(From
Add: Depreciation		(4) 67,500		operations,
Less: Gain on sale of land			(5) 20,000 ⎱	$127,500)
Sale of land		(5) 70,000		
Issuance of long-term notes payable		(6) 150,000		
Sale of capital stock		(9) 65,000		
Uses of working capital:				
Cash dividends declared			(2) 40,000	
Purchase of land in exchange for long-term note payable			(6) 150,000	
Purchase of equipment			(7) 90,000	
Retirement of bonds payable			(8) 75,000	
Total sources and uses of working capital		432,500	375,000	
Increase in working capital during Year 4			(x) 57,500	
		432,500	432,500	

Explanation of transactions for Year 4:

(1) Net income, $80,000 (including nonoperating gain of $20,000 on sale of land), is transferred to Retained Earnings and is classified as a tentative source of working capital [to be adjusted by entries (4) and (5), below].

(2) Cash dividends declared, $40,000, reduce retained earnings and are a use of working capital.

(3) A 50% stock dividend had no effect on working capital.

(4) Depreciation, $67,500, is added to net income in arriving at working capital provided by operations.

(5) Sale of land for $70,000. Explains a $50,000 credit change in the Land account. The $20,000 nonoperating gain on the sale is reclassified within the sources of working capital from the "operations" section to "sale of land."

(6) A $150,000 long-term note payable was issued (a source of funds) to acquire land (a use of funds).

(7) Working capital of $90,000 was used to purchase equipment.

(8) Working capital of $75,000 was used to retire bonds payable.

(9) Issued capital stock, increasing working capital by $65,000.

(x) Balancing figure—increase in working capital during year 4.

Step 2: Complete the computation of working capital provided by operations

(4) The $80,000 net income figure appearing in the bottom portion of the working papers is only a tentative measure of the working capital provided by operations. Depreciation expense, for example, must be added back to this figure, because the recording of depreciation expense reduced net income but did not reduce working capital. Entry (4) shows that depreciation expense explains the $67,500 credit change in the Accumulated Depreciation account and adds this amount to net income as a step in determining working capital provided by operations.

(5) To complete the computation of working capital provided by operations, we must remove from net income the $20,000 nonoperating gain arising from the sale of land. Entry (5) removes the $20,000 gain from the "operations" section of the working paper and shows the entire $70,000 proceeds from the sale as a separate source of funds. In the top portion of the working paper, entry (5) shows that the sale of land caused a $50,000 credit change in the Land account.

We have now determined that working capital of $127,500 was provided by operations ($80,000 net income + $67,500 depreciation expense − $20,000 nonoperating gain).

Step 3: Explain any remaining changes in noncurrent accounts

(6) The issuance of a $150,000 long-term note payable in exchange for land is an exchange transaction, representing both a source and a use of working capital. First, an entry is made in the top portion of the working paper explaining the $150,000 increase in the Notes Payable account and an offsetting entry is made below showing a $150,000 source of funds. Next, a debit entry is made in the upper portion of the working paper explaining the $150,000 increase in the Land account, and an offsetting entry is made below showing this $150,000 use of funds.

(7) The purchase of equipment explains the $90,000 debit change in the Equipment account and is a use of working capital.

(8) During Year 4, Allison Corporation retired $75,000 of bonds payable at par. A reduction in long-term debt is a use of working capital. This transaction is recorded in the working paper by a debit to the Bonds Payable account and an offsetting entry describing the use of funds.

(9) The sale of capital stock in February for $65,000 is recorded in the upper section of the working paper by credits to Capital Stock, $10,000 (2,000 shares with a $5 par value), and to Paid-in Capital in Excess of Par, $55,000. The issuance of capital stock is a source of funds; therefore, the offsetting entry in the lower section of the working papers is entered in the Sources column.

At this point we should check carefully to determine that our entries in the Debit and Credit columns correctly explain the difference between the beginning and ending balances of each noncurrent account. If the top section of the working paper explains the change in every noncurrent account, the bottom section should include all of the sources and uses of working capital for the year.

(x)   We now total the Sources column ($432,500) and the Uses column ($375,000) in the bottom section of the working paper. The $57,500 difference between these column totals represents the net change in working capital during Year 4. Since working capital increased, this $57,500 is entered as a debit to Working Capital on the top line of the working paper and as the balancing figure in the Uses column at the bottom of the working paper.

Totals can now be determined for the Debit and Credit columns in the top section of the working paper. If these totals agree, we know that our analysis is correct, at least so far as the mechanics are concerned.

Preparation of statement of changes in financial position   The preceding working paper analysis explained all changes in noncurrent accounts that took place during Year 4. In making this analysis, we listed the sources and uses of working capital in the lower section of the working paper on page 599. The increase of $57,500 in working capital has been confirmed and a statement of changes in financial position, including a schedule showing the changes in the components of working capital, can now be prepared as shown below:

ALLISON CORPORATION

Statement of Changes in Financial Position

For Year Ended December 31, Year 4

Sources of working capital:		
Operations:		
Net income		$ 80,000
Add: Expense not requiring the use of working capital—		
depreciation	$ 67,500	
Less: Nonoperating gain on sale of land	20,000	47,500
Total working capital provided by operations		$127,500
Sale of land		70,000
Issuance of long-term notes payable		150,000
Sale of capital stock		65,000
Total sources of working capital		$412,500
Uses of working capital:		
Declaration of cash dividends	$ 40,000	
Purchase of land in exchange for long-term notes payable	150,000	
Purchase of equipment	90,000	
Retirement of bonds payable	75,000	
Total uses of working capital		355,000
Increase in working capital		$ 57,500

Changes in Composition of Working Capital

This supporting
schedule shows
the change in
each working
capital account

	End of Year 4	End of Year 3	Increases or (Decreases) in Working Capital
Current assets:			
Cash	$ 15,000	$ 35,000	$(20,000)
Accounts receivable (net)	105,000	85,000	20,000
Inventory	200,000	120,000	80,000
Short-term prepayments	25,000	12,000	13,000
Total current assets	$345,000	$252,000	
Current liabilities:			
Accounts payable	$145,000	$ 90,000	(55,000)
Accrued liabilities	22,500	42,000	19,500
Total current liabilities	$167,500	$132,000	
Working capital	$177,500	$120,000	
Increase in working capital			$ 57,500

The schedule entitled Changes in Composition of Working Capital should accompany a formal statement of changes in financial position. The purpose of this supporting schedule is to help readers of the financial statements to evaluate the *quality* of the company's working capital. Working capital that includes adequate amounts of highly liquid assets, such as cash and marketable securities, is regarded as being of higher quality than working capital that consists primarily of inventory. If the economy enters a recession, for example, a company with a large inventory may have difficulty in converting this asset into cash. Even a company with a large amount of working capital can experience at least temporary insolvency if it runs short of cash.

CASH FLOW ANALYSIS

A statement of changes in financial position is designed to provide stockholders and other outsiders with an overview of the company's liquid resources. Managers, however, are often more concerned with having enough cash available to meet the company's maturing liabilities. To help managers plan and control cash balances, most companies prepare *cash flow statements*. These statements explain the change in the company's cash balance by summarizing the cash receipts and cash disbursements occurring over the accounting period.

Cash flow statements often are prepared monthly as well as annually. In addition, many companies prepare *projected* cash flow statements (called *cash budgets* or *cash forecasts*) which forecast the cash receipts and cash disbursements of future accounting periods. These forecasts enable managers to plan the company's borrowing and investment activities so as to avoid cash shortages or excessively high cash balances.

Cash flow statements usually do not appear in the annual report to stockholders and other outsiders; they are prepared only for internal use by management. However, banks often insist that a company applying for a loan include both a cash flow statement and a cash forecast with the loan application.

Preparation of a cash flow statement

The cash flow statement of Allison Corporation for Year 4 is illustrated below:

ALLISON CORPORATION
Cash Flow Statement
For Year Ended December 31, Year 4

Complete summary of cash movements for Year 4

Cash receipts:		
Cash generated from operations (see schedule on page 606)		$ 50,000
Sale of land		70,000
Sale of capital stock		65,000
Total cash receipts		$185,000
Cash payments:		
Purchase of equipment	$90,000	
Retirement of bonds payable	75,000	
Payment of cash dividends	40,000	
Total cash payments		205,000
Decrease in cash during the year		$ 20,000

Much of this statement was developed from our preceding discussion (page 600) of Allison Corporation's transactions in Year 4. For example, we already know that cash was received from the sale of land ($70,000) and from the sale of capital stock ($65,000). We also know that cash was paid to purchase equipment ($90,000), to retire bonds payable ($75,000), and to *pay* cash dividends ($40,000). (Notice that no cash payment occurs until a dividend is *paid,* whereas working capital is decreased as soon as a cash dividend is *declared.*) The remaining item, cash generated from operations, requires explanation and is discussed in the following paragraphs.

Cash flow from operations

Cash generated from operations is equal to the cash receipts from customers, less the cash payments for purchases of merchandise and for operating expenses and income taxes. If a company maintained its accounting records on a strict cash basis, these cash flows would appear as the balances of the revenue and expense accounts in the general ledger.[5] However, virtually all businesses maintain their accounting records on the accrual basis. To find the cash flows from operations, we must therefore *convert the accrual basis measurements of revenue and expense to the cash basis.* The conversion of net sales, cost of goods sold, and operating expenses from the accrual basis to the cash basis is illustrated in the following sections of this chapter.

Cash receipts from customers   Sales on account are an important factor in most companies. The relationship between the amount of cash collected from custom-

---

[5]The cash basis of accounting was explained in Chapter 3. Under the cash basis, revenue is not recorded until cash is collected from the customer; purchases of merchandise and expenses are recorded in the period in which payment is made. Under the accrual basis, on the other hand, revenue is recognized at the date of sale and expenses are recorded when the related goods or services are used.

ers and the net sales reported in the income statement depends on the change in accounts receivable during the period. If accounts receivable have increased during the period, we know that credit sales are being made faster than the cash is being collected from the customers. If accounts receivable have decreased, cash is being collected faster than credit sales are being made. The relationship between net sales and cash collections from customers may be stated as follows:

Converting sales to cash basis

$$\text{Net sales} \begin{cases} + \text{ decrease in accounts receivable} \\ \text{or} \\ - \text{ increase in accounts receivable} \end{cases} = \begin{array}{l} \text{cash receipts from} \\ \text{customers} \end{array}$$

In the Allison Corporation example, a glance at the comparative balance sheet on page 596 tells us that net accounts receivable increased from $85,000 to $105,000 during Year 4, an increase of $20,000. Therefore, the cash receipts from customers during Year 4 can be determined as follows:

Net sales on cash basis

Net sales	$900,000
Less: Increase in net accounts receivable during the year	20,000
Cash receipts from customers	$880,000

Cash payments for purchases   The relationship between the cost of goods sold for a period and the cash payments for the purchase of merchandise depends both on the change in inventory and the change in accounts payable to merchandise suppliers during the period. The relationship may be stated, in two stages, as follows:

Converting cost of goods sold to cash basis

$$\text{Cost of goods sold} \begin{cases} + \text{ increase in inventory} \\ \text{or} \\ - \text{ decrease in inventory} \end{cases} = \text{net purchases}$$

$$\text{net purchases} \begin{cases} + \text{ decrease in notes and} \\ \quad \text{accounts payable} \\ \text{or} \\ - \text{ increase in notes and} \\ \quad \text{accounts payable} \end{cases} = \begin{array}{l} \text{cash payments} \\ \text{for purchases} \end{array}$$

Again referring to the Allison Corporation example, we can see that the company increased its inventory by $80,000 and that accounts payable to merchandise suppliers increased by $55,000 during the year. The cash payments for purchases during Year 4 would be computed as follows:

Cost of goods sold on cash basis

Cost of goods sold	$500,000
Add: Increase in inventory	80,000
Net purchases (accrual basis)	$580,000
Less: Increase in accounts payable to suppliers	55,000
Cash payments for purchases	$525,000

Let us review the logic behind this computation. If a company is increasing its inventory, it will be buying more merchandise than it sells during the period; furthermore, if the company is increasing its accounts payable to merchandise creditors, it is not paying cash for all of these purchases.

Cash payments for expenses   Expenses in the income statement arise from three major sources: cash expenditures, the write-off of prepayments, and obligations incurred for accrued expenses. The relationship between operating expenses and cash payments, therefore, depends on changes in asset accounts representing the prepayment of expenses, and on changes in accrued liability accounts. These relationships may be summarized as follows:

Converting an expense on accrual basis to cash basis

$$\text{Expense} \begin{Bmatrix} + \text{ increase in related} \\ \text{prepayment} \\ \text{or} \\ - \text{ decrease in related} \\ \text{prepayment} \end{Bmatrix} \text{and} \begin{Bmatrix} + \text{ decrease in related} \\ \text{accrued liability} \\ \text{or} \\ - \text{ increase in related} \\ \text{accrued liability} \end{Bmatrix} = \begin{matrix} \text{cash payments} \\ \text{for expense} \end{matrix}$$

Recording depreciation expense causes a decrease in the book value of a depreciable asset, such as buildings or equipment. This depreciable asset may be viewed as a long-term prepayment. Thus, the amount of depreciation recorded during the period must be deducted from the accrual based operating expenses as a step in computing cash payments for expense. This is consistent with the fact that recording depreciation expense does not involve any cash payment.

Using the information for the Allison Corporation, we can summarize the relationship between the operating expenses and income taxes reported in the income statement and cash payments for these expenses during Year 4 as follows:

Expenses on cash basis

Total operating expenses and income taxes in the income statement		$340,000
Add: Decrease in accrued liabilities	$19,500	
Increase in short-term prepayments	13,000	32,500
Subtotal		$372,500
Less: Decrease in long-term prepayments (depreciation)		67,500
Cash payments for operating expenses and income taxes		$305,000

Conversion of an income statement to cash basis   The differences between an accrual basis income statement and the cash generated from operations are summarized in the following schedule. Notice that this schedule includes the same adjustments to net sales, cost of goods sold, and operating expenses that were illustrated in the preceding paragraphs.

ALLISON CORPORATION
Conversion of Income Statement from Accrual to Cash Basis
For Year Ended December 31, Year 4

<table>
<tr><td></td><td>Income Statement (Accrual Basis)</td><td>Add (Deduct)</td><td>Cash Basis</td></tr>
<tr><td>Net sales ....</td><td>$900,000</td><td></td><td></td></tr>
<tr><td>Less: Increase in accounts receivable ....</td><td></td><td>$(20,000)</td><td>$880,000</td></tr>
<tr><td>Cost of goods sold ....</td><td>500,000</td><td></td><td></td></tr>
<tr><td>Add: Increase in inventory ....</td><td></td><td>80,000</td><td></td></tr>
<tr><td>Less: Increase in notes and accounts payable to merchandise creditors ....</td><td></td><td>(55,000)</td><td>525,000</td></tr>
<tr><td>Gross profit on sales ....</td><td>$400,000</td><td></td><td>$355,000</td></tr>
<tr><td>Operating expenses and income taxes ....</td><td>340,000</td><td></td><td></td></tr>
<tr><td>Add: Decrease in accrued liabilities ....</td><td></td><td>19,500</td><td></td></tr>
<tr><td>Increase in short-term prepayments ....</td><td></td><td>13,000</td><td></td></tr>
<tr><td>Less: Depreciation expense ....</td><td></td><td>(67,500)</td><td>305,000</td></tr>
<tr><td>Income before gain on sale of land (accrual basis) ....</td><td>$ 60,000</td><td></td><td></td></tr>
<tr><td>Cash generated from operations ....</td><td></td><td></td><td>$ 50,000</td></tr>
</table>

How much cash was generated from operations in Year 4?

The Allison Corporation example was sufficiently simple that we could develop cash flow information from a direct inspection of the income statement and comparative balance sheets. In more complex situations, the accountant will use a working paper to convert the income statement from an accrual to a cash basis and to develop cash flow information in a systematic fashion. Familiarity with these working-paper procedures is not necessary in order to be able to understand and interpret cash flow information; therefore, discussion of this process is reserved for more advanced accounting courses.

KEY TERMS INTRODUCED OR EMPHASIZED IN CHAPTER 15

Cash basis   A method of summarizing operating results in terms of cash receipts and cash payments rather than revenue earned and expenses incurred.

Cash flow statement   A statement showing the sources of cash receipts and purposes of cash payments during an accounting period. This statement is useful for explaining changes in the balance of the Cash account, but it is not a substitute for an income statement.

Exchange transaction   In the context of a statement of changes in financial position, exchange transactions are financing or investing activities which do not directly affect working capital accounts. An example of such a transaction is the purchase of plant assets by issuing common stock. Such transactions should be shown in a funds statement as both a source and a use of working capital.

Funds   In the context of a statement of changes in financial position, "funds" are usually defined as working capital.

Noncurrent account   Any balance sheet account *other than* a current asset or a current liability. Noncurrent accounts include long-term investments, plant assets, intangible assets, long-term liabilities, and stockholders' equity accounts.

Statement of changes in financial position   A financial statement showing the sources and uses of working capital during the accounting period. In addition, this statement shows financing and investing activities, such as exchange transactions, which do not directly affect working capital.

Working capital   Current assets minus current liabilities. Working capital represents the net amount of liquid resources available to a business.

DEMONSTRATION PROBLEM FOR YOUR REVIEW

The comparative financial data for Liquid Gas Company for the last two years are shown below:

Debits	December 31 Year 2	Year 1
Cash	$ 39,220	$ 15,800
Receivables (net of allowance for doubtful accounts)	41,400	24,000
Inventories, lower of cost or market	27,600	36,800
Short-term prepayments	4,180	4,400
Land	9,000	19,000
Buildings	270,000	250,000
Equipment	478,600	450,000
Total debits	$870,000	$800,000

Credits	Year 2	Year 1
Accumulated depreciation: buildings	$ 95,000	$ 77,000
Accumulated depreciation: equipment	153,000	120,000
Accounts payable	59,200	30,000
Accrued liabilities	20,000	10,000
Bonds payable	90,000	90,000
Premium on bonds payable	2,800	3,000
Preferred stock ($100 par)	70,000	100,000
Common stock ($25 par)	260,000	250,000
Paid-in capital in excess of par	45,000	40,000
Retained earnings	75,000	80,000
Total credits	$870,000	$800,000

Other data

(1) During Year 2, the board of directors of the company authorized a transfer of $15,000 from retained earnings to reflect a 4% stock dividend on the common stock.
(2) Cash dividends of $6,000 were paid on the preferred stock, and cash dividends of $50,000 were paid on the common stock.
(3) Three hundred shares of preferred stock were retired at par value.
(4) The only entries recorded in the Retained Earnings account were for dividends and to close the Income Summary account, which had a credit balance of $66,000 after the loss of the sale of the land.
(5) There were no sales or retirements of building and equipment during the year; land was sold for $8,000, resulting in a loss of $2,000.

Instructions

a Compute the change in working capital during Year 2. You may use totals for current assets and current liabilities.

b Prepare a working paper for a statement of changes in financial position for Year 2.

c Prepare a statement of changes in financial position for Year 2, without showing the composition of working capital.

d Prepare a cash flow statement, with a supporting schedule converting the net income from the accrual basis to the cash basis.

SOLUTION TO DEMONSTRATION PROBLEM

a Computation of decrease in working capital:

	As of December 31	
	Year 2	Year 1
Current assets	$112,400	$81,000
Less: Current liabilities	79,200	40,000
Working capital	$ 33,200	$41,000
Decrease in working capital during Year 2	7,800	
	$ 41,000	$41,000

LIQUID GAS COMPANY
Working Paper for Statement of Changes in Financial Position
For Year 2

Debits	Account Balances, Dec. 31, Year 1	Analysis of Transactions for Year 2 — Debit		Analysis of Transactions for Year 2 — Credit		Account Balances, Dec. 31, Year 2
Working capital	41,000			(x)	7,800	33,200
Land	19,000			(5)	10,000	9,000
Buildings	250,000	(6)	20,000			270,000
Equipment	450,000	(7)	28,600			478,600
Total	760,000					790,800
Credits						
Accumulated depreciation: buildings	77,000			(4)	18,000	95,000
Accumulated depreciation: equipment	120,000			(4)	33,000	153,000
Bonds payable	90,000					90,000
Premium on bonds payable	3,000	(8)	200			2,800
Preferred stock, $100 par	100,000	(9)	30,000			70,000
Common stock, $25 par	250,000			(2)	10,000	260,000
Paid-in capital in excess of par	40,000			(2)	5,000	45,000
Retained earnings	80,000	(2)	15,000	(1)	66,000	75,000
		(3)	56,000			
Total	760,000		149,800		149,800	790,800

		Sources		Uses		
Sources of working capital:						
Operations—net income		(1)	66,000			
Add: Depreciation		(4)	51,000			(From operations, $118,800)
Loss on sale of land		(5)	2,000			
Less: Amortization of premium on bonds						
payable				(8)	200	
Sale of land		(5)	8,000			
Uses of working capital:						
Payment of cash dividends				(3)	56,000	
Purchase of buildings				(6)	20,000	
Purchase of equipment				(7)	28,600	
Retirement of preferred stock				(9)	30,000	
Total sources and uses of						
working capital			127,000		134,800	
Decrease in working capital		(x)	7,800			
			134,800		134,800	

Explanation of transactions for Year 2:
(1) Net income, $66,000, including a loss of $2,000 on sale of land, transferred to Retained Earnings.
(2) Entry to record 4% stock dividend; no effect on working capital.
(3) Cash dividends declared, $56,000 (preferred stock, $6,000, and common, $50,000).
(4) Depreciation, $51,000, is added to net income because it is an expense which did not reduce working capital.
(5) To record sale of land for $8,000; the loss of $2,000 had no effect on working capital.
(6) To record working capital used for purchase of buildings.
(7) To record working capital used for purchase of equipment.
(8) Amortization of premium on bonds payable increased net income but had no effect on working capital.
(9) To record working capital applied to retirement of preferred stock.
(x) Balancing figure—decrease in working capital during Year 2.

c

LIQUID GAS COMPANY
Statement of Changes in Financial Position
For Year 2

Sources of working capital:
  Operations:

Net income		$ 66,000
Add: Expense not requiring the use of working capital—		
depreciation	$51,000	
Nonoperating loss on sale of land	2,000	
Less: Increase in net income which did not provide working		
capital—amortization of premium on bonds payable	(200)	52,800
Total working capital provided by operations		$118,800
Sale of land		8,000
Total sources of working capital		$126,800

Uses of working capital:

Declaration of cash dividends	$56,000	
Purchase of buildings	20,000	
Purchase of equipment	28,600	
Retirement of preferred stock	30,000	
Total uses of working capital		134,600
Decrease in working capital		$ 7,800

d

LIQUID GAS COMPANY
Cash Flow Statement
For Year 2

Cash receipts:

Cash generated from operations (see Schedule A below)		$150,020
Sale of land		8,000
Total cash receipts		$158,020

Cash payments:

Payment of cash dividends	$56,000	
Purchase of buildings	20,000	
Purchase of equipment	28,600	
Retirement of preferred stock	30,000	
Total cash payments		134,600
Increase in cash during the year		$ 23,420

Schedule A—Cash generated from operations:

Working capital provided by operations—part c		$118,800
Add: Decrease in inventories	$ 9,200	
Decrease in short-term prepayments	220	
Increase in accounts payable	29,200	
Increase in accrued liabilities	10,000	48,620
Less: Increase in receivables		(17,400)
Cash generated from operations		$150,020

REVIEW QUESTIONS

1 Explain why an adequate amount of working capital is essential to the successful operation of a business.

2 What are the primary ways in which a firm generates working capital and the primary ways in which a firm uses working capital?

3 List four transactions which are neither a source nor a use of working capital and which are not disclosed in a statement of changes in financial position.

4 Source of funds include borrowing, sale of noncurrent assets, operations, and sale of capital stock. Which of these possible sources of funds do you consider to be most important to the long-run survival of a business?

5 What information can a reader gain from a statement of changes in financial position that is not apparent from reading an income statement?

6 In preparing a statement of changes in financial position, business transactions may be classified into three categories. List these categories and indicate which category results in changes in working capital.

7 Give examples of expenses, other than depreciation expense, which reduce net income but which do not result in the use of working capital during the period.

8 Give an example of an increase in net income which does not result in an increase in working capital during the period.

9 The following quotation appeared in the annual report of a large corporation: "Depreciation, depletion, and amortization charges provide funds which cause our working capital provided by operations to consistently exceed our net income." Evaluate this quotation.

10 Although extraordinary and nonoperating gains and losses may be included in net income, what reason can you give for excluding such gains and losses in computing the working capital provided by operations? Use the following facts to illustrate your point: Net income including gain on sale of land, $100,000; sale of land, with a book value of $70,000, for $150,000.

11 Miller Corporation acquired a building for $300,000, paying $60,000 cash and issuing a long-term note payable for the balance. What is the effect of this transaction upon the working capital of Miller Corporation? How should the transaction be shown in a statement of changes in financial position?

12 During the year, holders of $4 million of Dallas Company convertible bonds converted their bonds into shares of Dallas Company common stock. The president of Dallas Company made the following statement: "By issuing common stock to retire these bonds, the company has saved $4 million in cash. Our statement of changes in financial position will not have to show the retirement of the bonds among the uses of working capital." Do you agree with this statement? Explain.

13 What is the major difference between the statement of changes in financial position and a cash flow statement?

14 Give several examples of transactions which can reduce the amount of cash generated by operations, as shown in a cash flow statement, without reducing working capital.

15 The president of Dexter Corporation was puzzled by the following statement made by the accountant: "Our working capital provided by operations amounted to $85,000 last year but our cash generated from operations was only $10,000 because of the increases in our inventory and receivables and the decrease in our accounts payable." Explain what the accountant meant.

16 An outside member of the board of directors of a small corporation made the following comment after studying the comparative financial statements for the past two years: "I have trouble understanding why our cash has increased steadily during the past two years, yet our profits have been negligible; we have paid no dividends; and inventories, receivables, payables, cost of plant and equipment, long-term debt, and capital stock have remained essentially unchanged." Write a brief statement explaining how this situation might occur.

EXERCISES

Ex. 15-1 Indicate the amount of the increase or decrease (if any) in working capital as a result of each of the following events:

a Purchase and retirement of bonds payable, $1,000,000, at 96. The unamortized premium on bonds payable at the time of the retirement was $50,000.

b Declaration of a 25% stock dividend on $600,000 of par value capital stock outstanding.

c Purchase of equipment costing $400,000 for $100,000 cash and $75,000 (plus interest) payable every six months over the next two years.

d A $40,000 write-down of inventory to a market value below cost.

Ex. 15-2 Briefly explain how each of the following situations should be reported in the statement of changes in financial position.

a Depreciation of $100,000 was recorded in Year 1.

b In July of Year 1, the 10,000 shares of $50 par value capital stock were split 3 for 1 and in November of Year 1, a 10% stock dividend was distributed.

c Cash of $50,000 was paid and capital stock with a market value of $450,000 was issued to acquire land worth $500,000.

Ex. 15-3 The Tri-State Corporation reports a net loss of $80,000 on its income statement. In arriving at this figure, the following items among others were included:

Amortization of patents	*$16,000*
Amortization of premium on bonds payable	*10,000*
Gain on sale of land	*40,000*
Depreciation expense	*50,000*
Uninsured fire damage to building	*88,400*

What was the working capital increase or decrease as a result of *operations?*

Ex. 15-4 A summary of the comparative financial position for Landscape Consultants, Inc., for the current year appears below:

	End of Current Year	Beginning of Current Year
Working capital	*$110,000*	*$125,000*
Land	*90,000*	*50,000*
Buildings	*160,000*	*100,000*
Less: Accumulated depreciation	*(40,000)*	*(35,000)*
	$320,000	*$240,000*

Notes payable, due in five years	$ 70,000	$ –0–
Capital stock, no-par value	200,000	200,000
Retained earnings	50,000	40,000
	$320,000	$240,000

The net income was $42,000 and included no nonoperating gains or losses. Depreciation expense for the current year was $5,000. A cash dividend of $32,000 was declared at the end of the current year.

Prepare a statement of changes in financial position for the current year without using a working paper.

Ex. 15-5 The data below are taken from the records of the Ferraro Company:

	End of Year	Beginning of Year
Accounts receivable	$ 20,200	$10,200
Inventories	32,000	40,000
Short-term prepayments	2,300	1,500
Accounts payable (merchandise creditors)	28,000	25,000
Accrued expenses payable	1,000	1,200
Net sales	300,000	
Cost of goods sold	180,000	
Operating expenses (includes depreciation of $10,000)	80,000	

From the foregoing information, compute the following:
a Cash collected from customers during the year
b Cash paid to merchandise creditors during the year
c Cash paid for operating expenses during the year

Ex. 15-6 The information below is taken from comparative financial statements for the Bear Corporation:

	Year 10	Year 9
Net income (there were no extraordinary items)	$60,000	$37,000
Depreciation expense	42,500	31,800
Inventory at end of year	15,000	28,000
Accounts receivable at end of year	9,000	12,000
Accounts payable at end of year	8,000	6,000
Cash dividends declared in December of each year, payable Jan. 15 of following year	22,500	15,000

From the data above, determine the following:
a The *working capital* provided by operations in Year 10
b The *cash* generated by operations in Year 10
c *Working capital* used for dividends in Year 10

PROBLEMS

15-1 Below is given a list of business transactions and adjustments. For each item you are to indicate the effect first on working capital, and second on cash. In each case the possible effects are an increase, a decrease, or no change.
   (1) Plant assets sold for cash at a price below their carrying values
   (2) Declaration of a cash dividend
   (3) Payment of a previously declared cash dividend
   (4) One-year fire insurance policy paid in advance
   (5) Inventory destroyed by fire; one-half of its carrying value covered by insurance and recorded as a receivable from the insurance company
   (6) Amortization of the portion of prepaid insurance expense which expired during the current year
   (7) An uncollectible account receivable written off against the Allowance for Doubtful Accounts
   (8) Purchase of patent, giving 200 shares of the company's common stock in exchange
   (9) Merchandise sold for cash at a price below cost
   (10) Prior period adjustment made to reflect additional income taxes due on income of a prior period
   (11) Marketable securities sold for cash at a price above cost
   (12) Amortization of premium on bonds payable

Instructions
a List the numbers 1 to 12 on your answer sheet, and set up two columns headed "working capital effect" and "cash effect." For each transaction, write the words *increase, decrease,* or *no change* in the appropriate column to indicate the effect of the transaction on working capital and cash.

b Are any of the transactions listed above considered "exchange transactions" which would be listed as both a source and use of working capital in a statement of changes in financial position? Explain.

15-2 During Year 6 Wildcat Tractor Company showed the following *changes* in amount for the groups of accounts listed below. For example, current assets increased by $30,000 during Year 6, and this amount therefore appears in the "Debit" change column.

	Changes during Year 6	
	Debit	Credit
Current assets	$ 30,000	
Plant and equipment	160,000	
Accumulated depreciation		$ 40,000
Current liabilities	58,000	
Capital stock, $10 par		128,000
Paid-in capital in excess of par		32,000
Retained earnings		48,000
	$248,000	$248,000

During Year 6 the company issued 12,800 shares of capital stock and applied the proceeds to the purchase of equipment. There were no retirements of plant and equipment during the year. Net income for Year 6 was $142,000 and cash dividends declared and paid during the year amounted to $94,000.

Instructions Prepare a statement of changes in financial position for Year 6, without using working papers.

15-3 The following information is taken from the annual report of El Toro Corporation.

	Year 2	Year 1
Working capital	$102,000	$114,000
Equipment	360,000	252,000
Less: Accumulated depreciation	(120,000)	(72,000)
Long-term investments	48,000	60,000
Capital stock	120,000	120,000
Retained earnings	270,000	234,000

Depreciation for Year 2 amounted to $48,000; no equipment items were sold; investments were sold at a gain of $6,000; and net income (including the $6,000 nonoperating gain) for Year 2 was $78,000. Cash dividends of $42,000 were declared and paid.

Instructions From the information given, prepare a statement of changes in financial position for Year 2, without using working papers.

15-4 **Instructions** Using the information provided in Problem 15-3, prepare a working paper for a statement of changes in financial position. (If you have already worked Problem 15-3, determine that your solutions to both problems are in agreement.)

15-5 Comparative after closing trial balances for Home Port, Inc., are shown below:

Debits	Year 2	Year 1
Cash	$ 72,000	$ 78,000
Marketable securities		96,000
Accounts receivable	120,000	228,000
Inventories	132,000	180,000
Prepaid expenses	36,000	24,000
Land	120,000	
Buildings	600,000	
	$1,080,000	$606,000

Credits	Year 2	Year 1
Allowance for doubtful accounts	$ 6,000	$ 12,000
Accounts payable	138,000	102,000
Accrued liabilities	102,000	78,000
Long-term notes payable	300,000	60,000
Capital stock, $10 par	396,000	246,000
Retained earnings	138,000	108,000
	$1,080,000	$606,000

During Year 1 Home Port, Inc., operated in rented space. Early in Year 2 the company acquired suitable land and made arrangements to borrow funds from a local bank on long-term notes to finance the construction of new buildings. The company also sold additional stock at par and all its marketable securities at book value. Construction of the buildings was not completed until the end of Year 2; therefore, no depreciation expense was recorded in Year 2. Net income for Year 2 was $78,000; cash dividends declared and paid during Year 2 amounted to $48,000.

Instructions

a Prepare a schedule of changes in components of working capital during Year 2. The schedule should show the balances of each current account at the beginning and at the end of Year 2 and the effect of the change in the account balance on working capital.

b Prepare a working paper for a statement of changes in financial position.

c Prepare a formal statement of changes in financial position for Year 2, showing first the uses of working capital followed by sources of working capital.

15-6 A comparative balance sheet for Sierra Redwood Tub Co. at the end of Year 1 and Year 2 is shown below:

	Year 2	Year 1
Cash	$ 36,000	$ 60,000
Accounts receivable (net)	90,000	105,000
Merchandise inventory	195,000	150,000
Land for future expansion	45,000	
Plant and equipment (see accumulated depreciation below)	480,000	375,000
Patents (net of amortization)	54,000	60,000
	$900,000	$750,000
Accumulated depreciation	$157,500	$120,000
Accounts payable	91,500	45,000
Dividends payable	6,000	
Notes payable due in Year 5	15,000	
Capital stock, $10 par	600,000	525,000
Retained earnings	30,000	60,000
	$900,000	$750,000

Other data

(1) The net *loss* for Year 2 amounted to $24,000.

(2) Cash dividends of $6,000 were declared.

(3) Land for future expansion was acquired.

(4) Equipment costing $105,000 was purchased for cash; $15,000 was borrowed for three years in order to pay for this equipment.

(5) Additional shares of capital stock were sold at par value.

(6) Other changes in noncurrent accounts resulted from the usual transactions recorded in such accounts.

Instructions

a Prepare a schedule computing the change in working capital during Year 2.

b Prepare a working paper for a statement of changes in financial position for Year 2.

c Prepare a formal statement of changes in financial position for Year 2.

15-7 The accounting records of Earth Movers, Inc., showed the following balances at the end of Year 4 and Year 5:

Debits	Year 5	Year 4
Cash	$ 93,000	$ 120,000
Accounts receivable	165,000	105,000
Merchandise inventory	285,000	450,000
Long-term investments	45,000	
Equipment	1,170,000	675,000
Accumulated depreciation	(240,000)	(180,000)
Land	240,000	105,000
	$1,758,000	$1,275,000

Credits	Year 5	Year 4
Accounts payable	$ 135,000	$ 60,000
Notes payable (current)	15,000	90,000
Bonds payable, due in Year 10	300,000	240,000
Unamortized premium on bonds payable	5,400	5,700
Capital stock, $10 par	600,000	450,000
Paid-in capital in excess of par	240,000	150,000
Retained earnings	462,600	279,300
	$1,758,000	$1,275,000

Net income for Year 5 amounted to $258,000. Cash dividends of $74,700 were declared and paid during Year 5. Additional purchases of investments, equipment, and land were completed during Year 5, financed in part through the sale of bonds at par and 15,000 shares of capital stock. Equipment costing $75,000 was sold at a price equal to its book value of $30,000.

Instructions

a Prepare a schedule of changes in working capital during Year 5.

b Prepare a working paper for a statement of changes in financial position for Year 5. See the solution to the demonstration problem in this chapter for proper handling of the premium on bonds payable.

c Prepare a formal statement of changes in financial position for Year 5.

15-8 The financial statements shown below are presented to you by Linda Kahn, owner of Linda's Fashion Boutique.

Balance Sheet

Assets	Year 2	Year 1
Cash	$ 10,000	$ 40,000
Marketable securities	15,000	20,000
Accounts receivable (net)	100,000	35,000
Inventory	80,000	60,000
Equipment (net of accumulated depreciation)	35,000	45,000
Total assets	$240,000	$200,000

Liabilities & Owner's Equity

Accounts payable	$ 37,000	$ 40,000
Accrued liabilities	8,000	2,500
Note payable to bank (due early in Year 2)		12,500
Linda Kahn, capital	195,000	145,000
Total liabilities & owner's equity	$240,000	$200,000

Income Statement for Year 2

Sales (net)..		$400,000
Cost of goods sold		300,000
Gross profit on sales		$100,000
Operating expenses (including $10,000 depreciation)	$60,000	
Loss on sale of marketable securities	500	60,500
Net income		$ 39,500
Drawings by owner		22,500
Increase in owner's equity as a result of operations		$ 17,000

Kahn is concerned over the decrease in her cash position during Year 2, especially in view of the fact that she invested an additional $33,000 in the business and had a net income of $39,500 during the year. She asks you to prepare a cash flow statement which will explain the decrease in the Cash account.

Instructions

a Prepare a schedule showing the conversion of the income statement from an accrual to a cash basis, thus determining the net cash outflow from operations. (Organize your schedule in the format illustrated on page 606.)

b Prepare a cash flow statement which explains the decrease of $30,000 in cash during Year 2.

BUSINESS DECISION PROBLEM 15

Olympic Sportwear has working capital of $6,150,000 at the beginning of Year 5. Restrictions contained in bank loans require that working capital not fall below $6,000,000. The following projected information is available for Year 5:

(1) Budgeted net income (including nonoperating items) is $7,500,000. The following items were included in estimating net income: depreciation, $2,100,000; amortization of premium on bonds payable, $150,000; uncollectible accounts expense, $180,000; and income taxes, $6,300,000. The estimate of net income also included the non-operating items described below.

(2) Sale of plant assets with a carrying value of $1,200,000 is expected to bring $1,500,000 net of income taxes.

(3) Additional plant assets costing $15,000,000 will be acquired. Payment will be as follows: 20% cash, 20% short-term note, and 60% through issuance of capital stock.

(4) Long-term investment will be sold at cost, $300,000.

(5) Bonds payable in the amount of $1,500,000, bearing interest at 11%, will be redeemed at 105 approximately 10 years prior to maturity in order to eliminate the high

interest expense of $165,000 per year. The elimination of this interest and the gain or loss on the retirement of bonds payable were taken into account in estimating net income for Year 5. These bonds had been issued at par.

(6) Tentative planned cash dividend, $4,500,000.

Instructions

a Consider all the information that has been given and prepare a projected statement of changes in financial position (without showing the composition of working capital) in order to determine the estimated increase or decrease in working capital for Year 5. Some of the information given may be irrelevant.

b The planned cash dividend of $4,500,000 represents the same dividend per share as paid last year. The company would like to maintain dividends at this level. Does it appear likely that the past dividend policy can be maintained in Year 5? What factors other than working capital position should be considered in determining the level of cash dividends declared by the board of directors?

16

ANALYSIS AND INTERPRETATION OF FINANCIAL STATEMENTS

After reading this chapter you should be able to:

- Put the dollar amount of a company's net income into perspective by relating it to the company's sales, assets, and stockholders' equity.
- Describe several sources of financial information about a business.
- Explain the uses and limitations of dollar and percentage changes, and of component percentages.
- Compute dollar and percentage changes and component percentages from a set of comparative financial statements.
- Compute the ratios widely used in financial statement analysis, and explain what each ratio attempts to measure.
- Discuss the "quality" of a company's earnings.

Financial statements are the instrument panel of a business enterprise. They constitute a report on managerial performance, attesting to managerial success or failure and flashing warning signals of impending difficulties. To read a complex instrument panel, one must understand the gauges and their calibration to make sense out of the array of data they convey. Similarly, one must understand the inner workings of the accounting system and the significance of various financial relationships to interpret the data appearing in financial statements. To a reader with a knowledge of accounting, a set of financial statements tells a great deal about a business enterprise.

The financial affairs of a business may be of interest to a number of different groups; management, creditors, investors, politicians, union officials, and government agencies. Each of these groups has somewhat different needs, and accordingly each tends to concentrate on particular aspects of a company's financial picture.

What is your opinion of the level of corporate profits?

As a college student who has completed (or almost completed) a course in accounting, you have a much better understanding of corporate profits than do people who have never studied accounting. The level of earnings of large corporations is a controversial topic, a favorite topic in many political speeches and at cocktail parties. Many of the statements one reads or hears from these sources are emotional rather than rational, and fiction rather than fact. Public opinion polls show that the public believes the average manufacturing company has an after-tax profit of about 30% of sales, when in fact such profit has been *about 5% of sales* in recent years. A widespread public belief that profits are six times the actual rate may lead to some unwise legislation.

An in-depth knowledge of accounting does not enable you to say at what level corporate earnings *should be;* however, a knowledge of accounting does enable you to read audited financial statements that show what the level of corporate earnings *actually is.* Moreover, you are aware that the information in published financial statements of corporations has been audited by CPA firms and has been reviewed in detail by government agencies, such as the Securities and Exchange Commission and the IRS. Consequently, you know that the profits reported in these published financial statements are reasonably reliable; they have been determined in accordance with generally accepted accounting principles and verified by independent experts.

When such troublesome problems as severe unemployment and rising prices for consumer goods and services affect so many people, it is not surprising that some political leaders look for a scapegoat to hold responsible. Often, the blame has been laid on corporate profits, which sometimes have been labeled as "excessive," "outrageous," and even "obscene." Usually the speaker who uses these emotional adjectives cites an absolute dollar amount of profits without relating it in any way to the volume of sales or the amount of assets necessary to produce the quoted profit figure.

Some specific examples of corporate earnings

A few examples of the profits earned by some well-known companies may help put dollar amounts of profit into a realistic perspective. General Motors in a recent annual report showed a net income of $321 million. As an absolute amount, this profit sounds enormous, but it was only *one-half of one percent of GM's sales.* Thus, of every dollar received as revenue, only ½ cent represented profit for GM. Actually, earning only $321 million in a year must be regarded as very poor performance for a corporation the size of General Motors.

As a more representative example, General Electric had a net income of about 6% of sales last year. The net income amounted to $1,650 million, or just over $1½ billion; that may sound large by itself, but sales for the year amounted to over $27 billion.

Not all leading corporations earn a profit every year. In one recent year, for example, General Motors incurred a net loss of more than $775 million. During a good part of the last decade, much of the airline industry operated at a loss. Net losses were incurred in one or more years by such well-known companies as American Airlines, Continental, Pan American, TWA, Western, and United Airlines.

The oil companies have been particularly subject to criticism for so-called excessive profits, so let us briefly look at the profits of Exxon, the world's largest oil company. A recent annual report of Exxon (audited by Price Waterhouse & Co.) shows that profits amounted to a little over $5½ billion. Standing alone, that figure seems enormous—but we need to look a little farther. The total revenue of Exxon was over $113 billion, so net income amounted to approximately 5% of sales. On the other hand, income taxes, excise taxes, and other taxes levied upon Exxon amounted to more than $23 billion, or about 4 times as much as the company's profit. Thus, taxation represents a far greater portion of the cost of a gallon of gasoline than does the oil company's profit.

There are many ways of appraising the adequacy of corporate earnings. Certainly, earnings should be compared with total assets and with invested capital as well as with sales. In this chapter we shall look at a number of ways of evaluating corporate profits and solvency.

Sources of financial information

For the most part, our discussion will be limited to the kind of analysis that can be made by "outsiders" who do not have access to internal accounting records. Investors must rely to a considerable extent on financial statements in published annual and quarterly reports. In the case of large publicly owned corporations, additional information is filed with the Securities and Exchange Commission and is available to the public. Financial information about most large corporations is also published by Moody's Investors Service, Standard & Poor's Corporation, and stock brokerage firms.

Bankers are usually able to secure more detailed information by requesting it as a condition for granting a loan. Trade creditors may obtain financial information for businesses of almost any size from credit-rating agencies such as Dun & Bradstreet, Inc.

Comparative financial statements   The change in financial data over time is best exhibited in statements showing data for two or more years placed side by side in adjacent columns. Such statements are called *comparative financial statements.*

The usefulness of comparative financial statements covering two or more years is well recognized. Published annual reports often contain comparative financial statements covering a period as long as 10 years. By observing the change in various items year by year, the analyst may gain valuable clues regarding growth and other important trends affecting the business. A highly condensed comparative balance sheet is shown at the top of the next page.

BENSON CORPORATION
Comparative Balance Sheet
As of December 31
(in thousands of dollars)

	Year 3	Year 2	Year 1
Assets:			
Current assets	$180	$150	$120
Plant and equipment (net)	450	300	345
Total assets	$630	$450	$465
Liabilities & Stockholders' Equity:			
Current liabilities	$ 60	$ 80	$120
Long-term liabilities	200	100	–0–
Capital stock	300	300	300
Retained earnings (deficit)	70	(30)	45
Total liabilities & stockholders' equity	$630	$450	$465

Condensed three-year balance sheet

Tools of analysis

Few figures in a financial statement are highly significant in and of themselves. It is their relationship to other quantities, or the amount and direction of change since a previous date, that is important. Analysis is largely a matter of establishing significant relationships and pointing up changes and trends. Three widely used analytical techniques are (1) dollar and percentage changes, (2) component percentages, and (3) ratios.

Dollar and percentage changes

The dollar amount of change from year to year is significant, but expressing the change in percentage terms adds perspective. For example, if sales this year have increased by $100,000, the fact that this is an increase of 10% over last year's sales of $1 million puts it in a different perspective than if it represented a 1% increase over sales of $10 million for the prior year.

The dollar amount of any change is the difference between the amount for a *comparison* year and for a *base* year. The percentage change is computed by dividing the amount of the change between years by the amount for the base year. This is illustrated in the tabulation below, using data from the comparative balance sheet above.

	In Thousands			Increase or (Decrease)			
				Year 3 over Year 2		Year 2 over Year 1	
	Year 3	Year 2	Year 1	Amount	%	Amount	%
Current assets	$180	$150	$120	$30	20%	$30	25%
Current liabilities	$ 60	$ 80	$120	($20)	(25%)	($40)	(33.3%)

Dollar and percentage changes

Although current assets increased $30,000 in both Year 2 and Year 3, the percentage of change differs because of the shift in the base year from Year 1 to Year 2. These calculations present no problems when the figures for the base year are positive amounts. If a negative amount or a zero amount appears in the base year, a percentage change cannot be computed. For example, in the comparative balance sheet on page 623, there were no long-term liabilities in Year 1; therefore the percentage change from Year 1 to Year 2 for this liability cannot be calculated.

Percentage changes in sales and earnings   Computing the percentage changes in sales, gross profit, and net income from one year to the next gives insight into a company's rate of growth. If a company is experiencing growth in its economic activities, sales and earnings should increase at more than the rate of inflation. Assume, for example, that a company's sales increase by 6% while the general price level rises by 10%. It is probable that the entire increase in sales may be explained by inflation, rather than by an increase in sales volume. In fact, the company may well have sold fewer goods than in the preceding year.

In measuring the dollar or percentage change in *quarterly* sales or earnings, it is customary to compare the results of the current quarter with those of the *same quarter in the preceding year.* Use of the same quarter of the preceding year as the base period prevents our analysis from being distorted by seasonal fluctuations in business activity.

Percentages become misleading when the base is small   Percentage changes may create a misleading impression when the dollar amount used as a base is unusually small. Occasionally we hear a television newscaster say that a company's profits have increased by a very large percentage, such as 900%. The initial impression created by such a statement is that the company's profits must now be excessively large. But assume, for example, that a company had net income of $100,000 in Year 1; that in Year 2 net income drops to $10,000; and that in Year 3, net income returns to the $100,000 level. In Year 3, net income has increased by $90,000, representing a 900% increase over the profits of Year 2. What needs to be added is that this 900% increase *exactly offsets* the 90% decline in profits in Year 2.

Few people realize that a 90% decline in earnings must be followed by a 900% increase just to get back to the starting point.

ILLUSTRATIVE CASE.   In the third quarter of 1979, General Motors earned $21.4 million, as compared with $527.9 million in the third quarter of 1978. This represented a 97% decline in third quarter profits, computed as follows:

Decline in profits ($527.9 − $21.4)	$506.5
Base period earnings (third quarter, 1978)	$527.9
Percentage decrease ($506.5 ÷ $527.9)	96%

How much of an increase in profits would be required in the third quarter of 1980 for profits to return to the 1978 level? Many people erroneously guess 96%. However, the correct answer is an astounding 2,367%, computed as follows:

Required increase to reach 1978 profit level (from $21.4 to $527.9) . .	$506.5
Base period earnings (third quarter, 1979)	$ 21.4
Required percentage increase ($506.5 ÷ $21.4)	2,367%

Unfortunately for GM, the company's 1980 profits did not return to 1978 levels. Instead, the company lost a record-setting $567 million in the third quarter of 1980.

Component percentages

Component percentages indicate the *relative size* of each item included in a total. For example, each item on a balance sheet could be expressed as a percentage of total assets. This shows quickly the relative importance of current and noncurrent assets as well as the relative amount of financing obtained from current creditors, long-term creditors, and stockholders. By computing component percentages for several successive balance sheets, we can see which items are increasing in importance and which are becoming less significant.

Common size income statement   Another application of component percentages is to express all items on an income statement as a percentage of net sales. Such a statement is sometimes called a common size income statement. A condensed income statement in dollars and in common size form is illustrated below.

Income Statement

	Dollars		Component Percentages	
	Year 2	Year 1	Year 2	Year 1
Net sales	$1,000,000	$600,000	100.0%	100.0%
Cost of goods sold	700,000	360,000	70.0	60.0
Gross profit on sales	$ 300,000	$240,000	30.0%	40.0%
Expenses (including income taxes)	200,000	150,000	20.0	25.0
Net income	$ 100,000	$ 90,000	10.0%	15.0%

How successful was Year 2?

Looking only at the component percentages, we see that the decline in the gross profit rate from 40 to 30% was only partially offset by the decrease in expenses as a percentage of net sales, causing net income to decrease from 15 to 10% of net sales. The dollar amounts in the first pair of columns, however, present an entirely different picture. It is true that net sales increased faster than net income, but the dollar amount of net income did increase in Year 2, a fact not apparent from a review of component percentages alone. This points out an important limitation in the use of component percentages. Changes in the component percentage may result from a change in the component, in the total, or in both. It is important to recognize that 10% of a large total may be a greater amount than 15% of a smaller total.

Ratios

A ratio is a simple mathematical expression of the relationship of one item to another. Ratios may be stated several ways. To illustrate, let us consider the current ratio, which expresses the relationship between current assets and current liabilities. If current assets are $100,000 and current liabilities are $50,000, we may say either that the current ratio is 2 to 1 (which is written as 2:1), or that current assets are 200% of current liabilities. Either statement correctly summarizes the relationship—that is, that current assets are twice as large as current liabilities.

In order to compute a meaningful ratio, there must be a *significant relationship* between the two figures. A ratio focuses attention on a relationship which is significant, but a full interpretation of the ratio usually requires further investigation of the underlying data. Ratios are an aid to analysis and interpretation; they are not a substitute for sound thinking.

Standards of comparison

In using dollar and percentage changes, component percentages, and ratios, financial analysts constantly search for some standard of comparison against which to judge whether the relationships that they have found are favorable or unfavorable. Two such standards are (1) the past performance of the company and (2) the performance of other companies in the same industry.

Past performance of the company Comparing analytical data for a current period with similar computations for prior years affords some basis for judging whether the position of the business is improving or worsening. This comparison of data over time is sometimes called *horizontal* or *trend* analysis, to express the idea of reviewing data for a number of consecutive periods. It is distinguished from *vertical* or *static* analysis, which refers to the review of the financial information for only one accounting period.

In addition to determining whether the situation is improving or becoming worse, horizontal analysis may aid in making estimates of future prospects. Since changes may reverse their direction at any time, however, projecting past trends into the future is always a somewhat risky statistical pastime.

A weakness of horizontal analysis is that comparison with the past does not afford any basis for evaluation in absolute terms. The fact that net income was 2% of sales last year and is 3% of sales this year indicates improvement, but if there is evidence that net income *should be* 7% of sales, the record for both years is unfavorable.

Industry standards The limitations of horizontal analysis may be overcome to some extent by finding some other standard of performance as a yardstick against which to measure the record of any particular firm.[1] The yardstick may be a comparable company, the average record of several companies in the same industry, or some predetermined standard.

Suppose that Y Company suffers a 5% drop in its sales during the current year. The discovery that the sales of all companies in the same industry fell an average of 20% would indicate that this was a favorable rather than an unfavor-

---

[1]For example, the Robert Morris Associates publishes *Annual Statement Studies* which contains detailed data obtained from 27,000 annual reports grouped in 223 industry classifications. Assets, liabilities, and stockholders' equity are presented as a percentage of total assets; income statement amounts are expressed as a percentage of net sales; and key ratios are given (expressed as the median for each industry, the upper quartile, and the lower quartile). Measurements, within each of the 223 industry groups, are grouped according to the size of the firm. Similarly, Dun & Bradstreet, Inc., annually publishes *Key Business Ratios* in 125 lines of business divided by retailing, wholesaling, manufacturing, and construction. A total of 14 ratios are presented for each of the 125 industry groups.

able performance. Assume further that Y Company's net income is 2% of net sales. Based on comparison with other companies in the industry, this would be substandard performance if Y Company were a manufacturer of farm equipment, but it would be a satisfactory record if Y Company were a grocery chain.

When we compare a given company with its competitors or with industry averages, our conclusions will be valid only if the companies in question are reasonably comparable. Because of the large number of diversified companies formed in recent years, the term *industry* is difficult to define, and companies that fall roughly within the same industry may not be comparable in many respects. For example, one company may engage only in the marketing of oil products; another may be a fully integrated producer from the well to the gas pump, yet both are said to be in the "oil industry."

Differences in accounting methods may lessen the comparability of financial data for two companies. For example, companies may employ different depreciation methods or estimates of the useful life of substantially similar assets; inventories may be valued by different methods; and the timing of revenue recognition may differ significantly among companies engaged in certain industries. Despite these limitations, studying comparative performances is a useful method of analysis if carefully and intelligently done.

Quality of earnings

Profits are the lifeblood of a business entity. No entity can survive for long and accomplish its other goals unless it is profitable. On the other hand, continuous losses will drain assets from the business, consume owners' equity, and leave the company at the mercy of creditors. In assessing the prospects of a company, we are interested not only in the total *amount* of earnings but also in the *rate* of earnings on sales, on total assets, and on owners' equity. In addition, we must look to the *stability* and *source* of earnings. An erratic earnings performance over a period of years, for example, is less desirable than a steady level of earnings. A history of increasing earnings is preferable to a "flat" earnings record.

A breakdown of sales and earnings by *major product lines* is useful in evaluating the future performance of a company. Publicly owned companies include with their financial statements supplementary schedules showing sales and profits by product line and by geographic area. These schedules assist financial analysts in forecasting the effect upon the company of changes in consumer demand for particular types of products.

Financial analysts often express the opinion that the earnings of one company are of higher quality than earnings of other similar companies. This concept of *quality of earnings* arises because each company management can choose from a variety of accounting principles and methods, all of which are considered generally acceptable. A company's management often is under heavy pressure to report rising earnings, and accounting policies may be tailored toward this objective. We have already pointed out the impact on current reported earnings of the choice between the lifo and fifo methods of inventory valuation and the choice of depreciation policies. In judging the quality of earnings, the financial analyst should consider whether the accounting principles and methods selected by management lead to a conservative measurement of earnings or tend to inflate reported earnings.

Quality of assets and the relative amount of debt

Although a satisfactory level of earnings may be a good indication of the company's long-run ability to pay its debts and dividends, we must also look at the composition of assets, their condition and liquidity, the relationship between current assets and current liabilities, and the total amount of debt outstanding. A company may be profitable and yet be unable to pay its liabilities on time; sales and earnings may be satisfactory but plant and equipment may be deteriorating because of poor maintenance policies; valuable patents may be expiring; substantial losses may be in prospect from slow-moving inventories and past-due receivables. Companies with large amounts of debt often are vulnerable to increases in interest rates.

ILLUSTRATIVE CASE.   The home building industry is especially vulnerable to increases in interest rates. When interest rates rise, people stop buying new homes. In addition, most construction companies have large amounts of debt, upon which the interest charges are adjusted monthly to reflect current interest rates. Thus, when interest rates rise, these companies face large increases in their interest expense as well as declining revenue. The sustained period of high interest rates in the early 1980s caused the bankruptcy of a great many construction companies.

Impact of inflation

During a period of severe inflation, financial statements which are prepared in terms of historical costs do not reflect fully the economic resources or the *real income* (in terms of purchasing power) of a business enterprise. We discussed in Chapter 14 the requirements by the Financial Accounting Standards Board for large corporations to disclose both current cost and price-level-adjusted data in their annual reports. Financial analysts should therefore attempt to evaluate the impact of inflation on the financial position and operating results of the company being studied. They should raise such questions as: How much of the net income can be attributed to the increase in the general price level? Will the company lose or gain from inflation because of its holdings of monetary assets and liabilities? Will the company be able to keep its "physical capital" intact by paying the higher prices necessary to replace plant assets as they wear out? The topics of developing and interpreting accounting information designed to measure the impact of inflation were discussed in Chapter 14.

Illustrative analysis for Seacliff Company

Keep in mind the above discussion of analytical principles as you study the illustrative financial analysis which follows. The basic information for our discussion is contained in a set of condensed two-year comparative financial statements for Seacliff Company shown on the following pages. Summarized statement data, together with computations of dollar increases and decreases, and component percentages where applicable, have been compiled. For convenience in this illustration, relatively small dollar amounts have been used in the Seacliff Company financial statements.

Using the information in these statements, let us consider the kind of analysis that might be of particular interest to (1) common stockholders, (2) long-term creditors, (3) preferred stockholders, and (4) short-term creditors.

SEACLIFF COMPANY
Condensed Comparative Balance Sheet*
December 31

Assets	Year 2	Year 1	Increase or (Decrease) Dollars	%	Percentage of Total Assets Year 2	Year 1
Current assets	$390,000	$288,000	$102,000	35.4	41.1	33.5
Plant and equipment (net)	500,000	467,000	33,000	7.1	52.6	54.3
Other assets (loans to officers)	60,000	105,000	(45,000)	(42.9)	6.3	12.2
Total assets	$950,000	$860,000	$ 90,000	10.5	100.0	100.0
Liabilities & Stockholders' Equity						
Liabilities:						
Current liabilities	$112,000	$ 94,000	$ 18,000	(19.1)	11.8	10.9
Long-term liabilities	200,000	250,000	(50,000)	(20.0)	21.1	29.1
Total liabilities	$312,000	$344,000	$ (32,000)	(9.3)	32.9	40.0
Stockholders' equity:						
9% preferred stock, $100 par, callable at 105	$100,000	$100,000			10.5	11.6
Common stock, $50 par	250,000	200,000	$ 50,000	25.0	26.3	23.2
Paid-in capital in excess of par	70,000	40,000	30,000	75.0	7.4	4.7
Retained earnings	218,000	176,000	42,000	23.9	22.9	20.5
Total stockholders' equity	$638,000	$516,000	$122,000	23.6	67.1	60.0
Total liabilities & stockholders' equity	$950,000	$860,000	$ 90,000	10.5	100.0	100.0

*In order to focus attention on important subtotals, this statement is highly condensed and does not show individual asset and liability items. These details will be introduced as needed in the text discussion. For example, a list of Seacliff Company's current assets and current liabilities appears on page 639.

SEACLIFF COMPANY
Comparative Income Statement
Years Ended December 31

	Year 2	Year 1	Increase or (Decrease) Dollars	%	Percentage of Net Sales Year 2	Year 1
Net sales	$900,000	$750,000	$150,000	20.0	100.0	100.0
Cost of goods sold	530,000	420,000	110,000	26.2	58.9	56.0
Gross profit on sales	$370,000	$330,000	$ 40,000	12.1	41.1	44.0
Operating expenses:						
Selling expenses	$117,000	$ 75,000	$ 42,000	56.0	13.0	10.0
Administrative expenses	126,000	95,000	31,000	32.6	14.0	12.7
Total operating expenses	$243,000	$170,000	$ 73,000	42.9	27.0	22.7
Operating income	$127,000	$160,000	$ (33,000)	(20.6)	14.1	21.3
Interest expense	24,000	30,000	(6,000)	(20.0)	2.7	4.0
Income before income taxes	$103,000	$130,000	$ (27,000)	(20.8)	11.4	17.3
Income taxes	28,000	40,000	(12,000)	(30.0)	3.1	5.3
Net income	$ 75,000	$ 90,000	$ (15,000)	(16.7)	8.3	12.0
Earnings per share of common stock (see page 631)	$13.20	$20.25	$ (7.05)	(34.8)		

SEACLIFF COMPANY
Statement of Retained Earnings
Years Ended December 31

	Year 2	Year 1	Increase or (Decrease) Dollars	%
Balance, beginning of year	$176,000	$115,000	$61,000	53.0
Net income	75,000	90,000	(15,000)	(16.7)
	$251,000	$205,000	$46,000	22.4
Less: Dividends on common stock	$ 24,000	$ 20,000	$ 4,000	20.0
Dividends on preferred stock	9,000	9,000		
	$ 33,000	$ 29,000	$ 4,000	13.8
Balance, end of year	$218,000	$176,000	$42,000	23.9

Analysis by common stockholders

Common stockholders and potential investors in common stock look first at a company's earnings record. Their investment is in shares of stock, so *earnings per share and dividends per share* are of particular interest.

Earnings per share of common stock   As indicated in Chapter 12, earnings per share of common stock are computed by dividing the income available to common stockholders by the number of shares of common stock outstanding. Any preferred dividend requirements must be subtracted from net income to determine income available for common stock, as shown in the following computations for Seacliff Company:

Earnings per Share of Common Stock

		Year 2	Year 1
Net income		$75,000	$90,000
Less: Preferred dividend requirements		9,000	9,000
Income available for common stock	(a)	$66,000	$81,000
Shares of common stock outstanding, during the year	(b)	5,000	4,000
Earnings per share of common stock (a ÷ b)		$13.20	$20.25

Earnings related to number of common shares outstanding

Earnings per share of common stock are shown in the income statement below the net income figure. When the income statement includes operations discontinued during the period, the earnings per share of common stock may be reported in the income statement in three amounts as follows: (1) income from continuing operations, (2) income (or loss) from discontinued operations, and (3) net income. Similar treatment may be appropriate for extraordinary items. Seacliff Company had no discontinued operations or extraordinary items and therefore the amount earned per share is computed by dividing the net income available for the common stock by the number of common shares outstanding during the year. The computation of earnings per share in more complicated situations was illustrated in Chapter 12.

Dividend yield and price-earnings ratio   Dividends are of prime importance to some stockholders, but a secondary factor to others. In other words, some stockholders invest primarily to receive regular cash income, while others invest in stocks principally with the hope of securing capital gains through rising market prices. If a corporation is profitable and retains its earnings for expansion of the business, the expanded operations should produce an increase in the net income of the company and thus tend to make each share of stock more valuable.

In comparing the merits of alternative investment opportunities, we should relate earnings and dividends per share to the *market value* of the stock. Dividends per share divided by market price per share determines the *yield* rate of a company's stock. Dividend yield is especially important to those investors whose objective is to maximize the dividend revenue from their investments.

Earnings performance of common stock is often expressed as a *price-earnings ratio* by dividing the market price per share by the annual earnings per share. Thus, a stock selling for $60 per share and earning $5 per share in the year just ended may be said to have a price-earnings ratio of 12 times earnings ($60 ÷ $5). The price-earnings ratio of the 30 stocks included in the Dow-Jones Industrial

Average has varied widely in recent years, ranging from a low of about 6 for the group to a high of about 20.

Assume that the 1,000 additional shares of common stock issued by Seacliff on January 1, Year 2, received the full dividend of $4.80 paid in Year 2. When these new shares were issued, Seacliff Company announced that it planned to continue indefinitely the $4.80 dividend per common share currently being paid. With this assumption and the use of assumed market prices of the common stock at December 31, Year 1 and Year 2, the earnings per share and dividend yield may be summarized as follows:

Earnings and Dividends per Share of Common Stock

Date	Assumed Market Value per Share	Earnings per Share	Price-Earnings Ratio	Dividends per Share	Dividend Yield, %
Dec. 31, Year 1	$125	$20.25	6	$5.00	4.0
Dec. 31, Year 2	$100	$13.20	8	$4.80	4.8

Earnings and dividends related to market price of common stock

The decline in market value during Year 2 presumably reflects the decrease in earnings per share. Investors appraising this stock at December 31, Year 2, would consider whether a price-earnings ratio of 8 and a dividend yield of 4.8% represented a satisfactory situation in the light of alternative investment opportunities. They would also place considerable weight on estimates of the company's prospective future earnings and the probable effect of such estimated earnings on the market price of the stock and on dividend payments.

Book value per share of common stock   The procedures for computing book value per share were fully described in Chapter 12 and will not be repeated here. We will, however, determine the book value per share of common stock for the Seacliff Company:

Book Value per Share of Common Stock

	Year 2	Year 1
Total stockholders' equity	$638,000	$516,000
Less: Equity of preferred stockholders (1,000 shares at call price of $105)	105,000	105,000
Equity of common stockholders ....(a)	$533,000	$411,000
Shares of common stock outstanding ....(b)	5,000	4,000
Book value per share of common stock (a ÷ b)	$106.60	$102.75

Why did book value per share decrease?

Book value per share was reduced by $9.35 in Year 2 as a result of dividend payments and the issuance of 1,000 additional shares of common stock at $80 per share, a figure significantly below the book value of $102.75 per share at the end of Year 1; book value was increased by earnings of $13.20 per share in Year 2, thus causing a net increase of $3.85 in the book value per share.

Revenue and expense anlaysis   The trend of earnings of Seacliff Company is unfavorable and stockholders will want to know the reasons for the decline in net income. The comparative income statement on page 630 shows that despite a 20% increase in net sales, net income fell from $90,000 in Year 1 to $75,000 in Year 2, a decline of 16.7%. The *net income as a percentage of net sales* went from 12% to only 8.3%. The primary causes of this decline were the increases in selling expenses (56.0%), in general and administrative expenses (32.6%), and in the cost of goods sold (26.2%), all exceeding the 20% increase in net sales.

These observations suggest the need for further investigation. Suppose we find that Seacliff Company cut its selling prices in Year 2. This would explain the decrease in *gross profit rate* from 44% to 41.1% and would also show that sales volume in physical units rose more than 20%, since it takes proportionally more sales at lower prices to produce a given increase in dollar sales. Since the dollar amount of gross profit increased $40,000 in Year 2, the strategy of reducing sales prices to increase volume would have been successful if there had been little change in operating expenses. However, operating expenses rose by $73,000, resulting in a $33,000 decrease in operating income.

The next step would be to find which expenses increased and why. An investor may be handicapped here, because detailed operating expenses are not usually shown in published financial statements. Some conclusions, however, can be reached on the basis of even the condensed information available in the comparative income statement for Seacliff Company shown on page 630.

The substantial increase in selling expenses presumably reflects greater selling effort during Year 2 in an attempt to improve sales volume. However, the fact that selling expenses increased $42,000 while gross profit increased only $40,000 indicates that the cost of this increased sales effort was not justified in terms of results. Even more disturbing is the increase in general and administrative expenses. Some growth in administrative expenses might be expected to accompany increased sales volume, but because some of the expenses are fixed, the growth generally should be *less than proportional* to any increase in sales. The increase in general and administrative expenses from 12.7 to 14% of sales would be of serious concern to informed investors.

Management generally has greater control over operating expenses than over revenue. The *operating expense ratio* is often used as a measure of management's ability to control its operating expenses. The unfavorable trend in this ratio for Seacliff Company is shown below:

Operating Expense Ratio

		Year 2	Year 1
Operating expenses	(a)	$243,000	$170,000
Net sales	(b)	$900,000	$750,000
Operating expense ratio (a ÷ b)		27.0%	22.7%

Does a higher operating expense ratio indicate higher net income?

If management were able to increase the sales volume while at the same time increasing the gross profit rate and decreasing the operating expense ratio, the effect on net income could be quite dramatic. For example, if Seacliff Company increased its sales in Year 3 by 11% to $1,000,000, increased its gross profit rate from 41.1 to 44%, and reduced the operating expense ratio from 27 to 24%, its operating income would increase from $127,000 to $200,000 ($1,000,000 − $560,000 − $240,000), an increase of over 57%.

Return on investment (ROI)

The rate of return on investment (often called ROI) is a test of management's efficiency in using available resources. Regardless of the size of the organization, capital is a scarce resource and must be used efficiently. In other words, management has a limited amount of dollars to work with, and a good manager is the one who can get the most out of the resources which are available. In judging the performance of branch managers or of company-wide management, it is reasonable to raise the question: What rate of return have you earned on the resources under your control? The concept of return on investment can be applied to a number of situations: for example, evaluating a branch, a total business, a product line, or an individual investment. A number of different ratios have been developed for the ROI concept, each well suited to a particular situation. We shall consider the return on total assets and the return on common stockholders' equity as examples of the return on investment concept.

Return on total assets   An important test of management's ability to earn a return on funds supplied from all sources is the rate of return on total assets.

The income figure used in computing this ratio should be *income before deducting interest expense,* since interest is a payment to creditors for money used to *acquire assets.* Income before interest reflects earnings throughout the year and therefore should be related to the *average* investment in assets during the year. The computation of this ratio for Seacliff Company is shown below:

Percentage Return on Total Assets

	Year 2	Year 1
Net income	$ 75,000	$ 90,000
Add back: Interest expense	24,000	30,000
Income before interest expense (a)	$ 99,000	$120,000
Total assets, beginning of year	$860,000	$820,000
Total assets, end of year	950,000	860,000
Average investment in assets (b)	$905,000	$840,000
Return on total assets (a ÷ b)	10.9%	14.3%

Earnings related to investment in assets

This ratio shows that earnings per dollar of assets invested have fallen off in Year 2. Before drawing conclusions as to the effectiveness of Seacliff's management, however, we should consider the trend in the return on assets earned by other companies of similar kind and size.

Return on common stockholders' equity   Because interest and dividends paid to creditors and preferred stockholders are fixed in amount, a company may earn a greater or smaller return on the common stockholders' equity than on its total assets. The computation of return on stockholders' equity for Seacliff Company is shown below:

Return on Common Stockholders' Equity

	Year 2	Year 1
Net income	$ 75,000	$ 90,000
Less: Preferred dividend requirements	9,000	9,000
Net income available for common stock ....(a)	$ 66,000	$ 81,000
Common stockholders' equity, beginning of year	$416,000	$355,000
Common stockholders' equity, end of year	538,000	416,000
Average common stockholders' equity ....(b)	$477,000	$385,500
Return on common stockholders' equity (a ÷ b)	13.8%	21.0%

Does the use of leverage benefit common stockholders?

In both years the rate of return to common stockholders was higher than the return on total assets, because the average combined rate of interest paid to creditors and dividends paid to preferred stockholders was less than the rate earned on each dollar of assets used in the business.

Leverage

When the return on total assets is higher than the average cost of borrowed capital, as was the case in Seacliff Company, the common stockholders may benefit from the use of leverage. *Leverage* (or *trading on the equity*) refers to buying assets with money raised by borrowing or by issuing preferred stock. If the borrowed capital can be invested to earn a return *greater* than the cost of borrowing, then the net income and the return on common stockholders' equity will *increase*. In other words, if you can borrow money at 12% and use it to earn 14%, you will benefit by doing so. However, leverage can act as a "double-edged sword"; the effects may be favorable or unfavorable to the holders of common stock. If the return on total assets should fall *below* the average cost of borrowed capital, leverage will *reduce* net income and the return on common stockholders' equity. When this unfavorable situation occurs, one possible solution would be to pay off the loans that carry high interest rates. However, most companies do not have sufficient amounts of cash to retire long-term debt or preferred stock on short notice. Therefore, the common stockholders may become "locked in" for a long period of time to the unfavorable effects of leverage.

When the return on assets exceeds the cost of borrowed capital, the extensive use of leverage can increase dramatically the return on common stockholders' equity. However, extensive leverage also increases the *risk* to common stockholders that their return may be reduced dramatically in future years. Furthermore, if a business incurs so much debt that it becomes unable to meet the required interest and principal payments, creditors may force liquidation or reorganization of the business, to the detriment of stockholders.

In deciding how much leverage is appropriate, the common stockholders should consider the *stability* of the company's return on assets, as well as the relationship of this return to the average cost of borrowed capital. Also, they should consider the amount of risk that they are willing to accept in the effort to increase the return on their investment.

Leverage most frequently is achieved through debt financing, including both current and long-term liabilities. One advantage of debt financing is that interest payments are deductible in determining taxable income. Leverage also can be achieved through the issuance of preferred stock. Since preferred stock dividends are *not* deductible for income tax purposes, however, the advantage gained in this respect will be much smaller than in the case of debt financing.

Equity ratio   One indicator of the amount of leverage used by a business is the equity ratio. This ratio measures the proportion of the total assets financed by stockholders, as distinguished from creditors. It is computed by dividing total stockholders' equity by total assets. A *low* equity ratio indicates an extensive use of leverage, that is, a large proportion of financing provided by creditors. A high equity ratio, on the other hand, indicates that the business is making little use of leverage.

The equity ratio at year-end for Seacliff is determined as follows:

Equity Ratio

		Year 2	Year 1
Total stockholders' equity	(a)	$638,000	$516,000
Total assets (or total liabilities & stockholders' equity)	(b)	$950,000	$860,000
Equity ratio (a ÷ b)		67.2%	60.0%

Proportion of assets financed by stockholders

Seacliff Company has a higher equity ratio in Year 2 than in Year 1. Is this favorable or unfavorable?

From the viewpoint of the common stockholder, a low equity ratio will produce maximum benefits if management is able to earn a rate of return on assets greater than the rate of interest paid to creditors. However, a low equity ratio can be very unfavorable if the return on assets falls below the rate of interest paid to creditors. Since the return on total assets earned by Seacliff Company has declined from 14.3% in Year 1 to a relatively low 10.9% in Year 2, the common stockholders should *not* favor a low equity ratio. The action by management in Year 2 of retiring $50,000 in long-term liabilities will help to protect the common stockholders from the unfavorable effects of leverage should the return on assets continue to decline.

Analysis by long-term creditors

Bondholders and other long-term creditors are primarily interested in three factors: (1) the rate of return on their investment, (2) the firm's ability to meet its interest requirements, and (3) the firm's ability to repay the principal of the debt when it falls due.

Yield rate on bonds   The yield rate on bonds or other long-term indebtedness cannot be computed in the same manner as the yield rate on shares of stock, because bonds, unlike stocks, have a definite maturity date and amount. The ownership of a 12%, 10-year bond represents the right to receive $1,000 at the end of 10 years and the right to receive $120 per year during each of the next 10 years. If the market price of this bond is $950, the yield rate on an investment in the bond is the rate of interest that will make the present value of these two contractual rights equal to $950. *The yield rate varies inversely with changes in the market price of the bond.* If interest rates rise, the market price of existing bonds will fall; if interest rates decline, the price of bonds will rise. If the price of a bond is above maturity value, the yield rate is less than the bond interest rate; if the price of a bond is below maturity value, the yield rate is higher than the bond interest rate.

Number of times interest earned   Long-term creditors have learned from experience that one of the best indications of the safety of their investment is the fact that, over the life of the debt, the company has sufficient income to cover its interest requirements by a wide margin. A failure to cover interest requirements may have serious repercussions on the stability and solvency of the firm.

A common measure of debt safety is the ratio of income available for the payment of interest to the annual interest expense, called *number of times interest earned.* This computation for Seacliff Company would be:

Number of Times Interest Earned

	Year 2	Year 1
Operating income (before interest and income taxes) ....(a)	$127,000	$160,000
Annual interest expense ....(b)	$ 24,000	$ 30,000
Times interest earned (a ÷ b)	5.3	5.3

Long-term creditors watch this ratio

The ratio remained unchanged at a satisfactory level during Year 2. A ratio of 5.3 times interest earned would be considered strong in many industries. In the electric utilities industry, for example, the interest coverage ratio for the leading companies presently averages about 3, with the ratio of individual companies varying from 2 to 6.

Debt ratio   Long-term creditors are interested in the amount of debt outstanding in relation to the amount of capital contributed by stockholders. The *debt ratio* is computed by dividing total liabilities by total assets, shown below for Seacliff Company.

Debt Ratio

	Year 2	Year 1
Total liabilities ....(a)	$312,000	$344,000
Total assets (or total liabilities & stockholders' equity) ....(b)	$950,000	$860,000
Debt ratio (a ÷ b)	32.8%	40.0%

What portion of total assets is financed by debt?

From a creditor's viewpoint, the lower the debt ratio (or the higher the equity ratio) the better, since this means that stockholders have contributed the bulk of the funds to the business, and therefore the margin of protection to creditors against a shrinkage of the assets is high.

Analysis by preferred stockholders

If preferred stock is convertible, the interests of preferred stockholders are similar to those of common stockholders. If preferred stock is not convertible, the interests of preferred stockholders are more closely comparable to those of long-term creditors.

Preferred stockholders are interested in the yield on their investment. The yield is computed by dividing the dividend per share by the market value per share. The dividend per share of Seacliff Company preferred stock is $9. If we assume that the market value at December 31, Year 2, is $60 per share, the yield rate at that time would be 15% ($9 ÷ $60).

The primary measurement of the safety of an investment in preferred stock is the ability of the firm to meet its preferred dividend requirements. The best test of this ability is the ratio of the net income available to pay the preferred dividend to the amount of the annual dividend, as follows:

Times Preferred Dividends Earned

		Year 2	Year 1
Net income available to pay preferred dividends .... (a)		$75,000	$90,000
Annual preferred dividend requirements .... (b)		$ 9,000	$ 9,000
Times dividends earned (a ÷ b)		8.3	10

Is the preferred dividend safe?

Although the margin of protection declined in Year 2, the annual preferred dividend requirement still appears well protected.

Weakness of preferred stocks when interest rates rise   Investors buy preferred stocks principally for the regular dividends they pay, just as investors buy bonds in order to receive regular interest payments. But what happens to the market price of an 8% preferred stock, originally issued at par of $100, if government policy and other factors cause interest rates to rise to, say, 18 or 20%? The market price of the preferred stock will decline to less than half its original issuance price. Unlike bonds, preferred stock does not have a maturity date. Bonds with relatively low interest rates tend to rise to their face value as they approach payoff at maturity. No such upward force affects preferred stocks.

In recent years new government bonds and U.S. Treasury bills, as well as corporate bonds and notes, have been offered at interest rates of 15% and more. Why should investors buy existing preferred stocks at prices and dividend rates that offer a lower yield than high-quality bonds and notes? The conclusion is that investors in preferred stocks should recognize the threat posed by a possible increase in interest rates.

Analysis by short-term creditors

Bankers and other short-term creditors share the interest of stockholders and bondholders in the profitability and long-run stability of a business. Their primary interest, however, is in the current position of the firm—its ability to generate sufficient funds (working capital) to meet current operating needs and to pay current debts promptly. Thus the analysis of financial statements by a banker considering a short-term loan, or by a trade creditor investigating the credit status of a customer, is likely to center on the working capital position of the prospective debtor.

Amount of working capital The details of the working capital of Seacliff Company are shown below:

SEACLIFF COMPANY
Comparative Schedule of Working Capital
As of December 31

	Year 2	Year 1	Increase or (Decrease) Dollars	%	Percentage of Total Current Items Year 2	Year 1
Current assets:						
Cash	$ 38,000	$ 40,000	$(2,000)	(5.0)	9.7	13.9
Receivables (net)	117,000	86,000	31,000	36.0	30.0	29.9
Inventories	180,000	120,000	60,000	50.0	46.2	41.6
Prepaid expenses	55,000	42,000	13,000	31.0	14.1	14.6
Total current assets	$390,000	$288.000	$102,000	35.4	100.0	100.0
Current liabilities:						
Notes payable to creditors	$ 14,600	$ 10,000	$ 4,600	46.0	13.1	10.7
Accounts payable	66,000	30,000	36,000	120.0	58.9	31.9
Accrued liabilities	31,400	54,000	(22,600)	(41.9)	28.0	57.4
Total current liabilities	$112,000	$ 94,000	$ 18,000	19.1	100.0	100.0
Working capital	$278,000	$194,000	$ 84,000	43.3		

The amount of working capital is measured by the *excess of current assets over current liabilities*. Thus, working capital represents the amount of cash, near-cash items, and cash substitutes (prepayments) on hand after providing for payment of all current liabilities.

This schedule shows that current assets increased $102,000, while current liabilities rose by only $18,000, with the result that working capital increased $84,000. There was a shift in the composition of the current assets and current liabilities; cash decreased from 13.9 to 9.7% of current assets, and inventory rose from 41.6 to 46.2%. Inventory is a less liquid resource than cash. Therefore, although the amount of working capital increased in Year 2, the quality of working capital is not as liquid as in Year 1. Although creditors want to see large amounts of high-quality working capital, management must consider that excess amounts of cash are not productive and do not generate a high return.

The current ratio One means of further evaluating these changes in working capital is to observe the relationship between current assets and current liabilities, a test known as the *current ratio*. The current ratio for the Seacliff Company is computed below:

Current Ratio

Does this indicate satisfactory debt-paying ability?

		Year 2	Year 1
Total current assets	(a)	$390,000	$288,000
Total current liabilities	(b)	$112,000	$ 94,000
Current ratio (a ÷ b)		3.5	3.1

Along with the increase of $84,000 in the amount of working capital in Year 2, current assets per dollar of current liabilities increased. The margin of safety (current ratio) appears quite strong.

In interpreting the current ratio, a number of factors should be kept in mind:

1 Creditors tend to feel that the higher the current ratio the better, although from a managerial view there is an upper limit. Too high a current ratio may indicate that capital is not being used productively in the business.

2 Because creditors tend to stress the current ratio as an indication of short-term solvency, some firms may take conscious steps to improve this ratio just before statements are prepared at the end of a fiscal period for submission to bankers or other creditors. This may be done by postponing purchases, pressing collections on accounts receivable, and using the cash collected to pay off current liabilities.

3 The current ratio computed at the end of a fiscal year may not be representative of the current position of the company throughout the year. Since many firms arrange their fiscal year to end during a low point in the seasonal swing of business activity, the current ratio at year-end is likely to be more favorable than at any other time during the year.

Use of both the current ratio and the amount of working capital helps to place debt-paying ability in its proper perspective. For example, if Company X has current assets of $200,000 and current liabilities of $100,000 and Company Y has current assets of $2,000,000 and current liabilities of $1,900,000, each company has $100,000 of working capital, but the current position of Company X is clearly superior to that of Company Y. The current ratio for Company X is quite satisfactory at 2 to 1, but Company Y's current ratio is very low—only slightly above 1 to 1.

As another example, assume that Company A and Company B both have current ratios of 3 to 1. However, Company A has working capital of $20,000 and Company B has working capital of $200,000. Although both companies appear to be good credit risks, Company B would no doubt be able to qualify for a much *larger* bank loan than would Company A.

A widely used rule of thumb is that a current ratio of 2 to 1 or better is satisfactory. As with all rules of thumb this is an arbitrary standard, subject to numerous exceptions and qualifications.

Adjustment for undervalued inventories   The cost of inventory is a major factor in the computation of the current ratio or the amount of working capital. If a company uses the *lifo* inventory method, the cost of inventory appearing in the balance sheet may be unrealistically low in terms of current replacement costs. In such cases, many financial analysts substitute the *current replacement cost* of inventories for the historical cost figure in computing the current ratio or amount of working capital. As explained in earlier chapters, the Financial Accounting Standards Board requires large corporations to disclose the current replacement cost of their inventories and other items as supplementary information in their financial statements.

Quick ratio   Because inventories and prepaid expenses are further removed from conversion into cash than other current assets, a ratio known as the *quick ratio* or *acid-test ratio* is sometimes computed as a supplement to the current ratio. This ratio compares the highly liquid current assets (cash, marketable securities, and receivables) with current liabilities. Seacliff Company has no marketable securities; its quick ratio is computed as follows:

Quick Ratio

		Year 2	Year 1
Quick assets (cash and receivables) ....(a)		$155,000	$126,000
Current liabilities ....(b)		$112,000	$ 94,000
Quick ratio (a ÷ b)		1.4	1.3

A measure of liquidity

Here again the analysis reveals a favorable trend and a strong position. The adequacy of the quick ratio should be judged in the light of the amount of receivables included among quick assets and the average time required to collect receivables as compared to the credit period extended by suppliers. If the credit periods extended to customers and granted by creditors are roughly equal, a quick ratio of 1.0 or better is considered satisfactory.

Some financial analysts compute a *liquidity ratio* as a measure of immediate ability to pay short-term debts. This ratio is computed by dividing the total of cash and marketable securities owned by the total current liabilities outstanding.

Inventory turnover   The cost of goods sold figure on the income statement represents the total cost of all goods that have been transferred out of inventories during any given period. Therefore the relationship between cost of goods sold and the average balance of inventories maintained throughout the year indicates the number of times that inventories "turn over" and are replaced each year.

Ideally we should total the inventories at the end of each month and divide by 12 to obtain an average inventory. This information is not always available, however, and the nearest substitute is a simple average of the inventory at the beginning and at the end of the year. This tends to overstate the turnover rate, since many companies choose an accounting year that ends when inventories are at a minimum.

Assuming that only beginning and ending inventories are available, the computation of inventory turnover for Seacliff Company may be illustrated as follows:

Inventory Turnover

		Year 2	Year 1
Cost of goods sold	(a)	$530,000	$420,000
Inventory, beginning of year		$120,000	$100,000
Inventory, end of year		180,000	120,000
Average inventory	(b)	$150,000	$110,000
Average inventory turnover per year (a ÷ b)		3.5 times	3.8 times
Average days to turn over (divide 365 days by inventory turnover)		104 days	96 days

What does inventory turnover mean?

The trend indicated by this analysis is unfavorable, since the average investment in inventories in relation to the cost of goods sold is rising. Stating this another way, the company required on the average 8 days more during Year 2 to turn over its inventories than during Year 1. Furthermore, the inventory status *at the end of the year* has changed even more: At the end of Year 1 there were 104 days' sales represented in the ending inventory ($120,000/$420,000 × 365 days) compared with 124 days' sales contained in the ending inventory at the end of Year 2 ($180,000/$530,000 × 365 days).

The relation between inventory turnover and gross profit per dollar of sales may be significant. A high inventory and a low gross profit rate frequently go hand in hand. This, however, is merely another way of saying that if the gross profit rate is low, a high volume of business is necessary to produce a satisfactory return on total assets. Although a high inventory turnover is usually regarded as a good sign, a rate that is high in relation to that of similar firms may indicate that the company is losing sales by a failure to maintain an adequate stock of goods to serve its customers promptly.

Accounts receivable turnover   The turnover of accounts receivable is computed in a manner comparable to that just described for inventories. The ratio between the net sales for the period and the average balance in accounts receivable is a rough indication of the average time required to convert receivables into cash. Ideally, a monthly average of receivables should be used, and only *sales on credit* should be included in the sales figure. For illustrative purposes, we shall assume that Seacliff Company sells entirely on credit and that only the beginning and ending balances of receivables are available:

Accounts Receivable Turnover

		Year 2	Year 1
Net sales on credit	(a)	$900,000	$750,000
Receivables, beginning of year		$ 86,000	$ 80,000
Receivables, end of year		117,000	86,000
Average receivables	(b)	$101,500	$ 83,000
Receivable turnover per year (a ÷ b)		8.9 times	9.0 times
Average age of receivables (divide 365 days by receivable turnover)		41 days	41 days

Are customers paying promptly?

There has been no significant change in the average time required to collect receivables. The interpretation of the average age of receivables would depend upon the company's credit terms and the seasonal activity immediately before year-end. If the company grants 30-day credit terms to its customers, for example, the above analysis indicates that accounts receivable collections are lagging. If the terms were for 60 days, however, there is evidence that collections are being made ahead of schedule.

In Chapter 5 we defined the term *operating cycle* as the average time period between the purchase of merchandise and the conversion of this merchandise back into cash. In other words, the merchandise acquired for inventory is gradually converted into accounts receivable by selling goods to customers on credit, and these receivables are converted into cash through the process of collection. The word *cycle* refers to the circular flow of capital from cash to inventory to receivables to cash again.

The *operating cycle* in Year 2 was approximately 145 days (computed by adding the 104 days required to turn over inventory and the average 41 days required to collect receivables). This compares to an operating cycle of only 137 days in Year 1, computed as 96 days to dispose of the inventory plus 41 days to collect the resulting receivables. A trend toward a longer operating cycle suggests that inventory and receivables are increasing relative to sales and that profits may be hurt because of lower sales volume and an increasing investment in current assets.

Summary of analytical measurements

The basic ratios and other measurements discussed in this chapter and their significance are summarized on pages 644 and 645.

The student should keep in mind the fact that the full significance of any of the foregoing ratios or other measurements depends on the *direction of its trend* and on its *relationship to some predetermined standard* or industry average.

Ratio or Other Measurement	Method of Computation	Significance
1 Earnings per share of common stock	$\dfrac{\text{Net income} - \text{preferred dividends}}{\text{Shares of common outstanding}}$	Gives the amount of earnings applicable to a share of common stock.
2 Dividend yield	$\dfrac{\text{Dividend per share}}{\text{Market price per share}}$	Shows the rate earned by stockholders based on current price for a share of stock.
3 Price-earnings ratio	$\dfrac{\text{Market price per share}}{\text{Earnings per share}}$	Indicates whether price of stock is in line with earnings.
4 Book value per share of common stock	$\dfrac{\text{Common stockholders' equity}}{\text{Shares of common outstanding}}$	Measures the recorded value of net assets behind each share of common stock.
5 Operating expense ratio	$\dfrac{\text{Operating expenses}}{\text{Net sales}}$	Indicates management's ability to control expenses.
6 Return on total assets	$\dfrac{\text{Net income} + \text{interest expense}}{\text{Average investment in assets}}$	Measures the productivity of assets regardless of capital structures.
7 Return on common stockholders' equity	$\dfrac{\text{Net income} - \text{preferred dividends}}{\text{Average common stockholders' equity}}$	Indicates the earning power of common stockholders' equity.
8 Equity ratio	$\dfrac{\text{Total stockholders' equity}}{\text{Total assets}}$	Shows the protection to creditors and the extent of leverage being used.
9 Number of times interest earned	$\dfrac{\text{Operating income}}{\text{Annual interest expense}}$	Measures the coverage of interest requirements, particularly on long-term debt.
10 Debt ratio	$\dfrac{\text{Total liabilities}}{\text{Total assets}}$	Indicates the percentage of assets financed through borrowing; it shows the extent of leverage being used.
11 Times preferred dividends earned	$\dfrac{\text{Net income}}{\text{Annual preferred dividends}}$	Shows the adequacy of current earnings to pay dividends on preferred stock.
12 Current ratio	$\dfrac{\text{Current assets}}{\text{Current liabilities}}$	Measures short-run debt-paying ability.
13 Quick (acid-test) ratio	$\dfrac{\text{Quick assets}}{\text{Current liabilities}}$	Measures the short-term liquidity of a firm.

(continued)

Ratio or Other Measurement	*Method of Computation*	*Significance*
14 Inventory turnover	$\dfrac{\text{Cost of goods sold}}{\text{Average inventory}}$	Indicates management's ability to control the investment in inventory.
15 Accounts receivable turnover	$\dfrac{\text{Net sales on credit}}{\text{Average receivables}}$	Indicates reasonableness of accounts receivable balance and effectiveness of collections.

KEY TERMS INTRODUCED OR EMPHASIZED IN CHAPTER 16

Common size financial statement   All items are stated in percentages rather than dollar amounts. In the balance sheet each item is expressed as a percentage of total assets; in the income statement each item is expressed as a percentage of net sales.

Comparative financial statements   Financial statement data for two or more successive years placed side by side in adjacent columns to facilitate study of changes.

Component percentage   The percentage relationship of any financial statement item to a total including that item. For example, each type of asset as a percentage of total assets.

Horizontal analysis   Comparison of the change in a financial statement item such as inventories during two or more accounting periods.

Leverage   Refers to the practice of financing assets with borrowed capital. Extensive leverage creates the possibility for the rate of return on common stockholders' equity to be substantially above or below the rate of return on total assets. When the rate of return on total assets exceeds the average cost of borrowed capital, leverage increases net income and the return on common stockholders' equity. However, when the return on total assets is less than the average cost of borrowed capital, leverage reduces net income and the return on common stockholders' equity. Leverage is also called *trading on the equity.*

Quality of assets   The concept that some companies have assets of better quality than others, such as well-balanced composition of assets, well-maintained plant and equipment, and receivables that are all current. A lower quality of assets might be indicated by poor maintenance of plant and equipment, slow-moving inventories with high danger of obsolescence, past-due receivables, and patents approaching an expiration date.

Quality of earnings   Earnings are said to be of high quality if they are stable, the source seems assured and the methods used in measuring income are conservative. The existence of this concept suggests that the range of alternative but acceptable accounting principles may still be too wide to produce financial statements that are comparable.

Rate of return on investment (ROI)   The overall test of management's ability to earn a satisfactory return on the assets under its control. Numerous variations of the ROI concept are used such as return on total assets, return on total equities, etc.

Ratios   See page 644 for list of ratios, methods of computation, and significance.

Vertical analysis   Comparison of a particular financial statement item to a total including that item, such as inventories as a percentage of current assets, or operating expenses in relation to net sales.

DEMONSTRATION PROBLEM FOR YOUR REVIEW

The accounting records of King Corporation showed the following balances at the end of Years 1 and 2:

	Year 2	Year 1
Cash	$ 35,000	$ 25,000
Accounts receivable (net)	91,000	90,000
Inventory	160,000	140,000
Short-term prepayments	4,000	5,000
Investment in land	90,000	100,000
Equipment	880,000	640,000
Less: Accumulated depreciation	(260,000)	(200,000)
	$1,000,000	$ 800,000
Accounts payable	$ 105,000	$ 46,000
Income taxes payable and other accrued liabilities	40,000	25,000
Bonds payable—8%	280,000	280,000
Premium on bonds payable	3,600	4,000
Capital stock, $5 par	165,000	110,000
Retained earnings	406,400	335,000
	$1,000,000	$ 800,000
Sales (net of discounts and allowances)	$2,200,000	$1,600,000
Cost of goods sold	1,606,000	1,120,000
Gross profit on sales	$ 594,000	$ 480,000
Expenses (including $22,400 interest expense)	(330,000)	(352,000)
Income taxes	(91,000)	(48,000)
Extraordinary loss	(6,600)	–0–
Net income	$ 166,400	$ 80,000

Cash dividends of $40,000 were paid and a 50% stock dividend was distributed early in Year 2. All sales were made on credit at a relatively uniform rate during the year. Inventory and receivables did not fluctuate materially. The market price of the company's stock on December 31, Year 2, was $86 per share; on December 31, Year 1, it was $43.50 (before the 50% stock dividend distributed in Year 2).

Instructions   Compute the following for Year 2 and Year 1:
(1) Quick ratio
(2) Current ratio
(3) Equity ratio
(4) Debt ratio
(5) Book value per share of capital stock (based on shares outstanding after 50% stock dividend in Year 2)
(6) Earnings per share of capital stock (including extraordinary loss)
(7) Price-earnings ratio
(8) Gross profit percentage
(9) Operating expense ratio
(10) Income before extraordinary loss as a percentage of net sales

(11) Inventory turnover (Assume an average inventory of $150,000 for both years.)
(12) Accounts receivable turnover (Assume average accounts receivable of $90,000 for Year 1.)
(13) Times bond interest earned (before interest expense and income taxes)

SOLUTION TO DEMONSTRATION PROBLEM

	Year 2	Year 1
(1) Quick ratio:		
$126,000 ÷ $145,000	.9 to 1	
$115,000 ÷ $71,000		1.6 to 1
(2) Current ratio:		
$290,000 ÷ $145,000	2 to 1	
$260,000 ÷ $71,000		3.7 to 1
(3) Equity ratio:		
$571,400 ÷ $1,000,000	57%	
$445,000 ÷ $800,000		56%
(4) Debt ratio:		
$428,600 ÷ $1,000,000	43%	
$355,000 ÷ $800,000		44%
(5) Book value per share of capital stock:		
$571,400 ÷ 33,000 shares	$17.32	
$445,000 ÷ 33,000* shares		$13.48
(6) Earnings per share of capital stock (including extraordinary loss of $0.20 per share in Year 2):		
$166,400 ÷ 33,000 shares	$5.04	
$80,000 ÷ 33,000* shares		$2.42
(7) Price-earnings ratio:		
$86 ÷ $5.04	17 times	
$43.50 ÷ 1.5* = $29, adjusted market price; $29 ÷ $2.42 ..		12 times
(8) Gross profit percentage:		
$594,000 ÷ $2,200,000	27%	
$480,000 ÷ $1,600,000		30%
(9) Operating expense ratio:		
($330,000 − $22,400) ÷ $2,200,000	14%	
($352,000 − $22,400) ÷ $1,600,000		20.6%
(10) Income before extraordinary loss as a percentage of net sales:		
$173,000 ÷ $2,200,000	7.9%	
$80,000 ÷ $1,600,000		5%
(11) Inventory turnover:		
$1,606,000 ÷ $150,000	10.7 times	
$1,120,000 ÷ $150,000		7.5 times

*Adjusted retroactively for 50% stock dividend.

(continued)

(12) *Accounts receivable turnover:*

$2,200,000 ÷ $90,500	24.3 times
$1,600,000 ÷ $90,000	17.8 times

(13) *Times bond interest earned:*

($166,400 + $22,400 + $91,000) ÷ $22,400	12.5 times
($80,000 + $22,400 + $48,000) ÷ $22,400	6.7 times

REVIEW QUESTIONS

1 **a** What groups are interested in the financial affairs of publicly owned corporations?
  b List some of the more important sources of financial information for investors.

2 In financial statement analysis, what is the basic objective of observing trends in data and ratios? Suggest some other standards of comparison.

3 In financial analysis, what information is produced by computing a ratio that is not available in a simple observation of the underlying data?

4 Explain the distinction between a *percentage change* and a *component percentage.*

5 "Although net income declined this year as compared with last year, it increased from 3% to 5% of net sales." Are sales increasing or decreasing?

6 Differentiate between *horizontal* and *vertical* analysis.

7 Assume that Chemco Corporation is engaged in the manufacture and distribution of a variety of chemicals. In analyzing the financial statements of this corporation, why would you want to refer to the ratios and other measurements of companies in the chemical industry? In comparing the financial results of Chemco Corporation with another chemical company, why would you be interested in the accounting procedures used by the two companies?

8 Explain how the following accounting practices will tend to raise or lower the quality of a company's earnings. (Assume the continuance of inflation.)
  a Adoption of an accelerated depreciation method rather than straight-line depreciation.
  b Adoption of fifo rather than lifo for the valuation of inventories.
  c Adoption of a 7-year life rather than a 10-year life for the depreciation of equipment.

9 What single ratio do you think should be of greatest interest to:
  a a banker considering a short-term loan?
  b a common stockholder?
  c an insurance company considering a long-term mortgage loan?

10 Modern Company earned a 16% return on its total assets. Current liabilities are 10% of total assets. Long-term bonds carrying a 13% coupon rate are equal to 30% of total assets. There is no preferred stock. Would you expect the rate of return on stockholders' equity to be greater or less than 16%? Explain.

11 In deciding whether a company's equity ratio is favorable or unfavorable, creditors and stockholders may have different views. Why?

12 Company A has a current ratio of 3 to 1. Company B has a current ratio of 2 to 1. Does this mean that A's operating cycle is longer than B's? Why?

13 An investor states, "I bought this stock for $50 several years ago and it now sells for $100. It paid $5 per share in dividends last year so I'm earning 10% on my investment." Criticize this statement.

14 Company C experiences a considerable seasonal variation in its business. The high point in the year's activities comes in November, the low point in July. During which month would you expect the company's current ratio to be higher? If the company were choosing a fiscal year for accounting purposes, how would you advise them?

15 Both the inventory turnover and accounts receivable turnover increased from 10 times to 15 times from Year 1 to Year 2, but net income decreased. Can you offer some possible reasons for this?

16 Is the rate of return on investment (ROI) intended primarily to measure liquidity, solvency, or some other aspect of business operations? Explain.

17 Mention three financial amounts to which corporate profits can logically be compared in judging their adequacy or reasonableness.

18 Under what circumstances would you consider a corporate net income of $1,000,000 for the year as being unreasonably low? Under what circumstances would you consider a corporate profit of $1,000,000 as being unreasonably high?

EXERCISES

Ex. 16-1 Selected information taken from financial statements of Young Company for two successive years is shown below. Compute the percentage change from the base year to the following year whenever possible.

	Year 2	Year 1
a Cash	$ 36,000	$ 30,000
b Sales	325,000	250,000
c Retained earnings (deficit)	20,000	(10,000)
d Current liabilities	120,000	80,000
e Notes payable	60,000	–0–
f Accounts receivable	80,000	50,000
g Net income	20,000	25,000

Ex. 16-2 Prepare *common size* income statements for Hart Company, a single proprietorship, for the two years shown below by converting the dollar amounts into percentages. In each year, sales will appear as 100%, and other items will be expressed as a percentage of sales. Round the figures to the nearest tenth of one percent. (Income taxes are not involved since the business is not incorporated.)

HART COMPANY
Comparative Income Statements
For the Year Ended December 31, Years 1 and 2

	Year 2	Year 1
Sales	$500,000	$400,000
Cost of goods sold	330,000	256,000
Gross profit	$170,000	$144,000
Operating expenses	139,500	128,000
Net income	$ 30,500	$ 16,000

Ex. 16-3 The information below relates to the activities of a retail store. Since monthly figures are not provided, the average amounts for inventories and for accounts receivable may be based on the amounts shown for the beginning and end of Year 2.

	Year 2	Year 1
Sales (terms 2/10, n/30)	$480,000	$360,000
Cost of goods sold	312,000	252,000
Inventory at end of year	57,000	63,000
Accounts receivable at end of year	70,000	58,000

Compute the following for Year 2:
a Gross profit percentage
b Inventory turnover
c Accounts receivable turnover

Ex. 16-4 Given below is a condensed balance sheet for the Walnut Company:

Assets		Liabilities & Stockholders' Equity	
Cash	$ 30,000	Current liabilities	$ 75,000
Accounts receivable	60,000	Long-term liabilities	150,000
Inventory	135,000	Capital stock, $10 par	300,000
Prepaid expenses	45,000	Retained earnings	75,000
Plant assets (net)	300,000		
Other assets	30,000		
Totals	$600,000	Totals	$600,000

During the latest year, the company earned a gross profit of $480,000 on sales of $1,200,000. Accounts receivable, inventory, and plant assets remained relatively constant during the year. From this information, compute the following:
a Current ratio
b Acid-test ratio
c Equity ratio
d Asset turnover
e Accounts receivable turnover (all sales are on credit)
f Inventory turnover
g Book value per share of capital stock

Ex. 16-5 The following information is available for the Otis Corporation:

	Year 2	Year 1
Total assets (40% of which are current)	$400,000	$325,000
Current liabilities	$ 80,000	$100,000
Bonds payable, 12%	100,000	50,000
Capital stock, $10 stated value	150,000	150,000
Retained earnings	70,000	25,000
Total liabilities & stockholders' equity	$400,000	$325,000

The average income tax rate is 40% and dividends of $6,000 were declared and paid in Year 2. Compute the following:

a Current ratio for Year 2 and Year 1

b Debt ratio for Year 2 and Year 1

c Earnings per share for Year 2

Ex. 16-6 The following information relates to the operations of the Lava Corporation:

Sales (60% on credit)	$2,500,000
Beginning inventory, Year 1	350,000
Purchases	2,100,000
Ending inventory, Year 1	?
Ending accounts receivable, Year 1	150,000

The corporation's gross profit rate is 20%. Compute:

a The inventory turnover for Year 1.

b Accounts receivable turnover for Year 1.

Ex. 16-7 Figures for two companies engaged in the same line of business are presented below for the latest year:

	A Company	B Company
Sales (all on credit)	$1,600,000	$1,200,000
Total assets	800,000	400,000
Total liabilities	200,000	100,000
Average receivables	200,000	100,000
Average inventory	240,000	140,000
Gross profit as a percentage of sales	40%	30%
Operating expenses as a percentage of sales	37%	25%
Net income as a percentage of sales	3%	5%

Compute the following for each company:

a Net income

b Net income as a percentage of total assets

c Net income as a percentage of stockholders' equity

d Accounts receivable turnover

e Inventory turnover

PROBLEMS

16-1 The information listed below was taken from the financial statements of Harding Corporation. At the beginning of Year 5, the company began buying merchandise from a new supplier.

	Year 5	Year 4
Gross profit on sales	$292,500	$231,000
Net income as a percentage of sales	2%	3%
Net income	$ 15,000	$ 21,000
Income taxes as a percentage of income before income taxes	25%	25%

Instructions

a Compute the net sales for each year.

b Compute the cost of goods sold in dollars and as a percentage of sales for each year.

c Compute the federal income taxes for each year.

d Prepare a condensed comparative income statement for Years 4 and 5. Include the following items: sales, cost of goods sold, gross profit on sales, operating expenses, income before income taxes, income taxes, and net income.

e What favorable trends and unfavorable trends do you see in this year-to-year comparison of the income statement data of Harding Corporation? Comment on any unusual changes.

16-2   Harvest King manufactures and distributes farm machinery. Shown below for Year 1 are the income statement for the company and a common size summary for the industry in which the company operates:

	Harvest King	Industry Average
Sales (net)	$2,000,000	100%
Cost of goods sold	1,440,000	68
Gross profit on sales	$ 560,000	32%
Operating expenses:		
Selling	$ 160,000	7%
General and administrative	180,000	10
Total operating expenses	$ 340,000	17%
Operating income	$ 220,000	15%
Income taxes	88,000	6
Net income	$ 132,000	9%

Instructions

a Prepare a two-column common size income statement. The first column should show for Harvest King all items expressed as a percentage of net sales. (Round all figures to the nearest whole percent.) The second column should show as an industry average the percentage data given in the problem. The purpose of this common size statement is to compare the operating results of Harvest King for Year 1 with the average for the industry.

b Comment specifically on differences between Harvest King and the industry average with respect to gross profit on sales, selling expenses, general and administrative expenses, operating income, income taxes, and net income. Suggest possible reasons for the more important disparities.

16-3   The following information is taken from the records of Frost Corporation at the end of Year 1:

Sales (all on credit)	$600,000
Cost of goods sold	360,000
Average inventory (fifo method)	60,000
Average accounts receivable	100,000
Interest expense	6,000

Income taxes expense	7,000
Net income for Year 1	24,000
Total assets	250,000
Total liabilities	140,000

The corporation did not declare dividends during the year and capital stock was neither issued nor retired.

Instructions From the information given, compute the following for Year 1: (Any answers expressed as percentages should be rounded to the nearest percent.)
a Inventory turnover.
b Accounts receivable turnover.
c Total operating expenses. (Interest expense and income taxes are *not* operating expenses.)
d Gross profit percentage.
e Rate earned on average stockholders' equity. Average stockholders' equity should be computed as the average of two amounts: (1) stockholders' equity at the beginning of Year 1, and (2) stockholders' equity at the end of Year 1. Both these amounts can be derived from information given in the problem.
f Rate earned on total assets. (Use end-of-year total.)
g Frost Corporation has an opportunity to obtain a long-term loan at an annual interest rate of 15% and could use this additional capital at the same rate of profitability as indicated above. Would obtaining the loan be desirable from the viewpoint of the stockholders? Explain.

16-4 At the end of Year 5, the following information was obtained from the accounting records of Craftsman Clocks.

Sales (all on credit)	$900,000
Cost of goods sold	585,000
Average inventory (fifo method)	117,000
Average accounts receivable	100,000
Interest expense	15,000
Income taxes	18,000
Net income for Year 5	63,000
Total assets	600,000
Total liabilities	253,500

The company declared no dividends of any kind during the year and did not issue or retire any capital stock.

Instructions From the information given, compute the following for Year 5:
a Inventory turnover.
b Accounts receivable turnover.
c Total operating expenses. (Interest expense is a nonoperating expense.)
d Gross profit percentage.

e Rate earned on average stockholders' equity. Average stockholders' equity should be computed as the average of two amounts: (1) stockholders' equity at the beginning of Year 5, and (2) stockholders' equity at the end of Year 5. Both these amounts can be derived from information given in the problem.

f Rate earned on total assets. (Use end-of-year total.)

g Craftsman Clocks has an opportunity to obtain a long-term loan at an annual interest rate of 11% and could use this additional capital at the same rate of profitability as indicated for Year 5. Would obtaining the loan be desirable from the viewpoint of the stockholders? Explain.

16-5 Listed in the left-hand column below is a series of business transactions and events relating to the activities of Potomac Mills. Opposite each transaction is listed a particular ratio used in financial analysis:

Transaction	Ratio
(1) Purchased inventory on open account.	Quick ratio
(2) A larger physical volume of goods was sold at smaller unit prices.	Gross profit percentage
(3) Corporation declared a cash dividend.	Current ratio
(4) An uncollectible account receivable was written off against the allowance account.	Current ratio
(5) Issued additional shares of common stock and used proceeds to retire long-term debt.	Debt ratio
(6) Paid stock dividend on common stock, in common stock.	Earnings per share
(7) Conversion of a portion of bonds payable into common stock. (Ignore income taxes.)	Times interest charges earned
(8) Appropriated retained earnings.	Rate of return on stockholders' equity
(9) During period of rising prices, company changed from fifo to lifo method of inventory pricing.	Inventory turnover
(10) Paid a previously declared cash dividend.	Debt ratio
(11) Purchased factory supplies on open account.	Current ratio (assume that ratio is greater than 1:1)
(12) Issued shares of capital stock in exchange for patents.	Equity ratio

Instructions What effect would each transaction or event have on the ratio listed opposite to it; that is, as a result of this event would the ratio increase, decrease, or remain unchanged? Your answer for each of the 12 transactions should include a brief explanation.

16-6 Listed below is the working capital information for the Washington Corporation at the end of Year 1:

Cash	$225,000
Temporary investments in marketable securities	120,000
Notes receivable—current	180,000
Accounts receivable	300,000
Allowance for doubtful accounts	15,000
Inventory	240,000
Prepaid expenses	30,000
Notes payable within one year	90,000
Accounts payable	247,500
Accrued liabilities	22,500

The following transactions are completed early in Year 2:
(0) Sold inventory costing $36,000 for a reduced price of $30,000.
(1) Declared a cash dividend, $120,000.
(2) Declared a 10% stock dividend.
(3) Paid accounts payable, $60,000.
(4) Purchased goods on account, $45,000.
(5) Collected cash on accounts receivable, $90,000.
(6) Borrowed cash on short-term note, $150,000.
(7) Issued additional shares of capital stock for cash, $450,000.
(8) Sold temporary investments costing $30,000 for $27,000 cash.
(9) Acquired temporary investments, $52,500. Paid cash.
(10) Wrote off uncollectible accounts, $9,000, against the allowance account.
(11) Sold inventory costing $37,500 for $48,000.
(12) Acquired plant and equipment for cash, $240,000.

Instructions
a Compute the amount of quick assets, current assets, and current liabilities at the end of Year 1.

b Use the data compiled in part **a** to compute: (1) current ratio; (2) acid-test ratio; and (3) working capital at the end of Year 1.

c Indicate the effect (increase, decrease, none) of each transaction listed above for *Year 2* on the current ratio, acid-test ratio, and working capital. Use the following four-column format (item *0* is given as an example):

	Effect on		
Item	**Current Ratio**	**Acid-Test Ratio**	**Working Capital**
0	Decrease	Increase	Decrease

16-7 The financial information shown on page 656 for Continental Transfer Co. and American Van Lines (except market price per share of stock) is stated in *thousands of dollars.* The figures are as of the end of the current year. The two companies are in the same industry and are quite similar as to operations, facilities, and accounting methods. Assume that both companies pay income taxes equal to 50% of income before income taxes.

Assets	Continental Transfer Co.	American Van Lines
Current assets	$ 97,450	$132,320
Plant and equipment	397,550	495,680
Less: Accumulated depreciation	(55,000)	(78,000)
Total assets	$440,000	$550,000

Liabilities & Stockholders' Equity		
Current liabilities	$ 34,000	$ 65,000
Bonds payable, 12%, due in 15 years	120,000	100,000
Capital stock, no par	150,000	200,000
Retained earnings	136,000	185,000
Total liabilities & stockholders' equity	$440,000	$550,000

Analysis of retained earnings:		
Balance, beginning of year	$125,200	$167,200
Net income for the year	19,800	37,400
Dividends	(9,000)	(19,600)
Balance, end of year	$136,000	$185,000
Market price of capital stock, per share	$30	$61
Number of shares of capital stock outstanding	6 million	8 million

Instructions

a Compute for each company:
  (1) The number of times bond interest was earned during the current year. (Remember to use *available income* rather than net income in determining the coverage of interest expense. Add back to net income both income taxes and bond interest.)
  (2) The debt ratio.

b In the light of the information developed in **a** above, write a paragraph indicating which company's bonds you think would trade in the market at the higher price. Which would probably provide the higher yield? Explain how the ratios developed influence your answer. (It may be assumed that the bonds were issued several years ago and are traded on an organized securities exchange.)

c For each company compute the dividend yield, the price-earnings ratio, and the book value per share. (Show supporting computations to determine dividends per share. Remember that dollar amounts in the problem are in thousands of dollars, that is, three zeros omitted.) In determining the price-earnings ratios, you must first compute earnings per share. Show this computation in a supporting note.

d Express an opinion, based on the data developed in **c** above, as to which company's stock is a better investment at the present market price.

BUSINESS DECISION PROBLEM 16

Holiday Greeting Cards is a local company organized late in July of Year 1. The company's net income for each of its first six calendar quarters of operations is summarized on the next page. The amounts are stated in thousands of dollars.

	Year 2	Year 1
First quarter (January through March)	$ 253	—
Second quarter (April through June)	308	—
Third quarter (July through September)	100	$ 50
Fourth quarter (October through December)	450	500
Total for the calendar year	$1,111	$550

Glen Wallace reports the business and economic news for a local radio station. On the day that Holiday Greeting Cards released the above financial information, you heard Wallace make the following statement during his broadcast: "Holiday Greeting Cards enjoyed a 350% increase in its profits for the fourth quarter, and profits for the entire year were up by over 100%."

Instructions

a Show the computations that Wallace probably made in arriving at his statistics. (Hint: Wallace did not make his computations in the manner recommended in this chapter. His figures, however, can be developed from the financial data above.)

b Do you believe that Wallace's percentage changes present a realistic impression of Holiday Greeting Cards' rate of growth in Year 2? Explain.

c What figure would you use to express the percentage change in Holiday's fourth quarter profits in Year 2? Explain why you would compute the change in this manner.

17

INCOME TAXES AND BUSINESS DECISIONS

After studying this chapter you should be able to:

- Differentiate between tax planning and tax evasion.
- Explain the progressive nature of income tax rates.
- Explain the formula for determining the taxable income of an individual.
- Explain the income tax treatment of capital gains and losses.
- Distinguish between a tax deduction and a tax credit.
- Determine the income tax liability of an individual.
- Contrast the determination of taxable income for a corporation with that for an individual.
- Explain the concept of interperiod income tax allocation.
- Discuss the tax considerations in choosing a form of business entity and in designing its capital structure.

"A penny saved is a penny earned," according to an old saying credited to Benjamin Franklin. However, now that many individuals are subject to approximately a 50% income tax rate, we can modify this bit of folklore to read: "A dollar of income tax saved is worth two dollars of income earned."

In other words, almost half of what a corporation earns, and half of what some individuals earn, must be paid to the federal government as income taxes. If advance tax planning will enable an individual to save a dollar of income taxes, that dollar saved may be the equivalent of two dollars of before-tax earnings. Furthermore, there are a good many perfectly legal actions which can be taken to save or at least to postpone income taxes.

COURSE REQUEST FORM FOR (Fall / Spring) SEMESTER

NAME _Jim Muehlhausen_   ID .._137-531-7_..

INDICATE COURSES DESIRED BY WRITING IN THE APPROPRIATE DEPARTMENTAL INFORMATION AS NOTED
BELOW: FOR DEPARTMENT ABBREVIATIONS, SEE THE LIST OF PROPOSED COURSES.

DEPT.	NO.	SECTION
ACCT	55	C ✓
GLM	62	AB ✓
CS	91	
ECON	123	
ENG	25	M
PE	10	
......	......	

Jim Muehlhausen
Student signature

M M Martin
Advisor signature

WHITE COPY -- to be returned to the registrar or academic dean.
YELLOW COPY -- to be retained by the student as a reference for registration.
PINK COPY -- to be retained by the advisor.

Tax planning

Individuals who plan their business affairs in a manner that will result in the lowest possible income tax are acting rationally and legally. They are using the techniques called *tax planning*. In the words of a distinguished jurist, Judge Learned Hand:

> Over and over again courts have said that there is nothing sinister in so arranging one's affairs as to keep taxes as low as possible. Everybody does so, rich or poor; and all do right, for nobody owes any public duty to pay more than the law demands: taxes are enforced exactions, not voluntary contributions. To demand more in the name of morals is mere cant.

To reduce and to postpone income taxes are the goals of tax planning. Almost every business decision involves a choice among alternative courses of action. For example, should we lease or buy business automobiles; should we obtain needed capital by issuing bonds or preferred stock; should we use straight-line depreciation or an accelerated method? Some of these alternatives will lead to much lower income taxes than others. Tax planning, therefore, means *determining in advance the income tax effect* of every proposed business action and then making business decisions which will lead to the smallest tax liability. Tax practice is an important element of the services furnished to clients by CPA firms. This service includes not only the computing of taxes and preparing of tax returns, but also tax planning.

Tax planning must begin early. Unfortunately, some people wait until the end of the year and then, faced with the prospect of paying a large amount of income tax, ask their accountants what can be done to reduce the tax liability. If we are to arrange transactions in a manner that will lead to the minimum income tax liability, the tax planning must be carried out *before* the date of a transaction, not after it is an accomplished fact. Because it is important for everyone to recognize areas in which tax savings may be substantial, a few of the major opportunities for tax planning are discussed in the final section of this chapter.

Tax avoidance and tax evasion

Newspaper stories tell us each year of some taxpayers who have deliberately understated their taxable income by failing to report a portion of income received or by claiming fictitious deductions such as an excess number of personal exemptions. Such purposeful understatement of taxable income is called *tax evasion* and is, of course, illegal. On the other hand, *tax avoidance* (the arranging of business and financial affairs in a manner that will minimize tax liability) is entirely legal.

The critical importance of income taxes

Taxes levied by federal, state, and local governments are a significant part of the cost of operating a typical household, as well as a business enterprise. The knowledge required to be expert in taxation has made it a field of specialization among professional accountants. However, every manager who makes business decisions, and every individual who makes personal investments, urgently needs some knowledge of income taxes. A general knowledge of income taxes will help any business manager or owner to benefit more fully from the advice of the professional tax accountant.

Some understanding of income taxes will also aid the individual citizen in voting intelligently, because a great many of the issues decided in every election have tax implications. Such issues as pollution, inflation, foreign policy, and employment are quite closely linked with income taxes. For example, the offering of special tax incentives to encourage businesses to launch massive programs to reduce pollution is one approach to protection of the environment.

In terms of revenue generated, the four most important kinds of taxes in the United States are *income taxes, sales taxes, property taxes,* and *excise taxes.* Income taxes exceed all others in terms of the amounts involved, and they also exert a pervasive influence on all types of business decisions. For this reason we shall limit our discussion to the basic federal income tax rules applicable to individuals, partnerships, and corporations.

Income taxes are usually determined from information contained in accounting records. The amount of income tax is computed by applying the appropriate tax rates (as set by federal, state, and some local governments) to *taxable income.* As explained more fully later in this chapter, *taxable income* is not necessarily the same as *accounting income* even though both are derived from the accounting records. Business managers can influence the amount of taxes they pay by their choice of form of business organization, methods of financing, and alternative accounting methods. Thus income taxes are inevitably an important factor in arriving at business decisions.

The federal income tax: history and objectives

The present federal income tax dates from the passage of the Sixteenth Amendment to the Constitution in 1913.[1] This amendment, only 30 words in length,[2] removed all questions of the constitutionality of income taxes and paved the way for the more than 50 revenue acts passed by Congress since that date. In 1939 these tax laws were first combined into what is known as the Internal Revenue Code. The administration and enforcement of the tax laws are duties of the Treasury Department, operating through a division known as the Internal Revenue Service (IRS). The Treasury Department publishes its interpretation of the tax laws in Treasury regulations; the final word in interpretation lies with the federal courts.

---

[1] A federal income tax was proposed as early as 1815, and an income tax law was actually passed and income taxes collected during the Civil War. This law was upheld by the Supreme Court, but it was repealed when the need for revenue subsided after the war. In 1894 a new income tax law was passed, but the Supreme Court declared this law invalid on constitutional grounds.

[2] It reads "The Congress shall have power to lay and collect taxes on incomes, from whatever source derived, without apportionment among the several States, and without regard to any census or enumeration."

Originally the purpose of the federal income tax was simply to obtain revenue for the government. And at first, the tax rates were quite low—by today's standards. In 1913 a married person with taxable income of $15,000 would have been subject to a tax rate of 1%, resulting in a tax liability of $150. Today, a married person with a $15,000 taxable income (worth far less in purchasing power) would pay over $2,000 in federal income tax. The maximum federal income tax rate in 1913 was 7%. Today it is 50%.

The purpose of federal income tax now includes several goals apart from raising revenue. Examples of these other goals are: influencing the rate of economic growth, encouraging full employment, combatting inflation, favoring small businesses, and redistributing national income on a more equal basis.

Classes of taxpayers

In the eyes of the income tax law, there are four major classes of taxpayers: *individuals, corporations, estates,* and *trusts.* Proprietorships and partnerships are not taxed as business units; their income is taxed directly to the individual proprietor or partners, *whether or not actually withdrawn from the business.* A single proprietor reports his or her business income on an individual tax return; the members of a partnership include on their individual tax returns their respective shares of the partnership net income. An individual taxpayer's income tax return must include not only any business income from a proprietorship or partnership, but also any salary or other income and any deductions affecting the tax liability. A partnership must file an *information return* showing the computation of total partnership net income and the allocation of this income to each partner.

A corporation is a separate taxable entity; it must file a corporate income tax return and pay a tax on its annual taxable income. In addition, individual stockholders must report dividends received from corporations as part of their personal taxable income. The taxing of corporate dividends has led to the charge that there is "double taxation" of corporate income—once to the corporation and again when it is distributed to stockholders.

The *income before taxes* earned by a corporation may be subject to a federal corporate income tax rate of 46%. To illustrate, let us consider the tax impact on one dollar of corporate earnings. First the corporation pays 46%, or 46 cents, out of the dollar to the Internal Revenue Service. That leaves 54 cents for the corporation. Next, assume that the 54 cents is distributed as dividends to individual stockholders. The dividend will be taxed to the stockholders personally at rates varying from 12 to 50%, depending on their individual tax brackets. Thus, the 54 cents of after-tax income to the corporation could be reduced by 50%, or 27 cents of individual income tax, leaving 27 cents of the original dollar for the shareholder. In summary, *federal income taxes can take as much as 73 cents out of a dollar earned by a corporation and distributed as a dividend to a shareholder.* The remaining 27 cents could be reduced further by state income taxes.

Special and complex rules apply to the determination of taxable income for estates and trusts. These rules will not be discussed in this chapter.

Cash basis of accounting for income tax returns

Almost all *individual* income tax returns are prepared on the cash basis of accounting. Many small service-type business concerns and professional firms also choose to prepare their tax returns on the cash basis. Revenue is recognized when collected in cash; expenses (except depreciation) are recognized when a cash payment is made. The cash basis (as prescribed in IRS rules) does not permit expenditures for plant and equipment to be deducted in the year of purchase. These capital expenditures are capitalized and depreciated for tax purposes, as previously discussed in Chapter 10. Also, the income tax laws do not permit use of the cash basis by companies in which inventories and the sale of merchandise are significant factors.

Although the cash basis of accounting does not measure income satisfactorily in the context of generally accepted accounting principles, it has much merit in the area of taxation. From the government's viewpoint, the logical time to collect tax on income is when the taxpayer receives the income in cash. At any earlier date, the taxpayer may not have the cash to pay income taxes; at any later date, the cash may have been used for other purposes.

The cash basis is advantageous for the individual taxpayer and for service-type businesses for several reasons. It is simple, and requires a minimum of records. The income of most individuals comes in the form of salaries, interest, and dividends. At the end of each year, an individual receives from his or her employer a W-2 form (page 507) showing the salary earned and income tax withheld during the year. This report is prepared on a cash basis without any accrual of unpaid wages. Persons receiving interest or dividends also receive from the paying companies Form 1099 summarizing amounts received for the year. Thus, most individuals are provided with reports prepared on a cash basis for use in preparing their individual tax returns.

The cash basis has other advantages for the individual taxpayer and for many professional firms and service-type businesses. It often permits tax savings by individuals who deliberately shift the timing of revenue and expense transactions from one year to another. For example, a dentist whose taxable income is higher than usual in the current year may decide in December to delay billing patients until January 1, and thus postpone the receipt of gross income to the next year. The timing of *expense payments* near year-end is also controllable by a taxpayer using the cash basis. A taxpayer who has received a bill for a deductible expense item in December may choose to pay it before or after December 31 and thereby influence the amount of taxable income in each year.

Any taxpayer who maintains a set of accounting records may *elect* to use the accrual basis in preparing a tax return, but very few taxpayers (individual or corporate) choose to do so if they are eligible to use the cash basis.

Tax rates

All taxes may be characterized as progressive, proportional, or regressive with respect to any given base. A *progressive* tax becomes a larger portion of the base as that base increases. Federal income taxes are *progressive* with respect to income, since a higher tax *rate* applies as the amount of taxable income increases. A *proportional* tax remains a constant percentage of the base no matter how that base changes. For example, a 6% sales tax remains a constant percentage of sales regardless of changes in the dollar amount of sales. A *regressive* tax becomes a smaller percentage of the base as the base increases. Regressive taxes, however, are extremely rare.

In 1981 the top tax rate on individuals was set at 50% on all types of income. The 50% maximum rate had applied to salaries for several years before that, but the tax rate on interest, dividends, rent, and other "unearned" income had been 70%. In the 1960s, the tax rates on individuals reached as high as 90%. When tax rates reach 70%, 80%, or 90%, the incentive to save and invest is greatly reduced. Little remains for the investor under such extreme tax rates.

Tax rate schedules

On pages 664 and 665 we have tax rate schedules for single taxpayers and for married taxpayers filing joint returns. Tax rates for individuals at present vary from 12 to 50%, depending on the amount of income. Persons with very low incomes pay no income tax. Different tax rate schedules apply to (1) single taxpayers, (2) married taxpayers filing joint returns, (3) married taxpayers filing separate returns, and (4) single taxpayers who qualify as the head of a household. In computing the amount of the tax, the tax rates are applied to *taxable income,* a term which means gross income less certain exclusions and deductions specified in the tax law. Income tax rates are subject to *frequent revision* by Congress; in fact, a revision was under consideration by Congress at the time this was written.

The steeply progressive nature of income taxes

To illustrate the steeply progressive nature of income taxes, let us compare two single taxpayers, one of whom has a relatively low income and the other a relatively high income. Assume that Tom Jones has taxable income of $5,000 a year and Mary Smith has taxable income of $50,000 a year. According to the tax rate schedule on page 664, Jones would owe tax of $368 and Smith would owe tax of $16,318. The tax owed by Jones is about 7% of his total taxable income of $5,000; the tax owed by Smith is about 33% of her total taxable income of $50,000.

Next, let us consider how much additional income tax each of these two individuals would have to pay on any additional income. According to the tax rate schedules, an increase of $100 in income for Jones would be taxed at 16%. However, an increase of $100 in income for Smith would be taxed at 50%.

Supporters of a highly progressive income tax argue that the system is fair because the taxpayers most able to pay are subject to the highest rates. Critics contend that the high rates on high incomes discourage individual initiative and penalize productivity. Another criticism is that high tax rates lead to an increasing amount of violation with a significant part of economic transactions going "underground."

Single Taxpayers			
Taxable Income		Tax	
Not over $2,300		–0–	
Over—	But not over—		of the amount over—
$2,300	$3,400	12%	$2,300
$3,400	$4,400	$132 + 14%	$3,400
$4,400	$6,500	$272 + 16%	$4,400
$6,500	$8,500	$608 + 17%	$6,500
$8,500	$10,800	$948 + 19%	$8,500
$10,800	$12,900	$1,385 + 22%	$10,800
$12,900	$15,000	$1,847 + 23%	$12,900
$15,000	$18,200	$2,330 + 27%	$15,000
$18,200	$23,500	$3,194 + 31%	$18,200
$23,500	$28,800	$4,837 + 35%	$23,500
$28,800	$34,100	$6,692 + 40%	$28,800
$34,100	$41,500	$8,812 + 44%	$34,100
$41,500	......	$12,068 + 50%	$41,500

Example: Find the tax for a single person having taxable income of $21,000.

Answer: Tax on $18,200 as shown on tax rate schedule $3,194

Tax on $2,800 excess at 31% 868

Tax on $21,000 for a single person $4,062

Marginal tax rates compared with average tax rates

In any analysis of income taxes, it is important to distinguish the *marginal* rate of tax from the taxpayer's *average* rate. The marginal rate is the rate that will apply to the next dollar of income to be earned. For example, assume that you are an unmarried executive with a taxable income of $34,100 and are considering changing to a new job that will pay $5,000 more per year in salary. Using the tax rate schedule above, your present tax is $8,812, an average rate of about 26%. However, your marginal tax rate on the proposed $5,000 salary increase is 44%. Your decision with respect to the new job may well be affected by the fact that you would be able to keep only slightly more than half ($2,800) of the $5,000 increase in salary.

Another way of looking at the impact of income taxes is from the viewpoint of the employer. A company that wants to increase the salary of an executive must pay about $2 for every $1 to be received by the executive in take-home pay.

The marginal tax rate is important in many business decisions. Often the decision is whether to invest additional money or to expend additional time and effort in order to earn an increased amount of income. However, an increase in income will cause an increase in income taxes *at the marginal rate*. The *after-tax* result of a proposed investment must be estimated by using the marginal tax

Married Taxpayers Filing Joint Returns			
Taxable Income		**Tax**	
Not over $3,400		–0–	
Over—	**But not over—**		**of the amount over—**
$3,400	$5,500	12%	$3,400
$5,500	$7,600	$252 + 14%	$5,500
$7,600	$11,900	$546 + 16%	$7,600
$11,900	$16,000	$1,234 + 19%	$11,900
$16,000	$20,200	$2,013 + 22%	$16,000
$20,200	$24,600	$2,937 + 25%	$20,200
$24,600	$29,900	$4,037 + 29%	$24,600
$29,900	$35,200	$5,574 + 33%	$29,900
$35,200	$45,800	$7,323 + 39%	$35,200
$45,800	$60,000	$11,457 + 44%	$45,800
$60,000	$85,600	$17,705 + 49%	$60,000
$85,600	......	$30,249 + 50%	$85,600

Example: **Find the tax for a married couple filing a joint return and having a taxable income of $50,000.**

Answer: **Tax on $45,800 as shown on tax rate schedule** **$11,457**

Tax on $4,200 excess at 44% **1,848**

Tax on $50,000 for a married couple filing a joint return **$13,305**

rate, and not the average tax rate. In other words, the attractiveness of an extra dollar of income depends on the marginal tax rate applicable to that particular dollar.

Income taxes and inflation

As salaries and prices in general have risen sharply in recent years, people find themselves in higher income tax brackets even though their higher salaries represent no increase in purchasing power. Because income tax rates are steeply progressive, this means that many people must pay a *higher percentage* of their earnings as income taxes solely as a result of inflation. Thus, income taxes are actually being increased in each year of inflation even though the schedule of tax rates remains unchanged. A $20,000 salary may buy no more today than a $10,000 salary some years ago, but a $20,000 salary is taxed at a much higher rate.

In 1981 Congress passed indexing legislation designed to prevent tax increases based solely on inflation. The law provides that beginning in 1985, the tax brackets, personal exemption, and the zero bracket amount (see page 669) will be increased to reflect annual changes in the Consumer Price Index.

Income tax formula for individuals

The federal government supplies standard income tax forms on which taxpayers are guided to a proper computation of their taxable income and the amount of the tax. It is helpful to visualize the computation in terms of an income tax formula. The general formula for the determination of taxable income for all taxpayers is outlined on the next page.

The actual sequence and presentation of material on income tax forms differs somewhat from the arrangement in this formula. However, it is easier to understand the structure and logic of the federal income tax and to analyze tax rules and their effect by referring to the tax formula.

Total income and gross income

Total income is an accounting concept; gross income is a tax concept. *Total income* includes, in the words of the law, "all income from whatever source derived." To determine whether an amount received by an individual taxpayer should be included in total income, one need only ask, "Is it income or is it a return of capital?"

Gross income for tax purposes is all income not excluded by law. Gross income therefore includes salaries, commissions, bonuses, dividends, interest, rent, and gains from sale of securities, real estate, and other property. To determine whether any given income item is included in gross income, one must ask, "Is there a provision in the tax law excluding this item of income from gross income?" Among the items *currently excluded from gross income* by statute are interest on state and municipal bonds, gifts and inheritances, life insurance proceeds, workmen's compensation, social security benefits and the portion of receipts from annuities that represents return of cost, pensions to veterans, compensation for damages, and the first $100 of dividends received ($200 on a joint tax return).

Among the items of miscellaneous income which must be *included* in gross income are prizes and awards won, tips received, and gains from sale of personal property. The fact that income arises from an illegal transaction does not keep it from being taxable.

Deductions to arrive at adjusted gross income

The deductions from *gross income* allowed in computing *adjusted gross income* are discussed below:

1 **Business expenses of a single proprietorship** These include all ordinary and necessary expenses of carrying on a trade, business, or profession (other than as an employee). For the actual tax computation, business expenses are deducted from business revenue, and net business income is then included in adjusted gross income.

2 **Business expenses of an employee** Some expenses incurred by employees in connection with their employment are allowed as a deduction if the employees

General Federal Income Tax Formula for Individuals

Use this formula to compute taxable income for individuals

Total Income —— All income and gains from whatever source derived

minus

Exclusions —— Income excluded by law from taxation (see list of items on page 666)

equals

Gross Income —— Income before deductions and exemptions listed below

minus

Deductions to Arrive at Adjusted Gross Income —— Business-related expenses and losses; 60% of net long-term capital gains; contribution to retirement plans; two-earner married couples (see discussion on pages 668–669)

equals

Adjusted Gross Income —— Significant because several deductible items are computed as a percentage of it

minus

Excess Itemized Deductions from Adjusted Gross Income —— Itemized deductions allowed by law (see pages 669–670) after being reduced by a standard amount

and minus

Personal Exemptions —— A deduction of $1,000 each for taxpayer, spouse, and dependents; an additional $1,000 for taxpayers over sixty-five years of age and for taxpayers who are blind

equals

Taxable Income —— Amount to which appropriate tax rates are applied

are not reimbursed by the employer. These include, for example, travel and transportation as part of employees' duties, expenses of "outside salespersons," and certain moving expenses. The costs of commuting from home to work are not deductible.

3 **Expenses attributable to rental properties** The owner of rental property, such as an apartment building, incurs a variety of operating expenses. Depreciation, property taxes, repairs, maintenance, interest on indebtedness related to

property, and any other expense incurred in connection with the earning of rental income are allowed as a deduction. This means that only the *net income* derived from rental property is included in adjusted gross income.

4 **Losses from the sale of property used in business** The loss resulting from the sale of property used in a trade or business may be deducted against other items of gross income.[3]

5 **Net capital losses** Up to $3,000 of net capital losses may be deducted to arrive at adjusted gross income. Capital gains and losses are discussed on pages 671–673.

6 **Long-term capital gain deduction** Sixty percent of the excess of net long-term capital gains over net short-term capital losses is a deduction to arrive at adjusted gross income. In other words, only 40% of a long-term capital gain is taxable.

7 **Net operating loss carry-over** Taxable income may be either positive or negative. If positive income were taxed and no allowance made for operating losses, a taxpayer whose business income fluctuated between income and loss would pay a relatively higher tax than one having a steady income averaging the same amount. Therefore, the tax law allows the carry-back and carry-over of net operating losses as an offset against the income of other years. At the present time a loss may be carried back against the income of the three preceding years, and then forward against the income of the next seven years.

8 **Contributions to retirement plans** Individuals who are *self-employed* are permitted to deduct from gross income the amounts they contribute to a retirement plan. The present limit on such contributions is the lower of $15,000 or 15% of the self-employed person's annual earnings. By taking a deduction for this contribution, a self-employed person earning $100,000 or more can reduce adjusted gross income by as much as $15,000 each year. The amounts contributed plus earnings on the fund are taxable when the taxpayer retires and begins making withdrawals from the fund. This type of retirement plan (often referred to as a *Keogh H.R.10 plan*) is intended to provide self-employed persons with opportunities similar to those of persons employed by organizations with pension or retirement plans.

Another type of retirement plan (distinct from the Keogh H.R.10 plan) is available to both employees and self-employed persons. This plan, called an Individual Retirement Arrangement (IRA), permits anyone with earned income to contribute to the plan and to deduct from gross income as much as $2,000 of compensation received.

9 **Deduction for two-earner married couples** Under the tax rate schedules in effect before 1982, a two-earner married couple was subject to a higher tax than would have been imposed if they were single and the lower-earning spouse provided at least 20% of the combined incomes. This aspect of the tax laws was referred to as the "marriage penalty" and was subject to much criticism. New legislation has now provided some relief through a new deduc-

---

[3]Losses arising from the sale of personal property, such as a home or personal automobile, are not deductible. On the other hand, gains from the sale of personal property are taxable. This appears inconsistent, until one realizes that a loss on the sale of personal property usually reflects depreciation through use, which is a personal expense.

tion in computing adjusted gross income for married couples. The deduction is limited to 10% of the lower-earning spouse's earned income up to $30,000; thus, the maximum deduction is $3,000 a year.

Deductions from adjusted gross income (itemized deductions)

Remember that there are two basic groups of deductions for individuals: (1) items deductible from gross income to arrive at adjusted gross income and (2) items deductible from adjusted gross income to arrive at taxable income. We are now considering the second group of items (such as charitable contributions, interest on home mortgage, and sales taxes) which an individual may deduct *from* adjusted gross income. These items are referred to as *itemized deductions.*

The importance of itemizing deductions lies in the fact that every deduction reduces the income subject to tax. The taxpayer should retain documentary evidence supporting the deductions claimed.

Zero bracket amount   For many years taxpayers were permitted to take a standard deduction computed as a percentage of adjusted gross income. This standard deduction was based on the concept that all taxpayers could be expected to claim some deductions, such as interest expense and charitable contributions. As an alternative to taking the standard deduction, taxpayers could *itemize* their deductions. The extra work to itemize deductions was worthwhile if the total was more than the standard deduction. In recent years the tax laws have been changed to provide a new *zero bracket amount* which replaced the standard deduction. This zero bracket amount was built into the tax tables in order to simplify the computation of tax liability. The result is to assure a given amount of tax-free income to all taxpayers. Presently, the zero bracket amount is $3,400 for married taxpayers filing a joint return, and $2,300 for single taxpayers. In effect, the law is assuming that every taxpayer could claim at least $2,300 of deductions ($3,400 if married); therefore the proof of those amounts need not be submitted. The zero bracket amount automatically allows for them.

Excess itemized deductions   We have seen that the zero bracket amount is the equivalent of a standard deduction from adjusted gross income. The amount of income subject to tax can be reduced further by single taxpayers who itemize deductions in excess of $2,300 and by married taxpayers filing a joint return who itemize deductions in excess of $3,400. In other words, a reduction in tax is possible if a taxpayer has relatively large amounts of such items as contributions, interest, and property taxes, and the combined amount of these itemized deductions is in excess of the zero bracket amount. The term *excess itemized deductions* means the excess of itemized deductions over the zero bracket amount.

The major categories of itemized deductions allowable under the law are described below and on the following page.

1 Interest   Interest on any indebtedness, within certain limits.

2 Taxes   State and local real and personal property taxes, state income taxes, and all sales taxes are deductible by the person on whom they are imposed. No federal taxes qualify as itemized deductions.

3 Contributions Contributions by individuals to charitable, religious, educational, and certain other nonprofit organizations are deductible, within certain limits. Gifts to friends, relatives, or other persons are not deductible.

4 Medical expenses Medical and dental expenses of the taxpayer and his or her family are deductible to the extent that they exceed 3% of adjusted gross income, subject to certain maximum limits, and limits on the deductibility of drugs and medicines. A taxpayer may deduct one-half of medical insurance costs up to $150 without regard to the 3% exclusion.

5 Casualty losses Losses in excess of $100 from any fire, storm, earthquake, theft, or other sudden, unexpected, or unusual causes are deductible.

6 Expenses related to the production of income In this category are included any necessary expenses in producing income or for the management of income-producing property, other than those deductible to arrive at adjusted gross income. Some examples of *miscellaneous deductible expenses* are union dues, work clothes, professional dues, subscriptions to professional periodicals, investment advisers' fees, legal fees relating to investments, fees paid to employment agencies to get a job, and fees for income tax advice and for preparation of tax returns. Examples of *miscellaneous nondeductible expenses* are the cost of going to and from work, gifts to needy friends, most living expenses, babysitting expenses, gasoline taxes, the cost of school tuition, and gambling losses in excess of gambling winnings.

Personal exemptions

In addition to itemized deductions, a deduction from adjusted gross income is allowed for *personal exemptions.* One exemption each is allowed for the taxpayer, the taxpayer's spouse, and each person who qualifies as a dependent of the taxpayer. At present the amount of each personal exemption is $1,000. The amount of the personal exemption may be changed by Congress at any time.

The term *dependent* has a particular meaning under tax law. Briefly stated, a dependent is a person who (1) receives over one-half of his or her support from the taxpayer, (2) is either closely related to the taxpayer or lives in the taxpayer's home, and (3) has gross income during the year of less than the current exemption amount unless he or she is a child of the taxpayer and is under nineteen years of age or is a full-time student.[4] A taxpayer and spouse may each claim an additional personal exemption if sixty-five years of age or over, and another exemption if blind. These additional exemptions do not apply to dependents.

Taxpayers who use the tax tables (described later in this chapter) must determine the *number* of personal exemptions to which they are entitled in order to select the appropriate column in the tax tables. However they do not use the $1,000 deduction *amount,* because these amounts have been taken into account in constructing the tax tables. The personal exemption, unlike itemized deductions, does not require any record keeping as supporting evidence.

---

[4]A child under nineteen or a full-time student who qualifies as a dependent in all other respects but who earns over the current exemption amount in any one year has, in effect, two personal exemptions. One may be taken by the taxpayer who claims him or her as a dependent; the other he will claim for himself on his own personal income tax return.

Taxable income

We have now traced the steps required to determine the taxable income of an individual. In brief, this process includes:

1 Computation of total income
2 Exclusion of certain items specified by law to determine gross income
3 Deduction of business-related expenses to arrive at adjusted gross income
4 Deduction of excess itemized deductions and personal exemptions to arrive at the key figure of taxable income.

The concept of taxable income is most important because it is the amount to which the appropriate tax rate is applied to determine the tax liability.

Capital gains and losses

Certain kinds of property are defined under the tax law as capital assets.[5] The most common types of capital assets owned by individuals are securities and real estate (including a personal residence). Gains and losses from the sale of such assets are granted special treatment for income tax purposes. Anyone who studies federal income tax laws carefully in search of ways to save taxes will be impressed by the favorable tax treatment of *long-term capital gains.* Stated briefly, this favorable treatment causes long-term capital gains to be taxed at *much lower rates* than income from other sources (ordinary income). From the standpoint of tax planning, this situation calls for taxpayers to invest in properties that offer possible capital gains.

The rationale underlying special treatment of capital gains is to strengthen the economy by encouraging long-term investment in equities by individuals and by business concerns. If our future economy is to be strong and healthy, investment capital must flow into new growth industries. New growth industries are speculative. They do not offer investors assured low-risk income, but do offer the possibility of capital appreciation. Our tax laws can provide an incentive for risk-taking by investors, if capital gains are taxed at much lower rates than low-risk income such as interest on bonds and insured bank deposits.

Amount of gain or loss   A gain from the sale of a capital asset occurs if the sales price exceeds the *basis* of the property sold. A loss occurs if the sales price is less than the basis of the asset. In general, the basis of purchased property is its *cost* reduced by the accumulated depreciation allowed or allowable in computing taxable income. The detailed rules for determining the basis of property are quite complex and will not be considered here. These rules depend in part on how the property was acquired (purchase, gift, or inheritance), whether it is personal or business property, and whether it is sold at a gain or a loss.

---

[5]The Internal Revenue Code defines capital assets to include all items of property except: (a) business inventories; (b) accounts and notes receivable; (c) plant and equipment used in a business; (d) intangible assets such as copyrights and artistic compositions; and (e) government bonds and notes issued at a discount and due within one year.

Long-term versus short-term   Long and short are relative terms; in income taxation the dividing line at present is one year. Long-term capital gains (or losses) result from the sale of capital assets held for *more than one year;* short-term capital gains and losses result when capital assets are held one year or less. (Legislation currently being debated in Congress would shorten to six months the required holding period for long-term capital gains and losses.)

Remember that long-term capital gains are the ones that receive favorable tax treatment; short-term capital gains are taxed as ordinary income. If an individual invests in a capital asset which rises greatly in market price, the classic mistake would be to sell it one day short of the holding period required to qualify the gain as long-term. That one-day error in timing would more than double the tax on the capital gain.

The term *net short-term gain* means short-term gains in excess of short-term losses. Net short-term gains must be reported in full and are taxed as ordinary income. Only 40% of long-term gains, reduced by any net short-term losses, are included in adjusted gross income.

ILLUSTRATIVE CASE   Bob Savage, a taxpayer subject to a marginal tax rate of 30%, has a $1,000 net long-term capital gain and no net short-term capital loss. Savage would include only $400 (40% of the net long-term gain) in adjusted gross income and pay only a $120 tax on the $1,000 gain (30% of $400). The tax rate applicable to the $1,000 long-term gain is 12% (computed as $120 ÷ $1,000). This is less than half of Salvage's marginal rate of 30%.

Limited deductibility of capital losses   In general, capital *losses,* either long-term or short-term, are deductible only against capital gains. If total capital losses exceed gains, however, individual taxpayers (but not corporations) may deduct capital losses against other gross income up to a maximum of $3,000 a year. For example, if an individual incurred a capital loss of $100,000 but also had a salary of $50,000, he or she would have gross income subject to taxation of $47,000. The unused capital loss could be carried forward and offset against capital gains, if any, in future years, or against other income at the rate of $3,000 a year. Thus, a great many years would be required to offset the $100,000 capital loss against other income.

Critics of our present tax laws point out that persons who save and invest are taxed in a similar manner to those who gamble on horse races. (Gambling gains are taxable; gambling losses cannot be offset against other income.) Similarly, gains from investment are taxed heavily and losses from investments are generally not permitted as deductions if they exceed gains. This policy may be inconsistent with the national goal of encouraging investment. Although the United States formerly had worldwide recognition for its high productivity, the ratio of capital investment to gross national product has now fallen far below many other nations. The tax laws of some other countries are more conducive to investment; for example, no tax on capital gains.

Only 50% of a net long-term capital loss can be used in arriving at the maximum which can be offset against other income in a single year. In other words, a net long-term capital loss of $4,000 would be required to entitle the taxpayer to take a $2,000 deduction. Although capital losses not deductible in any given year may be carried forward to future tax years, it is apparent that a large capital loss as in the preceding example probably will not be utilized fully in future years unless the taxpayer is fortunate enough to have a large capital gain.

Wash sales   When the prices of stocks or bonds drop sharply, some taxpayers may be inclined to sell their holdings in order to get the tax advantage of a capital loss to offset against other income. If a sale is made, the seller must not repurchase identical securities within 30 days or the capital loss will not be deductible. The IRA considers a "wash sale" to have occurred if substantially identical securities are purchased within 30 days before or after a sale.

Business plant and equipment   Buildings, machinery, and other depreciable property used in a trade or business are not capital assets under the tax law. This means that a net loss realized on the sale or disposal of such business property is fully deductible. However, under certain circumstances, a gain on the sale of such property held more than one year may be treated as a capital gain.

Tax tables

Earlier in this chapter we considered the *tax rate schedules* (pages 664–665) used by all taxpayers with incomes of $50,000 or more. However, most taxpayers with income below this level are required to compute their tax liability by using *tax tables* provided by the IRS. Our interest is in the basic concepts of the income tax structure rather than in the mechanics of filling out tax returns; consequently, these lengthy tax tables are not illustrated. The tax tables are derived from the tax rate schedules, but also incorporate the number of personal exemptions claimed. Consequently, the taxpayer using the tables does not make the deduction for exemptions. Instead the taxpayer calculates his or her *taxable income* and looks through the tax tables to determine the income tax liability.

Tax credits

Tax credits are deducted directly from the income tax owed. After the taxpayer has computed the gross income tax liability, the next step is to deduct any tax credits. Notice the difference between tax credits and the deductions previously discussed. A deduction (such as charitable contributions) is subtracted from adjusted gross income and thus leads to a smaller amount of taxable income to which the tax rate is applied. A tax credit, however, is subtracted directly from the tax owed. Thus, a tax credit of, say, $500, is worth much more to the taxpayer than a $500 deduction. If we assume a marginal tax rate of 30%, an additional tax deduction would decrease the tax liability by $150 ($500 × 30%), but a tax credit of $500 would reduce the tax liability by the full $500.

One of the most important tax credits is the *investment tax credit* arising from purchase of depreciable business property. The investment tax credit is an example of efforts to provide tax incentives as a means of stimulating business investment and thus increasing the level of economic activity. When a business buys new long-lived assets such as office equipment or machinery, it can take a credit of 10% of the cost of the property as a deduction from the income tax for the year. The use of an investment credit does not affect the depreciation of the asset.

The variety of tax credits currently available indicates the continuing efforts by government to use the tax laws to achieve various social goals. A few examples are the residential energy credit, the credit for wages paid in work incentive programs, credit for the elderly, credit for scientific research and development, and credit for political contributions.

Quarterly payments of estimated tax

For self-employed persons such as doctors, dentists, and owners of small businesses, there is of course no salary and no withholding. Other examples of income on which no withholding occurs are rental income, dividends, and interest received. To equalize the treatment of employees and self-employed persons, the tax law requires persons who have taxable income in excess of a given amount, from which no withholding has been made, to file a *declaration of estimated tax* and to pay estimated income taxes in quarterly installments. Any underpayment or overpayment is adjusted when the annual tax return is filed. Both estimated tax payments and the amount of income tax withholdings are tax prepayments to be deducted at year-end in determining the taxpayer's remaining tax liability.

A declaration of estimated tax is a statement which a taxpayer having *income not subject to withholding* must file with the IRS by April 15 each year. The declaration shows the taxable income expected for the current year and the quarterly payments of estimated tax to be made. The first of the quarterly payments must accompany the declaration.

Although salaried employees are subject to withholding, many have other income such as interest or rent which are not subject to withholding. These persons must therefore file a declaration of estimated tax and make quarterly payments if the income not subject to withholding is substantial.

Tax returns, tax refunds, and payment of the tax

Whether you must file a tax return depends upon the amount of your income and your filing status. At present, a single person with income of $3,300 or more (the personal exemption plus the zero bracket amount) must file a return. A married couple filing jointly and having income of $5,400 or more must file. However, for a self-employed person, net earnings from self-employment of as little as $400 impose a requirement to file a return. These dollar limits, along with tax rates, are likely to be changed from year to year. The tax return must be filed within 3½ months after the close of the taxable year. Most taxpayers are on a calendar-year basis; therefore, the deadline for filing is April 15.

Withholding makes the system work   The payment of federal income taxes is on a "pay as you go" basis. The procedure by which employers withhold income taxes from the salaries of employees has been discussed previously in Chapter 13. Without the withholding feature, the present income tax system would probably be unworkable. The high rate of income taxes would pose an impossible collection problem if employees received their total earnings in cash and were later called upon at the end of the year to pay the government a major portion of a year's salary.

The amounts withheld from an employee's salary for income tax can be considered as payments on account. If the amount of income tax as computed by preparing a tax return at the end of the year is less than the amount withheld during the year, the taxpayer is entitled to a refund. On the other hand, if the tax as computed at year-end is more than the amount withheld, the additional amount must be paid with the tax return. Persons who are entitled to a refund because withholdings or payments of estimated tax exceed the tax liability will of course file a tax return to obtain a refund, even though they might not have sufficient income to make the filing of a tax return compulsory.

The deceptive lure of a tax refund check   The majority of American taxpayers receive tax refunds each year. Apparently these 60 million or more persons so enjoy receiving a refund check that they are willing to have the government withhold excessive amounts of tax from their paychecks throughout the year. The IRS reports that millions of individual taxpayers declare fewer personal exemptions than they expect to claim at year-end. The result is over-withholding of billions of dollars on which the government pays no interest. It seems strange during a period of inflation and high interest rates that American taxpayers would choose to have the government hold their money throughout the year with no interest in order to be paid back at year-end in dollars worth less in purchasing power than when earned.

Computation of individual income tax illustrated

The computation of the federal income tax for Mary and John Reed is illustrated on page 676.

In this example it is assumed that the Reeds provide over one-half the support of their two children. John Reed is a practicing attorney who received $81,000 in gross fees from his law practice and incurred $32,000 of business expenses. Mary Reed earned $24,400 during the year as a CPA working for a national firm of accountants. During the year, $4,000 was withheld from her salary for federal income taxes. Just before the end of the year, John Reed contributed $3,000 to a Keogh H.R.10 retirement plan. The Reeds received $700 interest on municipal bonds, and $120 on savings accounts. Dividends received on stock jointly owned amounted to $8,440. During the year stock purchased several years ago by John Reed for $2,600 was sold for $3,600, net of brokerage fees, thus producing a $1,000 long-term capital gain.

The Reeds have total itemized deductions (contributions, interest expense, taxes, medical costs, etc.) of $17,120. They paid a total of $10,000 on their declaration of estimated tax during the year. John Reed is entitled to an investment credit of $1,000 on $10,000 worth of office equipment purchased during the year.

MARY AND JOHN REED
Illustrative Federal Income Tax Computation
For the Year 198X

Gross income (excluding $700 interest on municipal bonds):			
Gross fees from John Reed's law practice	$81,000		
Less: Expenses incurred in law practice	32,000	$49,000	
Salary received by Mary Reed		24,400	
Dividends received, $8,440 (less exclusion of $200)		8,240	
Interest received		120	
Long-term capital gain on stock held over one year		1,000	$82,760
Deductions to arrive at adjusted gross income:			
Long-term capital gain deduction (60% of $1,000)		$ 600	
Deduction for contribution to retirement plan		3,000	
Deduction for two-earner married couple		2,440	6,040
Adjusted gross income			$76,720
Deductions from adjusted gross income:			
Excess itemized deductions (itemized deductions,			
$17,120, minus $3,400 zero bracket amount)		$13,720	
Personal exemptions (4 × $1,000)		4,000	17,720
Taxable income			$59,000
Computation of tax (using tax rate schedule on page 665)			
Tax on $45,800 (joint return)		$11,457	
Tax on $13,200 at 44%		5,808	$17,265
Less: Investment tax credit (10% of $10,000)			1,000
Total tax			$16,265
Less: Advance payments and amounts withheld:			
Payments by Reeds on declaration of estimated tax		$10,000	
Tax withheld from Mary Reed's salary		4,000	14,000
Amount of tax remaining to be paid with return			$ 2,265

On the basis of these facts, the taxable income for the Reeds is shown to be $59,000. Since they file a joint return, the tax on this amount of taxable income may be computed from the tax rate schedule for married couples filing jointly and is $17,265. This tax is reduced by the $1,000 investment credit, producing a tax liability of $16,265. Taking withholdings and payments on declared estimated tax into account, the Reeds have already paid income taxes of $14,000 and thus owe $2,265 at the time of filing their tax return.

Partnerships

Partnerships are not taxable entities. Under the federal income tax law, a partnership is treated as a conduit through which taxable income flows to the partners. Although a partnership pays no income tax, it must file an *information return* showing the computation of net income or loss and the share of net income or loss allocable to each partner. The partners must include on their personal tax returns their respective shares of the net income or loss of the partnership.

Taxation of corporations

A corporation is a separate taxable entity. Our discussion is focused on the general business corporation and does not cover certain other types of corporations for which special tax treatment applies. Every corporation, unless specifically exempt from taxation, must file an income tax return whether or not it has taxable income or owes any tax.

The earning of taxable income inevitably creates a liability to pay income taxes. This liability and the related charge to expense must be entered in the accounting records before financial statements are prepared. The following journal entry is typical.

Income Taxes Expense	60,000	
Income Taxes Payable		60,000
To record corporate income taxes for the current period.		

Corporation tax rates

Tax rates for corporations are in a graduated five-step structure, shown below. These rates are subject to frequent change by Congress.

Corporate Income Tax Rates

Taxable Income	Rates
Up to $25,000	15%
Over $25,000 but not over $50,000	18%
Over $50,000 but not over $75,000	30%
Over $75,000 but not over $100,000	40%
Over $100,000	46%

Note that above $100,000 the income tax on corporations is not progressive. No matter how large taxable income may be, the rate remains the same for amounts above $100,000.

Computation of taxable income of corporations

The taxable income of corporations is computed in much the same way as for individuals: that is, by deducting ordinary business expenses from gross income. However, the following major differences from taxation of individuals must be considered:

1 **Dividends received** The dividends received by a corporation on its investments in stocks of other corporations are included in gross income, but 85% of
such dividends can be deducted from gross income. The net result is that only
15% of dividend income is taxable to the receiving corporation. Corporations
are not entitled to the dividend exclusion of $100 allowed to individual
taxpayers.

2 **Capital gains and losses** Net long-term capital gains of corporations are
subject to a maximum tax of 28%. A corporation is not entitled to the 60%
long-term capital gain deduction as is an individual. If a corporation's taxable
income (including any long-term capital gain) is below $50,000, the corpora-
tion pays only the regular rates of tax on the long-term capital gain rather
than the 28% maximum capital gain tax rate.

   The dividing line between long-term and short-term capital gains and
losses is one year—the same as for individuals. Corporations may deduct
capital losses only to the extent of capital gains. However, if capital losses
exceed capital gains, the net loss may be offset against any capital gains of the
three preceding years (carry-back) or the following five years (carry-forward).

3 **Other variations from taxation of individuals** The concept of adjusted gross
income is not applicable to a corporation. There is no deduction for personal
exemptions and no zero bracket amount. *Gross income* minus the deductions
allowed to corporations equals *taxable income.*

Illustrative tax computation for corporation

To illustrate some of the features of the income tax law as it applies to corporations, a *tax computation* for Stone Corporation is shown below and on the next
page. Remember that this illustration is not an income statement and does not
show items in the sequence of an income statement.

STONE CORPORATION
Illustrative Tax Computation

*Notice the
difference
between income
per accounting
records
($184,000) and
taxable income
($180,000)*

Revenue:		
Sales		$800,000
Dividends received from domestic corporations		20,000
Total revenue		$820,000
Expenses:		
Cost of goods sold	$536,000	
Other expenses (includes capital loss of $13,000)	100,000	636,000
Income per accounting records		$184,000
Add back (items not deductible for tax purposes):		
Capital loss deducted as part of operating expenses*		13,000
Subtotal		$197,000
Special deductions:		
Dividends received credit (85% of $20,000)		17,000
Taxable income		$180,000

*The capital loss can be carried back three years and offset against capital gains if any.

Tax computation:

15% of first $25,000	$ 3,750
18% of second $25,000	4,500
30% of third $25,000	7,500
40% of fourth $25,000	10,000
46% of $80,000 (taxable income above $100,000)	36,800
Total income tax	$ 62,550
Deduct: Quarterly payments of estimated tax	60,000
Balance of tax payable with tax return	$ 2,550

A shortcut method of computing the tax for a corporation with taxable income above $100,000 consists of multiplying the *entire amount* of taxable income by 46% and then subtracting $20,250. The $20,250 figure is the excess of 46% of $100,000 over the tax computed by applying the several rates of 15%, 18%, 30%, and 40% to the four $25,000 segments of the first $100,000.

For example, the shortcut method of computing the tax owed by Stone Corporation on its taxable income of $180,000 is as follows:

$180,000 × 46%	$82,800
Deduct	20,250
Total income tax	$62,550

Accounting income versus taxable income

In the determination of *accounting income,* the objective is to measure business operating results as accurately as possible in accordance with the generally accepted accounting principles summarized in Chapter 14. *Taxable income,* on the other hand, is a legal concept governed by statute and subject to sudden and frequent change by Congress. In setting the rules for determining taxable income, Congress is interested not only in meeting the revenue needs of government but in achieving certain public policy objectives. Since accounting income and taxable income are determined with different purposes in mind, it is not surprising that they often differ by material amounts.

Differences between taxable income and accounting income may result from special tax rules which are unrelated to accounting principles.

1 Some items included in accounting income are not taxable. For example, interest on state or municipal bonds is excluded from taxable income.
2 Some business expenses are not deductible. For example, goodwill is amortized in determining accounting income, but for income tax purposes goodwill is considered to have an indefinite life and amortization is not a deductible expense.
3 Special deductions in excess of actual business expenses are allowed some taxpayers. For example, depletion deductions in excess of actual cost are allowed taxpayers in some mining industries. However, the *statutory depletion* (or *percentage depletion*) allowance which formerly existed for income derived from oil and gas operations has been eliminated.

In addition, the *timing* of the recognition of certain revenue and expenses under tax rules differs from that under accounting principles. Some items of income received in advance may be taxed in the year of receipt while certain accrued expenses may not be deductible for income tax purposes until they are actually paid in cash.

Alternative accounting methods offering possible tax advantages

You are already aware from your study of various methods of depreciation and various methods of inventory valuation that the choice of accounting methods can have considerable effect on the net income a company reports for a given year. The tax law permits taxpayers to follow certain accounting methods in the computation of taxable income which differ from the methods used in the accounting records and financial statements. Business executives therefore are faced with the challenge of choosing accounting methods for income tax purposes that will result in minimizing their tax burdens—usually by postponing the tax to later years.

There are many examples of elective methods which postpone income taxes. Companies which sell merchandise on the installment basis may elect to report income on their tax returns in proportion to the cash received on the installment contracts rather that at the time of the sale of the merchandise. Taxpayers engaged in exploration for oil may charge the cost of drilling oil wells to expense as incurred rather than capitalizing these costs for later depreciation. Ranchers may treat the cost of cattle feed as expense in the year of purchase rather than in the year the feed is consumed. However, the tax laws require that a business electing the lifo method of inventory valuation must also use this method for financial reporting.

The accelerated cost recovery system (ACRS) created by Congress in 1981 replaced for tax purposes the useful-life depreciation concept which had been followed since the beginning of the federal income tax. For units of plant and equipment acquired in 1981 or later, depreciation under ACRS is based on a recovery period shorter than useful life. This arbitrary shorter recovery period is not in accordance with generally accepted accounting principles; consequently a different amount of depreciation expense based on useful life will appear in financial statements. Thus, another factor exists to cause taxable income to differ from accounting income. Under present tax laws, taxpayers have the option of using straight-line depreciation rather than the rapid write-off provided by ACRS. However, taxpayers generally choose for income tax purposes those accounting methods which cause expenses to be recognized as soon as possible and revenue to be recognized as late as possible.

Interperiod income tax allocation

We have seen that differences between generally accepted accounting principles and income tax rules can be material. Some businesses might consider it more convenient to maintain their accounting records in conformity with the tax rules, but the result would be to distort financial statements. It is clearly preferable to maintain accounting records by the principles that produce relevant information about business operations. The data contained in the records can then be adjusted by use of work sheets to arrive at taxable income.

When a corporation follows one method in its accounting records and financial statements but uses a different method for its income tax return, a financial reporting problem arises. The difference in method will usually have the effect of postponing the recognition of income on the tax return (either because an expense deduction is accelerated or because revenue recognition is postponed). The question is whether the income tax expense should be accrued when the income is recognized in the accounting records, or when it is actually subject to taxation.

To illustrate the problem, let us consider a very simple case. Suppose the Pryor Company has before-tax accounting income of $200,000 in each of two years. However, the company takes as a tax deduction in Year 1 an expense of $80,000 which is reported for accounting purposes in Year 2. The company's accounting and taxable income, and the actual income taxes due (assuming for convenience an average tax rate of 40%) are shown below:

	Year 1	Year 2
Accounting income (before income taxes)	$200,000	$200,000
Taxable income	120,000	280,000
Actual income taxes due each year, at assumed rate of 40% of		
taxable income	48,000	112,000

Let us assume the Pryor Company reports in its income statement in each year the amount of income taxes due for that year as computed on the company's income tax returns. The effect on reported net income as shown in the company's financial statements would be as follows:

	Year 1	Year 2
Accounting income (before income taxes)	$200,000	$200,000
Income taxes expense (amount actually due)	48,000	112,000
Net income	$152,000	$ 88,000

Company reports actual taxes

The readers of Pryor Company's income statement might well wonder why the same $200,000 accounting income before income taxes in the two years produced such widely varying amounts of tax expense and net income.

To deal with this distortion between pretax income and after-tax income, an accounting policy known as ***interperiod income tax allocation*** is required for financial reporting purposes.[6] Briefly, the objective of income tax allocation is to accrue income taxes in relation to accounting income, whenever differences

---

[6]For a more complete discussion of tax allocation procedures, see *APB Opinion No. 11,* "Accounting for Income Taxes," AICPA (New York: 1967).

between accounting and taxable income are caused by differences in the *timing* of revenue or expenses. In the Pryor Company example, this means we would report in the Year 1 income statement a tax expense based on $200,000 of accounting income even though a portion of this income ($80,000) will not be subject to income tax until Year 2. The effect of this accounting procedure is demonstrated by the following journal entries to record the income tax expense in each of the two years:

Entries to record income tax allocation

Year 1 Income Taxes Expense	80,000	
Current Income Tax Liability		48,000
Deferred Income Tax Liability		32,000
To record current and deferred income taxes at 40% of accounting income of $200,000.		
Year 2 Income Taxes Expense	80,000	
Deferred Income Tax Liability	32,000	
Current Income Tax Liability		112,000
To record income taxes of 40% of accounting income of $200,000 and to record actual income taxes due.		

Using tax allocation procedures, Pryor Company's financial statements would report net income during the two-year period as follows:

Company uses tax allocation procedure

	Year 1	Year 2
Income before income taxes	$200,000	$200,000
Income taxes expense (tax allocation basis)	80,000	80,000
Net income	$120,000	$120,000

In this example, the difference between taxable income and accounting income (caused by the accelerated deduction of an expense) was fully offset in a period of two years. In practice, differences between accounting and taxable income may persist over extended time periods and deferred tax liabilities may accumulate to significant amounts. For example, in a recent balance sheet of Sears, Roebuck and Co., deferred taxes of $690 million were reported as a result of the use of the installment sales method for income tax purposes while reporting net income in financial statements on the usual accrual method.

In contrast to the example for the Pryor Company in which income taxes were deferred, income taxes *may be prepaid* when taxable income exceeds accounting income because of timing differences. The portion of taxes paid on income deferred for accounting purposes would be reported as prepaid taxes in the balance sheet. When the income is reported as earned for accounting purposes in a later period, the *prepaid taxes are recognized as tax expense* applicable to the income currently reported but *taxed in an earlier period.*[7]

---

[7] A good example of this treatment is found in the annual report of the Ford Motor Company. A recent balance sheet showed "Income Taxes Allocable to the Following Year," $206.5 million, as a current asset. This large prepaid tax came about as a result of estimated car warranty expense being deducted from revenue in the period in which cars were sold; for income tax purposes, this expense is deductible only when it is actually incurred.

TAX PLANNING

Federal income tax laws have become so complex that detailed tax planning has become a way of life for most business firms. Almost all companies today engage professional tax specialists to review the tax aspects of major business decisions and to develop plans for legally minimizing income taxes. Because it is important for everyone to recognize areas in which tax savings may be substantial, a few of the major opportunities for tax planning are discussed in the following sections of this chapter.

Form of business organization

Tax factors should be carefully considered at the time a business is organized. As a single proprietor or partner, a business owner will pay taxes at individual rates, ranging currently from 12 to 50%, on the business income earned in any year *whether or not it is withdrawn from the business.* Corporations, on the other hand, are taxed on earnings at rates varying from 15 to 46%. In determining taxable income, corporations deduct salaries paid to owners for services but cannot deduct dividends paid to stockholders. Both *salaries and dividends* are taxable income to the persons receiving them.

These factors must be weighed in deciding in any given situation whether the corporate or noncorporate form of business organization is preferable. There is no simple rule of thumb, even considering only these basic differences. To illustrate, suppose that Able, a married man, starts a business which he expects will produce, before any compensation to himself and before income taxes, an average annual income of $80,000. Able plans to withdraw $20,000 yearly from the business. The combined corporate and individual taxes under the corporate and single proprietorship form of business organization are summarized on the next page.

Under these assumptions, the formation of a corporation is favorable from an income tax viewpoint. If the business is incorporated, the combined tax on the corporation and on Able personally will be $14,143. If the business is not incorporated, the tax will be $27,505, or almost twice as much. The key to the advantage indicated for choosing the corporate form of organization is that Able did not take much of the earnings out of the corporation.

If Able decides to operate as a corporation, the $48,750 of net income retained in the corporation will be taxed to Able as ordinary income *when and if* it is distributed as dividends. In other words, Able cannot get the money out of the corporation without paying personal income tax on it. An advantage of the corporation as a form of business organization is that Able can *postpone* payment of a significant amount of tax as long as the earnings remain invested in the business.

If all earnings of the business are to be withdrawn   Now let us change one of our basic assumptions and say that Able plans to withdraw all net income from the business each year. Under this assumption the single proprietorship form of organization would be better than a corporation from an income tax standpoint.

Form of Business Organization

	Corporation	Single Proprietorship
Business income	$80,000	$80,000
Salary to Able	20,000	
Taxable income	$60,000	$80,000
Corporate tax:		
15% of first $25,000 .... $3,750		
18% of next $25,000 4,500		
30% on excess of $10,000 3,000	11,250	
Net income	$48,750	$80,000
Combined corporate and individual tax:		
Corporate tax on $60,000 income (above)	$11,250	
Individual tax—joint return:*		
On Able's $20,000 salary	2,893	
On Able's $80,000 share of business income		$27,505
Total tax on business income	$14,143	$27,505

Which form of business organization produces a lower tax?

*Able's personal exemptions and deductions have been ignored, on the assumption that his other income equals personal exemptions and deductions. For convenience, we have used the tax rate schedule on page 665 to compute Able's personal tax rather than the tax tables.

If the business is incorporated and Able again is to receive a $20,000 salary plus dividends equal to the $48,750 of corporate net income, the total tax will be much higher. The corporate tax of $11,250 plus personal tax of $21,993 (based on $20,000 salary and $48,750 in dividends) would amount to $33,243. This is considerably higher than the $27,505 which we previously computed as the tax liability if the business operated as a proprietorship.

We have purposely kept our example as short as possible. You can imagine some variations which would produce different results. Perhaps Able might incorporate and set his salary at, say, $75,000 instead of $20,000. If this salary were considered reasonable by the IRS, the corporation's taxable income would drop to $5,000 rather than the $60,000 used in our illustration. This and other possible assumptions should make clear that the choice between a corporation and a single proprietorship requires careful consideration of a number of factors in each individual case. Both the marginal rate of tax to which individual business owners are subject and the extent to which profits are to be withdrawn are always basic issues in studying the relative advantages of one form of business organization over another.

Under certain conditions, small, closely held corporations may elect to be Subchapter S corporations, in which case the corporation pays no tax but the individual shareholders are taxed directly on the corporation's earnings.

Tax planning in the choice of financial structure

In deciding upon the best means of raising capital to start or expand a business, consideration should be given to income taxes. Different forms of business financing produce different amounts of tax expense. Interest on debt, for example, is *fully deductible,* but dividends on preferred or common stock are not. This factor operates as a strong incentive to finance expansion by borrowing.

Let us suppose that a company subject to a 46% marginal tax rate needs $100,000 to invest in productive assets on which it can earn a 20% annual return. If the company obtains the needed money by issuing $100,000 in 16% preferred stock, it will earn *after taxes* only $10,800, which is not even enough to cover the $16,000 preferred dividend. (This after-tax amount is computed as $20,000 income less taxes at 46% of $20,000.)

Now let us assume on the other hand that the company borrowed $100,000 at 16% interest. The additional gross income would be $20,000 but interest expense of $16,000 would be deducted, leaving taxable income of $4,000. The tax on the $4,000 at 46% would be $1,840, leaving after-tax income of $2,160. Analysis along these lines is also needed in choosing between debt financing and financing by issuing common stock.

The choice of financial structure should also be considered from the viewpoint of investors, especially in the case of a small, closely held corporation:

ILLUSTRATIVE CASE   Assume that the owners of a small incorporated business decide to invest an additional $50,000 in the business to finance expanded operations. Should the owners make a $50,000 loan to the corporation or purchase $50,000 worth of additional capital stock? The loan may be advantageous because the $50,000 cash invested will be returned by the corporation at the maturity date of the loan without imposing any individual income tax on the owners. The loan may be designated to mature in installments or at a single fixed date. Renewal of the note is easily arranged if desired.

If the $50,000 investment were made by purchase of additional shares of capital stock, the return of these funds to the owners would be more difficult. If the $50,000 came back to the owners in the form of dividends, a considerable portion would be consumed by individual income taxes. If the corporation repurchased $50,000 worth of its own capital stock, the retained earnings account would become restricted by this amount. In summary, it is easier for persons in control of a small corporation to get their money back if the investment takes the form of a loan to the corporation rather than the purchase of additional capital stock.

Tax shelters

A tax shelter is an investment which produces a loss for tax purposes in the near term but hopefully proves profitable in the long run. Near the close of each year, many newspaper advertisements offer an opportunity to invest in a program which promises to reduce the investor's present tax liability yet produce future profits. These programs have a particular appeal to persons in very high tax brackets who face the prospect of paying most of a year's net income as taxes.

A limited partnership organization is often used for tax shelter ventures, so that each investor may claim his or her share of the immediate losses. Typical of the types of ventures are oil and gas drilling programs and real estate investments offering higher leverage and accelerated depreciation. Unfortunately, many so-called tax shelters have proved to be merely unprofitable investments, in which the investors saved taxes but lost larger amounts of capital. A sound approach to tax shelters should probably be based on the premise that if an investment does not appear *worthwhile without the promised tax benefits, it should be avoided.*

Some tax shelters, on the other hand, are not of a high-risk nature. State and municipal bonds offer a modest rate of interest which is tax exempt. Investment in real estate with deductions for mortgage interest, property taxes, and depreciation will often show losses which offset other taxable income, yet eventually prove profitable because of rising market value, especially in periods of inflation.

KEY TERMS INTRODUCED OR EMPHASIZED IN CHAPTER 17

Accelerated cost recovery system (ACRS)   An accelerated depreciation method for income tax purposes for depreciable assets acquired after 1980. Such assets are depreciated over a period of 3, 5, 10, or 13 years. This method is not used in financial statements prepared in accordance with generally accepted accounting principles.

Adjusted gross income   A subtotal in an individual's tax return computed by deducting from gross income any business-related expenses and other deductions authorized by law. A key figure to which many measurements are linked.

Capital asset   Stocks, bonds, and real estate not used in a trade or business.

Capital gain or loss   The difference between the cost basis of a capital asset and the amount received from its sale.

Cash basis of accounting   Revenue is recorded when received in cash and expenses are recorded in the period in which payment is made. Widely used for individual tax returns and for tax returns of professional firms and service-type businesses. Gives taxpayers a degree of control over taxable income by deliberate timing of collections and payments. Not used in most financial statements because it fails to match revenue with related expenses.

Declaration of estimated tax   Self-employed persons and others with income not subject to withholding must file by April 15 each year a declaration of estimated tax for the current year and must make quarterly payments of such tax.

Excess itemized deductions   The excess of itemized deductions over the zero bracket amount.

Gross income   All income and gains from whatever source derived unless specifically excluded by law, such as interest on state and municipal bonds.

Interperiod tax allocation   Allocation of income tax expense among accounting periods because of timing differences between accounting income and taxable income. Causes income tax expense reported in financial statements to be in logical relation to accounting income.

Itemized deductions   Personal expenses deductible from adjusted gross income, such as interest, taxes, contributions, medical expenses, casualty losses, and expenses incurred in production of income.

Long-term capital gains and losses   Gains and losses resulting from sale of capital assets owned for more than a specified period (currently one year). A net long-term capital gain qualifies for a special lower tax rate.

Marginal tax rate   The rate to which a taxpayer is subject on the top dollar of income received.

Personal exemption   A deduction (currently $1,000) from adjusted gross income for the taxpayer, the taxpayer's spouse, and each dependent.

Tax credit   An amount to be subtracted from the tax itself. Examples are investment credit, residential energy credit, and credit for wages paid in work incentive programs.

Tax planning   A systematic process of minimizing income taxes by considering in advance the tax consequences of alternative business or investment actions. A major factor in choosing the form of business organization and capital structure, in lease-or-buy decisions, and in timing of transactions.

Tax shelters   Investment programs designed to show losses in the short term to be offset against other taxable income, but offering the hope of long-run profits.

Taxable income   The computed amount to which the appropriate tax rate is to be applied to arrive at the tax liability.

Zero bracket amount   A specified amount of income not subject to individual income tax. Currently $2,300 for single taxpayers and $3,400 for married taxpayers filing jointly. Replaced the standard deduction.

DEMONSTRATION PROBLEM FOR YOUR REVIEW

Robert and Helen Sands have been engaged in various businesses for many years and have always prepared their own joint income tax return. In Year 11 the Sands decided to ask a certified public accountant to prepare their income tax returns.

Early in Year 12, the Sands presented the following tax information for Year 11 to the CPA:

Personal revenue:

Salary from Sands Construction Company, after withholding of $3,168 federal income taxes and social security taxes of $1,140	$ 14,692
Dividends from Sands Construction Company (jointly owned)	16,675
Drawings from Northwest Lumber Company	6,000
Drawings from S & S Business Advisers	9,600
Interest income—City of Norwalk bonds	800
Interest income—savings account	1,150
Proceeds on sale of stock:	
Sale of stock acquired two years ago for $6,200	14,200
Sale of stock held for three months, cost $4,100	3,400
Sale of stock held for over six years, cost $3,500	1,800

Personal expenses:

Contribution to St. Jerome's Church	$ 610
Interest on mortgage, $2,996; on personal note, $400	3,396
Property taxes	3,480
Sales taxes, including $580 paid on purchase of new automobile for personal use	850
Income taxes paid to state	2,100
Medical expenses	1,100
Subscription to investment advisory service	385

Single proprietorship—wholesale lumber, doing business as Northwest Lumber Company:

Sales	118,000
Cost of goods sold	82,000
Operating expenses	38,800
Drawings by Sands	6,000

Partnership—engaged in business consulting under the name of S & S Business Advisers:

Fees earned	76,300
Gain on sale of vacant lot acquired four years ago	4,400
Salaries paid to employees	32,400
Supplies expense	3,500
Contributions to charity	1,000
Rent expense	4,800
Miscellaneous business expenses	7,100
Drawings (Sands, $9,600 and Sims, $6,400)	16,000

Corporation—engaged in construction under the name of Sands Construction Company:

Customer billings	230,000
Materials used	70,000
Construction labor	60,000
Officers' salaries expense	25,000
Legal and professional expense	3,500
Advertising expense	2,000
Other business expenses	19,800
Loss on sale of equipment	4,200
Cash dividends paid	22,500

The Sands have a 60% share in the profits of S & S Business Advisers and John Sims has a 40% share. The Sands own 75% of the stock of Sands Construction Company. Because of their controlling interest, they have assumed responsibility for the preparation of the income tax returns for these organizations.

The Sands are married, have three children, and support Robert's seventy-nine-year-old mother. Robert is fifty-five years old and Helen is younger but declines to give her date of birth. The oldest child, Bill, is twenty years old and attends school full time. The Sands provide all of their son's support, even though Bill earns approximately $1,400 per year from odd jobs and from investments inherited from his grandfather.

In April of Year 11, the Sands paid the $3,100 balance due on their federal income tax return for Year 10. In addition to the income taxes withheld by the Sands Construction Company, Robert and Helen Sands made four quarterly payments of $1,200 each on their estimated tax for Year 11.

Instructions Using the tax rate schedule on page 665, prepare the joint return for Robert and Helen Sands for last year, showing the amount of tax due (or refund coming). You should also prepare in summary form the information for the partnership tax return for S & S Business Advisers and the corporation income tax return for the Sands Construction Company. Assume that a personal exemption is $1,000, that the corporate tax rate is 15% on the first $25,000 of taxable income and 18% on the next $25,000, and that Sands Construction Company has not paid any part of its income tax for Year 11.

SOLUTION TO DEMONSTRATION PROBLEM

S & S BUSINESS ADVISERS (a partnership)
Computation of Ordinary Income
For Year Ended December 31, Year 11

Fees earned		$76,300
Operating expenses:		
Salaries paid to employees	$32,400	
Supplies expense	3,500	
Rent expense	4,800	
Miscellaneous business expenses	7,100	47,800
Ordinary income		$28,500

Ordinary income and other items are to be included in partners' individual tax returns as follows:

	Sands (60%)	Sims (40%)
Ordinary income, $28,500	$17,100	$11,400
Gain on sale of vacant lot, long-term capital gain, $4,400	2,640	1,760
Contributions to charity, $1,000	600	400

SANDS CONSTRUCTION COMPANY
Income Tax Return
For Year Ended December 31, Year 11

Customer billings		$230,000
Operating expenses:		
Materials used	$70,000	
Construction labor	60,000	
Officers' salaries expense	25,000	
Legal and professional expenses	3,500	
Advertising expense	2,000	
Other business expenses	19,800	
Loss on sale of equipment	4,200	184,500
Taxable income		$ 45,500
Total income tax: 15% of $25,000	$ 3,750	
18% of 20,500	3,690	$ 7,440

ROBERT AND HELEN SANDS
Joint Income Tax Return
For Year 11

Gross income:

Salary from Sands Construction Company ($14,692 + $3,168 + $1,140)	$19,000	
Dividends from Sands Construction Company (less $200 exclusion)	16,475	
Interest on savings account	1,150	
Income from S & S Business Advisers, a partnership	17,100	

Net long-term capital gain:

Stock acquired two years ago	$8,000		
Stock held over six years	(1,700)		
Gain on sale of vacant lot—from partnership return	2,640		
Total long-term capital gain	$8,940		
Less: Short-term loss on stock held for three months	700	8,240	$61,965

Deductions to arrive at adjusted gross income:

Loss incurred by Northwest Lumber Company, a single proprietorship ($118,000 − $82,000 − $38,800)	$ 2,800	
Long-term capital gain deduction (60% of $8,240)	4,944	7,744
Adjusted gross income		$54,221

Deductions from adjusted gross income:

Itemized deductions:

Contributions ($600 from partnership return and $610 to St. Jerome's Church)	$ 1,210	
Interest paid	3,396	
Property taxes	3,480	
Sales taxes	850	
Income taxes paid to state	2,100	
Subscription to investment advisory service	385	
Total itemized deductions	$11,421	
Less: Zero bracket amount	3,400	
Excess itemized deductions	$ 8,021	
Personal exemptions (6 × $1,000)	6,000	14,021
Taxable income for Year 11		$40,200

Computation of tax for Year 11:

Tax on $35,200 on joint return (see page 665)	$ 7,323	
Tax on $5,000 excess at 39%	1,950	$ 9,273

Deduct:

Tax withheld from salary	$ 3,168	
Payments on declaration of estimated tax ($1,200 × 4)	4,800	7,968
Tax payable with return for Year 11		$ 1,305

Notes applicable to income tax return on page 690

(1) The loss from the single proprietorship is properly deducted in arriving at adjusted gross income despite the fact that the Sands withdrew $6,000 from the business.

(2) The Sands' share of ordinary income from the partnership (S & S Business Advisers), $17,100, is fully taxable despite the fact that they withdrew only $9,600 from the partnership.

(3) The salary from the Sands Construction Company is included in gross income as $19,000, the gross salary before any deductions.

(4) The ordinary income for the partnership is determined without taking into account the contribution to charity of $1,000 or the long-term capital gain of $4,400. These items are reported by the partners on their personal income tax return on the basis of the profit- and loss-sharing ratio agreed upon by the partners.

(5) Medical expenses are less than 3% of adjusted gross income, and therefore none is deductible.

(6) The oldest son, Bill, qualifies as a dependent even though he earned $1,400, because he is a full-time student.

(7) Interest on City of Norwalk bonds, $800, is not taxable.

REVIEW QUESTIONS

1 Some of the decisions that business owners must make in the organization and operation of a business will affect the amount of income taxes to be paid. List some of these decisions which affect the amount of income taxes legally payable.

2 What is meant by the expression "tax planning"?

3 What are the four major classes of taxpayers under the federal income tax law?

4 It has been claimed that corporate income is subject to "double taxation." Explain the meaning of this expression.

5 Taxes are characterized as *progressive, proportional,* or *regressive* with respect to any given base. Describe an income tax rate structure that would fit each of these characterizations.

6 State whether you agree with the following statements and explain your reasoning:
  a A person in a very high tax bracket who makes a cash contribution to a college will reduce his or her tax liability by more than the amount of the gift.
  b A decision as to whether a person is willing to undertake additional work in order to obtain additional income should be influenced more by a person's *marginal* tax rate than by his or her *average* tax rate.

7 State in equation form the federal income tax formula for individuals, beginning with total income and ending with taxable income.

8 List some differences between the tax rules for corporations and the tax rules for individuals.

9 What are some objectives of the federal income tax structure other than providing revenue for the government?

10 Explain the difference between *tax avoidance* and *tax evasion,* and give an example of each.

11 Helen Bame, M.D., files her income tax return on a cash basis. During the current year she collected $12,600 from patients for medical services rendered in prior years, and billed patients $77,000 for services rendered this year. She has accounts receiv-

able of $16,400 relating to this year's billings at the end of the year. What amount of gross income from her practice should Bame report on her tax return?

12 Joe Gilmore, a single man, files his income tax return on a cash basis. During the current year $800 of interest was credited to him on his savings account; he withdrew his interest on January 18 of the following year. No other interest and no dividends were received by Gilmore.

In December of the current year Gilmore purchased some business equipment having an estimated service life of 10 years. He also paid a year's rent in advance on certain business property on December 29 of the current year. Explain how these items would be treated on Gilmore's income tax return for the current year.

13 From an individual taxpayer's viewpoint, it is better to have a $10,000 net long-term capital gain than $10,000 of ordinary income; however, ordinary losses are usually more advantageous than net capital losses. Explain.

14 Even when a taxpayer uses the accrual method of accounting, taxable income may differ from accounting income. Give four examples of differences between the tax treatment and accounting treatment of items that are included in the determination of income.

15 Under what circumstances is the accounting procedure known as *income tax allocation* appropriate? Explain the purpose of this procedure.

16 List some tax factors to be considered in deciding whether to organize a new business as a corporation or as a partnership.

17 Explain how the corporate income tax makes debt financing in general more attractive than financing through the issuance of preferred stock.

18 The depreciation expense computed by Zane Company under the accelerated cost recovery system (ACRS) appeared in the tax return as $150,000. In the accounting records and financial statements, Zane's depreciation was computed on the straight-line basis and amounted to $100,000. Under interperiod tax allocation procedures, would Zane Company's balance sheet show prepaid income taxes or deferred income taxes? Explain.

EXERCISES

Ex. 17-1   Some of the following items should be included in gross income; others on the list should be excluded. For each item listed, write the identifying letter and the word *included* or *excluded* to show whether the item belongs in gross income on the federal income tax return of an individual.

a Kickbacks received by automobile salespersons from insurance brokers to whom they referred customers

b Prize money received by participating in television quiz show

c Social security benefits

d Tips received by waiter

e Money inherited from estate of relative

f Interest received on investment in municipal bonds

g Profit on sale of sailboat purchased and renovated before being sold

h Gift from relative

   i Dividends of $45 received from investment in General Motors stock (no other dividends or interest received during year)

   j Interest of $90 received from investment in American Airlines bonds (no other interest or dividends during year)

   k Vacation trip received as prize in lottery

   l Compensation received for damages suffered in automobile accident

Ex. 17-2 Shirley Jones is single, employed as an engineer, and has an adjusted gross income of $22,000. She is in the process of determining whether to itemize deductions on her federal tax return and has prepared a preliminary list of transactions from her checkbook and other records. For each item listed, write the identifying letter and the word ***deductible*** or ***nondeductible.*** Finally, state whether it will be advantageous for Jones to itemize deductions on her tax return and give figures to support your decision. Assume a zero bracket amount of $2,300.

a	*Interest paid on installment contract on automobile*	$ 180
b	*Gift to an unemployed relative*	300
c	*Professional dues*	60
d	*Contribution to Red Cross*	25
e	*Cost of commuting between home and work*	800
f	*Property taxes*	1,200
g	*Contributions to college fund drive*	100
h	*State income taxes paid*	1,300
i	*Medical expenses (not covered by insurance)*	500
j	*Gasoline taxes*	150
k	*Subscriptions to professional journals*	40
l	*Cash stolen in a burglary*	80

Ex. 17-3 During the current year, Carl Davis, a bachelor, expects a taxable income of $45,000. Using the schedules on pages 664–665, determine how much federal income tax Davis would save were he to get married before the end of the year, assuming that his bride had no taxable income or itemized deductions and that the personal exemption is $1,000.

Ex. 17-4 From the tax rate schedules on pages 664–665, compute the tax for each of the following.

		Taxable Income
a	*Single taxpayer*	$ 16,000
b	*Single taxpayer*	125,000
c	*Married couple filing joint return*	16,000
d	*Married couple filing joint return*	125,000

Ex. 17-5 John and Mary are considering getting married. John is single and earns $22,000 a year. Mary is single and earns $21,000 a year. Each has one personal exemption and no excess itemized deductions. Refer to the tax rate schedules on pages 664–665 and determine how much tax John and Mary currently pay. If John and Mary get married and file a joint return, will their combined tax go up or down? By how much? (Assume that the two-earner married couple deduction is limited to 10% of the lower-earning spouse's earned income up to $30,000.)

Ex. 17-6   From the following information for William and Susan Jones, a married couple filing a joint tax return, compute the taxable income. (Use only the relevant information.)

Total income, including gifts, inheritances, interest on municipal bonds, etc.	$49,200
Exclusions (gifts, inheritances, interest on municipal bonds, etc.)	17,520
Deductions to arrive at adjusted gross income	1,680
Itemized deductions (assume zero bracket amount of $3,400)	6,690
Personal exemptions ($1,000 each)	5,000
Income taxes withheld from salary	4,320

Ex. 17-7   Malibu Corporation reports the following income during Year 1:

Operating income (taxable at regular rates)	$550,000
Long-term capital gain	250,000
Extraordinary item:	
Loss (fully deductible from operating income)	50,000

Assume that corporate tax rates are as follows:

On first $25,000 of taxable income	15%
On second $25,000 of taxable income	18%
On third $25,000 of taxable income	30%
On fourth $25,000 of taxable income	40%
On taxable income over $100,000	46%
On long-term capital gains	28%

Compute the total tax liability for Malibu Corporation for Year 1.

Ex. 17-8   Mission Bay Corporation deducted on its tax return for Year 5 an expense of $100,000 which was not recognized as an expense for accounting purposes until Year 6. The corporation's accounting income before income taxes in each of the two years was $425,000. The company uses tax allocation procedures.

a Prepare the journal entries required at the end of Year 5 and Year 6 to record income tax expense. Use the shortcut method of computing tax as illustrated on page 679; multiply the entire amount of taxable income by 46% and then subtract $20,250.

b Prepare a two-column schedule showing the net income to appear on the financial statements for Years 5 and 6, assuming tax allocation procedures are used. Also prepare a similar schedule on the assumption that tax allocation procedures are not used.

PROBLEMS

17-1   Tom and Kay Nelson, a married couple, file a joint return and claim one exemption each plus two exemptions for dependents. (Assume that each personal exemption is $1,000 and that Kay does not have earned income.) They have gathered the following information in getting ready to prepare their tax return.

Federal income taxes withheld from salary	$ 9,400
Payments of estimated tax	3,000
Itemized deductions (remember zero bracket amount)	3,480
Total income (including $800 interest on municipal bonds)	60,000
Business-related expenses	5,200

Instructions

a Compute gross income.

b Compute adjusted gross income.

c Compute taxable income.

d Compute the amount of tax remaining to be paid. (Use the tax rate schedule for married individuals filing joint returns, page 665, and assume a zero bracket amount of $3,400.)

17-2 **a** You are to consider the income tax status of each of the items listed below. List the numbers 1 to 15 on your answer sheet. For each item state whether it is *included in gross income* or *excluded from gross income* for federal income tax on individuals. Add explanatory comments if needed.

(1) Cash dividends received on stock of General Motors Corporation. (Assume taxpayer had no other dividend or interest income.)

(2) Value of a color TV set won as a prize in a quiz contest.

(3) Gain on the sale of an original painting.

(4) Inheritance received on death of a rich uncle.

(5) Interest received on Kansas City municipal bonds.

(6) Proceeds of life insurance policy received on death of husband.

(7) Tips received by a waitress.

(8) Value of U.S. Treasury bonds received as a gift from aunt.

(9) Rent received on personal residence while on extended vacation trip.

(10) Share of income from partnership in excess of drawings.

(11) Amount received as damages for injury in automobile accident.

(12) Salary received from a corporation by a stockholder who owns directly or indirectly all the shares of the company's outstanding stock.

(13) Gain on sale of Signal Company's capital stock.

(14) Taxpayer owed $1,000 on a note payable. During the current year the taxpayer painted a building owned by the creditor, and in return the creditor canceled the note.

(15) Las Vegas vacation given by employer as reward for outstanding service.

b Consider the deductibility status of each of the items listed below for the purpose of preparing an individual's income tax return. List the numbers 1 to 11 on your answer sheet. For each item state whether the item is *deducted to arrive at adjusted gross income; deducted from adjusted gross income;* or *not deductible.*

(1) Dave Carter uses his vacation to paint a house (not his residence) which he owns and rents to others. A professional painter had bid $1,200 to do the job.

(2) Cost of commuting between home and place of employment.

(3) State sales tax paid on purchase of sailboat.

(4) Uninsured damage to roof of house caused by tornado.

(5) Interest paid on gambling debts.

(6) Capital loss on sale of investment in securities sold three months after purchase.

(7) Gambling losses. No gambling gains during the year.

(8) Expenses incurred in moving across country to accept position with different employer. Not reimbursed.

(9) Travel expense incurred by sales personnel in calling on various customers. Not reimbursed.

(10) Fee paid to CPA for services in contesting assessment of additional income taxes by IRS.

(11) Net operating loss carry-over from business owned by single proprietor.

17-3   During the year just ended, John Smith, a single taxpayer with one personal exemption and no itemized deductions, earned a salary of $24,000. During the year Smith had the following transactions resulting in capital gains and losses.

(1) Sold 200 shares of Lockport, Inc., for $5,400 after holding this investment for 4 months. The basis to Smith was cost of $4,900.

(2) Sold 100 shares of Gary, Inc., for $4,200, after holding these shares for 5 months. Cost was $6,000.

(3) Sold 100 shares of Lee Company for $4,800 after holding these shares for 13 months. Cost was $8,200.

(4) Sold 50 shares of Trent Company for $3,300 after holding these shares for 14 months. Cost was $2,700.

Assume that the personal exemption is in the amount of $1,000. Smith had no capital loss carry-over from prior years.

Instructions

a Compute Smith's net short-term capital gain or loss, his net long-term capital gain or loss, and his capital loss deduction (if any) for the year.

b Compute Smith's federal income tax for the year by referring to the tax rate schedule on page 664. Arrange your solution in good order and show among other things the adjusted gross income, taxable income, and calculation of the tax liability.

c Assuming that Smith could have sold the 100 shares of Lee Company stock nine months sooner at the same price. Would this earlier sale have been better from a tax viewpoint? Explain.

17-4   James and Janet Baylor, a married couple with two minor children, had items of income and expense for the year just ended as shown below. Assume that James and Janet are both forty years of age, that a personal exemption is $1,000, and that the zero bracket amount is $3,400.

Salaries from JB Corporation	$60,000
Consulting fees earned (net of applicable expenses)	4,200
Dividends (jointly owned)	780
Interest on bonds of State of Maine	252
Long-term capital gains	6,700
Short-term capital losses	2,800
Unused short-term capital loss carry-over from previous year	2,100
Proceeds on insurance policy on life of uncle	7,000
Casualty loss, interest, taxes, and other expenditures (see list below)	51,700
Theft of furniture on July 20 while on vacation	$ 2,200
Interest paid on loans	2,900
Medical expenses	1,120
Insurance on home	252
Income taxes withheld from salaries	15,000
Miscellaneous deductible expenses	200
Sales taxes	500
Property taxes on home	1,100
State income taxes	1,900
Clothes, food, and other living expenses	26,528
Total (as listed above)	$51,700

Instructions   Compute the taxable income and the income tax liability for James and Janet Baylor who file a joint return. Use a format similar to that illustrated on page 676, but list itemized deductions in detail. Your solution should show the various elements of gross income, the adjusted gross income, itemized deductions, personal exemptions, and taxable income, followed by a section for computation of tax. Use the tax rate schedule on page 665 for married taxpayers filing joint returns. Add a note identifying any items listed in the problem which are not deductible.

17-5   Ryan Corporation is completing its first year of operation. The company has been successful and a tentative estimate by the controller indicates an income before taxes of $250,000 for the year. Among the items entering into the calculation of the taxable income were the following:

(1) Inventories were reported on a first-in, first-out basis and amounted to $132,500 at year-end.

(2) Accounts receivable of $3,250 considered to be worthless were written off (direct charge-off method) and recorded as uncollectible accounts expense.

(3) Depreciation of $15,000 was recorded using the straight-line method.

Officers of the corporation are concerned over the large amount of income taxes to be paid and decide to change accounting methods for both financial reporting and tax purposes as follows:

(1) Inventories on a last-in, first-out basis would amount to $100,000.

(2) An acceptable allowance for doubtful accounts, after the write-off of $3,250 mentioned above, would be $10,000.

(3) Use of the ACRS method of depreciation would increase depreciation expense from $15,000 to $28,750.

Instructions

a Determine the *taxable income* of Ryan Corporation on the revised basis.

b Assume that the tax rates on corporations are 15% on the first $25,000; 18% on the second $25,000; 30% on the third $25,000; 40% on the fourth $25,000; and 46% on taxable income in excess of $100,000. Compute the income tax liability for Ryan Corporation (1) before the accounting changes, and (2) after the accounting changes. Also compute the reduction in the current year's income tax liability resulting from the accounting changes.

17-6   The following two cases are independent of each other. The instructions for preparing your solution appear at the end of the second case.

Case A   During the current year Robert Jensen has total income of $80,000. He has personal exemptions of $4,000, deductions to arrive at adjusted gross income of $6,400, itemized deductions of $8,200, and exclusions from gross income of $1,600. Jensen is married and the zero bracket amount is assumed to be $3,400.

Case B   Ann Mason, an attorney conducting her own law practice, uses the accrual basis of accounting in maintaining accounting records and preparing financial statements. However, for income tax purposes, she uses the cash basis of accounting. During the current year, her business net income (computed on an accrual basis) was $75,400. Between the beginning and end of the current year, her financial statements showed that receivables from clients increased by $12,000, and current liabilities for rent and other operating expenses decreased by $6,800. The net income for the business included $1,200 of interest received on municipal bonds.

Mason has a personal savings account to which $720 in interest was credited during the year, none of which was withdrawn from the bank. In addition to business expenses taken into account in computing the net income of her law practice, Mason has $1,360 in deductions to arrive at adjusted gross income. Her personal exemption amounts to $1,000 and her itemized deductions are $5,900. The zero bracket amount is assumed to be $2,300.

Instructions For each of the two cases described above, prepare a separate schedule showing in appropriate order all the steps necessary to determine the taxpayer's *adjusted gross income* and the *taxable income* for the year. For Case B, your solution should show: (1) business net income (accrual basis), (2) the increases and/or decreases for conversion to the cash basis, (3) the amount of business net income on a cash basis; and (4) the steps to determine taxable income.

17-7 Bill and Hannah Bailey own a successful small company, Bailey Corporation. The outstanding capital stock consists of 1,000 shares of $100 par value, of which 400 shares are owned by Bill and 600 by Hannah. In order to finance a new branch operation, the corporation needs an additional $100,000 in cash. Bill and Hannah have this amount on deposit with a savings and loan association and intend to put these personal funds into the corporation in order to establish the new branch. They will either arrange for the corporation to issue to them at par an additional 1,000 shares of stock, or they will make a loan to the corporation at an interest rate of 12%.

   Income before taxes of the corporation has been consistently averaging $150,000 a year, and annual dividends of $64,000 have been paid regularly. It is expected that the new branch will cause *income before taxes* to increase by $30,000. If new common stock is issued to finance the expansion, the total annual dividend of $64,000 will be continued unchanged. If a loan of $100,000 is arranged, the dividend will be reduced by $12,000, the amount of annual interest on the loan.

Instructions
a From the standpoint of the individual income tax return which Bill and Hannah file jointly, would there be any savings as between the stock issuance and the loan? Explain.

b From the standpoint of getting their money out of the corporation (assuming that the new branch is profitable), should Bill and Hannah choose capital stock or a loan for the infusion of new funds to the corporation?

c Prepare a two-column schedule, with one column headed If New Stock Is Used and the other headed If Loan Is Used. For each of these proposed methods of financing, show (1) the present corporate income *before taxes;* (2) the corporate income *before taxes* after the expansion; (3) the corporate income taxes after the expansion; and (4) the corporate net income after the expansion.

17-8 Riverbend Corporation had total revenue for the year of $304,000. Included in this amount were dividends of $6,000 received from domestic corporations. Expenses of the company for the year were as follows:

Advertising expense	$ 18,800
Depreciation expense	6,400
Property taxes expense	4,500

Rent expense	34,000
Salaries expense	110,000
Travel expense	8,400
Utilities expense	6,900

Instructions

a Prepare an income statement for the corporation. Show Dividends Received as a separate item following Income from Operations. Reference the amount for Income Tax Expense to a separate supporting schedule as called for in **b** below.

b Compute Riverbend's total income tax for the year in a schedule which begins with "Income before income taxes," and shows all details of the tax computation.

c At a meeting of the board of directors of Riverbend Corporation late in December, the controller outlined the financial results for the year as shown above. A member of the board then offered the following suggestion.

"As I recall, the Corporation has an investment in General Motors stock which is worth about $15,000 less than we paid for it. Why don't we sell that stock on December 31 and buy back the same number of shares on the first business day in January? That will give us a capital loss this year, which will put us in a lower tax bracket and save several thousand dollars of income tax. By buying the stock back on January 2, we will maintain our investment position so if the stock goes up next year we won't have missed the boat."

Evaluate the director's suggestion from an income tax viewpoint.

BUSINESS DECISION PROBLEM

Gary and Joy Allen, a married couple, are in the process of organizing a business which is expected to produce, before any compensation to the Allens and before income taxes, an income of $72,000 per year. In deciding whether to operate as a single proprietorship or as a corporation, the Allens are willing to make the choice on the basis of the relative income tax advantage under either form of organization.

The Allens file a joint return, have no other dependents, and have itemized deductions that average around $9,100 per year.

If the business is operated as a single proprietorship, the Allens expect to withdraw the entire income of $72,000 each year.

If the business is operated as a corporation, the Allens will own all the shares; they will pay themselves salaries of $21,000 each and will withdraw as dividends the entire amount of the corporation's net income after income taxes. In computing adjusted gross income, assume that the deduction for two-earner married couples is 10% of $21,000, or $2,100.

It may be assumed that the accounting income and the taxable income for the corporation would be the same and that the personal exemption is $1,000. Mr. and Mrs. Allen have only minor amounts of nonbusiness income, which may be ignored.

Instructions Determine the relative income tax advantage to the Allens of operating either as a single proprietorship or as a corporation, and make a recommendation as to the form of organization they should adopt. Use the individual (joint return) and corporate tax rate schedules given on pages 665 and 677.

To provide a basis for this recommendation, you should prepare two schedules: one for operation as a single proprietorship, and one for operation as a corporation.

In the first schedule, compute the total income tax on the Allens' joint personal return when the business is operated as a proprietorship. Also show the Allens' disposable income, that is, the amount withdrawn minus personal income tax.

In the second schedule, compute the corporate income tax and the amount remaining for dividends. Also compute the Allens' *personal* income tax if the corporate form of business entity is used. From these two steps, you can determine the Allens' disposable income under the corporate form of operation.

FINANCIAL STATEMENTS OF A PUBLICLY OWNED COMPANY

The financial statements of The Coca-Cola Company, a corporation listed on the New York Stock Exchange, are presented on the following pages. These financial statements have been audited by Ernst & Whinney, an international firm of certified public accountants. The audit report is attached. This particular company was selected because its financial statements provide realistic illustrations of many of the financial reporting issues discussed in this book.

Notice that several pages of explanatory notes are included with the basic financial statements. These explanatory notes supplement the condensed information in the financial statements and are designed to carry out the disclosure principle discussed in Chapter 14 of this book. As indicated in Chapter 14, the disclosure principle means that all material and relevant facts should be communicated to the users of financial statements.

The final two pages of this section illustrate the impact of inflation on financial statements. Data adjusted for general inflation and current cost data as well are presented by The Coca-Cola Company in accordance with requirements of the Financial Accounting Standards Board.

CONSOLIDATED STATEMENTS OF INCOME (In thousands except per share data)
The Coca-Cola Company and Subsidiaries

YEAR ENDED DECEMBER 31,	1981	1980	1979
Net sales	$5,889,035	$5,620,749	$4,688,739
Cost of goods sold	3,307,574	3,197,733	2,583,210
GROSS PROFIT	2,581,461	2,423,016	2,105,529
Selling, administrative and general expenses	1,782,875	1,681,861	1,414,858
OPERATING INCOME	798,586	741,155	690,671
Interest income	70,632	40,099	36,304
Interest expense	38,349	35,102	10,602
Other deductions — net	23,615	9,425	2,783
INCOME FROM CONTINUING OPERATIONS BEFORE INCOME TAXES	807,254	736,727	713,590
Income taxes	360,184	330,409	318,443
INCOME FROM CONTINUING OPERATIONS	447,070	406,318	395,147
Discontinued operations:			
Income from discontinued operations (net of applicable income taxes of $7,271 in 1981, $11,782 in 1980, and $3,629 in 1979)	5,641	15,790	24,973
Gain on disposal of discontinued operations (net of applicable income taxes of $13,274)	29,071	—	—
NET INCOME	$ 481,782	$ 422,108	$ 420,120
PER SHARE:			
Continuing operations	$ 3.62	$ 3.29	$ 3.20
Discontinued operations	.28	.13	.20
Net income	$ 3.90	$ 3.42	$ 3.40

CONSOLIDATED STATEMENTS OF RETAINED EARNINGS
(In thousands except per share data)

YEAR ENDED DECEMBER 31,	1981	1980	1979
Balance at January 1	$1,914,547	$1,759,367	$1,581,406
Net income for the year	481,782	422,108	420,120
Dividends paid in cash (per share— 1981, $2.32; 1980, $2.16; 1979, $1.96)	286,787	266,928	242,159
BALANCE AT DECEMBER 31	$2,109,542	$1,914,547	$1,759,367

See Notes to Consolidated Financial Statements

CONSOLIDATED BALANCE SHEETS (In thousands except share data)
The Coca-Cola Company and Subsidiaries

	DECEMBER 31	
Assets	**1981**	1980
CURRENT		
Cash	$ **120,908**	$ 129,685
Marketable securities, at cost (approximates market)	**218,634**	101,401
Trade accounts receivable, less allowances of		
$8,579 in 1981 and $8,594 in 1980	**483,491**	523,123
Inventories	**750,719**	810,235
Prepaid expenses	**62,494**	57,809
TOTAL CURRENT ASSETS	**1,636,246**	1,622,253
INVESTMENTS AND OTHER ASSETS	**387,418**	302,184
PROPERTY, PLANT AND EQUIPMENT		
Land and improvements	**96,468**	96,567
Buildings	**570,356**	537,235
Machinery and equipment	**1,271,065**	1,183,438
Containers	**306,243**	314,349
	2,244,132	2,131,589
Less allowances for depreciation	**834,676**	790,749
	1,409,456	1,340,840
FORMULAE, TRADEMARKS, GOODWILL AND CONTRACT RIGHTS	**131,661**	140,681
	$3,564,781	$3,405,958

Liabilities and Stockholders' Equity	**1981**	1980
CURRENT		
Notes payable	$ **89,647**	$ 87,587
Current maturities of long-term debt	**5,515**	7,528
Accounts payable and accrued expenses	**672,049**	733,023
Accrued taxes — including income taxes	**239,114**	233,442
TOTAL CURRENT LIABILITIES	**1,006,325**	1,061,580
LONG-TERM DEBT	**137,278**	133,221
DEFERRED INCOME TAXES	**150,406**	136,419
STOCKHOLDERS' EQUITY		
Common stock, no par value — authorized 140,000,000 shares;		
issued 124,024,735 shares in 1981 and 123,989,854 shares in 1980	**62,389**	62,372
Capital surplus	**114,194**	113,172
Retained earnings	**2,109,542**	1,914,547
	2,286,125	2,090,091
Less 401,338 shares of stock held in treasury, at cost	**15,353**	15,353
	2,270,772	2,074,738
	$3,564,781	$3,405,958

See Notes to Consolidated Financial Statements

CONSOLIDATED STATEMENTS OF CHANGES IN FINANCIAL POSITION (In thousands)
The Coca-Cola Company and Subsidiaries

YEAR ENDED DECEMBER 31,	1981	1980	1979
SOURCE OF WORKING CAPITAL			
From operations:			
Income from continuing operations	$447,070	$ 406,318	$ 395,147
Add charges not requiring outlay of working capital during the year:			
Depreciation	136,868	131,042	110,288
Deferred income taxes	23,692	31,500	17,629
Other (principally amortization of goodwill and container adjustments)	61,009	37,932	29,370
TOTAL FROM CONTINUING OPERATIONS	668,639	606,792	552,434
Discontinued operations (excludes provisions for depreciation, amortization and deferred income taxes of $2,429 in 1981, $4,521 in 1980, and $(2,504) in 1979)	37,141	20,311	22,469
TOTAL FROM OPERATIONS	705,780	627,103	574,903
Increase in long-term debt	4,057	99,415	7,234
Disposals of property, plant and equipment	71,788	77,053	25,041
Other	1,090	854	1,133
	782,715	804,425	608,311
APPLICATION OF WORKING CAPITAL			
Cash dividends	286,787	266,928	242,159
Additions to property, plant and equipment	319,792	287,186	329,559
Acquisitions of purchased companies excluding net current assets:			
Property, plant and equipment—net	9,814	5,885	51,842
Other assets including goodwill, net of other liabilities	113	7,593	23,456
Increase in investments and other assets	85,131	95,254	25,223
Other	11,830	2,348	7,147
	713,467	665,194	679,386
INCREASE (DECREASE) IN WORKING CAPITAL	$ 69,248	$ 139,231	$ (71,075)
INCREASE (DECREASE) IN WORKING CAPITAL BY COMPONENT			
Cash	$ (8,777)	$ 22,799	$ (49,265)
Marketable securities	117,233	59,716	(123,655)
Trade accounts receivable	(39,632)	88,044	96,788
Inventories	(59,516)	140,621	131,353
Prepaid expenses	4,685	5,470	13,820
Notes payable	(2,060)	16,229	(55,573)
Current maturities of long-term debt	2,013	(3,144)	1,283
Accounts payable and accrued expenses	60,974	(156,161)	(66,830)
Accrued taxes—including income taxes	(5,672)	(34,343)	(18,996)
INCREASE (DECREASE) IN WORKING CAPITAL	$ 69,248	$ 139,231	$ (71,075)

See Notes to Consolidated Financial Statements

NOTES TO CONSOLIDATED FINANCIAL STATEMENTS

1. Accounting Policies. The major accounting policies and practices followed by the Company and its subsidiaries are as follows:

The consolidated financial statements include the accounts of the Company and its majority-owned subsidiaries. All significant intercompany accounts and transactions are eliminated in consolidation.

Inventories are valued at the lower of cost or market. The last-in, first-out (LIFO) method of inventory valuation is used for sugar and other sweeteners used in domestic beverages, for certain major citrus concentrate products, and for substantially all inventories of domestic bottling subsidiaries, wine products and certain other domestic and foreign operations. All other inventories are valued on the average or first-in, first-out (FIFO) method. The excess of current costs over LIFO stated values amounted to approximately $76,000,000 and $109,000,000 at December 31, 1981 and 1980, respectively.

Property, plant and equipment is stated at cost, less allowance for depreciation, except that foreign subsidiaries carry bottles and shells in service at amounts (less than cost) which, in general, correspond with deposit prices obtained from customers. Approximately 87% of depreciation expense was determined by the straight-line method for each of the three years in the period ended December 31, 1981. A portion of the depreciation determined by the straight-line method for financial statement purposes is calculated on accelerated methods for income tax purposes. Deferred income taxes are provided to recognize timing differences in reporting depreciation for accounting and tax purposes. Investment tax credits are accounted for by the flow-through method.

Formulae, trademarks, goodwill and contract rights are stated on the basis of cost and, if purchased subsequent to October 31, 1970, are being amortized, principally on a straight-line basis, over the estimated future periods to be benefited (not exceeding 40 years). Accumulated amortization amounted to $16,168,000 and $12,189,000 at December 31, 1981 and 1980, respectively.

At January 1, 1980, the Company began capitalizing interest cost as part of the cost of acquisition or construction of major assets as required by Statement of Financial Accounting Standards No. 34. The Company previously followed the policy of expensing interest costs as in-

curred. Interest capitalized was $7,893,000 in 1981 and $5,674,000 in 1980.

The financial statements of foreign operations are translated to United States dollars in accordance with the provisions of Statement of Financial Accounting Standards No. 8.

2. Inventories. The principal categories of inventories shown in the balance sheet are as follows (in thousands):

	DECEMBER 31	
	1981	1980
Finished products	**$259,391**	$214,108
Work in process	**92,464**	113,348
Raw materials and supplies	**398,864**	482,779
	$750,719	$810,235

3. Short-Term Borrowings and Credit Arrangements. Notes payable include amounts payable to banks of $61,122,000 and $87,587,000 at December 31, 1981 and 1980, respectively.

Under line of credit arrangements for short-term debt with various financial institutions, the Company and its subsidiaries may borrow up to $280,170,000. These lines of credit are subject to normal banking terms and conditions. At December 31, 1981, the unused portion of the credit lines was $219,048,000. Some of the financial arrangements require compensating balances which are not material.

4. Accounts Payable and Accrued Expenses are composed of the following amounts (in thousands):

	DECEMBER 31	
	1981	1980
Trade accounts payable	**$565,697**	$618,548
Deposits on bottles and shells	**67,489**	69,428
Other	**38,863**	45,047
	$672,049	$733,023

5. Accrued Taxes are composed of the following amounts (in thousands):

	DECEMBER 31	
	1981	1980
Income taxes	**$175,753**	$152,590
Sales, payroll and miscellaneous taxes	**63,361**	80,852
	$239,114	$233,442

NOTES TO CONSOLIDATED FINANCIAL STATEMENTS (continued)

6. Long-Term Debt consisted of the following amounts (in thousands):

| | DECEMBER 31 | |
	1981	1980
9⅞% notes due June 1, 1985	$ 99,898	$ 99,867
Other	42,895	40,882
	142,793	140,749
Less current portion	5,515	7,528
	$137,278	$133,221

The 9⅞% notes may not be redeemed before June 1, 1983. After that date the notes may be redeemed at the option of the Company in whole or in part at 100% of their principal amount, plus accrued interest. The notes include various restrictions, none of which is presently significant to the Company.

Other long-term debt consists of various mortgages and notes with maturity dates ranging from 1982 to 2010. Interest on a portion of this debt varies with the changes in the prime rate, and the weighted average interest rate applicable to the remainder is approximately 10.3%.

Maturities of long-term debt for the five years succeeding December 31, 1981, are as follows (in thousands):

1982	$ 5,515
1983	5,490
1984	5,745
1985	104,190
1986	2,266

The Company is contingently liable for guarantees of indebtedness by its independent bottling companies and others of approximately $39,000,000 at December 31, 1981.

7. Changes in Capital during 1981, 1980 and 1979 were as follows (in thousands):

| | Common Stock Issued | | Capital Surplus |
	Shares	Amount	
Balance January 1, 1979	123,925	$62,340	$111,217
Sale of stock to employees exercising stock options	35	17	904
Tax benefit from sale of option shares by employees	–	–	212
Balance December 31, 1979	123,960	62,357	112,333
Sale of stock to employees exercising stock options and appreciation rights	30	15	711
Tax benefit from sale of option shares by employees	–	–	128
Balance December 31, 1980	123,990	62,372	113,172
Sale of stock to employees exercising stock options and appreciation rights	35	17	841
Tax benefit from sale of option shares by employees	–	–	181
Balance December 31, 1981	124,025	$62,389	$114,194

NOTES TO CONSOLIDATED FINANCIAL STATEMENTS (continued)

8. Stock Options. The Company's 1979 stock option plan covering 1,000,000 shares of the Company's common stock provides for the granting of stock appreciation rights and stock options. Stock options and stock appreciation rights under the plan are granted to certain officers and employees of the Company and its subsidiaries. Stock appreciation rights permit the holder, upon surrendering all or part of his/her related stock option, to receive cash, common stock, or a combination thereof, up to 100% of the difference between the market price and the option price. Shares covered by such surrendered stock options or portions thereof are not available for the grant of further stock options. Options were held at December 31 by officers and employees to purchase shares of the Company's common stock under all stock option plans at prices ranging from $22.08 to $67.91 per share for 1981, from $19.16 to $67.91 per share for 1980, and from $19.16 to $67.91 per share for 1979. Option prices on options exercised ranged from $22.08 to $34.00 per share in 1981, from $19.16 to $24.97 per share in 1980, and from $9.09 to $41.38 per share in 1979. Further information relating to options is as follows:

	1981	1980	1979
Options outstanding at January 1	1,392,457	1,259,886	1,153,598
Options granted during the year	244,975	362,350	262,242
Options exercised during the year	(35,651)	(29,559)	(35,443)
Options cancelled during the year	(195,421)	(200,220)	(120,511)
Options outstanding at December 31	1,406,360	1,392,457	1,259,886
Options exercisable at December 31	755,598	728,067	718,912
Shares available at December 31 for options which may be granted	278,121	400,408	737,758

In 1980, an officer of the Company was granted options for 25,000 shares of the Company's common stock. The options are exercisable at fair market value on the date of the grant on a cumulative basis at the rate of 20% a year. Upon exercise of the options, shares will be made available from treasury stock. Such options are not a part of any stock option plan.

9. Pension Plans. The Company and its subsidiaries sponsor or contribute to various pension plans covering substantially all domestic employees and certain employees in foreign countries. Pension expense for continuing operations determined under various actuarial cost methods, principally the aggregate level cost method, amounted to approximately $35,000,000 in 1981, $32,000,000 in 1980 and $31,000,000 in 1979. Changes in the actuarial assumptions for one plan reduced pension expense by approximately $2,600,000 in 1980.

The actuarial present value of accumulated benefits, as estimated by consulting actuaries, and net assets available for benefits of Company and subsidiary-sponsored domestic plans are presented below (in thousands).

	JANUARY 1	
	1981	1980
Actuarial present value of accumulated plan benefits:		
Vested	**$146,884**	$152,772
Nonvested	**12,669**	13,001
	$159,553	$165,773
Net assets available for benefits	**$193,268**	$165,448

The assumed rates of return used in determining the actuarial present value of accumulated plan benefits were approximately 9% for 1981 and 8% for 1980. This change reduced the actuarial present value of accumulated plan benefits at January 1, 1981, by approximately $19,000,000.

The Company has various foreign pension plans which are not required to report to certain governmental agencies pursuant to the Employee Retirement Income Security Act (ERISA) and do not otherwise determine the actuarial value of accumulated plan benefits or net assets available for benefits as calculated and disclosed above. For those plans, the value of the pension funds and balance sheet accruals exceeded the actuarially computed value of vested benefits as of January 1, 1981 and 1980, as estimated by consulting actuaries.

NOTES TO CONSOLIDATED FINANCIAL STATEMENTS (continued)

10. Income Taxes. The components of income before income taxes for continuing and discontinued operations consisted of the following (in thousands):

	YEAR ENDED DECEMBER 31		
	1981	1980	1979
United States	**$309,654**	$251,807	$248,063
Foreign	**552,857**	512,492	494,129
	$862,511	$764,299	$742,192

Federal, state and foreign income taxes for continuing and discontinued operations consisted of the following amounts (in thousands):

	YEAR ENDED DECEMBER 31			
	Federal	State & Local	Foreign	Total
1981				
Current	$86,589	$22,461	$248,292	$357,342
Deferred	15,574	1,646	6,167	23,387
1980				
Current	$63,636	$17,438	$228,013	$309,087
Deferred	25,518	2,390	5,196	33,104
1979				
Current	$76,965	$13,858	$218,951	$309,774
Deferred	18,541	881	(7,124)	12,298

Total tax expense differed from the amount computed by applying the statutory federal income tax rate to income before income taxes due to investment tax credits which had the effect of reducing the tax provision by approximately $14,000,000, $11,000,000 and $15,000,000 in 1981, 1980 and 1979, respectively. Additionally, in 1979 income taxes were reduced by approximately $11,000,000 resulting from changes in United Kingdom tax legislation.

11. Acquisitions. In 1979, the Company acquired The Atlanta Coca-Cola Bottling Company for approximately $65,000,000 in cash. In addition, several other companies, primarily bottling operations, were acquired in exchange for cash and notes during 1979 and 1980. These transactions were accounted for as purchases, and the operations of the acquired companies have been included in the consolidated statement of income from the dates of purchase. The purchased companies had no significant effect on operating results in 1979 or 1980.

12. Discontinued Operations. In September 1981, the Company sold Aqua-Chem, Inc., a wholly-owned subsidiary which produced steam generators, industrial boilers and water treatment equipment. On February 4, 1982, the Company sold its Tenco Division for approximately book value. Tenco was an operating unit which manufactured and distributed private label instant coffees and teas.

Net sales of discontinued operations were $240,216,000, $291,846,000 and $272,663,000 in 1981, 1980 and 1979, respectively. At December 31, 1981, assets of $60,967,000 and liabilities of $16,308,000 applicable to discontinued operations are included in the consolidated balance sheet.

13. Foreign Operations. The Company's identifiable assets and liabilities outside the United States and Puerto Rico are shown below (in thousands):

	DECEMBER 31	
	1981	1980
Current assets	$ 751,835	$ 773,168
Property, plant and equipment—net	567,179	513,731
Other assets	121,903	121,677
	1,440,917	1,408,576
Liabilities	637,015	664,980
Net assets	$ 803,902	$ 743,596

Appropriate United States and foreign income taxes have been accrued on earnings of subsidiary companies which are expected to be remitted to the parent company in the near future. Accumulated unremitted earnings of foreign subsidiaries which are expected to be required for use in the foreign operations amounted to approximately $61,000,000 at December 31, 1981, exclusive of amounts which if remitted would result in little or no tax. Exchange adjustments were not material in amount in 1981, 1980 or 1979.

14. Industry Segment and Geographic Data. The industry segment and geographic data for 1981, 1980 and 1979 presented on pages 44 and 45 are an integral part of these financial statements.

15. Contemplated Acquisition. In January 1982, the Company announced agreements in principle whereby the Company would acquire Columbia Pictures Industries, Inc. and The Outlet Company for consideration, consisting of cash and shares of the Company's common stock, having an aggregate value of approximately $900,000,000. These acquisitions are subject to execution of definitive agreements, approvals of the Boards of Directors and shareholders of the parties and receipt of consents and approvals by governmental authorities and regulatory agencies. Subsequently, the Company announced that the Outlet transaction would be considered separately following a review of potential contingent liabilities of Outlet resulting from a third party bankruptcy.

REPORT OF INDEPENDENT ACCOUNTANTS
The Coca-Cola Company and Subsidiaries

Board of Directors and Stockholders
The Coca-Cola Company
Atlanta, Georgia

We have examined the consolidated balance sheets of The Coca-Cola Company and subsidiaries as of December 31, 1981 and 1980, and the related consolidated statements of income, retained earnings and changes in financial position for each of the three years in the period ended December 31, 1981. Our examinations were made in accordance with generally accepted auditing standards and, accordingly, included such tests of the accounting records and such other auditing procedures as we considered necessary in the circumstances.

In our opinion, the financial statements referred to above present fairly the consolidated financial position of The Coca-Cola Company and subsidiaries at December 31, 1981 and 1980, and the consolidated results of their operations and the changes in their financial position for each of the three years in the period ended December 31, 1981, in conformity with generally accepted accounting principles applied on a consistent basis.

Ernst & Whinney

Atlanta, Georgia
February 25, 1982

REPORT OF MANAGEMENT
The Coca-Cola Company and Subsidiaries

Management is responsible for the preparation and integrity of the consolidated financial statements appearing in this annual report. The financial statements were prepared in conformity with generally accepted accounting principles appropriate in the circumstances and, accordingly, include some amounts based on management's best judgements and estimates. Other financial information in this annual report is consistent with that in the financial statements.

Management is responsible for maintaining a system of internal accounting controls and procedures to provide reasonable assurance, at an appropriate cost/benefit relationship, that assets are safeguarded and that transactions are authorized, recorded and reported properly. The internal accounting control system is augmented by a program of internal audits and appropriate reviews by management, written policies and guidelines, careful selection and training of qualified personnel and a written Code of Business Conduct adopted by the Board of Directors, applicable to all employees of the Company and its subsidiaries. Management believes that the Company's internal accounting controls provide reasonable assurance that assets are safeguarded against material loss from unauthorized use or disposition and that the financial records are reliable for preparing financial statements and other data and maintaining accountability for assets.

The Audit Committee of the Board of Directors, composed solely of Directors who are not officers of the Company, meets with the independent accountants, management and internal auditors periodically to discuss internal accounting controls, auditing and financial reporting matters. The Committee reviews with the independent accountants the scope and results of the audit effort. The Committee also meets with the independent accountants without management present to ensure that the independent accountants have free access to the Committee.

The independent accountants, Ernst & Whinney, are recommended by the Audit Committee of the Board of Directors, selected by the Board of Directors and ratified by the shareholders. Ernst & Whinney are engaged to examine the financial statements of The Coca-Cola Company and subsidiaries and conduct such tests and related procedures as they deem necessary in conformity with generally accepted auditing standards. The opinion of the independent accountants, based upon their examination of the consolidated financial statements, is contained in this annual report.

Roberto C. Goizueta
Chairman, Board of Directors,
and Chief Executive Officer

Sam Ayoub
Senior Executive Vice President
and Chief Financial Officer

March 3, 1982

UNAUDITED QUARTERLY DATA (For the years ended December 31, 1981 and 1980)
The Coca-Cola Company and Subsidiaries

Quarterly Results of Operations
(In thousands except per share data)

	NET SALES		GROSS PROFIT	
	1981	1980	**1981**	1980
First quarter	**$1,346,462**	$1,173,532	**$ 584,925**	$ 525,244
Second quarter	**1,600,247**	1,500,460	**701,879**	650,813
Third quarter	**1,529,810**	1,509,580	**661,166**	631,813
Fourth quarter	**1,412,516**	1,437,177	**633,491**	615,146
	$5,889,035	$5,620,749	**$2,581,461**	$2,423,016

	INCOME FROM CONTINUING OPERATIONS		NET INCOME	
	1981	1980	**1981**	1980
First quarter	**$ 97,633**	$ 89,479	**$ 100,097**	$ 92,110
Second quarter	**126,992**	127,976	**128,876**	131,500
Third quarter	**116,219**	99,295	**146,581**	102,643
Fourth quarter	**106,226**	89,568	**106,228**	95,855
	$ 447,070	$ 406,318	**$ 481,782**	$ 422,108

	INCOME PER SHARE FROM CONTINUING OPERATIONS		NET INCOME PER SHARE	
	1981	1980	**1981**	1980
First quarter	**$ .79**	$ .72	**$ .81**	$ .75
Second quarter	**1.03**	1.04	**1.04**	1.06
Third quarter	**.94**	.81	**1.19**	.83
Fourth quarter	**.86**	.72	**.86**	.78
	$ 3.62	$ 3.29	**$ 3.90**	$ 3.42

Net sales and gross profit for 1980 and the first three quarters of 1981 have been restated to exclude the results of Aqua-Chem, Inc., and Tenco Division, which have been accounted for as discontinued operations. Income from continuing operations and net income for the second quarter is slightly less in 1981 than in 1980. The decrease was principally caused by foreign exchange adjustments.

Cash Dividends
Cash dividends were declared on common stock in 1981 and 1980 as follows:

	1981	1980
First quarter	**$ .58**	$ .54
Second quarter	**.58**	.54
Third quarter	**.58**	.54
Fourth quarter	**.58**	.54
Full year	**$ 2.32**	$ 2.16

Management expects to continue its policy of paying regular cash dividends.

Stock Market Information
The common stock of the Company is traded on the New York Stock Exchange, Inc. The number of record holders of the Company's common stock at February 18, 1982, was 76,883. The high and low prices of each quarter for the past two years are as follows:

	1981		1980	
	High	**Low**	High	Low
First quarter	**$37.875**	**$26.75**	$38.875	$28.875
Second quarter	**40.25**	**33.75**	35.875	29.75
Third quarter	**34.75**	**30.50**	38.375	32.00
Fourth quarter	**37.00**	**33.00**	34.125	29.125

INDUSTRY SEGMENTS
The Coca-Cola Company and Subsidiaries

The Company operates principally in the soft drink industry. Citrus, coffee, wine and plastic products are included in other industries. Inter-segment transfers are not material. Information concerning operations in different industries is as follows (in thousands):

	YEAR ENDED DECEMBER 31		
	1981	1980	1979
Net sales:*			
Soft drinks	**$4,683,467**	$4,522,048	$3,764,704
Other industries	**1,205,568**	1,098,701	924,035
Total net sales	**$5,889,035**	$5,620,749	$4,688,739
Income from industry segments:*			
Soft drinks	**$ 803,748**	$ 731,783	$ 686,283
Other industries	**113,759**	101,138	78,833
Total from industry segments	**917,507**	832,921	765,116
Other income, net of other deductions	**(37,671)**	(37,893)	(1,244)
General expenses	**(72,582)**	(58,301)	(50,282)
Income from continuing operations before income taxes	**$ 807,254**	$ 736,727	$ 713,590
Identifiable assets at year-end:*			
Soft drinks	**$2,472,533**	$2,436,192	$2,106,451
Other industries	**578,588**	529,184	482,461
Total by industry segments	**3,051,121**	2,965,376	2,588,912
Corporate assets (principally marketable securities and fixed assets)	**452,693**	289,202	209,642
Discontinued operations	**60,967**	151,380	139,487
Total assets at year-end	**$3,564,781**	$3,405,958	$2,938,041
Capital expenditures by industry segment:			
Soft drinks	**$ 251,539**	$ 224,152	$ 294,946
Other industries	**58,422**	40,924	48,527
Depreciation and amortization by industry segment: *			
Soft drinks	**$ 112,476**	$ 108,126	$ 88,786
Other industries	**22,817**	20,731	19,260

*Amounts for 1980 and 1979 have been restated to reflect the sale of the Company's Aqua-Chem, Inc., subsidiary and Tenco Division.

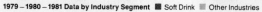

Net Sales (in thousands)

$4,688,739 — 1979: 19.7% / 80.3%
$5,620,749 — 1980: 19.6% / 80.4%
$5,889,035 — 1981: 20.5% / 79.5%

Income (in thousands)

$765,116 — 1979: 10.3% / 89.7%
$832,921 — 1980: 12.1% / 87.9%
$917,507 — 1981: 12.4% / 87.6%

Assets (in thousands)

$2,588,912 — 1979: 18.6% / 81.4%
$2,965,376 — 1980: 17.8% / 82.2%
$3,051,121 — 1981: 19.0% / 81.0%

1979 – 1980 – 1981 Data by Industry Segment ■ Soft Drink ■ Other Industries

OPERATIONS IN GEOGRAPHIC AREAS
The Coca-Cola Company and Subsidiaries

Information about the Company's operations in different geographic areas is presented below (in thousands). Africa, which is not a significant geographic area as defined by FAS 14, has been grouped with Europe in accordance with the Company's management organizational structure. The remaining insignificant geographic areas are combined as Canada and Pacific. Inter-company transfers between geographic areas are not material.

	YEAR ENDED DECEMBER 31		
	1981	1980	1979
Net sales:*			
United States and Puerto Rico	$3,238,673	$3,059,953	$2,470,911
Latin America	608,110	560,164	417,991
Europe and Africa	1,096,257	1,170,294	995,485
Canada and Pacific	945,995	830,338	804,352
Total net sales	$5,889,035	$5,620,749	$4,688,739
Income from geographic areas:*			
United States and Puerto Rico	$ 337,522	$ 279,315	$ 253,439
Latin America	179,739	148,055	100,541
Europe and Africa	248,802	278,707	267,360
Canada and Pacific	151,444	126,844	143,776
Total from geographic areas	917,507	832,921	765,116
Other income, net of other deductions	(37,671)	(37,893)	(1,244)
General expenses	(72,582)	(58,301)	(50,282)
Income from continuing operations before income taxes	$ 807,254	$ 736,727	$ 713,590
Identifiable assets at year-end:*			
United States and Puerto Rico	$1,631,123	$1,604,490	$1,407,059
Latin America	436,215	420,197	307,264
Europe and Africa	583,017	579,851	533,528
Canada and Pacific	400,766	360,838	341,061
Total by geographic areas	3,051,121	2,965,376	2,588,912
Corporate assets (principally marketable securities and fixed assets)	452,693	289,202	209,642
Discontinued operations	60,967	151,380	139,487
Total assets at year-end	$3,564,781	$3,405,958	$2,938,041

*Amounts for 1980 and 1979 have been restated to reflect the sale of the Company's Aqua-Chem, Inc., subsidiary and Tenco Division.

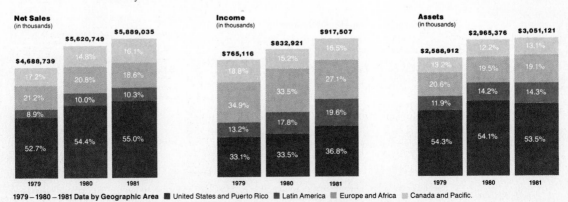

Net Sales (in thousands)

$4,688,739 — 1979
$5,620,749 — 1980
$5,889,035 — 1981

Income (in thousands)

$765,116 — 1979
$832,921 — 1980
$917,507 — 1981

Assets (in thousands)

$2,588,912 — 1979
$2,965,376 — 1980
$3,051,121 — 1981

1979 – 1980 – 1981 Data by Geographic Area ■ United States and Puerto Rico ■ Latin America ▨ Europe and Africa ▨ Canada and Pacific.

SUPPLEMENTAL INFORMATION ON THE EFFECTS OF CHANGING PRICES
(Unaudited)

In the 1970's, the United States experienced high rates of inflation. Many users of financial statements felt that the historical cost basis which is used in the primary financial statements did not adequately portray corporations' financial performance and well-being.

The Financial Accounting Standards Board adopted Statement No. 33, "Financial Reporting and Changing Prices," requiring major corporations to present supplemental information using two different methods intended to estimate the effects of inflation on the value of inventories, property, plant and equipment, and income from continuing operations as described below.

Constant Dollar. Under the constant dollar method for measuring the effect of inflation, historical amounts of depreciation expense and cost of goods sold valued on the average cost method are restated into dollars of the same (constant) general purchasing power using the average level of the U.S. Consumer Price Index for 1981. The amounts of revenues and other costs and expenses already approximate average 1981 constant dollars and generally remain unchanged from those amounts presented in the primary financial statements.

Current Cost. The current cost method attempts to measure the effect of increases in the specific prices of the Company's inventories and properties. It is in-

tended to estimate what it would cost in 1981 dollars to replace the Company's inventories and existing properties.

Under this method cost of goods sold valued on the average method is adjusted to reflect the current cost of inventories at the date of sale. That portion of cost of goods sold valued on the LIFO method approximates the current cost of inventory at the date of sale and generally remains unchanged from the amounts presented in the primary financial statements.

Current cost depreciation expense is based on the average current cost of properties during the year. The depreciation methods, salvage values and useful lives are the same as those used in the primary statements.

The current cost of finished products inventory was approximated by adjusting historical amounts to reflect current costs for material, labor and overhead expenses as well as current cost depreciation, where applicable. The current cost for inventories other than finished products was determined on the basis of price lists or appropriate supplier quotations and by other managerial estimates consistent with established purchasing and production procedures.

Direct supplier quotations, published price lists, engineering estimates, construction quotations, appraisals, published and internally developed indexes were the methods used to determine the current cost of property, plant and equipment.

Under current cost accounting, increases in specific prices (current cost) of inventories and properties held

Statement of Income Adjusted for Changing Prices
(In thousands except per share data)

Year Ended December 31, 1981	As Reported in the Primary Statements	Adjusted for General Inflation (Constant Dollar)	Adjusted for Changes in Specific Prices (Current Costs)
Net sales	$5,889,035	$5,889,035	$5,889,035
Cost of goods sold (excluding depreciation)	3,245,518	3,261,002	3,282,483
Depreciation and amortization	138,187	181,484	199,250
Other operating expenses	1,708,597	1,708,597	1,708,597
Net of other (income) and deductions	(10,521)	(3,558)	(12,149)
	5,081,781	5,147,525	5,178,181
Income from continuing operations before income taxes	807,254	741,510	710,854
Income taxes	360,184	360,184	360,184
Income from continuing operations	$ 447,070	$ 381,326	$ 350,670
Income from continuing operations per share	$ 3.62	$ 3.08	$ 2.84
Effective income tax rate	44.6%	48.6%	50.7%
Purchasing power gain from holding net monetary liabilities during the year		$ 24,476	$ 24,476
Increase in specific prices (current cost) of inventories and property, plant and equipment held during the year*			$ 77,435
Less effect of increase in general price level			284,477
Increase in specific prices over (under) increase in the general price level			$ (207,042)

*At December 31, 1981, current cost of inventory was $860,247 (historical amount, $750,719) and current cost of property, plant and equipment, net of accumulated depreciation, was $2,272,226 (historical amount, $1,409,456).

SUPPLEMENTAL INFORMATION ON THE EFFECTS OF CHANGING PRICES
(Unaudited) (continued)

during the year are not included in income from continuing operations.

Income Taxes. Taxes on income included in each of the supplementary statements of income are the same as reported in the primary financial statements. Present tax laws do not allow deductions for the effects of inflation. Thus, taxes are levied on the Company at rates which, in real terms, exceed established statutory rates.

Purchasing Power Gain. During periods of inflation, monetary assets, such as cash, marketable securities and accounts receivable, lose purchasing power since they will buy fewer goods when the general price level increases. The holding of monetary liabilities, such as accounts payable, accruals and debt, results in a gain of purchasing power because cheaper dollars will be used to repay the obligations. The Company has benefited from a net monetary liability position in recent years, resulting in a net gain in purchasing power. This gain neither represents an increase in funds available for distribution to stockholders nor does it necessarily follow that incurring more debt would be beneficial to the Company.

Management's Comments on Data Adjusted for Inflation. Management believes it is clear that high inflation rates significantly erode the purchasing power of corporate earnings and raise the effective tax rates on industry. However, it should be recognized that current methods to measure these effects are still experimental. The adjustments for general inflation, based on the Consumer Price Index, may not accurately reflect the effect of inflation on the Company's domestic and foreign operations. The Consumer Price Index is based on changes in costs to U.S. consumers of a wide range of goods and services. It is not intended to represent the effects of inflation on a specific corporation or individual. The validity of the use of this index is further questioned because a significant percentage of the Company's assets and operations are located outside the United States.

The adjustments for specific price changes involve a substantial number of judgements as well as the use of various estimating techniques employed to limit the cost of accumulating the data. The data reported should not be thought of as precise measurements of the assets and expenses involved, or of the amount at which the assets could be sold. Rather, they represent reasonable approximations of the price changes that have occurred in the business environment in which the Company operates.

In prior years current cost increases for inventories and properties have exceeded general inflation. In 1981, the current cost increases for inventories and properties were substantially less than general inflation, primarily because of lower sugar prices and lower foreign exchange rates used to translate the local currency value of foreign assets to U.S. dollars.

Five-Year Comparison of Selected Supplemental Financial Data Adjusted for Effects of Changing Prices (In Average 1981 Dollars) (In thousands except per share data)

	YEAR ENDED DECEMBER 31				
	1981	1980	1979	1978	1977
Net sales	**$5,889,035**	$6,206,054	$5,877,099	$5,711,229	$5,541,878
Historical cost information adjusted for general inflation					
Income from continuing operations	**381,326**	339,785	401,535		
Income from continuing operations per share	**3.08**	2.75	3.25		
Net assets at year-end	**2,885,059**	2,976,778	2,979,683		
Current cost information					
Income from continuing operations	**350,670**	292,375	347,184		
Income from continuing operations per share	**2.84**	2.36	2.81		
Increase in specific prices over (under) increase in the general price level	**(207,042)**	24,331	201,216		
Net assets at year-end	**3,137,313**	3,512,824	3,545,866		
Purchasing power gain on net monetary items	**24,476**	47,640	25,997		
Cash dividends declared per share*					
As reported	$ **2.32**	$ 2.16	$ 1.96	$ 1.74	$ 1.54
Adjusted for general inflation	**2.32**	2.38	2.46	2.43	2.31
Market price per common share at year- end*					
Historical amount	$ **34.75**	$ 33.375	$ 34.50	$ 43.875	$ 37.25
Adjusted for general inflation	**33.50**	36.85	43.24	61.19	55.93
Average Consumer Price Index — Urban	**272.5**	246.8	217.4	195.4	181.5

*Adjusted for a two-for-one stock split in 1977.

INDEX